The Global Information Technology Report

2003–2004

Towards an Equitable Information Society

Soumitra Dutta
Bruno Lanvin
Fiona Paua

New York • Oxford
Oxford University Press
2004

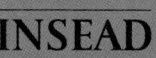

COMMITTED TO
IMPROVING THE STATE
OF THE WORLD

The Global Information Technology Report 2003–2004: Towards an Equitable Information Society (GITR)
is a special project within the framework of the Global Competitiveness Programme. The GITR is the result of a collaboration between the World Economic Forum, the World Bank, and INSEAD, France.

At the World Economic Forum:

Professor Klaus Schwab
Executive Chairman

José María Figueres-Olsen
Co-Chief Executive Officer

Dr Augusto Lopez-Claros
Director

Jennifer Blanke
Economist

Emma Loades
Manager

Fiona Paua
Economist

Catherine Vindret
Research Associate

Saadia Zahidi
Research Associate

At INSEAD:

Professor Soumitra Dutta
Roland Berger Professor of Business and Technology
Dean for Executive Education

Amit Jain
Research Program Manager

At the World Bank:

Bruno Lanvin
Manager of the Information for Development Program
(*info*Dev)

Heini Shi
Program Officer, *info*Dev

A special thank you to Mitchell & Company Graphic Design for their excellent work on the report cover.

Thank you to Pearl Jusem and her team at DBA Design for the great interior graphic design and layout.

We are very grateful to Victor Echevarria Icaza and Annette Heimlicher for invaluable research assistance.

The terms *country* and *nation* as used in this report do not in all cases refer to a territorial entity that is a state as understood by international law and practice. The term covers well-defined, geographically self-contained economic areas that may not be states but for which statistical data are maintained on a separate and independent basis.

Oxford University Press

Oxford   New York
Auckland   Bangkok   Buenos Aires   Cape Town
Chennai   Dar es Salaam   Delhi   Hong Kong
Istanbul   Karachi   Kolkata   Kuala Lumpur
Madrid   Melbourne   Mexico City   Mumbai
Nairobi   São Paulo   Shanghai   Singapore
Taipei   Tokyo   Toronto

Published by
Oxford University Press, Inc.
198 Madison Avenue
New York, New York 10016
http://www.oup.com

ISBN 0-19-517361-9

Printed in the United States of America
on acid-free paper

Contents

Preface

Professor Klaus Schwab
World Economic Forum

The release of the Global Information Technology Report 2003–2004 comes in a markedly different context than the two previous editions. The very first edition, the Global Information Technology Report 2001–2002 was released at a time when the technology sector was reeling from its peak and the global economy was entering a period of diminished growth expectations. Similarly, last year's Report was presented against the backdrop of continued consolidation in the technology sector and heightened uncertainty in the global economy.

In contrast, this year's Report comes at a time of rising optimism. Signs are quite clear that a nascent recovery of the global economy is underway. The technology sector, in particular, now exhibits visible indications of a turnaround, having benefited from the recent period of deep restructuring and extensive streamlining. These developments, together with the unmistakable gains achieved thus far under a more challenging environment, augur very well for creating the conditions necessary for promoting a global information society.

Poised at the threshold of a turning point, this is certainly not the time to be complacent. The use and application of information and communication technologies (ICT) remain the most powerful engines for economic growth. ICT also continues to be the best hope for developing countries to accelerate the development process. More than ever, we must all intensify our efforts to enable individuals, businesses, and governments to benefit more fully from the use and application of ICT.

Recognizing the importance of benchmarking performance and disseminating best practices, the Global Information Technology Report series of the World Economic Forum assesses the progress of networked readiness in countries, revealing the obstacles that prevent countries from fully capturing the benefits of ICT. Beyond just providing a yearly "snapshot" of networked readiness, what we want to do with the Report is establish a process whereby governments, businesses and other stakeholders can evaluate progress on a continual basis.

It is therefore most fitting that this year's Global Information Technology Report is being launched at a historic moment when leaders from around the world are gathering in Geneva on the occasion of the World Summit for Information Society. The theme of this year's Report, "Towards a More Equitable Information Society" is one that reflects the relevance of ICT to economic and social development. In keeping with our theme, we have made a special effort to include in this year's Report 20 more developing countries, mostly from sub-Saharan Africa. This brings the country coverage up to 102 countries, making the Report the most comprehensive assessment of networked readiness in the world.

We commend the contributors to this Report for their vision and commitment to producing a valuable resource for policymakers and business leaders who are engaged in the task of promoting networked readiness. We especially thank the editors of the Report, Soumitra Dutta of INSEAD, Bruno Lanvin of the infoDev Program of the World Bank, and Fiona Paua of the World Economic Forum for their leadership roles in this project. Appreciation also goes to Augusto Lopez-Claros, the Director of the Global Competitiveness Programme, and his team: Jennifer Blanke, Emma Loades, Catherine Vindret, and Saadia Zahidi. Finally, we would like to extend our appreciation to our global network of Partner Institutes who have provided an invaluable contribution in conducting our Executive Opinion Survey, without which this Report would not have been possible.

Introduction

José María Figueres-Olsen
World Economic Forum

Connectivity for the Next Five Billion

Helping the world to communicate has never been as important and as relevant as it is today. Working together to provide "Connectivity for the Next Five Billion" is the equivalent of giving the disenfranchised population of this world a technology-based passport out of poverty and into well-being! And today, when there are signs of renewed global economic activity, connectivity can also be a new engine of growth for a sustainable recovery by the technology sector.

On the supply side, we see constant increases in the offering of ICT products that cater to consumers in the developed world. They are the ones with the resources to buy. And they also have an insatiable appetite for the latest version of software, more powerful microprocessors, and the most newly designed personal computer.

In the case of technology, however, does it have to be the latest version all the time, for all markets? Or can we adequately "connect" and empower the poor of the world—at a good profit—with less than the most powerful version of everything?

We need to develop the connectivity equivalent of what Grameen Bank in Bangladesh or Banco Sol in Bolivia are to financial services, with their successful micro-credit programs. With this type of approach, other sectors of the global economy are not only creating new markets and capitalizing on new business opportunities, but they are also enabling people to unleash their sense of entrepreneurship and contribute to their own well-being!

On the demand side, there is increasing awareness about the importance of putting in place strong programs to deploy ICT for health, education, smart cards (thus lowering intermediation costs), environmental programs, and government services, and even to attracting foreign direct investment. This strategy pays off handsomely in terms of job creation and economic growth. There persists, however, a need to work collectively to broaden popular understanding in the developing world about what ICT can do. And there is also a need for committed leadership to spur initiatives and actions that will lead to greater connectivity.

The Global Information Technology Report 2003–2004 helps raise the profile of these issues, instill a healthy sense of competition amongst nations, and provide them with good insight on how to maximise return on their ICT investment. We are therefore proud to contribute to better livelihoods around the world through the findings and solutions that the GITR offers.

Executive Summary

Soumitra Dutta, INSEAD
Bruno Lanvin, *info*Dev
and
Fiona Paua, World Economic Forum

During the dot-com boom years, information and communication technologies (ICT) attracted a great deal of hype. Corporate executives, consultants, and academics believed that the primary reason for acquiring ICT was to achieve rapid, exponential growth and to penetrate new markets with radical new business models. Companies sought to replicate the "Amazon.com" model, and expectations from technology were unrealistically high. In the midst of this technology frenzy, governments raced to declare their e-visions and e-strategies; several projects and initiatives had as their intent the closing of the "digital divide," because ICT was seen as a critical enabler for the development of emerging economies.

The bursting of the technology bubble and the dot-com crash of the year 2000 was a brutal shock to many technology companies. The ensuing market turmoil and investor disenchantment led to widespread consolidation in many technology sectors. Corporate ICT budgets tightened, and spending on ICT-related projects slowed down. These changes in activity led to a paradigm shift and a realistic moderation of expectations; the focus of ICT projects shifted from achieving fast growth to enhancing productivity and e-enabling core business processes. Corporations began concentrating on the visible impact of and measurable return on their investments in ICT. Government ICT projects were similarly scrutinized for value and effectiveness.

The year 2003 has seen a reversal of the negative sentiments in the financial markets. Despite a turbulent geopolitical environment, markets have started a new and positive cycle. Initial signs of a global recovery are visible, and the ICT sector has benefited from this renewed positive sentiment. Investments in ICT are growing, albeit slowly. Technology stocks have benefited from renewed investment and have partly recovered, although most stocks are still quoted at a fraction of their peak values. After having made progress in e-enabling their core business processes, corporations are once again looking to exploit the transformational potential of ICT. Governments have also benefited from their own ICT investments—the use of ICT has spread rapidly amongst large segments of the world's population and the implementation of e-government projects has improved the effectiveness of many administrative processes.

It is in this setting and with an optimistic note that we publish the Global Information Technology Report 2003–2004. The third in the series of reports, this Report continues to provide a comprehensive assessment of the networked readiness of economies globally. Using the same framework as that used in last year's research, the current Report and research covers 102 of the world's leading economies. Networked readiness is examined by studying the environment for ICT in these economies—market, as well as political, regulatory, and infrastructure factors—and by analyzing the readiness and

Executive Summary | ix

usage of ICT from the perspective of three key stakeholders: individuals, businesses, and governments.

This Report is divided into three main sections: essays, country profiles, and data tables. The essay section draws upon the expertise of scholars, practitioners, policymakers, and business leaders. The country profiles section provides a detailed, relative snapshot of each economy's networked readiness. Data tables that contain rankings of economies for every variable discussed are presented at the final section of the Report.

The first chapter, "The Networked Readiness Index 2003–2004," by Soumitra Dutta and Amit Jain, presents the overall results of the research including the relative levels of networked readiness of different economies. After analyzing the performance of key economies in terms of the "Environment" for ICT, the "Readiness" of key stakeholders to benefit from ICT, and finally the level of "Usage" of ICT, the authors investigate the relation of networked readiness to levels of competition in industry and to GDP. The chapter also takes a look at the digital divide through the lens of networked readiness, and concludes that there is evidence to support the digital convergence of nations.

In her chapter, "Global Diffusion of ICT: A Progress Report," Fiona Paua of the World Economic Forum discusses the current state of diffusion of ICT across the world. Drawing on analysis of empirical data, Paua identifies current trends such as the rapid growth in ICT diffusion occurring in developing countries and the fact that the highest penetration rates are still in developed countries. She reveals that the leading markets for ICT today are a mix of developed and developing countries, and that there is vast market potential for ICT in the more populous developing countries. Aside from global trends, the analysis presents regional profiles that capture those countries that are significantly improving ICT access and those countries that are lagging behind. As the world gears up for economic recovery and the technology sector stands poised for a rebound, the chapter offers policymakers and regulators four policy imperatives and four market implications drawn from the analysis.

Bruno Lanvin and Christine Zhen-Wei Qiang of infoDev (The World Bank) present in their chapter, "Poverty 'e-Readication' Using ICT to Meet MDG: Direct and Indirect Roles of e-Maturity," the role of ICT in poverty eradication. Beginning with a discussion of the Millennium Development Goals of the United Nations General Assembly, they attempt to trace the trajectory of development and value-added resulting from the deployment of ICT. They argue that improving e-readiness gives rise successively to competitiveness, value/wealth creation, employment/ empowerment and, finally, the achievement of the goal of poverty eradication.

Four McKinsey consultants, Scott Beardsley, Ingo Beyer von Morgenstern, Luis Enriquez, and Walter Verbeke, present the chapter that follows, entitled, "Towards a New Regulatory Compact." This chapter describes four key trends in telecommunications that inevitably will have a tremendous impact on the future of the industry and its key stakeholders. They also point out the four regulatory issues that stakeholders such as operators, regulators, and policymakers need to consider in order to successfully manage industry trends and be better prepared for changes in the industry.

The final chapter, "Little Finland's Transformation to a Wireless Giant," by Petri Rouvinen and Pekka Ylä-Anttila, traces Finland's transformation from being one of the least ICT-specialized countries to being one of the most specialized ones. The authors point out that in pre-Nokia Finland, the dominant industries in the country were forestry and timber. They show how Finland, a country with a low technology base and small population, succeeded in transitioning into an information economy and becoming the current dominant player in the global mobile communications industry.

The second section of the Report contains the country profiles for each of the 102 economies assessed. This is followed by the third and final section, a presentation of the data tables and statistical methodology used to compute the Networked Readiness Index. These last two sections of the Report allow the reader to gain a deeper understanding of the networked readiness of a particular economy.

ICT leaders can use the essays and the two data-oriented sections as a guide for designing and structuring policy measures for the key ICT stakeholders—individuals, businesses, and governments—in order to capture the benefits of ICT. Moreover, given that this year's Report contains the third computation of the Networked Readiness Index rankings, we have the beginnings of valuable time-series data. This can help policymakers compute their current networked readiness trajectory and take measures to ensure that progress continues in the desired direction.

It is important to note that while ICT is an essential enabler of business growth and economic development, it also holds the potential for disruptive change. There are many examples of disruptive change, such as that which occurred in Finland, Singapore, Korea, and India, to name a few countries. These countries all succeeded in jump-starting development, productivity, and growth by leveraging the transformative potential of ICT. Our hope is that this Report will help readers to leverage ICT effectively for their chosen trajectories of progress.

The Networked Readiness Index Rankings

The Networked Readiness Index Rankings 2003

NRI RANK	COUNTRY	SCORE
1	United States	5.50
2	Singapore	5.40
3	Finland	5.23
4	Sweden	5.20
5	Denmark	5.19
6	Canada	5.07
7	Switzerland	5.06
8	Norway	5.03
9	Australia	4.88
10	Iceland	4.88
11	Germany	4.85
12	Japan	4.80
13	Netherlands	4.79
14	Luxembourg	4.76
15	United Kingdom	4.68
16	Israel	4.64
17	Taiwan	4.62
18	Hong Kong SAR	4.61
19	France	4.60
20	Korea	4.60
21	Austria	4.56
22	Ireland	4.55
23	New Zealand	4.48
24	Belgium	4.43
25	Estonia	4.25
26	Malaysia	4.19
27	Malta	4.15
28	Italy	4.07
29	Spain	4.01
30	Slovenia	3.99
31	Portugal	3.94
32	Chile	3.94
33	Czech Republic	3.80
34	Greece	3.76
35	Latvia	3.74
36	Hungary	3.74
37	South Africa	3.72
38	Thailand	3.72
39	Brazil	3.67
40	Tunisia	3.67
41	Slovak Republic	3.66
42	Lithuania	3.63
43	Mauritius	3.62
44	Mexico	3.57
45	India	3.54
46	Jordan	3.53
47	Poland	3.51
48	Croatia	3.48
49	Costa Rica	3.46
50	Argentina	3.45
51	China	3.38
52	Trinidad and Tobago	3.37
53	Jamaica	3.36
54	Uruguay	3.35
55	Botswana	3.34
56	Turkey	3.32
57	Dominican Republic	3.32
58	Panama	3.31
59	Namibia	3.28
60	Colombia	3.28
61	Romania	3.26
62	El Salvador	3.22
63	Russian Federation	3.19
64	Morocco	3.19
65	Egypt	3.19
66	Sri Lanka	3.15
67	Bulgaria	3.15
68	Vietnam	3.13
69	Philippines	3.10
70	Peru	3.09
71	Tanzania	3.09
72	Venezuela	3.09
73	Indonesia	3.06
74	Ghana	3.06
75	Macedonia, FYR	3.05
76	Pakistan	3.03
77	Serbia	2.98
78	Ukraine	2.96
79	Nigeria	2.92
80	Uganda	2.90
81	Senegal	2.90
82	Gambia	2.85
83	Cameroon	2.82
84	Kenya	2.81
85	Zambia	2.80
86	Guatemala	2.76
87	Algeria	2.75
88	Malawi	2.71
89	Ecuador	2.68
90	Bolivia	2.66
91	Paraguay	2.62
92	Madagascar	2.60
93	Bangladesh	2.57
94	Nicaragua	2.56
95	Zimbabwe	2.53
96	Mali	2.52
97	Mozambique	2.51
98	Honduras	2.41
99	Angola	2.32
100	Haiti	2.27
101	Ethiopia	2.13
102	Chad	2.09

Part 1
Chapters

Chapter 1

The Networked Readiness Index 2003–2004:
Overview and Analysis Framework

Soumitra Dutta, INSEAD
Amit Jain, INSEAD

Overview

The Networked Readiness Index (NRI) is defined as a nation's or community's degree of preparation to participate in and benefit from information and communication technology (ICT) developments. This is the third year that the NRI is being published. It represents a continuation of our efforts to better comprehend the impact of ICT on the competitiveness of nations. Building upon last year's collaboration between INSEAD, the World Bank (*info*dev), and the World Economic Forum, the current research provides a continuity of data and analysis for the evaluation of prior decisions and actions, and for the enhancement of planning for the future.

The ICT based dot-com boom and thriving global economy of the late 1990s gave way to economic stagnation in 2001–2002, and we now see the first few signs of recovery. In parallel, the perceived impact of ICT for companies and nations has also evolved. While the dot-com boom years were characterized by interest in the potential of ICT to transform industry business models, the focus in businesses over the last couple of years has shifted to productivity gains from ICT-enabled processes. Nevertheless, the fact remains that ICT forms the backbone of most industries such as banking, airlines, and publishing, and is an important value-adding component for others.

Governments and regulators also continue to see progress in ICT as fundamental to national progress. Policies are being put in place to increase ICT penetration in society and to reduce the digital divide. Tariffs continue to be reduced and levels of competition increased to provide incentives for businesses to invest effectively in ICT. Keeping this in mind, and realizing the value for decision makers of a reliable and consistent benchmark of networked readiness, the current research effort extends the set of 82 countries covered in the 2002–2003 study to a total of 102 countries.

This chapter presents the Networked Readiness Framework that has been used to assess the relative degree of networked readiness and compute the NRI of 102 countries. The discussion in this chapter is divided into five main sections. First, there is a brief recapitulation of the Networked Readiness Framework. Second, the results of the research and analysis are presented in the form of a relative ranking of nations based on their degrees of networked readiness. Third, we take a closer look at the three component indexes (and their constituent subindexes) composing the NRI, and how various countries have fared on each of these dimensions. In the fourth section, some key relationships are investigated: the relationship of Networked Readiness with GDP per capita; the link between ICT competition, the affordability of services and the NRI; the evolution of the NRI over the last three studies and a look at the evolution of the digital divide. In the fifth and concluding section, some of the key challenges faced while conducting the study are presented.

The Networked Readiness Framework 2003–2004

The Networked Readiness Index (NRI) is defined as "the degree of preparation of a nation or community to participate in and benefit from ICT developments." The NRI was introduced in 2001–2002 (Kirkman et al 2002) and was refined further in 2002–2003 (Dutta et al 2003). The Networked Readiness Framework used to compute the NRI rankings this year (2003–2004) remains identical to that used to compute the NRI rankings for 2002–2003.[1] The Networked Readiness Framework and its components provide not only a model for evaluating a country's relative development and use of ICT, but also allow for a better understanding of a nation's strengths and weaknesses with respect to ICT.

Figure 1 depicts the structure of the Networked Readiness Framework used in this research. The Networked Readiness Framework is based upon the following premises:

- There are three important stakeholders to consider in the development and use of ICT: individuals, businesses, and governments;

- There is a general macroeconomic and regulatory *environment* for ICT in which the stakeholders play out their respective roles;

- The degree of *usage* of ICT by (and hence the impact of ICT on) the three stakeholders is linked to their degrees of *readiness* (or capability) to use and benefit from ICT.

As shown in Figure 1, the NRI is a composite of three components: the environment for ICT offered by a given country or community, the readiness of the community's key stakeholders (individuals, businesses, and governments) to use ICT, and finally the usage of ICT amongst these stakeholders. A discussion in greater detail on the structure of the framework is presented in a later section entitled "Disaggregating the Networked Readiness Index."

NRI Results for 2003–2004

The overall results for the Networked Readiness Index 2003–2004 are presented in Table 1. The United States comes out with the top rank, followed by Singapore. The rapid evolution of Singapore[2] from the 8th rank in 2001–2002 to the 3rd rank in the 2002–2003 study and finally to 2nd place in the current ranking analysis is the consequence of the government's proactive efforts to promote ICT penetration and usage. Finland, Sweden, and Denmark occupy the 3rd, 4th, and 5th places, respectively. Canada gets the 6th position, followed by Switzerland, Norway, and Australia. Iceland comes in 10th place. Of note also are:

- In the top five places, three positions go to Scandinavian countries: Finland (3), Sweden (4), and Denmark (5).

- Luxembourg enters the top 25 moving from the 27th place in the 2002–2003 rankings to position 14.

- Korea, with its very high Internet penetration, and one of the highest usages of broadband in the world is ranked 20.

- Estonia is the leader amongst the eastern European countries with a rank of 25.

One sees in the top 25 rankings the following regional groupings:

Figure 1. **The Networked Readiness Index Framework**

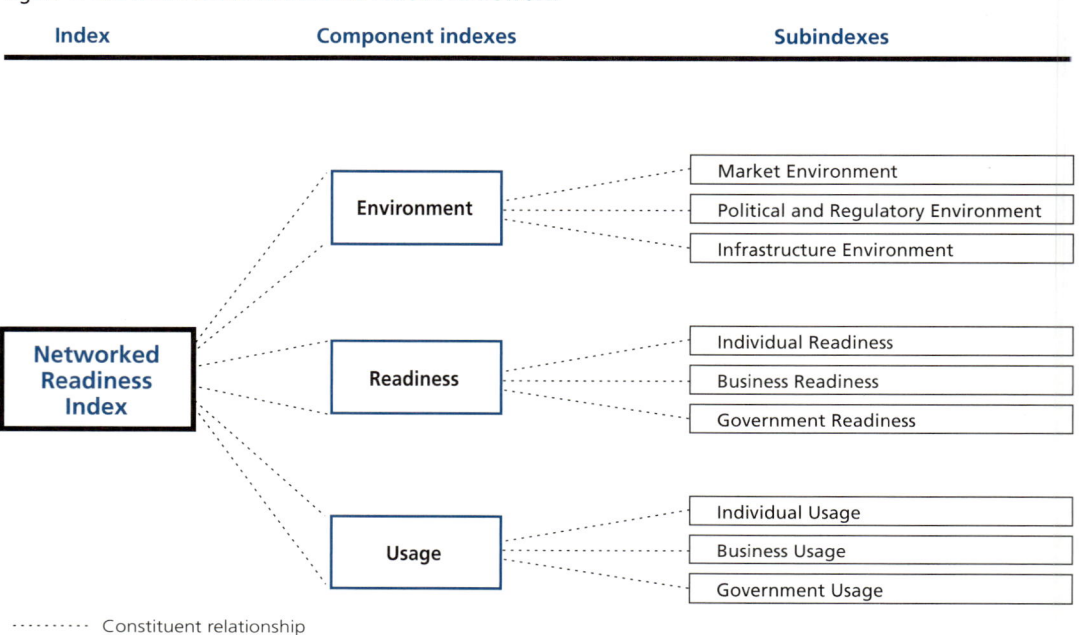

Index	Component indexes	Subindexes
		Market Environment
	Environment	Political and Regulatory Environment
		Infrastructure Environment
Networked Readiness Index	Readiness	Individual Readiness
		Business Readiness
		Government Readiness
		Individual Usage
	Usage	Business Usage
		Government Usage

·········· Constituent relationship

Source: INSEAD

Table 1. **The Networked Readiness Index Rankings**

COUNTRY	SCORE	NRI RANK	COUNTRY	SCORE	NRI RANK	COUNTRY	SCORE	NRI RANK
United States	5.50	1	Latvia	3.74	35	Philippines	3.10	69
Singapore	5.40	2	Hungary	3.74	36	Peru	3.09	70
Finland	5.23	3	South Africa	3.72	37	Tanzania	3.09	71
Sweden	5.20	4	Thailand	3.72	38	Venezuela	3.09	72
Denmark	5.19	5	Brazil	3.67	39	Indonesia	3.06	73
Canada	5.07	6	Tunisia	3.67	40	Ghana	3.06	74
Switzerland	5.06	7	Slovak Republic	3.66	41	Macedonia, FYR	3.05	75
Norway	5.03	8	Lithuania	3.63	42	Pakistan	3.03	76
Australia	4.88	9	Mauritius	3.62	43	Serbia	2.98	77
Iceland	4.88	10	Mexico	3.57	44	Ukraine	2.96	78
Germany	4.85	11	India	3.54	45	Nigeria	2.92	79
Japan	4.80	12	Jordan	3.53	46	Uganda	2.90	80
Netherlands	4.79	13	Poland	3.51	47	Senegal	2.90	81
Luxembourg	4.76	14	Croatia	3.48	48	Gambia	2.85	82
United Kingdom	4.68	15	Costa Rica	3.46	49	Cameroon	2.82	83
Israel	4.64	16	Argentina	3.45	50	Kenya	2.81	84
Taiwan	4.62	17	China	3.38	51	Zambia	2.80	85
Hong Kong SAR	4.61	18	Trinidad and Tobago	3.37	52	Guatemala	2.76	86
France	4.60	19	Jamaica	3.36	53	Algeria	2.75	87
Korea	4.60	20	Uruguay	3.35	54	Malawi	2.71	88
Austria	4.56	21	Botswana	3.34	55	Ecuador	2.68	89
Ireland	4.55	22	Turkey	3.32	56	Bolivia	2.66	90
New Zealand	4.48	23	Dominican Republic	3.32	57	Paraguay	2.62	91
Belgium	4.43	24	Panama	3.31	58	Madagascar	2.60	92
Estonia	4.25	25	Namibia	3.28	59	Bangladesh	2.57	93
Malaysia	4.19	26	Colombia	3.28	60	Nicaragua	2.56	94
Malta	4.15	27	Romania	3.26	61	Zimbabwe	2.53	95
Italy	4.07	28	El Salvador	3.22	62	Mali	2.52	96
Spain	4.01	29	Russian Federation	3.19	63	Mozambique	2.51	97
Slovenia	3.99	30	Morocco	3.19	64	Honduras	2.41	98
Portugal	3.94	31	Egypt	3.19	65	Angola	2.32	99
Chile	3.94	32	Sri Lanka	3.15	66	Haiti	2.27	100
Czech Republic	3.80	33	Bulgaria	3.15	67	Ethiopia	2.13	101
Greece	3.76	34	Vietnam	3.13	68	Chad	2.09	102

- The Americas: two countries (the United States and Canada)

- Western Europe: 14 countries, led by Scandinavia

- Asia and Oceania:[3] seven countries led by Singapore

- Middle-East and North Africa: one country (Israel)

- Central and Eastern Europe: one country (Estonia)

Furthermore, one can observe that

- The top ranked Latin American countries are Chile (32), Brazil (39), and Mexico (44).

- In Asia, Malaysia is ranked 26th and Thailand, 38th. India, with its immense pool of trained IT manpower, is ranked 45th. China is ranked 51st.

- Russia is ranked 63rd overall.

Interpreting the results

The NRI captures key factors relating to the environment, the readiness and the usage of the three stakeholders in the Networked Readiness Framework (individuals, businesses, and governments), and can be used to understand the performance of a nation or a region with regards to ICT readiness and usage. The component index and subindex rankings serve to identify key areas where a nation is under- or overperforming. One would, for instance, be able to identify relative imbalances in development across the three component indexes of Environment, Readiness and Usage, or even go one level deeper.[4]

We would like to emphasize that while rankings are useful as relative indicators of a nation's ICT excellence, there are several limitations to the analytic process. Caution should be exercised while comparing countries that are closely ranked. For instance, countries ranked close together can show very small variation in their index scores. Latvia (NRI score = 3.74, rank 35) and Hungary (NRI score = 3.74, rank = 36) even have the same overall scores. In this case, Latvia has an overall index score marginally higher than that of Hungary, but it is at the third decimal place. Additionally, small differences in the index may be outside the limits of statistical significance due to the fact that some missing observations were estimated using analytic techniques such as regression and clustering.

One must also keep in mind that while the number of countries included in the current study has increased from 82 in the 2002–2003 report to 102, a number of nations could not be included in the research due to limitations in the availability of reliable data. Ranking an even larger set of nations remains a challenge for the future. An overall global ranking needs to account for these missing countries, and any inferences drawn from the current analysis of 102 nations should be made with this limitation taken into consideration.

Finally, the complexity of ICT issues in a nation can get obscured behind the numerical score of the NRI. A country like India, for instance, shows enormous geographic and demographic divides in ICT readiness and usage. It has one of the largest ICT workforces in the world. One can find intense ICT usage in technology clusters such as Bangalore and Gurgaon (near New Delhi), or amongst the upper middle class. The other side of the story is that there is not even telephone connectivity in large parts of the country. Singapore, on the other hand, is a country where there is high ICT readiness and usage across all stakeholders—individuals, businesses, and governments.

Disaggregating the Networked Readiness Index

The NRI provides a relative benchmark of the overall success of a country in participating in and benefiting from ICT. While this is useful, one may need to gain further insights into areas of over- and underperformance of a nation, and to understand the key drivers determining the results. One can do so by looking at the component indexes: Environment, Readiness, and Usage. Table 2 presents the overall results of each component index. Further insight may be obtained by looking at the subindexes composing each Component Index. The final level of detail can be obtained by observing the 48 variables comprising the subindexes, which are presented in the Technical Appendix at the end of the chapter. Figure 2 gives a schematic diagram of the relationships between the various indexes, and how they add up to form the NRI.

Figure 2. **Disaggregating the Networked Readiness Index**

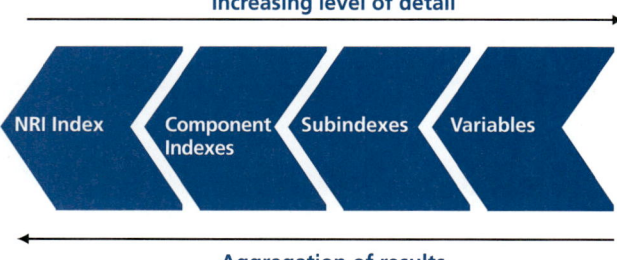

Environment

The Environment component index is designed to measure the degree of conduciveness of the environment that a country provides for the development and use of ICT. As can be seen from Table 2, the top countries with regards to the Environment are the United States, Singapore, and Finland; and the results are consistent with the overall index. Singapore owes its excellent performance in the Environment component index to the proactive policies and measures undertaken by the government to promote ICT, resulting in it being a unique center of excellence in the region.

Table 3 presents the detailed ranking and scores for each of the three subindexes comprising the Environment component index:

Market: This entails the assessment of the presence of the appropriate human resources and ancillary businesses to support a knowledge-based society. The forces that play an important role in determining the market environment for ICT are varied and include fundamental macroeconomic variables like GDP and import/export, commercial measures like availability of funding and skilled labor, and the level of development of the corporate environment. The leader for this subindex is Singapore, followed by the United States and Finland. Ireland and Israel, in the 4th and 5th positions, are notable for their performance on the Environment-Market subindex.

Political/Regulatory: The priorities of a nation are reflected in its policies and laws that in turn influence its rate of growth and direction of development. This component of the NRI measures the impact of a nation's polity, laws, and regulations, and their implementation on the development and use of ICT. The leaders from the Political/Regulatory perspective are Finland, Hong Kong SAR, and Estonia. Iceland manifests an exceptional performance and is highly ranked at 4th place, whereas Singapore is ranked 5th, which is not surprising, given the priority its government places on ICT.

Infrastructure: Infrastructure is defined as the level of availability and quality of the key access infrastructure for ICT within a country. A quality ICT access infrastructure facilitates the adoption, usage, and impact of these technologies, which again promote investment in ICT infrastructure. Infrastructure thus plays a critical role in influencing the networked readiness of a nation. The top ranks along this component go to Iceland, the United States, and Switzerland. One notes that India at 67th place for Infrastructure has a very low rank compared to its overall 44th position in the Environment component index—an indication of the heterogeneous proliferation of ICT across different socioeconomic and geographic segments of the country.

Readiness

The Readiness of a nation measures the capability of the principal agents of an economy (citizens, businesses, and governments) to leverage the potential of ICT. This capability is lent to the nation's community by a combination of factors like the presence of relevant skills for using ICT within individuals, access and affordability of ICT for corporations, and government use of ICT for its own services and processes. As shown in Table 2, Finland ranks highest on overall Readiness and shows a consistent performance across all three readiness subindexes. Sweden is in 2nd place and is supported by a very strong performance in Individual and Business Readiness. Third ranked United States benefits from high scores in Readiness for each of the three stakeholders.

Table 2. The Networked Readiness Index Component Indexes

Networked Readiness Index = 1/3 Environment Component index + 1/3 Readiness Component index + 1/3 Usage Component index

ENVIRONMENT COMPONENT INDEX

COUNTRY	SCORE	RANK	COUNTRY	SCORE	RANK	COUNTRY	SCORE	RANK
United States	5.17	1	Brazil	3.66	35	Bulgaria	2.88	69
Singapore	5.12	2	Tunisia	3.63	36	Gambia	2.85	70
Finland	4.98	3	Namibia	3.62	37	Peru	2.83	71
Switzerland	4.93	4	Latvia	3.61	38	Nigeria	2.82	72
Iceland	4.84	5	Slovenia	3.60	39	Russian Federation	2.82	73
Sweden	4.72	6	Hungary	3.60	40	Vietnam	2.80	74
Canada	4.67	7	Thailand	3.57	41	Romania	2.80	75
Taiwan	4.66	8	Jordan	3.56	42	Pakistan	2.80	76
Luxembourg	4.64	9	Botswana	3.49	43	Senegal	2.79	77
Denmark	4.61	10	India	3.45	44	Uganda	2.79	78
Hong Kong SAR	4.56	11	Lithuania	3.41	45	Serbia	2.78	79
Australia	4.56	12	Costa Rica	3.37	46	Mali	2.77	80
Israel	4.54	13	Mexico	3.36	47	Venezuela	2.75	81
United Kingdom	4.51	14	Mauritius	3.36	48	Philippines	2.67	82
Netherlands	4.46	15	Trinidad and Tobago	3.36	49	Cameroon	2.62	83
Norway	4.45	16	Poland	3.31	50	Guatemala	2.61	84
Germany	4.42	17	Slovak Republic	3.30	51	Bolivia	2.60	85
New Zealand	4.37	18	Uruguay	3.25	52	Zambia	2.59	86
Japan	4.34	19	Panama	3.24	53	Madagascar	2.59	87
Korea	4.34	20	Dominican Republic	3.23	54	Malawi	2.58	88
Austria	4.30	21	Croatia	3.22	55	Bangladesh	2.57	89
Ireland	4.28	22	Jamaica	3.20	56	Ecuador	2.57	90
France	4.27	23	Argentina	3.15	57	Kenya	2.55	91
Belgium	4.11	24	Turkey	3.14	58	Paraguay	2.53	92
Estonia	4.00	25	Macedonia, FYR	3.11	59	Ukraine	2.53	93
Malaysia	3.95	26	Egypt	3.08	60	Algeria	2.48	94
Portugal	3.89	27	Morocco	3.07	61	Mozambique	2.44	95
Italy	3.89	28	El Salvador	3.07	62	Honduras	2.29	96
Malta	3.87	29	China	3.03	63	Zimbabwe	2.29	97
Spain	3.86	30	Colombia	3.02	64	Nicaragua	2.23	98
Chile	3.85	31	Tanzania	3.01	65	Chad	2.19	99
Greece	3.76	32	Sri Lanka	2.99	66	Haiti	2.19	100
South Africa	3.68	33	Ghana	2.97	67	Angola	2.00	101
Czech Republic	3.66	34	Indonesia	2.92	68	Ethiopia	1.99	102

READINESS COMPONENT INDEX

COUNTRY	SCORE	RANK	COUNTRY	SCORE	RANK	COUNTRY	SCORE	RANK
Finland	6.07	1	Portugal	4.65	35	Indonesia	3.91	69
Sweden	5.95	2	Latvia	4.63	36	Morocco	3.87	70
United States	5.95	3	Thailand	4.59	37	Egypt	3.86	71
Singapore	5.85	4	Hungary	4.53	38	Philippines	3.84	72
Denmark	5.81	5	Greece	4.50	39	Namibia	3.81	73
Norway	5.71	6	Brazil	4.49	40	Ghana	3.81	74
France	5.66	7	Mauritius	4.47	41	Macedonia, FYR	3.80	75
Canada	5.66	8	Tunisia	4.47	42	Tanzania	3.70	76
Australia	5.56	9	Poland	4.44	43	Serbia	3.70	77
United Kingdom	5.54	10	Croatia	4.42	44	Pakistan	3.67	78
Japan	5.51	11	Colombia	4.34	45	Cameroon	3.61	79
Germany	5.50	12	South Africa	4.33	46	Algeria	3.59	80
Switzerland	5.44	13	Mexico	4.29	47	Zambia	3.54	81
Netherlands	5.36	14	Russian Federation	4.26	48	Nigeria	3.49	82
Austria	5.32	15	Argentina	4.24	49	Guatemala	3.48	83
Iceland	5.28	16	India	4.23	50	Bolivia	3.46	84
Taiwan	5.25	17	Jordan	4.19	51	Senegal	3.45	85
Ireland	5.24	18	Dominican Republic	4.18	52	Nicaragua	3.42	86
Korea	5.24	19	Uruguay	4.18	53	Paraguay	3.42	87
New Zealand	5.16	20	China	4.14	54	Malawi	3.42	88
Belgium	5.16	21	Costa Rica	4.14	55	Kenya	3.42	89
Estonia	5.11	22	Romania	4.13	56	Uganda	3.32	90
Israel	5.06	23	Jamaica	4.11	57	Zimbabwe	3.24	91
Spain	5.00	24	Ukraine	4.08	58	Gambia	3.23	92
Luxembourg	4.96	25	El Salvador	4.08	59	Ecuador	3.19	93
Italy	4.91	26	Bulgaria	4.06	60	Madagascar	3.05	94
Slovenia	4.90	27	Turkey	4.05	61	Bangladesh	3.00	95
Hong Kong SAR	4.87	28	Venezuela	4.02	62	Honduras	2.97	96
Malaysia	4.86	29	Panama	4.01	63	Angola	2.95	97
Chile	4.73	30	Sri Lanka	3.98	64	Haiti	2.92	98
Malta	4.70	31	Trinidad and Tobago	3.98	65	Mali	2.86	99
Lithuania	4.69	32	Peru	3.97	66	Mozambique	2.80	100
Czech Republic	4.68	33	Vietnam	3.93	67	Ethiopia	2.44	101
Slovak Republic	4.67	34	Botswana	3.91	68	Chad	2.32	102

Table 2. **The Networked Readiness Index Component Indexes (continued)**

USAGE COMPONENT INDEX

COUNTRY	SCORE	RANK	COUNTRY	SCORE	RANK	COUNTRY	SCORE	RANK
United States	5.39	1	Czech Republic	3.06	35	Russian Federation	2.49	69
Singapore	5.21	2	Mexico	3.05	36	Venezuela	2.49	70
Denmark	5.15	3	Mauritius	3.04	37	Sri Lanka	2.49	71
Norway	4.94	4	Greece	3.03	38	Peru	2.48	72
Sweden	4.94	5	Slovak Republic	3.02	39	Colombia	2.48	73
Canada	4.88	6	Thailand	3.00	40	Gambia	2.47	74
Switzerland	4.82	7	Latvia	2.99	41	Nigeria	2.47	75
Luxembourg	4.67	8	Argentina	2.97	42	Kenya	2.46	76
Finland	4.63	9	China	2.97	43	Serbia	2.45	77
Germany	4.62	10	India	2.94	44	Senegal	2.45	78
Japan	4.56	11	Tunisia	2.90	45	Namibia	2.41	79
Netherlands	4.53	12	Costa Rica	2.87	46	Ghana	2.39	80
Australia	4.53	13	Brazil	2.85	47	Indonesia	2.35	81
Iceland	4.52	14	Romania	2.85	48	Mozambique	2.30	82
Hong Kong SAR	4.39	15	Jordan	2.83	49	Ecuador	2.27	83
Israel	4.30	16	Philippines	2.80	50	Zambia	2.27	84
Korea	4.22	17	Croatia	2.79	51	Ukraine	2.26	85
Ireland	4.13	18	Poland	2.78	52	Cameroon	2.24	86
Austria	4.07	19	Lithuania	2.78	53	Macedonia, FYR	2.23	87
Belgium	4.02	20	Jamaica	2.78	54	Guatemala	2.19	88
United Kingdom	3.99	21	Trinidad and Tobago	2.76	55	Algeria	2.18	89
Taiwan	3.95	22	Turkey	2.76	56	Madagascar	2.17	90
New Zealand	3.90	23	Panama	2.68	57	Malawi	2.15	91
Malta	3.90	24	Vietnam	2.67	58	Bangladesh	2.14	92
France	3.87	25	Morocco	2.63	59	Zimbabwe	2.07	93
Malaysia	3.78	26	Botswana	2.63	60	Nicaragua	2.03	94
Estonia	3.65	27	Uruguay	2.63	61	Angola	2.01	95
Slovenia	3.47	28	Pakistan	2.62	62	Ethiopia	1.98	96
Italy	3.41	29	Egypt	2.62	63	Honduras	1.97	97
Portugal	3.29	30	Uganda	2.60	64	Mali	1.93	98
Chile	3.24	31	Tanzania	2.56	65	Bolivia	1.93	99
Spain	3.17	32	Dominican Republic	2.54	66	Paraguay	1.91	100
South Africa	3.15	33	El Salvador	2.52	67	Chad	1.75	101
Hungary	3.10	34	Bulgaria	2.50	68	Haiti	1.71	102

Detailed results for each of the subindexes used for measuring Readiness can be found in Table 4, and are listed below.

Individual Readiness: Individual Readiness measures the readiness of a nation's citizens to utilize and leverage ICT. Factors that are used to measure this include literacy rates, mode and locus of access to the Internet, and the degree of connectivity of individuals. This year's analysis leads to some interesting results; the top four positions on Individual Readiness go to the Scandinavian countries—Norway, Sweden, Denmark, and Finland. Another northern European country, Iceland, comes in 8th.

Business Readiness: Business Readiness measures the readiness of businesses to participate in and benefit from ICT. The aim is not to just focus on the largest corporations, but also to include small and medium-sized businesses and their willingness to exploit ICT and invest in the ICT skills of their employees. Finland and Sweden displace last year's leader, the United States, as the top 2 countries with regards to Business Readiness. The United States ranks 3rd, followed by Singapore.

Government Readiness: Government Readiness measures the readiness of a government to employ ICT. It is reflected in the policymaking machinery and internal processes of the government and in the availability of government services online. If the polity of a nation decides to make ICT a priority, this becomes visible in the short- and long-term policy measures and laws that help encourage ICT deployment and use. It is also reflected in the government's own use of ICT and the extent to which it equips its people to do the same. Singapore leads on Government Readiness, followed by Finland and the United States. France and Canada follow in 4th and 5th places, respectively. Of note also are Malaysia, in 6th place, and Korea, in 9th. The entry of developing countries such as Malaysia and Korea in the upper ranks on the government readiness dimension is a reflection of the policies and actions taken by member governments to promote ICT in the country and in particular in the government.

Usage

The Usage component aims to measure the degree of usage of ICT by the principal stakeholders of the NRI framework—individuals, businesses, and governments. In the absence of reliable data about the specific impact of ICT on the key stakeholders, the Usage component provides an indication of the changes in behaviors, lifestyles, and other economic and non-economic benefits brought about by the adoption of ICT. The United States, Singapore, and Denmark are the top three performers with regards to overall Usage, as shown in Table 2. One can observe variances in country performance across the three subindexes, reflecting uneven impact across

Table 3. **Environment Subindexes**

Environment Component = 1/3 Market Environment Subindex + 1/3 Political and Regulatory Subindex Environment + 1/3 Infrastructure Environment Subindex

MARKET ENVIRONMENT SUBINDEX

COUNTRY	SCORE	RANK	COUNTRY	SCORE	RANK	COUNTRY	SCORE	RANK
Singapore	5.06	1	Hungary	3.00	35	Serbia	2.45	69
United States	4.76	2	Greece	2.95	36	Jamaica	2.44	70
Finland	4.59	3	Czech Republic	2.94	37	Namibia	2.44	71
Ireland	4.37	4	Vietnam	2.91	38	Ghana	2.41	72
Israel	4.30	5	Estonia	2.89	39	Dominican Republic	2.40	73
Taiwan	4.29	6	Lithuania	2.89	40	Bulgaria	2.39	74
Japan	4.28	7	Malta	2.89	41	Pakistan	2.36	75
Luxembourg	4.27	8	Costa Rica	2.88	42	Macedonia, FYR	2.32	76
Sweden	4.17	9	Slovenia	2.87	43	Argentina	2.31	77
Switzerland	4.09	10	China	2.86	44	Philippines	2.30	78
Canada	3.96	11	South Africa	2.82	45	Algeria	2.27	79
Netherlands	3.93	12	Poland	2.82	46	Zimbabwe	2.26	80
United Kingdom	3.88	13	Jordan	2.78	47	Uruguay	2.24	81
Denmark	3.82	14	Russian Federation	2.78	48	Malawi	2.21	82
Germany	3.76	15	Egypt	2.77	49	Venezuela	2.19	83
Belgium	3.75	16	Indonesia	2.72	50	Madagascar	2.19	84
France	3.74	17	Slovak Republic	2.71	51	Bangladesh	2.18	85
Norway	3.74	18	Botswana	2.71	52	Senegal	2.18	86
Korea	3.61	19	Mauritius	2.69	53	Mali	2.17	87
Austria	3.61	20	Sri Lanka	2.66	54	Zambia	2.15	88
Australia	3.57	21	Mexico	2.66	55	Guatemala	2.15	89
Iceland	3.56	22	Trinidad and Tobago	2.65	56	Peru	2.11	90
Hong Kong SAR	3.50	23	Turkey	2.64	57	Ecuador	2.09	91
Italy	3.35	24	Panama	2.64	58	El Salvador	2.09	92
Spain	3.29	25	Croatia	2.62	59	Honduras	2.02	93
Malaysia	3.25	26	Morocco	2.60	60	Gambia	2.01	94
India	3.22	27	Romania	2.59	61	Mozambique	2.00	95
Thailand	3.16	28	Uganda	2.57	62	Ethiopia	2.00	96
Tunisia	3.15	29	Kenya	2.56	63	Nicaragua	1.94	97
Portugal	3.04	30	Tanzania	2.54	64	Bolivia	1.87	98
Chile	3.04	31	Nigeria	2.50	65	Chad	1.86	99
Latvia	3.03	32	Cameroon	2.46	66	Paraguay	1.82	100
New Zealand	3.02	33	Ukraine	2.45	67	Angola	1.75	101
Brazil	3.02	34	Colombia	2.45	68	Haiti	1.61	102

POLITICAL AND REGULATORY ENVIRONMENT SUBINDEX

COUNTRY	SCORE	RANK	COUNTRY	SCORE	RANK	COUNTRY	SCORE	RANK
Finland	5.74	1	Spain	4.37	35	Morocco	3.68	69
Hong Kong SAR	5.66	2	Belgium	4.36	36	Mali	3.65	70
Estonia	5.43	3	Japan	4.34	37	Indonesia	3.64	71
Iceland	5.33	4	Thailand	4.30	38	Senegal	3.64	72
Singapore	5.22	5	Ghana	4.25	39	Turkey	3.58	73
Switzerland	5.21	6	El Salvador	4.21	40	Pakistan	3.58	74
Denmark	5.20	7	Czech Republic	4.21	41	Kenya	3.56	75
United States	5.20	8	Italy	4.17	42	Peru	3.55	76
United Kingdom	5.18	9	Brazil	4.16	43	Argentina	3.50	77
Luxembourg	5.17	10	Namibia	4.16	44	Vietnam	3.43	78
Sweden	5.16	11	Dominican Republic	4.13	45	Macedonia, FYR	3.42	79
New Zealand	5.16	12	Hungary	4.09	46	Croatia	3.41	80
Australia	5.15	13	Trinidad and Tobago	4.08	47	Nicaragua	3.35	81
Netherlands	5.03	14	Greece	4.08	48	Bolivia	3.34	82
Israel	4.93	15	Malawi	4.07	49	Cameroon	3.30	83
Taiwan	4.88	16	Jamaica	4.05	50	Bangladesh	3.28	84
Germany	4.84	17	Slovenia	4.04	51	Bulgaria	3.28	85
Chile	4.82	18	Tanzania	4.00	52	Mozambique	3.28	86
Austria	4.81	19	Uruguay	3.93	53	Paraguay	3.27	87
Malta	4.78	20	Mauritius	3.90	54	Romania	3.23	88
Canada	4.78	21	Zambia	3.90	55	Madagascar	3.20	89
Norway	4.68	22	Poland	3.90	56	Honduras	3.20	90
South Africa	4.67	23	Costa Rica	3.89	57	Guatemala	3.18	91
Ireland	4.57	24	Lithuania	3.88	58	Serbia	3.16	92
Korea	4.56	25	Mexico	3.84	59	Ecuador	3.15	93
Jordan	4.56	26	Colombia	3.83	60	Algeria	3.10	94
Portugal	4.54	27	Slovak Republic	3.82	61	Russian Federation	3.02	95
Botswana	4.50	28	Sri Lanka	3.79	62	Venezuela	2.97	96
India	4.47	29	Philippines	3.78	63	Angola	2.95	97
Gambia	4.47	30	Panama	3.76	64	Ukraine	2.84	98
Malaysia	4.46	31	Nigeria	3.75	65	Haiti	2.81	99
France	4.44	32	Egypt	3.72	66	Zimbabwe	2.81	100
Latvia	4.43	33	Uganda	3.69	67	Chad	2.54	101
Tunisia	4.42	34	China	3.68	68	Ethiopia	2.49	102

Table 3. **Environment Subindexes (continued)**

Environment Component = 1/3 Market Environment Subindex + 1/3 Political and Regulatory Subindex Environment + 1/3 Infrastructure Environment Subindex

INFRASTRUCTURE ENVIRONMENT SUBINDEX

COUNTRY	SCORE	RANK	COUNTRY	SCORE	RANK	COUNTRY	SCORE	RANK
Iceland	5.61	1	Hungary	3.72	35	Bolivia	2.59	69
United States	5.55	2	Chile	3.69	36	Romania	2.58	70
Switzerland	5.48	3	Estonia	3.68	37	Senegal	2.57	71
Canada	5.26	4	Argentina	3.64	38	China	2.54	72
Singapore	5.09	5	Croatia	3.62	39	Sri Lanka	2.51	73
Australia	4.95	6	Macedonia, FYR	3.60	40	Guatemala	2.51	74
Norway	4.93	7	Uruguay	3.59	41	Paraguay	2.51	75
New Zealand	4.93	8	Mexico	3.59	42	Tanzania	2.49	76
Korea	4.85	9	South Africa	3.55	43	Mali	2.48	77
Taiwan	4.83	10	Mauritius	3.48	44	Pakistan	2.46	78
Sweden	4.83	11	Lithuania	3.45	45	Ecuador	2.46	79
Denmark	4.80	12	Latvia	3.39	46	Indonesia	2.40	80
Germany	4.65	13	Slovak Republic	3.36	47	Madagascar	2.38	81
France	4.63	14	Jordan	3.35	48	Ukraine	2.29	82
Finland	4.62	15	Costa Rica	3.34	49	Ghana	2.25	83
Hong Kong SAR	4.53	16	Trinidad and Tobago	3.34	50	Bangladesh	2.24	84
Austria	4.49	17	Panama	3.32	51	Nigeria	2.20	85
Luxembourg	4.48	18	Tunisia	3.31	52	Chad	2.19	86
United Kingdom	4.47	19	Botswana	3.26	53	Haiti	2.14	87
Netherlands	4.43	20	Thailand	3.25	54	Uganda	2.11	88
Japan	4.42	21	Turkey	3.20	55	Cameroon	2.08	89
Israel	4.38	22	Poland	3.20	56	Gambia	2.07	90
Namibia	4.27	23	Dominican Republic	3.16	57	Algeria	2.06	91
Greece	4.24	24	Jamaica	3.12	58	Vietnam	2.06	92
Belgium	4.23	25	Venezuela	3.09	59	Mozambique	2.03	93
Italy	4.15	26	Bulgaria	2.97	60	Philippines	1.92	94
Malaysia	4.14	27	Morocco	2.93	61	Zimbabwe	1.81	95
Portugal	4.10	28	El Salvador	2.91	62	Zambia	1.72	96
Malta	3.94	29	Peru	2.82	63	Honduras	1.67	97
Spain	3.91	30	Colombia	2.80	64	Kenya	1.54	98
Slovenia	3.90	31	Egypt	2.76	65	Ethiopia	1.46	99
Ireland	3.89	32	Serbia	2.74	66	Malawi	1.45	100
Czech Republic	3.84	33	India	2.65	67	Nicaragua	1.40	101
Brazil	3.82	34	Russian Federation	2.64	68	Angola	1.30	102

the three principal stakeholders. For example, Singapore ranks high for Business Usage (2) and Government Usage (1) but relatively low for Individual Usage (18). Another notable example is Estonia, with high Government Readiness (15) and Usage (13) but relatively low positions for Individual (26) and Business (39) Usage.

Table 5 gives the detailed results and scores for each of the three subindexes used for measuring Usage. These are listed below.

Individual Usage: Individual Usage gives an indication of the level of adoption and usage of ICT technologies by a nation's citizens. This is done by assessing the deployment of connectivity-enhancing technologies like telephones and Internet connections, levels of Internet usage, and money spent online. The Individual Usage rankings differ significantly from those of Individual Readiness. The top performers here are Luxembourg, Norway, the Netherlands, Switzerland, and Denmark.

Business Usage: Business Usage measures the level of deployment and use of ICT across businesses in a nation. Business usage is determined by factors such as the level of business-to-business and business-to-consumer e-commerce, the use of ICT for activities like marketing, and levels of online transactions. The top five performers are the United States, Singapore, Australia, Sweden, and Denmark.

Government Usage: Government Usage is the level of use of ICT technologies by the government of a given country. The government, besides making ICT a priority, can also benefit from the usage of ICT itself. This usage can help the government streamline services to its citizens and improve its overall functioning. Factors used to measure this include the volume of transactions that businesses have with governments and the presence of government services online. The top ranking countries on this measure are Singapore, the United States, Canada, Hong Kong SAR, and Denmark. Of note is Malaysia at 7th place and Estonia at 13th place, reflecting the fact that these countries' governments are taking active steps to promote ICT usage in their own functions.

Understanding Networked Readiness

The degree of networked readiness of a nation is the result of a multitude of effects. Our research started with a set of over 90 different variables or indicators for evaluating networked readiness. These 90 variables were narrowed down by statistical analysis to a set of 48 variables (see chapter entitled "The Networked Readiness Index: Methodology" later in this book). These 48 variables were grouped amongst the nine subindexes of the NRI framework. This provides us with an opportunity to study some of the interrelationships across the variables and the components/subindexes of the NRI framework.

Table 4. Readiness Subindexes

Readiness Component = 1/3 Individual Readiness Subindex + 1/3 Business Readiness Subindex + 1/3 Government Readiness Subindex

INDIVIDUAL READINESS SUBINDEX

COUNTRY	SCORE	RANK	COUNTRY	SCORE	RANK	COUNTRY	SCORE	RANK
Norway	6.53	1	Malta	4.74	35	El Salvador	3.96	69
Sweden	6.41	2	Ukraine	4.73	36	Zimbabwe	3.95	70
Denmark	6.05	3	Slovak Republic	4.73	37	Indonesia	3.94	71
Finland	5.98	4	Portugal	4.70	38	Egypt	3.91	72
United States	5.89	5	Poland	4.62	39	Vietnam	3.90	73
Australia	5.71	6	Bulgaria	4.62	40	Botswana	3.87	74
United Kingdom	5.66	7	Romania	4.57	41	Paraguay	3.84	75
Iceland	5.63	8	Uruguay	4.53	42	Algeria	3.79	76
Canada	5.59	9	Croatia	4.52	43	Namibia	3.76	77
Switzerland	5.56	10	Thailand	4.47	44	Morocco	3.68	78
France	5.53	11	Argentina	4.46	45	Honduras	3.66	79
Netherlands	5.48	12	Chile	4.45	46	India	3.65	80
Austria	5.47	13	Malaysia	4.43	47	Ecuador	3.65	81
Japan	5.44	14	Trinidad and Tobago	4.39	48	Ghana	3.62	82
New Zealand	5.37	15	Costa Rica	4.37	49	Zambia	3.54	83
Belgium	5.29	16	Macedonia, FYR	4.34	50	Kenya	3.54	84
Taiwan	5.26	17	Panama	4.25	51	Guatemala	3.52	85
Estonia	5.21	18	Colombia	4.25	52	Cameroon	3.51	86
Germany	5.21	19	Mexico	4.22	53	Nicaragua	3.50	87
Ireland	5.19	20	Jordan	4.21	54	Angola	3.49	88
Korea	5.18	21	Mauritius	4.19	55	Pakistan	3.26	89
Singapore	5.15	22	Tunisia	4.18	56	Nigeria	3.20	90
Italy	5.13	23	Serbia	4.17	57	Bangladesh	3.19	91
Hong Kong SAR	5.12	24	Turkey	4.16	58	Haiti	3.19	92
Latvia	5.08	25	Brazil	4.13	59	Malawi	3.19	93
Israel	5.07	26	Venezuela	4.12	60	Tanzania	3.12	94
Greece	5.06	27	Jamaica	4.12	61	Senegal	3.12	95
Luxembourg	5.04	28	China	4.06	62	Madagascar	3.08	96
Spain	5.01	29	Peru	4.02	63	Uganda	2.80	97
Slovenia	4.99	30	Dominican Republic	3.98	64	Mozambique	2.74	98
Russian Federation	4.92	31	Philippines	3.98	65	Mali	2.67	99
Lithuania	4.86	32	Bolivia	3.98	66	Gambia	2.53	100
Hungary	4.81	33	South Africa	3.97	67	Chad	2.45	101
Czech Republic	4.79	34	Sri Lanka	3.96	68	Ethiopia	2.37	102

BUSINESS READINESS SUBINDEX

COUNTRY	SCORE	RANK	COUNTRY	SCORE	RANK	COUNTRY	SCORE	RANK
Finland	6.49	1	Tunisia	4.72	35	Romania	3.96	69
Sweden	6.35	2	Czech Republic	4.70	36	Bulgaria	3.95	70
United States	6.34	3	Hungary	4.69	37	Macedonia, FYR	3.95	71
Singapore	6.23	4	Malaysia	4.68	38	Ukraine	3.88	72
Switzerland	6.22	5	Brazil	4.66	39	Botswana	3.87	73
Japan	6.15	6	Malta	4.63	40	Vietnam	3.85	74
Denmark	6.02	7	Latvia	4.63	41	Ghana	3.85	75
Norway	5.97	8	Jordan	4.62	42	Senegal	3.81	76
Germany	5.94	9	Russian Federation	4.61	43	Pakistan	3.79	77
Canada	5.90	10	Thailand	4.57	44	Malawi	3.61	78
France	5.89	11	Poland	4.46	45	Gambia	3.61	79
Australia	5.88	12	Morocco	4.43	46	Philippines	3.59	80
Belgium	5.78	13	India	4.43	47	Nigeria	3.56	81
United Kingdom	5.77	14	Dominican Republic	4.40	48	Zimbabwe	3.55	82
Netherlands	5.75	15	Mauritius	4.39	49	Algeria	3.51	83
Iceland	5.62	16	Mexico	4.38	50	Tanzania	3.48	84
Austria	5.55	17	Argentina	4.35	51	Bolivia	3.48	85
New Zealand	5.47	18	Colombia	4.34	52	Zambia	3.46	86
Taiwan	5.40	19	Croatia	4.34	53	Paraguay	3.42	87
Ireland	5.39	20	Uruguay	4.31	54	Serbia	3.40	88
Israel	5.37	21	El Salvador	4.25	55	Kenya	3.30	89
Spain	5.28	22	Turkey	4.25	56	Cameroon	3.26	90
Korea	5.28	23	Jamaica	4.25	57	Ecuador	3.25	91
Slovenia	5.22	24	Costa Rica	4.19	58	Nicaragua	3.23	92
Luxembourg	5.19	25	China	4.13	59	Uganda	3.16	93
Estonia	5.11	26	Egypt	4.10	60	Honduras	2.92	94
Slovak Republic	4.91	27	Peru	4.09	61	Angola	2.87	95
Chile	4.89	28	Indonesia	4.09	62	Bangladesh	2.84	96
Italy	4.89	29	Venezuela	4.07	63	Madagascar	2.80	97
Portugal	4.88	30	Panama	4.05	64	Mali	2.74	98
Hong Kong SAR	4.82	31	Guatemala	4.05	65	Haiti	2.71	99
Lithuania	4.77	32	Sri Lanka	4.04	66	Ethiopia	2.50	100
South Africa	4.72	33	Namibia	4.02	67	Chad	2.40	101
Greece	4.72	34	Trinidad and Tobago	3.98	68	Mozambique	2.36	102

Table 4. **Readiness Subindexes (continued)**
Readiness Component = 1/3 Individual Readiness Subindex + 1/3 Business Readiness Subindex + 1/3 Government Readiness Subindex

GOVERNMENT READINESS SUBINDEX

COUNTRY	SCORE	RANK	COUNTRY	SCORE	RANK	COUNTRY	SCORE	RANK
Singapore	6.17	1	Slovenia	4.51	35	Greece	3.71	69
Finland	5.72	2	Tanzania	4.50	36	Nigeria	3.71	70
United States	5.62	3	Tunisia	4.50	37	Uruguay	3.70	71
France	5.57	4	Lithuania	4.44	38	Indonesia	3.69	72
Canada	5.49	5	Colombia	4.44	39	Ukraine	3.64	73
Malaysia	5.46	6	Belgium	4.41	40	Namibia	3.64	74
Denmark	5.37	7	Croatia	4.40	41	Zambia	3.62	75
Germany	5.36	8	Portugal	4.38	42	Bulgaria	3.61	76
Korea	5.25	9	Slovak Republic	4.36	43	Egypt	3.57	77
United Kingdom	5.19	10	South Africa	4.31	44	Trinidad and Tobago	3.57	78
Ireland	5.14	11	Mexico	4.27	45	Gambia	3.54	79
Taiwan	5.10	12	Poland	4.25	46	Nicaragua	3.53	80
Sweden	5.10	13	China	4.23	47	Serbia	3.52	81
Australia	5.09	14	Latvia	4.19	48	Morocco	3.49	82
Estonia	5.00	15	Dominican Republic	4.16	49	Algeria	3.48	83
Austria	4.95	16	Hungary	4.10	50	Malawi	3.46	84
Japan	4.92	17	Cameroon	4.07	51	Senegal	3.43	85
Chile	4.86	18	Vietnam	4.03	52	Kenya	3.41	86
Netherlands	4.85	19	El Salvador	4.02	53	Mozambique	3.30	87
Mauritius	4.82	20	Botswana	4.00	54	Madagascar	3.26	88
Israel	4.75	21	Uganda	3.99	55	Russian Federation	3.26	89
Thailand	4.74	22	Philippines	3.96	56	Mali	3.17	90
Malta	4.72	23	Pakistan	3.96	57	Macedonia, FYR	3.12	91
Italy	4.72	24	Ghana	3.95	58	Paraguay	2.99	92
Spain	4.71	25	Jamaica	3.95	59	Bangladesh	2.97	93
Brazil	4.70	26	Sri Lanka	3.93	60	Bolivia	2.92	94
Hong Kong SAR	4.69	27	Argentina	3.90	61	Guatemala	2.88	95
Luxembourg	4.65	28	Romania	3.87	62	Haiti	2.85	96
New Zealand	4.65	29	Venezuela	3.86	63	Ecuador	2.69	97
Norway	4.64	30	Costa Rica	3.85	64	Angola	2.49	98
India	4.62	31	Peru	3.79	65	Ethiopia	2.45	99
Iceland	4.60	32	Turkey	3.74	66	Honduras	2.33	100
Switzerland	4.55	33	Jordan	3.73	67	Zimbabwe	2.22	101
Czech Republic	4.53	34	Panama	3.71	68	Chad	2.12	102

GDP and Networked Readiness

Any attempt to use a single measure to approximate the Networked Readiness of a nation would be a simplification. An interesting link to explore is that between NRI and the gross domestic product (GDP) per capita of a country. If one has a closer look at the NRI results, one would find that India, with a GDP per capita of USD 483, has an NRI score of 3.54 and is ranked 45 overall. Nicaragua, with a very similar GDP per capita of USD 485, has, on the other hand, a score of 2.56 and an overall ranking of 94. One thus sees a wide spread in the NRI score for a given GDP per capita. This is only one of many examples that could be cited.

Nevertheless, one can look at the relation between the NRI and GDP per capita in order to obtain a better understanding of trends, and also to identify over- and underperformers with respect to the trend. Figure 3 gives a plot between GDP per capita and the NRI. The partial log regression plot presents a projected trend line. One can note immediately the following points:

- For a given GDP per capita, there is a spread in the NRI scores around the regression plot as presented in Figure 3.

- The impact of GDP seems to be very high at low GDP values, and the NRI score increases rapidly with small increases in GDP.

- Around a GDP per capita of USD 6,000 to 9,000 the curve tapers off and the effect of increasing GDP is much less pronounced. Other factors become more relevant to the NRI score at higher values of GDP per capita.

Countries widely distanced from the regression plot could be examples of underperforming or overperforming countries. Thus one sees that the United States leads the NRI ranking, whereas Luxembourg, with a significantly higher GDP per capita, relatively underperforms on the overall NRI score. Similarly India and Estonia would be overperforming on their NRI scores with respect to their GDP per capita.

Does increased competition increase NRI?

Figure 4 shows the effect of increasing competition in the ICT sector on the ISP (Internet service provider) access charges. Intensity of competition in the ICT Sector is plotted against the ISP access charges, and one sees that there is a decrease in the cost of services with increasing competition. Thus the affordability of ICT services would tend to increase with increased competition.

One would expect that increased affordability of ICT services would stimulate the adoption and usage of ICT by the key stakeholders of the Networked Readiness Framework. Figure 5 plots the number of Internet users per 1,000 inhabitants

Table 5. Usage Subindexes

Usage Component = 1/3 Individual Usage Subindex + Business Usage Subindex + 1/3 Government Usage Subindex

INDIVIDUAL USAGE SUBINDEX

COUNTRY	SCORE	RANK	COUNTRY	SCORE	RANK	COUNTRY	SCORE	RANK
Luxembourg	6.00	1	Spain	2.06	35	India	1.17	69
Norway	5.80	2	Argentina	2.06	36	Jordan	1.17	70
Netherlands	5.44	3	Uruguay	2.02	37	Serbia	1.17	71
Switzerland	5.40	4	Latvia	1.98	38	Philippines	1.16	72
Denmark	4.98	5	Chile	1.97	39	Paraguay	1.13	73
Germany	4.75	6	Costa Rica	1.90	40	Algeria	1.13	74
Sweden	4.66	7	Mauritius	1.86	41	Bolivia	1.12	75
United States	4.63	8	Poland	1.81	42	Morocco	1.12	76
Iceland	4.40	9	Bulgaria	1.80	43	Egypt	1.11	77
Finland	4.19	10	Trinidad and Tobago	1.73	44	Zimbabwe	1.10	78
Canada	4.12	11	Lithuania	1.68	45	Vietnam	1.10	79
Japan	4.12	12	Romania	1.65	46	Nicaragua	1.08	80
Belgium	4.07	13	Jamaica	1.50	47	Madagascar	1.08	81
Australia	3.59	14	Croatia	1.50	48	Cameroon	1.08	82
Korea	3.56	15	Russian Federation	1.48	49	Honduras	1.07	83
Ireland	3.54	16	Panama	1.47	50	Indonesia	1.07	84
Austria	3.53	17	Peru	1.45	51	Haiti	1.07	85
Singapore	3.32	18	Dominican Republic	1.44	52	Senegal	1.06	86
Slovenia	3.30	19	Venezuela	1.43	53	Gambia	1.06	87
Malta	3.26	20	Mexico	1.41	54	Kenya	1.05	88
United Kingdom	3.16	21	China	1.37	55	Pakistan	1.04	89
Hong Kong SAR	3.10	22	Tunisia	1.36	56	Sri Lanka	1.04	90
Israel	3.03	23	South Africa	1.32	57	Tanzania	1.03	91
France	2.85	24	Brazil	1.32	58	Zambia	1.02	92
New Zealand	2.70	25	Macedonia, FYR	1.28	59	Angola	1.02	93
Estonia	2.59	26	Ukraine	1.27	60	Nigeria	1.02	94
Taiwan	2.53	27	El Salvador	1.25	61	Uganda	1.01	95
Portugal	2.51	28	Ecuador	1.25	62	Ghana	1.01	96
Italy	2.49	29	Turkey	1.23	63	Mozambique	1.01	97
Hungary	2.35	30	Colombia	1.22	64	Bangladesh	1.01	98
Malaysia	2.29	31	Thailand	1.21	65	Mali	1.01	99
Greece	2.19	32	Guatemala	1.20	66	Malawi	1.01	100
Slovak Republic	2.15	33	Botswana	1.20	67	Chad	1.00	101
Czech Republic	2.08	34	Namibia	1.19	68	Ethiopia	1.00	102

BUSINESS USAGE SUBINDEX

COUNTRY	SCORE	RANK	COUNTRY	SCORE	RANK	COUNTRY	SCORE	RANK
United States	6.02	1	Slovenia	4.02	35	China	3.43	69
Singapore	5.87	2	Costa Rica	4.01	36	Zimbabwe	3.41	70
Australia	5.85	3	Croatia	3.97	37	Colombia	3.39	71
Sweden	5.71	4	Portugal	3.96	38	Egypt	3.39	72
Denmark	5.44	5	Estonia	3.92	39	Ghana	3.35	73
Switzerland	5.42	6	India	3.92	40	Peru	3.33	74
Israel	5.40	7	Poland	3.88	41	Jamaica	3.32	75
Norway	5.37	8	Latvia	3.86	42	Pakistan	3.29	76
Iceland	5.32	9	Greece	3.86	43	Gambia	3.28	77
Japan	5.20	10	Panama	3.85	44	Uruguay	3.27	78
Finland	5.20	11	Slovak Republic	3.85	45	Russian Federation	3.17	79
Canada	5.12	12	Tunisia	3.81	46	Mozambique	3.14	80
New Zealand	5.08	13	Trinidad and Tobago	3.77	47	Guatemala	3.09	81
Hong Kong SAR	4.79	14	Dominican Republic	3.77	48	Serbia	3.05	82
Netherlands	4.75	15	Turkey	3.72	49	Ecuador	3.05	83
Germany	4.69	16	Lithuania	3.72	50	Zambia	3.04	84
Ireland	4.67	17	Hungary	3.71	51	Bangladesh	3.03	85
Korea	4.62	18	Jordan	3.69	52	Cameroon	3.01	86
Luxembourg	4.62	19	Vietnam	3.69	53	Bulgaria	3.00	87
United Kingdom	4.60	20	Botswana	3.64	54	Malawi	3.00	88
Taiwan	4.50	21	Argentina	3.61	55	Indonesia	2.99	89
Malaysia	4.48	22	Nigeria	3.59	56	Macedonia, FYR	2.99	90
France	4.45	23	Venezuela	3.58	57	Nicaragua	2.98	91
South Africa	4.40	24	Tanzania	3.58	58	Ukraine	2.98	92
Austria	4.37	25	Philippines	3.57	59	Algeria	2.97	93
Belgium	4.36	26	El Salvador	3.55	60	Honduras	2.86	94
Chile	4.18	27	Mauritius	3.52	61	Madagascar	2.85	95
Italy	4.15	28	Senegal	3.52	62	Angola	2.79	96
Malta	4.14	29	Namibia	3.50	63	Paraguay	2.66	97
Czech Republic	4.11	30	Morocco	3.50	64	Bolivia	2.65	98
Brazil	4.08	31	Uganda	3.50	65	Haiti	2.59	99
Mexico	4.05	32	Kenya	3.48	66	Chad	2.59	100
Thailand	4.05	33	Sri Lanka	3.46	67	Ethiopia	2.58	101
Spain	4.04	34	Romania	3.44	68	Mali	2.55	102

Table 5. **Usage Subindexes (continued)**
Usage component index = 1/3 Individual Usage + 1/3 Business Usage + 1/3 Government Usage

GOVERNMENT USAGE SUBINDEX

COUNTRY	SCORE	RANK	COUNTRY	SCORE	RANK	COUNTRY	SCORE	RANK
Singapore	6.45	1	Chile	3.58	35	Nigeria	2.79	69
United States	5.51	2	Tunisia	3.55	36	Trinidad and Tobago	2.79	70
Canada	5.38	3	Pakistan	3.53	37	Senegal	2.77	71
Hong Kong SAR	5.29	4	Jamaica	3.51	38	El Salvador	2.76	72
Denmark	5.05	5	Romania	3.45	39	Mozambique	2.76	73
Taiwan	4.83	6	Netherlands	3.42	40	Zambia	2.74	74
Malaysia	4.56	7	Spain	3.41	41	Bulgaria	2.71	75
Finland	4.51	8	Luxembourg	3.40	43	Panama	2.71	76
Israel	4.49	9	Portugal	3.40	42	Costa Rica	2.69	77
Korea	4.48	10	Egypt	3.37	44	Poland	2.67	78
Sweden	4.45	11	Turkey	3.33	45	Peru	2.65	79
Germany	4.43	12	Uganda	3.30	46	Cameroon	2.62	80
Estonia	4.42	13	Morocco	3.27	47	Uruguay	2.59	81
Japan	4.36	14	Argentina	3.25	48	Madagascar	2.58	82
Austria	4.32	15	Hungary	3.22	49	Namibia	2.55	83
France	4.29	16	Vietnam	3.22	50	Ecuador	2.53	84
Malta	4.29	17	Brazil	3.16	51	Ukraine	2.52	85
United Kingdom	4.20	18	Serbia	3.13	52	Venezuela	2.47	86
Ireland	4.17	19	Latvia	3.11	53	Malawi	2.44	87
Australia	4.16	20	Slovenia	3.08	54	Macedonia, FYR	2.43	88
China	4.12	21	Gambia	3.08	55	Algeria	2.42	89
New Zealand	3.92	22	Tanzania	3.07	56	Dominican Republic	2.40	90
Iceland	3.84	23	Slovak Republic	3.06	57	Bangladesh	2.37	91
Thailand	3.76	24	Botswana	3.04	58	Ethiopia	2.36	92
Mauritius	3.75	25	Greece	3.04	59	Guatemala	2.27	93
India	3.73	26	Indonesia	3.00	60	Mali	2.24	94
South Africa	3.72	27	Czech Republic	3.00	61	Angola	2.23	95
Mexico	3.70	28	Sri Lanka	2.97	62	Bolivia	2.02	96
Philippines	3.68	29	Lithuania	2.96	63	Nicaragua	2.02	97
Norway	3.64	30	Croatia	2.89	64	Honduras	1.99	98
Switzerland	3.64	31	Kenya	2.85	65	Paraguay	1.94	99
Belgium	3.64	32	Russian Federation	2.84	66	Zimbabwe	1.71	100
Jordan	3.64	33	Ghana	2.82	67	Chad	1.57	101
Italy	3.59	34	Colombia	2.82	68	Haiti	1.48	102

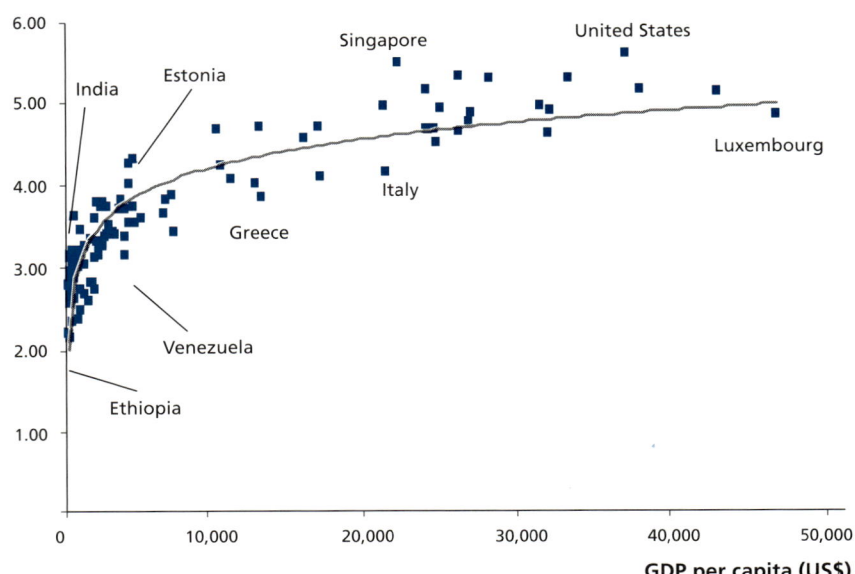

Figure 3. **Networked Readiness 2003–2004 vs Gross Domestic Product per Capita, Partial Log Regression**

Source: Authors' analysis of data from the World Bank

Figure 4. **Competition in the ICT Sector Gives Rise to Affordability of Services, Partial Logarithmic Regression**

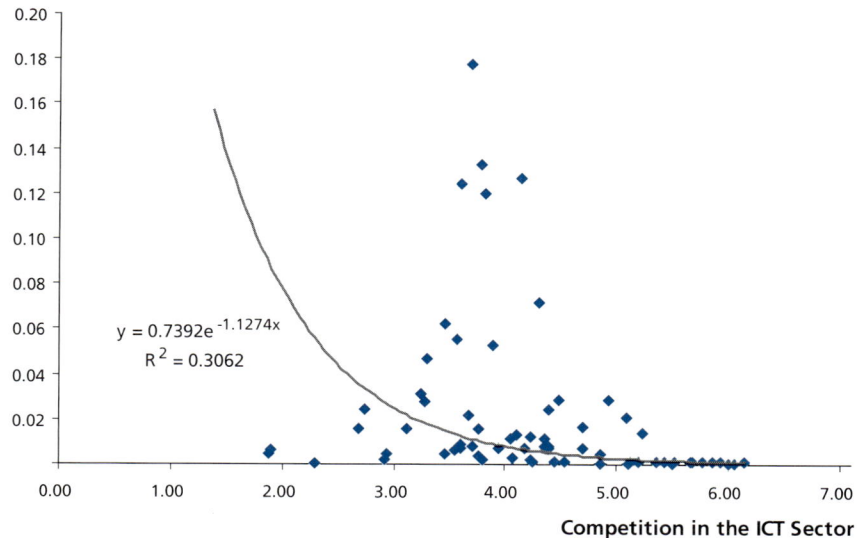

Internet service provider access charges (US$ per 30 off-peak hours) adjusted by GDP per capita

$y = 0.7392e^{-1.1274x}$

$R^2 = 0.3062$

Competition in the ICT Sector

Source: Authors' analysis of data from the World Economic Forum and The World Bank

Figure 5. **Internet Users per 1,000 inhabitants and Networked Readiness, Partial Logarithmic Regression**

Internet users per 1,000 inhabitants

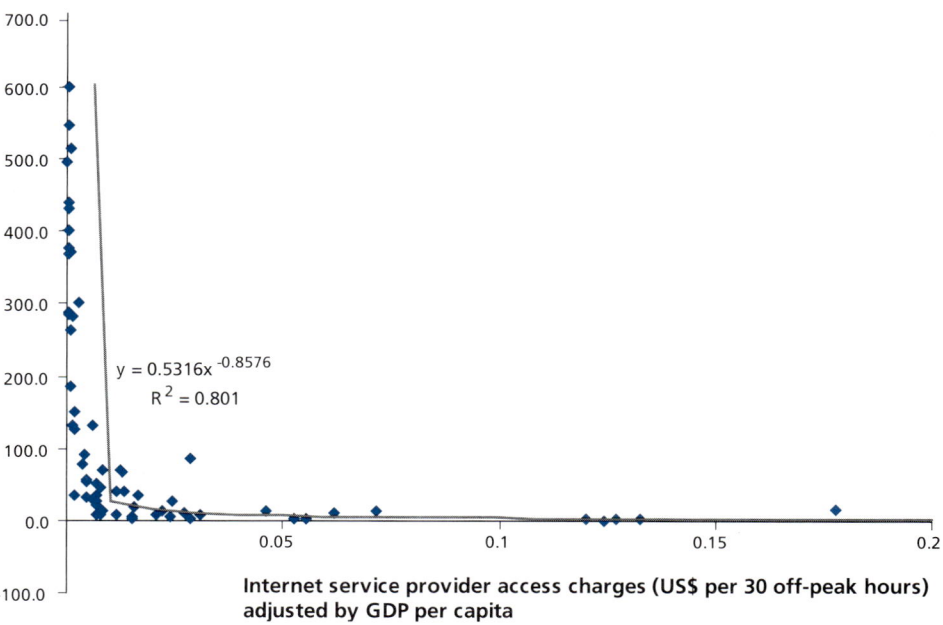

$y = 0.5316x^{-0.8576}$

$R^2 = 0.801$

Internet service provider access charges (US$ per 30 off-peak hours) adjusted by GDP per capita

Source: Authors' analysis of data from the World Bank

as a function of the ISP access charge adjusted by GDP per capita. One sees a decrease in the number of Internet users with increasing ISP access charges. Thus nations with more affordable ICT services would tend to have higher levels of ICT readiness and usage for their key stakeholders. This should lead to a higher level of NRI for the nation.

In Figure 6, the number of Internet users per 1,000 inhabitants is plotted against the overall NRI of a country. One sees that as the number of Internet users increases, there is a trend towards an increase in the NRI.

Plotting the intensity of ICT competition against the NRI provides a very interesting result as can be seen in Figure

Figure 6. **Internet Users per 1,000 Inhabitants and Networked Readiness, Partial Logarithmic Regression**

Networked Readiness score

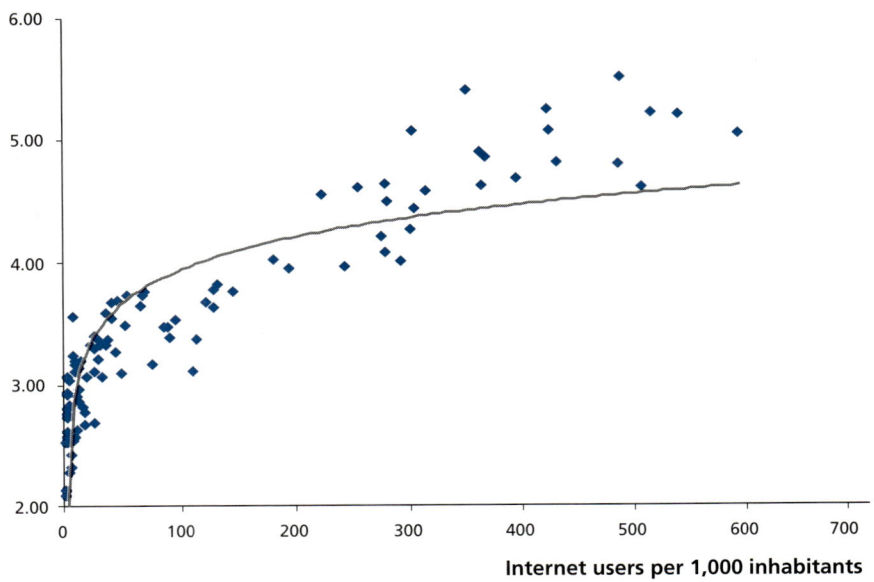

Internet users per 1,000 inhabitants

Sources: Authors' analysis of data from the World Economic Forum and from the World Bank

7. The NRI is seen to increase steadily as the degree of competition in the ICT sector increases. Thus one impact of policy on the NRI is clear. Competition in the ICT sector makes services more affordable, and the more affordable a service becomes, the more it is used by the key stakeholders—individuals, businesses, and governments. The increased readiness and usage of ICT increases the NRI of a country.

Our research provides empirical support for policymakers seeking to enhance their ICT competitiveness and overall levels of NRI; a key is to promote competition in the local ICT sector. An example of a country having followed this route is Japan. Japan's incumbent operator NTT actively promoted ISDN service, and reached significant penetration. At that moment, the government encouraged competition for entry by unbundling the local loop and, as a result, numerous players entered with DSL service. The result was a sharp decline in prices to half that of the incumbent NTT's initial offering, and a rapid take-off in the adoption of DSL. Japan today has one of the world's most competitive and cheapest broadband services. The uptake has grown exponentially since DSL was introduced.

Is there a threshold for Usage to take off?

One would expect the Readiness and Usage scores of a nation to move hand-in-hand. A country having a high degree of Readiness should be able to transform this ICT capability into usage statistics, and hence show a consequent high score on the Usage component index. For instance, the United States is among the highest in terms of Readiness component

index scores, and one sees this readiness translating into real ICT usage, as represented by high Usage scores (see Figure 8).

If one has a closer look at the trend of Readiness versus Usage, at lower values of Readiness, one sees that Usage remains rather flat with initial increases in Readiness. This leads us to believe that there is a threshold to Readiness: a country needs to have a certain level of Readiness with regards to ICT before there can be an effective usage of ICT, and a consequent impact. A certain critical mass in terms of number of users, or the availability of narrowband and broadband services, or of services online is essential before this is reflected in usage metrics. This is reflected in Figure 8.

- Haiti, with a Readiness score of 2.92, has a low Usage score of 1.71 and has still to increase its Readiness before Usage starts increasing significantly.

- Uganda is an over performer below the threshold level. It has a Readiness score of 3.32 and a corresponding Usage level of 2.60.

- Luxembourg and France find themselves above the threshold level. While Luxembourg overperforms, France has a lower Usage level than expected.

Evolution of the NRI over time

The Networked Readiness of a nation is a dynamic measure, and it evolves over time as a result of policy measures taken by government and business leaders, and as a result of changes occurring in the global environment. Looking at the changes in NRI rankings over time (see Table 6), one observes that 15 countries have shared the 10 top positions.

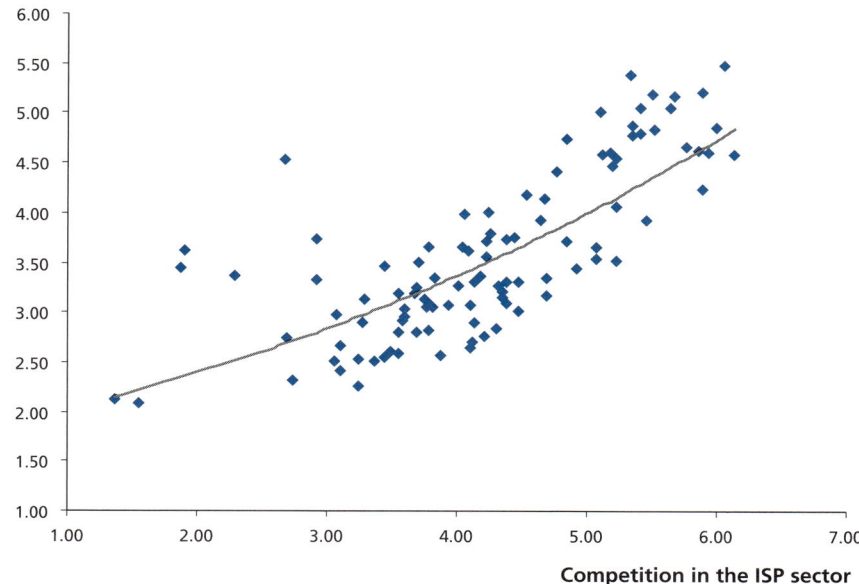

Figure 7. **Competition Promotes Networked Readiness, Partial Logarithmic Regression**

Networked Readiness Index score

Competition in the ISP sector

Sources: Authors' analysis of data from the World Economic Forum and from the World Bank

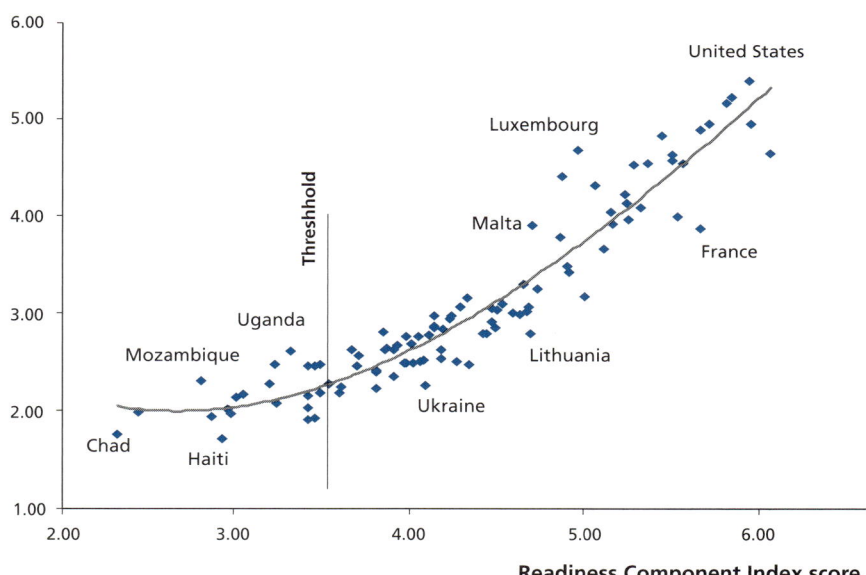

Figure 8. **Usage vs Readiness Component Indexes**

Usage Component Index score

Readiness Component Index score

Source: Technology Management Department, INSEAD

The United States and Finland have consistently been in the top three positions, whereas Singapore has rapidly progressed from 8th place in 2001–2002, to 3rd place in 2002–2003, and is currently in 2nd place.

Another constant is the performance of the northern European countries, with Finland, Sweden, Denmark, Norway, and Iceland present in the top 10 places in each of the three years.

One must add a note of caution to this analysis because the results of the three different research efforts are not directly comparable. The framework used in the 2001–2002 study is different (see Schwab et al 2002). Moreover, while the framework and methodology of analysis of the 2002–2003 and the 2003–2004 studies are identical, the underlying data variables used differ to a certain extent. This is in order to accomodate the larger set of countries considered in the current analysis and the availability of reliable and up-to-date information.

Table 6. Evolution of Networked Readiness from 2001–2003

Country	2003–2004	2002–2003	2001–2002
United States	1	2	1
Singapore	2	3	8
Finland	3	1	3
Sweden	4	4	4
Denmark	5	8	7
Canada	6	6	12
Switzerland	7	13	16
Norway	8	17	5
Australia	9	15	14
Iceland	10	5	2

The Digital Divide—Increasing or Decreasing?

The subject of digital divides across and within nations has received a lot of attention over the last years. Since ICT is seen as an important enabler of productivity and growth, leaders from business and government have embarked upon several plans to increase the adoption and usage of ICT among the key stakeholders—individuals, businesses, and governments.

In this context, frequently evoked questions have concerned changes in the digital divide: are the differences in the levels of digital development amongst nations increasing or decreasing? Is there a convergence or divergence in the digital divide?

Figure 9 shows the plot of the NRIs for the years 2002–2003 and 2003–2004 in descending order of NRI. The trend lines for the two sets of NRI are plotted also. The spread (distance between the higher and lower ends of the trend line) of the NRI is seen to decrease from the year 2002–2003 to the year 2003–2004, and this indicates a decrease in the digital divide across nations.

Figure 10 plots the weighted average NRI by region, normalized by taking the score of Africa (the region with the lowest NRI each year as 1). One sees that from 2001–2002 to the current study of 2003–2004, the weighted average NRI scores are tending to converge, indicating that the NRI of major regions of the world are converging over time.

Research Challenges

Finding the Facts

Lack of accurate and reliable data can pose seemingly insurmountable roadblocks to the implementation of even the best laid out frameworks. The goal of our research and analysis has been to provide a scientific and credible interpretation of reality. Thus, an important step in our research has been to collect a complete and high quality set of data relating to ICT. We used two types of data in our research: soft data, which are subjective data gathered from questionnaires (managed by the World Economic Forum as part of their research for the Global Competitiveness Report), and hard data, which are driven by statistics collected by international multilateral agencies (such as the World Bank and ITU). Both these sets of data play a crucial role in the overall analysis. The soft data are critical in determining the opinion of the decision makers and influencers who are intimately familiar with a nation's economy and ICT usage. On the other hand, the hard data capture fundamental elements related to the development of infrastructure, human capital and ICT.

Absence of Key Usage Metrics: Key ICT areas such as mobile telephony and the Internet are still undergoing rapid development. Owing to this, accurate and up-to-date usage metrics are difficult to obtain. For example, metrics on cost savings realized, on key measures of policy and regulation, and on the use of ICT by governments remain elusive.

Selection of Countries: The use of objective and reliable data is critical in preparing a report of this type. Availability of data has in fact been a key factor in selecting the 102 countries that form part of this study. As a consequence, regions suffering from a chronic lack of reliable statistics such as Africa and Central Asia find themselves underrepresented in the NRI index.

Ensuring Statistical Significance: Once solid and reliable facts had been accumulated, a comprehensive statistical analysis was conducted. Following the classic steps of any such analysis, correlation and factor analyses were conducted to determine interrelationships amongst variables and to drop variables if necessary. The variables were then classified along the lines of the NRI framework.

Data Estimation: Despite our best efforts to collect data from all major international sources, it has been necessary at times to cope with incomplete sets of data for the countries under consideration. In order to compensate for this, statistical procedures have been used to estimate missing data: mainly regression and clustering techniques. Control procedures and checks have been devised to ensure that estimations were reasonable and not overly favorable or disadvantageous in their representation of the countries in question.

Calculating the Index: In order to calculate the index, the data were first transformed on a scale of 1 to 7, in order that each piece of information would have an equal weight. Next, each of the subindexes was computed as the mathematical average of the variables composing it. The same approach was used to calculate the component indexes, averaging the subindexes. Finally, the NRI was computed as an average of the three component indexes. Details are provided in the technical appendix and in the later chapter titled "The Networked Readiness Index: Methodology."

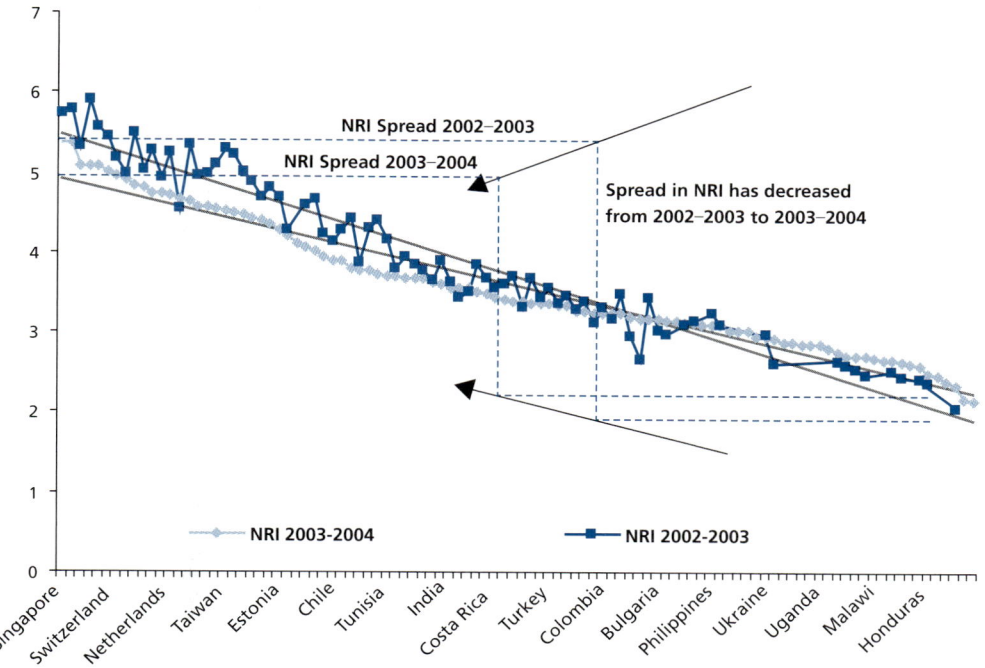

Figure 9. **Digital Convergence or Divergence?**

Networked Readiness score

Source: Technology Management Department, INSEAD

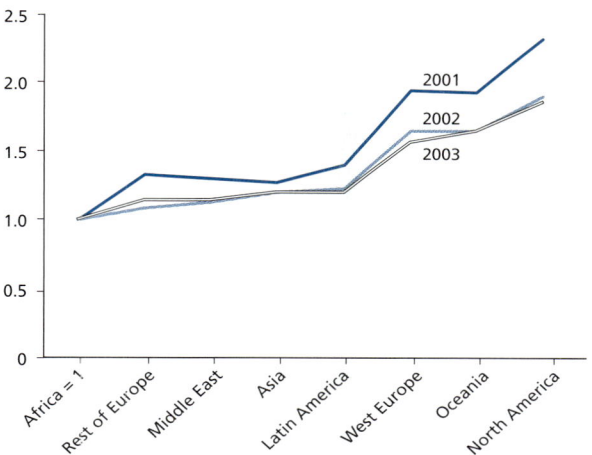

Figure 10. **Regional Weighted NRI, 3-Year Trend With Africa = 1**

The weighted average NRI is calculated as per the following formula: Weighted average NRI of Region = ($\sum$(NRI of Country*Population of country))/ Population of the region) over all the countries in the given region.

Source: Technology Management Department, INSEAD

Summary

Networked Readiness is a complex phenomena and the sum of diverse and interrelated forces. Measuring a country's Networked Readiness remains a significant challenge, and any framework or model representing Networked Readiness is a simplified representation at best. Further, limitations in the availability of reliable and current data restrict the measurement of the phenomena to a subset of countries, and also to a small number of the underlying forces.

Nevertheless the Networked Readiness Framework and Index are useful tools for key policy decision makers charting a country's strategic direction in order to enhance national competitiveness. The NRI Framework attempts to interpret the underlying complexity of the development and use of ICT in an intuitive and easy-to-comprehend model. The overall NRI is a summary measure of a nation's ability to participate in and benefit from ICT developments. The NRI provides guidance to business leaders and public policymakers for enhancing the impact of ICT on important stakeholders—individuals, businesses, and governments.

Governments and policymakers can have significant impact on the adoption and usage of ICT. For example, our research has demonstrated that promoting competition and deregulation in the ICT sector leads to decreasing service costs, and that lowered costs result in an increase in consumption of services.

The NRI allows a nation to benchmark its ICT performance, and to determine the effectiveness of policy. It also permits a country to learn from the policy and performance of other countries with similar profiles, and to identify best practice. The NRI serves to highlight the areas of over- and underperformance of a given country as compared to a similar set of countries, and to provide best practice examples.

Overperforming countries have put ICT on the national agenda, and have striven to make it an area of excellence, whereas other underperforming nations have not done so. The former countries have succeeded in going beyond individual measures of national income, or national ICT spending, in an effort to provide an optimal Environment for ICT development, thus promoting high levels of Readiness and Usage within all three key stakeholders. The United States, Singapore, and Finland are such leaders, and can serve as role models for other nations in their quest for ICT excellence.

Endnotes

1 For more information on the development of the Networked Readiness Framework and other efforts in the domain, refer to Dutta and Jain, "Networked Readiness of Nations" in Dutta et al 2003.

2 While the Networked Readiness Framework for 2003–2004 is identical to that used in 2002–2003, it is important to note that the underlying variables have evolved. The increase in the number of countries included in the NRI rankings from 82 in 2002–2003 to 102 this year limits the number of variables that can be considered. The research methodology imposes a 65 percent observation rate for each variable over the 102 countries. Variables with fewer observations than this have been dropped.

3 Oceania includes Australia and New Zealand.

4 For example, overall second ranked Singapore does well on the Readiness component index (4), supported by a strong Government Readiness (1) and Business Readiness (4), even though it has a relatively modest performance on Individual Readiness (22). See Table 4.

References

Dutta, S., B. Lanvin and F. Paua, eds. 2003. *The Global Information Technology Report 2002–2003: Readiness for the Networked World*. New York: Oxford University Press.

International Telecommunication Union. 2002. *World Telecommunication Indicators*. Online. http://www.itu.int/home/index.html

Kirkman, G., P. Cornelius, J. Sachs, and K. Schwab, eds. 2002. *The Global Information Technology Report 2001–2002: Readiness for the Networked World*. New York: Oxford University Press.

Organisation for Economic Co-operation and Development. 2001. *Science, Technology and Industry Outlook: Drivers of Growth: Information Technology, Innovation, and Entrepreneurship*. Online. http://www1.oecd.org/publications/e-book/9201131e.pdf

Pilat, D. and F. C. Lee. 2001. *Productivity Growth in ICT-Producing and ICT-Using Industries: A Source of Growth Differentials in the OECD?* Online. http://www.oecd.org

Schwab, K., M. Porter, J. Sachs, P. Cornelius, and J. McArthur, eds. 2002. *The Global Competitiveness Report 2001–2002*. New York: Oxford University Press.

United Nations Development Programme. 2001. *Human Development Report: Making New Technologies Work for Human Development*. New York: Oxford University Press.

Van Ark, B. 2001. *The Renewal of the Old Economy: An International Comparative Perspective*. Online. http://www.oecd.org

World Bank Group. 2002. *World Development Indicators 2001*. Online. http://www.worldbank.org/data/wdi/index.htm

Technical Appendix
Constructing the Networked Readiness Index

Definitions of the Networked Readiness Index, Component Indexes, and Subindexes

The Networked Readiness Index separates Environmental factors from ICT Readiness and Usage, and hence there are three component indexes. Starting from a set of over 90 ICT related variables, we have divided these variables amongst the 9 subindexes. We then eliminated variables on the basis of number of countries for which data were available and used analytical procedures such as correlation analysis. Our final index computation is based on a set of 48 variables.[†]

The Networked Readiness Index is defined as follows:
Networked Readiness Index = 1/3 Environment + 1/3 Readiness + 1/3 Usage

I. The Environment component index is defined as follows:
Environment Component = 1/3 Market Environment Subindex + 1/3 Political and Regulatory Environment Subindex + 1/3 Infrastructure Environment Subindex

I.1. Market Environment Subindex is defined by the following variables:
1.01   State of cluster development, 2003
1.02   Venture capital availability, 2003
1.03   Subsidies for firm-level R&D, 2003
1.04   Quality of scientific research institutions, 2003
1.05   Availability of scientists and engineers, 2003
1.06   Brain drain, 2003
1.07   Utility patents, 2002
1.08   ICT manufactured exports, 2001
1.09   ICT service exports, 2001

I.2. Political and Regulatory Environment Subindex is defined by the following variables:
2.01   Overall administrative burden, 2003
2.02   Quality of the legal system, 2003
2.03   Laws relating to ICT, 2003
2.04   Competition in the ISP sector, 2003
2.05   Foreign ownership restrictions, 2003
2.06   Efficiency of the tax system, 2003
2.07   Freedom of the press, 2003

I.3. Infrastructure Environment Subindex is defined by the following variables:
3.01   Overall infrastructure quality, 2003
3.02   Waiting time for telephone lines, 2000
3.03   Telephone mainlines, 2001
3.04   Public pay telephones, 2001
3.05   Internet servers, 2001

[†]Our research used the most recent data available from the concerned sources e.g., the Executive Opinion Survey 2003 from the World Economic Forum and data from the World Bank and International Telecommunication Union.

II. The Readiness component index is defined as follows:

Readiness Component = 1/3 Individual Readiness Subindex + 1/3 Business Readiness Subindex + 1/3 Government Readiness Subindex

II.1. Individual Readiness Subindex is defined by the following variables:

1.01   Public expenditure on education, 2000

1.02   Adult illiteracy, 2001

1.03   Tertiary enrollment, 2001

1.04   Radios, 2001

1.05   Television sets, 2001

1.06   Households online, 2001

1.07   Quality of math and science education, 2003

1.08   Affordability of local fixed line calls, 2001

1.09   Affordability of Internet telephone access, 2001

1.10   Affordability of Internet service provider fees, 2001

II.2. Business Readiness Subindex is defined by the following variables:

2.01   Ease of obtaining telephone lines, 2003

2.02   Cost of business phone subscription, 2002

2.03   Extent of staff training, 2003

2.04   Quality of business schools, 2003

2.05   Scientists and engineers in R&D, 2000

II.3. Government Readiness Subindex is defined by the following variables:

3.01   Government prioritization of ICT, 2003

3.02   Government procurement of ICT, 2003

3.03   Government online presence, 2003

III. The Usage component index is defined as follows:

Usage Component = 1/3 Individual Usage Subindex +1/3 Business Usage Subindex + 1/3 Government Usage Subindex

III.1. Individual Usage Subindex is defined by the following variables:

1.01   Personal computers, 2001

1.02   ISDN subscribers, 2001

1.03   Cable television subscribers, 2001

1.04   Internet users, 2001

III.2. Business Usage Subindex is defined by the following variables:

2.01   Computers installed in businesses, 2002

2.02   Firm-level technology absorption, 2003

2.03   Prevalence of foreign technology licensing, 2003

III.3. Government Usage Subindex is defined by the following variables:

3.01   Government success in ICT promotion, 2003

3.02   Government online services, 2003

Chapter 2

Global Diffusion of ICT:
A Progress Report

Fiona Paua, World Economic Forum

The views expressed here are the author's personal opinions and do not necessarily reflect those of the World Economic Forum. The author wishes to acknowledge invaluable research assistance from Catherine Vindret, Saadia Zahidi, and Victor Echevarria Icaza.

"Bridging the digital divide in and among countries has assumed a critical importance on our respective national agendas. Everyone should be able to enjoy access to information and communications networks."

"Okinawa Charter on Global Information Society," adopted at the G-8 summit meeting in Okinawa and Kyushu, July 2000

Recognizing the potential of information and communication technologies (ICT) for accelerating economic development and enhancing the lives of individuals, the international community has stressed the importance of improving access to technologies, particularly in the developing world. Attention to this issue reached a turning point in 2000, when the G-8 Digital Opportunity Taskforce (DOT Force) was created to focus on bridging the digital divide. It was also at this time that the World Economic Forum initiated work on the first *Global Information Technology Report*,[1] which focused on assessing the preparedness of individuals, businesses, and governments to participate in, and benefit more fully from, the global networked world.

Since 2000, however, much has changed in the global political, economic, and technological landscape. International geopolitical tensions have escalated at the same time that the engines of economic growth have slowed in many parts of the world. Meanwhile, the technology sector has undergone massive and widespread consolidation and restructuring, including painful reassessment of investment strategies and product deployment. Only recently have we begun to see the recovery of the global economy and signs of increased activity in the technology sector.

On the occasion of the World Summit for Information Society meetings to be held in Geneva (2003) and the launching of the third edition of the *Global Information Technology Report*, it is fitting to examine what has been accomplished in the last three years. Although a three-year time frame would appear short in most cases, it is a reasonable time frame when viewed in the context of the dynamism of ICT diffusion in the world.

The purpose of this progress report is to evaluate recent performance and ascertain the implications of the work that lies ahead. What is the global picture of the diffusion of ICT? What has been accomplished in the last three years? Which countries are performing well and which are lagging? How much remains to be done? What lessons can we glean?

This progress report is about access to ICT. It focuses on assessing the spread of key information and communication technologies. It examines the pervasiveness of Internet use in the world and traces the diffusion of personal computers, main telephone lines, cellular mobile telephones, television receivers, cable television, and home satellite antennas.

Among the important uses of these technologies is as tools for transmitting information that can be relevant for development purposes. But beyond the transmission of information, these same tools, when networked, enhance individual, firm, and national productivity, broaden the market access of entrepreneurs and businesses, and improve government service delivery. Significantly, these devices can improve overall individual well-being and transform the interaction between and among various stakeholders in society, transcending geographical and other boundaries.

This progress report analyzes information from the International Telecommunication Union (ITU),[2] which produces the most extensive database on relevant indicators. The database contains several decades' information for more than 200 countries and territories and is an excellent source not just because of the breadth of its scope, but also for the comparability of the data. The current analysis relates to data for 1999–2002 for 200 of the world's economies covering 99.98 percent of the world's population. Seven indicators are included: the number of Internet users (estimated), personal computers, main telephone lines in operation,[3] cellular mobile telephone subscribers[4] and, to a lesser extent, television receivers, cable television subscribers, and home satellite antennas. The data, although ending in 2002, appear to reflect the most current world status of these indicators.

The types of ICT assessed in this chapter were determined primarily by the availability of data. The selection does not, in any way, assert that these devices represent the technologies most relevant for the developmental requirements of countries worldwide. Indeed, beyond the scope of this report are other very important dimensions of the issue of ICT access, such as identifying appropriate technologies and relevant applications and ensuring affordability and ease of use, being particularly mindful of varied linguistic and learning capabilities.

Employing disaggregated data, this analysis is conducted at the global, regional, and country levels. The first part of the analysis focuses on the global picture, defining eight prevailing trends. The second part presents regional profiles that capture those countries that are significantly improving ICT access and those countries that are lagging behind. The third part of the analysis highlights policy considerations that are most relevant to promoting ICT access.

Part I. The Global Picture

Eight key findings sketch the global picture: (1) growth in ICT diffusion has been dramatic, with cellular mobile telephone subscribers exceeding the number of main telephone lines

Table 1. **Increase in Global ICT Diffusion at a Glance, 1999–2002**

	1999	2002	1999–2002 Increase	
	(in millions)	(in millions)	(in millions)	(in percent)
Population	5,962	6,192	229	4
Households	1,484	1,552	68	5
Internet users (estimated)	276	605	329	119
Personal computers	394	550	157	40
Main telephone lines in operation	906	1,098	192	21
Cellular mobile telephone subscribers	493	1,155	662	134
Television receivers	1,573	1,775	202	13
Cable television subscribers	288	359	71	25
Home satellite antennas	78	97	19	24

	% of Total population		% of Total households	
	1999	2002	1999	2002
Internet users (estimated)	5	10	19	39
Personal computers	7	9	27	35
Main telephone lines in operation	15	18	61	71
Cellular mobile telephone subscribers	8	19	33	74
Television receivers	26	29	106	114
Cable television subscribers	5	6	19	23
Home satellite antennas	1	2	5	6

	Ratio to population		Ratio to households	
	1999	2002	1999	2002
Internet users (estimated)	1 in 22	1 in 10	1 in 5	1 in 3
Personal computers	1 in 15	1 in 11	1 in 4	1 in 3
Main telephone lines in operation	1 in 7	1 in 6	1 in 2	1 in 1
Cellular mobile telephone subscribers	1 in 12	1 in 5	1 in 3	1 in 1
Television receivers	1 in 4	1 in 3	1 in 1	1 in 1
Cable television subscribers	1 in 21	1 in 17	1 in 5	1 in 4
Home satellite antennas	1 in 77	1 in 64	1 in 19	1 in 16

Source: Author's calculations based on data from the International Telecommunication Union, World Telecommunication Indicators Database, accessed July 2003

and with Internet users exceeding the number of personal computers; (2) the largest increases in ICT diffusion are in the most populous countries; (3) some of the fastest rates of growth and most sizeable increases in diffusion are in developing economies; (4) the best penetration rates are still in advanced economies with relatively small populations; (5) the less developed economies still have the poorest ICT penetration rates; (6) despite the dramatic increases in diffusion of ICT in the most populous countries, it is also in these very same countries where most of the work still needs to be done; and finally, (8) the "divide" in ICT access has narrowed but low income, particularly severely indebted economies in sub-Saharan Africa, still lag considerably.

1. Growth in global ICT diffusion has been dramatic.

While much remains to be done, it is indisputable that the diffusion of ICT access has been nothing less than dramatic over the three years under study. This improvement in ICT access has been achieved despite consolidation in the technology sector and an overall global economic growth slowdown.

The greatest dynamism was exhibited by the growth of cellular mobile telephone subscribers and the increase in the number of Internet users (see Table 1). Of the 6.2 billion people in the world, 1 in every 5 is a cellular mobile telephone subscriber, up from 1 in every 12 three years ago. In this period, the number of cellular mobile telephone subscribers grew 134 percent, outpacing the 21 percent growth of the number of main telephone lines in operation. Since 1999, there have been 662 million additional cellular mobile telephone subscribers, many more than the 192 million main lines added during the same period. As of 2002, the number of cellular mobile telephone subscribers (1.15 billion) exceeded the number of main telephone lines in operation (1.10 billion). Appendix 1 lists by income the 125 economies where the number of cellular mobile telephone subscribers exceeds the number of main telephone lines in operation. As

the table highlights, at least 85 of the 125 economies are from middle income and low income countries.[5]

The number of Internet users also multiplied exponentially—119 percent over the last three years. Since 1999, the world has added 329 million more Internet users, bringing the total estimated number of Internet users to 605 million as of 2002. This means that 10 percent or 1 person in every 10 in the world is an Internet user. Significantly, the number of Internet users in the world has exceeded the number of personal computers. There were 550 million personal computers in the world as of 2002, up 40 percent from nearly 400 million in 1999.

Television, however, retains the distinction of being the most pervasive device. There are 1.8 billion television receivers in the world, or 1 for every 3 persons and almost 1 for every household. Coming from a fairly high base, growth in television receivers was 13 percent over the last three years; in numerical terms, that is 202 million more television receivers, a figure higher than the increase in the number of main telephone lines in operation during the same period. But access to cable television and home satellite antennas remains limited. As of 2002, there were about 360 million cable television subscribers in the world, equivalent to 1 subscriber for every 4 households and 1 subscriber in every 17 persons. Meanwhile, home satellite antennas numbered 97 million in 2002, or 1 for every 16 households and 1 for every 64 persons. Both cable television and home satellite antennas grew at a comparable pace, about 25 percent for the three-year period.

2. The largest increases in ICT diffusion came from the most populous countries.

A large proportion of the improvement in ICT diffusion came from some of the most populous countries of the world (see Table 2). For the period 1999–2002, China is the most outstanding performer, posting the highest increase in many of the indicators. The country posted the highest increase in the number of main telephone lines in operation, cellular mobile telephone subscribers, television receivers, and cable

Table 2. **Increases in ICT Diffusion in the 7 Most Populous Countries, 1999–2002**

2002 Population (in millions)	Country	Increases, 1999–2002* (in millions)				
		Internet users (estimated)	Personal computers	Main telephone lines	Cellular mobile telephone subscribers	Television receivers
1,285	China	50	10	106	163	40
1,042	India	14	3	15	11	10
288	United States	53	37	6	55	34
212	Indonesia	7	0	2	9	2
174	Brazil	11	7	14	20	4
149	Pakistan	1	0	1	1	5
147	Russian Federation	5	8	5	16	5

Note: *or latest available data
Source: Author's calculations based on data from the International Telecommunication Union, World Telecommunication Indicators Database, accessed July 2003

Box 1. **ICT Diffusion in China and India**

Both China and India have posted remarkable improvements in ICT diffusion over the last decade. A close look at comparative historical data reveals different rates of ICT diffusion: each of the four diffusion rates for China appears to be a multiple of the corresponding rate for India. Differential rates such as these raise the question of what factors affect diffusion rates in countries.[6]

Figure 1. **Main Telephone Lines in Operation, 1992–2002**

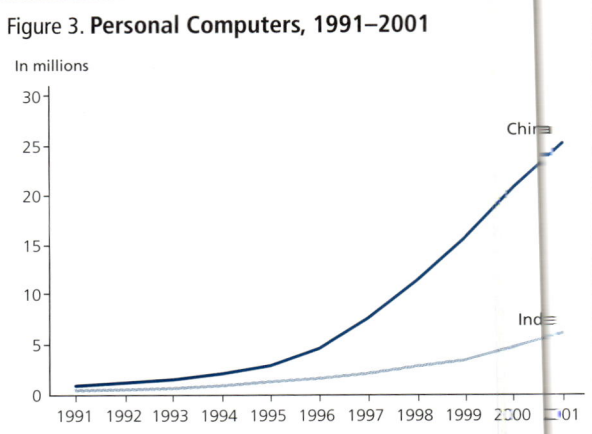

Figure 3. **Personal Computers, 1991–2001**

Figure 2. **Cellular Mobile Telephone Subscribers, 1992–2002**

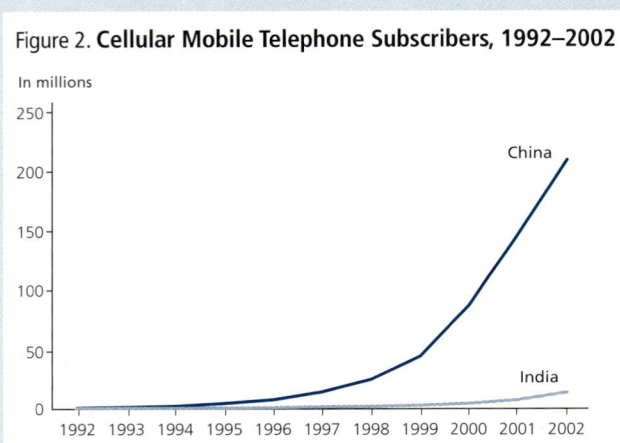

Figure 4. **Internet Users, 1992–2002**

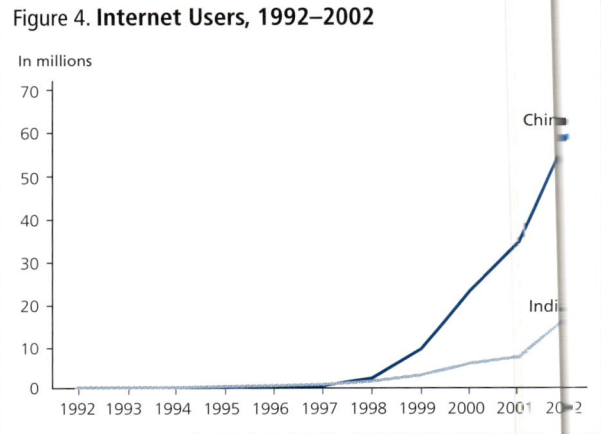

Source: International Telecommunication Union, World Telecommunication Indicators database, accessed July 2003

television subscribers. China also posted the second highest increase in the number of Internet users and the fifth highest increase in the number of personal computers.

Although it is tempting to chalk up the gains in penetration to the scale of China's population, the country's achievements over the last three years is best appreciated when juxtaposed with other populous countries (see Box 1 and Table 2). In terms of main telephone lines, for instance, China added 106 million while India, with the second highest increase, added 15 million. Likewise, China added 163 million cellular mobile telephone subscribers, while the United States, with the second highest increase, added 55 million. Similarly, China had 36 million new cable television subscribers in the three-

year period while Japan, with the second highest increase, added 6 million subscribers, a sixth of China's figure.

Of the most populous and developed economies, the United States, Japan, and Germany posted the highest increases. The United States, the third most populous country in the world, added the highest number of Internet users and personal computers at 53 million and 37 million, respectively. The United States is followed by Japan, the ninth most populous country, which posted the third highest increase in the number of Internet users and personal computers. Germany, the 12th most populous country in the world, posted the third highest increase in cellular mobile telephone subscribers, the fourth highest increases in Internet users personal computers, cable television subscribers, and home satellite antennas and the fifth highest increase in main telephone lines in operation.

Many of the most populous countries in the developing world also posted the largest increases over the last three years. Next to China and India, Brazil stands out as having added, since 1999, an additional 14 million main telephone lines, 20 million cellular mobile telephone subscribers, 11 million Internet users, and 7 million personal computers. Another notable performer is Russia, which, over the same period, added 8 million personal computers, 5 million main telephone lines, and 5 million television receivers.

Because the figure for main telephone lines in Table 2 includes public pay telephones, more access is being provided than the actual number of lines suggests. During the three-year period, Brazil added 638,100 public pay telephones, China added 488,562 pay phones and India added 442,000.

Indonesia also posted a significant increase in pay phones, adding 133,627 over the last three years.

3. Some of the fastest rates of growth and most sizeable increases are in developing economies.

Of the 200 economies included in the study, 180 economies, mostly developing economies, doubled their number of Internet users during this period, growing by as much as 44,400 percent (as in the case of Somalia). During this same period 61 economies doubled their number of personal computers; in the area of telecommunications, 26 economies doubled their number of main telephone lines in operation and at least 69 economies doubled their number of cellular mobile telephone subscribers. Twenty-one economies also doubled their number of television receivers, while 20 economies doubled their number of cable television subscribers and 32 economies doubled their number of home satellite antennas.

Table 3. **Most Significant Increases in ICT Diffusion, 1999–2002***

Country	(millions)	% of World increase	Country	% change	(thousands)
Internet users (estimated)					
United States	53	16	Somalia	44,400	89
China	50	15	Azerbaijan	3,650	292
Japan	30	9	Uzbekistan	3,567	268
Germany	18	5	Zimbabwe	2,400	480
Korea, Republic of	15	5	Lesotho	2,000	20
India	14	4	Myanmar	1,900	10
France	13	4	Pakistan	1,775	1,420
United Kingdom	12	4	Sao Tome and Principe	1,700	9
Brazil	11	3	Libya	1,686	118
Italy	9	3	Sudan	1,580	79
Personal computers					
United States	37	24	Yemen	383	115
Korea, Republic of	15	10	Zimbabwe	300	450
Japan	12	8	Equatorial Guinea	250	3
Germany	12	7	Bangladesh	246	320
China	10	6	Paraguay	233	140
Russian Federation	8	5	Bhutan	233	7
Brazil	7	4	Togo	200	100
France	5	3	Maldives	167	13
Canada	4	3	Croatia	153	460
Italy	4	3	Saudi Arabia	150	1,803
Main telephone lines in operation					
China	106	55	Somalia	186	65
India	15	8	Sudan	167	420
Brazil	14	7	China	97	105,704
United States	6	3	Mauritania	94	15
Germany	6	3	Ethiopia	89	174
Iran	5	2	Haiti	86	60
Russian Federation	5	2	Guinea-Bissau	84	5
Mexico	4	2	Yemen	79	226
Egypt	3	1	Malawi	77	32
Korea, Republic of	3	1	Lao, PDR	76	27

Table 3. **Most Significant Increases in ICT Diffusion, 1999–2002* (continued)**

In terms of figures			In terms of growth rates		
Country	(millions)	% of World increase	Country	% change	(thousands)
Cellular mobile telephone subscribers					
China	163	25	Syria	9,900	3_
United States	55	8	Cameroon	9,283	5_
Germany	36	5	Albania	7,167	7_
Japan	24	4	Nigeria	6,432	1,60_
United Kingdom	23	3	Burundi	6,400	5_
Italy	22	3	Kenya	5,478	1,30_
Brazil	20	3	Djibouti	5,257	1_
Spain	18	3	Equatorial Guinea	4,400	2_
Mexico	18	3	Congo, DR	4,336	21_
Television receivers					
China	40	20	Burkina Faso	631	82
United States	34	17	Togo	500	50_
Turkey	13	6	Namibia	314	38_
India	10	5	Eritrea	233	14_
Japan	9	4	Dem. People's Rep. of Korea	195	2,53_
Sudan	8	4	Sudan	151	7,57_
United Kingdom	7	4	Mali	15	21_
Philippines	6	3	Tanzania	117	81_
Pakistan	5	3	Albania	115	52_
Russian Federation	5	2	Jamaica	98	481
Cable television subscribers					
China	36	57	Spain	466	484
Japan	6	9	Thailand	449	654
United States	5	7	Lebanon	426	81_
Germany	3	5	Kyrgyzstan	389	10_
India	3	5	Georgia	308	46_
Philippines	2	3	Azerbaijan	275	3_
Korea, Republic of	1	2	Indonesia	250	50_
Australia	1	1	Philippines	145	1,740
United Kingdom	1	1	Australia	143	825
Thailand	1	1	Nigeria	115	32_
Home satellite antennas					
United States	5	28	New Zealand	466	247
United Kingdom	2	10	Tunisia	338	1,198
Canada	2	10	Canada	295	1,635
Germany	1	8	Sudan	291	64
Tunisia	1	7	Malta	277	7
Hungary	1	5	Chile	209	85
Syria	1	5	Syria	191	330
Spain	1	5	Sri Lanka	183	0.1
Italy	1	4	Maldives	176	2
Turkey	1	4	Switzerland	157	440

Note: *or latest available data
Source: Author's calculations based on data from the International Telecommunication Union, World Telecommunication Indicators Database, accessed July 2003

Table 3 shows numerous examples of developing economies that are making exemplary progress. Somalia, for instance, posted the largest rate of growth of main telephone lines and Internet users. Syria has the highest rates of growth of cellular mobile telephone subscribers while Yemen posted the highest rates of increase in personal computers. For many of these economies, the dramatic growth rates stem partly from having come from a relatively low base in 1999. But the fact remains that these tremendous growth rates represent huge increases in numbers in many economies. Indeed, over the three-year period and of the 200 economies in the study, 66 economies added at least 1 million cellular mobile telephone subscribers, 43 economies added at least 1 million Internet users, 31 economies added at least 1 million television receivers, 22 economies added at least 1 million personal computers, and 18 economies added at least 1 million main telephone lines.

In addition to China, India, Russia, and Brazil, several developing economies registered a combination of dramatic growth rates and an equally remarkable increase in the number of users. In South Asia, Pakistan is notable for increasing the number of Internet users despite having a fairly low personal computer base. In 1999 the country had only 80,000 Internet users but over three years 1.4 million users were added, amounting to a growth of 1,775 percent. Pakistan also added 5.4 million television receivers and over 900,000 cellular mobile telephone subscribers; Bangladesh likewise added a similar number of cellular mobile telephone subscribers as Pakistan, as well as 3.2 million new television receivers.

In the Middle East and North Africa region, rapid diffusion occurred in several economies. Iran, Saudi Arabia, and Egypt posted widespread increases. In the last three years, Iran, for instance, added 4.7 million main telephone lines, 2.9 million Internet users, 1.8 million cellular mobile telephone subscribers, 1 million personal computers, and 1 million television receivers. During the same period, Saudi Arabia increased its Internet user base from 100,000 to 1.6 million users. In addition, Saudi Arabia added 4.2 million cellular mobile telephone users, and 1.8 million personal computers. Also remarkable is Egypt's performance over the last three years: an additional 4 million cellular mobile telephone subscribers, 2.7 million main telephone lines, 1.4 million television receivers, and 1.3 million Internet users. Other economies posted spectacular performances for specific indicators: Morocco added 5.8 million cellular mobile telephone subscribers, Tunisia added 1.2 million home satellite antennas, while Syria added half a million more main telephone lines and television receivers.

In Latin America, Mexico posted impressive additions in the last three years: 18 million cellular mobile telephone subscribers, 4 million main telephone lines, 2.8 million Internet users, 2.6 million personal computers, and 1.8 million television receivers. Similarly, over the same period Chile added 4.2 million cellular mobile telephone subscribers, 3.7 million television receivers, and 3 million Internet users. Argentina, despite its economic difficulties during the last three years, added 2.9 million Internet users, 2.1 million cellular mobile telephone subscribers, and nearly 1 million personal computers. In the Caribbean, Jamaica is notable for doubling the numbers of its television receivers and Internet users while posting an 870 percent increase in the number of cellular phones from about 144,000 in 1999 to 1.4 million by 2002.

While there are fewer economies that posted across-the-board improvements in sub-Saharan Africa, the region nonetheless has many remarkable examples of improvements

in ICT diffusion. In the last three years, South Africa added 6.9 million cellular mobile telephone subscribers, 2 million television receivers, and 1.2 million Internet users. Over the same period Nigeria, the region's most populous country, added 4.5 million television receivers and 1.6 million cellular mobile telephone subscribers; the latter figure constitutes a 6,432 percent increase over its 1999 subscriber base of 25,000. Kenya, too, multiplied the number of its cellular mobile telephone subscribers from 24,000 in 1999 to 1.3 million in 2002. Another area where Kenya demonstrated significant improvement is in the number of Internet users, adding 465,000 users over the last three years from a base of only 35,000 users. Similarly, Zimbabwe added 480,000 new Internet users to its 1999 base of only 20,000 while increasing its personal computer base by 450,000. Sudan is outstanding in terms of television receivers, having added 7.5 million in the last three years. Also notable is Burkina Faso, which added 820,000 television receivers over the same period. Several notable improvements can also be found in the increases in the number of cellular mobile telephone subscribers in Cameroon, Senegal, and Côte d'Ivoire, which posted increases of 9,283 percent (557,000 subscribers), 530 percent (465,000 subscribers), and 299 percent (770,000 subscribers), respectively.

In Asia, different economies posted varying magnitudes of increases for different indicators. The largest increase in the number of Internet users was in the Republic of Korea, which added 15 million new users in the three-year period. Indonesia added 7 million Internet users, a 21-fold increase, while Taiwan added nearly 4 million new users, out of its population of about 22 million. Increases in personal computers were most notable in the Republic of Korea, which added 15 million units, and in Malaysia, which increased its number of units by 1.8 million, a doubling of the 1999 level. In terms of main telephone lines, Vietnam and Thailand posted the most remarkable increases: the former added 1.6 million lines while the latter added 1.2 million. Growth of cellular mobile telephone subscribers was most dramatic in Thailand, with nearly 14 million new subscribers added during the three-year period. Taiwan and the Philippines added 12.4 and 11.4 million new subscribers, respectively. Diffusion of television receivers expanded by 195 percent in the Democratic Republic of Korea while the Philippines added 6.3 million units. The latter is also notable for increasing the number of cable television subscribers by 1.7 million, nearly tripling the 1999 figure. Finally, the increase of home satellite antennas was most remarkable in New Zealand, which registered a 466 percent increase.

4. Best penetration rates are still in advanced economies with relatively small populations.

In Internet penetration, Iceland has the highest rate; its number of users is equivalent to 61 percent of its population (see Table 4). Iceland is succeeded by Liechtenstein, Sweden, and Republic of Korea with Internet penetration rates of 58 percent, 57 percent, and 55 percent of the population, respectively. Singapore, with an Internet penetration of 54 percent of its population, stands out as having the highest household Internet penetration at 227 percent of its households.

For personal computer penetration, the United States takes the lead, with a penetration rate of 62 percent of its population. The United States is followed by Denmark at 58 percent penetration, and both Sweden and Republic of Korea at 56 percent. In addition, there are five other economies with a personal computer penetration of at least 50 percent of their population: Switzerland, Luxembourg, Australia, Norway, and Singapore.

In terms of main telephone lines, Monaco and Bermuda have the highest penetration rates in the world, while Taiwan and Luxembourg have the best penetration rates in terms of cellular phones. For television receivers, Bermuda and the Faroe Islands have the highest penetration rates while Monaco and Liechtenstein have the highest penetration rate of cable television. Faroe Islands and Kuwait have the best penetration rate in the world for home satellite antennas.

Table 4. **Highest Penetration Rates, 2002***

Country	as % of Population
Internet users (estimated)	
Iceland	61
Liechtenstein	58
Sweden	57
Korea, Republic of	55
Singapore	54
United States	54
Netherlands	53
Finland	51
Norway	50
New Zealand	48
Personal computers	
United States	62
Denmark	58
Sweden	56
Korea, Republic of	56
Switzerland	54
Luxembourg	51
Australia	51
Norway	50
Singapore	50
Bermuda	49
Main telephone lines in operation	
Monaco	92
Bermuda	86
Luxembourg	77
Switzerland	73
Norway	73
Sweden	72
Denmark	70
United States	66
Germany	65
Canada	64
Cellular mobile telephone subscribers	
Taiwan	106
Luxembourg	101
Israel	95
Hong Kong SAR	93
Italy	93
Iceland	89
Sweden	89
Czech Republic	85
Greece	85
Finland	85

Country	as % of Population
Television receivers	
Bermuda	108
Faroe Islands	102
United Kingdom	97
Sweden	96
United States	93
Norway	88
Qatar	87
Denmark	86
Latvia	85
Japan	78
Cable television subscribers	
Monaco	59
Liechtenstein	40
Netherlands	40
Belgium	37
Switzerland	37
Luxembourg	31
Germany	26
Virgin Islands (US)	26
United States	25
Canada	25
Home satellite antennas	
Faroe Islands	42
Kuwait	27
Austria	19
Hungary	17
Germany	16
Tunisia	16
Denmark	15
Slovenia	14
Sweden	12
Slovak Republic	12

Note: *or latest available data
Source: Author's calculations based on data from the International Telecommunication Union, World Telecommunication Indicators Database, accessed July 2003

5. The least developed economies still have the poorest ICT penetration rates.

The economies that rank as having among the poorest penetration rates are quite dispersed around the world, with the exception of North America (see Table 5). In the Asia and the Pacific region, Myanmar and Cambodia are most notable: Myanmar has dismal penetration rates in terms of Internet users, personal computers, cellular mobile telephone subscribers, and television, and Cambodia also has low penetration of main telephone lines, television receivers, and personal computers. In the Middle East, Afghanistan has low penetration rates of main telephone lines and cellular mobile telephones while Iraq has a low penetration rate of Internet users and cellular mobile telephones. In Europe, Tajikistan is among the economies with the lowest Internet penetration while Turkmenistan is on the list of those with the lowest penetration rate of cellular mobile telephones. In Latin America and the Caribbean, Haiti ranks among the economies with the world's lowest penetration rates in television receivers while Cuba is among the economies with the poorest cellular mobile telephone penetration. In South Asia, Pakistan and Sri Lanka are among those with the lowest penetration rates of cable television, while Nepal has among the lowest penetration rates for television and cellular phones.

Most of the economies that appear to have the lowest penetration rates are from sub-Saharan Africa. It is notable that with the exception of Kenya, the World Bank has rated as severely indebted nearly all of the sub-Saharan African countries in the list in Table 5.

6. Despite the dramatic increases in diffusion of ICT in the most populous countries, it is also in these very same countries where the greatest number of people can potentially still be connected.

Table 6 lists the 15 most populous countries in the world and displays the numbers of people that are potentially still a market for technologies. The reality is that universal access for individuals is unlikely to be a goal in these countries. In many economies, and for many of these technologies, shared access is not only the norm but is perhaps the optimal and most pragmatic mode. Each country will have to ascertain its own optimal penetration level.

With the two largest populations in the world, China and India face the greatest challenges in ICT diffusion. Both China and India have a combined population of 2 billion people who were not cellular mobile telephone subscribers as of 2002; of the same magnitude are the numbers of main telephone lines in operation, Internet users and personal computers, and television receivers. Next to China and India,

Table 5. Lowest Penetration Rates, 2002: Priority Countries*

Country	Ratio (per population)
Internet users (estimated)	
Congo, DR	1 per 8,774
Myanmar	1 per 4,899
Liberia	1 per 3,238
Tajikistan	1 per 1,822
Ethiopia	1 per 1,347
Central African Rep.	1 per 1,319
Niger	1 per 979
Iraq	1 per 970
Burundi	1 per 832
Sierra Leone	1 per 707
Personal computers	
Niger	1 per 1,958
Burundi	1 per 1,398
Myanmar	1 per 891
Malawi	1 per 803
Mali	1 per 759
Cambodia	1 per 689
Ethiopia	1 per 673
Chad	1 per 656
Burkina Faso	1 per 629
Benin	1 per 599
Main telephone lines in operation	
Congo, DR	1 per 2,632
Afghanistan	1 per 705
Chad	1 per 665
Niger	1 per 542
Liberia	1 per 476
Uganda	1 per 449
Central African Rep.	1 per 444
Cambodia	1 per 412
Rwanda	1 per 380
Burundi	1 per 316
Cellular mobile telephone subscribers	
Niger	1 per 5,525
Myanmar	1 per 3,555
Afghanistan	1 per 1,941
Liberia	1 per 1,619
Ethiopia	1 per 1,337
Iraq	1 per 1,212
Nepal	1 per 1,060
Cuba	1 per 632
Turkmenistan	1 per 594
Papua New Guinea	1 per 511
Television receivers	
Congo, DR	1 per 526
Chad	1 per 525
Comoros	1 per 282
Malawi	1 per 261
Ethiopia	1 per 182
Central African Rep.	1 per 174
Haiti	1 per 166
Cambodia	1 per 135
Myanmar	1 per 134
Nepal	1 per 120

Note: *or latest available data
Source: Author's calculations based on data from the International Telecommunication Union, World Telecommunication Indicators Database, accessed July 2003

Table 6. **Potential Market for ICT Diffusion, 2002***

Rank according to population	Country	Population that are non-Internet users (in millions)	Population without personal computers (in millions)	Population less the number of main telephone lines (in millions)	Population without cellular phones (in millions)	Population without television receivers (in millions)	Population without cable television subscribers (in millions)
1	China	1,225	1,260	1,070	1,078	875	1,185
2	India	1,025	1,036	1,000	1,029	957	1,002
3	United States	133	110	98	148	21	215
4	Indonesia	204	210	204	200	180	215
5	Brazil	160	161	135	139	114	162
6	Pakistan	147	148	145	148	127	148
7	Russian Federation	141	134	111	129	68	135
8	Bangladesh	133	133	132	132	125	14
9	Japan	70	79	56	46	28	114
10	Nigeria	120	119	119	118	108	120
11	Mexico	97	95	87	76	74	93
12	Germany	48	47	29	23	34	44
13	Vietnam	80	80	78	79	66	79
14	Philippines	76	78	77	66	65	77
15	Ethiopia	67	67	67	67	67	68

Note: *or latest available data
Source: Author's calculations based on data from the International Telecommunication Union, World Telecommunication Indicators Database, accessed July 2003

significant proportions of the populations of Indonesia, Pakistan, Brazil, and Bangladesh are still unconnected. Significantly, even the United States has considerable work ahead. As of 2002, 147 million people in the country were not cellular mobile telephone subscribers and 133 million people were not Internet users.

7. The largest markets for ICT applications and content are now a mixture of developed and developing economies.

When assessing which among the economies in the world now have the largest number ICT users and devices, it is significant to find that China, Republic of Korea, India, Brazil, and Russia have risen to the top leagues of economies with the largest ICT base. Table 7 depicts the top 10 economies in terms of the number of users for each ICT indicator, along with the proportion of the world market represented by the country. Even for these economies, however, there remains the challenge of creating relevant applications for the different markets.

8. The "divide" in ICT access has narrowed, but low income economies still lag considerably, particularly in sub-Saharan Africa.

Table 8 demonstrates that middle and low income economies have posted faster growth rates than high income economies for most of the technologies included in this study. Faster growth rates for middle and low income economies are certainly evident in the increases in the number of Internet users and cellular mobile telephone subscribers.

With the exception of the Internet and personal computers, middle and low income economies posted larger increases than high income economies. In terms of the number of main telephone lines in operation, the increase in the number of lines in middle and low income economies was seven times higher than the increase in high income economies. In the case of television receivers, the increase in middle and low income economies was twice the increase in high income economies. Even in terms of cellular mobile telephone subscribers, low and middle income economies added 1.4 times the number added by high income economies.

Other signs of a narrowing divide in ICT access are evident when examining how much the low and middle income economies account for the overall global penetration of ICT. Low and middle income economies are inhabited by 84 percent of world population. It is notable that as of 2002, this category accounted for 61 percent of all television receivers, 52 percent of all cable television subscribers, 48 percent of all main telephone lines, 45 percent of cellular mobile telephone subscribers, 30 percent of Internet users and home satellite antennas, and 22 percent of personal computers. These figures are particularly striking when compared to those of 1999, when low and middle income economies accounted for only 15 percent of the world's Internet users and 26 percent of cellular mobile telephone subscribers.

Table 7. Largest Markets for ICT Applications and Content, 2002

Internet users (estimated)	(in millions)	% of World total
United States	155	26
China	59	10
Japan	57	9
Germany	35	6
Korea	26	4
United Kingdom	24	4
France	19	3
Italy	17	3
India	17	3
Canada	15	3

Main telephone lines in operation	(in millions)	% of World total
China	214	15
United States	190	19
Japan	71	8
Germany	54	5
India	41	3
Brazil	39	3
Russian Federation	36	3
United Kingdom	35	4
France	34	3
Italy	27	3

Television receivers	(in millions)	% of World total
China	410	24
United States	267	14
Japan	100	6
India	85	5
Russian Federation	79	5
Brazil	60	4
United Kingdom	57	3
Germany	48	3
France	38	2
Indonesia	32	2

Home satellite antennas	(in millions)	% of World total
United States	18	19
Germany	13	15
Japan	12	13
United Kingdom	7	6
Indonesia	4	5
Algeria	4	4
France	3	3
Italy	3	3
Poland	3	3
Canada	2	1

Personal computers	(in millions)	% of World total
United States	178	35
Japan	49	9
Germany	36	6
Korea, Republic of	26	4
China	25	4
United Kingdom	22	4
France	21	4
Canada	15	3
Italy	13	2
Brazil	13	2

Cellular mobile telephone subscribers	(in millions)	% of World total
China	207	12
United States	141	15
Japan	81	9
Germany	59	7
Italy	52	6
United Kingdom	50	6
France	39	4
Brazil	35	3
Spain	33	3
Korea, Republic of	32	4

Cable television subscribers	(in millions)	% of World total
China	96	25
United States	73	22
India	40	12
Japan	23	6
Germany	22	6
Russian Federation	11	4
Korea, Republic of	8	3
Canada	8	2
Netherlands	7	2
Argentina	6	2

Source: Author's calculations based on data from the International Telecommunication Union, World Telecommunication Indicators Database, accessed July 2003

It is of great concern, however, that the low income economies still lag considerably behind in terms of penetration rates of their population. Of the 2.5 billion total population of low income economies (41 percent of the world's population), only 2 percent are cellular mobile telephone subscribers, and only 1 percent are Internet users and have access to cellular mobile telephones.

Part II. Regional Profiles

When the global picture is disaggregated into different regions, the results present an interesting mix, as shown in Table 9. Of all the regions, the United States and Canada combined ("North America") has the highest number of personal computers, equivalent to 35 percent of the world's

Table 8. The "Divide" in ICT Diffusion (According to Income Level), 1999–2002*

	1999 (in millions)	2002 (in millions)	1999–2002 Increase (in percent)	(in millions)	% of Total population 1999	2002
Internet users (estimated)						
High income	235	423	80	187	25	44
Upper middle income	16	51	213	34	3	10
Lower middle income	20	99	398	79	1	5
Low income	5	32	575	28	0	1
World	276	605	119	329	5	10
Personal computers						
High income	321	429	34	108	34	45
Upper middle income	25	43	75	19	5	
Lower middle income	38	63	64	25	2	
Low income	10	15	56	5	0	
World	394	550	40	156	7	
Main telephone lines in operation						
High income	542	567	4	23	58	
Upper middle income	85	107	25	22	17	
Lower middle income	221	345	57	125	10	
Low income	58	80	38	22	2	
World	906	1,098	21	192	15	
Cellular mobile telephone subscribers						
High income	363	637	76	274	39	
Upper middle income	49	138	181	89	10	
Lower middle income	73	335	357	262	3	
Low income	7	44	532	37	0	
World	493	1,155	134	662	8	
Television receivers						
High income	629	695	11	66	66	
Upper middle income	154	167	9	14	31	
Lower middle income	583	663	14	80	27	
Low income	207	250	21	43	9	
World	1,573	1,775	13	202	26	
Cable television subscribers						
High income	153	172	12	19	16	3
Upper middle income	19	21	11	2	4	4
Lower middle income	79	119	50	39	4	5
Low income	37	47	8	3	2	2
World	288	359	22	64	5	6
Home satellite antennas						
High income	57	68	18	10	6	7
Upper middle income	9	12	29	3	2	2
Lower middle income	8	13	42	3	0	1
Low income	4	5	12	0	0	0
World	78	97	22	17	1	2

Note: *or latest available data
Source: Author's calculations based on data from the International Telecommunication Union, World Telecommunication Indicators Database, accessed July 2003

Table 9. **The "Divide" in ICT Diffusion (Geographic Perspective), 1999–2002***

	1999 (in millions)	2002 (in millions)	1999–2002 Increase (in percent)	1999–2002 Increase (in millions)	% of Total population 1999	% of Total population 2002
Internet users (estimated)						
Asia and the Pacific	67.1	192.5	187	125.5	3	9
Canada and the United States	113.0	170.2	51	57.2	37	53
Europe	77.6	168.5	117	90.8	9	19
Latin America and the Caribbean	10.5	36.2	245	26.2	2	7
North Africa and the Middle East	2.6	12.8	383	9.6	1	4
South Asia	3.0	18.6	512	15.5	0	1
Sub-Saharan Africa	2.3	6.0	156	3.6	0	1
World	276.2	604.8	119	328.5	5	10
Personal computers						
Asia and the Pacific	90.3	137.3	52	47.0	4	7
Canada and the United States	152.1	193.3	27	41.2	49	60
Europe	114.7	159.4	39	44.7	13	18
Latin America and the Caribbean	19.1	32.6	71	13.5	4	6
North Africa and the Middle East	8.7	13.6	51	4.4	3	4
South Asia	4.2	7.4	77	3.2	0	1
Sub-Saharan Africa	4.7	6.8	42	2.0	1	1
World	393.9	550.5	40	156.1	7	9
Main telephone lines in operation						
Asia and the Pacific	251.7	368.0	46	116.3	12	18
Canada and the United States	203.6	210.0	3	6.4	66	66
Europe	314.3	334.5	6	20.2	36	38
Latin America and the Caribbean	67.4	89.4	33	22.1	13	17
North Africa and the Middle East	29.0	38.9	34	9.9	10	12
South Asia	30.9	47.1	52	16.2	2	3
Sub-Saharan Africa	9.2	10.2	11	1.0	1	2
Cellular mobile telephone subscribers						
World	492.7	1,154.8	134	662.1	8	19
Asia and the Pacific	160.0	423.7	165	263.6	8	20
Canada and the United States	93.0	152.6	64	59.7	30	48
Europe	182.2	404.9	122	222.7	21	46
Latin America and the Caribbean	40.9	101.5	148	60.6	8	19
North Africa and the Middle East	7.6	33.4	340	25.8	3	10
South Asia	2.6	16.0	520	13.4	0	1
Sub-Saharan Africa	6.5	22.8	253	16.3	1	3
World	906.1	1,098.0	21	191.9	15	18
Television receivers						
Asia and the Pacific	583.5	648.5	11	65.0	29	31
Canada and the United States	253.3	288.5	14	35.2	82	90
Europe	414.5	460.8	11	46.3	48	53
Latin America and the Caribbean	136.5	150.1	10	13.5	27	28
North Africa and the Middle East	57.6	63.0	8	4.9	19	20
South Asia	98.1	117.0	19	18.9	7	8
Sub-Saharan Africa	29.4	47.3	61	17.9	5	7
World	1,572.8	1,775.1	13	201.8	26	29
Cable television subscribers						
Asia and the Pacific	91.8	139.0	51	47.1	5	7
Canada and the United States	76.6	81.0	6	4.4	25	25
Europe	67.9	78.4	10	6.9	8	9
Latin America and the Caribbean	13.3	15.5	14	1.9	3	3
North Africa and the Middle East	1.3	1.4	12	0.1	0	0
South Asia	37.1	43.7	8	3.0	3	3
Sub-Saharan Africa	0.1	0.2	38	0.1	0	0
World	288.1	359.2	22	63.6	5	6
Home satellite antennas						
Asia and the Pacific	19.5	17.5	-11	-2.1	1	1
Canada and the United States	13.7	20.1	47	6.4	4	6
Europe	33.8	43.6	26	8.7	4	5
Latin America and the Caribbean	1.6	2.7	62	1.0	0	1
North Africa and the Middle East	8.9	11.9	29	2.6	3	4
South Asia	0.0	0.0	177	0.0	0	0
Sub-Saharan Africa	0.4	1.2	83	0.3	0	0
World	77.9	96.8	22	16.8	1	2

Note: *or latest available data
Source: Author's calculations based on data from the International Telecommunication Union, World Telecommunication Indicators Database, accessed July 2003

Table 10. **Regional Profiles in ICT Diffusion, 1999–2002***

	1999 (in millions)	2002 (in millions)	1999–2002 Increase (in percent)	(in millions)	% of Total population 1999	2002
Asia						
Population	2,031.7	2,080.3	2	48.6		
Internet users (estimated)	67.1	192.5	187	125.5	3	
Personal computers	90.3	137.3	52	47.0	4	
Main telephone lines in operation	251.7	368.0	46	116.3	12	1
Cellular mobile telephone subscribers	160.0	423.7	165	263.6	8	2
Television receivers	583.5	648.5	11	65.0	29	3
Cable television receivers	91.8	139.0	51	47.1	5	
Home satellite antennas	17.1	17.5	2	0.4	1	
Europe						
Population	868.1	874.0	1	5.8		
Internet users (estimated)	77.6	168.5	117	90.9	9	1
Personal computers	114.7	159.4	39	44.7	13	1
Main telephone lines in operation	314.3	334.5	6	20.2	36	3
Cellular mobile telephone subscribers	182.2	404.9	122	222.7	21	4
Television receivers	414.5	460.8	11	46.3	48	5
Cable television receivers	67.9	78.4	15	10.4	8	
Home satellite antennas	33.8	43.6	29	9.7	4	
Latin America						
Population	509.8	530.8	4	21.0		
Internet users (estimated)	10.5	36.2	245	25.7	2	
Personal computers	19.1	32.6	71	13.5	4	
Main telephone lines in operation	67.4	89.4	33	22.1	13	
Cellular mobile telephone subscribers	40.9	101.5	148	60.6	8	
Television receivers	136.5	150.1	10	13.5	27	
Cable television receivers	13.3	15.5	17	2.2	3	
Home satellite antennas	1.6	2.7	66	1.1	0	
North Africa and the Middle East						
Population	300.9	320.3	6	19.4		
Internet users (estimated)	2.6	12.8	388	10.2	1	
Personal computers	8.7	13.6	56	4.9	3	
Main telephone lines in operation	29.0	38.9	34	9.9	10	
Cellular mobile telephone subscribers	7.6	33.4	340	25.8	3	
Television receivers	57.6	63.0	9	5.4	19	
Cable television receivers	1.3	1.4	12	0.1	0	
Home satellite antennas	8.9	11.9	34	3.0	3	
South Asia						
Population	1,322.9	1,390.2	5	67.3		
Internet users (estimated)	3.0	18.6	512	15.5	0	
Personal computers	4.2	7.4	77	3.2	0	0
Main telephone lines in operation	30.9	47.1	52	16.2	2	
Cellular mobile telephone subscribers	2.6	16.0	520	13.4	0	
Television receivers	98.1	117.0	19	18.9	5	6
Cable television receivers	37.1	43.7	18	6.6	2	2
Home satellite antennas	0.0	0.0	192	0.0	0	0
Sub-Saharan Africa						
Population	621.5	676.2	9	54.7		
Internet users (estimated)	2.3	6.0	156	3.6	0	
Personal computers	4.7	6.8	43	2.0	1	
Main telephone lines in operation	9.2	10.2	11	1.0	1	2
Cellular mobile telephone subscribers	6.5	22.8	253	16.3	1	3
Television receivers	29.4	47.3	61	17.9	5	7
Cable television receivers	0.1	0.2	38	0.1	0	
Home satellite antennas	0.4	1.2	228	0.8	0	

Note: *or latest available data
Source: Author's calculations based on data from the International Telecommunication Union, World Telecommunication Indicators Database, accessed July 2003

personal computers. In 1999, North America also had the highest number of Internet users and cellular mobile telephone subscribers but by 2002, this was no longer the case. By 2002, because of dynamic growth in overall ICT diffusion, the Asia-Pacific region had the highest number not only of Internet users and cellular mobile telephone subscribers but also of main telephone lines, television receivers, and cable television subscribers. Europe takes the lead in terms of the number of home satellite antennas. These three regions—North America, Asia and the Pacific, and Europe—account for at least 60 percent of the global penetration for each device.

In terms of penetration rates, Europe is a distant second to North America with the exception of cellular mobile telephone subscribers where Europe, with a 46 percent rate, nearly matches North America's 48 percent rate. The Asia and the Pacific region, despite its dynamism, actually has a penetration rate below the world average in terms of numbers of Internet users and personal computers. The remaining regions, Latin America and the Caribbean, North Africa and the Middle East, South Asia, and sub-Saharan Africa, have single digit penetration rates for both Internet users and personal computers. A particularly distressing figure is the main telephone line penetration rate in sub-Saharan Africa, which barely improved since 1999 and remains low at 2 percent of its total population and 8 percent of total households.

North America—Canada and the United States

Canada and the United States, with a combined population of 320 million people, have an estimated 170.2 million Internet users. This is equivalent to a 53 percent penetration rate of the population and 28 percent of the world's Internet users. About a third of the estimated number of Internet users were added in the last three years alone, when the number of Internet users in the region increased by 57.2 million, a 51 percent increase.

Compared to the growth in the number of Internet users, the growth in personal computers was slower although these two economies combined still have the largest number compared to any other region in the world. As of 2002, these two economies together had 193 million personal computers, of which 41.2 million were added in the last three years, equivalent to a 27 percent increase. The current individual penetration rate is 60 percent.

With already high penetration rates in the number of main telephone lines in operation, the United States and Canada posted a 3 percent increase in the number of telephone lines, adding 6.4 million lines in the last three years. By 2002, the number of main telephone lines reached 210 million, equivalent to a 66 percent individual penetration rate.

Cellular mobile telephone penetration is lower at 48 percent but the growth rate in the diffusion of this device has been much higher. In the last three years, the number of cellular mobile telephone subscribers increased by 64 percent, or 59.7 million. As of 2002, Canada and the United States had 153 million cellular mobile telephone subscribers, a figure that exceeds the number of cellular mobile telephone subscribers in Latin America and the Caribbean.

Despite an already high television penetration rate at 82 percent of its individual population as of 1999, Canada and the United States added a combined 35.2 million television receivers in the three-year period, a 14 percent increase. As of 2002, these two economies had a total of 288.5 television receivers, significantly more than 3.5 times the number of cable television subscribers, and 14.4 times the number of home satellite antennas. In the last three years, cable television subscribers increased by 4.4 million, a relatively lackluster growth of 6 percent when compared to the growth of home satellite antennas which increased by 47 percent or 6.4 million.

Europe

Looking at the 52 economies of the region with a combined population of 874 million, Europe, as of 2002, had 461 million television receivers, 405 million cellular mobile telephone subscribers, 335 million main telephone lines, and 168 million Internet users (see Table 10). In addition, the region had 159 million personal computers, 78 million cable television subscribers, and 44 million home satellite antennas.

Over the last three years, the most dramatic growth rates in the region are the number of cellular mobile telephone subscribers, up 122 percent, and the number of Internet users, up 117 percent. Diffusion of other devices was more moderate, with growth of television receivers at 11 percent and main telephone lines at 6 percent over the three-year period. The relatively mild growth in the diffusion of these two technologies is largely because of the fairly high 1999 penetration rates: television receivers at 48 percent of total population and main telephone lines at 36 percent of the population.

In Europe, Germany, as of 2002, had the largest number of Internet users and personal computers, as well as main telephone lines, cellular mobile telephone subscribers, cable television subscribers, and home satellite antennas. Over the last three years, Germany also posted the largest increases in nearly all the devices under study except for television receivers and home satellite antennas. In actual numbers, Germany added nearly 18 million new Internet users, an increase of 105 percent and nearly 12 million personal computers, a growth of 47 percent. During the same period, the country added 5.5 million main telephone lines and nearly six times that number, or 36 million, new cellular mobile telephone subscribers, equivalent to a 152 percent

Table 11. Regional Highlights: Leading Countries in Growth and Penetration, Europe

	Change (units), 1999–2002			Change (%), 1999–2002			Penetration rate (% of Population), 2002
Internet users (estimated)							
1	Germany	17,900,000	1	Azerbaijan	3,650	1	Iceland	61
2	France	13,346,000	2	Uzbekistan	3,567	2	Liechtenstein	58
3	United Kingdom	11,500,000	3	Belarus	1,517	3	Sweden	57
4	Italy	8,800,000	4	Kyrgyzstan	1,420	4	Netherlands	53
5	Spain	5,026,000	5	Bosnia and Herzegovina	1,329	5	Finland	51
6	Russian Federation	4,500,000	6	Serbia	700	6	Norway	50
7	Turkey	3,400,000	7	Lithuania	385	7	Denmark	47
8	Netherlands	2,390,000	8	Russian Federation	300	8	Monaco	46
9	Portugal	2,200,000	9	Albania	300	9	Germany	42
10	Belgium	2,000,000	10	Turkmenistan	300	10	Estonia	41
Personal computers							
1	Germany	11,520,940	1	Croatia	153	1	Denmark	58
2	Russian Federation	7,500,000	2	Russian Federation	136	2	Sweden	56
3	France	5,020,000	3	Latvia	100	3	Switzerland	54
4	Italy	4,025,000	4	Moldova	100	4	Luxembourg	51
5	United Kingdom	4,000,000	5	Bulgaria	84	5	Norway	50
6	Spain	2,000,000	6	Armenia	75	6	Iceland	45
7	Netherlands	1,200,000	7	Lithuania	73	7	Finland	44
8	Sweden	1,000,000	8	Slovak Republic	64	8	Germany	43
9	Austria	913,000	9	Georgia	56	9	Netherlands	43
10	Poland	900,000	10	Albania	50	10	Ireland	38
Main telephone lines in operation							
1	Germany	5,510,000	1	Albania	57	1	Monaco	92
2	Russian Federation	4,551,000	2	Azerbaijan	36	2	Luxembourg	77
3	Spain	2,225,170	3	Bosnia and Herzegovina	33	3	Switzerland	73
4	Poland	1,224,800	4	Kazakhstan	18	4	Norway	73
5	United Kingdom	1,124,000	5	Moldova	15	5	Sweden	72
6	Italy	949,950	6	Croatia	15	6	Denmark	70
7	Turkey	860,810	7	Russian Federation	15	7	Germany	65
8	Ukraine	595,600	8	Macedonia, FYR	14	8	Iceland	63
9	Netherlands	387,000	9	Ireland	14	9	Netherlands	62
10	Romania	376,000	10	Spain	14	10	Cyprus	61
Cellular mobile telephone subscribers							
1	Germany	35,754,000	1	Albania	7,167	1	Luxembourg	101
2	United Kingdom	22,736,000	2	Tajikistan	2,012	2	Italy	93
3	Italy	22,020,000	3	Kazakhstan	1,975	3	Iceland	89
4	Spain	18,471,290	4	Kyrgyzstan	1,962	4	Sweden	89
5	France	17,151,800	5	Belarus	1,883	5	Czech Republic	85
6	Russian Federation	16,297,500	6	Bosnia and Herzegovina	1,323	6	Greece	85
7	Turkey	15,252,843	7	Russian Federation	1,189	7	Finland	85
8	Poland	10,043,500	8	Moldova	1,150	8	United Kingdom	84
9	Czech Republic	6,665,624	9	Ukraine	927	9	Norway	84
10	Greece	5,410,260	10	Croatia	672	10	Slovenia	84
Television receivers							
1	Turkey	12,725,620	1	Albania	115	1	Faroe Islands	102
2	United Kingdom	7,400,000	2	Turkey	81	2	United Kingdom	97
3	Russian Federation	5,000,000	3	Sweden	76	3	Sweden	96
4	Sweden	3,700,000	4	Georgia	74	4	Norway	88
5	Netherlands	2,000,000	5	Kazakhstan	39	5	Denmark	86
6	Kazakhstan	1,540,110	6	Norway	38	6	Latvia	85
7	Romania	1,500,000	7	Azerbaijan	36	7	Monaco	76
8	Poland	1,298,000	8	Netherlands	24	8	Finland	68
9	Norway	1,100,000	9	Romania	21	9	Luxembourg	66
10	France	1,000,000	10	Austria	21	10	Netherlands	65

Note: *or latest available data
Source: Author's calculations based on data from the International Telecommunication Union, World Telecommunication Indicators Database, accessed July 2003

growth. Germany also added 3.2 million cable television subscribers and 1.3 million home satellite antennas during the three-year period.

The United Kingdom is second in Europe in the number of Internet users, personal computers, television receivers, and home satellite antennas. It is the third in the region in the number of main telephone lines in operation and cellular mobile telephone subscribers, and fourth in the region in terms of cable television subscribers. Over the last three years, the United Kingdom has added nearly 12 million Internet users, 4 million personal computers, 1 million main telephone lines, 23 million cellular mobile telephone subscribers, more than 7 million television receivers, 760,000 cable television subscribers, and nearly 1.8 million home satellite antennas.

France is third in the region in the number of Internet users, personal computers, and home satellite antennas while ranking fourth in the region in terms of main telephone lines in operation, cellular mobile telephone subscribers, and television receivers. In the three-year period, France added more than 13 million Internet users, a growth of nearly five times the 1999 figure, bringing the total number of Internet users in the country to more than 18.7 million.

In the region, Italy has the fourth largest number of Internet users and personal computers, at 17 million and 13 million, respectively. Italy is fifth in the region in terms of the number of main telephone lines but is second in the number of cellular mobile telephone subscribers. Italy is sixth in the number of television receivers and fourth in home satellite antennas. In the last three years, Italy has added 8.8 million Internet users, 4 million personal computers and, notably, 22 million cellular mobile telephone subscribers.

Russia stands out in Europe as having the largest number of television receivers and the second largest number of main telephone lines and cable television subscribers in the region. Russia has also demonstrated tremendous increases over the last three years: a 300 percent increase in the number of Internet users, 136 percent increase in the number of personal computers and, notably, a 1,189 percent increase in the number of cellular mobile telephone subscribers.

In terms of population penetration rates, six economies in the region have over 50 percent of their population using the Internet: Iceland, Liechtenstein, Sweden, the Netherlands, Finland, and Norway, in descending order. For personal computers, five economies have over 50 percent penetration rates: Denmark, Sweden, Switzerland, Luxembourg, and Norway, also in descending order. Regarding main telephone line penetration rates, 19 economies have over 50 percent penetration rates; in the lead are Monaco, Luxembourg, Switzerland, Norway, and Sweden. In terms of cellular mobile

telephone subscribers, at least 27 economies in the region have a penetration rate greater than 50 percent; Luxembourg, Italy, Iceland, Sweden, and the Czech Republic have the highest penetration rates in the region. For television receivers, 24 economies in the region have over 50 percent penetration, led by the Faroe Islands, the United Kingdom, Sweden, and Norway; among the middle income economies in this list are Latvia, Malta, the Czech Republic, Russia, and Estonia. For cable television, only Monaco has more than 50 percent penetration; the other leading economies in this regard are Liechtenstein, the Netherlands, Belgium, and Switzerland. For home satellite antennas, Faroe Island has the highest penetration rate at 42 percent of its population, followed by Austria at 19 percent penetration, Hungary at 17 percent, and Germany at 16 percent.

As of 2002, there were 20 economies in the region that had Internet penetration rates lower than 10 percent, which is the world average. The three raising the most concern are Tajikistan, where 1 person in every 1,822 is an Internet user; Turkmenistan, which has a ratio of 1 user for every 606 persons; and Albania, which has a ratio of 1 Internet user for every 403 persons. In terms of personal computers, data were missing for 12 economies in the region, but among those that had available data, Albania had the lowest penetration rate with 1 computer for every 134 persons, and Armenia followed with 1 personal computer for every 109 persons. In terms of main telephone lines, only five economies in the region had less than 10 percent penetration rate: Turkmenistan, Kyrgyzstan, Uzbekistan, Albania, and Tajikistan. The last in the list, Tajikistan, had a 4 percent penetration rate. For cellular mobile telephone subscribers, nine economies in the region had a less than 10 percent penetration rate; Turkmenistan and Tajikistan have among the lowest penetration rates, both with less than 1 percent. In terms of television penetration, only one country in the region has less than a 10 percent penetration—Kyrgyzstan, with a 5 percent rate.

One of the economies in the region with among the lowest penetration rates but that has made considerable progress over the last three years is Albania. Between 1999 and 2002, Albania increased its number of Internet users by 300 percent, personal computers by 50 percent, main telephone lines by 57 percent, television receivers by 115 percent and, notably, the number of cellular mobile telephone subscribers by 7,167 percent.

Asia and the Pacific

Asia and the Pacific, a region comprising 33 economies, has a combined population of 2.1 billion, of which 193 million, or 9 percent, are Internet users and 137 million, or 7 percent, have personal computers (see Table 10). There are more cellular mobile telephone subscribers in the region than there are main telephone lines: about 424 million cellular mobile telephone subscribers compared to 368 million main telephone lines. In terms of television, the region has 648 million television receivers, 139 million cable television subscribers, and 17 million home satellite antennas.

Over the period 1999–2002, the number of Internet users in the region surged by 187 percent while the number of cellular mobile telephone subscribers jumped by 165 percent. The growth in cellular mobile telephone subscribers has increased the penetration rate from 8 percent to 20 percent in three years, the latter rate being higher than the main line penetration rate of 18 percent. Slowest growth rates in the region were in television receivers, up 11 percent, and home satellite antennas, which only increased by 2 percent. Television, however, is the most pervasive device in the region, with a 31 percent penetration rate.

In terms of actual numbers, China leads the region in Internet users, main telephone lines, cellular mobile telephone subscribers, television receivers, and cable television subscribers. China also leads the region in terms of growth rates in many of these technologies. In the 1999–2002 period, China increased its number of main telephone lines by 97 percent, cellular mobile telephone subscribers by 377 percent, and the number of Internet users by 564 percent. Overall penetration rates, however, still have much room for improvement: main telephone and cellular mobile telephone penetration rates are below 20 percent while Internet user and personal computer penetration rates are in the low single digits.

Japan leads the region in the number of personal computers and home satellite antennas. It is second to China in the number of Internet users, the number of main telephone lines in operation, cellular mobile telephone subscribers, television receivers and cable television subscribers. Despite relatively high levels of penetration, Japan continued to post significant increases. Over the period 1999–2002, Japan added 30 million new Internet users, 12 million personal computers, 24 million cellular mobile telephone subscribers, 9 million television receivers, and more than 5 million cable television subscribers. In terms of penetration rates, Japan leads the region in television receivers and home satellite antennas.

In actual numbers, as of 2002, the Republic of Korea is second in the region in terms of personal computers, with more than 26 million units. The country is third in the region in the number of Internet users, the number of main telephone lines, cellular mobile telephone subscribers, and cable television subscribers.

Next to China, Japan, and the Republic of Korea is Taiwan, which is fourth in terms of total number of Internet users, main telephone lines, cellular mobile telephone subscribers and cable television subscribers, and fifth in the penetration of personal computers. Australia is fourth in terms of

numbers of personal computers and home satellite antennas but fifth in numbers of Internet users and main telephone lines. Indonesia is third in the region for numbers of television receivers and second for home satellite antennas, and Thailand is fourth in the region in terms of television receivers and fifth in terms of cellular mobile telephone subscribers and home satellite antennas. Malaysia is third in numbers of home satellite antennas while the Philippines is fifth in the region in terms of the number of cable television subscribers.

In terms of Internet users, two economies in the region have greater than 50 percent penetration rates: Republic of Korea and Singapore. These two economies are followed by New Zealand, Japan, Hong Kong, and Australia, all of which have penetration rates higher than 40 percent. For personal computers, three economies, Republic of Korea, Australia, and Singapore have penetration rates above 50 percent, followed by Taiwan at a 40 percent penetration rate. In terms of main telephone line penetration, Taiwan, Hong Kong, Japan, Australia, and Guam have the highest rates, all exceeding 50 percent. Similarly, Taiwan also leads in the region in terms of cellular mobile telephone penetration, but this time followed by Hong Kong, Singapore, and Republic of Korea. Significantly, 9 out of 33 economies in the region have cellular mobile telephone penetration rates greater than 60 percent. Television penetration rates are also significantly high in the region, with Japan at 78 percent, Australia at 72 percent, Guam at 71 percent and Brunei at 61 percent. For cable television, Taiwan, followed by Guam and Japan, has the highest penetration rates while for home satellite antennas, Japan leads, followed by New Zealand.

As of 2002, 19 of the 33 economies have Internet penetration rates below 10 percent, including China, Indonesia, the Philippines, Thailand, and Vietnam. Of the 19 economies with single-digit Internet penetration rates, four have penetration rates below 1 percent: Solomon Islands, Laos, Cambodia, and Myanmar (there is no figure for the Democratic People's Republic of Korea). The latter three economies also have personal computer penetration rates below 1 percent. In terms of main telephone line penetration, 15 economies have a less than 10 percent penetration rate, with Cambodia having the lowest rate of less than 1 percent. For cellular mobile telephone penetration rates, 13 economies have less than a 10 percent penetration rate (data are missing for two economies). Television penetration rates tend to be higher, with 11 economies having penetration rates of less than 10 percent.

Of concern is Myanmar, which ranks among those with the lowest penetration rates in the region across various indicators. The country has 1 television for every 134 persons, 1 main telephone line for every 166 persons, 1 personal computer for every 891 persons, 1 cellular mobile

Table 12. Regional Highlights: Leading Countries in Growth and Penetration, Asia and the Pacific

	Change (units), 1999–2002			Change (%), 1999–2002			Penetration rate (% of Population), 2002
Internet users (estimated)							
1	China	50,200,000	1	Myanmar	1,900	1	Korea, Republic of	55
2	Japan	30,140,000	2	Reunion	1,400	2	Singapore	54
3	Korea, Republic of	15,410,000	3	Vietnam	1,400	3	New Zealand	48
4	Indonesia	7,100,000	4	Indonesia	789	4	Japan	45
5	Malaysia	4,700,000	5	Samoa	700	5	Hong Kong SAR	43
6	Taiwan	3,790,000	6	Lao, PDR	650	6	Australia	43
7	Thailand	3,500,000	7	Cambodia	650	7	Taiwan	38
8	Australia	2,800,000	8	Vanuatu	600	8	Malaysia	31
9	Philippines	2,410,000	9	China	564	9	Guam	30
10	Hong Kong SAR	1,518,800	10	French Polynesia	338	10	Macau	26
Personal computers							
1	Korea, Republic of	14,928,000	1	Korea, Republic of	129	1	Korea, Republic of	56
2	Japan	12,400,000	2	Mongolia	108	2	Australia	51
3	China	9,500,000	3	Malaysia	100	3	Singapore	50
4	Taiwan	2,226,100	4	Marshall Islands	100	4	Taiwan	40
5	Australia	2,000,000	5	Thailand	78	5	Hong Kong SAR	38
6	Malaysia	1,800,000	6	Philippines	75	6	Japan	38
7	Thailand	1,079,000	7	China	61	7	New Zealand	38
8	Philippines	940,000	8	Vietnam	60	8	French Polynesia	28
9	Hong Kong SAR	600,000	9	Cambodia	54	9	Macau	21
10	Singapore	400,000	10	Macau	53	10	Malaysia	15
Main telephone lines in operation							
1	China	105,704,200	1	China	97	1	Taiwan	58
2	Korea, Republic of	2,738,910	2	Lao, PDR	76	2	Hong Kong SAR	57
3	Indonesia	1,669,842	3	Vietnam	74	3	Japan	56
4	Vietnam	1,558,861	4	Indonesia	27	4	Australia	54
5	Thailand	1,284,206	5	Thailand	25	5	Guam	50
6	Taiwan	1,055,660	6	Mongolia	24	6	Korea, Republic of	49
7	Australia	830,000	7	Tonga	23	7	Singapore	46
8	Japan	619,000	8	Cambodia	21	8	New Zealand	45
9	Philippines	446,491	9	Samoa	21	9	Reunion	40
10	Malaysia	239,201	10	Vanuatu	20	10	Macau	40
Cellular mobile telephone subscribers							
1	China	163,324,000	1	Tonga	2,296	1	Taiwan	106
2	Japan	24,272,410	2	Vanuatu	1,533	2	Hong Kong SAR	93
3	Thailand	13,777,599	3	Thailand	589	3	Singapore	79
4	Taiwan	12,364,270	4	Mongolia	525	4	Korea, Republic of	68
5	Philippines	11,366,250	5	Vietnam	479	5	Reunion	66
6	Indonesia	9,479,031	6	Indonesia	427	6	Australia	64
7	Korea, Republic of	8,899,280	7	Philippines	399	7	Japan	64
8	Australia	6,264,000	8	China	377	8	Macau	63
9	Malaysia	6,255,000	9	Lao, PDR	357	9	New Zealand	62
10	Hong Kong SAR	2,022,493	10	Reunion	341	10	Brunei Darussalam	39
Television receivers							
1	China	40,000,000	1	Dem. People's Rep. of Korea	195	1	Japan	78
2	Japan	9,000,000	2	Papua New Guinea	83	2	Australia	72
3	Philippines	6,300,000	3	Philippines	77	3	Guam	71
4	Dem. People's Rep. of Korea	2,535,000	4	Solomon Islands	71	4	Brunei Darussalam	61
5	Indonesia	2,000,000	5	Kiribati	35	5	New Zealand	54
6	Thailand	1,700,000	6	Tonga	27	6	Hong Kong SAR	50
7	Australia	768,000	7	Malaysia	13	7	New Caledonia	50
8	Taiwan	760,000	8	Myanmar	13	8	Taiwan	44
9	Vietnam	609,000	9	China	11	9	Korea, Republic of	36
10	Malaysia	555,000	10	Thailand	10	10	China	32

Source: Author's calculations based on data from the International Telecommunication Union, World Telecommunication Indicators Database, accessed July 2003

telephone subscriber in every 3,555 persons, and 1 Internet user in every 4,899 persons.

Latin America and the Caribbean

Of the 531 million people in the 38 economies in the Latin America and the Caribbean region, 36 million (7 percent of the population) are Internet users and a slightly lower figure, 33 million (6 percent of the population), have personal computers (see Table 10). As in Europe and Asia, the region has more cellular mobile telephone subscribers (102 million) than the number of main telephone lines (89 million). The region has 150 million television receivers, 15 million cable television subscribers, and 2.7 million home satellite antennas.

From 1999–2002, the region has experienced a 245 percent increase in the number of Internet users and a 148 percent increase in the number of cellular mobile telephone subscribers. Personal computers grew by 71 percent while home satellite antennas increased by 66 percent. Growth of television receivers was relatively mild at 10 percent, and brought the television penetration rate to 28 percent of total population. The region's cellular mobile telephone penetration rate of 19 percent exceeds the main telephone line penetration rate of 17 percent. Internet and personal computer penetration in the region, at 7 percent and 6 percent respectively, is below the world average of 10 percent and 9 percent, respectively.

In terms of actual numbers, Brazil leads the region in the number of Internet users, personal computers, main telephone lines in operation, cellular mobile telephone subscribers, television receivers, and home satellite antennas. Brazil is succeeded by Mexico, which holds the second highest number for all the indicators. Argentina is first for the number of cable television subscribers and third for Internet users, personal computers, main telephone lines, cellular mobile telephones, and home satellite antennas. Chile is fourth in the number of Internet users and home satellite antennas, and fifth for numbers of personal computers, main telephone lines, cellular mobile telephone subscribers, television receivers, and cable television subscribers. Colombia is fourth in terms of personal computers and number of main telephone lines in operation and fifth in terms of numbers of home satellite antennas. Venezuela is fourth in numbers of cellular mobile telephone subscribers and cable television subscribers.

For both Internet users and personal computers, no economy in the region has a penetration rate higher than 50 percent. Twenty-seven economies in the region, including Brazil, Mexico, Colombia, Venezuela, and Peru have less than a 10 percent penetration rate for Internet and personal computers. In terms of main telephone lines, the region has two economies, Bermuda and the Virgin Islands, with penetration rates above 50 percent, while nine economies have main telephone line penetration rates below 10 percent. Cuba,

Honduras, Paraguay, Nicaragua, and Haiti have among the lowest main telephone penetration rates. For cellular mobile telephones, three economies have penetration rates above 50 percent—Martinique, Guadeloupe, and Jamaica—while seven economies have penetration rates below 10 percent. Honduras, Nicaragua, Haiti, and Cuba have among the lowest cellular mobile telephone penetration rates. In terms of television receivers, five economies in the region, including Chile and Uruguay, have penetration rates above 50 percent, and only two economies have penetration rates below 10 percent.

Of the economies in the region, Cuba has one of the lowest penetration rates for some indicators. The country has a 1 percent Internet penetration rate, with 1 Internet user in every 94 persons. In terms of telephone lines, Cuba has a 5 percent penetration rate, with 1 main telephone line for every 20 persons. Perhaps the most striking statistic is the number of cellular mobile telephone subscribers, which, at 17,851, is equivalent to 1 subscriber in every 632 persons.

South Asia

South Asia, a region of eight economies and a combined population of 1.4 billion, has 18.6 million Internet users and 7.4 million personal computers (see Table 10). The region has 47 million main telephone lines and 16 million cellular mobile telephone subscribers. Television receivers are more prevalent than any other device—there are 117 million television receivers in the region and 44 million cable television subscribers but less than 4,000 home satellite antennas.

In the last three years, the region added nearly 19 million television receivers and more than 16 million main telephone lines. In the same period there were 15 million new Internet users, a growth of 512 percent. The region also increased the number of cellular mobile telephone subscribers by 13.4 million, equivalent to a growth of 520 percent, and added 3.2 million personal computers and 6.6 million cable television subscribers during the three-year period.

Overall, regional penetration rates have been quite low, the highest being the television penetration rate at 6 percent of total population. Penetration rates of main telephone lines and cable television subscribers are in the 2 percent range, while the region's cellular mobile telephone penetration is at 1 percent. The penetration rate of personal computers is less than 1 percent.

As the largest economy in the region in terms of weight and population, India also has the highest numbers for the various devices and user indicators. The scale in which India has been improving in the last three years is quite remarkable—the country added nearly 15 million main telephone lines, nearly 14 million Internet users, 103 million cellular mobile telephone subscribers, 10 million television receivers, 3 million cable television subscribers, and 2.7 million personal computers.

Table 13. Regional Highlights: Leading Countries in Growth and Penetration, Latin America and the Caribbean

Internet users (estimated)

#	Change (units), 1999–2002		#	Change (%), 1999–2002		#	Penetration rate (% of Population), 2002	
1	Brazil	10,800,000	1	Haiti	1,233	1	Bermuda	46
2	Chile	2,950,000	2	Martinique	700	2	Chile	24
3	Argentina	2,900,000	3	Dominica	525	3	Aruba	22
4	Mexico	2,841,166	4	Guatemala	515	4	Dominica	16
5	Peru	1,500,000	5	Aruba	500	5	Puerto Rico	16
6	Colombia	1,318,000	6	El Salvador	500	6	Virgin Islands (US)	15
7	Venezuela	594,429	7	Chile	472	7	Uruguay	12
8	Ecuador	403,315	8	Honduras	471	8	Argentina	11
9	Puerto Rico	400,000	9	Ecuador	403	9	Guyana	11
10	Guatemala	335,000	10	Paraguay	400	10	Trinidad and Tobago	11

Personal computers

#	Change (units), 1999–2002		#	Change (%), 1999–2002		#	Penetration rate (% of Population), 2002	
1	Brazil	6,900,000	1	Paraguay	233	1	Bermuda	49
2	Mexico	2,600,000	2	Brazil	113	2	Guadeloupe	22
3	Argentina	900,000	3	Cuba	100	3	Costa Rica	17
4	Colombia	733,000	4	Bolivia	90	4	Belize	14
5	Chile	641,814	5	Costa Rica	75	5	Martinique	13
6	Peru	350,000	6	Ecuador	61	6	Grenada	12
7	Costa Rica	300,000	7	Mexico	60	7	St. Vincent and the Grenadines	12
8	Venezuela	300,000	8	Chile	56	8	Chile	12
9	Ecuador	152,652	9	Colombia	52	9	Uruguay	11
10	Paraguay	140,000	10	Nicaragua	50	10	Barbados	9

Main telephone lines in operation

#	Change (units), 1999–2002		#	Change (%), 1999–2002		#	Penetration rate (% of Population), 2002	
1	Brazil	13,825,000	1	Haiti	86	1	Bermuda	86
2	Mexico	4,014,240	2	Brazil	55	2	Virgin Islands (US)	63
3	Colombia	1,100,578	3	Guatemala	39	3	Barbados	48
4	Argentina	652,672	4	Mexico	37	4	Antigua and Barbuda	48
5	Chile	358,403	5	El Salvador	35	5	Guadeloupe	45
6	Peru	334,265	6	Cuba	32	6	Martinique	42
7	Ecuador	296,660	7	Costa Rica	29	7	Bahamas	41
8	Venezuela	290,982	8	Ecuador	26	8	Netherlands Antilles	37
9	Costa Rica	235,389	9	Guyana	26	9	Puerto Rico	34
10	Guatemala	235,267	10	Peru	20	10	Aruba	34

Cellular mobile telephone subscribers

#	Change (units), 1999–2002		#	Change (%), 1999–2002		#	Penetration rate (% of Population), 2002	
1	Brazil	19,848,300	1	Guyana	3,001	1	Martinique	79
2	Mexico	18,196,625	2	Dominica	1,070	2	Guadeloupe	70
3	Chile	4,185,011	3	Jamaica	870	3	Jamaica	53
4	Venezuela	2,678,826	4	Trinidad and Tobago	836	4	Aruba	48
5	Colombia	2,630,465	5	Belize	697	5	Chile	43
6	Argentina	2,066,000	6	Bahamas	665	6	Bahamas	39
7	Peru	1,286,686	7	St. Vincent and the Grenadines	603	7	Virgin Islands (US)	37
8	Jamaica	1,255,612	8	Haiti	460	8	Antigua and Barbuda	32
9	Guatemala	1,239,285	9	Nicaragua	442	9	Puerto Rico	31
10	Paraguay	1,231,407	10	Suriname	397	10	Paraguay	29

Television receivers

#	Change (units), 1999–2002		#	Change (%), 1999–2002		#	Penetration rate (% of Population), 2002	
1	Brazil	4,000,000	1	Jamaica	98	1	Bermuda	108
2	Chile	3,668,711	2	Chile	87	2	Virgin Islands (US)	65
3	Mexico	1,800,000	3	Guyana	42	3	Uruguay	52
4	Colombia	1,499,020	4	Haiti	19	4	Chile	52
5	Jamaica	481,000	5	Honduras	18	5	Antigua and Barbuda	45
6	Ecuador	424,633	6	Ecuador	16	6	Jamaica	37
7	Argentina	400,000	7	Suriname	15	7	Grenada	35
8	Venezuela	214,258	8	Guatemala	13	8	Brazil	35
9	Peru	200,000	9	Colombia	13	9	Trinidad and Tobago	34
10	Guatemala	200,000	10	Barbados	13	10	Puerto Rico	34

Source: Author's calculations based on data from the International Telecommunication Union, World Telecommunication Indicators Database, accessed July 2003

Table 14. **Regional Highlights: Leading Countries in Growth and Penetration, South Asia**

		Change (units), 1999–2002			Change (%), 1999–2002			Penetration rate (% of Population) 2002
Internet users (estimated)								
1	Maldives	12,000	1	Maldives	400	1	Maldives	5
2	India	13,780,000	2	India	492	2	India	2
3	Bhutan	9,250	3	Bhutan	1,233	3	Bhutan	1
4	Sri Lanka	135,000	4	Sri Lanka	208	4	Sri Lanka	1
5	Pakistan	1,420,000	5	Pakistan	1,775	5	Pakistan	1
6	Nepal	25,000	6	Nepal	71	6	Nepal	0
7	Bangladesh	154,000	7	Bangladesh	308	7	Bangladesh	0
8	Afghanistan	n/a	8	Afghanistan	n/a	8	Afghanistan	n/a
Personal computers								
1	Maldives	12,500	1	Maldives	167	1	Maldives	7
2	Bhutan	7,000	2	Bhutan	233	2	Bhutan	1
3	Sri Lanka	145,000	3	Sri Lanka	138	3	Sri Lanka	1
4	India	2,700,000	4	India	82	4	India	1
5	Pakistan	20,000	5	Pakistan	3	5	Pakistan	0
6	Nepal	20,000	6	Nepal	33	6	Nepal	0
7	Bangladesh	320,000	7	Bangladesh	246	7	Bangladesh	0
8	Afghanistan	n/a	8	Afghanistan	n/a	8	Afghanistan	n/a
Main telephone lines in operation								
1	India	14,908,660	1	Bhutan	64	1	Maldives	10
2	Pakistan	703,893	2	Bangladesh	58	2	Sri Lanka	5
3	Bangladesh	249,032	3	India	56	3	India	4
4	Sri Lanka	211,192	4	Sri Lanka	31	4	Bhutan	3
5	Nepal	74,638	5	Nepal	29	5	Pakistan	2
6	Bhutan	7,625	6	Maldives	29	6	Nepal	1
7	Maldives	6,472	7	Pakistan	24	7	Bangladesh	1
8	Afghanistan	4,050	8	Afghanistan	14	8	Afghanistan	0
Cellular mobile telephone subscribers								
1	India	10,803,329	1	Maldives	1,332	1	Maldives	15
2	Pakistan	940,170	2	Bangladesh	621	2	Sri Lanka	5
3	Bangladesh	926,000	3	India	573	3	India	1
4	Sri Lanka	674,925	4	Pakistan	337	4	Pakistan	1
5	Maldives	38,973	5	Nepal	298	5	Bangladesh	1
6	Nepal	16,381	6	Sri Lanka	263	6	Nepal	0
7	Afghanistan	12,000	7	Afghanistan	n/a	7	Afghanistan	0
8	Bhutan	0	8	Bhutan	n/a	8	Bhutan	0
Television receivers								
1	India	10,000,000	1	Bangladesh	68	1	Pakistan	14
2	Pakistan	5,390,000	2	Maldives	41	2	Maldives	13
3	Bangladesh	3,171,102	3	Bhutan	38	3	Sri Lanka	12
4	Sri Lanka	300,000	4	Pakistan	34	4	India	8
5	Nepal	43,000	5	Nepal	29	5	Bangladesh	6
6	Afghanistan	20,000	6	Sri Lanka	16	6	Bhutan	3
7	Maldives	10,700	7	India	13	7	Afghanistan	1
8	Bhutan	5,000	8	Afghanistan	7	8	Nepal	1

Note: *or latest available data
Source: Author's calculations based on data from the International Telecommunication Union, World Telecommunication Indicators Database, accessed July 2003

None of the economies in the region has a penetration rate of more than 20 percent for any of the indicators. The penetration rates are notably high for television receivers, where Pakistan at 14 percent has the highest rate percent, followed by Maldives at 13 percent and Sri Lanka at 12 percent; the rest of the economies have single-digit penetration rates. In terms of main telephone lines only the Maldives reaches the 10 percent mark, with India at a 4 percent penetration rate, Pakistan at 2 percent, and Bangladesh at 1 percent. In terms of cellular mobile telephone penetration, Maldives has a 15 percent penetration rate followed by Sri Lanka at 5 percent while India, Pakistan, and Bangladesh post a 1 percent penetration rate.

In this region, penetration rates for Bangladesh, Nepal, and Afghanistan are cause for concern. In Bangladesh, only 1 person in every 653 is an Internet user; there is 1 personal computer for every 296 persons and 1 main telephone line for every 195 persons. Similarly, Nepal has 1 television for every 120 persons, 1 personal computer for every 290 persons, 1 Internet user in every 387 persons, and 1 cellular mobile telephone subscriber in every 1,060 persons. Finally, Afghanistan has 1 main telephone line for every 705 persons and 1 cellular mobile telephone subscriber in every 1,941 persons.

Middle East and North Africa

The Middle East and North Africa, a region of 20 economies, has a combined population of 320 million, roughly equivalent to the combined population of the United States and Canada (see Table 10). Of the region's 320 million people, about 13 million, or 4 percent, are Internet users and about 14 million have personal computers. The Middle East and North Africa region is one of the few regions where the number of personal computers exceeds the estimated number of Internet users. In terms of telecommunications, the region has 39 million main telephone lines (12 percent individual penetration) and 33 million cellular mobile telephone subscribers (10 percent individual penetration). The region also has 63 million television receivers, and a far higher number of home satellite antennas, nearly 12 million, than cable television subscribers, which number 1.4 million.

Between 1999 and 2002 the region posted a 388 percent increase in the number of Internet users, equivalent to 10.2 million new users, and a 340 percent increase in cellular mobile telephone subscribers, equivalent to 25.8 million new subscribers. Personal computers increased by 56 percent while main telephone lines and home satellite antennas both grew by 34 percent. At a slower pace were increases in cable television at 12 percent and television receivers at 9 percent.

Television penetration rate in the region is 20 percent. Main telephone lines and cellular mobile telephone subscriber penetration rates are slightly lower at 12 percent and 10 percent, respectively. Penetration rates of both Internet users and personal computers are both at 4 percent, leaving much room for improvement.

In the region, Iran has the highest number of Internet users, personal computers, and main telephone lines. Over the last three years Iran has added 2.9 million Internet users, a 1,167 percent increase. During the same period, Iran also increased the number of personal computers by 1 million, main telephone lines by 4.7 million, and cellular mobile telephone subscribers by 1.8 million.

Israel has the highest number of cellular mobile telephone subscribers and cable television subscribers, and the second highest number of Internet users. In the last three years, Israel added 1.2 million Internet users, a 150 percent increase. During the same period, Israel also added 3.4 million cellular mobile telephone subscribers, a 120 percent increase.

Saudi Arabia is second in the region in terms of the number of personal computers and home satellite antennas. It ranks third in the region in the number of Internet users, main telephone lines in operation, television receivers and cable television subscribers. Notably, during the period 1999–2002 the number of Internet users in Saudi Arabia rose by 1.5 million, an increase of 1,500 percent. Similarly, the country increased its number of personal computers by 150 percent or 1.8 million. Saudi Arabia also posted a notable increase in the number of cellular mobile telephone subscribers, adding 4 million over the last three years, which is equivalent to a growth of 499 percent.

Egypt has the second highest number of telephone lines in the region, and the fourth highest number of cellular mobile telephone subscribers, Internet users, and personal computers. Over the last three years, Egypt expanded its number of Internet users by 650 percent, adding 1.3 million new users. The country also added more than 2.7 million main telephone lines and more than 4 million new cellular mobile telephone subscribers.

In terms of Internet penetration rates, at 37 percent the United Arab Emirates has the highest in the region. The United Arab Emirates is followed by Israel at 30 percent penetration, Bahrain at 25 percent, and Lebanon at 12 percent. In terms of personal computers, Israel has the highest penetration rate at 24 percent, followed by Qatar at 18 percent and Bahrain at 16 percent. In terms of main telephone lines, Israel has the highest penetration rate at 47 percent, followed by the United Arab Emirates at 34 percent and Qatar at 29 percent. Similarly, Israel has the highest cellular mobile telephone penetration at 95 percent followed by the United Arab Emirates with a 76 percent penetration rate and Bahrain at 58 percent. In terms of television penetration, Qatar has the highest rate at 87 percent, followed by Oman at 55 percent and Bahrain at 43 percent. For cable television, Israel has the highest penetration rate at 18 percent, and for home satellite antennas Kuwait has the highest penetration rate of 27 percent.

Table 15. **Regional Highlights: Leading Countries in Growth and Penetration, Middle East and North Africa**

	Change (units), 1999–2002			Change (%), 1999–2002			Penetration rate (% of Population), 2002	
Internet users (estimated)								
1	Iran	2,918,000	1	Libya	1,686	1	United Arab Emirates	37
2	Saudi Arabia	1,500,000	2	Saudi Arabia	1,500	2	Israel	30
3	Egypt	1,300,000	3	Iran	1,167	3	Bahrain	25
4	Israel	1,200,000	4	Syria	1,000	4	Lebanon	12
5	United Arab Emirates	717,615	5	Morocco	900	5	Qatar	11
6	Morocco	450,000	6	Algeria	733	6	Kuwait	11
7	Algeria	440,000	7	Egypt	650	7	Saudi Arabia	7
8	Tunisia	355,500	8	Djibouti	500	8	Oman	7
9	Lebanon	200,000	9	Bahrain	450	9	Jordan	6
10	Syria	200,000	10	Yemen	300	10	Tunisia	5
Personal computers								
1	Saudi Arabia	1,803,000	1	Yemen	383	1	Israel	24
2	Iran	1,000,000	2	Saudi Arabia	150	2	Qatar	18
3	Egypt	370,000	3	Jordan	122	3	Bahrain	16
4	Israel	240,000	4	Tunisia	107	4	United Arab Emirates	14
5	Tunisia	155,000	5	Lebanon	83	5	Saudi Arabia	13
6	United Arab Emirates	150,000	6	Djibouti	67	6	Kuwait	12
7	Lebanon	125,000	7	United Arab Emirates	50	7	Lebanon	8
8	Yemen	115,000	8	Egypt	49	8	Iran	7
9	Jordan	110,000	9	Oman	46	9	Jordan	4
10	Syria	100,000	10	Syria	43	10	Oman	4
Main telephone lines in operation								
1	Iran	4,703,833	1	Yemen	79	1	Israel	47
2	Egypt	2,743,639	2	Egypt	59	2	United Arab Emirates	34
3	Saudi Arabia	611,361	3	Iran	56	3	Qatar	29
4	Syria	498,955	4	Tunisia	35	4	Bahrain	26
5	Algeria	308,000	5	West Bank and Gaza	34	5	Kuwait	20
6	Tunisia	297,619	6	Syria	31	6	Iran	20
7	Yemen	225,704	7	Saudi Arabia	23	7	Lebanon	20
8	Israel	222,000	8	Jordan	22	8	Saudi Arabia	14
9	Jordan	122,325	9	Libya	20	9	Jordan	13
10	United Arab Emirates	118,476	10	Algeria	19	10	Syria	12
Cellular mobile telephone subscribers								
1	Morocco	5,829,496	1	Syria	9,900	1	Israel	95
2	Saudi Arabia	4,171,337	2	Djibouti	5,257	2	United Arab Emirates	76
3	Egypt	4,013,726	3	Yemen	1,707	3	Bahrain	58
4	Israel	3,454,000	4	Morocco	1,579	4	Kuwait	52
5	Iran	1,829,082	5	Jordan	930	5	Qatar	44
6	United Arab Emirates	1,595,804	6	Egypt	834	6	Jordan	23
7	Jordan	1,101,180	7	Tunisia	812	7	Lebanon	23
8	Kuwait	927,000	8	Saudi Arabia	499	8	Saudi Arabia	22
9	Yemen	472,323	9	Algeria	456	9	Morocco	21
10	Tunisia	448,653	10	Iran	373	10	Oman	17
Television receivers								
1	Egypt	1,400,000	1	Syria	28	1	Qatar	87
2	Iran	1,000,000	2	Jordan	11	2	Oman	55
3	Syria	674,300	3	Tunisia	11	3	Bahrain	43
4	Saudi Arabia	407,000	4	Egypt	10	4	Kuwait	40
5	Yemen	310,000	5	Iran	10	5	Lebanon	35
6	Morocco	293,381	6	Israel	8	6	Israel	32
7	Tunisia	200,000	7	Saudi Arabia	7	7	Yemen	27
8	Israel	150,000	8	Morocco	6	8	Saudi Arabia	26
9	Jordan	95,000	9	Yemen	6	9	United Arab Emirates	24
10	Oman	85,000	10	Oman	6	10	Egypt	23

Source: Author's calculations based on data from the International Telecommunication Union, World Telecommunication Indicators Database, accessed July 2003

For television, only two economies, Iraq and Djibouti, have penetration rates below 10 percent. For main telephone lines, seven economies have single-digit penetration rates, including Algeria and Morocco. For cellular mobile telephone subscribers, 10 economies have less than 10 percent penetration rates, including Egypt, Tunisia, Iran, Yemen, and Syria. In terms of Internet users, Saudi Arabia, Jordan, and Tunisia are among the 14 economies in the region with penetration rates that are lower than the world average of 10 percent. In the region, Yemen has the lowest Internet penetration, with 1 Internet user for every 485 persons. In terms of personal computers, Morocco, Iraq, Yemen, and Algeria have penetration rates of about 1 percent of population.

Sub-Saharan Africa

Sub-Saharan Africa, a region with 47 economies and a combined population of 676 million, has about 6 million Internet users and nearly 7 million personal computers (see Table 10). There are nearly 23 million cellular mobile telephone subscribers, which is more than twice the 10.2 million main telephone lines in operation. Like other regions, television is the most prevalent of the ICT devices included in the study. There are 47 million television receivers in the region, and about 1.2 million home satellite antennas and 188,000 cable television subscribers.

Over the last three years, cellular mobile telephones increased by 253 percent in the region, an addition of 16.3 million. During the same period, only 1 million lines were added, an 11 percent increase. Consequently, in 20 economies of the region, the number of cellular mobile telephone subscribers exceeds the number of main telephone lines.

Regional Internet growth, although it was an increase of 156 percent, amounted to only 3.6 million new users. This means that in the last three years, the region added slightly fewer users than what Taiwan, an economy with about 22 million people, added during the same period. Personal computers in the region also rose by only 2 million during the three-year period, an increase of 43 percent. While the increase is certainly welcome, it is disappointing when one takes into account that it is slightly less than the increase in the number of personal computers in Taiwan.

South Africa has the highest number of Internet users, personal computers, main telephone lines in operation, cellular mobile telephone subscribers, and home satellite antennas in the region. The country added nearly 1.3 million Internet users over the last three years, a 70 percent increase. In terms of the number of cellular mobile telephone subscribers, the country added 6.9 million, an increase of 133 percent.

Other economies in the region with notable ICT bases are Nigeria, Kenya, Zimbabwe, and Sudan. Nigeria has the highest number of cable television subscribers in the region,

and the second highest number of personal computers, main telephone lines in operation, and cellular mobile telephone subscribers. Kenya has the second highest number of Internet users (tied with Zimbabwe) and the third highest number of cellular mobile telephone subscribers. Zimbabwe has the second highest number of Internet users, the third highest number of personal computers, and the third highest number of cable television subscribers. Sudan has the largest number of television receivers in the region, the third largest number of main telephone lines, and the fifth largest number of personal computers.

In terms of penetration rates, Mauritius and the Seychelles interchange for the top 2 slots for most of the technologies. Mauritius has the highest Internet penetration rate at 15 percent of its population, followed by the Seychelles at 11 percent and South Africa at 7 percent. For personal computers, the Seychelles has the highest penetration rate at 14 percent of the population, Mauritius is second with 11 percent penetration and Cape Verde is third, with 8 percent penetration. In terms of the number of cellular mobile telephone subscribers, the Seychelles registered a 53 percent penetration rate, followed by Mauritius at 29 percent and South Africa at 27 percent. For television receivers, Sudan has the highest penetration rate at 39 percent, followed by Gabon and Mauritius at 30 percent

The penetration rates for the majority of the economies in the region are cause for concern. Forty-three economies in the region have a less than 5 percent penetration rate for Internet users. Of the 43 economies, 30 of them have penetration rates below 1 percent. The Central African Republic, Ethiopia, Liberia, and the Democratic Republic of Congo have among the worst Internet penetration rates. In the latter, for example, only 1 in every 8,774 persons is an Internet user, a far cry from the world average of 1 in every 10 persons.

Personal computers present a similar picture. Only two economies, the Seychelles and Mauritius, post penetration rates higher than 10 percent. The rest of the region either has less than 10 percent, or no data are available. Of those where data are available, at least 17 have penetration rates below 1 percent. Among those with the lowest penetration rates for personal computers is Niger, with 1 personal computer for every 1,958 persons.

In terms of main telephone lines, 41 out of 47 economies in sub-Saharan Africa have a penetration rate below 5 percent. At least 31 of these economies have penetration rates of 1 percent or less. Some of the worst rates are in the Democratic Republic of the Congo, where there is an estimated 1 main telephone line for every 2,632 persons.

For cellular mobile telephone subscribers, 33 economies have a penetration rate below 5 percent. Of these 33 economies,

Table 16. **Regional Highlights: Leading Countries in Growth and Penetration, Sub-Saharan Africa**

	Change (units), 1999–2002			Change (%), 1999–2002			Penetration rate (% of Population), 2002	
Internet users (estimated)								
1	South Africa	1,280,000	1	Somalia	44,400	1	Mauritius	15
2	Zimbabwe	480,000	2	Zimbabwe	2,400	2	Seychelles	11
3	Kenya	465,000	3	Lesotho	2,000	3	South Africa	7
4	Togo	170,000	4	Sao Tome and Principe	1,700	4	Sao Tome and Principe	6
5	Nigeria	150,000	5	Sudan	1,580	5	Zimbabwe	4
6	Mauritius	125,000	6	Chad	1,400	6	Togo	4
7	Somalia	88,800	7	Kenya	1,329	7	Cape Verde	4
8	Sudan	79,000	8	Congo, DR	1,100	8	Botswana	3
9	Senegal	75,000	9	Eritrea	900	9	Namibia	2
10	Tanzania	75,000	10	Congo, DR	900	10	Swaziland	2
Personal computers								
1	South Africa	700,000	1	Zimbabwe	300	1	Seychelles	14
2	Zimbabwe	450,000	2	Equatorial Guinea	250	2	Mauritius	11
3	Sudan	115,000	3	Togo	200	3	Cape Verde	8
4	Togo	100,000	4	Sudan	135	4	South Africa	7
5	Nigeria	100,000	5	Gabon	127	5	Namibia	5
6	Senegal	60,000	6	Angola	125	6	Zimbabwe	5
7	Ethiopia	55,000	7	Ethiopia	122	7	Botswana	4
8	Namibia	50,000	8	Comoros	110	8	Togo	3
9	Kenya	50,000	9	Namibia	100	9	Senegal	2
10	Tanzania	40,000	10	Eritrea	79	10	Gabon	2
Main telephone lines in operation								
1	Sudan	420,422	1	Somalia	186	1	Mauritius	27
2	Nigeria	251,828	2	Sudan	167	2	Seychelles	26
3	Ethiopia	173,705	3	Mauritania	94	3	Cape Verde	16
4	Côte d'Ivoire	116,846	4	Ethiopia	89	4	South Africa	11
5	Ghana	83,567	5	Guinea-Bissau	84	5	Botswana	8
6	Mauritius	70,126	6	Malawi	77	6	Namibia	6
7	Somalia	65,000	7	Rwanda	70	7	Sao Tome and Principe	4
8	Senegal	58,749	8	Lesotho	58	8	Swaziland	3
9	Zimbabwe	48,898	9	Comoros	57	9	Gambia	3
10	Malawi	31,738	10	Nigeria	56	10	Zimbabwe	2
Cellular mobile telephone subscribers								
1	South Africa	6,893,000	1	Cameroon	9,283	1	Seychelles	53
2	Nigeria	1,608,060	2	Nigeria	6,432	2	Mauritius	29
3	Kenya	1,301,465	3	Burundi	6,400	3	South Africa	27
4	Côte d'Ivoire	769,924	4	Kenya	5,478	4	Botswana	24
5	Cameroon	557,000	5	Equatorial Guinea	4,400	5	Gabon	22
6	Senegal	465,548	6	Congo, DR	4,336	6	Cape Verde	10
7	Tanzania	376,014	7	Gabon	3,057	7	Mauritania	9
8	Uganda	336,952	8	Mozambique	2,326	8	Namibia	8
9	Ghana	334,974	9	Gambia	1,784	9	Gambia	7
10	Botswana	323,000	10	Burkina Faso	1,685	10	Congo, DR	7
Television receivers								
1	Sudan	7,571,630	1	Burkina Faso	631	1	Sudan	39
2	Nigeria	4,500,000	2	Togo	500	2	Gabon	31
3	South Africa	2,053,000	3	Namibia	314	3	Mauritius	30
4	Burkina Faso	820,000	4	Eritrea	233	4	Namibia	27
5	Tanzania	810,000	5	Sudan	151	5	Seychelles	20
6	Togo	500,000	6	Mali	150	6	South Africa	18
7	Namibia	382,480	7	Tanzania	117	7	Togo	13
8	Mali	210,000	8	Burundi	83	8	Cape Verde	10
9	Kenya	152,928	9	Mozambique	79	9	Nigeria	10
10	Eritrea	140,000	10	Nigeria	60	10	Mauritania	10

Source: Author's calculations based on data from the International Telecommunication Union, World Telecommunication Indicators Database, accessed July 2003

24 economies have a penetration rate of 1 percent or lower. Niger's penetration rate is particularly worrisome, with 1 cellular mobile telephone subscriber in every 5,525 persons.

Television penetration rates are, on the whole, higher than that for the other technologies. Ten of the 47 economies have television penetration rates higher than 10 percent. Only four economies have penetration rates below 1 percent. Chad and the Democratic Republic of the Congo are among those with the lowest television penetration rates. Chad has 1 television for every 525 persons while the Democratic Republic of the Congo has 1 television for every 526 persons.

Breaking down the aggregate figures according to levels of indebtedness, the picture reveals the tendency that the greater the level of indebtedness, the lower the penetration rates. In the region, 64 percent of the population live in what are classified as severely indebted economies, 24 percent of the population belong to economies classified as moderately indebted economies, while 12 percent belong to less indebted economies. In sub-Saharan Africa, less indebted economies have on average 1 Internet user in every 22 persons. This is in stark contrast to severely indebted economies that have, on average, 1 Internet user in every 471 persons. Similarly, less indebted economies have on average 1 personal computer for every 20 persons, while severely indebted economies have 1 personal computer for every 277 persons. Less indebted economies also have 1 main telephone line for every 13 persons, while severely indebted economies have 1 main telephone line for every 149 persons. In terms of cellular mobile telephones there is 1 cellular mobile telephone subscriber in every 6 persons in less indebted economies while in severely indebted economies there is 1 subscriber in every 87.

Box 2. Crafting the Right Framework

It is more important than ever for each economy to determine what types of policies are needed to create an environment and network infrastructure that would facilitate greater ICT access and overall networked readiness. Setting the "right" framework is difficult because it requires policy coherence among various areas.

The framework below outlines the elements that should be considered in crafting an environment for networked readiness:

PART I. MARKET ENVIRONMENT

HUMAN RESOURCES

Education
- Infrastructure-related: computerization and networking of schools and libraries
- Content-related: training of educators and integration of ICT in the curriculum
- Government expenditures in education

Labor
- Certification and accreditation of ICT literacy levels
- Skills development
- Skills matching through appropriate recruitment tools and centers
- Reversing the brain drain

CAPITAL
- Early-stage financing: access to venture capital
- Later-stage financing: access to capital markets

TECHNOLOGY
Technological Diffusion
- Role of trade in technology transfer
- Role of foreign direct investment in technology transfer

Technological Innovation
- Financing: grants, subsidies, tax concessions, loans
- Academia-business collaboration
- Industry clusters
- Ease of patent registration

PART II. LEGAL AND REGULATORY FRAMEWORK

LEGAL FRAMEWORK
- Basic legal framework: property rights, contract law
- Revising and creating relevant legislation: e-commerce
- Harmonization with international law

REGULATORY FRAMEWORK
- Regulatory capacity: establishing an independent and effective regulatory agency
- Degree of regulation: choosing an appropriate level of regulation
- Regulatory process: licensing/auctions, standards setting, dispute resolution: interconnection

PART III. INFRASTRUCTURE

- Market Structure: privatization, liberalization
- Pricing: choice or regulatory pricing regime, metered vs. non-metered, subsidies vs. no subsidies, Internet telephony
- Universal Service/Access
- Content: local content, content regulation, taxation, privacy, and consumer data protection
- Network quality: network service and support, quality of service monitoring, security
- Supporting infrastructure: electricity, postal systems, customs, transport logistics
- Financial: payment gateway, identification, authentication

Source: Figueres-Olsen, J-M and F. Paua. 2003. "Crafting the Environment for Networked Readiness." In *Global Information Technology Report 2002–2003*. New York: Oxford University Press for the World Economic Forum.

Box 3. Promoting ICT Diffusion Through e-Government: Presence and Services

ICT diffusion flourishes best when governments make it a priority to promote the use of technologies. One of the ways governments can do this is through e-government, such as increasing government presence on the web and providing relevant information and services online.

To benchmark the presence of national governments on the web and to assess the quality and sophistication of online government services, the World Economic Forum conducted a survey of national government websites from June to July 2003. Significantly, many developing economies are making inroads in e-government. Low income economies such as Tanzania and Nicaragua have remarkable online government presence. Moreover, several middle income economies, including Argentina, China, Estonia, Mexico, Philippines, South Africa, Guatemala, and Malta are increasing the level of sophistication of their e-government services websites (Figure E).

The result of the survey is captured in two e-government indicators that have been incorporated this year in the Networked Readiness Index Rankings. The first measure (Data table II.3.03) pertains to the presence of national governments on the web and this includes assessment of the websites of the chief executive, the judiciary, the main legislative body, ministries, embassies, and finally, the main government online portal, if available. The second measure (Data table III.3.02) evaluates the sophistication of online government service delivery. For each country, the availability and quality of five e-government services were assessed: filing of personal taxes, application for car registration, application for passports, application for business permits and, finally, electronic public procurement.

Of the five e-government services assessed, application for business permits and electronic public procurement cater mostly to business while the other three services cater to individual citizens.

In terms of online government presence, it is remarkable that all 102 economies have at least one branch of government online. Of the 102 economies, 101 economies have at least one ministry website, 94 economies have a website for the national parliament and 89 economies have a website for the judiciary. Of the 94 economies with a website for the national parliament, 79 economies have old bills and the constitution online. Of the 89 economies with a website for the judiciary, 66 economies post information on bills and pending cases online. Finally, of the 102 economies covered in the survey, 83 economies have a central site for the government, and of this number, 25 economies have single-entry portals to electronic services for citizens.

In terms of the sophistication of online government services, many countries, including developing countries, are making significant inroads. For business permits, only 14 economies can conduct electronic payments, but at least 90 economies had procedure details online, of which 52 economies allow downloading of forms. For electronic procurement, only 10 economies can do the entire transaction online but at least 78 economies have a related website with procedure details. For passport applications, at least 70 economies have simple contact information and procedure details while for car registration, at least 49 economies provide procedure details, of which 31 allow downloading of forms. Finally, for filing personal taxes, 72 economies have relevant web pages with downloadable forms while 17 countries, including developing countries like Guatemala, allow electronic payment.

Figure 5. **Matrix of Sophistication of Online Government Service Delivery vs Country Income Classification**

	Stage 1	Stage 2	Stage 3
HIGH INCOME		Greece	Australia
		Luxembourg	Austria
		Slovenia	Canada
			Denmark
			Finland
			France
			Germany
			Hong Kong SAR
			Ireland
			Israel
			Japan
			Korea, Republic of
			New Zealand
			Singapore
			Spain
			Sweden
			Taiwan
			United Kingdom
			United States
MIDDLE INCOME	Bolivia	Algeria	Argentina
	Botswana	Brazil	China
	Honduras	Bulgaria	Estonia
	Macedonia	Chile	Guatemala
	Namibia	Colombia	Malta
	Trinidad and Tobago	Costa Rica	Mexico
		Croatia	Philippines
		Czech Republic	South Africa
		Dominican Republic	
		Ecuador	
		Egypt	
		El Salvador	
		Hungary	
		Jamaica	
		Jordan	
		Latvia	
		Lithuania	
		Malaysia	
		Mauritius	
		Morocco	
		Panama	
		Paraguay	
		Peru	
		Poland	
		Romania	
		Russian Federation	
		Serbia	
		Slovak Republic	
		Sri Lanka	
		Thailand	
		Tunisia	
		Turkey	
		Uruguay	
		Venezuela	
LOW INCOME	Chad	Angola	
	Ethiopia	Bangladesh	
	Gambia	Cameroon	
	Ghana	India	
	Haiti	Indonesia	
	Madagascar	Kenya	
	Malawi	Mozambique	
	Mali	Nigeria	
	Nicaragua	Pakistan	
	Senegal	Tanzania	
	Vietnam	Uganda	
	Zimbabwe	Ukraine	
		Zambia	

Stage 1. Information stage: e-government services websites, where available, provide basic information

Stage 2. Interactive stage: e-government services websites allow submitting and downloading forms

Stage 3. Transaction stage: at least one e-government service enables electronic payment for the transaction

Source: World Economic Forum, Survey of National Government Websites, accessed June–July 2003

Nonetheless, the gains are apparent across the board, particularly in the area of Internet users and cellular mobile telephone subscribers. In 1999, 1 in every 266 persons was an Internet user in sub-Saharan Africa; by 2002, this ratio improved to 1 in every 113 persons. For the severely indebted economies, this ratio moved from 1 Internet user in every 1,996 persons to 1 in every 471 persons. In terms of cellular mobile telephone subscribers, the region improved its 1999 ratio of 1 subscriber in every 96 persons to 1 in 30 by 2002. At the same time, the penetration rate of cellular mobile telephone subscribers in severely indebted economies dramatically improved from 1 subscriber in every 797 persons to 1 subscriber in 87.

Policy Imperatives and Market Implications

The analysis above has painted the global picture of ICT diffusion as well as presented the profiles of ICT penetration in the different regions of the world. Evaluating the progress of ICT diffusion over the last three years, the analysis clearly shows that much has been achieved in improving access to information and communication technologies in the world, particularly in many developing economies.

That much of this remarkable growth in ICT diffusion has been achieved in a difficult environment makes it even more extraordinary. The last three years marked the peaking of the Internet bubble and consolidation in the technology industry. It was also a period marked by a synchronized downturn in the global economy.

Today, the technology industry is increasingly showing signs of a pick-up in activity. The information and communication technology sector in general is also benefiting from the consolidation that has occurred during the last three years: debt levels have been reduced, operations have been streamlined, and much of the excess has been minimized. Research and development activities are accelerating and more innovations are coming to market. All these positive developments in the sector augur very well for continued dramatic improvements in ICT diffusion.

These positive developments come at an opportune time because, as the above analysis also shows, much still needs to be done to improve global ICT diffusion. Many members of the global community have yet to gain access to some of the most basic information and communication technologies. Even in the context of shared access in developing economies, the disparities of ICT access remain glaring. The lingering gap will continue to exist unless international and national policymakers as well as business leaders and other stakeholders exert concerted efforts to close it.

The task before us all is twofold: apply the lessons we have learned, particularly in the last three years, and seize the opportunities of improved economic prospects in order to reduce the gaps in access to ICT. As the world gears up for economic recovery and the technology sector stands poised for a rebound, there are four policy considerations and another four market implications for policymakers, business leaders, and civil society to bear in mind.

Four Policy Imperatives

The first policy imperative is that it is more important than ever to craft the right framework. As the variations in country performance in ICT diffusion reveals there is no simple blueprint for crafting the right environment for fostering increased ICT access. A particular policy and regulatory framework that is most suitable for one country may not be applicable to another due to a myriad of variations, ranging from geographic terrains to differing economic, political, social, and institutional contexts.

Yet the fact remains that the most appropriate framework for an economy must be in place to enable it to fully capture the benefits of ICT (see Box 2). On the policy side, this means assessing several aspects of the framework: market structure, pricing, universal service/access, content, network quality, and supporting infrastructure. With so many aspects involved in the framework, it is important to ensure policy coherence as well as flexibility in adapting to rapidly changing technologies and shifting global trade and investment patterns. Moreover, there must be in place a clear and up-to-date legal framework that is consistent with international law. It is also important to ensure that an independent regulator who is empowered and equipped to implement regulatory policy, allocate scarce resources, adjudicate disputes, and balance goals of efficiency, equity, and innovation oversees a country's regulatory regime.

The second important policy imperative is that the issue of ICT access is ultimately about developing human capacity. The willingness to acquire technological devices depends on the expected utility of these devices, which in turn depends on an individual's capacity to use these devices. For policymakers, this means that attention must be placed on education and labor policies. A country's educational system and policies must provide the relevant knowledge and skills needed by individuals in the knowledge economy. Likewise, labor policies must ensure timely upgrading of the knowledge and skill base of the workforce. Significantly, both education and labor policies must entail the allocation of sufficient resources and investment from governments.

It is important, however, that efforts to enhance human capacity be pursued concurrently with efforts to ensure that appropriate technologies are being developed. Policymakers and business leaders must continually assess whether existing technologies are relevant to the needs and abilities of the intended users.

The third important policy imperative is that ICT diffusion flourishes best when governments make it a priority to promote the use of technologies. When one looks at economies with low penetration rates, one of the questions that immediately come to mind is: what, if anything, are the governments doing to promote ICT access? There are many reasons that developing country governments may be unable to focus on ICT promotion. Some governments are unfortunately caught in wars and various forms of political instability. There are others that simply do not have the resources to address the issue of ICT access because of pressing requirements in the area of food, security, or healthcare; these cases clearly provide opportunities for donor economies and international and nongovernmental organizations to offer assistance. In yet other cases the problem is lack of attention to policy and resource allocation; policymakers are then called upon to adopt a longer-term perspective and to look at effective ICT promotion as an investment in the future.

Beyond establishing policy and regulatory frameworks conducive to creating a network infrastructure, governments must also promote the use of these technologies, either by example through e-government (see Box 3), or through proactive policies to promote local content. Production of local content and relevant applications are important elements when encouraging individuals to acquire and use ICT. In advanced economies, there are cases where it is lack of interest, rather than lack of affordability, that deters a potential Internet user.

Equally as important as producing local content, government also must foster the creation of an environment that allows information exchanges, that is, freedom of communication and expression. Freedom of the press is curtailed in many countries, and this constraint often extends into Internet content regulation.

The fourth policy imperative is that international trade plays a very important role in ICT diffusion. International trade allows domestic producers and consumers to have access to a greater variety of ICT products and services at prices lower than would otherwise be possible. To facilitate ICT diffusion, policymakers must liberalize trade by lowering tariff and non-tariff barriers to ICT.

Four Market Implications

In addition to policy considerations, this progress report on global ICT diffusion indicates important market implications. The first is that there is a significantly large market that is yet to be connected. Ninety percent of the world's 6.2 billion population are not Internet users. There are 1.5 billion households in the world but there are only half a billion personal computers. Moreover, despite the rapid adoption of cellular mobile telephones, more than 5.5 billion people in the world are not cellular mobile telephone subscribers.

The second implication is that there is a potentially large market for technologies and applications other than what is available today. One of the caveats noted in the introduction of this study is that indicators monitored in this analysis may not be the most relevant or the most affordable technologies, particularly for developing economies. For instance, is a desktop personal computer practical for a farmer who works in the field all day? Or can more appropriate technologies be developed? Beyond the question of relevance, more user-friendly technologies must also be developed to cater to the varying educational, linguistic, and ability levels of people. Technologies must also be developed that are affordable for the intended users. There are clearly unmet needs and opportunities to innovate upon existing technologies.

The third implication revealed by the analysis of global ICT diffusion is that it is important to study demand and take-up patterns. In the face of rapidly shifting technologies, companies and governments are often faced with the difficult task of choosing technology platforms. As policymakers strive towards promoting ICT access and providing information and relevant online services, it is important that they choose a platform that is broadly used by their constituency and that can be best used to connect to the networked economy. For companies, this task has the added component of having to ascertain the projected demand for these technologies.

Three years ago, it would have been difficult to predict that cellular mobile telephone subscribers would exceed the number of main telephones lines in 125 economies (Appendix 1). There are many reasons for the rapid take-up of cellular mobile telephone subscribers; among these reasons is the waiting time in many developing economies to get a telephone line connected. Two other very important reasons are the introduction of pre-paid cards, which dramatically reduced the cost of access, and the popularity and affordability of short messaging service, which allows the sending of text messages through a mobile telephone. Indeed, determining which technologies are spreading rapidly and assessing what is driving the spread can provide important lessons that may be applicable to existing and emerging technologies.

Beyond examining where growth is coming from, it is equally important to examine the varying take-up patterns of technologies. What does this mean for developing economies seeking the easiest, most affordable way to connect to the Internet? It is also interesting to see that amidst the emergence of various new devices, television remains among the most pervasive ICT in the world. What implication does this have for delivering time-sensitive information? Worldwide over the last three years, purchases of personal computers grew by 40 percent, which pales in comparison to the 119 percent growth in the number of Internet users. What does this say about the price structure and appeal of the current design of personal computers? What impact would Wi-Fi, and other new technologies, have on improving Internet access?

The fourth market implication is that we have barely begun to tap the possibilities of the current network. In the world today, for example, there are at least 1.5 billion cellular mobile telephone subscribers. What kind of applications can be created for this subscriber base? What opportunities do a network of more than 600 million Internet users present? Moreover, what implications would convergence have on the current network and array of applications? The rate of growth of ICT diffusion and the rapid take-up of newer technologies certainly provide us with strong reasons to be optimistic about tapping the potential of an increasingly networked world.

Conclusion

As a progress report on the global diffusion of ICT, the analysis of the empirical data clearly shows that globally, access to ICT has increased dramatically, particularly in terms of cellular mobile telephones and the Internet. That a significant proportion of the growth came from emerging market economies is remarkable. What makes the overriding high rate and diffusion of ICT even more extraordinary is that it occurred at a time that was marked by a synchronized downturn in the global economy and deep consolidation in the technology sector.

Yet analysis at the regional and country level, particularly when disaggregated according to income levels, reveals the persistence of a significant gap between the penetration rates in high income economies and low income economies, particularly those economies in sub-Saharan Africa that are severely indebted. Even in the context of shared access in developing economies, the disparities of ICT access still remain glaring. The lingering gap will continue to exist unless international and national policymakers as well as business leaders and other stakeholders exert a concerted effort to apply the lessons that have been learned, particularly over the last three years. It is equally important to seize the opportunities of improved economic prospects in order to reduce the gaps in access to ICT.

The analysis of the global diffusion of ICT leads us to four policy imperatives and four market implications for policymakers, business leaders, and civil society. To promote greater diffusion of ICT it is important, first, to craft the right framework in terms of policy and regulatory environments. The second policy consideration is to develop human capacity in order to encourage individuals to use ICT and enable them to maximize the benefits of having access to ICT. The

third is for governments to promote the use of ICT through a national ICT strategy, e-government initiatives, promotion of local content, and the creation of an environment where freedom of communication and expression can prevail. The fourth policy imperative is that international trade plays a very important role in ICT diffusion, and governments must reduce tariff and non-tariff barriers to ICT imports.

As the world gears up for economic recovery and the technology sector stands poised for a rebound, the analysis highlights four market implications. The first is that a large proportion of the world is yet to be connected and this represents a tremendous market opportunity. The second implication is that since most of those yet to be connected are in the developing world, there is a potentially large market for new and more affordable technology as well as applications that are more relevant and user friendly. Clearly there are opportunities to innovate and improve upon existing technologies. Related to the second implication is the third, which highlights the importance of studying demand and take-up patterns in order to anticipate future requirements. And the final implication is that the world has barely begun to tap the possibilities of the current network, which has more than 600 million Internet users, and more than 2 billion main telephone lines and cellular mobile telephone subscribers. The rate of growth of ICT diffusion and the rapid take-up of newer technologies certainly provide strong reasons for optimism as we continue to tap the potential of an increasingly networked world.

Endnotes

1 The first *Global Information Technology Report* was a collaboration between the World Economic Forum, the Center for International Development at Harvard University, and *info*Dev of the World Bank.

2 Data are primarily from the International Telecommunication Union (ITU) World Telecommunication Indicators Database, accessed July 2003. Public information is available at the ITU website:http://www.itu.int/ITU-D/ict/

3 "Main telephone lines" is defined by the ITU as "telephone lines connecting a customer's equipment (e.g., telephone set, facsimile machine) to the Public Switched Telephone Network (PSTN) and which have a dedicated port on a telephone exchange." ITU also notes that, "for most countries, main lines also include public payphones." More information can be found on the Technical Notes page of the ITU website: http://www.itu.int/ITU-D/ict/statistics/at_glance/main02.pdf

4 "Cellular mobile telephone subscribers" is defined by the ITU as "users of portable telephones subscribing to an automatic public mobile telephone service using cellular technology that provides access to the PSTN." More information can be found on the Technical Notes page of the ITU website: http://www.itu.int/ITU-D/ict/statistics/at_glance/main02.pdf

5 Classification of economies according to income is based on the World Bank's Country Classification whereby economies are divided according to 2002 GNI per capita, calculated using the World Bank Atlas method. The groups are: low income, USD 735 or less; lower middle income, USD 736 to 2,935; upper middle income, USD 2,936 to 9,075; and high income, USD 9,076 or more. For the purposes of Appendix 1, "lower middle income" and "upper middle income" were merged into one "middle income" category. More information on the World Bank Country Classification can be found on the World Bank website: http://www.worldbank.org/data/countryclass/countryclass.html

6 The historical perspective on the China and India experiences in ICT diffusion was first explored in Paua, F., E. J. Lee, A. Padmanabhan, et al. 2001. "Information Infrastructure Development in China and India: Comparative Analysis, 1986–2000." Unpublished paper, Harvard University.

References

Cornelius, P., F. von Kirchbach, F. Paua and N. Semine. 2002. "Trade in ICT Products: The Global Framework and Empirical Evidence." In *Global Information Technology Report 2001–2002*. New York: Oxford University Press.

Figueres-Olsen, J.M. and F. Paua. 2003. "Crafting the Environment for Networked Readiness." In Dutta, S., F. Paua, and B. Lanvin, eds., *Global Information Technology Report 2002–2003*. New York: Oxford University Press for the World Economic Forum.

International Telecommunication Union (ITU). World Telecommunication Indicators Database. Online. Accessed July 2003.

Appendix 1. **Countries Where the Number of Cellular Mobile Telephones Subscribers Exceeds the Number of Main Telephones Lines in Operation, 2002***

High income economies	Difference**
Italy	24,864,050
United Kingdom	14,776,000
Spain	14,769,400
Taiwan	10,805,990
Japan	9,969,000
Korea, Republic of	9,085,000
Germany	5,480,000
France	4,656,560
Portugal	4,167,900
Greece	3,706,534
Israel	3,234,000
Belgium	3,003,085
Hong Kong SAR	2,454,598
Austria	2,427,000
Netherlands	2,100,000
Australia	1,989,000
Finland	1,550,000
Sweden	1,474,000
Singapore	1,364,900
United Arab Emirates	1,334,417
Ireland	994,000
Slovenia	855,565
Kuwait	745,109
Denmark	738,898
New Zealand	671,000
Norway	517,000
Switzerland	399,000
Bahrain	213,544
Reunion	189,800
Martinique	147,900
Guadeloupe	113,500
Luxembourg	108,237
Macau	100,032
Qatar	90,184
Iceland	75,310
Brunei Darussalam	48,560
French Polynesia	37,480
New Caledonia	29,291
Aruba	15,868
Liechtenstein	2,077

Middle income economies	Difference**
Mexico	10,986,630
Philippines	10,877,304
Thailand	9,617,158
South Africa	7,186,000
Morocco	5,071,223
Czech Republic	4,749,334
Malaysia	4,575,000
Turkey	4,459,500
Venezuela	3,621,790
Chile	2,978,496
Hungary	2,895,555
Poland	2,600,000
Saudi Arabia	1,690,422
Slovak Republic	1,520,658
Paraguay	1,393,800
Jamaica	950,000
Guatemala	731,117
Lithuania	695,674
Albania	580,000
Jordan	531,999
Estonia	406,000
Croatia	399,000
Dominican Republic	314,937
Bolivia	308,735
Peru	277,735
Botswana	272,400
Bosnia and Herzegovina	258,555
Serbia	257,434
Gabon	248,584
El Salvador	221,119
Oman	218,000
Latvia	215,985
Ecuador	134,673
Panama	98,855
Lebanon	96,264
Malta	69,590
Sri Lanka	48,472
Trinidad and Tobago	36,857
Namibia	32,602
Swaziland	27,940
Mauritius	22,775
Seychelles	22,734
West Bank and Gaza	21,500
Belize	20,860
Maldives	13,248
Suriname	9,634
Guyana	6,859
Djibouti	4,875
Honduras	4,011

Low income economies	Difference**
Indonesia	3,949,965
Kenya	997,118
Nigeria	931,060
Côte d'Ivoire	690,929
Cameroon	461,558
Bangladesh	393,000
Cambodia	346,506
Uganda	338,334
Senegal	328,804
Tanzania	278,500
Mauritania	213,733
Mozambique	207,512
Congo	199,800
Ghana	162,878
Congo, DR	130,000
Togo	108,844
Madagascar	103,569
Mongolia	88,000
Rwanda	68,500
Nicaragua	68,295
Benin	65,702
Zimbabwe	65,146
Guinea	64,783
Gambia	61,650
Lesotho	57,964
Zambia	50,617
Angola	45,000
Sierra Leone	43,505
Burundi	29,916
Burkina Faso	27,992
Chad	22,365
Equatorial Guinea	18,200
Malawi	12,947
Haiti	10,000
Mali	2,909
Central African Republic	2,083

Note: *or latest available data
** indicates the difference between the number of cellular mobile telephone subscribers and the number of telephone main lines in operation.
Source: Author's calculations based on data from the International Telecommunication Union, World Telecommunication Indicators Database, accessed July 2003

## Chapter 3

Poverty "e-Readication"

Using ICT to Meet MDG: Direct and Indirect Roles of e-Maturity

Bruno Lanvin and
Christine Zhen-Wei Qiang

Respectively Manager, Information for Development Program (*info*Dev), and Economist, Global Information and Communications Technology Department, the World Bank. The views expressed here should be considered as the authors personal opinions. They do not necessarily reflect those of the World Bank or *info*Dev.

Overview

For policymakers, the acronym ICT covers a complex set of technical, legal, and regulatory issues that they sometimes have difficulty relating to broader social and economic objectives. Efforts to bring ICT to the forefront of economic and social thinking (in particular in the area of development) are still relatively recent. However, because some of those efforts have been initiated close enough to decision-making circles, they are starting to bear fruit at the policy level. This is all the more remarkable because the increased awareness of the crucial social and economic roles of ICT has taken place against the background of depressed ICT markets and significant downsizing in related industries. Among the major challenges that the pursuit and expansion of those efforts now have to face, two interrelated ones require immediate attention. These are (1) the involvement of civil society and local communities in supporting greater resource allocation to ICT as a means of achieving broad economic and social objectives such as poverty reduction, and (2) the production of credible indicators through which action in this area can be measured and rewarded. This chapter offers a few practical proposals for dealing with these challenges.

Introduction

The year 2000 saw the launch of two major international efforts, which are now expected to converge. One was the "Digital Opportunity Task Force" (DOT Force), initiated by the G-8. The other was the adoption by the UN General Assembly of a new set of development targets, called "Millennium Development Goals" or MDG, to be achieved by 2015.[1]

The DOT Force concluded that "when wisely applied, ICT offer enormous opportunities to narrow social and economic inequalities and support sustainable local wealth creation, and thus help to achieve the broader development goals that the international community has set. . . . ICT can provide new and more efficient methods of production, bring previously unattainable markets within the reach of local producers, improve the delivery of government services, and increase access to basic social goods and services. There need therefore be no trade-off between investment in ICT and the achievement of development objectives" (G8 DOT Task Force 2001, p. 4).

As the world prepares for the World Summit on the Information Society (WSIS), to be held in Geneva (2003) and Tunis (2005), businesses and governments now seek the operational tools that will enable them to link their respective decisions, strategies, and policies to the broader objective of reducing the gap between rich and poor. In this context, indicators measuring e-readiness and network readiness are attracting growing attention. They are powerful guides for action and have attracted the attention of the media, civil society, and analysts interested in finding out "what and who works well in reducing the digital divide."

From a development point of view, this means that when poverty reduction is the objective, e-readiness has the potential to bring us closer to the ultimate goal, that is, poverty eradication. This is what the neologism *Poverty e-Readication* is meant to encapsulate.

E-Readiness and Poverty Eradication

On the multidimensional scale of e-readiness and e-maturity, the way in which various countries move from one level to the next is significantly more interesting (at least from a policy point of view) than their "absolute" rankings vis-à-vis each other. However, both the "dynamics" and the "ranking" of e-readiness may look very different, depending on the axes of reference which are used to measure them.

Box 1. Millennium Development Goals and Related Targets

GOAL 1—Eradicate extreme poverty and hunger
Halve, between 1990 and 2015, the proportion of people whose income is less than US$1 per day Halve, between 1990 and 2015, the proportion of people who suffer from hunger

GOAL 2—Achieve universal primary education
Ensure that, by 2015, children everywhere, boys and girls alike, will be able to complete a full course of primary schooling

GOAL 3—Promote gender equality and empower women
Eliminate gender disparity in primary and secondary education, preferably by 2005, and in all levels of education no later than 2015

GOAL 4—Reduce child mortality
Reduce by two-thirds, between 1990 and 2015, the under-five mortality rate

GOAL 5—Improve maternal health
Reduce by three-quarters, between 1990 and 2015, the maternal mortality rate

GOAL 6—Combat HIV/AIDS, malaria, and other diseases
Have halted by 2015, and begun to reverse the spread of HIV/AIDS
Have halted by 2015, and begun to reverse the incidence of malaria and other major diseases

GOAL 7—Ensure environmental sustainability
Integrate the principles of sustainable development into country policies and program and reverse the loss of environmental resources
Halve, by 2015, the proportion of people without sustainable access to safe drinking water
Have achieved, by 2020, a significant improvement in the lives of at least 100 million slum dwellers

GOAL 8—Develop a global partnership for development
Develop further an open, rule-based, predictable, nondiscriminatory trading and financial system (includes a commitment to good governance, development, and poverty reduction—both nationally and internationally)

Official development assistance
Address the special needs of the least developed countries (includes tariff-and quota-free access for exports, enhanced program of debt relief for HIPC and cancellation of official bilateral debt, and more generous ODA for countries committed to poverty reduction)

Market access
Address the special needs of landlocked countries and small island developing states (through the Barbados Programme and 22nd General Assembly provisions)

Debt sustainability
Deal comprehensively with the debt problems of developing countries through national and international measures in order to make debt sustainable in the long term

Other
In cooperation with developing countries, develop and implement strategies for decent and productive work for youth
In cooperation with pharmaceutical companies, provide access to affordable, essential drugs in developing countries
In cooperation with the private sector, make available the benefits of new technologies, especially information and communications

Figure 1. **The e-Readiness Ripple Effect**

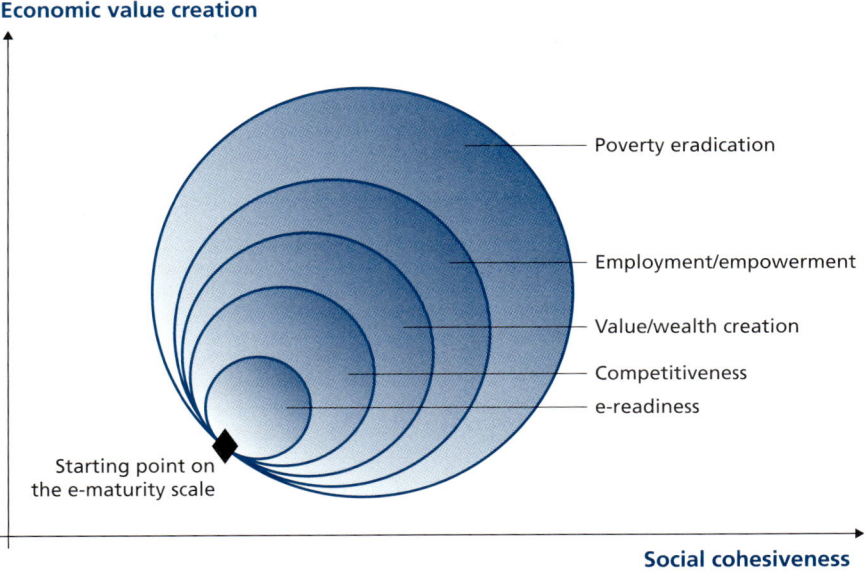

Economic value creation

Poverty eradication

Employment/empowerment

Value/wealth creation

Competitiveness

e-readiness

Starting point on
the e-maturity scale

Social cohesiveness

Figure 2. **From e-Readiness to Poverty Eradication**

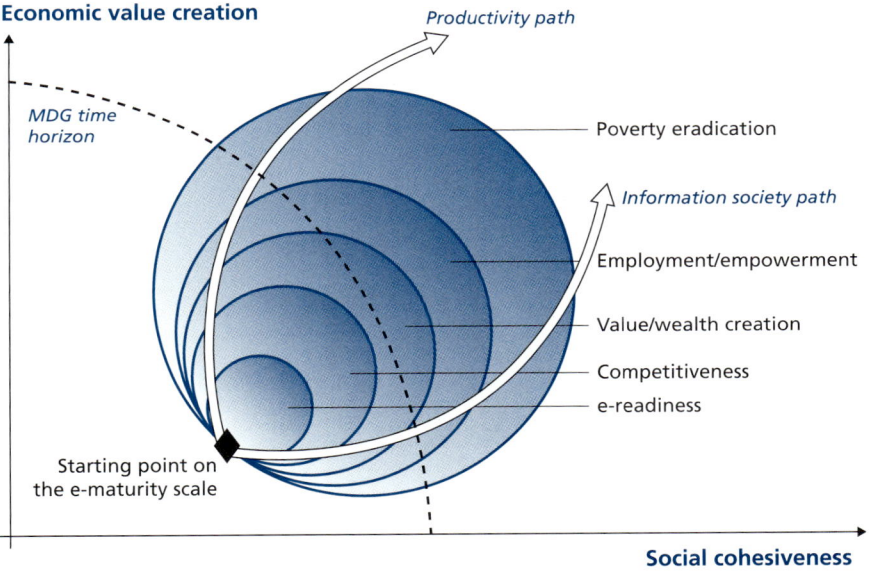

Economic value creation

Productivity path

MDG time
horizon

Poverty eradication

Information society path

Employment/empowerment

Value/wealth creation

Competitiveness

e-readiness

Starting point on
the e-maturity scale

Social cohesiveness

This simple fact becomes particularly relevant when one considers that e-readiness is not an end in itself. Both from the point of view of economic value creation and from that of social cohesiveness, the ripple effect of greater e-readiness pervades increasingly broad policy and social objectives. These include the competitiveness of national economies and enterprises, the ability of such economies and enterprises to create wealth and hence, employment and empowerment to local communities, and, finally, contributions to the elimination of poverty (see Figure 1).

Seen from this point of view, e-readiness can be used as an instrument to eradicate poverty in many different ways. The path that a particular country will follow from e-readiness

to poverty eradication will depend very narrowly on the relative importance that its society and decision makers grant to economic indicators on one hand (e.g., economic value creation) and social objectives (e.g., reducing income disparities) on the other. Although the two paths may eventually converge and contribute efficiently to poverty eradication (see Figure 2), medium-term time horizons (such as that of the MDG, which focus on 2015) may give a "divergent picture" of such paths.

So, is there a "techno-economic" vision and a "social" vision of *e-readication*? Although it has yet to be expressed in those terms, this debate is at the very core of the World Summit on the Information Society (Geneva 2003, Tunis 2005). In that controversial context, the MDG framework offers a unique set of references and objectives, around which both paths can be reconciled.

Information Societies and the Millennium Development Goals

The old debate of the 1990s about choosing between ICT and other development imperatives (e.g., by stating that, in poor countries, investment in ICT draws precious resources away from more urgent development needs), has now shifted from one of trade-offs to one of complementarity (Accenture, Markle Foundation, and UNDP 2001). These new technologies, it is now clear, are not an end in themselves. Nor will a one-size-fits-all approach work—the challenges faced by developing countries vary too greatly by geography, culture, and level of economic attainment. ICT can not eliminate the need for political stability, physical infrastructure, human capacity, and basic health care, nor can it offer a panacea for all development problems. But evidence is growing that ICT is a potentially powerful tool when used in the right way as part of an overall development strategy. This is clearly an approach that will require innovative and close partnership between governments, business, and civil society.

In the context of the MDG, this means that Goal 8 (which covers both ICT and partnerships) can increase the efficiency with which the international community will pursue Goals 1 to 7. Considering the fact that Goals 2 to 7 are actually fundamental components of a concerted strategy to achieve Goal 1 (poverty eradication), one can represent a simplified dynamic model of the pursuit of MDG as follows:

Assessing the potential of using ICT, as measured by the e-economy maturity ranking[2] (e-readiness) in achieving the MDG, requires addressing the three different channels through which it could work (see Figure 4):

- *Social empowerment*—its part in helping to achieve specific social development objectives;

- *Economic empowerment*—its role in fostering broader economic development; and

- *Political empowerment*—its worth in bringing the poor into the process of making policies that affect their lives.

First, ICT applications have already proved their value in addressing several specific challenges identified in the MDG. By mainstreaming ICT into a broader development context, ICT may be leveraged to achieve such core social objectives.[3] Sustainable poverty reduction is not achieved by short-sighted miracle cures, such as universal Internet access. For solutions to be credible, useful, and sustainable, they must respond to demand. A prerequisite for success is that people be aware of the possibilities that ICT offers in traditional development sectors such as education, good governance, health, livelihood opportunities (e.g., agriculture), and environment.

Figure 3. **Pursuing MDG: A Dynamic Model**

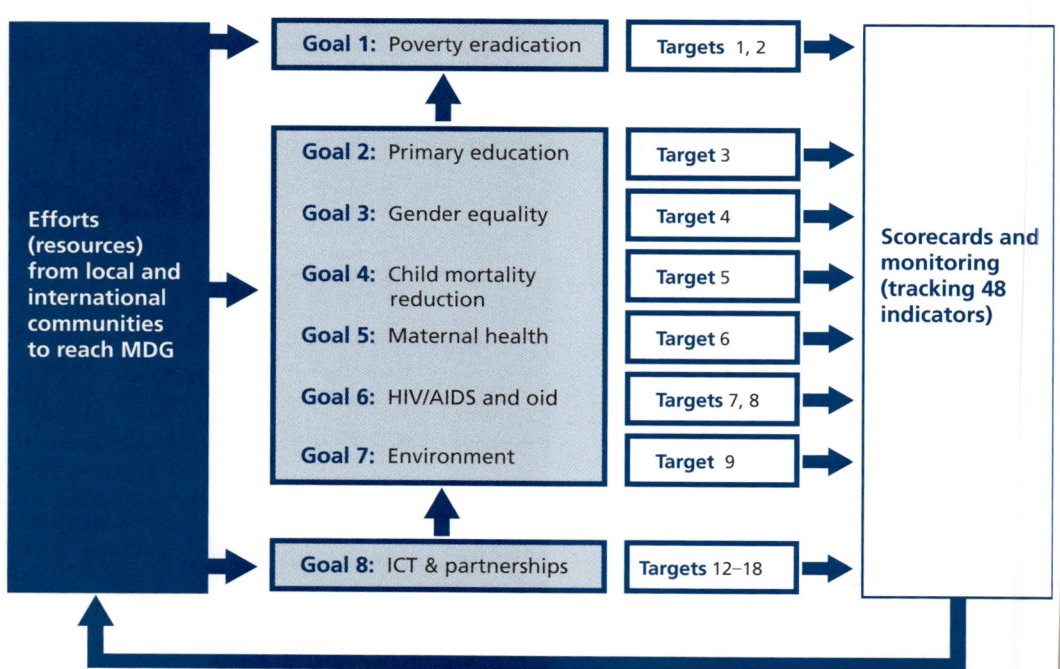

Figure 4. **From e-Readiness to Achieving MDG**

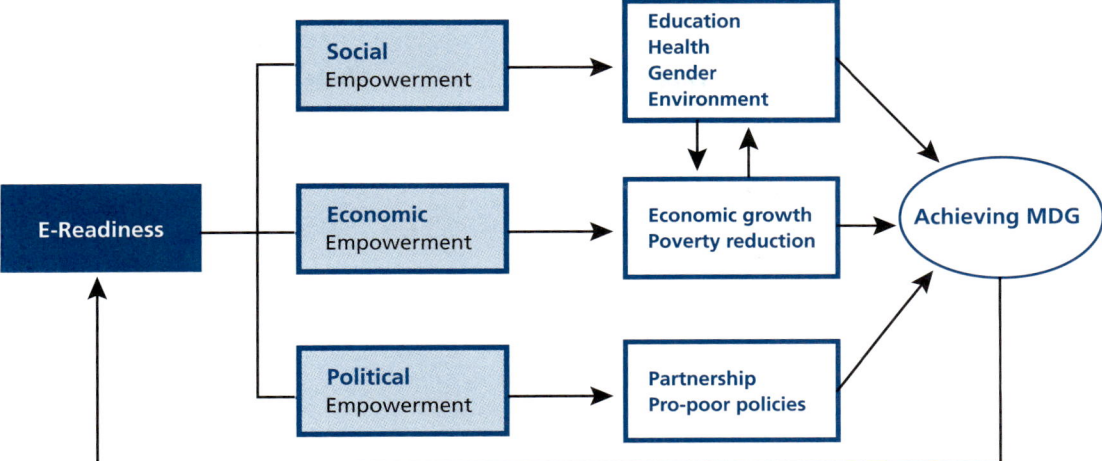

Second, the key to self-sustaining development, in the end, is economic growth. ICT can make a significant contribution to economic growth by increasing labor productivity through high growth of total factor productivity (TFP) in ICT-producing industries, through increase in the real ICT capital stock per worker, and through the overall productivity growth arising from reorganization across the entire economy (Qiang and Pitt 2003).

Third, ICT has the potential to help bring ideas and experience to even the most isolated, opening to them the world outside their village, city, or country. It also allows people to share their experience with the world at large with a tap on a keyboard or a touch on a cellular phone keypad. ICT can also empower individuals to participate in the political institutions and policymaking of their community, giving voice to those who have traditionally been excluded.

Naturally, meeting MDG can in turn improve a country's e-maturity/e-readiness. This relies on four components: (1) the readiness of a community's key stakeholders (individuals, businesses, and governments) to use ICT, (2) access to, and availability of ICT, (3) usage of ICT amongst those stakeholders, and (4) the impact of ICT on the key stakeholders. The actions required to achieve social and economic objectives (such as those contained in the MDG) often include the adaptation of ICT applications for local use and to local conditions, and the promotion of local content. Such a process, because it involves all key players and makes their respective impacts mutually reinforcing, can be a critical way to empower and involve civil society in building information societies.

However, one must be careful to avoid technological determinism in considering the role of ICT in reaching the MDG. If policies (e.g., in the legal and regulatory fields) do not create the right incentives, or if institutions are too weak to implement those policies, ICT can only make a limited

contribution to addressing relevant social and societal issues. Moreover, access to ICT should not be seen as an end in itself. The measure of success remains the progress towards reaching the MDG, rather than the spread of technologies.[4]

In the following discussion, the focus is primarily on the opportunities opened by ICT for achieving the MDG and sustainable development, provided that the appropriate policies and institutions are existent or forthcoming.

Using ICT to Achieve MDG

Social Empowerment

Characterizing ICT
Before exploring the power of ICT to improve efficiency in delivering each of the MDG social goals, an appreciation of the characteristics and the economy-wide effects of ICT may facilitate a greater understanding of their potential as a development tool.

ICT is a general purpose technology (GPT) and has the features characterized by new growth theorists and economic historians: (1) wide scope for improvement and elaboration; (2) applicability across a broad range of uses and in a wide variety of products and processes; and (3) strong complementarities with existing or potential new technologies. GPT play the role of "enabling technologies," opening up new opportunities rather than offering complete solutions (Hanna 2003). Their characteristics are:

- *Interactive, permanent, and global reach*—ICT includes effective synchronous and asynchronous two-way communication technologies. Once one has access to ICT, it is available around the clock and permits communication independent of the physical movement of individuals and geographic distances between them.

Figure 5. **Role of ICT in Social Sectors**

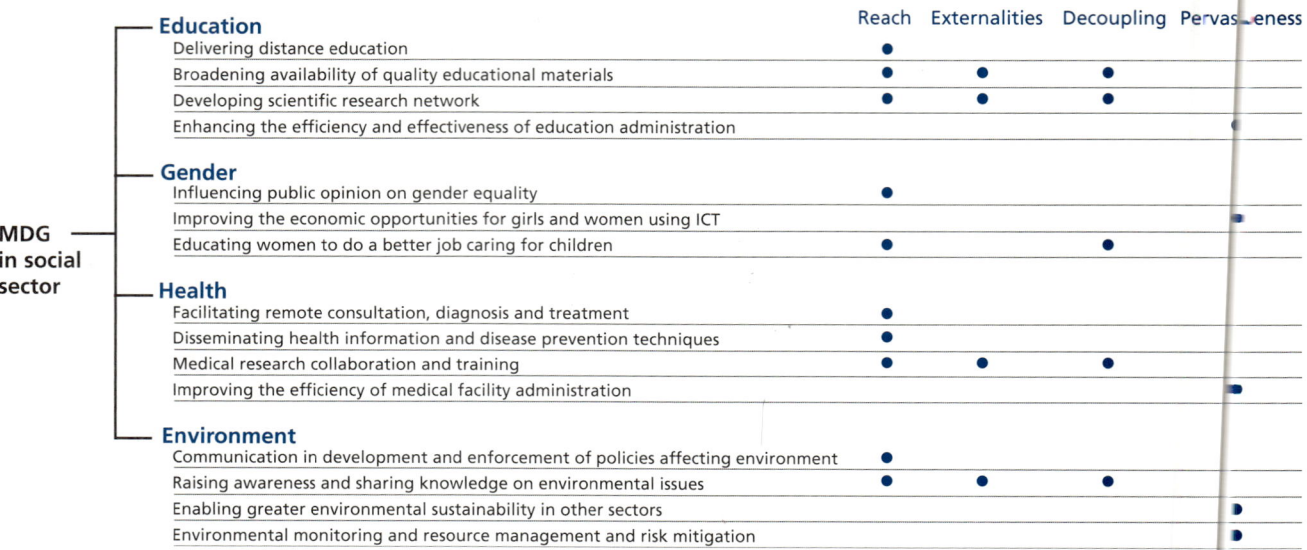

Source: World Bank, 2003

- *Externalities*—As inputs into the development process, ideas, knowledge, and information are non-rival in nature and can potentially be treated as global public goods, with significant external effects on the economy as a whole. In addition to these content-related externalities, there are also externalities related to the size of the ICT networks and applications. Once a critical mass of investments is reached, network externalities[5] come into effect and marginal returns on ICT investment increase, at least up to a point (Qiang and Pitt 2003).

- *Decoupling property*—ICT is able to serve as information channels due to its ability to support the decoupling of information from its physical repository (Bedi 1999). This revolutionary aspect allows the immediate transmission of information, unhindered by the volume or the nature (voice, video, or data). The capacity to support information separation is the key attribute underlying the wide range of activities and services offered through ICT.

- *Pervasiveness*—A technology may have pervasive economic effects[6] if it (1) generates a wide range of new products and services; (2) generates strong industrial interests as a means for profitability and competitive advantage; and (3) reduces the costs and improves the performance of the processes, services, and products of many sectors of the economy. The widespread applications of ICT and the possibility of tailoring them to adapt to individual, corporate, and government needs clearly qualify ICT as pervasive technologies.

Linking ICT to the Social Objectives of the MDG

Rather than being treated as an isolated sector , ICT should be used as a lens to re-think development strategies, as a tool to enable all sectors, and as a new and powerful means to help reach development objectives. This does not mean that ICT is a panacea, but that an understanding of the promise and implications of the ongoing ICT revolution is necessary in order to realize its potential for development; this goes far beyond its contribution as a sector.

Figure 5 provides examples of linkages between ICT applications and each one of the social sector MDG (Goals 2 to 7). This is done by identifying which of the above-mentioned GPT characteristics of ICT apply to any particular social objective.

Over the last few years, many ICT-for-development initiatives have contributed analytical and empirical evidence illustrating the developmental role of ICT. An action-oriented international consensus now needs to be built on the basis of such evidence.

Economic and Political Empowerment— Foundations of Achieving MDG

As stressed earlier, eradication of extreme poverty and hunger is the first of the MDG, while most of the other seven goals are mutually reinforcing and focus on reducing poverty in all its forms. The poor are not just deprived of basic food, education, and health services; their lack of access to knowledge and their low political visibility reinforce their vulnerability to constraints and challenges. This, in turn, forces them into social exclusion, powerlessness, and poverty traps.

Lack of access to ICT is clearly not an element of poverty in the way that insufficient nutrition or inadequate shelter are (Kenny, Navas-Sabater, and Qiang 2002), but it can be seen both as a cause and an outcome of low level of human development. As shown in Figure 6, the correlation between the human development index (HDI)[8] and the networked readiness index (NRI)[9] is very high (greater than 80 percent).

Figure 6. **NRI and HDI, 2003**

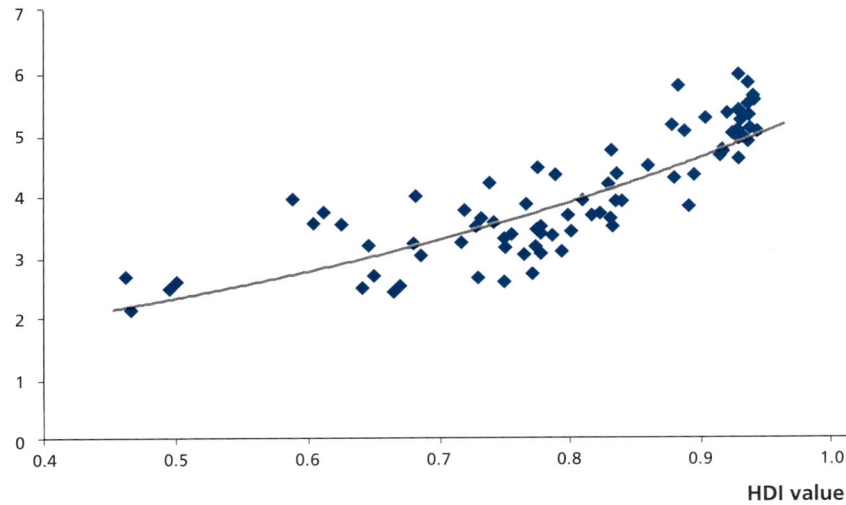

Source: UNDP (2003c), Dutta, Lanvin and Paua ed. (2003)

If ICT are appropriately deployed by the users, governments, civil society, and donors to take into consideration people's differing needs, they can become powerful economic and political tools for the poor. Policies and projects targeting poverty reduction and involving ICT may promote opportunities for poor people by (1) providing information about access to resources and managing them efficiently, (2) stimulating economic growth and reducing the digital divide, (3) educating citizens about their rights and helping them to voice their needs, and (4) facilitating political involvement. These are all key ingredients of economic and political empowerment.

Economic Empowerment

RESOURCE MANAGEMENT

Resource management aims at influencing the use and distribution of assets. A more poor-supportive distribution of assets would not only increase the income of the poor, but also their aggregate growth (see Box 2). ICT's relevance lies in managing resources (e.g, humanitarian aid in emergencies) as well as in providing information about access to resources (e.g., micro-credit, credit schemes, land allocation). In a knowledge-based economy, the distribution of information via ICT is strategically important.

GROWTH

While growth is not all that is required to improve equality, it can be argued that growth-enhancing policies generally benefit the poor.[10]

The contribution of increased ICT production and utilization to economic growth appears significant. A recent survey on this topic by Qiang and Pitt (2003) suggests that ICT is contributing to labor productivity through both increases

Box 2. **Targeting the Poor**

Although the poverty line in Brazil dropped sharply in the mid 1990s, there still exists a "hard core" of 40 million people (nearly a quarter of the population), who live on less than half the minimum wage of 240 reais (US$80) a month. The government-linked Institute of Applied Economic Research estimates the number of those in extreme poverty (lacking the money to feed themselves properly) at 23 million.

The government used information technology to identify the needy and make sure that resources reached them: beneficiaries collect their income transfer from the bank through electronic cards. This not only reduces the scope for corruption or political favoritism, but also generates a stream of information that can be used for designing, targeting, and monitoring programs.

The government wants to boost spending on income support next year by up to 1.5 billion reais. The goal is to eradicate hunger in Brazil by the end of 2006.

Source: *After The Economist* vol. 268 no. 8337, page 31–33 (August 16, 2003)

in the level of ICT capital, and through growth of TFP in ICT production. Empirical results also show that, during the 1990s, the contribution of ICT to economic growth through these two channels increased in a significant number of countries. The most diffusive and profound long-term effects—namely the productivity growth arising from reorganization of production and creation of new products, markets, and operations around ICT goods and services—appear to be spreading, particularly in some sectors such as transport, tourism, financial services, and retail.

INEQUALITY AND REDISTRIBUTION

Developing countries need to capture growth opportunities. However, gains from national growth do not automatically trickle down to benefit the poor. A well-balanced development strategy should seek to target more directly opportunities for the poor and marginalized groups in the society.

The distribution of the welfare gains from ICT is a subject of debate among both academics and practitioners. Critics have pointed to the emergence of a "digital divide" between the information "haves" and "have-nots." In contrast to most free market advocates, critics of globalization claim that ICT could exacerbate the extremes of wealth already observable in the world economy and increase relative, if not absolute, poverty. The probability of exclusion is seen as high and the implications significant.

At present, data are not sufficient to support any firm conclusions as to whether ICT is diminishing or increasing income inequalities at the national level. But there is country-level anecdotal evidence in some developing countries that highlights a growing urban-rural digital divide and inequality, with economic opportunities being unevenly spread (see Qiang and Smith 2003).

Political Empowerment

There are also non-economic dimensions to ICT. Communication is a basic requirement of social interaction. The key lies in determining the crucial information and communication needs of the poor and how communication can address such quality-of-life issues as social exclusion, marginalization, isolation, alienation, humiliation, vulnerability (to external shocks and internal conflicts), and insecurity (the risk of being subjected to physical violence because of social status, gender, or ethnic identity). Because of the particular issues they face as a result of their poverty, poor people need additional support in terms of physical and economic access to information.

Pro-poor policies should not only take a "do no harm" approach to ICT strategies, but should be proactive. Policies need to include specific objectives and indicators, such as the promotion of universal access to ICT, and the adaptation of ICT applications to local needs and conditions, including languages and cultures. For instance, if private industry were to be the starting point in the telecom sector, strong conditions and commitments would be required to ensure that supply also goes to rural districts and to the poor.

RIGHTS AND CHOICES

Development is also about fulfillment of entitlements and rights. Lack of efficient information and communication processes makes public institutions slow and unresponsive, and shifts much of the burden of transactions onto citizens, particularly the poor. The latter do not know their rights and choices and lack knowledge of the political and development

processes that shape their lives. Moreover, poor people and communities are often isolated and lack means to take collective action. The disadvantaged cannot assert their rights unless they are organized. Thus, the notion "organization is power" carries as much weight as "knowledge is power" (see Gerster and Zimmermann 2003). ICT have a great deal of potential for increasing the efficiency of organization.[11] Local communities and civil society can play a critical role in enabling the poor to access relevant information and tools for communication with others, making their own choices, articulating their interests, engaging in social learning and having more decision power over their lives.

POLITICAL PARTICIPATION/LOCAL EMPOWERMENT

Local empowerment and the redistribution of political power are aimed at introducing social change and making poverty reduction sustainable. Political participation is now being redefined by the use of multi-way communications, through electronic and non-electronic ICT networks. Information and communication flow both vertically (top-down and bottom-up), and horizontally (between networks, communities, and individuals).

Using ICT, governments can improve the quality and responsiveness of the services they provide to their citizens, coordinate among various agencies, and expand the reach and accessibility of services and public infrastructure. Citizens are encouraged to participate in the democratic process through ICT mechanisms such as electronic forums and bulletin boards, which enable participation in public discussions. This is especially relevant for marginalized communities and groups such as rural citizens, women, and ethnic minorities who can exchange information of mutual interest, share knowledge on best practices, strengthen their collective power, and shape their own development solutions. This gives the citizens a greater sense of ownership in decision-making processes.

Reaching the MDG Requires Both Money and Efficiency

In order to reach the targets set by the MDG, countries can either increase the resources they allocate to specific objectives, or increase the efficiency with which they use their available resources. At the core of the discussion about ICT

Figure 7. **Financing MDG: Resource Allocation and Efficiency**

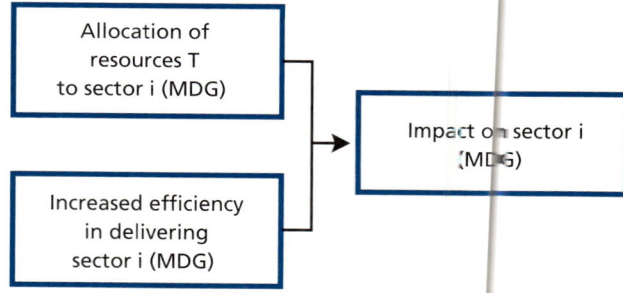

Figure 8. **Efficiency in Deliverying MDG: Introducing the ICT Factor**

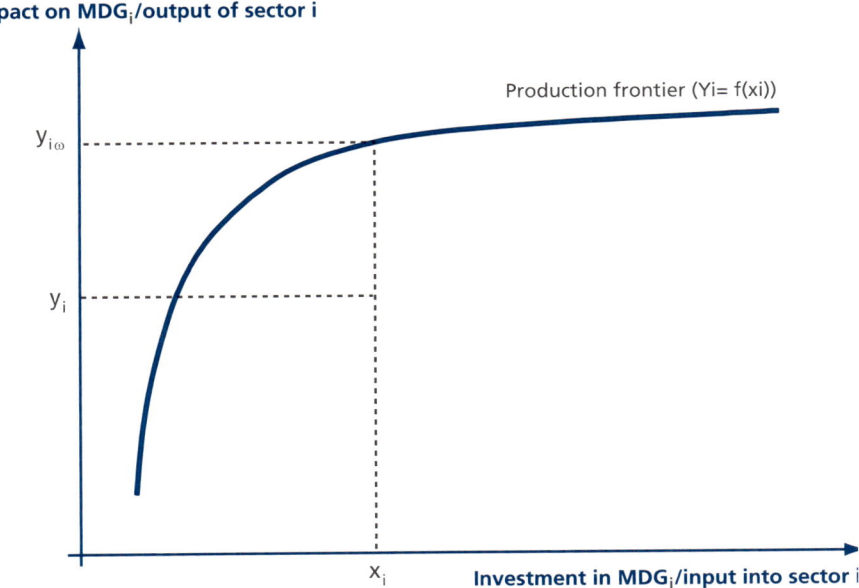

and MDG is the question of whether ICT can contribute to improving efficiency in delivering the MDG.

The Jayasuriya-Wodon Model

As Ruwan Jayasuriya and Quentin Wodon (2003) remark, efficiency in delivering a particular MDG[12] can be measured as the ratio between "actual delivery" and "optimal delivery" (see Figure 8, in which $y_i = f(x_i)$, where y_i is the output generated in sector i by allocating x_i to the sector).

If, however, one introduces the possibility of allocating available resources (T) between a direct allocation to sector i (e.g., health or education), x_i on one hand and a partial allocation to the ICT sector, x_T on the other hand, the following chain of causalities is generated (see Figure 9 below).

This simplified model can be translated into the following set of equations:

$x_i + x_{T=T}$ *(resource allocation frontier)*

$y'_i = f(x_i, x_{T})$, *where y'_i is the output generated in sector i by allocating x_i to the sector and x_T to ICT*

Graphically, we now have to consider three dimensions: two are contained in the resource allocation plane (between sector i and ICT), and the third one allows us to represent the final impact on sector I and its corresponding MDG. (See Figure 10 on next page.)

Figure 9. **Investing in ICT to Reach MDG**

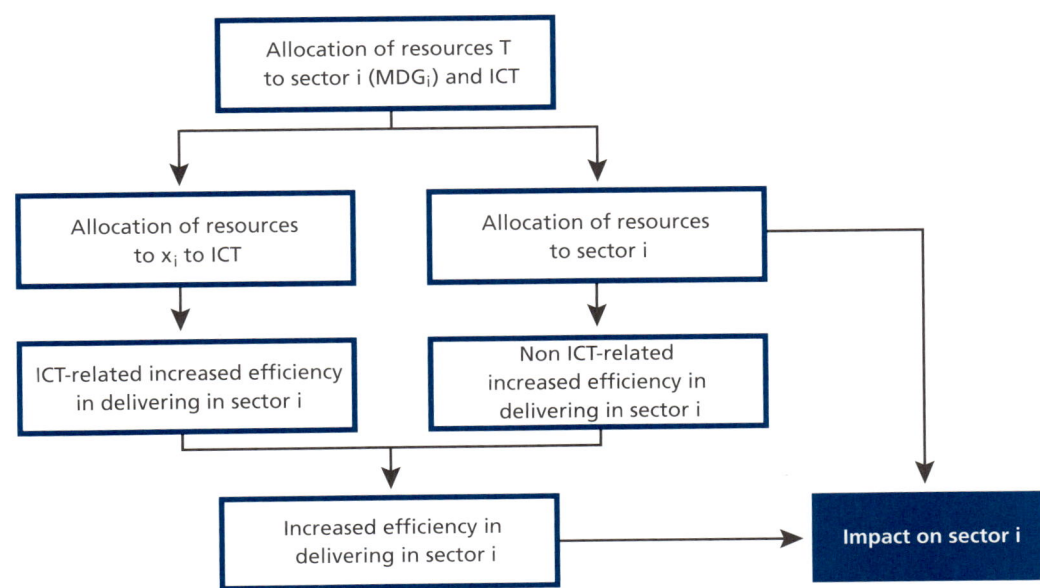

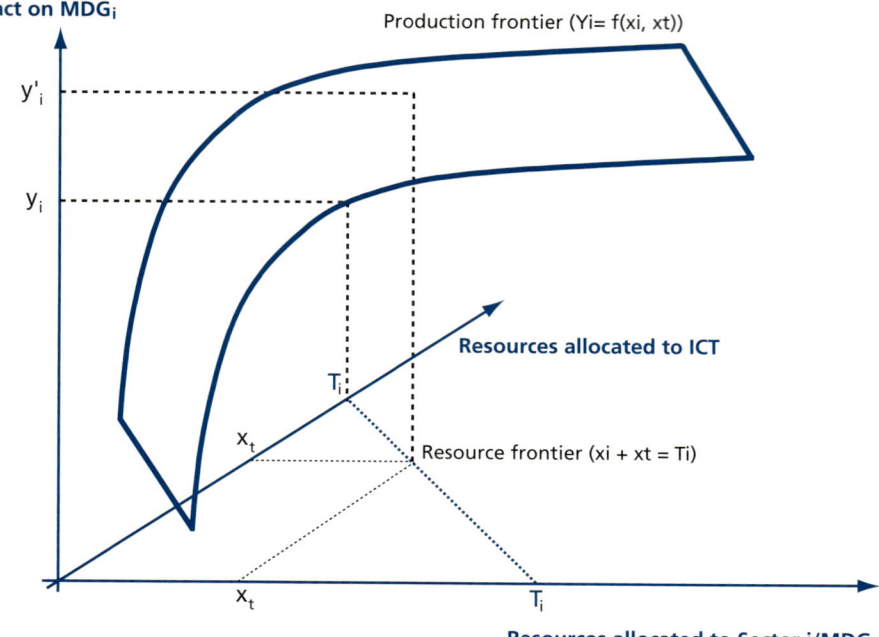

Figure 10. **Investing in ICT to Enchance Efficiency in Delivering in MDG**

This way of representing ICT investment as a source of increased efficiency in pursuing MDG 2 to 7 (and hence 1) opens a number of policy and strategic avenues. Additional efforts will be required from statisticians and econometricians to help quantify the relevant elasticities and dynamic linkages between various variables, which may vary from one country to another. International efforts are hence required to collect relevant data at the local, regional and global levels.

Conclusion: The Measure of All Things

Over the last few years, policymakers have paid increased attention to ICT and the extent to which it can help to achieve the MDG while also fostering inclusion and equity. The international community currently has at its disposal a rare combination of tools to turn the information revolution into a powerful instrument to fight poverty and inequality at the global level. This combination consists of (1) an agreed-upon framework of references (the MDG and their related targets), and (2) a higher level of awareness among decision makers of the economic and social importance of ICT. So, what is missing to trigger action and generate impact at the policy level ?

The analysis and discussion provided in this chapter and elsewhere in the *Global Information Technology Report* indicate that the additional key ingredients necessary include the following :

1. A conceptual frame of reference with which decision and policymakers can (1) get the big picture, (2) identify causalities between their actions and anticipated effects, and (3) choose the political paths, relative emphases, and sequencings according to which they want their own actions and those of their partners (public and private, local or not) to be organized. Such a framework should in particular provide examples, references, and methodologies for estimating the effects of higher investments in ICT on various social and economic objectives (including the MDG).

2. A set of "scorecards" with which policymakers, local players, and international observers and contributors can (1) measure[13] the efforts made at different levels of decision-making, (2) evaluate their impact along the chain of causalities contained in the framework described above, and (3) attract attention and mobilize energies and support whenever any "missing link," sluggishness, or imbalance is identified that might imperil the pursuit of established objectives (including the MDG and ultimately poverty eradication).

3. Feedback mechanisms through which the intensity of efforts made (in particular at the local level) by the public and private sector to promote ICT as a tool for development and growth can be valued and rewarded.

In the broad context of the pursuit of the Millennium Development Goals, these elements can be schematically included in the following diagram :

Figure 11. The Roles of Policy Decisions and Scorecards in "e-Readication"

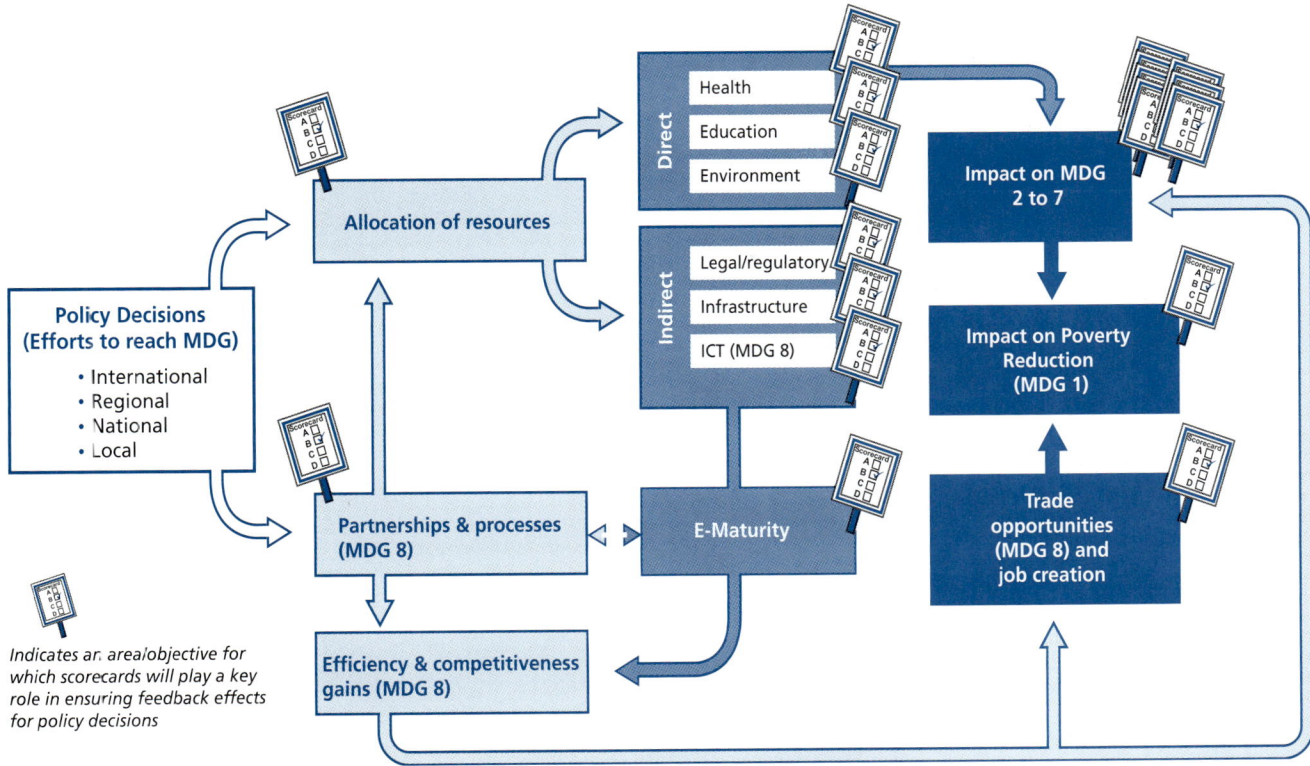

Indicates an area/objective for which scorecards will play a key role in ensuring feedback effects for policy decisions

IDENTIFYING THE RIGHT PLAYERS AND GIVING THEM THE RIGHT TOOLS

As the world prepares for the World Summit on the Information Society (WSIS), an opportunity and a challenge arise. How will the international community provide the necessary "scorecards," giving them the credibility and legitimacy they require to be effective tools for policymakers? Identifying the right "issuer" of such scorecards will be an important and difficult exercise. Such an issuer should combine a rare set of qualities including (1) technical competence, (2) acceptance among all users of such scorecards (governments, international organizations, business, and civil society), and (3) the visibility and outspokenness necessary to make such scorecards a universally accepted reference and support for action.

The Global Information Technology Report and its various "e-maturity" indices are among the better recognized tools for assessing how ready national economies are to benefit from the information revolution and the emergence of a global networked economy. Improving its country coverage and refining its methodology will be necessary and other statistical and econometric tools will be required in order to offer the complete set of scorecards that decision and policymakers will need to justify their decisions to do more and better in the field of information technology. Such tools will need to be sophisticated enough to reflect the complexity of the direct and indirect effects of ICT on various social and economic fields. They will also have to be user-friendly so that governments can make use of them in budget discussions and business leaders can relate them to their bottom line.

This is definitely a tall order, and one that will require significant efforts and attention in the coming few years. It is also one in which all members of the information society have a role to play. The more we all know about the ways in which e-readiness and e-maturity can contribute effectively to poverty eradication, the faster we shall be able to move towards the building of a vibrant, open, and equitable information society. As its name suggests, *poverty e-readication* may very well be a shortcut to this destination.

Appendix. **Some Initiatives Illustrating the Link Between ICT and Sectoral MDG**

Initiative and Application Model	Impact
EDUCATION **Enlaces—Chilean ICT in Education Initiative** In 1990, the Chilean government embarked on a major educational reform program, known as Enlaces. It included an initiative to integrate ICT as learning and teaching resources for all students and teachers within the public school system. Enlaces began as a pilot project interconnecting 100 schools and by 1995, became a nationwide initiative. The hallmark of the program is to provide both connectivity in the classroom and training and support for teachers. http://www.mirandanet.ac.uk/ftp/enlaces.pdf	• By 2000, over 5,300 primary and secondary schools had received computers, local networks, educational and productivity software, and free/unlimited Internet access. • Also by 2000, 70,000 teachers (50 percent of all teachers) had received technical training. Enlaces had reached 90 percent of the student population attending state subsidized institutions.
GENDER Training for African Women in Internet Working Technology is a training course for African women offered at the Information Technology Center of the United Nations Economic Commission for Africa (UNECA) in Addis Ababa, Ethiopia. The training course, sponsored by *info*Dev, Cisco Systems, and UNECA, aims to increase opportunities for African women to enter the field of ICT and to empower women through entrepreneurship and management training. http://wbln0018.worldbank.org/ict/projects.nsf	• The training course includes 280 instructional hours over a six-month period, and leads to independent certification as a Certified Networking Associate or a Certified Networking Professional. • In addition to networking courses, participants take part in training on gender and development, entrepreneurship, and management for African women.
HEALTH **RESCUER** (The Rural Extended Services and Care for Ultimate Emergency Relief) was initiated by the Ugandan Ministry of Health, UNFPA, and the Uganda Population Secretariat in 1996. Its objective is to improve maternal health within the country, where the maternal mortality rate (506 per 100,000) is one of the highest in the world. Due to the unavailability of electric power in most rural areas, lack of fixed telephone lines and 24-hour service requirements, radio technology was employed via fixed base stations, mobile walkie-talkies, and vehicle radios.	• This project connects traditional rural community health providers with a cost-effective formal health delivery system that provides responsive maternal health care. • Three years after project implementation, a study sample of the Iganga district concluded that the maternal mortality rate had decreased by nearly 50 percent
ENVIRONMENT **SIDSNet** is a medium of communication for 43 Small Island Developing States (SIDS) on common issues such as biodiversity, climate change, coastal and marine management, energy sources, and trade. It is promoting the sharing of SIDS experiences and the development of the global SIDS agenda. http://www.sidsnet.org/	• The website receives an average of 300,000 hits per month from over 100 countries, including donors and SIDS • The site contributes to the increasing level of awareness and understanding of the link between the environment and human development among SIDS decision makers.

Source: World Bank (2003)

References

Accenture, Markle Foundation, and United Nations Development Programme. 2001. *Creating a Development Dynamic: Final Report of the Digital Opportunity Initiative*. Online. http://www.opt-init.org/framework/pages/contents.html

Avgerou, C. 1998. "How Can ICT Enable Growth in Developing Countries," *Information Technology for Development* 8, pp. 15–28.

Bedi, A. S. 2001. "The Role of ICT in Economic Development—A Partial Survey," ZEF Discussion Paper on Development Policy No. 7. Bonn, Germany: Center for Development Research (ZEF). Online. http://www.developmentgateway.org/download/164685/zef_dp7–99.pdf

Dollar, D. and A. Kraay. 2001. "Growth is Good for the Poor," Policy Research Working Paper No. 2587. Washington, D.C.: The World Bank. Online. http://econ.worldbank.org/files/1696_wps2587.pdf

Dutta, S., B. Lanvin, and F. Paua eds. 2003. *Global Information Technology Report 2002–2003*. New York: Oxford University Press.

Flore, A. G. 2001. "ICT and Poverty: the Indisputable Link," Paper presented at Third Asia Development Forum on Regional Economic Cooperation in Asia and the Pacific, Asian Development Bank, Bangkok, June 11–14, 2001. Online. http://www.worldbank.org/html/extdr/offrep/eap/eapprem/infoalexan.pdf

G-8 Digital Opportunity Task Force (DOT Force). 2001. "Digital Opportunities for All," final report of the DOT Force presented at the Genoa G-8 Summit, July 2001. Online. http://www.dotforce.org/reports/DOT_Force_Report_V_0h.html

Gerster, R. and S. Zimmermann. 2003. "Information and Communication Technologies (ICT) for Poverty Reduction?" Swiss Agency for Development and Cooperation Discussion Paper. Online. http://www.gersterconsulting.ch/docs/ICT_for_Poverty_Reduction.pdf

Kenny, C., J. Navas-Sabater, and C. Qiang. 2002. Chapter 24. "Information and Communication Technologies and Poverty." In *A Source Book for Poverty Reduction Strategy Paper*. Washington, D.C.: The World Bank.

Nagy, H. 2003. "Why ICT Matters for Growth and Poverty Reduction." Mimeographed, the World Bank. Online. http://www.developmentgateway.org/node/133831/sdm/docview?docid=510867

*info*Dev. 2002. *Annual Report*. Washington, D.C.: The World Bank. Online. http://www.infodev.org

Jayasuriya, R. and Q. Wodon. 2003. "Efficiency in Reaching the Millennium Development Goals," World Bank Working Paper No 9. Washington, D.C.: The World Bank.

Lanvin, B. 2002. "La fracture numérique n'est pas une fatalité." In J.F. Soupizet and L. Gille, eds., *Nord et Sud Numeriques (Les cahiers du numérique 2, no. 3–4, 2001)*. Online. http://www.lavoisier.fr/fr/livres/index.asp?texte=2746204120&select=isbn&from=Hermes

Lanvin, B. 2003. "Leaders and Facilitators—The New Roles of Governments in Digital Economies." In S. Dutta, B. Lanvin, and F. Paua, eds., *Global Information Technology Report 2002–2003*. New York: Oxford University Press. Online. http://www.weforum.org/pdf/Global_Competitiveness_Reports/Reports/GITR_2002_2003/Leaders_and_Facilitators.pdf

Marker, P., K. McNamara, and L. Wallace. 2002. *The Significance of ICT for Reducing Poverty*, Department for International Development. Online. http://www.dfid.gov.uk/Pubs/files/ict_poverty.pdf

Organization for Economic Co-operation and Development (OECD, 2003). "How ICTs Can Help Achieve the Millennium Development Goals," Table presented at meeting on Integrating ICT in Development Programmes. Online. http://www.oecd.org/dataoecd/54/4/2500199.xls

Pilat, D. 2003. "Digital Economy—Going for Growth," *OECD Observer* 237.

Qiang, C. Z.-W., A. Pitt, with S. Ayers. 2003. "Contribution of ICT to Growth," World Bank Working Paper. Washington, D.C.: the World Bank.

Qiang, C. Z.-W. and P. L. Smith. 2003. "Digital Divide in China." Mimeographed, the World Bank.

Samiullah, Y. and S. Rao. 2003. *Role of ICTs in Urban and Rural Poverty Reduction*. Department for International Development. Online. http://www.teri.res.in/icteap/present/session4/sami.doc

Steinberg, J. 2003. "Information Technology and Development Beyond 'either/or'," *Brookings Review* 21, no. 2, pp. 45–48.

United Nations Development Programme (UNDP). 2003a. "The Role of ICT in Enhancing the Achievement of Millennium Development Goals," A Contribution to the Work of Millennium Project, Task Force 10 on Science and Technology. Mimeographed, UNDP.

———. 2003b. "ICT for Development: Elements of an Action Framework for Implementing the MDG," Discussion Paper, Task Force on Science, Technology and Innovation of the UN Millennium Project. Online. http://infolac.ucol.mx/eventos/reunion-varadero/task_force.pdf

———. 2003c. *Millennium Development Goals: A Compact Among Nations to End Human Poverty*. Human Development Report 2003. Online. http://www.undp.org/hdr2003

United Nations Information Communications Technology (UNICT Task Force). 2003. "Using ICT to achieve the MDG," Paper presented by Richard Simpson (Canada) at the Fifth Meeting of the UNICT Task Force, Geneva, September 2003.

World Bank. 2003. "ICT and MDG: The WBG Experiences." Mimeographed, the World Bank.

Endnotes

1   The MDG and associated targets come from the Millennium Declaration signed by the representatives of 189 countries, including 147 Heads of States, in 2000. The eight goals (see Box 1) represent a partnership among the developed countries, the developing countries, and international agencies determined, as the Declaration states, "to create an environment—at the national and global levels alike—which is conducive to development and the elimination of poverty" (see Box 2).

2   As defined in *The Global Information Technology Report 2002–2003*, page 9. Addressing the Joint OECD/UN/World Bank Global Forum on the Knowledge Economyntegrating ICT in Development Programmes (Paris, 4–5 March 2003), Jean-François Rischard, Vice-President of the World Bank, recalled that there are at least three ways in which ICT can be mainstreamed in development, namely (1) integrating ICT in topical development solutions, (2) integrating ICT in overall development solutions, and (3) integrating ICT in advanced development thinking; he also noted that, although significant progress had been made on the first of those three elements, much remained to be done on (2) and even more about (3).

3   This implies that the ICT targets of MDG 8 (telephony and Internet connectivity) should not be considered in isolation. It also reflects the growing consensus that the so-called digital divide is less about equipment and connectivity than about content, applications, and the ability of local communities to create and derive socio-economic value from the use of ICT.

4   Network externalities are considered to be generated when, as the total number of connections increases, the average benefit obtained from connecting to the network also increases. Metcalfe's Law states that the usefulness (or utility) of a network grows with the square of the number of its users.

5   As described, for example, by Avgerou 1998.

6   See DOT Force (2001), *info*Dev (2002) and UNICT Task Force (2003) for example. This chapter's appendix lists some examples of the positive transformational impact of ICT in each of the social sectors.

7   The human development index is a composite index measuring average achievement in three basic dimensions of human development—a long and healthy life (as measured by life expectancy at birth); knowledge (as measured by the adult literacy rate and the combined primary, secondary, and tertiary gross enrollment ratio); and a decent standard of living (as measured by GDP per capita).

8   The networked economy index is a composite of three components: the environment for enabling ICT; the readiness of a community's key stakeholders (individuals, businesses, and governments) to use ICT; and finally, the usage of ICT amongst these stakeholders.

9   IMF (2000). A research report by Dollar and Kraay (2001) analyzes 80 countries over the past four decades and concludes that growth in the overall economy is reflected one for one by income growth for the poor (defined as the bottom one-fifth of the income distribution). See also Ferreira, (1999). Qiang and Smith (2003).

10 In Kenya, for instance, a group of women used videos to raise their voices and inform the decision makers about their needs. See http://www.itdg.org

11 The Jayasuriya/Wodon study encompasses goals 1 to 7, its authors considering that Goal 8 is out of the scope of their analysis.

12 One could argue that measurement, which is always a delicate affair in economics and other social sciences, is particularly difficult in the field of ICT, where innovation is so fast-paced, and effects so unpredictable. One of the best possible answers to this worry has been provided by Ken Adler in his report of the odyssey of Jean-Baptiste-Joseph Delambre and Pierre-François-André Méchain, the two scientists sent by the French Revolutionary Government of 1792 to measure the earth and establish the legal length of the meter: "How do you measure the earth while the world is turning beneath your feet? How do you establish a new order when the countryside is in chaos? How do you set standards at a time when everything is up for grabs? Or is there, in fact, no better time to do so?" (from K. Adler, *The Measure of All Things*, Free Press, 2002).

Chapter 4

Towards a New Regulatory Compact

Scott Beardsley, Ingo Beyer von Morgenstern, Luis Enriquez, and Walter Verbeke

McKinsey & Company

Thanks to Nicole Kozera Almonte and Wim Torfs of McKinsey & Company for researching the facts supporting the findings of this chapter.

Regulatory moves and evolving technology are reshaping the telecom landscape. Most affected are Bell companies such as SBC. SBC lost customers for 1.8 million local phone lines (10 percent) from April 2002 through June 30 of this year (in California alone). They jumped to long-distance carriers and cable companies that barged into the local-phone business after state regulators made it far cheaper for outside companies to use SBC's network.

—*The Wall Street Journal,* August 13, 2003

Introduction

Over the past decade, the telecom industry has been dramatically reshaped by the wave of liberalization and privatization that has swept across the world. State-owned monopolies have been privatized, and incumbent operators have had to cope with substantial price declines and losses in their shares of key markets such as long distance, international carriage, and data services. In many market segments, incumbents' market shares have dropped to below 50 percent. This has been accompanied by the explosive growth in mobile penetration and usage—in some countries, mobile voice traffic has surpassed that of traditional fixed-line networks and in many countries, mobile penetration is greater than fixed. However, despite these changes, one area has remained firmly dominated by incumbents: the "last mile" of access to the vast majority of users. Even in countries that have seen liberalization here, such as the United States and the United Kingdom, there has not yet been any substantial dent in local operators' market share—until now.

As the cited *Wall Street Journal* excerpt notes, incumbent providers are beginning to see their last-mile market share erode, driven by two forces. Technology has allowed cable networks to capture increasing shares of broadband subscribers and of telephony subscribers. Technology has also increased infrastructure availability and reduced the price of mobile calls, driving latent demand as well as substitution of both traffic and access (particularly in developing countries). Regulators have provided a second impetus to these forces by pushing incumbents to open their fixed networks to entrants at relatively low costs. These two forces support several major trends that are slowly eroding incumbents' dominance and will transform the industry in the coming years.

This chapter describes four trends in the telecommunications (telecom) industry that will have a tremendous impact on the future of the industry and its key stakeholders: fixed-mobile substitution, increasing competition in fixed-access, take-up of voice-over-IP (VoIP), and growth of broadband access. In the medium term, these trends will gradually but significantly alter the traditional fixed-telephony business model. Regulation will play a key role in determining the pace of these trends and the freedom that incumbents will have to respond to them.

Successfully managing the evolution of these trends requires that key industry stakeholders address four critical dimensions: a regulatory shift towards focusing on the economics of telecom players; the variation between national structures in terms of starting conditions and network readiness; the constraints to change; and the tailoring of the regulatory approach such that it offers mutually consistent solutions for governments, society, and telecom operators.

This chapter contains several key points, outlined below:

1. *Four major economic trends* will substantially reduce the overall importance of incumbent-provided traditional voice telephony:

   - *Fixed-mobile* traffic and access *substitution* will continue. However, the degree of substitution will substantially vary by country, as it is primarily driven by relative fixed/mobile penetration and corresponding price differentials.

   - Incumbents' *losses* of market share in PSTN (public switched telephone network) *fixed-access* to cable and LLU (local-loop unbundling) attackers remains relatively small with a few exceptions but could increase significantly in certain countries, particularly in North America and, to a lesser extent, the United Kingdom, the Benelux countries, and other upgraded cable environments.

   - *VoIP* is poised to take off and could have a significant impact on the volume of PSTN voice traffic in the medium term, especially in countries with high broadband penetration.

   - The growth in *broadband* will reshape the revenue model for both incumbents and attackers in the medium term but could also prompt new regulatory intervention to support wider adoption.

2. Together, these trends will have a *substantial effect on industry structure*, despite the fact that the impact of each individual trend is moderate. Although this impact will vary by country, the countries at highest risk could see their share of traditional voice-line access decline from 83 percent today (end of 2002) to less than 50 percent by the end of 2007.

3. *Broadband penetration* is becoming significant in many countries, some of them achieving household penetration rates of more than 50 percent. However, penetration growth will probably level off, since consumer spending on telecom is limited and prices are not likely to come down very quickly.

4. *Regulation will have a major influence* on the extent of the impact and will determine a substantial allocation of value among key industry players and consumers. This will shape the evolution of the sector and determine the rate at which the sector is able to generate further economic benefits.

5. There are *four regulatory dimensions* in which stakeholders such as operators, regulators, and policymakers need to work in order to manage these industry trends successfully and be better prepared for a reshaped industry:

   - Regulation has to ensure that business decisions by players can be based on *business economics*.

   - Regulatory change should be a function of market and starting conditions and can therefore be expected to *vary by country*.

   - *Constraints to regulatory change* should be recognized and understood.

   - Regulatory approaches should be tailored towards *mutually consistent solutions*.

The first section of this chapter summarizes those trends that are having the greatest impact on the traditional telephony voice model and outlines their underlying economics. The second section outlines the role of regulation in setting the pace of these trends. The final section defines the four critical dimensions within which operators, regulators, and policymakers will need to work in order to manage the trends successfully. Supporting case studies and insights are drawn from McKinsey's extensive experience serving major stakeholders within the telecom industry.

Four Trends Reshaping Traditional Voice Telephony

Traditional fixed-line, incumbent-dominated networks are coming under increasing pressure. Four trends in particular will substantially reduce the overall importance of incumbent-provided traditional voice telephony, each adding approximately 1 to 2 percent annually to the erosion of incumbents' access lines. As a result, incumbents' narrowband access lines now account for nearly 80 percent of the total in the United States and in those European countries at the highest risk of share erosion. As Figure 1 indicates, by the end of 2007, estimates suggest that less than half of fixed access lines will be incumbent-provided narrowband voice. This is a major evolution in the traditional fixed-line access model that will fundamentally alter the economics of the business and put significant pressure on prices and costs for all players, thereby placing substantial value at risk for all stakeholders in the industry.

The "death of a thousand cuts" can be broken down into four key trends, as outlined below:

To date, *fixed-mobile traffic substitution* has mostly affected voice traffic in advanced countries as mobile networks have become ubiquitous and perceived price differentials between fixed and mobile considerably

Figure 1. Substantial Erosion of the Traditional Fixed-Line Incumbents' Market Share in Voice

Total number of fixed-access lines (narrow- and broadband) in US, UK, Spain, Germany, Japan, Belgium

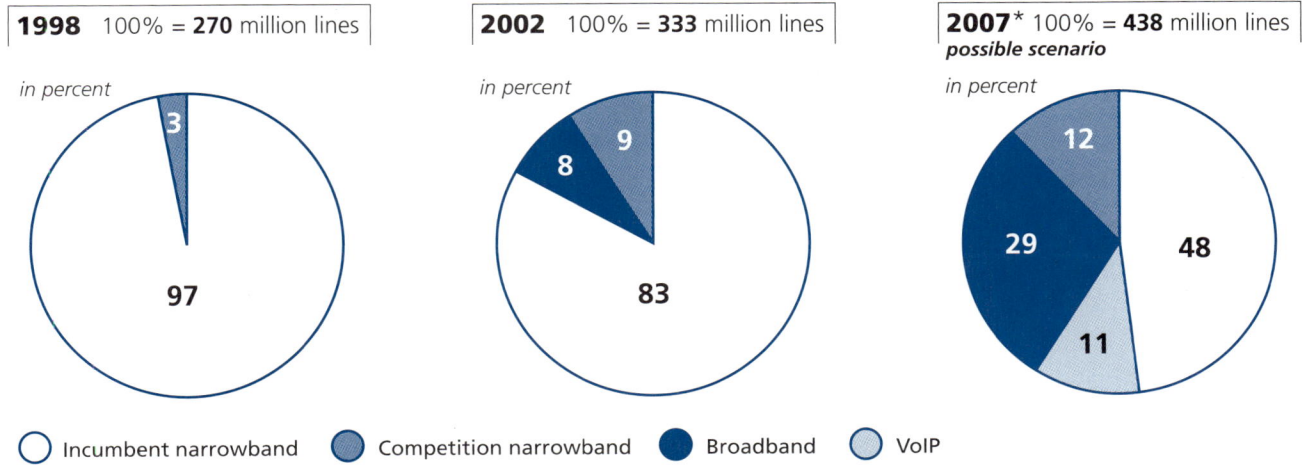

1998 100% = 270 million lines

in percent
- 3
- 97

2002 100% = 333 million lines

in percent
- 9
- 8
- 83

2007* 100% = 438 million lines
possible scenario

in percent
- 12
- 29
- 48
- 11

○ Incumbent narrowband ◉ Competition narrowband ● Broadband ○ VoIP

Sources: ECTA; Analysys; Ovum; regulators; company data; McKinsey analysis

decline. In addition, more countries are seeing access substitution starting to emerge, driven primarily by the growing traffic substitution. In developing economies, mobile infrastructure is in many cases leapfrogging ahead of fixed, rapidly fulfilling latent demand and suppressing the building of a fixed network.

Attackers' market share of fixed-access remains rather limited—usually around 5 percent. This is mostly due to the regulatory conditions of LLU and cable penetration. However, in the United States and the United Kingdom, fixed-line attackers have managed to capture roughly 13 percent of the local-access market.

Thus far, *VoIP take-up* has been in the business segment, driven by the cost savings offered on internal company calls. In Europe, nearly one-fifth of enterprises already use VoIP, with Spain (24 percent) and the United Kingdom (22 percent) having an especially high take-up. In addition to further business-user growth, a major breakthrough in residential usage seems very likely, as significant cost savings could make VoIP very attractive.

Broadband penetration has been growing steadily, primarily among higher-income households, reaching levels of 20 to 30 percent in higher-adoption countries such as the United States, Canada, Japan, Sweden, and Benelux. At today's prices, broadband growth is likely to slow down as penetration reaches 45 percent in the United States and 15 percent in Europe (although many richer European countries are likely to see a much higher leveling-off point), as it is still relatively expensive (USD 30 to 50 per month). However, South Korea's 66 percent penetration level demonstrates that a comprehensive policy of supply support and demand

encouragement can push broadband penetration well beyond expected saturation levels.

In a number of countries, these four trends threaten to put significant value at risk, particularly for incumbents, depending upon market structure, starting position, and the regulatory environment. Given the interrelated and mutually reinforcing character of these trends, their combined effect could still be significant in an even wider group of countries. An initial assessment, shown in Figure 2, indicates that certain high-risk countries may experience an extremely significant impact of a particular trend in the next five years:

- In the Czech Republic, fixed-mobile substitution could hit an incumbents' EBIT (earnings before interest and taxes) by more than 40 percent.

- In the United States, competition on local PSTN access could remove between 40 and 80 percent of an incumbent's EBIT, depending upon the type of customer.

- In the United Kingdom, VoIP telephony could represent 8 percent of total voice-market revenues.

- In Japan, broadband penetration could reach up to 80 percent, 55 percentage points more than today.

In most of the medium- and lower-risk countries, no individual trend is likely to have the degree of impact shown above. However, as illustrated in Figure 3, the four trends are interrelated, and it is likely that they will often reinforce each other. The resulting effect could, therefore, still be important and put substantial value at stake.

VoIP growth and broadband are certainly mutually reinforcing. VoIP-related services are more attractive over broadband access and will increase the attractiveness of

Figure 2. **Impact of Trends Varies Substantially, Putting Significant Value at Risk in Some Countries**

Trend		Description	Potential impact in highest-risk countries		
			Example market	Unit	Amount at stake (%)
1	Voice-over-IP growth	Significant savings via VoIP over broadband over existing PSTN line or upgrades to IP-terminal	UK	% of PSTN residential voice market revenues in 2007	8
2	Fixed-mobile substitution	Voice traffic shifts from fixed to mobile, and access lines are switched off or not installed	Czech Republic	% of EBIT of fixed business in 2005	43
3	Competition on local fixed-access	Incumbents lose most profitable customers through cable and LLU competition	US	% of EBIT of fixed business in 2007	40-84
4	Broadband	Achieving Korea's levels of penetration by increasing households' willingness to spend on broadband	EU	% of household market penetration in 2007*	25-30

Source: McKinsey analysis

Figure 3. **Trends Are Interrelated, in Many Cases Reinforcing Each Other**

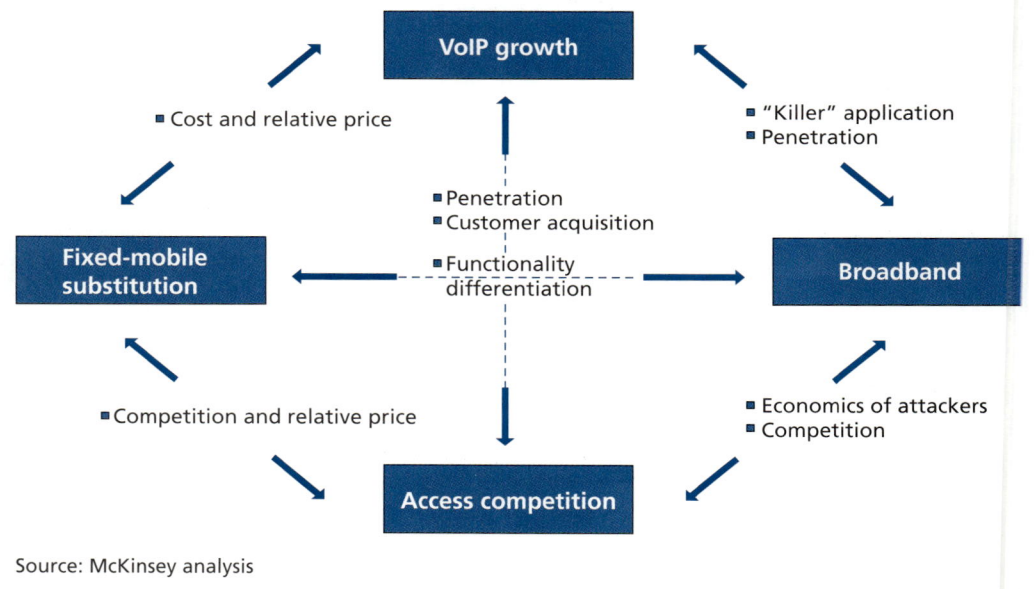

Source: McKinsey analysis

broadband to some users, thereby pushing deeper broadband penetration. Consequently, increasing broadband penetration could swell the potential pool of VoIP users. This, in turn, could increase savings to all other VoIP users, since VoIP-to-VoIP could be very low-cost, thereby prompting further penetration of residential VoIP. VoIP also mutually reinforces access competition, as VoIP could be instrumental in helping operators acquire new customers.

Broadband and access competition are also mutually reinforcing trends, since broadband can benefit attackers' economics and thereby support an attacker's distinctive value proposition.

The increasing substitution of mobile telephony for both traffic and access substantially reinforces overall access competition. Finally, fixed-mobile substitution and broadband could potentially reinforce each other on the basis of functional differentiation, whereby data-related services would use broadband, while voice-related products would use mobile technology, resulting in the further cancellation of traditional narrowband access lines.

To understand these trends in greater depth, we will now tackle the underlying economics of each one in turn.

Fixed-Mobile Substitution

In an increasing majority of countries, mobile-telephony markets are maturing and mobile access is beginning to exceed fixed-line penetration. In Europe, a recent newspaper article reported that average mobile penetration in the EU hit 80 percent, vastly exceeding the fixed penetration of 40 to 60 percent of the population. With the ubiquity of mobile networks and the drop in perceived mobile-call prices relative to fixed-line calls, increasingly large segments of users have become used to making most phone calls on mobile telephones. Consequently, mobile telephony is completing its transition from a premium niche product to a direct mainstream substitute for traditional fixed-line voice traffic.

As shown in Figure 4, the degree of fixed-mobile substitution varies considerably among countries, with Italy, Portugal,

the Czech Republic, and Finland having a high degree of substitution at between 36 and 51 percent of total potential fixed traffic. Countries such as Norway, France, and Spain, with between 15 and 25 percent, still experience medium substitution, whereas in countries such as the United Kingdom, Sweden, and Germany levels remain below 10 percent.

The key drivers for traffic substitution in developed countries are high levels of mobile penetration and relative price differentials. These determine how often consumers have a choice between fixed and mobile (structural substitution); and, when given the choice, which technology they use (behavioral substitution).

In countries with low fixed-line penetration relative to mobile penetration, structural substitution occurs more often than in markets with relatively high fixed-line penetration, because consumers often have no choice but to use their mobile phones. In countries with low perceived price differentials between fixed and mobile, behavioral substitution also occurs more often because consumers prefer to use their mobile phones as they may be cheaper and are more convenient. Once the "substitution wheel" starts to spin, it triggers an exponential trend (i.e., as mobile usage increases, the likelihood of preferring mobile over fixed grows), explained by a networking effect and the fact that even those who were initially attracted only by price, start valuing the convenience highly.

As Figure 5 demonstrates, there are also growing indications that fixed-mobile substitution is occurring, not only in traffic, but also increasingly in access, whereby the former drives the latter. This access substitution appears to be primarily significant in lower-income countries where fixed-line penetration was not that high to begin with. In Portugal, Jordan, Malaysia, and the Czech Republic, for instance, fixed-line penetration effectively dropped over the past five years, in the latter even by 5 percent, while it remained stable or even grew in other countries. Mobile penetration, by contrast, has enjoyed relatively robust growth.

The more consumers use their mobile phones, the lower the perceived value of their fixed line and the greater chance that they eventually disconnect. The trend is exacerbated by high broadband penetration in countries such as the United States, where millions of customers have cancelled their fixed line and use their mobiles for voice calls and broadband for Internet access. The introduction and growth of VoIP telephony over broadband connections is expected to fuel even more access-line cancellations.

The implication is that traditional fixed line voice infrastructure investment is becoming increasingly unattractive and will need to shift to new services and technologies in emerging countries, but such a shift may never happen.

Figure 4. **Traffic Substitution Varies Substantially by Country**

Traffic substitution

Loss of fixed traffic to mobile as percent of total potential fixed traffic, 2002

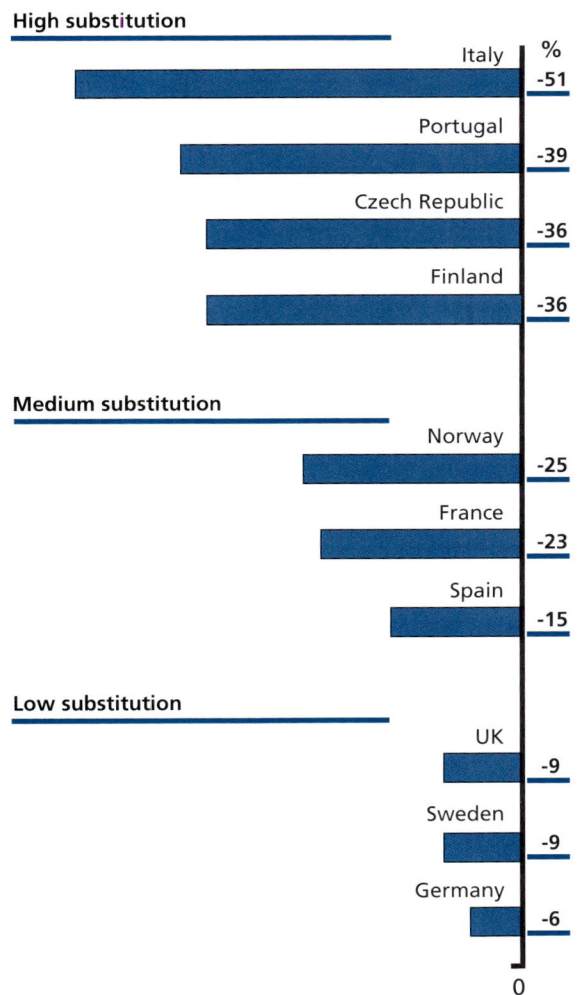

High substitution

	%
Italy	-51
Portugal	-39
Czech Republic	-36
Finland	-36

Medium substitution

Norway	-25
France	-23
Spain	-15

Low substitution

UK	-9
Sweden	-9
Germany	-6

0

Sources: Regulators; McKinsey analysis

Figure 5. **Fixed-Access Stagnation or Decline Due to Fixed-Mobile Access Substitution**

Developed countries
Penetration (percent of population)

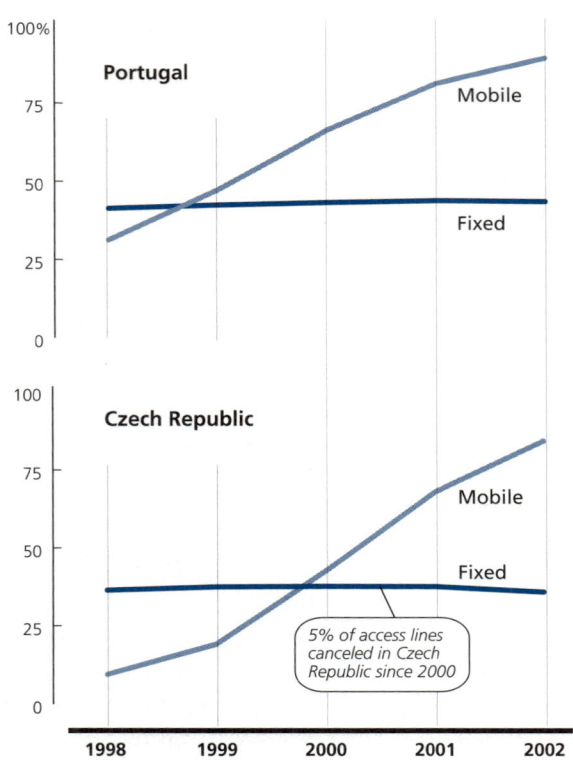

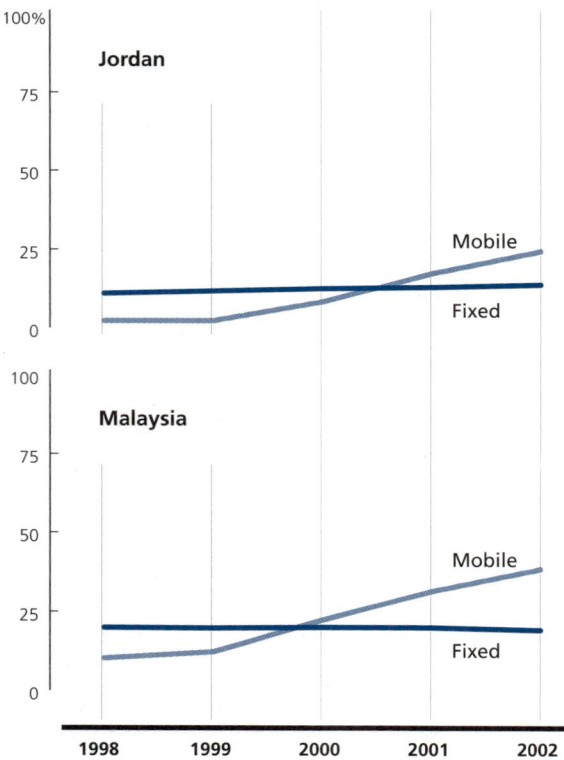

Developing countries
Penetration (percent of population)

Sources: Regulators; ITU; company annual reports; McKinsey analysis

Figure 6. **Loss In Fixed-Access Networks Remains Relatively Small**

Fixed competitors' market share in local access, 200_

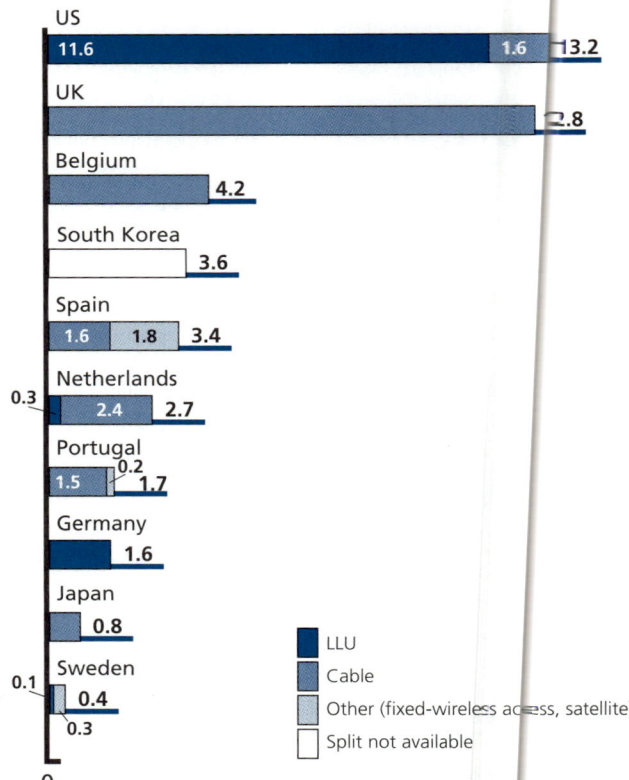

Sources: Regulators; Ovum; Analysys; company data; ECTA; McKinsey analysis

Fixed-Access Competition: A Limited, but Increasing Threat to 'Incumbents' Profits

Following the liberalization of many telecom markets, attackers entered the fray. They typically acted as a service provider, using another operator's—usually the incumbent's—network, or they operated their own network on which telecom services are provided. In the latter situation, depending upon market and regulatory conditions, attackers would employ LLU (Germany), upgrade cable networks (e.g., Benelux and the United Kingdom), or use other access technologies such as FTTX (fiber, ethernet to the building in Italy and Sweden) and fixed-wireless access and satellite (e.g., Italy, New Zealand, South Korea, and Sweden).

As illustrated in Figure 6, attackers' market share in fixed-access has remained rather limited, leaving incumbents with only minor losses in market share. The United States and the United Kingdom are the exceptions—fixed-line competitors already hold 13 percent of the local-access market. In Europe and Asia, typical fixed-access market share losses to attackers have been less than 5 percent.

However, these relatively low percentages hide potentially higher revenue and profit losses. Loss of access market share appears to be disproportionately concentrated in

Figure 7. 40 to 84 Percent of Incumbents' Fixed EBIT at Risk If Losses Continue at Current Pace in High-Risk Countries

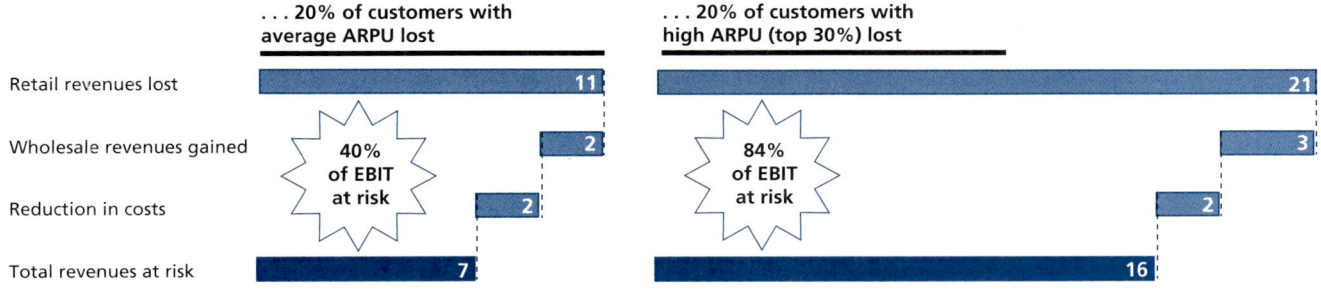

Value at risk for fixed-line incumbents if . . .

Sources: Company data; Wall Street Journal; McKinsey analysis

Figure 8. Business Can Capture Benefits of VoIP Today

Savings on fixed-to-fixed voice traffic bill

EUR per user, per year

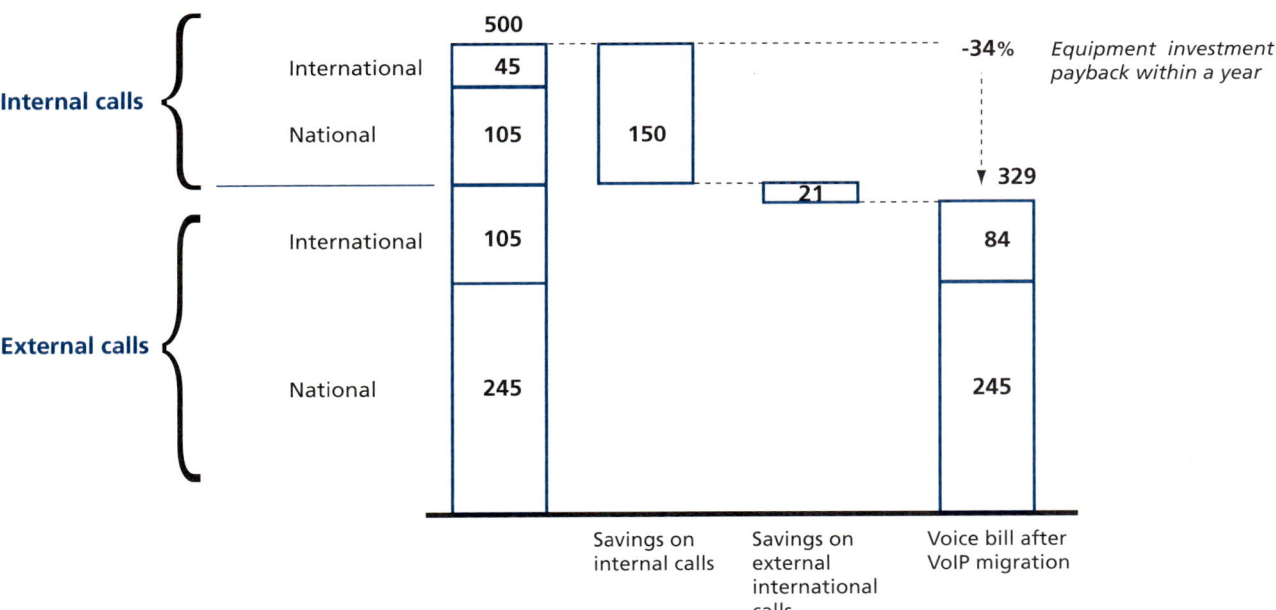

Sources: IDC European IP user survey; company data; McKinsey analysis

urban and suburban areas where small businesses and high average revenue per user (ARPU) customers represent a significantly higher share of incumbents' revenues and profits. As illustrated in Figure 7, if share losses in access continue at their current pace, based on average ARPU numbers, 40 percent of an incumbent's EBIT could be at stake in high-risk countries. If the trend of higher-end ARPU customers canceling their access line accelerates, this EBIT impact could double to more than 80 percent.

VoIP: Gradually Eroding PSTN Telephony

Following a number of years of uncertainty about its future, IP telephony finally appears poised to take off as a partial replacement for PSTN telephony. As broadband penetration, which is a key enabler to support high quality VoIP connections, increases, the potential market for VoIP has grown. Initial assessments indicate that IP telephony could put up to USD 10 billion at risk for the traditional incumbents by 2007. To date, VoIP has been adopted mostly by business customers, thanks to the savings it can offer on internal company calls (see Figure 8). In Europe, VoIP has already penetrated nearly one-fifth of all companies, with Spain (24 percent) and the United Kingdom (22 percent) at the high end. Finance and manufacturing, in particular, have been very quick to adopt, with the media and travel industries expected to migrate to VoIP in the near future.

Figure 9. **VoIP Could Potentially Cannibalize Significant PSTN Revenues**

	Average monthly savings US$	Broadband residential users that might switch to VoIP Percent of total by 2007	PSTN revenue at stake Billion US$
UK	2.8–4.2	8–11	0.5–0.7
Spain	2.7–4.0	5–7	0.1–0.2
Italy	2.5–3.8	5–8	0.2–0.3
France	2.2–3.2	4–7	0.2–0.3
Sweden	1.8–2.5	8–13	<0.1
US	7.2–10.7	18–23	4.3–5.5
Japan	2.6–3.8	19–26	2.0–2.7

Rationale

▲ Based on savings of 20–30% of traffic bills; could be higher if IP-to-IP connectivity obstacles are resolved

▲ Assumes 50% of users to whom VoIP is attractive and who have broadband will switch (e.g., 75% of Yahoo Japan DSL subscribers use VoIP)

Sources: IDC; McKinsey analysis

VoIP could offer population segments as well as broadband penetration, important discounts over the current voice telephony tariffs. However, growth is likely to be gradual unless a major breakthrough in IP-to-IP connection is achieved. Without that breakthrough, the ability of a VoIP user to call another VoIP user is somewhat limited by the inability of the VoIP phone to recognize whether the recipient of that call is an IP device. This would limit any savings to be gained by an IP-phone user, since in this case the call would most likely have to go through the more costly PSTN network, thus limiting the adoption of VoIP among broadband users.

Assuming a breakthrough in IP-to-IP is realized, and taking into consideration the calling patterns of different population segments, as well as broadband penetration of those segments, an estimate was made of the number of users by country that would benefit from using VoIP for some or all of their traffic. A determination of the market share at risk was then based on the assumption that half of those users would actually switch.

An assessment, illustrated in Figure 9, indicates that dramatic changes would be likely in the United Kingdom, the United States, and Japan, where 10 to 20 percent of users could switch to VoIP. In terms of PSTN revenues, the value at risk by 2007 would amount to USD 500 to 700 million in the United Kingdom, USD 4.3 to 5.5 billion in the United States, and USD 2 to 2.7 billion in Japan.

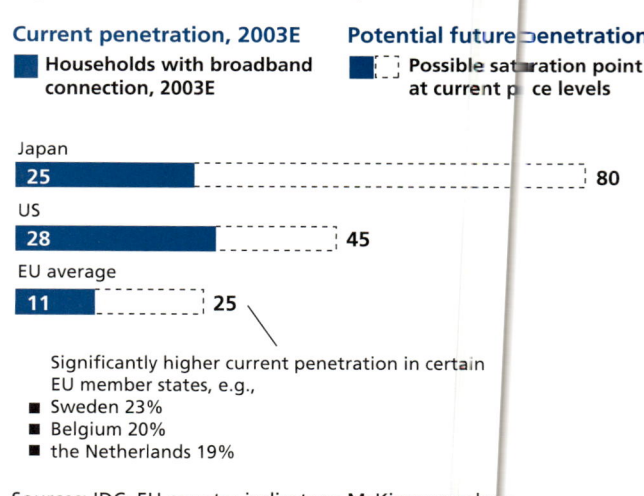

Figure 10. **Broadband Penetration Grows Steadily, but Will Top Off Unless Price/Value Perception Is Addressed**

Current penetration, 2003E
■ Households with broadband connection, 2003E

Potential future penetration
◻ Possible saturation point at current price levels

Japan — 25 ... 80
US — 28 ... 45
EU average — 11 ... 25

Significantly higher current penetration in certain EU member states, e.g.,
■ Sweden 23%
■ Belgium 20%
■ the Netherlands 19%

Sources: IDC; EU country indicators; McKinsey analysis

Broadband: Growing Steadily or Leveling Out?

Broadband penetration has been growing rapidly in recent years, primarily among higher-income households. By the end of 2003, broadband will have reached 20 to 30 percent of households in countries such as the United States, Japan, Sweden, and Benelux. In South Korea, a staggering two-thirds of households have broadband, while the EU average lags well behind at just 11 percent.

Figure 11. **South Korean Example Shows Regulation/Government Policy Can Encourage Penetration Beyond Market Equilibrium**

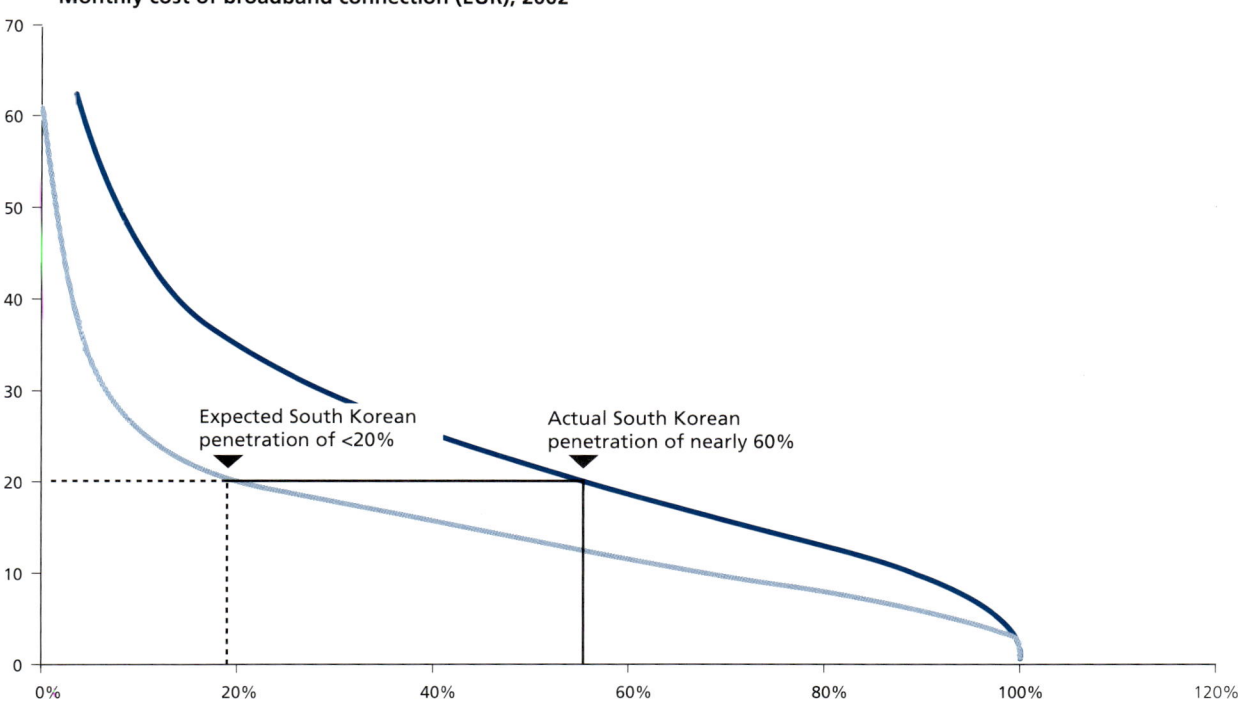

Monthly cost of broadband connection (EUR), 2002

Expected South Korean penetration of <20%

Actual South Korean penetration of nearly 60%

Households to whom broadband price < 1% of monthly disposable income (percent)

Sources: EU country indicators; IDC; McKinsey analysis

Penetration is expected to increase in the medium term. However, broadband is relatively expensive, costing from USD 30 to 50 per month. Therefore, early adopters have tended to be higher-income households, but saturation will be reached when this monthly fee becomes too expensive for the average household adopting it. If one assumes that households would be willing to spend up to 1 percent of their income on broadband, then at current price levels, broadband penetration could rise to 80 percent in Japan, more than tripling the current penetration level. In the United States, penetration could increase from 28 percent today to 45 percent, while average broadband penetration in Europe would be expected to reach approximately 25 percent (Figure 10) although levels could be much higher in some richer European countries.

The message is clear: in the foreseeable future broadband saturation levels will be far below the 100 percent of households that have telephones today and may even fall below the number of households that could have access to a broadband-enabled line. Over the next few years saturation is likely to be somewhere between 10 and 50 percent for most of the developed world—with Japan and South Korea as the exceptions. Beyond that point, broadband will simply be too expensive, particularly considering that a personal computer is required as well. If there is a public policy desire

to increase broadband beyond this level (and there may be, once close to half of a country's subscribers adopt the service and applications such as VoIP grow), then a combination of steps to support further supply and encourage demand would probably be needed. This is exactly what has happened in South Korea (Figure 11).

South Korea not only subsidizes infrastructure (which is well known and has resulted in broadband subscription prices that are among the lowest in the world), but also promoted the take-up of broadband services (for example, by highlighting the value of broadband or education and promoting personal computers). This has resulted in a penetration of about 66 percent, higher than would be suggested by the underlying household incomes.

This example highlights the importance of comprehensive policies that address all aspects of broadband adoption. As saturation is reached, the easy way out for regulators is to continue to push lower prices by forcing the incumbent telephone provider to offer cheap infrastructure to attackers. This does not directly address the willingness-to-pay issue (which is probably best tackled at a governmental level) and runs the risk of reducing, rather than increasing, infrastructure investment. This is particularly important if there is a large cable infrastructure that can compete with the incumbent. If attackers get a good deal from regulated incumbent prices, this will reduce cable operators' incentive to push broadband everywhere.

Going forward, alternative technologies with broadband performance such as 3G or 800.11 (Wi-Fi) may provide for their availability and penetration, particularly when combined with per use, rather than fixed fee business models. They will also be facilitated by the availability of alternative handsets or variants of personal assistant devices. But here again, regulations governing licensing of spectrum and wholesale conditions, among others will impact price levels and thus affordability and penetration.

Regulation's Significant Impact on Outcome

Regulation will have a substantial, even defining, role to play in accelerating or decelerating the pace of the trends previously outlined. There are a number of overarching critical regulatory areas that will impact the future evolution of these specific industry trends, which include licensing conditions, LLU, retail-pricing flexibility, interconnection (mainly mobile termination), treatment of attackers (primarily cable and VoIP), and cross-subsidy possibilities in the industry. The following section addresses in further detail how these and other regulatory factors will impact each of the four major industry trends.

Fixed-Mobile Substitution

The extent to which regulation will have an impact on fixed-mobile substitution will differ greatly by country.

In developed countries, the primary lever for influencing fixed-mobile voice substitution is pricing—both end-user and interconnection rates. Regulators could allow fixed-line players greater flexibility in competing against their mobile counterparts by, for example, permitting incumbents to bundle voice, mobile, and broadband services or by allowing the kind of "same network" on-net price discounts that mobile operators offer. In the mobile industry, regulators could remove or reduce the cross-subsidy between "cross-network" and "on-network" calls in European markets by lowering the high mobile termination rate that currently enables this subsidization. However, changing the mobile termination rate could have negative implications for the fixed-line industry and thus a cost/benefit analysis would be needed for each country before any attempt to unilaterally lower termination rates. Finally, the licensing regime is likely to affect the degree of competition in mobile, impacting pricing and further influencing the degree of substitution.

The situation in developing countries is very different. The increase in mobile penetration has not only resulted in

substitution, but also in a leapfrogging of technologies, as many users never acquired a fixed line but went directly to mobile. Fixed-line penetration was relatively low, so when growth in mobile penetration surged, fixed-line penetration stalled and even declined. In Malaysia, fixed-line penetration has fallen in the past two years and hovers below 20 percent, while mobile penetration has reached 40 percent and is growing rapidly.

This slowing of fixed-access growth has huge implications for incumbents in developing markets. Countries have always expected penetration levels to grow over time as their GDP per capita increases. However, with rapidly growing mobile penetration, fixed-line penetration may not go much beyond its current levels and as a result, incumbents could be deprived of large revenue streams.

In such markets, regulators and policymakers can play a major role, but the appropriate course of action will depend on the objectives laid out for the sector. Applying regulatory frameworks from developed countries could result in the mobile industry dominating the voice services market, while fixed-line incumbents—especially those without mobile subsidiaries—will continue to be heavily regulated, burdened with costly universal service obligations, and faced with reduced economic surplus as liberalization pushes prices down. This, combined with the flexibility of mobile operators who can have more refined pricing and can acquire new customers quickly, could result in poor financial performance or eventual bankruptcy for fixed-line incumbents.

Severe economic hardship for fixed-line incumbents could well mean that no significant data infrastructure would be built up, given the lack of demand for the fixed-access network and the incumbent's inability to finance further investments in its core network. If regulators want to avoid such a scenario, they have three main options for doing so:

Support fixed-line. Preserve fixed-line incumbents' solvency by treating fixed-line networks as a public good, similar to roads and railways, and heavily subsidize the build-out of the access network. This would ensure the development of basic data infrastructure and would maintain some degree of competition between mobile and fixed-line technologies.

Go fully mobile. Allow fixed-line incumbents to go bankrupt and rely on mobile operators to build-out the entire access network for both voice and data. This would mean regulating the mobile industry similarly to the ways the fixed-line industry is regulated that is, by introducing universal service obligations (USO) and/or other means to ensure widespread build-out of a mobile data infrastructure (possibly including 3G) at generally accessible prices.

Let the markets decide. Regulators could level the playing field between the two industries and let them compete for customers. To improve the fixed-line incumbents' ability to compete, regulators should balance the degree of regulation between the two industries. This could be done by increasing price flexibility for the fixed-line sector, shifting some of the USO burden to mobile operators, or by applying equally stringent cost-based pricing obligations to the mobile sector.

Fixed-Access Competition

Competition in fixed-access has been driven thus far by local loop unbundling (LLU) and cable penetration. Depending upon the regulatory regime, substantial differences in the degree and type of fixed-access competition can be identified. Other forms of access-based competition may eventually come in the form of 802.11b and 3G deployments, or with the broadband wireless spectrum. The New Zealand government, for example, has launched an initiative to use wireless broadband technology to serve rural areas. This will allow the government to offer broadband for USD 30 per month to consumers.

LLU conditions and prices have had a tremendous impact on attackers' economics. In the United States, for example, attackers can rent the entire platform—local-loop and transmission/switching equipment—at TELRIC (cost methodology based on long-run incremental costs) prices. This results in an entirely variable cost (on a per-customer basis) for the attacker and leaves the incumbents responsible for the bulk of the costs for the required capacity increase. In other words, attackers can enter the market gradually without large upfront investments. As a result, the United States has seen the greatest amount of competition through LLU with up to 13 percent of unbundled local-access lines now held by attackers. In Europe, attackers can rent just the local loop as far as the main distribution frame, which means they have to invest in switching and transmission equipment for narrowband access at each local switch, regardless of the initial traffic volume or number of customers. As a result, competition in local access has remained low in Europe and is centered around broadband DSL-type services, where margins are tight but potential revenue streams are higher.

In parallel with LLU, attackers have entered the fixed-line market in countries with high cable penetration by upgrading the cable networks, which allows cable companies to offer voice telephony. Nevertheless, substantial investment is still required (e.g., backbone, local nodes, switching, and transmission equipment). The market potential may justify it in selected countries. In the United States, Benelux, and Canada (with high cable penetration) as well as the United Kingdom (despite having only 30 percent cable penetration), cable providers have captured 13 percent of overall market

share in local access, converting up to one-third of homes with potential cable access into telecom fixed-access customers.

The impact of regulation on fixed-access competition as a result of addressing LLU and cable will vary greatly by market:

In *high-risk markets* (those with high cable penetration and an LLU regime attractive to attackers) such as the United States, the incumbents' share of access may continue to decline. Combined with fixed-mobile substitution in some markets, incumbent share access losses could reach 15 to 20 percent of access lines by 2007—enough to virtually bankrupt the incumbent. Regulators could adjust wholesale conditions under which incumbents must provide access to their local loop, as in the United States, where the LLU regime is discussed at the state level. However, there are other regulatory levers to compensate for the revenue loss. These include such things as allowing for relative retail price increases. Increasing interconnection fees (as real costs per traffic minute used rise), unbundling cable, and reconsidering the USO regime by expanding components to the cable industry.

In *medium-risk markets* (those with high cable penetration but either an unattractive LLU regime or strong incumbent driven broadband initiatives) such as Belgium and the Netherlands, LLU could be made more attractive by lowering prices or shifting some of the cost burden to incumbents. This could be done, for example, through more attractive co-location requirements or by giving attackers access to the entire platform, as the United States does. Furthermore, competition through cable could be encouraged by allowing operators to provide telecom services (as was the case in Europe, following liberalization in 1998), subsidizing cable upgrades, deregulating (increasing) prices for cable television packages, or even taking a share in the cable company to help finance the conversion of the cable network into a telephone network. This last approach was used in Belgium, where the government-owned Flemish Investment Company became a shareholder in the upgraded cable networks in the northern part of the country.

In *low-risk markets* (those with low cable penetration and unattractive LLU regimes) such as Spain and Italy, regulators can encourage fixed-access competition by changing the terms for LLU. Without fundamental changes to the current offer, competition in fixed-access is unlikely to develop. Fixed-mobile substitution could result in an alternative form of access competition and would lead to a certain loss of access lines in some markets (e.g., Portugal and Italy). Alternatively, government could consider direct public subsidies to promote alternative infrastructure.

Going forward in all three rich markets, fixed access competition will also be heavily influenced by the development of alternative wireless technologies such as 3G, WCDMA, and 802.11, among others. Competition and infrastructure development can be spurred by attractive licensing conditions and industry structure. Huge licensing fees levied on 3G in many countries run counter to the goal of economically viable competition, but ongoing decisions permitting infrastructure sharing, and ensuring MVNOs cannot ??? arbitrage rates will stimulate alternative infrastructure growth. Low-cut licensing of the 802.11MHz spectrum may also stimulate competition, if incumbents can develop this spectrum as an alternative to 3G and extend the fixed network.

VoIP

If VoIP is to fulfill its potential, a number of key regulatory issues still need to be resolved. These concern broadband penetration, interconnection, numbering, IP-to-IP calls, and interoperability with PSTN networks.

Broadband access is the most critical enabler of VoIP telephony, offering countries with high broadband penetration the greatest potential. In some cases—Japan, for example—it is the demand for VoIP that will drive growth in broadband penetration. (Regulatory issues surrounding broadband will be discussed further in the following section on broadband trends.)

There are several regulatory approaches to the interconnection of IP networks and traditional PSTN networks. VoIP providers can be treated as regular voice providers, benefiting from relatively low interconnection rates and relying on standard incumbent reference interconnection offers, as, for example, in Sweden. Alternatively, regulators can require individual interconnection agreements (as in Japan and the United States) between VoIP providers and incumbents, although this could result in lengthy negotiations and even potentially higher interconnection rates. Another option is to exclude VoIP from standard interconnection, treating it as a data connection through nongeographic numbers, as in France. However, removing it from the scope of the strict traditional interconnection regimes may lead to less attractive conditions, including higher rates and customers having to adopt a nongeographic number.

Numbering is another key regulatory issue. The ability to keep a number is a critical switching factor for customers. As a result, customers are more likely to switch to a VoIP provider in markets with regulated VoIP number portability, as is the case in Sweden. Assigning nongeographic numbers to VoIP services could impose an additional hurdle, since the geographic character of the number is lost. This was the case in France and it resulted in lower VoIP take-up.

Another factor in the penetration of VoIP is the ability of users to make IP-to-IP calls over a data network, thereby completely bypassing the more costly PSTN network. This occurs when IP customers have a special number or means of identifying their number as IP, thereby avoiding routing through the PSTN network. A solution would be to assign an IP address to all phone numbers in order to heavily promote VoIP, for example through efforts such as e-num. VoIP customers would keep their traditional phone number, but receive the maximum IP-to-IP savings when they call other IP phones. This approach is not feasible at present, in part due to technology, in part due to regulation. Therefore, interim approaches must work around the difficulty of identifying a receiving number as an IP phone.

One approach would be to enable IP-to-IP calls, but route them through the PSTN network. This provides the flexibility to call any PSTN or IP number, but does not give customers the full benefit of savings on all IP-to-IP calls. Another option is to allow IP-to-IP calls only within the customer's own IP network, as is done in Japan.

A last critical enabler for VoIP telephony growth is the interoperability with PSTN networks, that is, the ability to receive calls from PSTN networks on IP phones. Sweden and the United States have this ability already, and it is expected to be rolled out by the end of 2003 in Japan. In each case, interoperability was mandated by a regulatory body without such mandates, interoperability appears very unlikely.

These obstacles suggest that VoIP phones will probably grow gradually as the technological and regulatory obstacles are overcome. However, its dependence, at least for now, on broadband to ensure adequate quality of services means that, unless mandated by regulators/governments, VoIP is unlikely to fully replace PSTN phones in the near future.

Broadband

Broadband penetration has grown rapidly in the past few years, primarily driven by higher-income early adopters and infrastructure-based competition, particularly cable. At current prices and perceived value, the broadband demand curve is expected to eventually level off as the high-income segment becomes saturated and broadband penetration spreads further to medium-and lower-income households.

Countries at the top of the broadband penetration race—South Korea, the United States, Canada, Singapore, Hong Kong, and Belgium, among others—have one attribute in common: robust infrastructure-based competition. Generally, this competition comes from cable companies not owned by the telcos that have aggressively upgraded their infrastructure.

Based on experience in several developed markets, households typically cannot justify spending more than 1 percent of their disposable income on broadband, given that they do not spend more than 3 to 4 percent of their disposable income on overall telecom services. Using this metric, at current broadband prices penetration growth could be expected to slow down at approximately 25 percent in the EU (although strong variations exist by country), at 45 percent in the United States, and at nearly 80 percent in Japan. These differences are driven by income levels and substantial price differences, with Japan having the lowest average price of USD 20 and Europe the highest with USD 40.

Increasing broadband penetration will probably require lowering prices, particularly in Europe. However, the challenging industry economics make it unlikely that operators will be in a hurry to do so, unless forced by competition. Only the larger providers (e.g., incumbents) may be able to reduce prices—and this only after justification by customer numbers and certain economies of scale (e.g., marketing and acquisition).

The increasing importance of broadband to reducing fixed line access churn for incumbents, combined with rapidly filling equipment prices, the need of government to show top-line reserve growth, and pressure from regulators and policymakers to achieve broadband and networked readiness, mean that broadband prices will trend downward.

Nevertheless, the example of South Korea indicates that there are other levers that can be used to attain higher broadband penetration. Two-thirds of South Korean households have broadband, which is three times the expected rate (based on the 1 percent of household income constraint)—even allowing for the fact that at just USD 30 a month, the country has among the lowest broadband subscription prices in the world. This situation is driven by several factors: (1) initial price decreases fueled by strong infrastructure-based competition from cable; (2) government-supported broadband growth through indirect subsidies, public awareness campaigns, and allowing facilities-based competition in last-mile access; (3) strong Internet demand by schools, promoted by the government; (4) favorable population demographics with high user concentration, creating scale economies; and finally, (5) a strong demand for content and applications due to South Koreans' interest in online gaming and brokerage. The example illustrates that rapid broadband growth can be driven by a combination of regulatory, political, cultural, and demographic factors.

This highlights the importance of comprehensive policies that address all aspects of broadband adoption. As saturation is reached, the easy option for regulators is to continue to push for lower prices by forcing the incumbent telephone providers to offer cheap infrastructure to attackers. However, reaching saturation is not guaranteed. Forced price reductions do not directly address the willingness-to-pay issue (which is probably best tackled at the governmental level) and run the risk of reducing, rather than increasing, infrastructure

investment. This is particularly important if there is a large cable infrastructure that can compete with the incumbent. If attackers get a good deal from regulated incumbent prices, this will reduce the attractiveness for cable operators to push broadband everywhere.

In many countries, however, there remains the challenge of making broadband infrastructure available. In countries with a weak fixed line infrastructure that is under attack from mobile and VoIP, the challenge is to create economically viable conditions under which broadband can be deployed. In many markets with low spending, or in rural environments that may be unprofitable for fixed line deployment, it may require public sector funding and/or regulatory stimulus to achieve broad penetration or deployment of alternative wireless broadband technologies.

The Critical Nature of Execution Along Four Regulatory Dimensions

The previously discussed industry trends and their implications pose a potential economic threat to the traditional voice telephony incumbents. As illustrated in Figure 12, there are four regulatory dimensions in which stakeholders such as operators, regulators, and policymakers need to work in order to manage these industry trends successfully and be better prepared for the reshaped industry: (1) regulation has to ensure that players' business decisions can be based on business economics, (2) regulatory change should be a function of market and starting conditions and therefore vary by country, (3) constraints to change should be well understood, and (4) regulatory approaches should be tailored towards mutually consistent solutions.

Figure 12. **For Stakeholders, Executing Along Four Regulatory Dimensions Is Critical in Order to Manage Industry Trends**

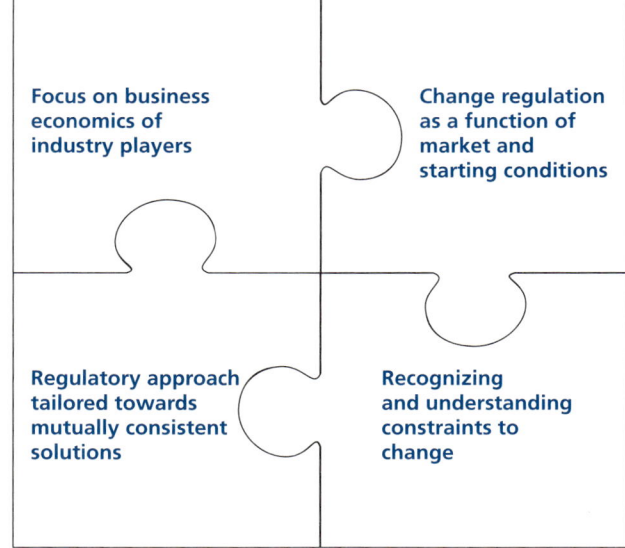

Source: McKinsey analysis

Focus on Business Economics of Industry Players

Within today's regulatory frameworks, the trends under discussion could be detrimental to the economics of key players in the industry, thereby potentially distorting the market. Therefore, regulation needs to be adjusted to allow operators to make decisions based on business economics. This will contribute to ensuring a sustainable market and ongoing network readiness for society. The focus of regulation would thus need to be shifted as follows:

Drastically reduce telecom-specific regulation and apply general economic law as competition progressively takes shape in the different markets. This is particularly the case with international and long-distance communications. Incumbents, although they have lost their key market positions, are still required to follow lengthy regulatory filing processes to launch new pricing schemes or service bundles, while their competitors are allowed to change products and services at their own discretion. Additionally, in assessing competition in the local loop and the need for specific regulation, national regulators must take into account local voice services that are becoming increasingly competitive. This is especially important because mobile phone services are rapidly maturing and cable is getting its foot in the door of a number of developed markets.

Focus regulatory intervention more on overall value creation within the market. This requires a significant policy shift from the initial years of liberalization. Policy goals have typically included the redistribution of value towards consumers (via price reductions) and operators/shareholders (i.e., profit through market share). Regulations must become less incumbent- and price-focused at a time when incumbents are systematically losing access lines and EBITs are coming under increased pressure. South Korea's successful broadband penetration was driven by a proactive government approach that encouraged both supply and demand for broadband services.

Make regulation more dynamic. As the telecom market's structure and operating conditions are continually evolving, and consumers are rapidly changing service providers, it will become increasingly challenging to adequately deal with issues and adjust regulations accordingly. Issues include how to deal with interconnection rates when incumbents' access lines gradually erode, pushing unit costs upwards; and how to treat consolidation in mobile markets, following the awarding of 3G licenses. To date, regulation has been substantially focused on locking-in the market into pre-set models. Aligning regulations with market economics and conditions will require greater empowerment of regulatory authorities, as they are well positioned to understand market needs and adequately act on them. While this is ostensibly one of the key components of the EU telecom reform, the jury is still out on whether this will mean a shift in the regulatory approaches followed up to now.

Re-equilibrate regulation, moving away from asymmetric regulation that primarily targets incumbent operators. At one time, it was logical to impose asymmetric rules to force monopolists to open up the market to new entrants. The pendulum has now swung the other way, and attackers have been allowed to grab market share, while incumbent-oriented restrictive regulation remained unaltered. Regulation should now move towards a middle-ground position, equalizing the regulatory pressure across all players. Should, for instance, mobile interconnection rates remain a multiple of fixed-line rates in an era where mobile is surpassing fixed-line penetration?

Until quite recently, investments in the highly capital intensive telecom industry were typically financed through cross-subsidies. Long distance calls financed local calls, business calls financed residential calls, and fixed-line revenues ensured the rollout of mobile networks through high interconnection fees. This is no longer the case under today's liberalized telecom regulations. Strict retail and wholesale price regulations are aimed primarily at transferring surplus to the customer and at stimulating re-usage of existing networks. Increasingly, incumbents are prevented from creating additional surplus to reinvest in future-oriented fine-mazed broadband networks, and this evolution could fundamentally put future network readiness at risk.

Incumbent operators need to fully understand the impact of policies and regulations on their business models and work with policymakers and regulatory authorities to steer future regulations in a more favorable direction.

Change Regulation as a Function of Market and Starting Conditions

The need for regulatory change according to the principles described above will most certainly vary by country as a function of the respective market structure, starting conditions, and degree of network readiness. In this respect, policymakers and regulators should avoid too linear an application of developed country telecom regulation to developing countries. Adaptation to country and market specificities is essential; without it, regulatory reform could, in many cases, significantly distort the sector. For example, under a developed country's regulations, a developing country incumbent's business case could substantially deteriorate, as there is simply less value available to share among the stakeholders.

Regulatory reform that does not appropriately take into account the major industry trends previously outlined runs a substantial risk of fostering an environment that will lead to structural under-investment in fixed-line infrastructure, or even bankruptcy of incumbent fixed-line operators. High-risk countries can be identified both in developed and developing markets:

In *developed markets* with a developed fixed-line infrastructure, incumbents are particularly at risk in countries where upgraded cable penetration is high, as local-access competition and the risk of fixed-line infrastructure erosion to cable is substantial (e.g., the United States, Canada, and Benelux). In these cases, the regulatory change should ensure a sustainable incumbent business case, without which enduring network readiness would be at risk.

In developed markets lacking adequate local loop competition, measures should focus on enabling economically viable cable competition via non-telco ownership and relaxing video pricing constraints, local loop unbundling to serve as a competition catalyst, and stimulating deployment of alternative technologies such as 3G or wireless broadband.

In *developing markets* where fixed-line penetration and infrastructure are limited, and mobile telephony is substantially present, there is a high probability that considerable mobile traffic and especially access substitution will occur (e.g., the Czech Republic, India). Here, the regulatory focus should be on ensuring that, next to the fixed-line infrastructure, the mobile networks effectively contribute to society's network readiness, which includes general Internet access. The challenge will be to ensure that mobile networks are Internet-enabled and that, for example, mobile intermediate devices for personal computers and handsets are adequately stimulated.

Recognizing and Understanding Constraints to Change

Recognizing constraints will be crucial to the eventual success of any form of regulatory change. In this respect, it is essential to assess whether proposed regulatory change will allow for challenges stemming from the major industry trends to be properly addressed and determine the likelihood that change will effectively occur.

The recently defined European telecom regulatory reform may become a case in point. Over the past few years, the EU conducted a major telecom regulatory reform that culminated on July 25, 2003, the deadline for EU countries to introduce the new regulatory compact into member state law. After years of debate about policy objectives and preferred approach, the question today is whether the new EU regulatory framework will allow and drive EU countries to effectively deal with the telecommunications industry's major challenges.

Several initial observations may lead us to draw a different conclusion:

Regulatory pressure to further reduce mobile rates for residential customers continues, consequently boosting fixed-mobile substitution. However, this approach neglects to take into account the significant revenue decrease that mobile operators will experience in the coming years due to a substantial reduction in interconnection and roaming revenues. Therefore, mobile operators may be forced to raise retail prices to compensate for lost revenues.

Pressure on fixed-line incumbents' wholesale offers will most probably continue, both in terms of further rate reductions (e.g., in interconnection, LLU) and by requiring incumbents to mirror their retail products in wholesale offers, thus allowing attackers to provide similar services.

Incumbent-oriented asymmetric regulation is not likely to change. Fixed-line incumbent operators in many markets still hold 45 percent market share. Therefore, changing the SMP (significant market power, i.e., market share of approximately 25 percent) threshold for regulation to a dominance threshold (i.e., approximately 45 percent market share), represents a *de facto* case in which specific regulation will apply to fixed-line incumbents, since fixed-line attackers and mobile operators rarely reach such a market share percentage. However, this means that regulators will have to be clever about appropriately defining the relevant markets in which dominance is assessed. Perhaps more appropriate would be a subtler, more dynamic definition that recognizes contestability via different modes of communications in relevant customer segments. (This may be especially relevant, for example, in the inter-modal competition between fixed and mobile networks.) This would most likely need to be done on a case-by-case, country-by-country basis. Merger authorities in the US (the Department of Justice) already take this approach; however, its role in overseeing the market is vastly different from that of a telecom regulator.

Regulatory Approach Tailored Towards Mutually Consistent Solutions

The final critical cornerstone for regulatory success involves addressing the challenges resulting from the key industry trends, while at the same time finding the middle ground that meets stakeholders' expectations with regard to those challenges. Policymakers and regulatory authorities will need to tailor their approach so as to move the industry towards solutions that are mutually consistent for the key stakeholders. This means finding solutions that tread a middle road between the objectives of the government, the interests of the incumbents (still the primary provider of fixed-line infrastructure and access in all countries), the economic needs of entrants, and the customers' needs for choice, improved quality, and innovative services.

This will be difficult, since there will be multiple competitive models (which will differ by country). Moreover, the road map is not as clear as it was in the early stages of liberalization, when the focus was to open the market to competitors, leverage the incumbents' infrastructure, and eliminate cross-subsidies in order to achieve lower consumer prices.

At the time of liberalization, many regulatory regimes took either anti- or pro-incumbent stances—sometimes by accident, sometimes by design. The resulting regimes may or may not have led to sharp declines in prices in the short term or encouraged the emergence of infrastructure-based attackers (such as in the United Kingdom and United States). Accidental regulation could work as long as the emphasis was on simply lowering prices and removing cross-subsidies in key industry segments, such as international long-distance and other distance-based services. However, today's focus is very different and more complex. Existing substantial issues involve completely different topics, including infrastructure issues (broadband, 3G, data-enabling mobile lines, local-access competition); ensuring a level playing field in inter-modal competition (mobile vs. fixed); and addressing disruptive technologies and their long-term impact on infrastructure economics (VoIP). The road map for addressing these issues is not evident and the path to efficient markets is unclear. None of the issues achieves an economically efficient outcome simply by lower prices—in fact, the opposite is true: simply pushing down prices may actually distort some choices.

The industry challenges raise a number of questions that will need to be addressed, among them being:

- Should governments abandon fixed-line networks and favor mobile—particularly in the case of developing countries? If governments decide not to go this route, what are the implications of taking a neutral role?

- What role, if any, should governments play when broadband penetration levels out?

- What should developing countries do to enable primary telephone access or the mobile network for data?

- How should regulated prices be adjusted as incumbent market shares decline? Should these changes occur before the traditional incumbent thresholds currently used by regulators are reached (e.g., 25 percent, 45 percent, and so on)?

- What role, if any, should the government take in addressing VoIP?

The power of regulatory inertia is tremendous. But the gradual erosion of the traditional fixed-line model suggested by the trends discussed in this document indicate that this inertia can interfere with an efficient evolution of the industry. Mutual consistency between the objectives of all key stakeholders will be critical to the eventual realization of an efficient outcome.

Conclusion

Traditional fixed-line incumbent operators will face significant challenges as the telecommunications industry continues to redefine itself. A global wave of liberalization and privatization of telecom providers, combined with new and dynamic technologies, continues to dramatically reshape the industry. This calls for action from all industry stakeholders to protect the economic interests of both developed and emerging markets. Fixed-mobile substitution, fixed-access competition, the growth in VoIP, and the growth of broadband access are major trends that will have an enormous impact on the face of the telecom industry. Regulation will play a determining role in how these trends will affect the industry, how readily the incumbents will be allowed to respond to them, and in how well competition develops. While telecom industry players can prepare themselves for and, to a certain extent, even influence these trends, they will have to learn how to successfully manage the evolution of the trends. In order to achieve this, all industry key stakeholders must address the issues of a regulatory shift toward the economics of players, local market conditions, and network readiness, recognizing the constraints to change, and tailoring the regulatory approach to arrive at mutually consistent solutions for all parties.

## Chapter 5

CASE STUDY:
Little Finland's Transformation to a Wireless Giant

Petri Rouvinen and Pekka Ylä-Anttila

ETLA, The Research Institute of the Finnish Economy

Introduction—The 21st Century in Beta?

In the "new economy" boom, Finland became labeled as a country where ". . . the 21st century is in beta" (Wired magazine, September 1999) and, for a time, its corporate icon Nokia was Europe's most valuable company. Technology enthusiasts expected Linux, an open source operating system with Finnish roots, to replace Windows on virtual desktops.

In a decade, Finland went from being one of the least information and communication technologies (ICT) specialized countries to becoming the single most specialized one. Currently the Finnish ICT sector, with Nokia as its locomotive, consists of some 6 thousand firms and accounts for approximately 10 percent of Finland's GDP. Although in what follows ICT is discussed at large, the Finnish story is mostly one of (digital) mobile telecommunications.

In the early 1990s, Finland's prospects seemed gloomy. In 1990, it was hit by the most severe economic crisis in any OECD country since World War II. Real GDP dropped by over 10 percent in just three years, and unemployment had risen to nearly 20 percent by 1994 (Honkapohja and Koskela 1999). Among the factors contributing to the crisis were a downturn in the nationally vital forest-related industries, disruption in the country's sizable eastern trade due to the collapse of the Soviet Union, a speculative bubble in the domestic securities and real estate markets fueled by uncontrolled credit expansion and favorable terms of trade, and mismanaged financial liberalization, which eventually led to credit crunch and excessive private sector indebtedness (Kiander and Vartia 1996).

In the latter half of the 1990s, Finland was nevertheless one of the fastest growing countries in the world. Its remarkable recovery and stellar performance are in considerable part attributable to developments in the ICT sector. But how did Finland become a success story in ICT? Does the Finnish experience hold lessons for other countries?

Section Two provides background information on Finland and its macroeconomic developments as well as a discussion of the country's transformation from a factor- to an innovation-driven economy. Section Three discusses ICT-related history and developments in Finland, with an emphasis primarily on mobile telecommunications. Section Four briefly outlines the key factors underlying the "Finnish miracle." Section Five discusses future prospects for the ICT sector. Finally, Section Six concludes with general considerations of the "Finnish model" and related policy issues.

From Factor- to Innovation-Driven Economy

Historical Backdrop

During the 20th century, Finnish GDP per capita grew at an annual rate of close to 3 percent, that is, faster than in any other European country. Admittedly, as compared to the countries in the vanguard of the first industrial revolution in the late 1800s, the starting point was relatively low. Many of the basic preconditions for growth were nevertheless in place at that time. Institutions such as well-functioning educational and banking systems, as well as a good transportation infrastructure, were important in the take-off phase. Similarly, national identity and culture were strong enough to facilitate economic growth. After completing the liberalization of both internal and external trade by the end of the 1870s, the path for industrial growth and new business activity had opened.

The role of institutions was important, not only in the take-off phase of industrial growth, but also later when the economy moved from factor- to investment-, and later, innovation-driven stages of industrial development.

Finland's most important—and virtually only—endowment of natural resources, forests, proved to be the decisive factor in the take-off phase. Quick advancement in prosperity towards the end of the 1800s and in the early 20th century was based on rapidly growing exports of forest-related products—first timber and later, pulp and paper. From the late 1950s to the late 1970s, the Finnish forest industry carried out massive investments and transformed itself gradually into a global technology leader with the most modern and efficient production capacity in the world (see Raumolin 1992). By the late 1980s, the forest sector had developed into a competitive industrial cluster that today provides high value-added paper grades, as well as forestry technologies and consulting services (Hernesniemi, Lammi, and Ylä-Anttila 1996; Ojainmaa 1994; Rouvinen and Ylä-Anttila 1999).

The latest phase of forest cluster development is the integration of ICT into pulp and paper making processes and maintenance services. The strong forest cluster with roots in traditional factor-driven industries is finding interfaces with the knowledge-driven ICT cluster. Furthermore, the global consolidation in pulp and paper, as well as in other traditional industries, has spawned new ICT markets as the demand for electronic means of integrating geographically dispersed activities has grown.

A Small Nordic Welfare State

Geographically, Finland is about the size of Germany or the US state of New Mexico. Yet with only 5.2 million inhabitants, it is sparsely populated. The climate is cold, but not quite as harsh as might be expected from the second most northerly country in the world.

Finland's economic and social institutions are similar to those of other Nordic countries. It can be appropriately characterized as a Nordic welfare state: it is an egalitarian country with relatively even income distribution and minimal class distinctions.

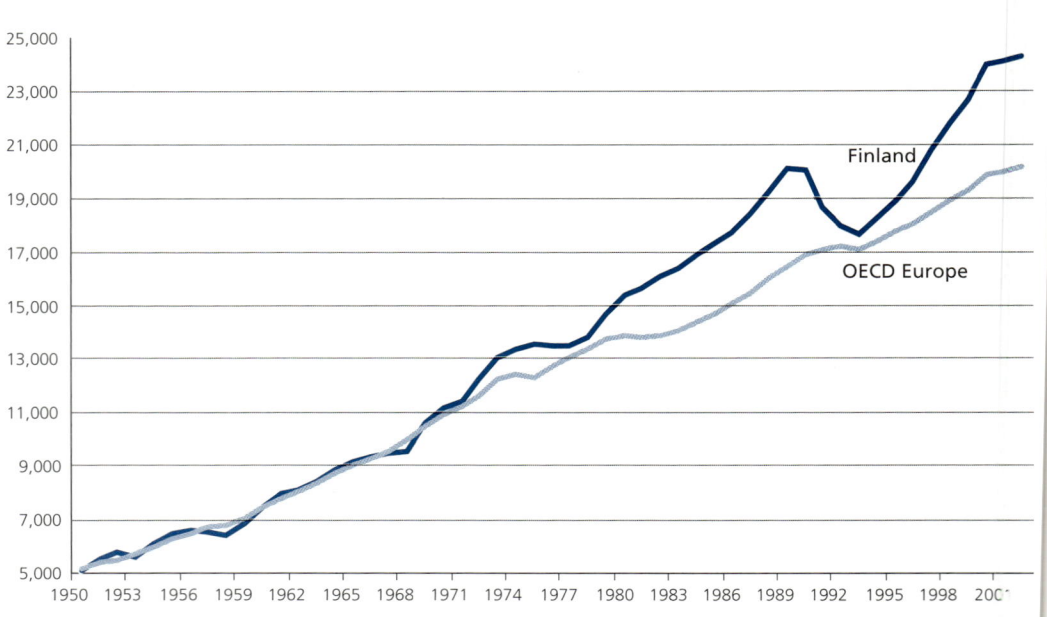

Figure 1. **The Fastest Growing European Country in the Postwar Era: GDP Volume in Finland and OECD-Europe (in 1995 prices and purchasing power parity exchange rates)**

Sources: www.SourceOECD.org, Penn World Tables.

Smallness is both an advantage and a disadvantage. There is some evidence in the economic literature that smallness retards economic growth. Small countries have less scope for utilizing scale economies in production and marketing. On the other hand, small home markets drive firms to specialize and seek foreign markets. Most small countries can be described as open economies with large exporting sectors. In Finland the share of exports in GDP is currently close to 50 percent.

Smallness and a homogeneous society might also be beneficial for the diffusion of new knowledge in specific areas such as ICT; in the world of rapid technological change this could be a competitive advantage.

While smallness and specialization increase a country's sensitivity to external shocks, small economies have developed various ways to cope with the problem. These include not only macroeconomic policies but also many kinds of networks and social security systems. Networking and cooperation in society in general, and in the business sector in particular, have proven to be important in developing new technologies. In many ways Finland can be characterized as a "network society" (see Castells and Himanen 2002). Of course, social networks, often labeled social capital, can become too tight and finally an obstacle for change and industrial transformation. Thus far, however, networking and cooperation have been an advantage rather than a disadvantage in Finnish industrial development.

Structural Transformation

In addition to the aforementioned immediate reasons for the recession of the early 1990s, rigidities in economic and political systems and corporatist structures were among the underlying causes. The deep recession led to a clear shift in policy thinking. Greater emphasis was put on long-term microeconomic as opposed to short-term macroeconomic policies in an acknowledgment that the foundations of sustained national competitiveness are largely created at the micro level—in firms, financial institutions, and various innovative policy agencies.

The European integration process also fueled the shift in policy. Finland joined the European Union in 1995 and, unlike the other Scandinavian countries, adopted the euro from the outset. However, this also meant that the scope for national macroeconomic policies was considerably reduced.

The recession of the early 1990s was a watershed between the investment- and innovation-driven stages of national development. The country's R&D intensity grew rapidly as the business sector increased expenditures on innovative activity. Public R&D funding also rose at a time when virtually all other public expenditures were cut in the midst of the recession.

The transition to innovation-driven growth was considerably aided by widespread telecommunications deregulation in Europe and elsewhere, as well as by technological developments in the ICT sector. Both of these developments have contributed to the booming demand felt since the early 1990s.

Figure 2. **Explosive Growth in Electronics Since the Early 1990s:**
Finnish Manufacturing Production Volume by Industry (€ billions in 2000 prices)

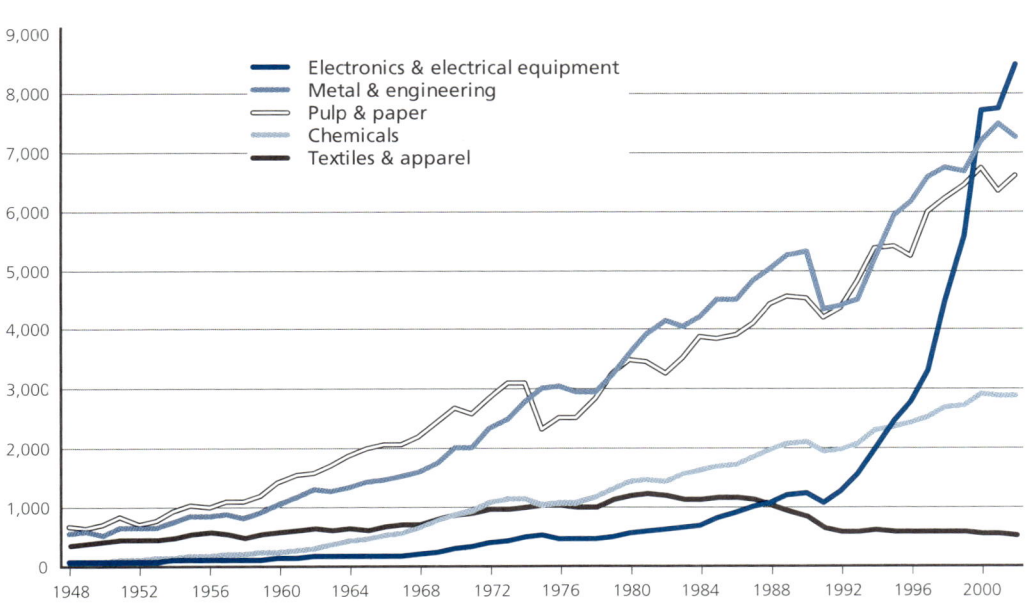

Sources: ETLA database, Hjerppe et al. (1976), National industrial statistics by *Statistics Finland*.

Figure 3. **The Second Most R&D-Intensive Country in the World**

Gross domestic expenditure on R&D
(GERD) per GDP %

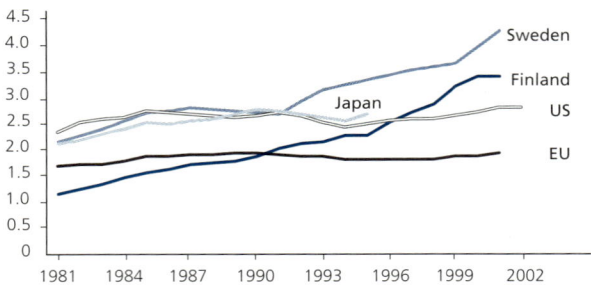

Share of GERD financed by government
%

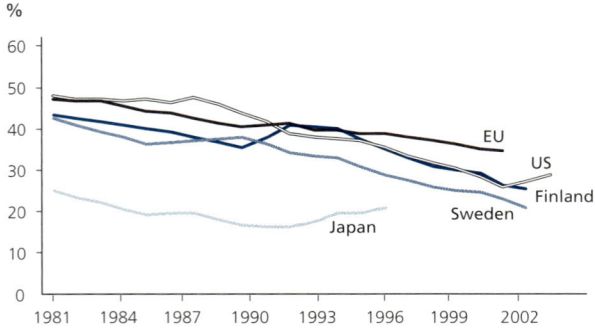

Share of GERD performed by the business sector
%

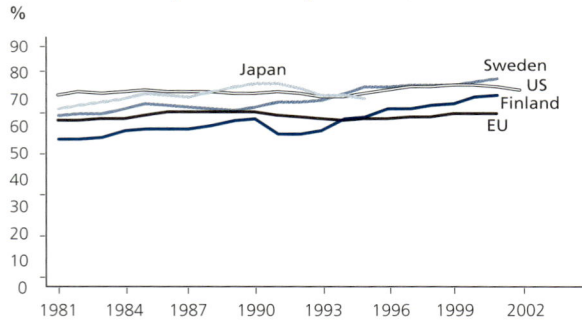

Share of communications equipment manufacturing (ISIC 32) in total business enterprise R&D (BERD)
%

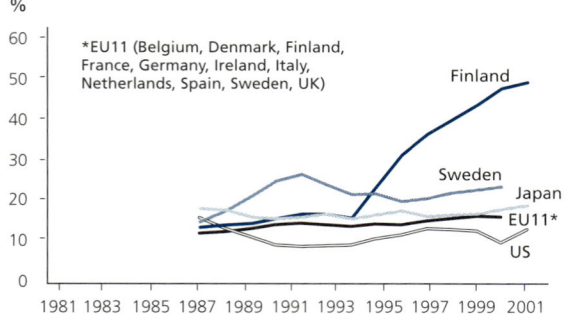

Sources: OECD Main Science and Technology Indicators Vol. 2003 release 01; OECD R&D Expenditure in Industry (ISIC Rev.3) Vol. 2002 release 01 (for the lowest pane).

The change in the 1990s in Finnish industrial structure and exports was unique both nationally and internationally. In less than a decade, electronics became the most important single branch in production and exports. The Finnish industrial structure that was previously raw material-, capital-, energy-, and scale-intensive, is now primarily knowledge-intensive. Finland's relative R&D intensity—the share of the gross domestic research and development expenditure (GERD) of GDP—is the second highest in the world (3.5 percent in 2002), with only neighboring Sweden surpassing it.

Innovation-Intensive Growth

Entering a phase of innovation-driven development presumes the interplay of several factors. High social cohesion, a consistent and predictable policy environment, sound basic infrastructure, as well as a just and efficient legislative and juridical environment are necessary preconditions. While these were all in place in Finland before the boom, the key factors were rising investments in R&D and a strong commitment to education.

Due to increased investments in the education system, by the late 1980s, younger generations of Finns were among the most educated in the world. Education that would enhance technological change was prioritized in the policies of the 1960s and 1970s. Among the OECD countries, the Finnish educational system lags behind only the Korean and German systems in terms of its relative emphasis on natural sciences and engineering. It is not only graduate level science and technology education that matters; a high general level of education is equally important for adopting and utilizing new technologies. Basic education continues to be the focal point of the Finnish educational system.

As will be discussed below, most of the structural change is attributable to the ICT sector. And within that sector, mobile telecommunications equipment manufacturing and Nokia dominate. In the latter half of 1990s the Finnish economy grew at an annual rate of approximately 5 percent. The contribution of Nokia to that growth was on average more than half a percentage point. In 2000 it peaked at one and a half percentage points, when the GDP growth was 6 percent.

World's Most ICT-Intensive Country

Initially Competitive ICT Markets

Up until the worldwide deregulation and liberalization boom of the 1990s, Finland had been one of the most competitive telecommunications operators and equipment markets in the world—a position it had occupied for over a hundred years.

Figure 4. **Heavy Emphasis on Natural Sciences and Engineering Education**

(a) Finnish postgraduate degrees in natural sciences and engineering

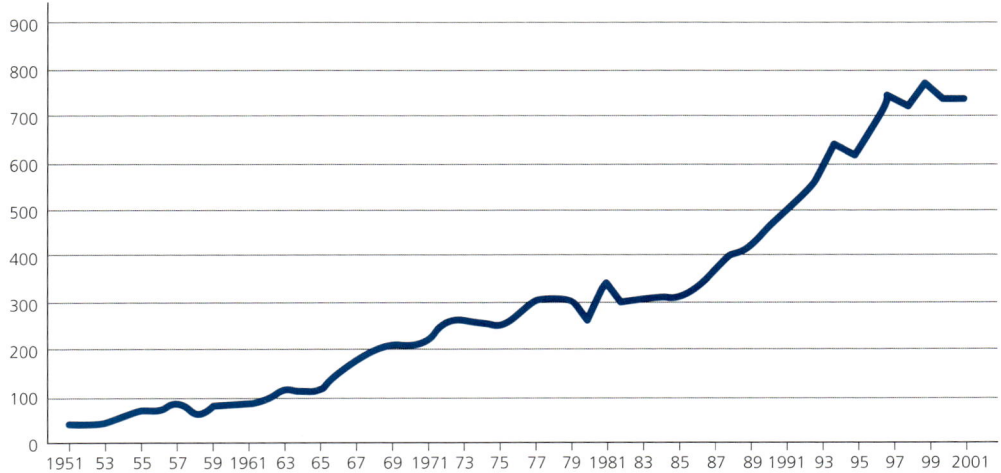

(b) Share of tertiary type A graduates in engineering, manufacturing, construction, life sciences, physical sciences, mathematics and statistics, and computing in all graduates

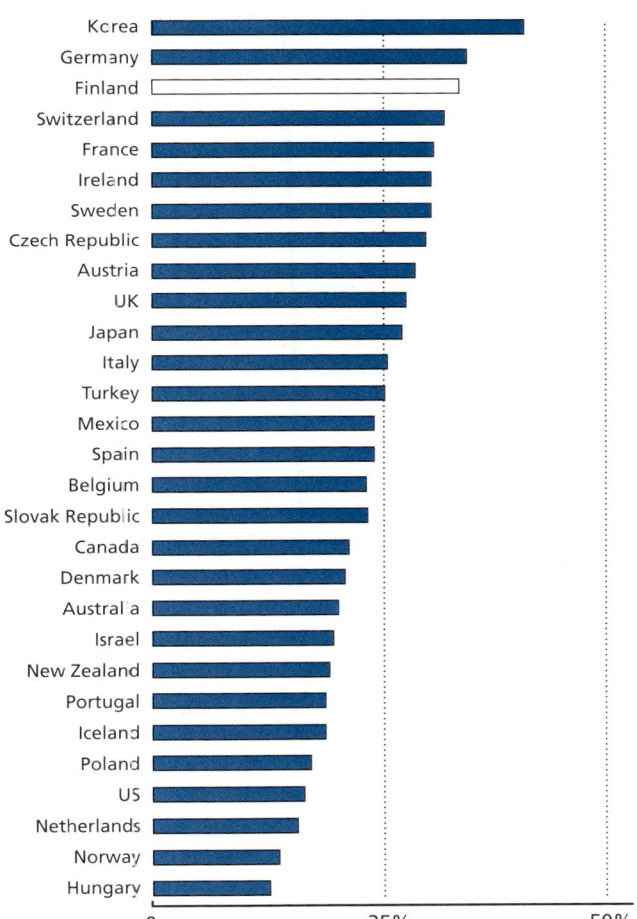

Sources: KOTA OnLine (top, www.csc.fi/kota/) and OECD (2002a).

The origins of this exceptional market structure can be traced back to the Telephony Decree of the Finnish Senate in 1886, which distributed numerous private operator licenses in order to circumvent Russian telegraph regulations.[1] Upon gaining independence in 1917,[2] an additional public

telephony operator (PTO) and regulator was established to operate the telegraph and military telephone network left behind by the Russians. In the 1930s there were over 800 private telecommunications operators in Finland. Even today there are some 40 significant operators.[3]

From the outset, Finnish telecommunications equipment markets were open to foreign suppliers. Thanks to its small multi-operator market, Finland became a test market for the latest technology. Private operators' interest in state-of-the-art technology was fueled by the threat of being taken over by the PTO in case of underperformance. In order to integrate different manufacturers' network equipment, operators had to develop technological expertise, which was later exploited by the emerging domestic equipment industry.

Table 1. **In the mid 1970s the Equipment Market was Dominated by Foreign Suppliers:** Finnish Telephone Exchange Equipment Market Shares in 1975, a Total of 161 million (2000 prices)

Ericsson (Sweden)	60%
Siemens (Germany)	25%
Televa (Finland)	8%
ITT (United States)	7%

Source: Häikiö (2001a, p. 162—countries of origin added by the authors).

Emergence of Wireless Communications

Applications of radio technology were developed in three companies around 1920: Salora (a Finnish consumer electronics company), Suomen Kaapelitehdas (Finnish Cable Works), and Radio Laboratory (under the Ministry of Defense). Fervent engineers, often objects of suspicion and

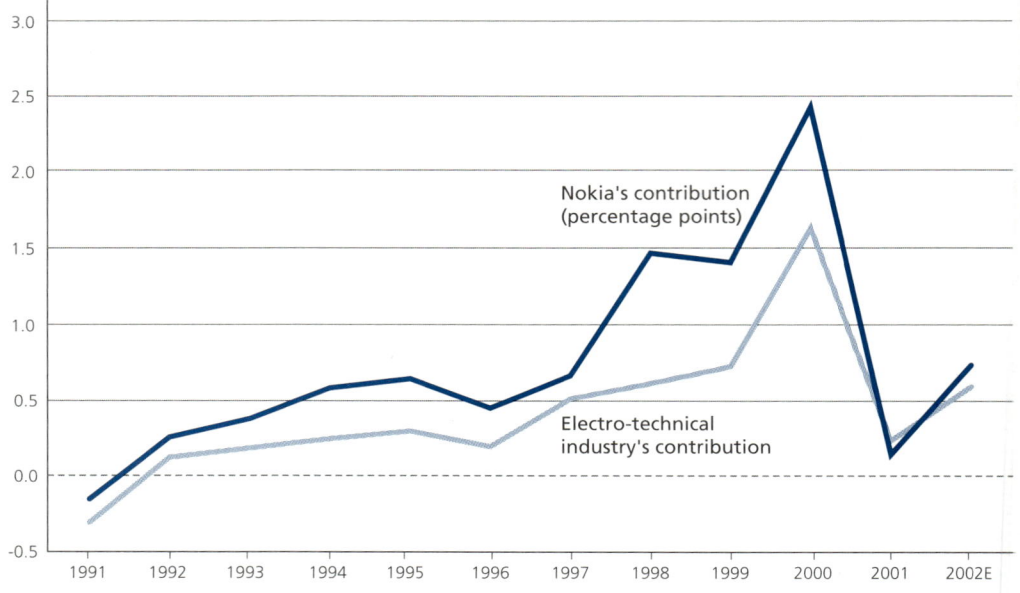

Figure 5. **In the Peak Year of 2000 Nokia Accounted for One and a Half Percentage Points of Overall GDP Growth:** Contribution of Nokia and the Electro-Technical Industry to GDP Growth in Finland (percentage points)

Source: Authors' update of Ali-Yrkkö and Hermans (2002).

Figure 6. **Rapid Worldwide Transition to Open Competition in Telecommunications:** Fixed Telecommunications Network Operator Market Structure in the OECD Area

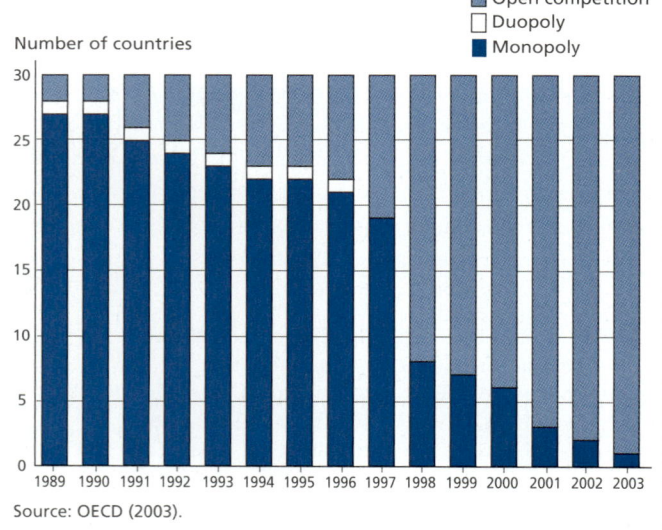

Source: OECD (2003).

Table 2. **Nordic Suppliers and Global Heavyweights Competed in NMT Handsets:** Market Shares in NMT Handsets in 1985 (83,525 units in total)[4]

Mobira (Finland)	27.7%
Ericsson (Sweden)	15.9%
Panasonic (Japan)	13.9%
Storno (United States, until 1977 Denmark)	7.1%
Dancall (Denmark)	6.5%
Mitsubishi (Japan)	6.1%
NEC (Japan)	6.0%
Siemens (Germany)	5.6%
Motorola (United States)	5.6%
Simonsen (Norway)	2.3%

Source: Nokia Mobile Phones (as cited in Häikiö, 2001c, p. 1??—countries of origin added by the authors).

opposition by conservative colleagues and managers, worked on applications of radio technology on the sidelines of main business activities.

In 1963, a call for tenders by the Finnish army for a battlefield radio spurred companies to give physical expression to their accumulated expertise. Ultimately the army did not have the resources to purchase the system, but the prototypes served as the forerunners of commercial handsets.

The Auto Radio Puhelin (ARP, Car Radio Telephone) network was introduced in 1971 as the country's first mobile telephone network providing nationwide service. It provided good geographical coverage but was not technologically sophisticated. In the mid 1970s the service had some 10 thousand subscribers. Although ARP did not turn mobile communications into a major business, it provided experience and customer interfaces for companies such as Nokia, Salora, and Televa, the main suppliers of terminals and network equipment in Finland. It also indicated that there was commercial potential in mobile services.

The telecommunications industry is characterized by generations of new standards with the potential to alter the competitive landscape. The GSM standard was especially discontinuous in this respect, since it marked a clear break in technological developments and regulatory regimes. GSM set the stage for Nokia's global breakthrough, and thereby provides an important snapshot of how the Finnish ICT industry managed to enter mobile telephony, master the technologies and regulatory challenges, and transform itself into a global leader.

In the software communities of the 1980s, the GSM acronym was translated into the "Global Software Monster" due to the technological challenges involved in living up to the demanding specifications of the standard. The standard was based on many years of European collaboration within the Groupe Spécial Mobile, founded in 1983 under the Conférence Européenne des Administrations des Postes et des Télécommunications (CEPT) and subsequently transferred to the European Telecommunications Standardisation Institute (ETSI). Initially, this collaboration included the major European PTOs—this was the regulatory regime that had been a successful one in the NMT era. However, due to increasing technological complexity and IPR clashes, collaboration was subsequently opened to the equipment suppliers as well. This was largely facilitated through political coordination at the European level, whereby the "basket model" of standardization was introduced.

In the basket model the interfaces between the subsystems of the cellular network were standardized, while the detailed choice of the internal component technologies was left to the equipment suppliers. Accordingly, competition was enhanced because equipment suppliers could contribute to the standard with their own technological solutions. This also invited the formation of constellations of R&D alliances around competing component technologies. One such alliance was the ECR900, which provided Nokia and Finland with an entry ticket through the back door into the large firms' oligopoly alongside such players as Ericsson, Alcatel, and Siemens.

The technological challenges of the GSM were foremost related to the digitalization of radio transmissions, and the exponential increase in the complexity of the signalling and control software. In Finland, meeting these challenges involved the interplay of various developments, some of which were based on bold managerial choices, others of which were highly coincidental.

A key precondition for the timely entry into GSM markets was the accumulated competencies that Nokia had developed in the field of digital software processing and transmissions in the 1970s and 1980s. A peculiarity was that Nokia had gained a very significant market position in the data modem business in the 1980s, based on interactions with an advanced banking sector in the Nordic countries as the key customer. Data modems and early personal computers made Nokia a leading user of digitalized integrated circuits (ICs) in collaboration with such giants as AT&T and Texas Instruments in the United States. Likewise, Nokia was an early mover in the field of digital transmission systems with such global industry firsts as the delivery of a 30-channel transmission system to the Finnish PTO in the late 1960s. Later on, further collaboration with the PTO, various local telecom operators, the State Railways, and advanced customers in the Soviet Union gave way to voluminous orders for the DX200, a digital switching system. In the early 1980s, following the strong market position of Mobira in NMT, a clear vision of the future potential of mobile telephony became evident throughout Nokia. These competencies found unintentional applications in the digital cellular environment of the GSM.

Apart from being an "accidental incumbent" in digital signal processing, transmission, and switching, Nokia also managed to coordinate scarce resources and combine various technologies very efficiently and at the right time. The first step towards Nokia's consolidation of competencies in Finland was its outsourcing of some R&D to the Oulu region. As a result of regional initiatives to proliferate Oulu as an important ICT center in Finland, a vibrant software community was emerging there. This outsourcing was subsequently internalized through the founding of Nokia's R&D centers in the Helsinki and Tampere regions, in close collaboration with technical universities.

At the same time, Nokia reorganized its telecom divisions through the founding of Nokia Cellular Systems. Instituted in 1988, Nokia Cellular Systems was designed to cater solely to the envisioned GSM-based growth in the cellular systems business. This reorganization was meant to contribute to the goal of making the deadline for the inauguration of the GSM service in Europe in 1991. The tight deadline was met in Finland through the world's first GSM call in June of 1991, even though the pan-European inauguration of the service was delayed due to technical problems.

However, Nokia was also lucky in many respects. In hindsight the decentralized microprocessor architecture of the DX200 digital switching platform was optimal for the GSM software extensions, although this decision was made primarily due to limited resources in the 1970s. Moreover, the fact that Nokia had collaborated and provided technological solutions to a range of different local operators, PTO, and other state agencies in Finland as well as the Soviets, meant that a whole arsenal of technological solutions were readily available also for the extensions to the global GSM markets. The collapse of the Soviet markets in the late 1980s was a further "lucky" coincidence. It struck the digital DX200 switching business hard but at the same time, enabled the transfer of resources from fixed to mobile telephony at a time when these resources were needed the most. Likewise, the GSM standardization process took many turns favorable to Nokia, one of which was the basket-model compromise that facilitated the formation of competing R&D alliances.

Presently, standardization is increasingly open and primarily in the domain of large multi-technology firms due to the further increase in technological complexity, number of participants, and the importance of multiple patents. This trend is best illustrated through the growth in the number of patents deemed as essential to the GSM and to the UMTS standard (see Table). As a consequence, the competitive landscape is changing once again.

Firms and Their Share Essential Patents in the GSM and UMTS Standard

	Number of essential patents	Number of firms holding essential patents	Key players' shares of the essential patents							
			Nokia	Ericsson	Philips	Motorola	Alcatel	Siemens	Qualcomm	Other
GSM	2,024	24	41%	18%	9%	4%	4%	2%	–	22%
UMTS	3,499	30	27%	8%	–	12%	3%	1%	45%	4%

Source: ETSI (2002).

The GSM has defined one technological and regulatory path towards next generations of mobile telephony, through the GRPS, EDGE, and UMTS standards. The future will tell to which degree this present stronghold of Finland in GSM technologies and markets will also support further advances and standardization paths in the rapidly changing and increasingly multi-layered and competitive landscape of the ICT industry.

Source: Kindly provided by Christopher Palmberg on the basis of Palmberg and Martikainen (2003).

The development of the *Nordisk Mobil Telefon* (NMT, Nordic Mobile Telephone) standard in the 1970s was a highly valuable outcome of the traditional cooperation of Nordic authorities and industry. It aimed at creating a Nordic market for mobile telephony and inducing competition. The standard was open to third-country suppliers as well. Openness promoted competition in network equipment and handsets. Advanced features such as roaming were included, and fortunately, the diffusion-promoting "caller pays" practice was also adopted.

In the early 1980s, the Nordic countries formed the largest mobile communication market worldwide in terms of the number of subscribers. Mobira, a joint venture of Nokia and Salora, supplied the first NMT handsets.[5] In contrast, Finnish companies were neither ready nor willing to supply network technology at the starting phase of the NMT project. Eventually, under pressure from PTO, and motivated by the need to curb Swedish Ericsson's market power and equipment prices in general, Mobira, and later Tele-Nokia, started to manufacture network equipment (Palmberg 2002).

In 1988, the telecommunication authorities of the European Community published the *Groupe Spécial Mobile* (GSM, Digital Global System for Mobile Communication) standard. Nokia and Ericsson were among the first to adopt GSM, which eventually became almost universally accepted—with the major exceptions of the United States, Canada, and leading Latin American countries. Recently GSM has also gained ground in these markets.

PTO was the sole NMT operator in Finland. The liberalization of the wireless operation culminated in the granting of a GSM license to Radiolinja (a private operator). In 1991, PTO and Radiolinja were among the few who opened their GSM networks in accordance with the original schedule set up by the GSM development group's memorandum of understanding. Nokia made its global GSM premiere by providing Radiolinja's network.

Although the foundations of domestic equipment manufacturing were laid in the 1920s, up until the 1980s, foreign manufacturers dominated the market. During the 1970s and 1980s, Finland was advancing rapidly in digital and mobile technologies. Nokia participated in these developments and since the 1970s, it has become a central force in the consolidation of the industry. By the late 1980s, the bulk of the Finnish telecommunications equipment industry had merged into Nokia.

Nokia's Transformation into a Global Mobile Communications Giant

The merger of Suomen Kaapelitehdas (Finnish Cable Works), Suomen Gummitehdas (Finnish Rubber Works) and Nokia in 1967 may be seen as the birth of the current Nokia Corporation. Although the wood-grinding mill lent the name, the cable company provided the core knowledge base to the new entity: in 1960 it had established an electronics department reselling computers, providing computing services, and also manufacturing some its own

Figure 7. **The Evolution of the Finnish Mobile Communications Industry**

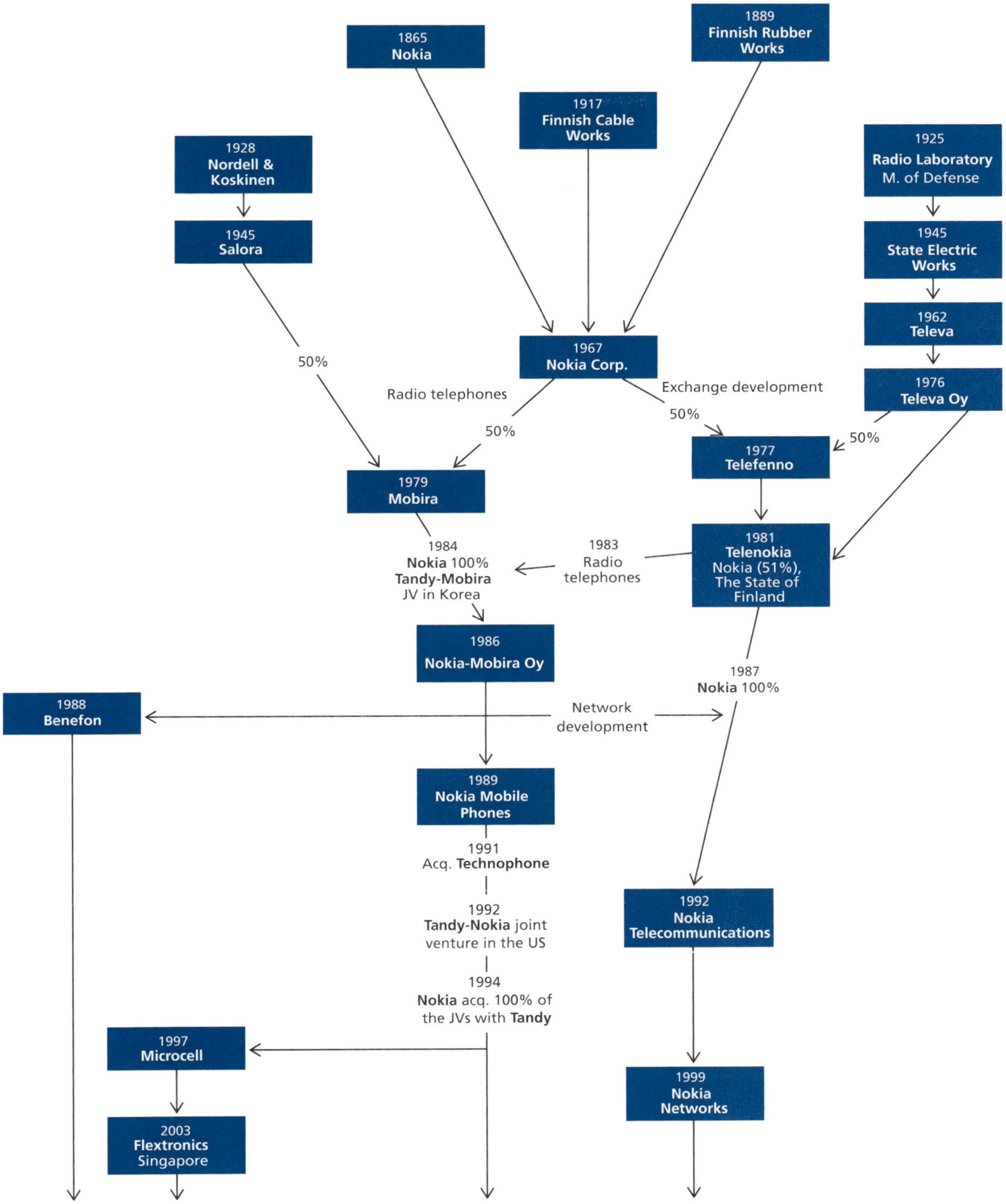

Source: Derived by the authors from an earlier version by Paija (2001, p. 25).

electronic devices. It also assumed an important role in educating its own staff—and Finns more generally—on digital technologies.

Nokia was still pursuing a conglomerate strategy in the 1980s and made several sizable acquisitions in consumer electronics (i.e., televisions such as Swedish Luxor in 1984 and German Standard Elektrik Lorenz in 1987), information systems

(e.g., Swedish Ericsson Information Systems in 1988), and other fields not directly related to telecommunications.[6] This conglomerate strategy, together with managerial and ownership problems, caused—along with the early 1990s recession—a deep crisis. Jorma Ollila became the CEO in 1992. Under his leadership, activities outside mobile communications were divested. The process was completed by the late 1990s.

Figure 8. **From a Multi-Branch Conglomerate to a Mobile Handset Company in a Decade**: Nokia's Sales by Industry[7]

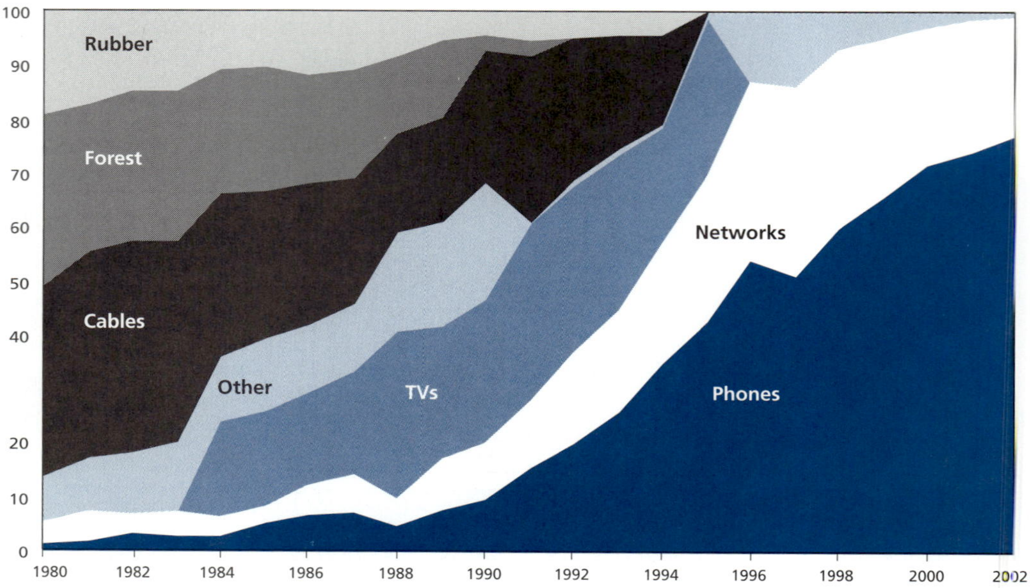

Sources: Derived by the authors from an earlier version by Paija (2001, p. 27) with additional data from Häikiö (2001b) and Nokia's annual reports.

With the exception of UK-based Technophone in 1991,[8] Nokia has not made major foreign acquisitions in its current core businesses. In fact, it retreated from its acquisition strategy almost completely after the early 1990s. But alliances were important from early on: in handsets, Nokia established joint ventures with American Tandy, and did private labeling with Tandy-owned Radio Shack, AT&T, and others; on the network side, it initially partnered with Alcatel (France) and AEG (Germany) to provide GSM solutions.[9]

With a nearly 40 percent market share, Nokia is currently a clear market leader in mobile handsets, and is one of the dominant players in mobile network infrastructure equipment. It has been riding the wave of exploding global mobile telecommunication markets, fueled by worldwide deregulation in telecommunications. Thanks to its narrowly defined and globally orientated strategy, it has been able to meet the market challenge somewhat better than its closest competitors. Furthermore, the management has been able to build an innovation-driven culture and supporting organizational structure, flexibly exploiting both internal and external networking.

Nokia has had its share of problems and challenges as well. It was nearly bankrupted in the early 1990s, primarily as a consequence of its overly ambitious and costly acquisition and internationalization strategy.[10] The mid 1990s logistics crisis and the mismatch of product mix and market demand led to a major revision in organizational structure. What seems to set Nokia apart from many other gigantic corporations is its ability to react quickly and improvise in a moment of crisis.

There Is More to the Finnish ICT Cluster than Nokia

Koski, Rouvinen, and Ylä-Anttila (2002) show that international ICT manufacturing exhibited an intensifying concentration tendency in the 1990s, and that laggards rarely catch up, let alone leapfrog, the leaders. Thus, originally ICT-specialized countries tend to become more so. Finland is a rare exception to this rule. During the 1990s, it went from being one of the least ICT-specialized industrialized countries to becoming the single most specialized one.

The broadly understood Finnish ICT sector (or cluster) —from digital content provision and packing via network infrastructure equipment manufacturing and operation to end-user terminals and portals—is comprised of 6,000 firms (Paija and Rouvinen 2003), including 300 first-tier subcontractors of Nokia (Ali-Yrkkö 2003).

The impact of the ICT cluster on the Finnish economy can hardly be exaggerated. In the 1990s its GDP share rose from 4 to 10 percent.[12] Nokia's share is an estimated 3 percent. ICT has indeed become the country's third industrial pillar at the expense of the traditional metal and engineering as well as forest-based sectors. Nokia alone accounts for an estimated one-fifth of Finnish exports.

Finland is quite dependent on Nokia, but at least now the Finnish economy has a second major pillar alongside the traditional forest-related industries. Should anything go wrong, the country has a proven ability to adapt. As compared to a dependence on natural resources such as oil, it seems

Table 3. Siemens Remains the Biggest Communications Equipment Providing Corporation:
Some ICT-Related Companies in Fortune Global 500

Communications Equipment Providers						
Firm	Country	Revenues (US$ billion in 2002)	Profit margin (profits/revenues, % in 2002)	Employees (thousands in 2002)	R&D intensity (expenditure/ revenue, % in 2001)	Worldwide market share in mobile phones (% in 2002)
Siemens	Germany	77	3	426	10	8
Samsung Electronics	Korea	48	12	80	6	10
NEC	Japan	39	-1	146	7	
Fujitsu	Japan	38	-3	157	7	
Nokia	Finland	28	11	52	10	36
Motorola	United States	27	-9	97	14	15
Cisco	United States	19	10	36	18	
LG Electronics	Korea	18	2	55	5	
Alcatel	France	16	-29	76	11	
Ericsson	Sweden	15	-13	65	20	6
Lucent	United States	14	-86	47	17	
Nortel	Canada	11	-34	37	19	

Major Operators						
Firm	Country	Revenues (US$ billion in 2002)	Profit margin (profits/revenues, % in 2002)	Employees (thousands in 2002)	R&D intensity (expenditure/ revenue, % in 2001)	Worldwide market share in mobile phones (% in 2002)
NTT	Japan	90	2	207	3	
Verizon Communications	United States	68	6	229		
Deutsche Telekom	Germany	51	-46	256	2	
AT&T	United States	47	-28	71	1	
France Telecom	France	44	-44	244	1	
SBC Communications	United States	43	13	176		
Olivetti	Italy	30	-2	107		
BT	UK	29	14	105	2	

Other ICT Firms						
Firm	Country	Revenues (US$ billion in 2002)	Profit margin (profits/revenues, % in 2002)	Employees (thousands in 2002)	R&D intensity (expenditure/ revenue, % in 2001)	Worldwide market share in mobile phones (% in 2002)
IBM	United States	83	4	316		
Hitachi	Japan	67	0	340		
Sony	Japan	61	2	161		
HP	United States	57	-2	141		
Vivendi	France	55	-40	284		
AOL Time Warner	United States	42	-237	91		
Microsoft	United States	28	28	51		
Intel	United States	21	2	79		

Sources: Fortune (2003), R&D figures for communications companies and some operators from OECD (2003, pp. 80–81), mobile phone market shares of major suppliers from *Gartner Dataquest's* website (*www.gartner.com*, Ericsson refers to SonyEricsson).

plausible to argue that the knowledge accumulated in ICT-related activities could be more easily applied elsewhere. Obviously, such a small country can probably never hold a well-diversified portfolio of internationally competitive business activities.

Although other Finnish ICT companies are gaining ground in global markets, there have not been major breakthroughs in broader ICT market segments. In recent years Finland has nevertheless been able to attract R&D activities of such firms as Ericsson, Fujitsu, IBM, HP, and Siemens, which may be interpreted as a sign of the viability of its ICT cluster.

Jalava and Pohjola (2002) show that the absolute macroeconomic effects of ICT in the late 1990s were quite similar in Finland and in the United States (see, for example, Jorgenson 2001). As distinct from the situation of the United States, however, the effects in Finland are mostly mediated via

Figure 9. **Heavy Specialization in ICT and Communications Equipment Manufacturing**[11]

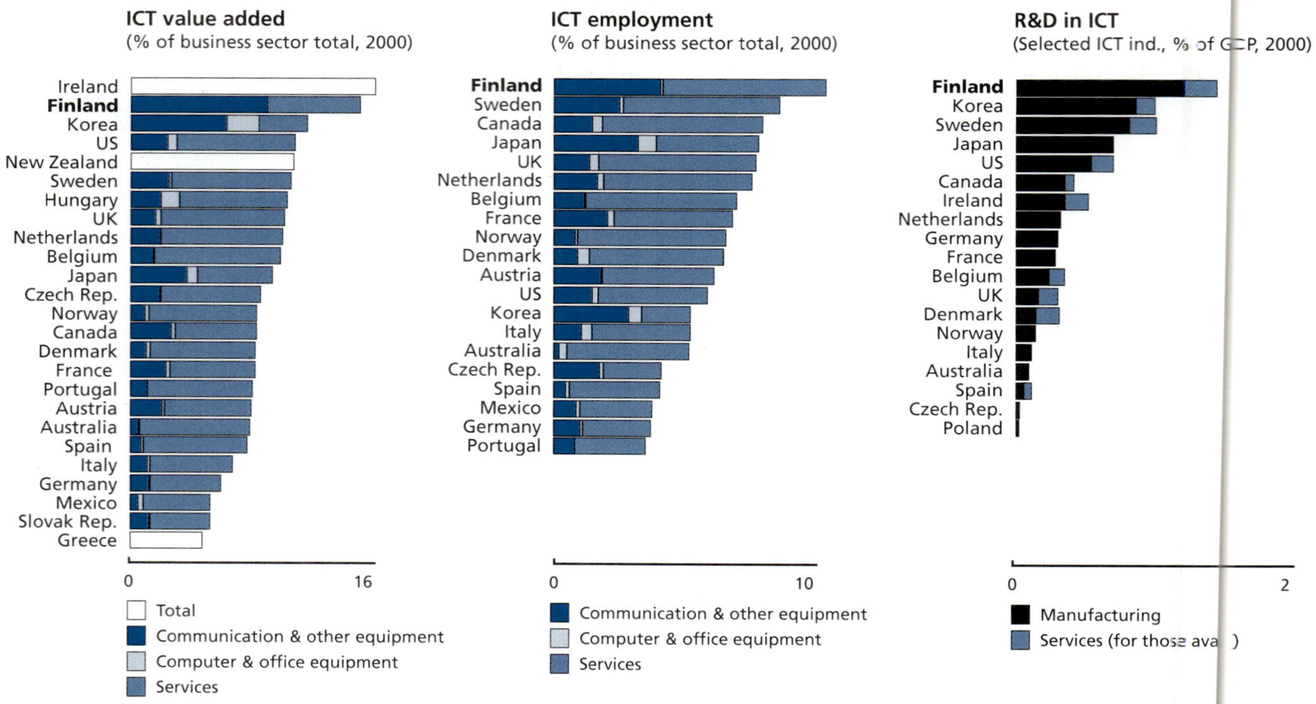

ICT value added
(% of business sector total, 2000)

Ireland
Finland
Korea
US
New Zealand
Sweden
Hungary
UK
Netherlands
Belgium
Japan
Czech Rep.
Norway
Canada
Denmark
France
Portugal
Austria
Australia
Spain
Italy
Germany
Mexico
Slovak Rep.
Greece

0 — 16

ICT employment
(% of business sector total, 2000)

Finland
Sweden
Canada
Japan
UK
Netherlands
Belgium
France
Norway
Denmark
Austria
US
Korea
Italy
Australia
Czech Rep.
Spain
Mexico
Germany
Portugal

0 — 10

R&D in ICT
(Selected ICT ind., % of GDP, 2000)

Finland
Korea
Sweden
Japan
US
Canada
Ireland
Netherlands
Germany
France
Belgium
UK
Denmark
Norway
Italy
Australia
Spain
Czech Rep.
Poland

0 — 2

Legend (ICT value added):
☐ Total
■ Communication & other equipment
☐ Computer & office equipment
■ Services

Legend (ICT employment):
■ Communication & other equipment
☐ Computer & office equipment
■ Services

Legend (R&D in ICT):
■ Manufacturing
■ Services (for those available)

Source: OECD (2002b).

Table 4. **Some ICT Companies on the Main List of the Helsinki Stock Exchange**

Company	Self description	Net sales in 2002 (€ millions)	Profit margin in 2002 (%, net sales per operating profit)	Personnel in 2002
Nokia Oyj	The world leader in mobile communications	30,016	15.9	52,700
TeliaSonera AB (Sweden, figures for Sonera)	The leading telecommunications group in the Nordic and Baltic regions	2,241	2.9	8,170
Elisa Oyj	One of the leading European operators in applying new technology	1,563	-4.5	8,120
Tietoenator Oyj	One of leading suppliers of high value-added IT services in Europe	1,271	7.5	11,600
Perlos Oyj	The world's largest supplier of mobile phone precision components, powder inhalers for pharmaceuticals	365	0.4	3,640
Novo Group Oyj	One of the largest providers of business-to-business IT services in the Nordic countries	309	3.0	2,260
Eimo Oyj	A leading manufacturer of precision plastic components for communications, automotive, and healthcare	252	1.2	1,940
Aspocomp Group Oyj	A high-tech circuits and mechanics manufacturer for communications, automotive, and other industries	183	-12.8	3,080
Teleste Oyj	A technology-leading provider of video and broadband cable networks	67	-6.4	506
Aldata Solution Oyj	A leading European retail software company	66	6.4	448
Yomi Oyj	A significant provider of software for communications networks and terminals	58	6.7	621
Comptel Oyj	The global market leader in mediation software for operators and service providers	49	-13.4	595
Tecnomen Oyj	A worldwide supplier of messaging and intelligent network systems for operators and service providers	40	-35.4	457
F-Secure	The leading provider of centrally managed security solutions for the mobile enterprise	39	-4.5	306
Stonesoft Oyj	A global supplier of security platform software	30	-75.3	336
Sysopen Oyj	One of the leading independent integrated e-Business solution providers	29	10.0	323
TJ Group Oyj	A European provider of Extended CRM solutions	28	-57.6	321
SSH Communications Security	A world-leading supplier of managed security middleware (cryptography and authentication)	17	-83.9	147

Sources: Helsinki Stock Exhange (www.hex.com), Top 500 database by Talouselämä business periodical, companies' websites.

Nokia and Finland

Nokia is by far the biggest company in Finland. It accounts for one-fifth of the country's total exports and close to 3 percent of its GDP. But its role is even more important in strategically important activities like R&D and internationalization of business. Nokia's share in total business sector R&D is 50 percent, and of total national research and development some one third. Hence, as a performer of R&D, Nokia is bigger than the whole Finnish university sector. More than 60 percent of Nokia's R&D (€3 billion in 2002) is conducted in Finland. Nokia employs 20,000 people in Finland, of which more than half are in R&D.

Nokia in the Finnish Economy

Nokia's 2002 Share in	
GDP	2.7%
R&D (GERD)	35%
Exports	21%
Employment	1%
Employment, manufacturing	5%
Market valuation of Helsinki Stock Exhange	60%

Source: ETLA estimates.

ICT provision. ICT penetration rates are nevertheless quite high and the country is a leader in certain types of ICT usage, for example, online banking and mobile payments.

Maliranta and Rouvinen (2003) use firm-level data to study the effects of ICT usage. The average effect in Finland is almost exactly the same as the mean estimate calculated across tens of similar international studies. There is, however, huge variation across firms. Although in most respects Finland is also an advanced user of ICT, it nevertheless seems that as a user it is not as exceptional as it is as a producer. This is somewhat alarming, as the long-run economic effects of ICT are mostly mediated via its use.

Can We Explain It?

New Markets, Reduced Financial Constraints

The liberalization of global markets for goods, services, capital, and technology, initiated by developments in the United Kingdom and the United States in the late 1970s, led to a globalization boom in the mid 1980s. Finnish companies gained access to new markets, dependency on domestic banks for finance was reduced, and capital constraints were relaxed. Larger Finnish companies gained direct access to foreign investors. There was a huge influx of capital to Finland in the mid 1990s, and for a couple of years the Helsinki Stock

Exchange was the most internationalized one in the world, as measured by market value owned by foreigners. Contrary to the Israeli case, for example, smaller Finnish companies have not made initial public offerings in NASDAQ or other foreign markets. They have nevertheless benefited from the rapidly increasing availability of venture capital finance since the early 1990s (Hyytinen and Pajarinen 2002).[13]

Creative Destruction

Clearly, a country's historical developments and macroeconomic environment provide the general conditions for its economic development and microeconomic restructuring. For Finland, World War II and the recession of the early 1990s provided clear breaks from the past. These events, together with the country's natural environment and lack of natural resources, fostered pragmatism and a straightforward culture in both politics and business. The relatively poor Finns simply could not afford inflexibility or bureaucracy—they had to adapt to the challenges imposed by the internationalizing world. Even in the deepest crisis, political and economic institutions remained functional, and thus the necessary adjustments took place in an orderly manner.

Vast unemployment in the 1990s gave the ICT cluster the large recruitment pool necessary for its expansion. The public educational system also responded to the content and volume needs in ICT-related education. Furthermore, the collapse of the eastern trade relaxed resource constraints within firms, which could then be targeted to the development of ICT (including GSM) and the expansion that followed.

Role of Public Policies

The institutionalization and strengthening of science and technology policies began in the early 1960s. Important changes that contributed to the knowledge-driven growth and expansion of the ICT sector took place throughout the following decades. The main target of these policies was to strengthen the science and technology base of industry (Lemola 2002).

In the beginning of the 1980s, technology policy became increasingly target-oriented and systematic. The National Technology Agency (Tekes) was established in 1982 to coordinate public R&D support and related efforts, such as national technology programs. Technology transfer and commercialization of research results were emphasized. Tekes and its programs became important instruments for implementing policies. The focus of the new agency's operations was information technology. In fact, two extensive information technology programs had already been initiated before Tekes was established.

Towards the end of the 1980s, a more systemic view on policymaking was adopted. In the 1990s, the Science and Technology Policy Council, a high-level body advising the Cabinet and the President on science and technology matters, introduced the national innovation system as a basic framework for policymaking. Innovation was seen as having a systemic character, contrary to the traditional linear innovation model. This enhanced cooperation between various policy agencies and improved possibilities for making use of emerging complex ICT. The systemic view also emphasized the role of education in adopting, diffusing, and utilizing new technologies (see Georghiou, Smith, Toivanen, and Ylä-Anttila 2003).

Booming Demand

During and prior to the cold war era, telecommunications operation was considered a natural monopoly and equipment manufacturing was largely kept national for strategic reasons. Since then, both operation and equipment markets have been almost completely deregulated and liberalized. Finnish ICT firms had ample experience operating in a competitive environment with diverse customer needs, unlike many of their international competitors. Besides having a history of telecommunications competition that dated back over a hundred years, Finland was also some three years ahead of other industrialized countries in taking the final steps towards completely deregulated communications markets.

In mobile telecommunications in particular, deregulation brought about eager "second-tier" operators and service providers that wanted to deploy new networks rapidly and with a minimum of technical problems. Former monopoly operators were forced to respond by upgrading their networks. Competition, and resulting lower prices, fueled demand, which in turn led to further investments. Thus, the industry was indeed in a virtuous cycle in the 1990s.

The non-telecom ICT market was also booming. The geographically dispersed multinational enterprises had new demands for ICT-related equipment and services. Rapidly falling equipment prices boosted both business and consumer use. The Internet went mainstream in the mid 1990s; the mobile phone became a mass-market product around the same time, although initially these two developments were not directly related.

Technological Opportunity

Digitalization was a major technological breakthrough in voice and data storage, processing, and transmission. It was important for Finland, as it provided an opportunity for new players with no experience or vested interests in computing or communication. Finland had sufficient expertise in digital technologies at large and in telecommunications in particular, both of which were absolutely vital for the big GSM breakthrough.[14]

Radio technology, in addition to a profound understanding of telecommunications, was one of the prerequisites for building a mobile telephone system. University-level education in radio technology had started in the early 1920s. As suggested above, it "lurked in the shadows" in many Finnish firms well before it had commercial applications. This was driven by the fact that amateur radio was a popular hobby in Finland.

NMT and GSM—Winning Standards

Telecommunications standardization in the Nordic and European contexts may be the single biggest explanatory factor in the Finnish ICT success. Finland was an early adopter of first NMT and then GSM, both of which eventually proved to be the "winning technologies" in their eras.

Early on, NMT provided critical mass and relatively high penetration rates, which led to early recovery of development costs as well as accumulation of hands-on knowledge and scale benefits. Network benefits of both production and consumption also accumulated quickly.

Upon the transition to digital technologies, Nokia bet heavily on GSM as the second-generation (2G) standard, which eventually commanded three-quarters of the worldwide user base. Nokia managed to capitalize on its early lead in both GSM networks and handsets.

The fact that mobile telecommunications standards were agreed beforehand rather than being completely or in part determined by market forces, clearly aided entrants and market creation. The settlement of these and subsequent standards was in part based on demonstrations, where the benefits of a given technological solution could be shown in an open competition. Nokia has been quite successful in these competitions, and thus it has considerably influenced the formation of these standards.

Advanced Users

Scandinavians seem to be accustomed, and therefore quite willing, to test new technologies. In the early years of mobile telecommunications, new generations of phones always caused quite a stir and "forced" many users to shop for an upgrade. Fortunately, customer needs in these markets preceded those elsewhere, thus giving somewhat of a first-mover advantage to the Scandinavian firms. Thus, the Scandinavian market was a rather happy marriage of technological competence in both production and use.

As shown above, all of the Scandinavian countries were present in the early NMT markets, but only Nokia and Ericsson stood the test of time. One of the reasons for this may be the fact that these two also had a strong presence on the network side, giving them a thorough understanding of the whole system.

Nokia's expertise in networks was considerably enhanced by technologically advanced domestic operators who were interested in the latest gadgets but at the same time quite

Box 3. **Nokia Success Factors**

Nokia's sales were €30 billion (31 billion USD) in 2002, thus exceeding the annual budget of the state of Finland. At the end of 2002 it had three business groups: Mobile Phones (77 percent of net sales), Networks (22 percent of net sales), and Ventures Organization. It employed over 50,000 people in 2002, of which more than 40 percent were in Finland. Ninety percent of its shares were held abroad. At the end of 2002 it had production centers in nine and R&D centers in 15 countries.

In a decade, Nokia's (nominal) sales have grown 10-fold and its share price has grown over 70-fold. How did Nokia do it? The underlying market trends and general factors are considered in the text; in this box we look for explanations inside the company.

Nokia—Key Figures

	1992	2002
Market value (€ billions, end of year)	1,028	72,300
Net sales (€ billions)	3,056	30,016
of which abroad (%)	80.0	98.8
Profit margin (%, operating profit per net sales)	1.7	19.0
Employment	26,770	52,700
of which abroad (%)	48.6	57.1
R&D (%, R&D expenditure per net sales)	6.1	10.2
of which abroad (%, authors' estimates)	30.0	35.0

Sources: Top 500 database by Talouselämä business periodical, Nokia's annual reports, ETLA estimates.

SUCCESS FACTORS

The Foundations—Technology

Technology at Nokia consists of many things, including, first and foremost, its own R&D. Also important have been efforts to promote prevailing and new industry standards, a broad patenting strategy, as well as technology at production, including its "platform thinking" and logistics to and from the factory.

The initial impetus for much of Nokia's R&D effort has been direct or indirect (e.g., standards) customer needs. Oftentimes the work was conducted with outside partners or in joint ventures. In the late 1980s Nokia Research Center was established to coordinate and support R&D efforts in various business groups. Currently the center primarily serves the business units. The business units also have their own R&D centers.

NMT, GSM, and UMTS standards—all vitally important for Nokia—are discussed in the text. The company's latest efforts in promoting standards go beyond telecommunications protocols. In a combined effort with other manufacturers, Symbia is being promoted as a standard handset operating system. In Open Mobile Alliance, more than 300 companies promote open standard solutions for interoperable mobile services.

Jacques Noels, a Frenchman leading Nokia Consumer Electronics from 1988 to 1992, drew the attention of Nokia's management to the important role of a solid patenting strategy (Häikiö 2001, pp. 21–22, 153). He noted that in the late 1980s, Japanese, Korean, and Taiwanese ICT companies were preyed upon by some US manufacturers with strong patent portfolios. In 1988, after reaching a 10 percent market share in the United States, Nokia was predictably sued by Motorola for alleged patent violations. The case was settled out of court. After the incident, Nokia started to take determined actions to expand its patent portfolio.

"Platform thinking" is one of the cornerstones of Nokia Mobile Phone's R&D and production strategy. Its aim is to develop a manageable set of standard subsystems or platforms, a combination of which then forms a specific handset. A platform includes necessary design, technical, and commercial specifications. The number of specialized, as opposed to industry standard, components is kept to a minimum. As a consequence of this strategy, Nokia has been able to outsource most of its component production and assembly, while focusing itself primarily on brand management, logistics, and key software components (SEC 2001).

Focus—From Technology to Lifestyle-Driven Consumption

Nokia has carefully attended to customer needs and has valued long-term customer relationships. In practice this has shown in the company's close cooperation with operators in the business side, and in offering desirable features, design, and branding on the consumer side.

In handsets Nokia was among the first to offer curvy "pocket-fitting" designs with integrated antennas, screens with sufficient contrast and size for comfortable reading, end-user customization such as exchangeable covers, and downloadable ring tones and logos, as well as entertainment such as off- and online games. While all of these seem obvious now, it took surprisingly long before they became part of the standard setup.

Surprisingly enough, Nokia's head designer is not a Finn. Since 1987, American Frank Nuovo (at first as a consultant, and since 1995 as the head of the Nokia Design Center in Los Angeles) has led handset designing.

The name Nokia became the centerpiece of the company's branding strategy in 1991. Relatively early, "lifestyle consumption," as opposed to, for example, technological excellence, became the focal point in branding. A decade later, Nokia had become the strongest brand in the mobile market and one of the ten most valuable brands in the world.

price conscious and always benchmarking domestic offerings against foreign competition.

Cooperation and Visionary Management

Competition brings about efficient and lean organization. Somewhat paradoxically, cooperation has been equally important for the success of ICT in Finland. Indeed, international comparisons (EU 2000; OECD 1999) suggest that intense inter-organizational cooperation is one of the essential features of the Finnish national innovation system.

As shown above, a diverse set of Finnish communications expertise was eventually merged into Nokia. In the 1980s it was relatively similar to some other Finnish conglomerates, but in the 1990s it transformed itself to something exceptional. Despite its roots, Nokia was able to give up its forest-related activities and seems to have realized quite early that the Soviet trade was best treated as a "cash cow" used to finance developments elsewhere. Focusing on mobile communications was a rather bold move on Nokia's behalf in the early 1990s, but it has paid off handsomely.

Although Finns are often accused of being too engineer-oriented, Nokia has been less so than its closest competitors, Swedish Ericsson and US Motorola. This may be due to its historically somewhat broader customer interface in both the operator and end-user side, Nokia's early lead in the handset market, and early industry developments. Nokia started to emphasize design and branding before the competitors—it anticipated that the mobile phone was going to become a mass-market consumer product. It seems that from early on Ericsson has envisioned itself as a system company, while Nokia always identified itself as a handset company, although at times the network side commanded a large share of the turnover. As compared to Ericsson and Motorola with long traditions in the field, Nokia was clearly the challenger, and thus it had to be humble.

What's Ahead?

All-IP World

One of the key challenges of the Finnish ICT cluster is the on-going convergence of voice and data communications, information systems, consumer electronics, and digital content that is being tailored for these various channels and devices. Mobile Internet or perhaps more appropriately "whatever, wherever, and however desired," will introduce a new playing field with diverse and seemingly different players. Indeed, participants in the respective industries are already competing in both handsets and networks, and this tendency will only strengthen as Internet protocols (IP) increasingly form the basis for *all* electronic communication. Over time the focus on equipment weakens as it becomes more diffused, and shifts to applications and content.

Finland has two major weaknesses in the all-IP future. First, it has little clout outside mobile telecommunication equipment. Thus, at least domestically, it cannot leverage market power in other domains as the industry is being transformed. Second, the all-IP world is not likely to favor the integrated and closed architectures and business models of the telecommunications world. The first problem has been addressed by acquiring a broader set of competencies and forming alliances with the leaders of the respective industries. The second problem can only be addressed by actually competing in the ever more open and fragmented operating environment.[15]

Next Generation Networks

In the mid 1980s, the International Telecommunications Union (ITU) assumed an active role in the introduction of the next generation (third, 3G) standards. Although ITU pushed for one worldwide standard, eventually three became accepted in International Mobile Telecommunications (IMT-2000) guidelines: W-CDMA (better known as UMTS, Universal Mobile Telecommunication System), CDMA2000 (promoted in particular by American Qualcomm) and the Chinese TD-SCDMA. Originally ITU's decision was considered a win for the Nokia-Ericsson camp promoting UMTS, but early market developments seem to suggest that CDMA2000 is progressing faster than expected.

Europe attempted to maintain its lead in mobile telecommunications by pushing for rapid deployment of UMTS. In many European countries radio spectrums for 3G operations were auctioned for over €100 billion in total. It soon became clear that deployment and diffusion would be slower, network building costs higher, and expected revenue per user lower than the licensees had anticipated. While the auctions were designed to maximize the immediate pay-off for the public good (radio spectrum), the long-term effects were unanticipated. The rules of the auction explicitly prohibited secondary trading and defined how, when, by whom, and with what standard the 3G networks were to be set up. Thus, the operators were not making a technology or even a business decision—they were deciding whether or not they wanted to be in the (mobile) telecommunications business; this was a question of their very existence. Currently the operators' indebtedness due to auctions, combined with the bearish financial market, is holding back the deployment of 3G networks.

With the 3G auctions, Europe effectively did the exact opposite of what was intended; in effect, it taxed the UMTS standard over its rivals. In any case, by making a public decision favoring one technology over another, the auctions did away with technology neutrality, which is often considered one of the golden rules in technology policymaking. The regulatory failure in the 3G rollout has recently sparked requests for public actions "reversing" the damage.

The main benefit of the first generation digital (as compared to analog) system was improved voice quality. The key promise of 3G is improved data communication. So far voice has been the key driver of mobile communication, although data is gaining ground. Upon bidding for a spectrum, the operators seem to have assumed a rapid and large shift from voice to data. This shift is indeed taking place, but from the European point of view, somewhat differently than they had expected.

Whereas Europeans seem to have assumed that the mobile Internet would be an extension of mobile telecommunications, the American route of extending wire-line data communications architectures to wireless local area networks (WLANs, also known as Wi-Fi or 802.11*x*, where *x* refers to the incarnation) seems to have an early market lead.

Arguably, a combination of WLAN and an intermediate generation (2.5G, e.g., GPRS, general packet radio service) mobile telecommunications system having the "always on" feature could be used to reach the goals of 3G. WLAN nevertheless has a number of unsolved problems such as control for log-in and access rights, payment, and coverage, which have already been solved in 3G. It is too early to say how the market will unfold, but most likely 3G and WLAN will coexist with in-between roaming as desired.

Industry Turbulence

There was an over-investment in virtually all ICT-related activities in the late 1990s. In part these were driven by one-time events, such as deregulation and liberalization in major markets, the Y2K computer glitch, the introduction of the euro, and commercialization of the Internet—not to mention the new economy bubble. In hindsight it is easy to say that the market participants should have anticipated some leveling-off in demand. But nobody could have anticipated the collapse of the ICT market that has taken place. The current market situation has taken a heavy toll on the companies involved. The underlying factors of the recent boom are nevertheless still there: real prices of digital computing power and communications drop at double-digit annual rates, new applications of ICT that are discovered every day and continue to boost productivity in business and to improve our daily lives. Thus, while the medium-term prospects of the industry are gloomy, the longer-term prospects are considerably brighter. However, only some of the current businesses will live to see the dawn of these prospects.

What Kind of Mobile Culture?

In a sense, the discussion of 3G vs. WLAN is also about how the culture of using the technology evolves. Will a typical user eventually require broadband access at all times and locations for streaming video and similar applications, or is s/he going to be happy having hotspots in areas of peak demand and limited communication ability elsewhere? And perhaps more importantly, for what and how much is s/he willing to pay?

For the majority of us, the office or home desktop computer remains the most important means for storing the flow of our lives. A number of small electronic appliances, mobile phones, along with personal digital assistants, electronic organizers as well as lap- and palmtops, are trying to take over the personal computer in this respect and to become all-encompassing "personal trusted devices," perhaps even replacing our wallets and passports.

Depending on the actual configuration, Finland may stay on the cutting edge and continue to serve as a useful testing ground for new applications, or it may have to play catch-up with respect to some other lead-user concentrations such as Japan or some US regions. Individuals, both as consumers and business representatives, will ultimately decide who wins in the market place.

Conclusion

Viability of the Finnish Model

Upon its birth as an independent nation, Finland had a somewhat disadvantageous starting point. But as Porter (1990), among others, has noted, in the long run selective disadvantages can be turned to sources of national competitiveness. Decades of a relatively stable political and economic environment, as well as a shared national vision on how to build the country, have been important factors in Finland's success.

Finland was lagging behind the rest of Europe in industrial development after World War II. It consciously upgraded its skills and competencies and in half a century caught up with the leaders. The most recent push in the country's development nevertheless involves many coincidental factors and good timing. Thus, Finland has been fortunate, but the fact that it was well-positioned when the opportunity arose had nothing to do with luck. Historically Finland has played catch-up; now it is slowly learning that it is considerably harder to be one of the leaders.

As shown above, the confluence of several factors led to the ICT boom in Finland. The country itself provided particularly fertile framework conditions and had accumulated a great deal of ICT-related expertise. Due to unfavorable macroeconomic shocks, it had resources available and a desperate need for something new. Digitalization presented a technological opportunity. Furthermore, the country had early exposure to two successive generations of winning standards. Finnish firms had already "laboratory tested" competition when deregulation created a wide open world market. On top of this, there was a company that had the vision and a strategy to make it happen. These factors, combined with quite a few lucky breaks, served to put Finland out in front of the pack.

Although the scope of the Finnish ICT cluster has broadened in recent years, it remains highly specialized in mobile communications. The cluster has benefited greatly from having a powerful locomotive and system integrator, Nokia. Although smaller Finnish companies have made efforts to decrease their dependency on their key customer, in many cases their fortunes are still tied to it. Nokia has been able to maintain and even strengthen its position in global competition, and to a limited extent can influence developments in the market place. However, the fact remains that the whole sector is in turbulence.

Major future challenges for the Finnish economy include an aging population and increasing needs for flexibility in the labor market. The working population will inevitably start to decline in only a couple of years. This will weaken one of the economy's most important competitive advantages as the growth of a highly educated labor force slows down.

Changing Policy Priorities

The performance of the Finnish economy in the 1990s was remarkable. It looked as though the economy had found a unique way to combine high social security, dynamism and growth. Successful policies contributing to the Finnish success story were equated with a new economic model for the information society (see Castells and Himanen 2002).

While in hindsight the Finnish public policies of the 1990s were successful, the "Finnish miracle" can only be partially explained by public policies pursued in the 1990s. The necessary policy changes had already been made in the 1980s, with some having come as early as the 1970s. Building competitive advantages takes time. There was no master plan to restructure the Finnish economy and industry; rather, an array of policy measures were working to the same end over an extended period of time (see Georghiou et al. 2003).

However, policies pursued since the early 1990s have had their role as well. There was a major shift in priorities as a consequence of European integration and changes in comparative advantages of the economy; focus shifted from short-term macroeconomic to long-term microeconomic policies. It is nevertheless true that sound but stringent macroeconomic policies contributed to the recovery. By the end of 1990s the high double-deficit of the current account and public sector finances vanished and unemployment had started to fall. While joining the EU and EMU narrowed the scope of macroeconomic policies, it also brought new stability with moderate inflation, low real interest rates, and increasing predictability of fiscal policies.

Under these circumstances, the increased emphasis on microeconomic and especially innovation policies has been a successful choice. These new policies are based on indirect measures aimed at influencing firm behavior. Policies concentrate on rectifying market failures, promoting competition, and improving framework conditions. These types of enabling policies fit well to the economic environment of the 21st century. The key priorities today are innovation policies and policies for enhancing the functioning of capital markets.

Although the high-road strategy of innovation and technology has been emphasized only recently, it was initiated in the 1970s and 1980s. In the 1980s, long before the rise and fall of the "new economy," Finnish technology policy began to give high priority to ICT. These policies were continued in the following decade and they undoubtedly contributed to the success story of the 1990s. Finnish R&D investment and networking between public and private actors rose to new heights.

What Is to Be Learned?

The Finnish experience suggests that a deep crisis often precedes considerable and lasting shifts in economic and social structures. In general, people seldom have a desire to take great leaps forward into the unknown, but a crisis may bring about a willingness to accept the inevitable. Major adjustments in "mental models" may also make one better able to adapt to further changes.

Moreover, it appears that small countries with greater homogeneity and closer interaction (networking) among economic agents may well have an advantage in adjusting to new technologies and, hence, in generating economic growth. This is a kind of a small country paradox, since most of the economic literature (including new growth theories) suggests that larger countries grow faster than smaller ones, and should thus achieve higher levels of income (see Lundvall 1999).

The Finnish response to the most recent crisis was to open up the economy, modernize social structures, strengthen public finance, and shift policies from direct business involvement to building framework conditions for private business.

The rapid turnaround of the Finnish economy would not have been possible without the rise of the ICT cluster, which in turn was facilitated by the convergence of a number of factors. Unfortunately we cannot perform real world experiments to see what would have happened in a different environment, but it is our belief that even slight changes in events or their timing would have made a big difference. For instance, had the remaining bits and pieces of the Finnish communications sector, deregulated and liberalized from 1988 to 1994, been opened up a few years earlier, later, or even in a different order, the situation would have been quite different. If, for example, Radiolinja had built an analog NMT network or, along with PTO, postponed its GSM introduction a few years, Nokia's international GSM premiere and a progressive market as a homebase would have been endangered. Had Finland not experienced the recession, there would have been fewer resources targeted to the at-the-time uncertain ICT business. Other aspects of recent developments provoke similar thought exercises and conclusions.

Although the history of Finnish ICT-related policymaking is full of right decisions at the right time, they have mostly been made for the wrong reasons. For instance, the political wrangling over GSM licenses did not even touch upon the economic and social benefits that would be gained by competition in and early adoption of digital mobile telephony.

Because there are no universally applicable policies that every country should adopt, the Finnish model cannot be replicated as such. There are nevertheless some general principles of sound policymaking that can and should be imitated. Policies should adapt to changes in operating environment and should take into account lessons learned from experiences elsewhere. At the same time, they should build on national strengths and not be swayed by wishful thinking. Innovation policy must have a long-term strategic perspective. Hence, policies must be consistent over the long term and not dictated by short-term cyclical or political considerations. Constant benchmarking of performance is necessary for the assessment of policies.

The case of Finland is a good example of the interaction of several growth-generating factors. Favorable factor conditions and a high level of investment are not sufficient. In order to achieve sustained growth, more emphasis has to be put on adoption of innovations, learning, and increasing specialization. Growth that is not based on constantly rising productivity is unsustainable.

Reading Guide

Pajarinen, Rouvinen, and Ylä-Anttila (1998) consider Finnish competitiveness in the globalizing world. Hernesniemi, Lammi, and Ylä-Anttila (1996) discuss the micro-foundations of Finnish competitiveness and provide an overview of the Finnish industrial clusters. Some of this work has been summarized by Rouvinen and Ylä-Anttila (1999) Castells and Himanen (2002) discuss the "Finnish model" (reviewed in Ylä-Anttila 2003).

The *National Industrial Strategy* by the Ministry of Trade and Industry of Finland (Pietarinen and Ranki 1993) may be seen as the starting point and original documentation of the country's current industrial policy. In their evaluation of the Finnish national innovation system, Georghiou, Smith, Toivanen, and Ylä-Anttila (2003) summarize recent developments in policymaking and consider future prospects.

Paija (2001) provides a comprehensive overview of the Finnish ICT cluster. This work has partly been updated in Paija and Rouvinen (2003). Koski, Rouvinen, and Ylä-Anttila (2002) have a comparative perspective on ICT in the EU countries, but they also touch upon the Finnish case. Steinbock (2002) has a global perspective, but he also discusses Finnish experiences.

The three volume *magnum opus* by Häikiö (2001a; 2001b; 2001c) is the most authoritative piece of writing on the history of Nokia. With unrestricted access to the company's internal archives and personnel, he provides an unmatched level of detail. An abbreviated version is also available in English (Häikiö 2002). Ali-Yrkkö, Paija, Reilly, and Ylä-Anttila (2000) discuss the role of Nokia in the Finnish economy. Ali-Yrkkö (2003) discusses the role of Nokia in the Finnish national innovation system. Ali-Yrkkö (2001) takes a detailed look at the company's partner network in Finland. Ali-Yrkkö,

Paija, Rouvinen, and Ylä-Anttila (2003) look at the company from a global management perspective.

Palmberg (2002) examines the cases of DX200 and NMT from a public procurement perspective. Palmberg and Martikainen (2003) discuss the role of GSM and related technologies in Finland.

Acknowledgements

This chapter was written as a part of the Wireless Communication Research Program (brie-etla.org) of BRIE, the Berkeley Roundtable on the International Economy at the University of California at Berkeley, and ETLA, the Research Institute of the Finnish Economy. It has benefited from earlier work and insights of Jyrki Ali-Yrkkö and Laura Paija. Christopher Palmberg and Olli Martikainen have provided detailed comments and suggestions, and Palmberg has kindly provided the box on GSM.

Notes

1   Recall that from the 13th century until 1809 Finland was under Swedish reign, after which it was a semi-autonomous grand duchy of Imperial Russia until it gained independence in 1917. Due to its strategic importance, the Tsar had established a telegraph monopoly in the country shortly after Morse's original patent in 1837. Fortunately, the Tsar's reaction to Bell's 1876 patent for telephone was somewhat different, perhaps because the telephone was considered "an instrument of entertainment." Interestingly, at the time that Finnish telephony was being established, nearby Stockholm had more telephones than any other city in the world (Holst 2003).

2   Coincidently, in the very same year, Eric Tigerstedt, a Finnish inventor who was well ahead of his time, attempted to patent a "pocketsize folding telephone with a very thin carbon microphone."

3   There are also three or more significant operators in each of the following: long distance, international telecommunication services, and mobile telephony.

4   Mobira was the fourth in the global handset market after Motorola, NEC, and OKI.

5   Weighing approximately five kilograms, the original NMT terminals were not quite the handsets of today.

6   Indeed, in the late 1980s Nokia was the biggest manufacturer of personal computers and color television sets in the Nordic countries and was among the top 10 in Europe. In 1986 Nokia had 10 divisions, 45 business units, and 180 lines of business.

7   The area in the middle of the figure indicates Nokia's disastrous attempt to buy its way into television manufacturing; cumulative losses amounted to €1.3 billion in year 2000 prices (Häikiö 2001b, p. 126). Although it seems plausible to argue the experiences gained aided Nokia in its mobile communications businesses, there is no evidence to support the argument (see, e.g., Häikiö 2001b, pp. 115, 254). There was little exchange of personnel between the units. The communications business separately built its production facilities, logistics, and distribution channels. There is also no evidence of sharing ideas in branding, design, or management between the two lines of business. The failures in television

nevertheless had the indirect effect of making Nokia very cautious in its acquisitions, emphasizing cost-efficiency and profitability and the importance of maintaining a narrow business focus.

8   At the time, Technophone was the second largest mobile phone manufacturer in Europe.

9   According to a Nokia director Kari-Pekka Wilska, the Tandy cooperation considerably enhanced the company's customer orientation. In the leading Finnish daily newspaper *Helsingin Sanomat* (7 April 2002, p. E3—in Finnish, translated by the authors), he notes: "We had a Finnish engineer's mindset. As a major distributor of consumer products, Tandy's view was totally different. . . . We learned that even though the product can command a high price in the market place, it does not have to be expensive to produce."

10   There was even an attempt to sell the company to Ericsson, which in hindsight unwisely showed no interest, although it had made a proposal for a joint venture in the mid 1980s; Siemens showed interest in the company but negotiations were discontinued.

11   ICT sectors as defined at the source. The reference year may vary. See the original source for further notes.

12   We approximate the ICT cluster with the following NACE industries: 30 office, accounting and computing machinery, 32 radio, Television and communications equipment, 64 post and telecommunications, 72 computer and related activities. This is considerably narrower than Paija's (2001) "original" ICT cluster definition.

13   The recruitment of Mr. Jorma Ollila (Nokia's current CEO) from the London office of American Citibank in 1985 was motivated by the increasing role of international finance. The following year he took the first steps towards implementing Nokia's current ownership structure by managing a directed share issue to one of George Soros' funds (Häikiö 2001, pp. 75, 78). After Finland removed the remaining restrictions on foreign ownership in 1993, Nokia started sizable equity issues in international markets. In 1994 it was listed to the New York Stock Exchange. According to Häikiö (2001b, p. 195), Nokia is the least domestically-owned company among the hundred biggest companies in the world.

14   Nokia electronics, established in 1960, resold computers, provided computing services, and also manufactured some of its own electronic devices. Sales were modest, but the 1960s may be seen as an era of competence building in digital technologies. The real breakthrough and expansion came in the 1970s. In 1972 Nokia signed a contract to deliver a large computer system for the Loviisa nuclear plant. In 1973 Nokia decided to start its own computer manufacturing after a major order from a local bank (Kansallis Banking Group). In order to capitalize on accumulated computer expertise and to leverage its phone cable business, Nokia became involved in fixed-line digital telecommunications by acquiring a license for a central telephone exchange from CIT-Alcatel in 1976. Its own (in part developed at Televa) digital exchange, the now legendary DX200, was introduced in 1982. It was based on a standard Intel microprocessor and was thus easily programmable and upgradeable. With its distributed processing power, all-digital silicon architecture, and industry-standard components and programming language, it went against prevailing beliefs about telecommunications. DX200 was amazingly profitable in fixed networks and later formed the foundations of Nokia's wireless network systems. With altogether 2 thousand person-years of R&D effort spanning over 10 years (Keijo Olkkola, as cited in Häikiö 2001a, p. 275), it may be the biggest single R&D project in Finnish history (see also Palmberg 2002).

15 The management of Nokia understood opportunities and threats in the all-IP world quite clearly in the mid 1990s. Internally its business impact was likened to that of digitalization some years earlier. Partly as a response, a corporate venturing unit New Ventures Organization was established in 1998.

References

Ali-Yrkkö, J. 2001. *Nokia's Network—Gaining Competitiveness from Co-Operation*. Helsinki: Taloustieto (ETLA B 174).

Ali-Yrkkö, J. 2003. "Nokia—A Giant in the Finnish Innovation System." In G. Schienstock, ed., *Catching Up and Forging Ahead: The Finnish Success Story*. Albershot, Hants, UK: Edward Elgar.

Ali-Yrkkö, J. and R. Hermans. 2002. "Nokia in the Finnish Innovation System," ETLA Discussion Papers No. 811. Helsinki: The Research Institute of the Finnish Economy.

Ali-Yrkkö, J., L. Paija, C. Reilly, and P. Ylä-Anttila. 2000. *NOKIA—A Big Company in a Small Country*. Helsinki: Taloustieto (ETLA B 162).

Ali-Yrkkö, J., L. Paija, P. Rouvinen, and P. Ylä-Anttila. 2003. "Nokia: An Extended Compnay with Local and Global Operations." In P. N. Gooderham and O. Nordhaug, *International Management: Cross-Boundary Challenges*. Oxford and Boston: Blackwell.

Castells, M. and P. Himanen. 2002. *The Information Society and the Welfare State—The Finnish Model*. New York: Oxford University Press (Sitra 250).

Day, J. D., P. Y. Mang, A. Richter, and J. Roberts. 2001. "The Innovative Organization: Why New Ventures Need More than a Room of Their Own." *The McKinsey Quarterly* 2, pp. 21–31.

European Telecommunications Standards Institute (ETSI). 2002. *Intellectual Property Rights (IPRs); Essential, or Potentially Essential, IPRs Notified to ETSI in Respect to ETSI Standards*. Sophia Antipolis, France: ETSI (ETSI SR 000 314 V1.9.1 (2002–11)).

European Union. 2000. *Towards a European Research Area*. Brussels: European Commission (COM (2000)6).

Georghiou, L., K. Smith, O. Toivanen, and P. Ylä-Anttila. 2003. *Evaluation of the Finnish Innovation Support System*. Helsinki: Ministry of Trade and Industry (Publications 5/2003).

Häikiö, M. 2001a. *Nokia Oyj:n historia*, vol. 1, *Fuusio*. Helsinki: Edita.

———. 2001b. *Nokia Oyj:n historia*, vol. 3, *Globalisaatio*. Helsinki: Edita.

———. 2001c. *Nokia Oyj:n historia*, vol. 2, *Sturm und Drang*. Helsinki: Edita.

———. 2002. *Nokia: The Inside Story*. London: Prentice Hall (for Financial Times).

Hernesniemi, H., M. Lammi, and P. Ylä-Anttila. 1996. *Advantage Finland: The Future of Finnish Industries*. Helsinki: Taloustieto (ETLA B 113, Sitra 149).

Hjerppe, R., R. Hjerppe, K. Mannermaa, O. E. Niitamo, and K. Siltari. 1976. *Suomen teollisuus ja teollinen käsityö 1900–1965*. Helsinki: Bank of Finland.

Holst, G.-M. 2003. *Information and Communication Technology in Finland and Sweden—Addicted Users Pushing Creative Engineers to "Killer Applications"*. Stockholm: TELDOK (Report 147).

Honkapohja, S. and E. Koskela. 1999. "The Economic Crisis of the 1990s in Finland," *Economic Policy* 14, no. 29, pp. 399–436.

Hyytinen, A.and M. Pajarinen. 2002. "Financing of Technology-Intensive Small Businesses: Some Evidence of the Uniqueness of the ICT Industry," ETLA Discussion Paper No. 813. Helsinki: The Research Institute of the Finnish Economy.

Jalava, J. and M. Pohjola. 2002. "Economic Growth in the New Economy: Evidence from Advanced Economies," *Information Economics And Policy* 14, no. 2, pp. 189–210.

Jorgenson, D. W. 2001. "Information Technology and the U.S. Economy," *American Economic Review* 91, no. 1, pp. 1–42.

Kiander, J. and P. Vartia. 1996. "The Great Depression of the 1990s in Finland," *Finnish Economic Papers* 9, no. 1, pp. 72–88.

Koski, H., P. Rouvinen, and P. Ylä-Anttila. 2002. "ICT Clusters in Europe: The Great Central Banana and Small Nordic Potato," *Information Economics and Policy* 14, no. 2, pp. 145–165.

Lemola, T. 2002. "Convergence of National Science and Technology Policies: the case of Finland," Research Policy 31, nos. 8–9, pp. 1481–1490.

Lundvall, B.-Å. 1999. "Nation States, Social Capital and Economic Development—A Systems's Approach to Knowledge Creation and Learning," Paper presented at the Innovation, Competitiveness and Environment in Central America: A Systems of Innovation Approach, conference in Costa Rica, February 22–23, 1999.

Maliranta, M., and P. Rouvinen. 2003. "Productivity Effects of ICT in Finnish Business," ETLA Discussion Paper No. 852. Helsinki: The Research Institute of the Finnish Economy.

Ojainmaa, K. 1994. *International Competitive Advantage of the Finnish Chemical Forest Industry*. Helsinki: Taloustieto (ETLA C 66).

Organisation for Economic Co-operation and Development (OECD). 1999. *Science, Technology and Industry Scoreboard— Benchmarking Knowledge-based Economies*. Paris: Organisation for Economic Co-operation and Development.

———. 2002a. *Education at Glance*. Paris: Organization for Economic Co-operation and Development.

———. 2002b. *Measuring the Information Economy*. Paris: Organization for Economic Co-operation and Development.

———. 2003. *Communications Outlook*. Paris: Organization for Economic Co-operation and Development.

Paija, L. 2001. "The ICT Cluster in Finland—Can We Explain It?" In L. Paija, ed., *Finnish ICT Cluster in the Digital Economy*. Helsinki: Taloustieto (ETLA B 176).

Paija, L. and P. Rouvinen. 2003. "Evolution of the Finnish ICT cluster." In G. Schienstock, ed., *Catching Up and Forging Ahead: The Finnish Success Story*. Albershot, Hants, UK: Edward Elgar.

Pajarinen, M., P. Rouvinen, and P. Ylä-Anttila. 1998. *Small Country Strategies in Global Competition—Benchmarking the Finnish Case*. Helsinki: Taloustieto (ETLA B 144, Sitra 203).

Palmberg, C. 2002. "Technological Systems and Competent Procurers—The Transformation of Nokia and the Finnish Telecom Industry Revised?" *Telecommunications Policy* 26, nos. 3–4, pp. 129–148.

Palmberg, C. and O. Martikainen. 2003. "Overcoming a Technological Discontinuity—The Case of the Finnish Telecom Industry and the GSM," ETLA Discussion Paper No. 855. Helsinki: The Research Institute of the Finnish Economy.

Pietarinen, M. and R. Ranki. 1993. *National Industrial Strategy for Finland*. Helsinki: Ministry of Trade and Industry (Publications 3/1993).

Porter, M. E. 1990. *The Competitive Advantage of Nations*. London: MacMillan.

Raumolin, J. 1992. "The Diffusion of Technology in the Forest and Mining Sector in Finland." In S. Vuori and P. Ylä-Anttila, eds., *Mastering Technology Diffusion—The Finnish Experience*. Helsinki: Taloustieto (ETLA B 82).

Rouvinen, P. and P. Ylä-Anttila. 1999. "Finnish Clusters and New Industrial Policymaking." In OECD Proceedings, *Boosting Innovation: The Cluster Approach*. Paris: Organisation for Economic Co-operation and Development.

Securities and Exchange Commission (SEC). 2001. FORM 20-F REPORT—Nokia Corporation." Washington D.C.: Securities and Exchange Commission.

Steinbock, D. 2002. *Wireless Horizon: Strategy and Competition in the Worldwide Mobile Marketplace*. New York: AMACOM.

"The 500 Largest Corporations in the World," 2003. *Fortune*. (European edition) 48, no. 2, pp. F1–F10.

Ylä-Anttila, P. 2003. The Information Society and the Welfare State—The Finnish Model (Book review). *Research Policy 32*, no. 8, pp. 1533–1534.

Part 2
Country Profiles

How to Read the Country Tables

The Country Tables section presents the rankings of the 102 countries analyzed in the *Global Information Technology Report 2003–2004*. It provides a snapshot of a country's level of ICT development by grouping information under the following sections:

1. **Key indicators concerning the level of ICT diffusion** includes indicators of population, the number of households, main telephone lines, cellular phones, television receivers, cable television subscribers, personal computers, Internet users, and public pay telephones. The International Telecommunication Union is the source of the data in the Key Indicators section.

2. **Overall Networked Readiness Index (NRI)** ranking for 2003–2004 gives immediate insight into the overall preparedness of a country to participate in and benefit from the networked world. Where available, the country's historical rank is provided for comparison.

3. **Component indexes** is divided into three sections corresponding to the index components: Environment, Readiness, and Usage. Rankings for a country can be found for each of the component indexes and for the subindexes comprising the component indexes. A listing of the variables is provided under each of the component indexes. Detailed country rankings for each variable are presented.

By looking at this information, and by identifying key areas of relative over- and underperformance, one can gain a rapid understanding of a country's networked readiness. For example, one can identify key parameters contributing to a country's performance in the environment component index by looking at the rankings of the variables contributing to it, such as venture capital availability or the state of cluster development.

The inferences that one draws from the ranking of a given country can be put into perspective by taking a closer look at the relative performance of other countries. This can be done by examining the Data Rankings section of the *Report*, where one can study the performance of all 102 countries.

By analyzing the performance of two countries that are similar, one can quickly assess their relative strengths and weaknesses, as well as identify the key areas requiring improvement.

Algeria.dz

Key Indicators

Population, 2002	31,293,000
Main telephone lines in operation, 2002	1,908,000
growth (%) 1999–2002	19%
Cellular mobile telephone subscribers, 2002	400,000
growth (%) 1999–2002	456%
Personal computers, 2002	220,000
growth (%) 1999–2002	22%
Internet users (estimated), 2002	500,000
growth (%) 1999–2002	733%

Source: Data from International Telecommunication Union STARS database

Networked Readiness Index Rank
2003–2004 (102 countries) **87**

Readiness Component Index	80
Individual Readiness	76
Business Readiness	83
Government Readiness	83
Public expenditure on education (per capita), 2000	59
Adult illiteracy (%), 2001	86
Tertiary enrollment (gross %), 2001 or most recent available	67
Radios (per 1,000 inhabitants), 2001 or most recent available	73
Television sets (per 1,000 inhabitants), 2001	79
Households online (as % of households with computers), 2002	88
Quality of math and science education, 2003	73
Affordability of local fixed line calls (as % of per capita GDP), 2001	39
Affordability of Internet telephone access (as % of per capita GDP), 2001	18
Affordability of Internet service provider fees (as % of per capita GDP), 2001	71
Ease of obtaining telephone lines, 2003	90
Cost of business telephone monthly subscription (as % of per capita GDP), 2002	40
Extent of staff training, 2003	87
Quality of business schools, 2003	86
Scientists and engineers in R&D (per 1,000 inhabitants), 2000	52
Government prioritization of ICT, 2003	80
Government online presence, 2003	80
Government procurement of ICT, 2003	52

RANK/102

Environment Component Index	94
Market Environment	79
Political and Regulatory Environment	94
Infrastructure Environment	91
State of cluster development, 2003	97
Venture capital availability, 2003	101
Subsidies for firm-level R&D, 2003	59
Quality of scientific research institutions, 2003	88
Availability of scientists and engineers, 2003	23
Brain drain, 2003	88
Utility patents granted (per 1,000,000 inhabitants), 2002	72
ICT manufactured exports (per capita), 2001	80
ICT service exports (per capita), 2001	57
Overall administrative burden, 2003	99
Quality of the legal system, 2003	76
Laws relating to ICT, 2003	100
Competition in the ISP sector, 2003	96
Foreign ownership restrictions, 2003	96
Efficiency of the tax system, 2003	54
Freedom of the press, 2003	56
Overall infrastructure quality, 2003	69
Waiting time for telephone lines (years), 2000	90
Telephone mainlines (per 1,000 inhabitants), 2001	73
Public pay phones (per 1,000 inhabitants), 2001	92
Internet servers (per 1,000,000 inhabitants), 2001	61

Usage Component Index	89
Individual Usage	74
Business Usage	93
Government Usage	89
Personal computers (per 1,000 inhabitants), 2001	85
ISDN subscribers (per 1,000 inhabitants), 2001	56
Cable TV subscribers (per 1,000 inhabitants), 2001	57
Internet users (per 1,000 inhabitants), 2001	96
Computers installed in businesses (per 1,000 inhabitants), 2002	76
Firm-level technology absorption, 2003	76
Prevalence of foreign technology licensing, 2003	92
Government success in ICT promotion, 2003	91
Government online services, 2003	68

List of Countries

Algeria.dz

Key Indicators

Population, 2002	**31,293,000**
Main telephone lines in operation, 2002	**1,908,000**
growth (%) 1999–2002	19%
Cellular mobile telephone subscribers, 2002	**400,000**
growth (%) 1999–2002	456%
Personal computers, 2002	**220,000**
growth (%) 1999–2002	22%
Internet users (estimated), 2002	**500,000**
growth (%) 1999–2002	733%

Source: Data from International Telecommunication Union

Networked Readiness Index Rank

2003–2004 (102 countries) 87

RANK/102

Environment Component Index	94
Market Environment	79
Political and Regulatory Environment	94
Infrastructure Environment	91
State of cluster development, 2003	97
Venture capital availability, 2003	101
Subsidies for firm-level R&D, 2003	59
Quality of scientific research institutions, 2003	88
Availability of scientists and engineers, 2003	23
Brain drain, 2003	88
Utility patents granted (per 1,000,000 inhabitants), 2002	72
ICT manufactured exports (per capita), 2001	80
ICT service exports (per capita), 2001	57
Overall administrative burden, 2003	99
Quality of the legal system, 2003	76
Laws relating to ICT, 2003	100
Competition in the ISP sector, 2003	96
Foreign ownership restrictions, 2003	96
Efficiency of the tax system, 2003	54
Freedom of the press, 2003	56
Overall infrastructure quality, 2003	69
Waiting time for telephone lines (years), 2000	90
Telephone mainlines (per 1,000 inhabitants), 2001	73
Public pay telephones (per 1,000 inhabitants), 2001	92
Internet servers (per 1,000,000 inhabitants), 2001	61

Readiness Component Index	80
Individual Readiness	76
Business Readiness	83
Government Readiness	83
Public expenditure on education (per capita), 2000	59
Adult illiteracy (%), 2001	86
Tertiary enrollment (gross %), 2001 or most recent available	67
Radios (per 1,000 inhabitants), 2001 or most recent available	73
Television sets (per 1,000 inhabitants), 2001	79
Households online (as % of households with computers), 2002	88
Quality of math and science education, 2003	73
Affordability of local fixed line calls (as % of per capita GDP), 2001	39
Affordability of Internet telephone access (as % of per capita GDP), 2001	18
Affordability of Internet service provider fees (as % of per capita GDP), 2001	71
Ease of obtaining telephone lines, 2003	90
Cost of business telephone monthly subscription (as % of per capita GDP), 2002	40
Extent of staff training, 2003	87
Quality of business schools, 2003	86
Scientists and engineers in R&D (per 1,000 inhabitants), 2000	52
Government prioritization of ICT, 2003	80
Government online presence, 2003	80
Government procurement of ICT, 2003	52

Usage Component Index	89
Individual Usage	74
Business Usage	93
Government Usage	89
Personal computers (per 1,000 inhabitants), 2001	85
ISDN subscribers (per 1,000 inhabitants), 2001	56
Cable television subscribers (per 1,000 inhabitants), 2001	57
Internet users (per 1,000 inhabitants), 2001	96
Computers installed in businesses (per 1,000 inhabitants), 2002	76
Firm-level technology absorption, 2003	76
Prevalence of foreign technology licensing, 2003	92
Government success in ICT promotion, 2003	91
Government online services, 2003	68

Angola.ao

Key Indicators

Population, 2002	13,937,000
Main telephone lines in operation, 2002	85,000
growth (%) 1999–2002	26%
Cellular mobile telephone subscribers, 2002	130,000
growth (%) 1999–2002	442%
Personal computers, 2002	27,000
growth (%) 1999–2002	125%
Internet users (estimated), 2002	41,000
growth (%) 1999–2002	733%

Source: Data from International Telecommunication Union

Networked Readiness Index Rank

2003–2004 (102 countries) 99

RANK/102

Environment Component Index	101
Market Environment	101
Political and Regulatory Environment	97
Infrastructure Environment	102
State of cluster development, 2003	102
Venture capital availability, 2003	97
Subsidies for firm-level R&D, 2003	96
Quality of scientific research institutions, 2003	99
Availability of scientists and engineers, 2003	102
Brain drain, 2003	57
Utility patents granted (per 1,000,000 inhabitants), 2002	72
ICT manufactured exports (per capita), 2001	40
ICT service exports (per capita), 2001	75
Overall administrative burden, 2003	35
Quality of the legal system, 2003	91
Laws relating to ICT, 2003	97
Competition in the ISP sector, 2003	95
Foreign ownership restrictions, 2003	60
Efficiency of the tax system, 2003	70
Freedom of the press, 2003	100
Overall infrastructure quality, 2003	100
Waiting time for telephone lines (years), 2000	99
Telephone mainlines (per 1,000 inhabitants), 2001	92
Public pay telephones (per 1,000 inhabitants), 2001	93
Internet servers (per 1,000,000 inhabitants), 2001	73

Readiness Component Index	97
Individual Readiness	88
Business Readiness	95
Government Readiness	98
Public expenditure on education (per capita), 2000	83
Adult illiteracy (%), 2001	63
Tertiary enrollment (gross %), 2001 or most recent available	100
Radios (per 1,000 inhabitants), 2001 or most recent available	99
Television sets (per 1,000 inhabitants), 2001	94
Households online (as % of households with computers), 2002	67
Quality of math and science education, 2003	102
Affordability of local fixed line calls (as % of per capita GDP), 2001	85
Affordability of Internet telephone access (as % of per capita GDP), 2001	73
Affordability of Internet service provider fees (as % of per capita GDP), 2001	79
Ease of obtaining telephone lines, 2003	96
Cost of business telephone monthly subscription (as % of per capita GDP), 2002	93
Extent of staff training, 2003	93
Quality of business schools, 2003	102
Scientists and engineers in R&D (per 1,000 inhabitants), 2000	48
Government prioritization of ICT, 2003	97
Government online presence, 2003	93
Government procurement of ICT, 2003	96

Usage Component Index	95
Individual Usage	93
Business Usage	96
Government Usage	95
Personal computers (per 1,000 inhabitants), 2001	99
ISDN subscribers (per 1,000 inhabitants), 2001	63
Cable television subscribers (per 1,000 inhabitants), 2001	84
Internet users (per 1,000 inhabitants), 2001	87
Computers installed in businesses (per 1,000 inhabitants), 2002	89
Firm-level technology absorption, 2003	85
Prevalence of foreign technology licensing, 2003	96
Government success in ICT promotion, 2003	90
Government online services, 2003	86

Argentina.ar

Key Indicators

Population, 2002	**36,600,000**
Main telephone lines in operation, 2002	**8,009,446**
growth (%) 1999–2002	9%
Cellular mobile telephone subscribers, 2002	**6,500,000**
growth (%) 1999–2002	47%
Personal computers, 2002	**3,000,000**
growth (%) 1999–2002	43%
Internet users (estimated), 2002	**4,100,000**
growth (%) 1999–2002	242%

Source: Data from International Telecommunication Union

RANK/102

Environment Component Index — 57

Market Environment	77
Political and Regulatory Environment	77
Infrastructure Environment	38
State of cluster development, 2003	83
Venture capital availability, 2003	98
Subsidies for firm-level R&D, 2003	82
Quality of scientific research institutions, 2003	73
Availability of scientists and engineers, 2003	41
Brain drain, 2003	73
Utility patents granted (per 1,000,000 inhabitants), 2002	37
ICT manufactured exports (per capita), 2001	50
ICT service exports (per capita), 2001	68
Overall administrative burden, 2003	95
Quality of the legal system, 2003	95
Laws relating to ICT, 2003	71
Competition in the ISP sector, 2003	28
Foreign ownership restrictions, 2003	38
Efficiency of the tax system, 2003	99
Freedom of the press, 2003	54
Overall infrastructure quality, 2003	45
Waiting time for telephone lines (years), 2000	35
Telephone mainlines (per 1,000 inhabitants), 2001	49
Public pay telephones (per 1,000 inhabitants), 2001	16
Internet servers (per 1,000,000 inhabitants), 2001	48

Networked Readiness Index Rank

2003–2004 (102 countries) — 50

2002–2003 (82 countries)	45
2001–2002 (75 countries)	32

Readiness Component Index — 49

Individual Readiness	45
Business Readiness	51
Government Readiness	61
Public expenditure on education (per capita), 2000	54
Adult illiteracy (%), 2001	39
Tertiary enrollment (gross %), 2001 or most recent available	28
Radios (per 1,000 inhabitants), 2001 or most recent available	32
Television sets (per 1,000 inhabitants), 2001	44
Households online (as % of households with computers), 2002	93
Quality of math and science education, 2003	65
Affordability of local fixed line calls (as % of per capita GDP), 2001	63
Affordability of Internet telephone access (as % of per capita GDP), 2001	36
Affordability of Internet service provider fees (as % of per capita GDP), 2001	82
Ease of obtaining telephone lines, 2003	51
Cost of business telephone monthly subscription (as % of per capita GDP), 2002	90
Extent of staff training, 2003	57
Quality of business schools, 2003	25
Scientists and engineers in R&D (per 1,000 inhabitants), 2000	46
Government prioritization of ICT, 2003	98
Government online presence, 2003	16
Government procurement of ICT, 2003	89

Usage Component Index — 42

Individual Usage	36
Business Usage	55
Government Usage	48
Personal computers (per 1,000 inhabitants), 2001	40
ISDN subscribers (per 1,000 inhabitants), 2001	38
Cable television subscribers (per 1,000 inhabitants), 2001	16
Internet users (per 1,000 inhabitants), 2001	43
Computers installed in businesses (per 1,000 inhabitants), 2002	41
Firm-level technology absorption, 2003	70
Prevalence of foreign technology licensing, 2003	49
Government success in ICT promotion, 2003	93
Government online services, 2003	17

Australia.au

Key Indicators

Population, 2002	19,662,780
Main telephone lines in operation, 2002	10,590,000
growth (%) 1999–2002	9%
Cellular mobile telephone subscribers, 2002	12,579,000
growth (%) 1999–2002	99%
Personal computers, 2001	10,000,000
growth (%) 1999–2001	25%
Internet users (estimated), 2002	8,400,000
growth (%) 1999–2002	50%

Source: Data from International Telecommunication Union

RANK/102

Environment Component Index	12
Market Environment	21
Political and Regulatory Environment	13
Infrastructure Environment	6
State of cluster development, 2003	34
Venture capital availability, 2003	7
Subsidies for firm-level R&D, 2003	13
Quality of scientific research institutions, 2003	9
Availability of scientists and engineers, 2003	14
Brain drain, 2003	30
Utility patents granted (per 1,000,000 inhabitants), 2002	21
ICT manufactured exports (per capita), 2001	33
ICT service exports (per capita), 2001	33
Overall administrative burden, 2003	22
Quality of the legal system, 2003	3
Laws relating to ICT, 2003	3
Competition in the ISP sector, 2003	16
Foreign ownership restrictions, 2003	39
Efficiency of the tax system, 2003	40
Freedom of the press, 2003	5
Overall infrastructure quality, 2003	9
Waiting time for telephone lines (years), 2000	1
Telephone mainlines (per 1,000 inhabitants), 2001	16
Public pay telephones (per 1,000 inhabitants), 2001	30
Internet servers (per 1,000,000 inhabitants), 2001	3

Networked Readiness Index Rank

2003–2004 (102 countries) 9

2002–2003 (82 countries)	15
2001–2002 (75 countries)	14

Readiness Component Index	9
Individual Readiness	6
Business Readiness	12
Government Readiness	14
Public expenditure on education (per capita), 2000	20
Adult illiteracy (%), 2001	1
Tertiary enrollment (gross %), 2001 or most recent available	9
Radios (per 1,000 inhabitants), 2001 or most recent available	4
Television sets (per 1,000 inhabitants), 2001	7
Households online (as % of households with computers), 2002	23
Quality of math and science education, 2003	9
Affordability of local fixed line calls (as % of per capita GDP), 2001	24
Affordability of Internet telephone access (as % of per capita GDP), 2001	27
Affordability of Internet service provider fees (as % of per capita GDP), 2001	17
Ease of obtaining telephone lines, 2003	14
Cost of business telephone monthly subscription (as % of per capita GDP), 2002	24
Extent of staff training, 2003	12
Quality of business schools, 2003	13
Scientists and engineers in R&D (per 1,000 inhabitants), 2000	10
Government prioritization of ICT, 2003	30
Government online presence, 2003	9
Government procurement of ICT, 2003	27

Usage Component Index	13
Individual Usage	14
Business Usage	3
Government Usage	20
Personal computers (per 1,000 inhabitants), 2001	6
ISDN subscribers (per 1,000 inhabitants), 2001	16
Cable television subscribers (per 1,000 inhabitants), 2001	44
Internet users (per 1,000 inhabitants), 2001	16
Computers installed in businesses (per 1,000 inhabitants), 2002	2
Firm-level technology absorption, 2003	16
Prevalence of foreign technology licensing, 2003	3
Government success in ICT promotion, 2003	45
Government online services, 2003	11

Austria.at

Key Indicators

Population, 2002	8,159,000
Main telephone lines in operation, 2002	3,988,000
growth (%) 1999–2002	3%
Cellular mobile telephone subscribers, 2002	6,415,000
growth (%) 1999–2002	51%
Personal computers, 2002	3,013,000
growth (%) 1999–2002	43%
Internet users (estimated), 2002	3,340,000
growth (%) 1999–2002	82%

Source: Data from International Telecommunication Union

RANK/102

Environment Component Index — 21

Market Environment	20
Political and Regulatory Environment	19
Infrastructure Environment	17
State of cluster development, 2003	19
Venture capital availability, 2003	47
Subsidies for firm-level R&D, 2003	14
Quality of scientific research institutions, 2003	23
Availability of scientists and engineers, 2003	26
Brain drain, 2003	23
Utility patents granted (per 1,000,000 inhabitants), 2002	17
ICT manufactured exports (per capita), 2001	16
ICT service exports (per capita), 2001	5
Overall administrative burden, 2003	12
Quality of the legal system, 2003	19
Laws relating to ICT, 2003	31
Competition in the ISP sector, 2003	21
Foreign ownership restrictions, 2003	20
Efficiency of the tax system, 2003	69
Freedom of the press, 2003	11
Overall infrastructure quality, 2003	13
Waiting time for telephone lines (years), 2000	1
Telephone mainlines (per 1,000 inhabitants), 2001	25
Public pay telephones (per 1,000 inhabitants), 2001	43
Internet servers (per 1,000,000 inhabitants), 2001	13

Networked Readiness Index Rank

2003–2004 (102 countries) — 21

2002–2003 (82 countries)	16
2001–2002 (75 countries)	9

Readiness Component Index — 15

Individual Readiness	13
Business Readiness	17
Government Readiness	16
Public expenditure on education (per capita), 2000	8
Adult illiteracy (%), 2001	30
Tertiary enrollment (gross %), 2001 or most recent available	16
Radios (per 1,000 inhabitants), 2001 or most recent available	25
Television sets (per 1,000 inhabitants), 2001	23
Households online (as % of households with computers), 2002	15
Quality of math and science education, 2003	7
Affordability of local fixed line calls (as % of per capita GDP), 2001	22
Affordability of Internet telephone access (as % of per capita GDP), 2001	72
Affordability of Internet service provider fees (as % of per capita GDP), 2001	14
Ease of obtaining telephone lines, 2003	17
Cost of business telephone monthly subscription (as % of per capita GDP), 2002	18
Extent of staff training, 2003	16
Quality of business schools, 2003	22
Scientists and engineers in R&D (per 1,000 inhabitants), 2000	20
Government prioritization of ICT, 2003	56
Government online presence, 2003	7
Government procurement of ICT, 2003	43

Usage Component Index — 19

Individual Usage	17
Business Usage	25
Government Usage	15
Personal computers (per 1,000 inhabitants), 2001	20
ISDN subscribers (per 1,000 inhabitants), 2001	11
Cable television subscribers (per 1,000 inhabitants), 2001	20
Internet users (per 1,000 inhabitants), 2001	18
Computers installed in businesses (per 1,000 inhabitants), 2002	18
Firm-level technology absorption, 2003	37
Prevalence of foreign technology licensing, 2003	74
Government success in ICT promotion, 2003	40
Government online services, 2003	7

Bangladesh.bd

Key Indicators

Population, 2002	133,132,000
Main telephone lines in operation, 2002	682,000
growth (%) 1999–2002	58%
Cellular mobile telephone subscribers, 2002	1,075,000
growth (%) 1999–2002	621%
Personal computers, 2002	450,000
growth (%) 1999–2002	246%
Internet users (estimated), 2002	204,000
growth (%) 1999–2002	308%

Source: Data from International Telecommunication Union

RANK/102

Environment Component Index	89
Market Environment	85
Political and Regulatory Environment	84
Infrastructure Environment	84
State of cluster development, 2003	50
Venture capital availability, 2003	94
Subsidies for firm-level R&D, 2003	94
Quality of scientific research institutions, 2003	85
Availability of scientists and engineers, 2003	62
Brain drain, 2003	95
Utility patents granted (per 1,000,000 inhabitants), 2002	72
ICT manufactured exports (per capita), 2001	88
ICT service exports (per capita), 2001	94
Overall administrative burden, 2003	96
Quality of the legal system, 2003	74
Laws relating to ICT, 2003	99
Competition in the ISP sector, 2003	63
Foreign ownership restrictions, 2003	61
Efficiency of the tax system, 2003	83
Freedom of the press, 2003	75
Overall infrastructure quality, 2003	90
Waiting time for telephone lines (years), 2000	79
Telephone mainlines (per 1,000 inhabitants), 2001	95
Public pay telephones (per 1,000 inhabitants), 2001	55
Internet servers (per 1,000,000 inhabitants), 2001	102

Networked Readiness Index Rank

2003–2004 (102 countries) **93**

2002–2003 (82 countries)	77
2001–2002 (75 countries)	73

Readiness Component Index	95
Individual Readiness	91
Business Readiness	96
Government Readiness	93
Public expenditure on education (per capita), 2000	91
Adult illiteracy (%), 2001	98
Tertiary enrollment (gross %), 2001 or most recent available	79
Radios (per 1,000 inhabitants), 2001 or most recent available	100
Television sets (per 1,000 inhabitants), 2001	95
Households online (as % of households with computers), 2002	75
Quality of math and science education, 2003	87
Affordability of local fixed line calls (as % of per capita GDP), 2001	83
Affordability of Internet telephone access (as % of per capita GDP), 2001	81
Affordability of Internet service provider fees (as % of per capita GDP), 2001	86
Ease of obtaining telephone lines, 2003	100
Cost of business telephone monthly subscription (as % of per capita GDP), 2002	83
Extent of staff training, 2003	98
Quality of business schools, 2003	93
Scientists and engineers in R&D (per 1,000 inhabitants), 2000	94
Government prioritization of ICT, 2003	43
Government online presence, 2003	96
Government procurement of ICT, 2003	97

Usage Component Index	92
Individual Usage	98
Business Usage	85
Government Usage	91
Personal computers (per 1,000 inhabitants), 2001	97
ISDN subscribers (per 1,000 inhabitants), 2001	93
Cable television subscribers (per 1,000 inhabitants), 2001	88
Internet users (per 1,000 inhabitants), 2001	97
Computers installed in businesses (per 1,000 inhabitants), 2002	102
Firm-level technology absorption, 2003	83
Prevalence of foreign technology licensing, 2003	83
Government success in ICT promotion, 2003	88
Government online services, 2003	74

Belgium.be

Key Indicators

Population, 2002	10,346,000
Main telephone lines in operation, 2002	5,132,427
growth (%) 1999–2002	-2%
Cellular mobile telephone subscribers, 2002	8,135,512
growth (%) 1999–2002	155%
Personal computers, 2002	2,500,000
growth (%) 1999–2002	11%
Internet users (estimated), 2002	3,400,000
growth (%) 1999–2002	143%

Source: Data from International Telecommunication Union

RANK/102

Environment Component Index	**24**
Market Environment	16
Political and Regulatory Environment	36
Infrastructure Environment	25
State of cluster development, 2003	38
Venture capital availability, 2003	21
Subsidies for firm-level R&D, 2003	17
Quality of scientific research institutions, 2003	15
Availability of scientists and engineers, 2003	22
Brain drain, 2003	19
Utility patents granted (per 1,000,000 inhabitants), 2002	15
ICT manufactured exports (per capita), 2001	9
ICT service exports (per capita), 2001	6
Overall administrative burden, 2003	93
Quality of the legal system, 2003	28
Laws relating to ICT, 2003	39
Competition in the ISP sector, 2003	31
Foreign ownership restrictions, 2003	18
Efficiency of the tax system, 2003	86
Freedom of the press, 2003	9
Overall infrastructure quality, 2003	17
Waiting time for telephone lines (years), 2000	1
Telephone mainlines (per 1,000 inhabitants), 2001	18
Public pay telephones (per 1,000 inhabitants), 2001	66
Internet servers (per 1,000,000 inhabitants), 2001	23

Networked Readiness Index Rank

2003–2004 (102 countries) **24**

2002–2003 (82 countries)	22
2001–2002 (75 countries)	18

Readiness Component Index	**21**
Individual Readiness	16
Business Readiness	13
Government Readiness	40
Public expenditure on education (per capita), 2000	9
Adult illiteracy (%), 2001	30
Tertiary enrollment (gross %), 2001 or most recent available	18
Radios (per 1,000 inhabitants), 2001 or most recent available	23
Television sets (per 1,000 inhabitants), 2001	22
Households online (as % of households with computers), 2002	39
Quality of math and science education, 2003	2
Affordability of local fixed line calls (as % of per capita GDP), 2001	25
Affordability of Internet telephone access (as % of per capita GDP), 2001	85
Affordability of Internet service provider fees (as % of per capita GDP), 2001	16
Ease of obtaining telephone lines, 2003	19
Cost of business telephone monthly subscription (as % of per capita GDP), 2002	19
Extent of staff training, 2003	10
Quality of business schools, 2003	15
Scientists and engineers in R&D (per 1,000 inhabitants), 2000	13
Government prioritization of ICT, 2003	60
Government online presence, 2003	31
Government procurement of ICT, 2003	56

Usage Component Index	**20**
Individual Usage	13
Business Usage	26
Government Usage	32
Personal computers (per 1,000 inhabitants), 2001	24
ISDN subscribers (per 1,000 inhabitants), 2001	12
Cable television subscribers (per 1,000 inhabitants), 2001	2
Internet users (per 1,000 inhabitants), 2001	19
Computers installed in businesses (per 1,000 inhabitants), 2002	22
Firm-level technology absorption, 2003	41
Prevalence of foreign technology licensing, 2003	53
Government success in ICT promotion, 2003	61
Government online services, 2003	24

Bolivia.bo

Key Indicators

Population, 2002	8,341,000
Main telephone lines in operation, 2002	563,941
growth (%) 1999–2002	12%
Cellular mobile telephone subscribers, 2002	872,676
growth (%) 1999–2002	108%
Personal computers, 2002	190,000
growth (%) 1999–2002	90%
Internet users (estimated), 2002	270,000
growth (%) 1999–2002	238%

Source: Data from International Telecommunication Union

RANK/102

Environment Component Index	85
Market Environment	98
Political and Regulatory Environment	82
Infrastructure Environment	69
State of cluster development, 2003	93
Venture capital availability, 2003	88
Subsidies for firm-level R&D, 2003	99
Quality of scientific research institutions, 2003	98
Availability of scientists and engineers, 2003	91
Brain drain, 2003	76
Utility patents granted (per 1,000,000 inhabitants), 2002	72
ICT manufactured exports (per capita), 2001	72
ICT service exports (per capita), 2001	89
Overall administrative burden, 2003	80
Quality of the legal system, 2003	98
Laws relating to ICT, 2003	95
Competition in the ISP sector, 2003	57
Foreign ownership restrictions, 2003	82
Efficiency of the tax system, 2003	42
Freedom of the press, 2003	57
Overall infrastructure quality, 2003	98
Waiting time for telephone lines (years), 2000	38
Telephone mainlines (per 1,000 inhabitants), 2001	72
Public pay telephones (per 1,000 inhabitants), 2001	71
Internet servers (per 1,000,000 inhabitants), 2001	72

Networked Readiness Index Rank

2003–2004 (102 countries) **90**

2002–2003 (82 countries)	78
2001–2002 (75 countries)	67

Readiness Component Index	84
Individual Readiness	66
Business Readiness	85
Government Readiness	94
Public expenditure on education (per capita), 2000	72
Adult illiteracy (%), 2001	68
Tertiary enrollment (gross %), 2001 or most recent available	40
Radios (per 1,000 inhabitants), 2001 or most recent available	33
Television sets (per 1,000 inhabitants), 2001	75
Households online (as % of households with computers), 2002	94
Quality of math and science education, 2003	88
Affordability of local fixed line calls (as % of per capita GDP), 2001	86
Affordability of Internet telephone access (as % of per capita GDP), 2001	45
Affordability of Internet service provider fees (as % of per capita GDP), 2001	67
Ease of obtaining telephone lines, 2003	56
Cost of business telephone monthly subscription (as % of per capita GDP), 2002	89
Extent of staff training, 2003	100
Quality of business schools, 2003	95
Scientists and engineers in R&D (per 1,000 inhabitants), 2000	87
Government prioritization of ICT, 2003	94
Government online presence, 2003	72
Government procurement of ICT, 2003	101

Usage Component Index	99
Individual Usage	75
Business Usage	98
Government Usage	96
Personal computers (per 1,000 inhabitants), 2001	69
ISDN subscribers (per 1,000 inhabitants), 2001	63
Cable television subscribers (per 1,000 inhabitants), 2001	76
Internet users (per 1,000 inhabitants), 2001	69
Computers installed in businesses (per 1,000 inhabitants), 2001	74
Firm-level technology absorption, 2003	102
Prevalence of foreign technology licensing, 2003	95
Government success in ICT promotion, 2003	93
Government online services, 2003	93

Botswana.bw

Key Indicators

Population, 2002	1,720,000
Main telephone lines in operation, 2001	142,600
growth (%) 1999–2001	15%
Cellular mobile telephone subscribers, 2002	415,000
growth (%) 1999–2002	351%
Personal computers, 2002	65,000
growth (%) 1999–2002	30%
Internet users (estimated), 2001	50,000
growth (%) 1999–2001	163%

Source: Data from International Telecommunication Union

RANK/102

Environment Component Index	43
Market Environment	52
Political and Regulatory Environment	28
Infrastructure Environment	53
State of cluster development, 2003	59
Venture capital availability, 2003	42
Subsidies for firm-level R&D, 2003	58
Quality of scientific research institutions, 2003	53
Availability of scientists and engineers, 2003	87
Brain drain, 2003	17
Utility patents granted (per 1,000,000 inhabitants), 2002	72
ICT manufactured exports (per capita), 2001	55
ICT service exports (per capita), 2001	51
Overall administrative burden, 2003	26
Quality of the legal system, 2003	11
Laws relating to ICT, 2003	73
Competition in the ISP sector, 2003	93
Foreign ownership restrictions, 2003	25
Efficiency of the tax system, 2003	3
Freedom of the press, 2003	55
Overall infrastructure quality, 2003	28
Waiting time for telephone lines (years), 2000	46
Telephone mainlines (per 1,000 inhabitants), 2001	68
Public pay telephones (per 1,000 inhabitants), 2001	62
Internet servers (per 1,000,000 inhabitants), 2001	46

Networked Readiness Index Rank

2003–2004 (102 countries) **55**

2002–2003 (82 countries)   44

Readiness Component Index	68
Individual Readiness	74
Business Readiness	73
Government Readiness	54
Public expenditure on education (per capita), 2000	36
Adult illiteracy (%), 2001	78
Tertiary enrollment (gross %), 2001 or most recent available	84
Radios (per 1,000 inhabitants), 2001 or most recent available	91
Television sets (per 1,000 inhabitants), 2001	90
Households online (as % of households with computers), 2002	49
Quality of math and science education, 2003	59
Affordability of local fixed line calls (as % of per capita GDP), 2001	29
Affordability of Internet telephone access (as % of per capita GDP), 2001	10
Affordability of Internet service provider fees (as % of per capita GDP), 2001	43
Ease of obtaining telephone lines, 2003	77
Cost of business telephone monthly subscription (as % of per capita GDP), 2002	31
Extent of staff training, 2003	61
Quality of business schools, 2003	83
Scientists and engineers in R&D (per 1,000 inhabitants), 2000	92
Government prioritization of ICT, 2003	36
Government online presence, 2003	75
Government procurement of ICT, 2003	25

Usage Component Index	60
Individual Usage	67
Business Usage	54
Government Usage	58
Personal computers (per 1,000 inhabitants), 2001	58
ISDN subscribers (per 1,000 inhabitants), 2001	46
Cable television subscribers (per 1,000 inhabitants), 2001	79
Internet users (per 1,000 inhabitants), 2001	59
Computers installed in businesses (per 1,000 inhabitants), 2002	59
Firm-level technology absorption, 2003	69
Prevalence of foreign technology licensing, 2003	12
Government success in ICT promotion, 2003	29
Government online services, 2003	74

Brazil.br

Key Indicators

Population, 2002	173,879,000
Main telephone lines in operation, 2002	38,810,000
growth (%) 1999–2002	55%
Cellular mobile telephone subscribers, 2002	34,881,000
growth (%) 1999–2002	132%
Personal computers, 2002	13,000,000
growth (%) 1999–2002	113%
Internet users (estimated), 2002	14,300,000
growth (%) 1999–2002	309%

Source: Data from International Telecommunication Union

RANK/102

Environment Component Index	35
Market Environment	34
Political and Regulatory Environment	43
Infrastructure Environment	34
State of cluster development, 2003	25
Venture capital availability, 2003	54
Subsidies for firm-level R&D, 2003	35
Quality of scientific research institutions, 2003	49
Availability of scientists and engineers, 2003	46
Brain drain, 2003	22
Utility patents granted (per 1,000,000 inhabitants), 2002	48
ICT manufactured exports (per capita), 2001	46
ICT service exports (per capita), 2001	59
Overall administrative burden, 2003	53
Quality of the legal system, 2003	52
Laws relating to ICT, 2003	37
Competition in the ISP sector, 2003	26
Foreign ownership restrictions, 2003	42
Efficiency of the tax system, 2003	101
Freedom of the press, 2003	17
Overall infrastructure quality, 2003	47
Waiting time for telephone lines (years), 2000	44
Telephone mainlines (per 1,000 inhabitants), 2001	50
Public pay telephones (per 1,000 inhabitants), 2001	5
Internet servers (per 1,000,000 inhabitants), 2001	49

Networked Readiness Index Rank

2003–2004 (102 countries) **39**

2002–2003 (82 countries)	29
2001–2002 (75 countries)	38

Readiness Component Index	40
Individual Readiness	59
Business Readiness	39
Government Readiness	26
Public expenditure on education (per capita), 2000	53
Adult illiteracy (%), 2001	66
Tertiary enrollment (gross %), 2001 or most recent available	62
Radios (per 1,000 inhabitants), 2001 or most recent available	47
Television sets (per 1,000 inhabitants), 2001	41
Households online (as % of households with computers), 2002	87
Quality of math and science education, 2003	75
Affordability of local fixed line calls (as % of per capita GDP), 2001	42
Affordability of Internet telephone access (as % of per capita GDP), 2001	56
Affordability of Internet service provider fees (as % of per capita GDP), 2001	59
Ease of obtaining telephone lines, 2003	34
Cost of business telephone monthly subscription (as % of per capita GDP), 2002	58
Extent of staff training, 2003	27
Quality of business schools, 2003	34
Scientists and engineers in R&D (per 1,000 inhabitants), 2000	65
Government prioritization of ICT, 2003	66
Government online presence, 2003	11
Government procurement of ICT, 2003	53

Usage Component Index	47
Individual Usage	58
Business Usage	31
Government Usage	51
Personal computers (per 1,000 inhabitants), 2001	48
ISDN subscribers (per 1,000 inhabitants), 2001	42
Cable television subscribers (per 1,000 inhabitants), 2001	69
Internet users (per 1,000 inhabitants), 2001	51
Computers installed in businesses (per 1,000 inhabitants), 2002	38
Firm-level technology absorption, 2003	40
Prevalence of foreign technology licensing, 2003	7
Government success in ICT promotion, 2003	38
Government online services, 2003	58

Bulgaria.bg

Key Indicators

Population, 2002	**7,801,000**
Main telephone lines in operation, 2002	**2,922,028**
growth (%) 1999–2002	3%
Cellular mobile telephone subscribers, 2001	**1,550,000**
growth (%) 1999–2001	343%
Personal computers, 2002	**405,000**
growth (%) 1999–2002	84%
Internet users, (estimated), 2002	**700,000**
growth (%) 1999–2002	198%

Source: Data from International Telecommunication Union

RANK/102

Environment Component Index	**69**
Market Environment	74
Political and Regulatory Environment	85
Infrastructure Environment	60
State of cluster development, 2003	77
Venture capital availability, 2003	75
Subsidies for firm-level R&D, 2003	77
Quality of scientific research institutions, 2003	70
Availability of scientists and engineers, 2003	31
Brain drain, 2003	91
Utility patents granted (per 1,000,000 inhabitants), 2002	50
ICT manufactured exports (per capita), 2001	61
ICT service exports (per capita), 2001	48
Overall administrative burden, 2003	65
Quality of the legal system, 2003	78
Laws relating to ICT, 2003	70
Competition in the ISP sector, 2003	70
Foreign ownership restrictions, 2003	94
Efficiency of the tax system, 2003	89
Freedom of the press, 2003	78
Overall infrastructure quality, 2003	74
Waiting time for telephone lines (years), 2000	81
Telephone mainlines (per 1,000 inhabitants), 2001	34
Public pay telephones (per 1,000 inhabitants), 2001	46
Internet servers (per 1,000,000 inhabitants), 2001	54

Networked Readiness Index Rank

2003–2004 (102 countries) **67**

2002–2003 (82 countries)	68
2001–2002 (75 countries)	53

Readiness Component Index	**60**
Individual Readiness	40
Business Readiness	70
Government Readiness	76
Public expenditure on education (per capita), 2000	63
Adult illiteracy (%), 2001	25
Tertiary enrollment (gross %), 2001 or most recent available	35
Radios (per 1,000 inhabitants), 2001 or most recent available	38
Television sets (per 1,000 inhabitants), 2001	31
Households online (as % of households with computers), 2002	85
Quality of math and science education, 2003	29
Affordability of local fixed line calls (as % of per capita GDP), 2001	73
Affordability of Internet telephone access (as % of per capita GDP), 2001	2
Affordability of Internet service provider fees (as % of per capita GDP), 2001	38
Ease of obtaining telephone lines, 2003	72
Cost of business telephone monthly subscription (as % of per capita GDP), 2002	50
Extent of staff training, 2003	91
Quality of business schools, 2003	87
Scientists and engineers in R&D (per 1,000 inhabitants), 2000	38
Government prioritization of ICT, 2003	88
Government online presence, 2003	56
Government procurement of ICT, 2003	79

Usage Component Index	**68**
Individual Usage	43
Business Usage	87
Government Usage	75
Personal computers (per 1,000 inhabitants), 2001	54
ISDN subscribers (per 1,000 inhabitants), 2001	50
Cable television subscribers (per 1,000 inhabitants), 2001	24
Internet users (per 1,000 inhabitants), 2001	44
Computers installed in businesses (per 1,000 inhabitants), 2002	48
Firm-level technology absorption, 2003	95
Prevalence of foreign technology licensing, 2003	91
Government success in ICT promotion, 2003	85
Government online services, 2003	54

Cameroon.cm

Key Indicators

Population, 2002	15,752,000
Main telephone lines in operation, 2001	101,442
growth (%) 1999–2001	7%
Cellular mobile telephone subscribers, 2002	563,000
growth (%) 1999–2002	9283%
Personal computers, 2001	60,000
growth (%) 1999–2001	50%
Internet users (estimated), 2001	45,000
growth (%) 1999–2001	125%

Source: Data from International Telecommunication Union

Networked Readiness Index Rank
2003–2004 (102 countries) **83**

Readiness Component Index	79
Individual Readiness	86
Business Readiness	90
Government Readiness	51
Public expenditure on education (per capita), 2000	89
Adult illiteracy (%), 2001	82
Tertiary enrollment (gross %), 2001 or most recent available	83
Radios (per 1,000 inhabitants), 2001 or most recent available	87
Television sets (per 1,000 inhabitants), 2001	89
Households online (as % of households with computers), 2002	69
Quality of math and science education, 2003	61
Affordability of local fixed line calls (as % of per capita GDP), 2001	89
Affordability of Internet telephone access (as % of per capita GDP), 2001	80
Affordability of Internet service provider fees (as % of per capita GDP), 2001	94
Ease of obtaining telephone lines, 2003	98
Cost of business telephone monthly subscription (as % of per capita GDP), 2002	65
Extent of staff training, 2003	85
Quality of business schools, 2003	76
Scientists and engineers in R&D (per 1,000 inhabitants), 2000	74
Government prioritization of ICT, 2003	46
Government online presence, 2003	69
Government procurement of ICT, 2003	22

RANK/102

Environment Component Index	83
Market Environment	66
Political and Regulatory Environment	83
Infrastructure Environment	89
State of cluster development, 2003	94
Venture capital availability, 2003	78
Subsidies for firm-level R&D, 2003	49
Quality of scientific research institutions, 2003	50
Availability of scientists and engineers, 2003	36
Brain drain, 2003	80
Utility patents granted (per 1,000,000 inhabitants), 2002	72
ICT manufactured exports (per capita), 2001	100
ICT service exports (per capita), 2001	67
Overall administrative burden, 2003	79
Quality of the legal system, 2003	72
Laws relating to ICT, 2003	87
Competition in the ISP sector, 2003	68
Foreign ownership restrictions, 2003	49
Efficiency of the tax system, 2003	73
Freedom of the press, 2003	92
Overall infrastructure quality, 2003	84
Waiting time for telephone lines (years), 2000	92
Telephone mainlines (per 1,000 inhabitants), 2001	91
Public pay telephones (per 1,000 inhabitants), 2001	38
Internet servers (per 1,000,000 inhabitants), 2001	74

Usage Component Index	86
Individual Usage	82
Business Usage	86
Government Usage	80
Personal computers (per 1,000 inhabitants), 2001	91
ISDN subscribers (per 1,000 inhabitants), 2001	73
Cable television subscribers (per 1,000 inhabitants), 2001	64
Internet users (per 1,000 inhabitants), 2001	90
Computers installed in businesses (per 1,000 inhabitants), 2002	85
Firm-level technology absorption, 2003	84
Prevalence of foreign technology licensing, 2003	88
Government success in ICT promotion, 2003	73
Government online services, 2003	81

Canada.ca

Key Indicators

Population, 2002	**31,414,000**
Main telephone lines in operation, 2002	**19,962,070**
growth (%) 1999–2002	0%
Cellular mobile telephone subscribers, 2002	**11,849,020**
growth (%) 1999–2002	71%
Personal computers, 2002	**15,300,000**
growth (%) 1999–2002	38%
Internet users (estimated), 2002	**15,200,000**
growth (%) 1999–2002	38%

Source: Data from International Telecommunication Union

RANK/102

Environment Component Index — 7

Market Environment	11
Political and Regulatory Environment	21
Infrastructure Environment	4
State of cluster development, 2003	12
Venture capital availability, 2003	11
Subsidies for firm-level R&D, 2003	5
Quality of scientific research institutions, 2003	13
Availability of scientists and engineers, 2003	5
Brain drain, 2003	26
Utility patents granted (per 1,000,000 inhabitants), 2002	9
ICT manufactured exports (per capita), 2001	17
ICT service exports (per capita), 2001	18
Overall administrative burden, 2003	34
Quality of the legal system, 2003	20
Laws relating to ICT, 2003	16
Competition in the ISP sector, 2003	10
Foreign ownership restrictions, 2003	55
Efficiency of the tax system, 2003	53
Freedom of the press, 2003	19
Overall infrastructure quality, 2003	14
Waiting time for telephone lines (years), 2000	1
Telephone mainlines (per 1,000 inhabitants), 2001	5
Public pay telephones (per 1,000 inhabitants), 2001	15
Internet servers (per 1,000,000 inhabitants), 2001	5

Networked Readiness Index Rank

2003–2004 (102 countries) **6**

2002–2003 (82 countries)	6
2001–2002 (75 countries)	12

Readiness Component Index — 8

Individual Readiness	9
Business Readiness	10
Government Readiness	5
Public expenditure on education (per capita), 2000	12
Adult illiteracy (%), 2001	37
Tertiary enrollment (gross %), 2001 or most recent available	12
Radios (per 1,000 inhabitants), 2001 or most recent available	10
Television sets (per 1,000 inhabitants), 2001	10
Households online (as % of households with computers), 2002	12
Quality of math and science education, 2003	13
Affordability of local fixed line calls (as % of per capita GDP), 2001	21
Affordability of Internet telephone access (as % of per capita GDP), 2001	65
Affordability of Internet service provider fees (as % of per capita GDP), 2001	10
Ease of obtaining telephone lines, 2003	12
Cost of business telephone monthly subscription (as % of per capita GDP), 2002	32
Extent of staff training, 2003	17
Quality of business schools, 2003	3
Scientists and engineers in R&D (per 1,000 inhabitants), 2000	12
Government prioritization of ICT, 2003	19
Government online presence, 2003	1
Government procurement of ICT, 2003	16

Usage Component Index — 6

Individual Usage	11
Business Usage	12
Government Usage	3
Personal computers (per 1,000 inhabitants), 2001	10
ISDN subscribers (per 1,000 inhabitants), 2001	36
Cable television subscribers (per 1,000 inhabitants), 2001	5
Internet users (per 1,000 inhabitants), 2001	9
Computers installed in businesses (per 1,000 inhabitants), 2002	8
Firm-level technology absorption, 2003	18
Prevalence of foreign technology licensing, 2003	52
Government success in ICT promotion, 2003	17
Government online services, 2003	4

Chad.td

Key Indicators

Population, 2002	7,871,778
Main telephone lines in operation, 2002	11,835
growth (%) 1999–2002	22%
Cellular mobile telephone subscribers, 2002	34,200
growth (%) 1999–2002	n/a
Personal computers, 2001	12,000
growth (%) 1999–2001	20%
Internet users (estimated), 2002	15,000
growth (%) 1999–2002	1,400%

Source: Data from International Telecommunication Union

RANK/102

Environment Component Index	99
Market Environment	99
Political and Regulatory Environment	101
Infrastructure Environment	86
State of cluster development, 2003	89
Venture capital availability, 2003	102
Subsidies for firm-level R&D, 2003	83
Quality of scientific research institutions, 2003	100
Availability of scientists and engineers, 2003	99
Brain drain, 2003	66
Utility patents granted (per 1,000,000 inhabitants), 2002	72
ICT manufactured exports (per capita), 2001	93
ICT service exports (per capita), 2001	90
Overall administrative burden, 2003	43
Quality of the legal system, 2003	96
Laws relating to ICT, 2003	93
Competition in the ISP sector, 2003	101
Foreign ownership restrictions, 2003	97
Efficiency of the tax system, 2003	97
Freedom of the press, 2003	95
Overall infrastructure quality, 2003	102
Waiting time for telephone lines (years), 2000	43
Telephone mainlines (per 1,000 inhabitants), 2001	102
Public pay telephones (per 1,000 inhabitants), 2001	102
Internet servers (per 1,000,000 inhabitants), 2001	86

Networked Readiness Index Rank

2003–2004 (102 countries) 102

Readiness Component Index	102
Individual Readiness	101
Business Readiness	101
Government Readiness	102
Public expenditure on education (per capita), 2000	101
Adult illiteracy (%), 2001	96
Tertiary enrollment (gross %), 2001 or most recent available	98
Radios (per 1,000 inhabitants), 2001 or most recent available	75
Television sets (per 1,000 inhabitants), 2001	102
Households online (as % of households with computers), 2002	82
Quality of math and science education, 2003	100
Affordability of local fixed line calls (as % of per capita GDP), 20—	101
Affordability of Internet telephone access (as % of per capita GDP), 2001	101
Affordability of Internet service provider fees (as % of per capita GDP), 2001	97
Ease of obtaining telephone lines, 2003	95
Cost of business telephone monthly subscription (as % of per capita GDP), 2002	97
Extent of staff training, 2003	97
Quality of business schools, 2003	101
Scientists and engineers in R&D (per 1,000 inhabitants), 2000	99
Government prioritization of ICT, 2003	96
Government online presence, 2003	102
Government procurement of ICT, 2003	99

Usage Component Index	101
Individual Usage	101
Business Usage	100
Government Usage	101
Personal computers (per 1,000 inhabitants), 2001	98
ISDN subscribers (per 1,000 inhabitants), 2001	89
Cable television subscribers (per 1,000 inhabitants), 2001	96
Internet users (per 1,000 inhabitants), 2001	101
Computers installed in businesses (per 1,000 inhabitants), 2002	82
Firm-level technology absorption, 2003	99
Prevalence of foreign technology licensing, 2003	100
Government success in ICT promotion, 2003	98
Government online services, 2003	99

Chile.cl

Key Indicators

Population, 2002	15,050,340
Main telephone lines in operation, 2002	3,467,202
growth (%) 1999–2002	12%
Cellular mobile telephone subscribers, 2002	6,445,698
growth (%) 1999–2002	185%
Personal computers, 2002	1,795,814
growth (%) 1999–2002	56%
Internet users (estimated), 2002	3,575,000
growth (%) 1999–2002	472%

Source: Data from International Telecommunication Union

RANK/102

Environment Component Index	31
Market Environment	31
Political and Regulatory Environment	18
Infrastructure Environment	36
State of cluster development, 2003	65
Venture capital availability, 2003	37
Subsidies for firm-level R&D, 2003	44
Quality of scientific research institutions, 2003	48
Availability of scientists and engineers, 2003	39
Brain drain, 2003	3
Utility patents granted (per 1,000,000 inhabitants), 2002	45
ICT manufactured exports (per capita), 2001	65
ICT service exports (per capita), 2001	43
Overall administrative burden, 2003	30
Quality of the legal system, 2003	38
Laws relating to ICT, 2003	30
Competition in the ISP sector, 2003	13
Foreign ownership restrictions, 2003	10
Efficiency of the tax system, 2003	19
Freedom of the press, 2003	30
Overall infrastructure quality, 2003	31
Waiting time for telephone lines (years), 2000	27
Telephone mainlines (per 1,000 inhabitants), 2001	46
Public pay telephones (per 1,000 inhabitants), 2001	33
Internet servers (per 1,000,000 inhabitants), 2001	43

Networked Readiness Index Rank

2003–2004 (102 countries) — 32

2002–2003 (82 countries)	35
2001–2002 (75 countries)	34

Readiness Component Index	30
Individual Readiness	46
Business Readiness	28
Government Readiness	18
Public expenditure on education (per capita), 2000	47
Adult illiteracy (%), 2001	40
Tertiary enrollment (gross %), 2001 or most recent available	38
Radios (per 1,000 inhabitants), 2001 or most recent available	24
Television sets (per 1,000 inhabitants), 2001	51
Households online (as % of households with computers), 2002	51
Quality of math and science education, 2003	67
Affordability of local fixed line calls (as % of per capita GDP), 2001	50
Affordability of Internet telephone access (as % of per capita GDP), 2001	22
Affordability of Internet service provider fees (as % of per capita GDP), 2001	44
Ease of obtaining telephone lines, 2003	15
Cost of business telephone monthly subscription (as % of per capita GDP), 2002	49
Extent of staff training, 2003	36
Quality of business schools, 2003	17
Scientists and engineers in R&D (per 1,000 inhabitants), 2000	62
Government prioritization of ICT, 2003	33
Government online presence, 2003	14
Government procurement of ICT, 2003	55

Usage Component Index	31
Individual Usage	39
Business Usage	27
Government Usage	35
Personal computers (per 1,000 inhabitants), 2001	38
ISDN subscribers (per 1,000 inhabitants), 2001	27
Cable television subscribers (per 1,000 inhabitants), 2001	51
Internet users (per 1,000 inhabitants), 2001	31
Computers installed in businesses (per 1,000 inhabitants), 2002	32
Firm-level technology absorption, 2003	24
Prevalence of foreign technology licensing, 2003	30
Government success in ICT promotion, 2003	41
Government online services, 2003	32

China.cn

Key Indicators

Population, 2002	1,284,530,000
Main telephone lines in operation, 2002	214,420,000
growth (%) 1999–2002	97%
Cellular mobile telephone subscribers, 2002	206,620,000
growth (%) 1999–2002	377%
Personal computers, 2001	25,000,000
growth (%) 1999–2001	61%
Internet users (estimated), 2002	59,100,000
growth (%) 1999–2002	564%

Source: Data from International Telecommunication Union

RANK/102

Environment Component Index	63
Market Environment	44
Political and Regulatory Environment	68
Infrastructure Environment	72
State of cluster development, 2003	30
Venture capital availability, 2003	58
Subsidies for firm-level R&D, 2003	22
Quality of scientific research institutions, 2003	28
Availability of scientists and engineers, 2003	68
Brain drain, 2003	51
Utility patents granted (per 1,000,000 inhabitants), 2002	55
ICT manufactured exports (per capita), 2001	44
ICT service exports (per capita), 2001	87
Overall administrative burden, 2003	21
Quality of the legal system, 2003	62
Laws relating to ICT, 2003	51
Competition in the ISP sector, 2003	52
Foreign ownership restrictions, 2003	81
Efficiency of the tax system, 2003	29
Freedom of the press, 2003	99
Overall infrastructure quality, 2003	55
Waiting time for telephone lines (years), 2000	88
Telephone mainlines (per 1,000 inhabitants), 2001	57
Public pay telephones (per 1,000 inhabitants), 2001	48
Internet servers (per 1,000,000 inhabitants), 2001	82

Networked Readiness Index Rank

2003–2004 (102 countries) — 51

2002–2003 (82 countries)	43
2001–2002 (75 countries)	64

Readiness Component Index	54
Individual Readiness	62
Business Readiness	59
Government Readiness	47
Public expenditure on education (per capita), 2000	79
Adult illiteracy (%), 2001	69
Tertiary enrollment (gross %), 2001 or most recent available	78
Radios (per 1,000 inhabitants), 2001 or most recent available	62
Television sets (per 1,000 inhabitants), 2001	46
Households online (as % of households with computers), 2002	89
Quality of math and science education, 2003	46
Affordability of local fixed line calls (as % of per capita GDP), 2001	77
Affordability of Internet telephone access (as % of per capita GDP, 2001	30
Affordability of Internet service provider fees (as % of per capita GDP, 2001	49
Ease of obtaining telephone lines, 2003	57
Cost of business telephone monthly subscription (as % of per capita GDP), 2002	70
Extent of staff training, 2003	55
Quality of business schools, 2003	72
Scientists and engineers in R&D (per 1,000 inhabitants), 2000	51
Government prioritization of ICT, 2003	32
Government online presence, 2003	76
Government procurement of ICT, 2003	9

Usage Component Index	43
Individual Usage	55
Business Usage	69
Government Usage	21
Personal computers (per 1,000 inhabitants), 2001	71
ISDN subscribers (per 1,000 inhabitants), 2001	53
Cable television subscribers (per 1,000 inhabitants), 2001	45
Internet users (per 1,000 inhabitants), 2001	63
Computers installed in businesses (per 1,000 inhabitants), 2002	65
Firm-level technology absorption, 2003	58
Prevalence of foreign technology licensing, 2003	70
Government success in ICT promotion, 2003	24
Government online services, 2003	18

Colombia.co

Key Indicators

Population, 2002	43,290,000
Main telephone lines in operation, 2002	7,766,000
growth (%) 1999–2002	17%
Cellular mobile telephone subscribers, 2002	4,597,000
growth (%) 1999–2002	134%
Personal computers, 2002	2,133,000
growth (%) 1999–2002	52%
Internet users (estimated), 2002	1,982,000
growth (%) 1999–2002	198%

Source: Data from International Telecommunication Union

Networked Readiness Index Rank

2003–2004 (102 countries) **60**

2002–2003 (82 countries)	59
2001–2002 (75 countries)	57

Readiness Component Index	45
Individual Readiness	52
Business Readiness	52
Government Readiness	39
Public expenditure on education (per capita), 2000	60
Adult illiteracy (%), 2001	55
Tertiary enrollment (gross %), 2001 or most recent available	55
Radios (per 1,000 inhabitants), 2001 or most recent available	37
Television sets (per 1,000 inhabitants), 2001	51
Households online (as % of households with computers), 2002	91
Quality of math and science education, 2003	58
Affordability of local fixed line calls (as % of per capita GDP), 2001	46
Affordability of Internet telephone access (as % of per capita GDP), 2001	31
Affordability of Internet service provider fees (as % of per capita GDP), 2001	69
Ease of obtaining telephone lines, 2003	48
Cost of business telephone monthly subscription (as % of per capita GDP), 2002	48
Extent of staff training, 2003	52
Quality of business schools, 2003	41
Scientists and engineers in R&D (per 1,000 inhabitants), 2000	86
Government prioritization of ICT, 2003	57
Government online presence, 2003	24
Government procurement of ICT, 2003	64

RANK/102

Environment Component Index	64
Market Environment	68
Political and Regulatory Environment	60
Infrastructure Environment	64
State of cluster development, 2003	58
Venture capital availability, 2003	69
Subsidies for firm-level R&D, 2003	71
Quality of scientific research institutions, 2003	64
Availability of scientists and engineers, 2003	74
Brain drain, 2003	58
Utility patents granted (per 1,000,000 inhabitants), 2002	59
ICT manufactured exports (per capita), 2001	63
ICT service exports (per capita), 2001	86
Overall administrative burden, 2003	64
Quality of the legal system, 2003	70
Laws relating to ICT, 2003	41
Competition in the ISP sector, 2003	45
Foreign ownership restrictions, 2003	79
Efficiency of the tax system, 2003	72
Freedom of the press, 2003	49
Overall infrastructure quality, 2003	66
Waiting time for telephone lines (years), 2000	71
Telephone mainlines (per 1,000 inhabitants), 2001	55
Public pay telephones (per 1,000 inhabitants), 2001	72
Internet servers (per 1,000,000 inhabitants), 2001	59

Usage Component Index	73
Individual Usage	64
Business Usage	71
Government Usage	68
Personal computers (per 1,000 inhabitants), 2001	55
ISDN subscribers (per 1,000 inhabitants), 2001	41
Cable television subscribers (per 1,000 inhabitants), 2001	71
Internet users (per 1,000 inhabitants), 2001	62
Computers installed in businesses (per 1,000 inhabitants), 2002	53
Firm-level technology absorption, 2003	59
Prevalence of foreign technology licensing, 2003	75
Government success in ICT promotion, 2003	56
Government online services, 2003	74

Costa Rica.cr

Key Indicators

Population, 2002	4,143,000
Main telephone lines in operation, 2001	1,037,986
growth (%) 1999–2001	29%
Cellular mobile telephone subscribers, 2002	528,047
growth (%) 1999–2002	282%
Personal computers, 2001	700,000
growth (%) 1999–2001	75%
Internet users (estimated), 2001	384,000
growth (%) 1999–2001	156%

Source: Data from International Telecommunication Union

RANK/102

Environment Component Index	**46**
Market Environment	42
Political and Regulatory Environment	57
Infrastructure Environment	49
State of cluster development, 2003	64
Venture capital availability, 2003	68
Subsidies for firm-level R&D, 2003	75
Quality of scientific research institutions, 2003	30
Availability of scientists and engineers, 2003	34
Brain drain, 2003	9
Utility patents granted (per 1,000,000 inhabitants), 2002	44
ICT manufactured exports (per capita), 2001	29
ICT service exports (per capita), 2001	40
Overall administrative burden, 2003	28
Quality of the legal system, 2003	54
Laws relating to ICT, 2003	62
Competition in the ISP sector, 2003	100
Foreign ownership restrictions, 2003	33
Efficiency of the tax system, 2003	41
Freedom of the press, 2003	21
Overall infrastructure quality, 2003	72
Waiting time for telephone lines (years), 2000	41
Telephone mainlines (per 1,000 inhabitants), 2001	47
Public pay telephones (per 1,000 inhabitants), 2001	27
Internet servers (per 1,000,000 inhabitants), 2001	33

Networked Readiness Index Rank

2003–2004 (102 countries) **49**

2002–2003 (82 countries)	49
2001–2002 (75 countries)	45

Readiness Component Index	**55**
Individual Readiness	49
Business Readiness	58
Government Readiness	64
Public expenditure on education (per capita), 2000	46
Adult illiteracy (%), 2001	41
Tertiary enrollment (gross %), 2001 or most recent available	64
Radios (per 1,000 inhabitants), 2001 or most recent available	20
Television sets (per 1,000 inhabitants), 2001	55
Households online (as % of households with computers), 2002	44
Quality of math and science education, 2003	48
Affordability of local fixed line calls (as % of per capita GDP), 2001	33
Affordability of Internet telephone access (as % of per capita GDP), 2001	6
Affordability of Internet service provider fees (as % of per capita GDP), 2001	39
Ease of obtaining telephone lines, 2003	92
Cost of business telephone monthly subscription (as % of per capita GDP), 2002	41
Extent of staff training, 2003	30
Quality of business schools, 2003	26
Scientists and engineers in R&D (per 1,000 inhabitants), 2000	53
Government prioritization of ICT, 2003	77
Government online presence, 2003	61
Government procurement of ICT, 2003	46

Usage Component Index	**46**
Individual Usage	40
Business Usage	36
Government Usage	77
Personal computers (per 1,000 inhabitants), 2001	28
ISDN subscribers (per 1,000 inhabitants), 2001	60
Cable television subscribers (per 1,000 inhabitants), 2001	36
Internet users (per 1,000 inhabitants), 2001	42
Computers installed in businesses (per 1,000 inhabitants), 2001	47
Firm-level technology absorption, 2003	17
Prevalence of foreign technology licensing, 2003	11
Government success in ICT promotion, 2003	63
Government online services, 2003	81

Croatia.hr

Key Indicators

Source: Data from International Telecommunication Union

Population, 2002	**4,844,000**
Main telephone lines in operation, 2002	**1,879,000**
growth (%) 1999–2002	15%
Cellular mobile telephone subscribers, 2002	**2,278,000**
growth (%) 1999–2002	672%
Personal computers, 2002	**760,000**
growth (%) 1999–2002	153%
Internet users (estimated), 2002	**789,000**
growth (%) 1999–2002	295%

Networked Readiness Index Rank

2003–2004 (102 countries) **48**

2002–2003 (82 countries) 48

RANK/102	
Environment Component Index	**55**
Market Environment	59
Political and Regulatory Environment	80
Infrastructure Environment	39
State of cluster development, 2003	78
Venture capital availability, 2003	65
Subsidies for firm-level R&D, 2003	52
Quality of scientific research institutions, 2003	42
Availability of scientists and engineers, 2003	43
Brain drain, 2003	71
Utility patents granted (per 1,000,000 inhabitants), 2002	32
ICT manufactured exports (per capita), 2001	39
ICT service exports (per capita), 2001	31
Overall administrative burden, 2003	85
Quality of the legal system, 2003	79
Laws relating to ICT, 2003	61
Competition in the ISP sector, 2003	83
Foreign ownership restrictions, 2003	92
Efficiency of the tax system, 2003	38
Freedom of the press, 2003	74
Overall infrastructure quality, 2003	81
Waiting time for telephone lines (years), 2000	56
Telephone mainlines (per 1,000 inhabitants), 2001	33
Public pay telephones (per 1,000 inhabitants), 2001	13
Internet servers (per 1,000,000 inhabitants), 2001	34

Readiness Component Index	**44**
Individual Readiness	43
Business Readiness	53
Government Readiness	41
Public expenditure on education (per capita), 2000	43
Adult illiteracy (%), 2001	28
Tertiary enrollment (gross %), 2001 or most recent available	46
Radios (per 1,000 inhabitants), 2001 or most recent available	61
Television sets (per 1,000 inhabitants), 2001	50
Households online (as % of households with computers), 2002	37
Quality of math and science education, 2003	34
Affordability of local fixed line calls (as % of per capita GDP), 2001	45
Affordability of Internet telephone access (as % of per capita GDP), 2001	16
Affordability of Internet service provider fees (as % of per capita GDP), 2001	41
Ease of obtaining telephone lines, 2003	42
Cost of business telephone monthly subscription (as % of per capita GDP), 2002	45
Extent of staff training, 2003	74
Quality of business schools, 2003	79
Scientists and engineers in R&D (per 1,000 inhabitants), 2000	39
Government prioritization of ICT, 2003	49
Government online presence, 2003	25
Government procurement of ICT, 2003	74

Usage Component Index	**51**
Individual Usage	48
Business Usage	37
Government Usage	64
Personal computers (per 1,000 inhabitants), 2001	41
ISDN subscribers (per 1,000 inhabitants), 2001	32
Cable television subscribers (per 1,000 inhabitants), 2001	54
Internet users (per 1,000 inhabitants), 2001	49
Computers installed in businesses (per 1,000 inhabitants), 2002	40
Firm-level technology absorption, 2003	35
Prevalence of foreign technology licensing, 2003	21
Government success in ICT promotion, 2003	64
Government online services, 2003	63

Czech Republic.cz

Key Indicators

Population, 2002	10,144,000
Main telephone lines in operation, 2001	3,860,843
growth (%) 1999–2001	1%
Cellular mobile telephone subscribers, 2002	8,610,177
growth (%) 1999–2002	343%
Personal computers, 2001	1,500,000
growth (%) 1999–2001	36%
Internet users (estimated), 2002	2,500,000
growth (%) 1999–2002	257%

Source: Data from International Telecommunication Union

RANK/102

Environment Component Index	**34**
Market Environment	37
Political and Regulatory Environment	41
Infrastructure Environment	33
State of cluster development, 2003	76
Venture capital availability, 2003	38
Subsidies for firm-level R&D, 2003	42
Quality of scientific research institutions, 2003	34
Availability of scientists and engineers, 2003	33
Brain drain, 2003	35
Utility patents granted (per 1,000,000 inhabitants), 2002	30
ICT manufactured exports (per capita), 2001	26
ICT service exports (per capita), 2001	27
Overall administrative burden, 2003	57
Quality of the legal system, 2003	46
Laws relating to ICT, 2003	35
Competition in the ISP sector, 2003	47
Foreign ownership restrictions, 2003	35
Efficiency of the tax system, 2003	75
Freedom of the press, 2003	32
Overall infrastructure quality, 2003	38
Waiting time for telephone lines (years), 2000	34
Telephone mainlines (per 1,000 inhabitants), 2001	31
Public pay telephones (per 1,000 inhabitants), 2001	39
Internet servers (per 1,000,000 inhabitants), 2001	26

Networked Readiness Index Rank

2003–2004 (102 countries)	**33**
2002–2003 (82 countries)	28
2001–2002 (75 countries)	28

Readiness Component Index	**33**
Individual Readiness	34
Business Readiness	36
Government Readiness	34
Public expenditure on education (per capita), 2000	33
Adult illiteracy (%), 2001	7
Tertiary enrollment (gross %), 2001 or most recent available	45
Radios (per 1,000 inhabitants), 2001 or most recent available	21
Television sets (per 1,000 inhabitants), 2001	25
Households online (as % of households with computers), 2002	34
Quality of math and science education, 2003	17
Affordability of local fixed line calls (as % of per capita GDP), 2001	43
Affordability of Internet telephone access (as % of per capita GDP), 2001	93
Affordability of Internet service provider fees (as % of per capita GDP), 2001	28
Ease of obtaining telephone lines, 2003	45
Cost of business telephone monthly subscription (as % of per capita GDP), 2002	28
Extent of staff training, 2003	50
Quality of business schools, 2003	44
Scientists and engineers in R&D (per 1,000 inhabitants), 2000	37
Government prioritization of ICT, 2003	62
Government online presence, 2003	21
Government procurement of ICT, 2003	51

Usage Component Index	**35**
Individual Usage	34
Business Usage	30
Government Usage	61
Personal computers (per 1,000 inhabitants), 2001	33
ISDN subscribers (per 1,000 inhabitants), 2001	28
Cable television subscribers (per 1,000 inhabitants), 2001	31
Internet users (per 1,000 inhabitants), 2001	34
Computers installed in businesses (per 1,000 inhabitants), 2002	29
Firm-level technology absorption, 2003	53
Prevalence of foreign technology licensing, 2003	17
Government success in ICT promotion, 2003	77
Government online services, 2003	47

Denmark.dk

Key Indicators

Population, 2002	5,374,255
Main telephone lines in operation, 2002	3,739,247
growth (%) 1999–2002	3%
Cellular mobile telephone subscribers, 2002	4,478,145
growth (%) 1999–2002	70%
Personal computers, 2002	3,100,000
growth (%) 1999–2002	29%
Internet users (estimated), 2002	2,500,000
growth (%) 1999–2002	54%

Source: Data from International Telecommunication Union

Networked Readiness Index Rank

2003–2004 (102 countries) **5**

2002–2003 (82 countries)	8
2001–2002 (75 countries)	7

Environment Component Index	RANK/102 **10**
Market Environment	14
Political and Regulatory Environment	7
Infrastructure Environment	12
State of cluster development, 2003	11
Venture capital availability, 2003	13
Subsidies for firm-level R&D, 2003	32
Quality of scientific research institutions, 2003	7
Availability of scientists and engineers, 2003	11
Brain drain, 2003	24
Utility patents granted (per 1,000,000 inhabitants), 2002	13
ICT manufactured exports (per capita), 2001	10
ICT service exports (per capita), 2001	10
Overall administrative burden, 2003	14
Quality of the legal system, 2003	4
Laws relating to ICT, 2003	4
Competition in the ISP sector, 2003	9
Foreign ownership restrictions, 2003	15
Efficiency of the tax system, 2003	80
Freedom of the press, 2003	1
Overall infrastructure quality, 2003	3
Waiting time for telephone lines (years), 2000	1
Telephone mainlines (per 1,000 inhabitants), 2001	4
Public pay telephones (per 1,000 inhabitants), 2001	76
Internet servers (per 1,000,000 inhabitants), 2001	16

Readiness Component Index	**5**
Individual Readiness	3
Business Readiness	7
Government Readiness	7
Public expenditure on education (per capita), 2000	2
Adult illiteracy (%), 2001	1
Tertiary enrollment (gross %), 2001 or most recent available	15
Radios (per 1,000 inhabitants), 2001 or most recent available	8
Television sets (per 1,000 inhabitants), 2001	4
Households online (as % of households with computers), 2002	5
Quality of math and science education, 2003	28
Affordability of local fixed line calls (as % of per capita GDP), 2001	5
Affordability of Internet telephone access (as % of per capita GDP), 2001	71
Affordability of Internet service provider fees (as % of per capita GDP), 2001	18
Ease of obtaining telephone lines, 2003	8
Cost of business telephone monthly subscription (as % of per capita GDP), 2002	4
Extent of staff training, 2003	1
Quality of business schools, 2003	23
Scientists and engineers in R&D (per 1,000 inhabitants), 2000	9
Government prioritization of ICT, 2003	10
Government online presence, 2003	15
Government procurement of ICT, 2003	13

Usage Component Index	**3**
Individual Usage	5
Business Usage	5
Government Usage	5
Personal computers (per 1,000 inhabitants), 2001	4
ISDN subscribers (per 1,000 inhabitants), 2001	7
Cable television subscribers (per 1,000 inhabitants), 2001	10
Internet users (per 1,000 inhabitants), 2001	2
Computers installed in businesses (per 1,000 inhabitants), 2002	7
Firm-level technology absorption, 2003	13
Prevalence of foreign technology licensing, 2003	16
Government success in ICT promotion, 2003	10
Government online services, 2003	5

Dominican Republic.do

Key Indicators

Population, 2002	8,707,500
Main telephone lines in operation, 2001	955,145
growth (%) 1999–2001	16%
Cellular mobile telephone subscribers, 2001	1,270,082
growth (%) 1999–2001	199%
Personal computers, 2002	n/a
growth (%) 1999–2002	n/a
Internet users (estimated), 2001	186,000
growth (%) 1999–2001	94%

Source: Data from International Telecommunication Union

RANK/102

Environment Component Index	54
Market Environment	73
Political and Regulatory Environment	45
Infrastructure Environment	57
State of cluster development, 2003	82
Venture capital availability, 2003	48
Subsidies for firm-level R&D, 2003	80
Quality of scientific research institutions, 2003	83
Availability of scientists and engineers, 2003	90
Brain drain, 2003	33
Utility patents granted (per 1,000,000 inhabitants), 2002	61
ICT manufactured exports (per capita), 2001	59
ICT service exports (per capita), 2001	63
Overall administrative burden, 2003	46
Quality of the legal system, 2003	60
Laws relating to ICT, 2003	40
Competition in the ISP sector, 2003	42
Foreign ownership restrictions, 2003	21
Efficiency of the tax system, 2003	44
Freedom of the press, 2003	60
Overall infrastructure quality, 2003	44
Waiting time for telephone lines (years), 2000	67
Telephone mainlines (per 1,000 inhabitants), 2001	61
Public pay telephones (per 1,000 inhabitants), 2001	25
Internet servers (per 1,000,000 inhabitants), 2001	66

Networked Readiness Index Rank

2003–2004 (102 countries) — **57**

2002–2003 (82 countries)	57
2001–2002 (75 countries)	47

Readiness Component Index	52
Individual Readiness	64
Business Readiness	48
Government Readiness	49
Public expenditure on education (per capita), 2000	67
Adult illiteracy (%), 2001	73
Tertiary enrollment (gross %), 2001 or most recent available	56
Radios (per 1,000 inhabitants), 2001 or most recent available	84
Television sets (per 1,000 inhabitants), 2001	56
Households online (as % of households with computers), 2002	55
Quality of math and science education, 2003	84
Affordability of local fixed line calls (as % of per capita GDP), 2001	61
Affordability of Internet telephone access (as % of per capita GDP), 2001	57
Affordability of Internet service provider fees (as % of per capita GDP), 2001	50
Ease of obtaining telephone lines, 2003	31
Cost of business telephone monthly subscription (as % of per capita GDP), 2002	68
Extent of staff training, 2003	43
Quality of business schools, 2003	63
Scientists and engineers in R&D (per 1,000 inhabitants), 2000	54
Government prioritization of ICT, 2003	74
Government online presence, 2003	36
Government procurement of ICT, 2003	63

Usage Component Index	66
Individual Usage	52
Business Usage	48
Government Usage	90
Personal computers (per 1,000 inhabitants), 2001	50
ISDN subscribers (per 1,000 inhabitants), 2001	81
Cable television subscribers (per 1,000 inhabitants), 2001	42
Internet users (per 1,000 inhabitants), 2001	67
Computers installed in businesses (per 1,000 inhabitants), 2002	58
Firm-level technology absorption, 2003	33
Prevalence of foreign technology licensing, 2003	31
Government success in ICT promotion, 2003	74
Government online services, 2003	93

Ecuador.ec

Key Indicators

Population, 2002	**12,941,500**
Main telephone lines in operation, 2002	**1,426,188**
growth (%) 1999–2002	26%
Cellular mobile telephone subscribers, 2002	**1,560,861**
growth (%) 1999–2002	307%
Personal computers, 2002	**402,652**
growth (%) 1999–2002	61%
Internet users (estimated), 2002	**503,315**
growth (%) 1999–2002	403%

Source: Data from International Telecommunication Union

Networked Readiness Index Rank

2003–2004 (102 countries) **89**

RANK/102

Environment Component Index	90
Market Environment	91
Political and Regulatory Environment	93
Infrastructure Environment	79
State of cluster development, 2003	71
Venture capital availability, 2003	81
Subsidies for firm-level R&D, 2003	92
Quality of scientific research institutions, 2003	94
Availability of scientists and engineers, 2003	86
Brain drain, 2003	75
Utility patents granted (per 1,000,000 inhabitants), 2002	72
ICT manufactured exports (per capita), 2001	76
ICT service exports (per capita), 2001	76
Overall administrative burden, 2003	88
Quality of the legal system, 2003	94
Laws relating to ICT, 2003	81
Competition in the ISP sector, 2003	90
Foreign ownership restrictions, 2003	91
Efficiency of the tax system, 2003	85
Freedom of the press, 2003	51
Overall infrastructure quality, 2003	78
Waiting time for telephone lines (years), 2000	73
Telephone mainlines (per 1,000 inhabitants), 2001	64
Public pay telephones (per 1,000 inhabitants), 2001	87
Internet servers (per 1,000,000 inhabitants), 2001	69

Readiness Component Index	93
Individual Readiness	81
Business Readiness	91
Government Readiness	97
Public expenditure on education (per capita), 2000	77
Adult illiteracy (%), 2001	57
Tertiary enrollment (gross %), 2001 or most recent available	61
Radios (per 1,000 inhabitants), 2001 or most recent available	50
Television sets (per 1,000 inhabitants), 2001	57
Households online (as % of households with computers), 2002	98
Quality of math and science education, 2003	92
Affordability of local fixed line calls (as % of per capita GDP), 2001	98
Affordability of Internet telephone access (as % of per capita GDP), 2001	33
Affordability of Internet service provider fees (as % of per capita GDP), 2001	56
Ease of obtaining telephone lines, 2003	87
Cost of business telephone monthly subscription (as % of per capita GDP), 2002	76
Extent of staff training, 2003	90
Quality of business schools, 2003	90
Scientists and engineers in R&D (per 1,000 inhabitants), 2000	89
Government prioritization of ICT, 2003	95
Government online presence, 2003	87
Government procurement of ICT, 2003	94

Usage Component Index	83
Individual Usage	62
Business Usage	83
Government Usage	84
Personal computers (per 1,000 inhabitants), 2001	66
ISDN subscribers (per 1,000 inhabitants), 2001	55
Cable television subscribers (per 1,000 inhabitants), 2001	56
Internet users (per 1,000 inhabitants), 2001	65
Computers installed in businesses (per 1,000 inhabitants), 2002	67
Firm-level technology absorption, 2003	90
Prevalence of foreign technology licensing, 2003	80
Government success in ICT promotion, 2003	94
Government online services, 2003	49

Egypt.eg

Key Indicators

Population, 2002	**65,643,000**
Main telephone lines in operation, 2002	**7,430,000**
growth (%) 1999–2002	59%
Cellular mobile telephone subscribers, 2002	**4,494,700**
growth (%) 1999–2002	834%
Personal computers, 2002	**1,120,000**
growth (%) 1999–2002	49%
Internet users (estimated), 2002	**1,500,000**
growth (%) 1999–2002	650%

Source: Data from International Telecommunication Union

RANK/102

Environment Component Index	60
Market Environment	49
Political and Regulatory Environment	66
Infrastructure Environment	65
State of cluster development, 2003	26
Venture capital availability, 2003	44
Subsidies for firm-level R&D, 2003	45
Quality of scientific research institutions, 2003	60
Availability of scientists and engineers, 2003	57
Brain drain, 2003	54
Utility patents granted (per 1,000,000 inhabitants), 2002	64
ICT manufactured exports (per capita), 2001	91
ICT service exports (per capita), 2001	56
Overall administrative burden, 2003	49
Quality of the legal system, 2003	59
Laws relating to ICT, 2003	63
Competition in the ISP sector, 2003	33
Foreign ownership restrictions, 2003	70
Efficiency of the tax system, 2003	57
Freedom of the press, 2003	90
Overall infrastructure quality, 2003	43
Waiting time for telephone lines (years), 2000	70
Telephone mainlines (per 1,000 inhabitants), 2001	64
Public pay telephones (per 1,000 inhabitants), 2001	83
Internet servers (per 1,000,000 inhabitants), 2001	81

Networked Readiness Index Rank

2003–2004 (102 countries) **65**

2002–2003 (82 countries)	65
2001–2002 (75 countries)	60

Readiness Component Index	71
Individual Readiness	72
Business Readiness	60
Government Readiness	77
Public expenditure on education (per capita), 2000	70
Adult illiteracy (%), 2001	92
Tertiary enrollment (gross %), 2001 or most recent available	37
Radios (per 1,000 inhabitants), 2001 or most recent available	62
Television sets (per 1,000 inhabitants), 2001	59
Households online (as % of households with computers), 2002	99
Quality of math and science education, 2003	66
Affordability of local fixed line calls (as % of per capita GDP), 2001	35
Affordability of Internet telephone access (as % of per capita GDP), 2001	25
Affordability of Internet service provider fees (as % of per capita GDP), 2001	52
Ease of obtaining telephone lines, 2003	64
Cost of business telephone monthly subscription (as % of per capita GDP), 2002	38
Extent of staff training, 2003	66
Quality of business schools, 2003	75
Scientists and engineers in R&D (per 1,000 inhabitants), 2000	55
Government prioritization of ICT, 2003	42
Government online presence, 2003	89
Government procurement of ICT, 2003	48

Usage Component Index	63
Individual Usage	77
Business Usage	72
Government Usage	44
Personal computers (per 1,000 inhabitants), 2001	74
ISDN subscribers (per 1,000 inhabitants), 2001	80
Cable television subscribers (per 1,000 inhabitants), 2001	n/a
Internet users (per 1,000 inhabitants), 2001	80
Computers installed in businesses (per 1,000 inhabitants), 2002	70
Firm-level technology absorption, 2003	71
Prevalence of foreign technology licensing, 2003	64
Government success in ICT promotion, 2003	35
Government online services, 2003	44

El Salvador.sv

Key Indicators

Population, 2002	6,457,500
Main telephone lines in operation, 2002	667,699
growth (%) 1999–2002	35%
Cellular mobile telephone subscribers, 2002	888,818
growth (%) 1999–2002	74%
Personal computers, 2001	140,000
growth (%) 1999–2001	40%
Internet users (estimated), 2002	300,000
growth (%) 1999–2002	500%

Source: Data from International Telecommunication Union

Networked Readiness Index Rank

2003–2004 (102 countries) **62**

2002–2003 (82 countries)	63
2001–2002 (75 countries)	55

RANK/102

Environment Component Index	62
Market Environment	92
Political and Regulatory Environment	40
Infrastructure Environment	62
State of cluster development, 2003	87
Venture capital availability, 2003	50
Subsidies for firm-level R&D, 2003	100
Quality of scientific research institutions, 2003	96
Availability of scientists and engineers, 2003	97
Brain drain, 2003	49
Utility patents granted (per 1,000,000 inhabitants), 2002	72
ICT manufactured exports (per capita), 2001	64
ICT service exports (per capita), 2001	62
Overall administrative burden, 2003	29
Quality of the legal system, 2003	75
Laws relating to ICT, 2003	74
Competition in the ISP sector, 2003	43
Foreign ownership restrictions, 2003	50
Efficiency of the tax system, 2003	9
Freedom of the press, 2003	29
Overall infrastructure quality, 2003	50
Waiting time for telephone lines (years), 2000	72
Telephone mainlines (per 1,000 inhabitants), 2001	67
Public pay telephones (per 1,000 inhabitants), 2001	44
Internet servers (per 1,000,000 inhabitants), 2001	64

Readiness Component Index	59
Individual Readiness	69
Business Readiness	55
Government Readiness	53
Public expenditure on education (per capita), 2000	71
Adult illiteracy (%), 2001	76
Tertiary enrollment (gross %), 2001 or most recent available	60
Radios (per 1,000 inhabitants), 2001 or most recent available	45
Television sets (per 1,000 inhabitants), 2001	60
Households online (as % of households with computers), 2002	56
Quality of math and science education, 2003	81
Affordability of local fixed line calls (as % of per capita GDP), 2001	58
Affordability of Internet telephone access (as % of per capita GDP), 2001	44
Affordability of Internet service provider fees (as % of per capita GDP), 2001	62
Ease of obtaining telephone lines, 2003	26
Cost of business telephone monthly subscription (as % of per capita GDP), 2002	73
Extent of staff training, 2003	49
Quality of business schools, 2003	64
Scientists and engineers in R&D (per 1,000 inhabitants), 2000	95
Government prioritization of ICT, 2003	72
Government online presence, 2003	51
Government procurement of ICT, 2003	57

Usage Component Index	67
Individual Usage	61
Business Usage	60
Government Usage	72
Personal computers (per 1,000 inhabitants), 2001	67
ISDN subscribers (per 1,000 inhabitants), 2001	68
Cable television subscribers (per 1,000 inhabitants), 2001	50
Internet users (per 1,000 inhabitants), 2001	83
Computers installed in businesses (per 1,000 inhabitants), 2002	62
Firm-level technology absorption, 2003	52
Prevalence of foreign technology licensing, 2003	58
Government success in ICT promotion, 2003	62
Government online services, 2003	74

Estonia.ee

Key Indicators

Population, 2002	1,355,000
Main telephone lines in operation, 2002	475,000
growth (%) 1999–2002	-8%
Cellular mobile telephone subscribers, 2002	881,000
growth (%) 1999–2002	128%
Personal computers, 2002	285,000
growth (%) 1999–2002	46%
Internet users (estimated), 2002	560,000
growth (%) 1999–2002	180%

Source: Data from International Telecommunication Union

RANK/102

Environment Component Index	25
Market Environment	39
Political and Regulatory Environment	3
Infrastructure Environment	37
State of cluster development, 2003	74
Venture capital availability, 2003	27
Subsidies for firm-level R&D, 2003	55
Quality of scientific research institutions, 2003	31
Availability of scientists and engineers, 2003	52
Brain drain, 2003	38
Utility patents granted (per 1,000,000 inhabitants), 2002	29
ICT manufactured exports (per capita), 2001	24
ICT service exports (per capita), 2001	26
Overall administrative burden, 2003	6
Quality of the legal system, 2003	22
Laws relating to ICT, 2003	6
Competition in the ISP sector, 2003	5
Foreign ownership restrictions, 2003	29
Efficiency of the tax system, 2003	4
Freedom of the press, 2003	20
Overall infrastructure quality, 2003	32
Waiting time for telephone lines (years), 2000	63
Telephone mainlines (per 1,000 inhabitants), 2001	35
Public pay telephones (per 1,000 inhabitants), 2001	63
Internet servers (per 1,000,000 inhabitants), 2001	18

Networked Readiness Index Rank

2003–2004 (102 countries) | 25

2002–2003 (82 countries)	24
2001–2002 (75 countries)	23

Readiness Component Index	22
Individual Readiness	18
Business Readiness	26
Government Readiness	15
Public expenditure on education (per capita), 2000	31
Adult illiteracy (%), 2001	10
Tertiary enrollment (gross %), 2001 or most recent available	17
Radios (per 1,000 inhabitants), 2001 or most recent available	9
Television sets (per 1,000 inhabitants), 2001	13
Households online (as % of households with computers), 2002	31
Quality of math and science education, 2003	15
Affordability of local fixed line calls (as % of per capita GDP), 2001	48
Affordability of Internet telephone access (as % of per capita GDP), 2001	28
Affordability of Internet service provider fees (as % of per capita GDP), 2001	40
Ease of obtaining telephone lines, 2003	27
Cost of business telephone monthly subscription (as % of per capita GDP), 2002	42
Extent of staff training, 2003	40
Quality of business schools, 2003	28
Scientists and engineers in R&D (per 1,000 inhabitants), 2000	25
Government prioritization of ICT, 2003	18
Government online presence, 2003	18
Government procurement of ICT, 2003	33

Usage Component Index	27
Individual Usage	26
Business Usage	39
Government Usage	13
Personal computers (per 1,000 inhabitants), 2001	27
ISDN subscribers (per 1,000 inhabitants), 2001	25
Cable television subscribers (per 1,000 inhabitants), 2001	30
Internet users (per 1,000 inhabitants), 2001	21
Computers installed in businesses (per 1,000 inhabitants), 2002	45
Firm-level technology absorption, 2003	19
Prevalence of foreign technology licensing, 2003	41
Government success in ICT promotion, 2003	12
Government online services, 2003	16

Ethiopia.et

Key Indicators

Population, 2002	**67,347,000**
Main telephone lines in operation, 2002	**368,199**
growth (%) 1999–2002	89%
Cellular mobile telephone subscribers, 2002	**50,369**
growth (%) 1999–2002	647%
Personal computers, 2002	**100,000**
growth (%) 1999–2002	122%
Internet users (estimated), 2002	**50,000**
growth (%) 1999–2002	525%

Source: Data from International Telecommunication Union

RANK/102

Environment Component Index	102
Market Environment	96
Political and Regulatory Environment	102
Infrastructure Environment	99
State of cluster development, 2003	86
Venture capital availability, 2003	90
Subsidies for firm-level R&D, 2003	90
Quality of scientific research institutions, 2003	65
Availability of scientists and engineers, 2003	96
Brain drain, 2003	92
Utility patents granted (per 1,000,000 inhabitants), 2002	72
ICT manufactured exports (per capita), 2001	102
ICT service exports (per capita), 2001	96
Overall administrative burden, 2003	68
Quality of the legal system, 2003	87
Laws relating to ICT, 2003	101
Competition in the ISP sector, 2003	102
Foreign ownership restrictions, 2003	102
Efficiency of the tax system, 2003	76
Freedom of the press, 2003	94
Overall infrastructure quality, 2003	93
Waiting time for telephone lines (years), 2000	96
Telephone mainlines (per 1,000 inhabitants), 2001	95
Public pay telephones (per 1,000 inhabitants), 2001	101
Internet servers (per 1,000,000 inhabitants), 2001	96

Networked Readiness Index Rank

2003–2004 (102 countries) 101

Readiness Component Index	101
Individual Readiness	102
Business Readiness	100
Government Readiness	99
Public expenditure on education (per capita), 2000	102
Adult illiteracy (%), 2001	99
Tertiary enrollment (gross %), 2001 or most recent available	96
Radios (per 1,000 inhabitants), 2001 or most recent available	82
Television sets (per 1,000 inhabitants), 2001	97
Households online (as % of households with computers), 2002	86
Quality of math and science education, 2003	85
Affordability of local fixed line calls (as % of per capita GDP), 2001	95
Affordability of Internet telephone access (as % of per capita GDP), 2001	96
Affordability of Internet service provider fees (as % of per capita GDP), 2001	102
Ease of obtaining telephone lines, 2003	94
Cost of business telephone monthly subscription (as % of per capita GDP), 2002	98
Extent of staff training, 2003	101
Quality of business schools, 2003	97
Scientists and engineers in R&D (per 1,000 inhabitants), 2000	96
Government prioritization of ICT, 2003	86
Government online presence, 2003	100
Government procurement of ICT, 2003	95

Usage Component Index	96
Individual Usage	102
Business Usage	101
Government Usage	92
Personal computers (per 1,000 inhabitants), 2001	102
ISDN subscribers (per 1,000 inhabitants), 2001	97
Cable television subscribers (per 1,000 inhabitants), 2001	n/a
Internet users (per 1,000 inhabitants), 2001	102
Computers installed in businesses (per 1,000 inhabitants), 2002	99
Firm-level technology absorption, 2003	98
Prevalence of foreign technology licensing, 2003	99
Government success in ICT promotion, 2003	84
Government online services, 2003	86

Finland.fi

Key Indicators

Population, 2002	5,207,000
Main telephone lines in operation, 2002	2,850,000
growth (%) 1999–2002	0%
Cellular mobile telephone subscribers, 2002	4,400,000
growth (%) 1999–2002	34%
Personal computers, 2002	2,300,000
growth (%) 1999–2002	24%
Internet users (estimated), 2002	2,650,000
growth (%) 1999–2002	59%

Source: Data from International Telecommunication Union

RANK/102

Environment Component Index	3
Market Environment	3
Political and Regulatory Environment	1
Infrastructure Environment	15
State of cluster development, 2003	1
Venture capital availability, 2003	1
Subsidies for firm-level R&D, 2003	6
Quality of scientific research institutions, 2003	4
Availability of scientists and engineers, 2003	2
Brain drain, 2003	2
Utility patents granted (per 1,000,000 inhabitants), 2002	7
ICT manufactured exports (per capita), 2001	8
ICT service exports (per capita), 2001	15
Overall administrative burden, 2003	3
Quality of the legal system, 2003	1
Laws relating to ICT, 2003	1
Competition in the ISP sector, 2003	6
Foreign ownership restrictions, 2003	7
Efficiency of the tax system, 2003	12
Freedom of the press, 2003	8
Overall infrastructure quality, 2003	5
Waiting time for telephone lines (years), 2000	1
Telephone mainlines (per 1,000 inhabitants), 2001	14
Public pay telephones (per 1,000 inhabitants), 2001	65
Internet servers (per 1,000,000 inhabitants), 2001	11

Networked Readiness Index Rank

2003–2004 (102 countries) **3**

2002–2003 (82 countries)	1
2001–2002 (75 countries)	3

Readiness Component Index	1
Individual Readiness	4
Business Readiness	1
Government Readiness	2
Public expenditure on education (per capita), 2000	6
Adult illiteracy (%), 2001	1
Tertiary enrollment (gross %), 2001 or most recent available	1
Radios (per 1,000 inhabitants), 2001 or most recent available	5
Television sets (per 1,000 inhabitants), 2001	11
Households online (as % of households with computers), 2002	11
Quality of math and science education, 2003	4
Affordability of local fixed line calls (as % of per capita GDP), 2001	18
Affordability of Internet telephone access (as % of per capita GDP), 2001	51
Affordability of Internet service provider fees (as % of per capita GDP), 2001	15
Ease of obtaining telephone lines, 2003	1
Cost of business telephone monthly subscription (as % of per capita GDP), 2002	6
Extent of staff training, 2003	7
Quality of business schools, 2003	6
Scientists and engineers in R&D (per 1,000 inhabitants), 2000	2
Government prioritization of ICT, 2003	3
Government online presence, 2003	12
Government procurement of ICT, 2003	4

Usage Component Index	9
Individual Usage	10
Business Usage	11
Government Usage	8
Personal computers (per 1,000 inhabitants), 2001	12
ISDN subscribers (per 1,000 inhabitants), 2001	10
Cable television subscribers (per 1,000 inhabitants), 2001	12
Internet users (per 1,000 inhabitants), 2001	11
Computers installed in businesses (per 1,000 inhabitants), 2002	13
Firm-level technology absorption, 2003	1
Prevalence of foreign technology licensing, 2003	47
Government success in ICT promotion, 2003	5
Government online services, 2003	20

France.fr

Key Indicators

Population, 2002	59,637,000
Main telephone lines in operation, 2002	33,928,740
growth (%) 1999–2002	0%
Cellular mobile telephone subscribers, 2002	38,585,300
growth (%) 1999–2002	80%
Personal computers, 2002	20,700,000
growth (%) 1999–2002	32%
Internet users (estimated), 2002	18,716,000
growth (%) 1999–2002	249%

Source: Data from International Telecommunication Union

RANK/102

Environment Component Index — 23

Market Environment	17
Political and Regulatory Environment	32
Infrastructure Environment	14
State of cluster development, 2003	19
Venture capital availability, 2003	14
Subsidies for firm-level R&D, 2003	8
Quality of scientific research institutions, 2003	8
Availability of scientists and engineers, 2003	4
Brain drain, 2003	40
Utility patents granted (per 1,000,000 inhabitants), 2002	16
ICT manufactured exports (per capita), 2001	14
ICT service exports (per capita), 2001	17
Overall administrative burden, 2003	90
Quality of the legal system, 2003	42
Laws relating to ICT, 2003	13
Competition in the ISP sector, 2003	24
Foreign ownership restrictions, 2003	19
Efficiency of the tax system, 2003	79
Freedom of the press, 2003	25
Overall infrastructure quality, 2003	6
Waiting time for telephone lines (years), 2000	1
Telephone mainlines (per 1,000 inhabitants), 2001	13
Public pay telephones (per 1,000 inhabitants), 2001	35
Internet servers (per 1,000,000 inhabitants), 2001	25

Networked Readiness Index Rank

2003–2004 (102 countries) — 19

2002–2003 (82 countries)	19
2001–2002 (75 countries)	24

Readiness Component Index — 7

Individual Readiness	11
Business Readiness	11
Government Readiness	4
Public expenditure on education (per capita), 2000	10
Adult illiteracy (%), 2001	17
Tertiary enrollment (gross %), 2001 or most recent available	21
Radios (per 1,000 inhabitants), 2001 or most recent available	17
Television sets (per 1,000 inhabitants), 2001	12
Households online (as % of households with computers), 2002	17
Quality of math and science education, 2003	3
Affordability of local fixed line calls (as % of per capita GDP), 2001	28
Affordability of Internet telephone access (as % of per capita GDP), 2001	62
Affordability of Internet service provider fees (as % of per capita GDP), 2001	25
Ease of obtaining telephone lines, 2003	9
Cost of business telephone monthly subscription (as % of per capita GDP), 2002	15
Extent of staff training, 2003	15
Quality of business schools, 2003	2
Scientists and engineers in R&D (per 1,000 inhabitants), 2000	14
Government prioritization of ICT, 2003	26
Government online presence, 2003	3
Government procurement of ICT, 2003	6

Usage Component Index — 25

Individual Usage	24
Business Usage	23
Government Usage	16
Personal computers (per 1,000 inhabitants), 2001	19
ISDN subscribers (per 1,000 inhabitants), 2001	17
Cable television subscribers (per 1,000 inhabitants), 2001	47
Internet users (per 1,000 inhabitants), 2001	27
Computers installed in businesses (per 1,000 inhabitants), 2002	21
Firm-level technology absorption, 2003	27
Prevalence of foreign technology licensing, 2003	55
Government success in ICT promotion, 2003	26
Government online services, 2003	14

Gambia.gm

Key Indicators

Population, 2002	1,372,000
Main telephone lines in operation, 2002	38,350
growth (%) 1999–2002	31%
Cellular mobile telephone subscribers, 2002	100,000
growth (%) 1999–2002	1,784%
Personal computers, 2001	17,000
growth (%) 1999–2001	70%
Internet users (estimated), 2001	18,000
growth (%) 1999–2001	100%

Source: Data from International Telecommunication Union

RANK/102

Environment Component Index — 70

Market Environment	94
Political and Regulatory Environment	30
Infrastructure Environment	90
State of cluster development, 2003	68
Venture capital availability, 2003	79
Subsidies for firm-level R&D, 2003	89
Quality of scientific research institutions, 2003	87
Availability of scientists and engineers, 2003	100
Brain drain, 2003	89
Utility patents granted (per 1,000,000 inhabitants), 2002	72
ICT manufactured exports (per capita), 2001	99
ICT service exports (per capita), 2001	91
Overall administrative burden, 2003	8
Quality of the legal system, 2003	30
Laws relating to ICT, 2003	83
Competition in the ISP sector, 2003	46
Foreign ownership restrictions, 2003	14
Efficiency of the tax system, 2003	13
Freedom of the press, 2003	71
Overall infrastructure quality, 2003	53
Waiting time for telephone lines (years), 2000	91
Telephone mainlines (per 1,000 inhabitants), 2001	83
Public pay telephones (per 1,000 inhabitants), 2001	85
Internet servers (per 1,000,000 inhabitants), 2001	89

Networked Readiness Index Rank

2003–2004 (102 countries) — 82

Readiness Component Index — 92

Individual Readiness	100
Business Readiness	79
Government Readiness	79
Public expenditure on education (per capita), 2000	95
Adult illiteracy (%), 2001	101
Tertiary enrollment (gross %), 2001 or most recent available	95
Radios (per 1,000 inhabitants), 2001 or most recent available	54
Television sets (per 1,000 inhabitants), 2001	101
Households online (as % of households with computers), 2002	80
Quality of math and science education, 2003	83
Affordability of local fixed line calls (as % of per capita GDP), 2001	93
Affordability of Internet telephone access (as % of per capita GDP), 2001	102
Affordability of Internet service provider fees (as % of per capita GDP), 2001	90
Ease of obtaining telephone lines, 2003	67
Cost of business telephone monthly subscription (as % of per capita GDP), 2002	87
Extent of staff training, 2003	82
Quality of business schools, 2003	88
Scientists and engineers in R&D (per 1,000 inhabitants), 2000	75
Government prioritization of ICT, 2003	13
Government online presence, 2003	92
Government procurement of ICT, 2003	81

Usage Component Index — 74

Individual Usage	87
Business Usage	77
Government Usage	55
Personal computers (per 1,000 inhabitants), 2001	78
ISDN subscribers (per 1,000 inhabitants), 2001	90
Cable television subscribers (per 1,000 inhabitants), 2001	94
Internet users (per 1,000 inhabitants), 2001	73
Computers installed in businesses (per 1,000 inhabitants), 2002	61
Firm-level technology absorption, 2003	42
Prevalence of foreign technology licensing, 2003	90
Government success in ICT promotion, 2003	9
Government online services, 2003	96

Germany.de

Key Indicators

Population, 2002	**82,600,000**
Main telephone lines in operation, 2002	**53,720,000**
growth (%) 1999–2002	11%
Cellular mobile telephone subscribers, 2002	**59,200,000**
growth (%) 1999–2002	152%
Personal computers, 2002	**35,920,940**
growth (%) 1999–2002	47%
Internet users (estimated), 2002	**35,000,000**
growth (%) 1999–2002	105%

Source: Data from International Telecommunication Union

RANK/102

Environment Component Index — 17

Market Environment	15
Political and Regulatory Environment	17
Infrastructure Environment	13
State of cluster development, 2003	16
Venture capital availability, 2003	30
Subsidies for firm-level R&D, 2003	19
Quality of scientific research institutions, 2003	12
Availability of scientists and engineers, 2003	18
Brain drain, 2003	28
Utility patents granted (per 1,000,000 inhabitants), 2002	8
ICT manufactured exports (per capita), 2001	15
ICT service exports (per capita), 2001	16
Overall administrative burden, 2003	24
Quality of the legal system, 2003	8
Laws relating to ICT, 2003	14
Competition in the ISP sector, 2003	11
Foreign ownership restrictions, 2003	11
Efficiency of the tax system, 2003	102
Freedom of the press, 2003	4
Overall infrastructure quality, 2003	4
Waiting time for telephone lines (years), 2000	1
Telephone mainlines (per 1,000 inhabitants), 2001	7
Public pay telephones (per 1,000 inhabitants), 2001	75
Internet servers (per 1,000,000 inhabitants), 2001	17

Networked Readiness Index Rank

2003–2004 (102 countries) — 11

2002–2003 (82 countries)	10
2001–2002 (75 countries)	17

Readiness Component Index — 12

Individual Readiness	19
Business Readiness	9
Government Readiness	8
Public expenditure on education (per capita), 2000	17
Adult illiteracy (%), 2001	17
Tertiary enrollment (gross %), 2001 or most recent available	31
Radios (per 1,000 inhabitants), 2001 or most recent available	36
Television sets (per 1,000 inhabitants), 2001	16
Households online (as % of households with computers), 2002	6
Quality of math and science education, 2003	53
Affordability of local fixed line calls (as % of per capita GDP), 2001	12
Affordability of Internet telephone access (as % of per capita GDP), 2001	60
Affordability of Internet service provider fees (as % of per capita GDP), 2001	12
Ease of obtaining telephone lines, 2003	10
Cost of business telephone monthly subscription (as % of per capita GDP), 2002	8
Extent of staff training, 2003	4
Quality of business schools, 2003	19
Scientists and engineers in R&D (per 1,000 inhabitants), 2000	11
Government prioritization of ICT, 2003	38
Government online presence, 2003	2
Government procurement of ICT, 2003	14

Usage Component Index — 10

Individual Usage	6
Business Usage	16
Government Usage	12
Personal computers (per 1,000 inhabitants), 2001	16
ISDN subscribers (per 1,000 inhabitants), 2001	4
Cable television subscribers (per 1,000 inhabitants), 2001	6
Internet users (per 1,000 inhabitants), 2001	14
Computers installed in businesses (per 1,000 inhabitants), 2002	20
Firm-level technology absorption, 2003	11
Prevalence of foreign technology licensing, 2003	38
Government success in ICT promotion, 2003	37
Government online services, 2003	6

Ghana.gh

Key Indicators

Population, 2002	21,674,000
Main telephone lines in operation, 2001	242,122
growth (%) 1999–2001	53%
Cellular mobile telephone subscribers, 2002	405,000
growth (%) 1999–2002	478%
Personal computers, 2001	70,000
growth (%) 1999–2001	40%
Internet users (estimated), 2001	40,520
growth (%) 1999–2001	103%

Source: Data from International Telecommunication Union

Networked Readiness Index Rank

2003–2004 (102 countries) | 74

RANK/102

Environment Component Index	67
Market Environment	72
Political and Regulatory Environment	39
Infrastructure Environment	83
State of cluster development, 2003	55
Venture capital availability, 2003	72
Subsidies for firm-level R&D, 2003	62
Quality of scientific research institutions, 2003	40
Availability of scientists and engineers, 2003	80
Brain drain, 2003	96
Utility patents granted (per 1,000,000 inhabitants), 2002	72
ICT manufactured exports (per capita), 2001	98
ICT service exports (per capita), 2001	97
Overall administrative burden, 2003	27
Quality of the legal system, 2003	50
Laws relating to ICT, 2003	53
Competition in the ISP sector, 2003	65
Foreign ownership restrictions, 2003	34
Efficiency of the tax system, 2003	22
Freedom of the press, 2003	43
Overall infrastructure quality, 2003	71
Waiting time for telephone lines (years), 2000	75
Telephone mainlines (per 1,000 inhabitants), 2001	87
Public pay telephones (per 1,000 inhabitants), 2001	89
Internet servers (per 1,000,000 inhabitants), 2001	95

Readiness Component Index	74
Individual Readiness	82
Business Readiness	75
Government Readiness	58
Public expenditure on education (per capita), 2000	87
Adult illiteracy (%), 2001	81
Tertiary enrollment (gross %), 2001 or most recent available	89
Radios (per 1,000 inhabitants), 2001 or most recent available	27
Television sets (per 1,000 inhabitants), 2001	77
Households online (as % of households with computers), 2002	76
Quality of math and science education, 2003	70
Affordability of local fixed line calls (as % of per capita GDP), 2001	87
Affordability of Internet telephone access (as % of per capita GDP), 2001	87
Affordability of Internet service provider fees (as % of per capita GDP), 2001	91
Ease of obtaining telephone lines, 2003	91
Cost of business telephone monthly subscription (as % of per capita GDP), 2002	35
Extent of staff training, 2003	72
Quality of business schools, 2003	59
Scientists and engineers in R&D (per 1,000 inhabitants), 2000	44
Government prioritization of ICT, 2003	17
Government online presence, 2003	88
Government procurement of ICT, 2003	19

Usage Component Index	80
Individual Usage	96
Business Usage	73
Government Usage	67
Personal computers (per 1,000 inhabitants), 2001	93
ISDN subscribers (per 1,000 inhabitants), 2001	94
Cable television subscribers (per 1,000 inhabitants), 2001	90
Internet users (per 1,000 inhabitants), 2001	95
Computers installed in businesses (per 1,000 inhabitants), 2002	90
Firm-level technology absorption, 2003	57
Prevalence of foreign technology licensing, 2003	71
Government success in ICT promotion, 2003	22
Government online services, 2003	96

Greece.gr

Key Indicators

Population, 2002	11,018,000
Main telephone lines in operation, 2001	5,607,726
growth (%) 1999–2001	0%
Cellular mobile telephone subscribers, 2002	9,314,260
growth (%) 1999–2002	139%
Personal computers, 2001	860,000
growth (%) 1999–2001	34%
Internet users (estimated), 2002	1,704,936
growth (%) 1999–2002	127%

Networked Readiness Index Rank

2003–2004 (102 countries) **34**

2002–2003 (82 countries)	42
2001–2002 (75 countries)	31

RANK/102

Environment Component Index	32
Market Environment	36
Political and Regulatory Environment	48
Infrastructure Environment	24
State of cluster development, 2003	61
Venture capital availability, 2003	35
Subsidies for firm-level R&D, 2003	26
Quality of scientific research institutions, 2003	55
Availability of scientists and engineers, 2003	19
Brain drain, 2003	42
Utility patents granted (per 1,000,000 inhabitants), 2002	35
ICT manufactured exports (per capita), 2001	43
ICT service exports (per capita), 2001	35
Overall administrative burden, 2003	75
Quality of the legal system, 2003	35
Laws relating to ICT, 2003	64
Competition in the ISP sector, 2003	39
Foreign ownership restrictions, 2003	54
Efficiency of the tax system, 2003	88
Freedom of the press, 2003	24
Overall infrastructure quality, 2003	49
Waiting time for telephone lines (years), 2000	37
Telephone mainlines (per 1,000 inhabitants), 2001	15
Public pay telephones (per 1,000 inhabitants), 2001	10
Internet servers (per 1,000,000 inhabitants), 2001	38

Readiness Component Index	39
Individual Readiness	27
Business Readiness	34
Government Readiness	69
Public expenditure on education (per capita), 2000	28
Adult illiteracy (%), 2001	36
Tertiary enrollment (gross %), 2001 or most recent available	26
Radios (per 1,000 inhabitants), 2001 or most recent available	45
Television sets (per 1,000 inhabitants), 2001	27
Households online (as % of households with computers), 2002	9
Quality of math and science education, 2003	38
Affordability of local fixed line calls (as % of per capita GDP), 2001	30
Affordability of Internet telephone access (as % of per capita GDP), 2001	52
Affordability of Internet service provider fees (as % of per capita GDP), 2001	27
Ease of obtaining telephone lines, 2003	39
Cost of business telephone monthly subscription (as % of per capita GDP), 2002	16
Extent of staff training, 2003	46
Quality of business schools, 2003	57
Scientists and engineers in R&D (per 1,000 inhabitants), 2000	36
Government prioritization of ICT, 2003	68
Government online presence, 2003	65
Government procurement of ICT, 2003	76

Usage Component Index	38
Individual Usage	32
Business Usage	43
Government Usage	59
Personal computers (per 1,000 inhabitants), 2001	43
ISDN subscribers (per 1,000 inhabitants), 2001	20
Cable television subscribers (per 1,000 inhabitants), 2001	22
Internet users (per 1,000 inhabitants), 2001	35
Computers installed in businesses (per 1,000 inhabitants), 2002	36
Firm-level technology absorption, 2003	78
Prevalence of foreign technology licensing, 2003	10
Government success in ICT promotion, 2003	72
Government online services, 2003	49

Guatemala.gt

Key Indicators

Population, 2002	11,997,000
Main telephone lines in operation, 2002	845,968
growth (%) 1999–2002	39%
Cellular mobile telephone subscribers, 2002	1,577,085
growth (%) 1999–2002	367%
Personal computers, 2001	150,000
growth (%) 1999–2001	36%
Internet users (estimated), 2002	400,000
growth (%) 1999–2002	515%

Source: Data from International Telecommunication Union

RANK/102

Environment Component Index	84
Market Environment	89
Political and Regulatory Environment	91
Infrastructure Environment	74
State of cluster development, 2003	81
Venture capital availability, 2003	67
Subsidies for firm-level R&D, 2003	98
Quality of scientific research institutions, 2003	93
Availability of scientists and engineers, 2003	89
Brain drain, 2003	53
Utility patents granted (per 1,000,000 inhabitants), 2002	72
ICT manufactured exports (per capita), 2001	68
ICT service exports (per capita), 2001	64
Overall administrative burden, 2003	84
Quality of the legal system, 2003	90
Laws relating to ICT, 2003	92
Competition in the ISP sector, 2003	51
Foreign ownership restrictions, 2003	88
Efficiency of the tax system, 2003	95
Freedom of the press, 2003	72
Overall infrastructure quality, 2003	75
Waiting time for telephone lines (years), 2000	82
Telephone mainlines (per 1,000 inhabitants), 2001	71
Public pay telephones (per 1,000 inhabitants), 2001	42
Internet servers (per 1,000,000 inhabitants), 2001	65

Networked Readiness Index Rank

2003–2004 (102 countries) **86**

2002–2003 (82 countries)	73
2001–2002 (75 countries)	68

Readiness Component Index	83
Individual Readiness	85
Business Readiness	65
Government Readiness	95
Public expenditure on education (per capita), 2000	78
Adult illiteracy (%), 2001	84
Tertiary enrollment (gross %), 2001 or most recent available	77
Radios (per 1,000 inhabitants), 2001 or most recent available	98
Television sets (per 1,000 inhabitants), 2001	86
Households online (as % of households with computers), 2002	58
Quality of math and science education, 2003	101
Affordability of local fixed line calls (as % of per capita GDP), 20	72
Affordability of Internet telephone access (as % of per capita GDP), 2001	35
Affordability of Internet service provider fees (as % of per capita GDP), 2001	68
Ease of obtaining telephone lines, 2003	50
Cost of business telephone monthly subscription (as % of per capita GDP), 2002	53
Extent of staff training, 2003	75
Quality of business schools, 2003	66
Scientists and engineers in R&D (per 1,000 inhabitants), 2000	69
Government prioritization of ICT, 2003	102
Government online presence, 2003	63
Government procurement of ICT, 2003	100

Usage Component Index	88
Individual Usage	66
Business Usage	81
Government Usage	93
Personal computers (per 1,000 inhabitants), 2001	77
ISDN subscribers (per 1,000 inhabitants), 2001	75
Cable television subscribers (per 1,000 inhabitants), 2001	55
Internet users (per 1,000 inhabitants), 2001	70
Computers installed in businesses (per 1,000 inhabitants), 2002	66
Firm-level technology absorption, 2003	81
Prevalence of foreign technology licensing, 2003	87
Government success in ICT promotion, 2003	101
Government online services, 2003	49

Haiti.ht

Key Indicators

Population, 2002	8,298,000
Main telephone lines in operation, 2002	130,000
growth (%) 1999–2002	86%
Cellular mobile telephone subscribers, 2002	140,000
growth (%) 1999–2002	460%
Personal computers, 2002	n/a
growth (%) 1999–2002	n/a
Internet users (estimated), 2002	80,000
growth (%) 1999–2002	1,233%

Networked Readiness Index Rank

2003–2004 (102 countries) 100

2002–2003 (82 countries)   82

RANK/102

Environment Component Index	**100**
Market Environment	102
Political and Regulatory Environment	99
Infrastructure Environment	87
State of cluster development, 2003	101
Venture capital availability, 2003	89
Subsidies for firm-level R&D, 2003	101
Quality of scientific research institutions, 2003	102
Availability of scientists and engineers, 2003	94
Brain drain, 2003	102
Utility patents granted (per 1,000,000 inhabitants), 2002	72
ICT manufactured exports (per capita), 2001	85
ICT service exports (per capita), 2001	79
Overall administrative burden, 2003	59
Quality of the legal system, 2003	102
Laws relating to ICT, 2003	102
Competition in the ISP sector, 2003	88
Foreign ownership restrictions, 2003	98
Efficiency of the tax system, 2003	43
Freedom of the press, 2003	84
Overall infrastructure quality, 2003	101
Waiting time for telephone lines (years), 2000	85
Telephone mainlines (per 1,000 inhabitants), 2001	88
Public pay telephones (per 1,000 inhabitants), 2001	24
Internet servers (per 1,000,000 inhabitants), 2001	84

Readiness Component Index	**98**
Individual Readiness	92
Business Readiness	99
Government Readiness	96
Public expenditure on education (per capita), 2000	100
Adult illiteracy (%), 2001	93
Tertiary enrollment (gross %), 2001 or most recent available	97
Radios (per 1,000 inhabitants), 2001 or most recent available	102
Television sets (per 1,000 inhabitants), 2001	97
Households online (as % of households with computers), 2002	72
Quality of math and science education, 2003	98
Affordability of local fixed line calls (as % of per capita GDP), 2001	82
Affordability of Internet telephone access (as % of per capita GDP), 2001	76
Affordability of Internet service provider fees (as % of per capita GDP), 2001	89
Ease of obtaining telephone lines, 2003	101
Cost of business telephone monthly subscription (as % of per capita GDP), 2002	86
Extent of staff training, 2003	99
Quality of business schools, 2003	100
Scientists and engineers in R&D (per 1,000 inhabitants), 2000	83
Government prioritization of ICT, 2003	100
Government online presence, 2003	74
Government procurement of ICT, 2003	93

Usage Component Index	**102**
Individual Usage	85
Business Usage	99
Government Usage	102
Personal computers (per 1,000 inhabitants), 2001	70
ISDN subscribers (per 1,000 inhabitants), 2001	86
Cable television subscribers (per 1,000 inhabitants), 2001	81
Internet users (per 1,000 inhabitants), 2001	88
Computers installed in businesses (per 1,000 inhabitants), 2002	86
Firm-level technology absorption, 2003	89
Prevalence of foreign technology licensing, 2003	101
Government success in ICT promotion, 2003	100
Government online services, 2003	99

Honduras.hn

Key Indicators

Population, 2002	6,712,000
Main telephone lines in operation, 2002	322,497
growth (%) 1999–2002	16%
Cellular mobile telephone subscribers, 2002	326,508
growth (%) 1999–2002	315%
Personal computers, 2001	80,000
growth (%) 1999–2001	33%
Internet users (estimated), 2002	200,000
growth (%) 1999–2002	471%

Source: Data from International Telecommunication Union

RANK/102

Environment Component Index	96
Market Environment	93
Political and Regulatory Environment	90
Infrastructure Environment	97
State of cluster development, 2003	84
Venture capital availability, 2003	91
Subsidies for firm-level R&D, 2003	88
Quality of scientific research institutions, 2003	95
Availability of scientists and engineers, 2003	95
Brain drain, 2003	60
Utility patents granted (per 1,000,000 inhabitants), 2002	52
ICT manufactured exports (per capita), 2001	81
ICT service exports (per capita), 2001	69
Overall administrative burden, 2003	70
Quality of the legal system, 2003	93
Laws relating to ICT, 2003	91
Competition in the ISP sector, 2003	89
Foreign ownership restrictions, 2003	78
Efficiency of the tax system, 2003	68
Freedom of the press, 2003	67
Overall infrastructure quality, 2003	86
Waiting time for telephone lines (years), 2000	95
Telephone mainlines (per 1,000 inhabitants), 2001	75
Public pay telephones (per 1,000 inhabitants), 2001	86
Internet servers (per 1,000,000 inhabitants), 2001	71

Networked Readiness Index Rank

2003–2004 (102 countries) **98**

2002–2003 (82 countries)	81
2001–2002 (75 countries)	72

Readiness Component Index	96
Individual Readiness	79
Business Readiness	94
Government Readiness	100
Public expenditure on education (per capita), 2000	74
Adult illiteracy (%), 2001	80
Tertiary enrollment (gross %), 2001 or most recent available	68
Radios (per 1,000 inhabitants), 2001 or most recent available	50
Television sets (per 1,000 inhabitants), 2001	82
Households online (as % of households with computers), 2002	65
Quality of math and science education, 2003	99
Affordability of local fixed line calls (as % of per capita GDP), 2001	80
Affordability of Internet telephone access (as % of per capita GDP), 2001	68
Affordability of Internet service provider fees (as % of per capita GDP), 2001	70
Ease of obtaining telephone lines, 2003	102
Cost of business telephone monthly subscription (as % of per capita GDP), 2002	77
Extent of staff training, 2003	92
Quality of business schools, 2003	98
Scientists and engineers in R&D (per 1,000 inhabitants), 2001	48
Government prioritization of ICT, 2003	92
Government online presence, 2003	97
Government procurement of ICT, 2003	98

Usage Component Index	97
Individual Usage	83
Business Usage	94
Government Usage	98
Personal computers (per 1,000 inhabitants), 2001	79
ISDN subscribers (per 1,000 inhabitants), 2001	63
Cable television subscribers (per 1,000 inhabitants), 2001	78
Internet users (per 1,000 inhabitants), 2001	86
Computers installed in businesses (per 1,000 inhabitants), 2002	78
Firm-level technology absorption, 2003	101
Prevalence of foreign technology licensing, 2003	89
Government success in ICT promotion, 2003	95
Government online services, 2003	89

Hong Kong SAR.hk

Key Indicators

Population, 2002	6,773,000
Main telephone lines in operation, 2002	3,842,943
growth (%) 1999–2002	-1%
Cellular mobile telephone subscribers, 2002	6,297,541
growth (%) 1999–2002	47%
Personal computers, 2001	2,600,000
growth (%) 1999–2001	30%
Internet users (estimated), 2002	2,918,800
growth (%) 1999–2002	108%

Source: Data from International Telecommunication Union

RANK/102

Environment Component Index	11
Market Environment	23
Political and Regulatory Environment	2
Infrastructure Environment	16
State of cluster development, 2003	9
Venture capital availability, 2003	15
Subsidies for firm-level R&D, 2003	53
Quality of scientific research institutions, 2003	39
Availability of scientists and engineers, 2003	51
Brain drain, 2003	21
Utility patents granted (per 1,000,000 inhabitants), 2002	24
ICT manufactured exports (per capita), 2001	22
ICT service exports (per capita), 2001	4
Overall administrative burden, 2003	2
Quality of the legal system, 2003	17
Laws relating to ICT, 2003	18
Competition in the ISP sector, 2003	4
Foreign ownership restrictions, 2003	2
Efficiency of the tax system, 2003	1
Freedom of the press, 2003	39
Overall infrastructure quality, 2003	10
Waiting time for telephone lines (years), 2000	1
Telephone mainlines (per 1,000 inhabitants), 2001	12
Public pay telephones (per 1,000 inhabitants), 2001	74
Internet servers (per 1,000,000 inhabitants), 2001	15

Networked Readiness Index Rank

2003–2004 (102 countries) **18**

2002–2003 (82 countries) 18
2001–2002 (75 countries) 13

Readiness Component Index	28
Individual Readiness	24
Business Readiness	31
Government Readiness	27
Public expenditure on education (per capita), 2000	14
Adult illiteracy (%), 2001	47
Tertiary enrollment (gross %), 2001 or most recent available	51
Radios (per 1,000 inhabitants), 2001 or most recent available	31
Television sets (per 1,000 inhabitants), 2001	28
Households online (as % of households with computers), 2002	14
Quality of math and science education, 2003	16
Affordability of local fixed line calls (as % of per capita GDP), 2001	20
Affordability of Internet telephone access (as % of per capita GDP), 2001	64
Affordability of Internet service provider fees (as % of per capita GDP), 2001	23
Ease of obtaining telephone lines, 2003	11
Cost of business telephone monthly subscription (as % of per capita GDP), 2002	22
Extent of staff training, 2003	28
Quality of business schools, 2003	30
Scientists and engineers in R&D (per 1,000 inhabitants), 2000	88
Government prioritization of ICT, 2003	22
Government online presence, 2003	39
Government procurement of ICT, 2003	26

Usage Component Index	15
Individual Usage	22
Business Usage	14
Government Usage	4
Personal computers (per 1,000 inhabitants), 2001	15
ISDN subscribers (per 1,000 inhabitants), 2001	43
Cable television subscribers (per 1,000 inhabitants), 2001	35
Internet users (per 1,000 inhabitants), 2001	15
Computers installed in businesses (per 1,000 inhabitants), 2002	15
Firm-level technology absorption, 2003	28
Prevalence of foreign technology licensing, 2003	37
Government success in ICT promotion, 2003	31
Government online services, 2003	2

Hungary.hu

Key Indicators

Population, 2002	10,152,000
Main telephone lines in operation, 2002	3,666,443
growth (%) 1999–2002	-2%
Cellular mobile telephone subscribers, 2002	6,561,998
growth (%) 1999–2002	303%
Personal computers, 2002	1,100,000
growth (%) 1999–2002	47%
Internet users (estimated), 2002	1,600,000
growth (%) 1999–2002	167%

Source: Data from International Telecommunication Union

RANK/102

Environment Component Index	40
Market Environment	35
Political and Regulatory Environment	46
Infrastructure Environment	35
State of cluster development, 2003	72
Venture capital availability, 2003	41
Subsidies for firm-level R&D, 2003	37
Quality of scientific research institutions, 2003	22
Availability of scientists and engineers, 2003	24
Brain drain, 2003	46
Utility patents granted (per 1,000,000 inhabitants), 2002	28
ICT manufactured exports (per capita), 2001	20
ICT service exports (per capita), 2001	23
Overall administrative burden, 2003	58
Quality of the legal system, 2003	29
Laws relating to ICT, 2003	49
Competition in the ISP sector, 2003	94
Foreign ownership restrictions, 2003	12
Efficiency of the tax system, 2003	60
Freedom of the press, 2003	42
Overall infrastructure quality, 2003	58
Waiting time for telephone lines (years), 2000	31
Telephone mainlines (per 1,000 inhabitants), 2001	32
Public pay telephones (per 1,000 inhabitants), 2001	22
Internet servers (per 1,000,000 inhabitants), 2001	35

Networked Readiness Index Rank

2003–2004 (102 countries) **36**

2002–2003 (82 countries)	30
2001–2002 (75 countries)	30

Readiness Component Index	38
Individual Readiness	33
Business Readiness	37
Government Readiness	50
Public expenditure on education (per capita), 2000	32
Adult illiteracy (%), 2001	16
Tertiary enrollment (gross %), 2001 or most recent available	36
Radios (per 1,000 inhabitants), 2001 or most recent available	30
Television sets (per 1,000 inhabitants), 2001	32
Households online (as % of households with computers), 2002	30
Quality of math and science education, 2003	8
Affordability of local fixed line calls (as % of per capita GDP), 2001	40
Affordability of Internet telephone access (as % of per capita GDP), 2001	94
Affordability of Internet service provider fees (as % of per capita GDP), 2001	35
Ease of obtaining telephone lines, 2003	40
Cost of business telephone monthly subscription (as % of per capita GDP), 2002	47
Extent of staff training, 2003	65
Quality of business schools, 2003	40
Scientists and engineers in R&D (per 1,000 inhabitants), 2000	34
Government prioritization of ICT, 2003	50
Government online presence, 2003	60
Government procurement of ICT, 2003	34

Usage Component Index	34
Individual Usage	30
Business Usage	51
Government Usage	49
Personal computers (per 1,000 inhabitants), 2001	39
ISDN subscribers (per 1,000 inhabitants), 2001	21
Cable television subscribers (per 1,000 inhabitants), 2001	18
Internet users (per 1,000 inhabitants), 2001	33
Computers installed in businesses (per 1,000 inhabitants), 2002	35
Firm-level technology absorption, 2003	68
Prevalence of foreign technology licensing, 2003	65
Government success in ICT promotion, 2003	65
Government online services, 2003	40

Iceland.is

Key Indicators

Population, 2002	**288,000**
Main telephone lines in operation, 2002	**180,690**
growth (%) 1999–2002	-4%
Cellular mobile telephone subscribers, 2002	**256,000**
growth (%) 1999–2002	48%
Personal computers, 2002	**130,000**
growth (%) 1999–2002	30%
Internet users (estimated), 2002	**175,000**
growth (%) 1999–2002	17%

Source: Data from International Telecommunication Union

RANK/102

Environment Component Index	**5**
Market Environment	22
Political and Regulatory Environment	4
Infrastructure Environment	1
State of cluster development, 2003	37
Venture capital availability, 2003	20
Subsidies for firm-level R&D, 2003	31
Quality of scientific research institutions, 2003	21
Availability of scientists and engineers, 2003	6
Brain drain, 2003	10
Utility patents granted (per 1,000,000 inhabitants), 2002	20
ICT manufactured exports (per capita), 2001	37
ICT service exports (per capita), 2001	11
Overall administrative burden, 2003	5
Quality of the legal system, 2003	6
Laws relating to ICT, 2003	9
Competition in the ISP sector, 2003	3
Foreign ownership restrictions, 2003	93
Efficiency of the tax system, 2003	6
Freedom of the press, 2003	12
Overall infrastructure quality, 2003	11
Waiting time for telephone lines (years), 2000	1
Telephone mainlines (per 1,000 inhabitants), 2001	9
Public pay telephones (per 1,000 inhabitants), 2001	58
Internet servers (per 1,000,000 inhabitants), 2001	1

Networked Readiness Index Rank

2003–2004 (102 countries) 10

2002–2003 (82 countries)	5
2001–2002 (75 countries)	2

Readiness Component Index	**16**
Individual Readiness	8
Business Readiness	16
Government Readiness	32
Public expenditure on education (per capita), 2000	7
Adult illiteracy (%), 2001	7
Tertiary enrollment (gross %), 2001 or most recent available	27
Radios (per 1,000 inhabitants), 2001 or most recent available	7
Television sets (per 1,000 inhabitants), 2001	9
Households online (as % of households with computers), 2002	7
Quality of math and science education, 2003	26
Affordability of local fixed line calls (as % of per capita GDP), 2001	6
Affordability of Internet telephone access (as % of per capita GDP), 2001	53
Affordability of Internet service provider fees (as % of per capita GDP), 2001	6
Ease of obtaining telephone lines, 2003	4
Cost of business telephone monthly subscription (as % of per capita GDP), 2002	12
Extent of staff training, 2003	14
Quality of business schools, 2003	21
Scientists and engineers in R&D (per 1,000 inhabitants), 2000	21
Government prioritization of ICT, 2003	20
Government online presence, 2003	50
Government procurement of ICT, 2003	21

Usage Component Index	**14**
Individual Usage	9
Business Usage	9
Government Usage	23
Personal computers (per 1,000 inhabitants), 2001	9
ISDN subscribers (per 1,000 inhabitants), 2001	8
Cable television subscribers (per 1,000 inhabitants), 2001	11
Internet users (per 1,000 inhabitants), 2001	10
Computers installed in businesses (per 1,000 inhabitants), 2002	11
Firm-level technology absorption, 2003	7
Prevalence of foreign technology licensing, 2003	22
Government success in ICT promotion, 2003	11
Government online services, 2003	39

India.in

Key Indicators

Population, 2002	1,041,846,000
Main telephone lines in operation, 2002	41,420,000
growth (%) 1999–2002	56%
Cellular mobile telephone subscribers, 2002	12,687,640
growth (%) 1999–2002	573%
Personal computers, 2001	6,000,000
growth (%) 1999–2001	82%
Internet users (estimated), 2002	16,580,000
growth (%) 1999–2002	492%

Source: Data from International Telecommunication Union

RANK/102

Environment Component Index	44
Market Environment	27
Political and Regulatory Environment	29
Infrastructure Environment	67
State of cluster development, 2003	17
Venture capital availability, 2003	28
Subsidies for firm-level R&D, 2003	21
Quality of scientific research institutions, 2003	20
Availability of scientists and engineers, 2003	3
Brain drain, 2003	65
Utility patents granted (per 1,000,000 inhabitants), 2002	54
ICT manufactured exports (per capita), 2001	82
ICT service exports (per capita), 2001	77
Overall administrative burden, 2003	67
Quality of the legal system, 2003	25
Laws relating to ICT, 2003	36
Competition in the ISP sector, 2003	26
Foreign ownership restrictions, 2003	41
Efficiency of the tax system, 2003	59
Freedom of the press, 2003	26
Overall infrastructure quality, 2003	70
Waiting time for telephone lines (years), 2000	53
Telephone mainlines (per 1,000 inhabitants), 2001	79
Public pay telephones (per 1,000 inhabitants), 2001	34
Internet servers (per 1,000,000 inhabitants), 2001	85

Networked Readiness Index Rank

2003–2004 (102 countries) **45**

2002–2003 (82 countries)	37
2001–2002 (75 countries)	54

Readiness Component Index	50
Individual Readiness	80
Business Readiness	47
Government Readiness	31
Public expenditure on education (per capita), 2000	84
Adult illiteracy (%), 2001	91
Tertiary enrollment (gross %), 2001 or most recent available	72
Radios (per 1,000 inhabitants), 2001 or most recent available	95
Television sets (per 1,000 inhabitants), 2001	83
Households online (as % of households with computers), 2002	101
Quality of math and science education, 2003	14
Affordability of local fixed line calls (as % of per capita GDP), 2001	66
Affordability of Internet telephone access (as % of per capita GDP), 2001	49
Affordability of Internet service provider fees (as % of per capita GDP), 2001	75
Ease of obtaining telephone lines, 2003	45
Cost of business telephone monthly subscription (as % of per capita GDP), 2002	94
Extent of staff training, 2003	45
Quality of business schools, 2003	8
Scientists and engineers in R&D (per 1,000 inhabitants), 2000	80
Government prioritization of ICT, 2003	12
Government online presence, 2003	36
Government procurement of ICT, 2003	71

Usage Component Index	44
Individual Usage	69
Business Usage	40
Government Usage	26
Personal computers (per 1,000 inhabitants), 2001	88
ISDN subscribers (per 1,000 inhabitants), 2001	82
Cable television subscribers (per 1,000 inhabitants), 2001	53
Internet users (per 1,000 inhabitants), 2001	85
Computers installed in businesses (per 1,000 inhabitants), 2002	80
Firm-level technology absorption, 2003	31
Prevalence of foreign technology licensing, 2003	6
Government success in ICT promotion, 2003	16
Government online services, 2003	40

Indonesia.id

Key Indicators

Population, 2002	212,110,000
Main telephone lines in operation, 2002	7,750,035
growth (%) 1999–2002	27%
Cellular mobile telephone subscribers, 2002	11,700,000
growth (%) 1999–2002	427%
Personal computers, 2001	2,300,000
growth (%) 1999–2001	21%
Internet users (estimated), 2002	8,000,000
growth (%) 1999–2002	789%

Source: Data from International Telecommunication Union

RANK/102

Environment Component Index	68
Market Environment	50
Political and Regulatory Environment	71
Infrastructure Environment	80
State of cluster development, 2003	33
Venture capital availability, 2003	49
Subsidies for firm-level R&D, 2003	28
Quality of scientific research institutions, 2003	62
Availability of scientists and engineers, 2003	85
Brain drain, 2003	45
Utility patents granted (per 1,000,000 inhabitants), 2002	69
ICT manufactured exports (per capita), 2001	52
ICT service exports (per capita), 2001	100
Overall administrative burden, 2003	15
Quality of the legal system, 2003	67
Laws relating to ICT, 2003	48
Competition in the ISP sector, 2003	69
Foreign ownership restrictions, 2003	95
Efficiency of the tax system, 2003	36
Freedom of the press, 2003	89
Overall infrastructure quality, 2003	51
Waiting time for telephone lines (years), 2000	84
Telephone mainlines (per 1,000 inhabitants), 2001	81
Public pay telephones (per 1,000 inhabitants), 2001	64
Internet servers (per 1,000,000 inhabitants), 2001	78

Networked Readiness Index Rank

2003–2004 (102 countries) **73**

2002–2003 (82 countries)	64
2001–2002 (75 countries)	59

Readiness Component Index	69
Individual Readiness	71
Business Readiness	62
Government Readiness	72
Public expenditure on education (per capita), 2000	76
Adult illiteracy (%), 2001	65
Tertiary enrollment (gross %), 2001 or most recent available	69
Radios (per 1,000 inhabitants), 2001 or most recent available	89
Television sets (per 1,000 inhabitants), 2001	71
Households online (as % of households with computers), 2002	92
Quality of math and science education, 2003	62
Affordability of local fixed line calls (as % of per capita GDP), 2001	51
Affordability of Internet telephone access (as % of per capita GDP), 2001	42
Affordability of Internet service provider fees (as % of per capita GDP), 2001	72
Ease of obtaining telephone lines, 2003	81
Cost of business telephone monthly subscription (as % of per capita GDP), 2002	61
Extent of staff training, 2003	47
Quality of business schools, 2003	71
Scientists and engineers in R&D (per 1,000 inhabitants), 2000	33
Government prioritization of ICT, 2003	83
Government online presence, 2003	73
Government procurement of ICT, 2003	27

Usage Component Index	81
Individual Usage	84
Business Usage	89
Government Usage	60
Personal computers (per 1,000 inhabitants), 2001	82
ISDN subscribers (per 1,000 inhabitants), 2001	83
Cable television subscribers (per 1,000 inhabitants), 2001	90
Internet users (per 1,000 inhabitants), 2001	68
Computers installed in businesses (per 1,000 inhabitants), 2002	71
Firm-level technology absorption, 2003	96
Prevalence of foreign technology licensing, 2003	81
Government success in ICT promotion, 2003	69
Government online services, 2003	53

Ireland.ie

Key Indicators

Population, 2002	3,931,000
Main telephone lines in operation, 2002	1,975,000
growth (%) 1999–2002	14%
Cellular mobile telephone subscribers, 2002	2,969,000
growth (%) 1999–2002	77%
Personal computers, 2001	1,500,000
growth (%) 1999–2001	27%
Internet users (estimated), 2002	1,065,000
growth (%) 1999–2002	160%

Source: Data from International Telecommunication Union

RANK/102

Environment Component Index	22
Market Environment	4
Political and Regulatory Environment	24
Infrastructure Environment	32
State of cluster development, 2003	7
Venture capital availability, 2003	9
Subsidies for firm-level R&D, 2003	11
Quality of scientific research institutions, 2003	14
Availability of scientists and engineers, 2003	20
Brain drain, 2003	20
Utility patents granted (per 1,000,000 inhabitants), 2002	23
ICT manufactured exports (per capita), 2001	2
ICT service exports (per capita), 2001	3
Overall administrative burden, 2003	18
Quality of the legal system, 2003	26
Laws relating to ICT, 2003	22
Competition in the ISP sector, 2003	97
Foreign ownership restrictions, 2003	2
Efficiency of the tax system, 2003	20
Freedom of the press, 2003	48
Overall infrastructure quality, 2003	64
Waiting time for telephone lines (years), 2000	1
Telephone mainlines (per 1,000 inhabitants), 2001	20
Public pay telephones (per 1,000 inhabitants), 2001	52
Internet servers (per 1,000,000 inhabitants), 2001	12

Networked Readiness Index Rank

2003–2004 (102 countries) **22**

2002–2003 (82 countries)	21
2001–2002 (75 countries)	19

Readiness Component Index	18
Individual Readiness	20
Business Readiness	20
Government Readiness	11
Public expenditure on education (per capita), 2000	11
Adult illiteracy (%), 2001	30
Tertiary enrollment (gross %), 2001 or most recent available	30
Radios (per 1,000 inhabitants), 2001 or most recent available	29
Television sets (per 1,000 inhabitants), 2001	37
Households online (as % of households with computers), 2002	21
Quality of math and science education, 2003	20
Affordability of local fixed line calls (as % of per capita GDP), 2001	16
Affordability of Internet telephone access (as % of per capita GDP), 2001	61
Affordability of Internet service provider fees (as % of per capita GDP), 2001	8
Ease of obtaining telephone lines, 2003	43
Cost of business telephone monthly subscription (as % of per capita GDP), 2002	10
Extent of staff training, 2003	23
Quality of business schools, 2003	16
Scientists and engineers in R&D (per 1,000 inhabitants), 2000	23
Government prioritization of ICT, 2003	31
Government online presence, 2003	10
Government procurement of ICT, 2003	18

Usage Component Index	18
Individual Usage	16
Business Usage	17
Government Usage	19
Personal computers (per 1,000 inhabitants), 2001	14
ISDN subscribers (per 1,000 inhabitants), 2001	9
Cable television subscribers (per 1,000 inhabitants), 2001	19
Internet users (per 1,000 inhabitants), 2001	29
Computers installed in businesses (per 1,000 inhabitants), 2001	16
Firm-level technology absorption, 2003	29
Prevalence of foreign technology licensing, 2003	54
Government success in ICT promotion, 2003	20
Government online services, 2003	18

Israel.il

Key Indicators

Population, 2002	**6,635,600**
Main telephone lines in operation, 2002	**3,100,000**
growth (%) 1999–2002	8%
Cellular mobile telephone subscribers, 2002	**6,334,000**
growth (%) 1999–2002	120%
Personal computers, 2001	**1,600,000**
growth (%) 1999–2001	18%
Internet users (estimated), 2002	**2,000,000**
growth (%) 1999–2002	150%

Source: Data from International Telecommunication Union

RANK/102

Environment Component Index	13
Market Environment	5
Political and Regulatory Environment	15
Infrastructure Environment	22
State of cluster development, 2003	26
Venture capital availability, 2003	4
Subsidies for firm-level R&D, 2003	4
Quality of scientific research institutions, 2003	2
Availability of scientists and engineers, 2003	1
Brain drain, 2003	18
Utility patents granted (per 1,000,000 inhabitants), 2002	6
ICT manufactured exports (per capita), 2001	12
ICT service exports (per capita), 2001	9
Overall administrative burden, 2003	31
Quality of the legal system, 2003	2
Laws relating to ICT, 2003	21
Competition in the ISP sector, 2003	7
Foreign ownership restrictions, 2003	23
Efficiency of the tax system, 2003	77
Freedom of the press, 2003	22
Overall infrastructure quality, 2003	25
Waiting time for telephone lines (years), 2000	25
Telephone mainlines (per 1,000 inhabitants), 2001	22
Public pay telephones (per 1,000 inhabitants), 2001	18
Internet servers (per 1,000,000 inhabitants), 2001	21

Networked Readiness Index Rank

2003–2004 (102 countries) **16**

2002–2003 (82 countries)	12
2001–2002 (75 countries)	22

Readiness Component Index	23
Individual Readiness	26
Business Readiness	21
Government Readiness	21
Public expenditure on education (per capita), 2000	15
Adult illiteracy (%), 2001	44
Tertiary enrollment (gross %), 2001 or most recent available	22
Radios (per 1,000 inhabitants), 2001 or most recent available	40
Television sets (per 1,000 inhabitants), 2001	43
Households online (as % of households with computers), 2002	25
Quality of math and science education, 2003	21
Affordability of local fixed line calls (as % of per capita GDP), 2001	2
Affordability of Internet telephone access (as % of per capita GDP), 2001	4
Affordability of Internet service provider fees (as % of per capita GDP), 2001	19
Ease of obtaining telephone lines, 2003	5
Cost of business telephone monthly subscription (as % of per capita GDP), 2002	11
Extent of staff training, 2003	24
Quality of business schools, 2003	10
Scientists and engineers in R&D (per 1,000 inhabitants), 2000	32
Government prioritization of ICT, 2003	58
Government online presence, 2003	35
Government procurement of ICT, 2003	7

Usage Component Index	16
Individual Usage	23
Business Usage	7
Government Usage	9
Personal computers (per 1,000 inhabitants), 2001	23
ISDN subscribers (per 1,000 inhabitants), 2001	24
Cable television subscribers (per 1,000 inhabitants), 2001	14
Internet users (per 1,000 inhabitants), 2001	24
Computers installed in businesses (per 1,000 inhabitants), 2002	10
Firm-level technology absorption, 2003	4
Prevalence of foreign technology licensing, 2003	20
Government success in ICT promotion, 2003	21
Government online services, 2003	8

Italy.it

Key Indicators

Population, 2002	56,464,000
Main telephone lines in operation, 2002	27,451,950
growth (%) 1999–2002	4%
Cellular mobile telephone subscribers, 2002	52,316,000
growth (%) 1999–2002	73%
Personal computers, 2002	13,025,000
growth (%) 1999–2002	45%
Internet users (estimated), 2002	17,000,000
growth (%) 1999–2002	107%

Source: Data from International Telecommunication Union

RANK/102

Environment Component Index	28
Market Environment	24
Political and Regulatory Environment	42
Infrastructure Environment	26
State of cluster development, 2003	2
Venture capital availability, 2003	29
Subsidies for firm-level R&D, 2003	33
Quality of scientific research institutions, 2003	44
Availability of scientists and engineers, 2003	29
Brain drain, 2003	50
Utility patents granted (per 1,000,000 inhabitants), 2002	25
ICT manufactured exports (per capita), 2001	25
ICT service exports (per capita), 2001	21
Overall administrative burden, 2003	73
Quality of the legal system, 2003	43
Laws relating to ICT, 2003	34
Competition in the ISP sector, 2003	20
Foreign ownership restrictions, 2003	72
Efficiency of the tax system, 2003	84
Freedom of the press, 2003	34
Overall infrastructure quality, 2003	40
Waiting time for telephone lines (years), 2000	1
Telephone mainlines (per 1,000 inhabitants), 2001	23
Public pay telephones (per 1,000 inhabitants), 2001	17
Internet servers (per 1,000,000 inhabitants), 2001	29

Networked Readiness Index Rank

2003–2004 (102 countries) **28**

2002–2003 (82 countries) 26
2001–2002 (75 countries) 25

Readiness Component Index	26
Individual Readiness	23
Business Readiness	29
Government Readiness	24
Public expenditure on education (per capita), 2000	22
Adult illiteracy (%), 2001	26
Tertiary enrollment (gross %), 2001 or most recent available	25
Radios (per 1,000 inhabitants), 2001 or most recent available	19
Television sets (per 1,000 inhabitants), 2001	29
Households online (as % of households with computers), 2002	19
Quality of math and science education, 2003	40
Affordability of local fixed line calls (as % of per capita GDP), 2001	23
Affordability of Internet telephone access (as % of per capita GDP), 2001	77
Affordability of Internet service provider fees (as % of per capita GDP), 2001	22
Ease of obtaining telephone lines, 2003	47
Cost of business telephone monthly subscription (as % of per capita GDP), 2002	23
Extent of staff training, 2003	33
Quality of business schools, 2003	27
Scientists and engineers in R&D (per 1,000 inhabitants), 2000	40
Government prioritization of ICT, 2003	65
Government online presence, 2003	13
Government procurement of ICT, 2003	40

Usage Component Index	29
Individual Usage	29
Business Usage	28
Government Usage	34
Personal computers (per 1,000 inhabitants), 2001	26
ISDN subscribers (per 1,000 inhabitants), 2001	13
Cable television subscribers (per 1,000 inhabitants), 2001	83
Internet users (per 1,000 inhabitants), 2001	24
Computers installed in businesses (per 1,000 inhabitants), 2002	25
Firm-level technology absorption, 2003	61
Prevalence of foreign technology licensing, 2003	15
Government success in ICT promotion, 2003	58
Government online services, 2003	27

Jamaica.jm

Key Indicators

Population, 2002	**2,618,000**
Main telephone lines in operation, 2002	**450,000**
growth (%) 1999–2002	-8%
Cellular mobile telephone subscribers, 2002	**1,400,000**
growth (%) 1999–2002	870%
Personal computers, 2001	**130,000**
growth (%) 1999–2001	18%
Internet users (estimated), 2001	**100,000**
growth (%) 1999–2001	67%

Source: Data from International Telecommunication Union

RANK/102

Environment Component Index	**56**
Market Environment	70
Political and Regulatory Environment	50
Infrastructure Environment	58
State of cluster development, 2003	62
Venture capital availability, 2003	74
Subsidies for firm-level R&D, 2003	70
Quality of scientific research institutions, 2003	37
Availability of scientists and engineers, 2003	76
Brain drain, 2003	79
Utility patents granted (per 1,000,000 inhabitants), 2002	43
ICT manufactured exports (per capita), 2001	89
ICT service exports (per capita), 2001	39
Overall administrative burden, 2003	92
Quality of the legal system, 2003	48
Laws relating to ICT, 2003	59
Competition in the ISP sector, 2003	32
Foreign ownership restrictions, 2003	16
Efficiency of the tax system, 2003	64
Freedom of the press, 2003	53
Overall infrastructure quality, 2003	56
Waiting time for telephone lines (years), 2000	93
Telephone mainlines (per 1,000 inhabitants), 2001	52
Public pay telephones (per 1,000 inhabitants), 2001	4
Internet servers (per 1,000,000 inhabitants), 2001	56

Networked Readiness Index Rank

2003–2004 (102 countries) **53**

2002–2003 (82 countries)	60
2001–2002 (75 countries)	56

Readiness Component Index	**57**
Individual Readiness	61
Business Readiness	57
Government Readiness	59
Public expenditure on education (per capita), 2000	44
Adult illiteracy (%), 2001	67
Tertiary enrollment (gross %), 2001 or most recent available	63
Radios (per 1,000 inhabitants), 2001 or most recent available	22
Television sets (per 1,000 inhabitants), 2001	65
Households online (as % of households with computers), 2002	50
Quality of math and science education, 2003	72
Affordability of local fixed line calls (as % of per capita GDP), 2001	60
Affordability of Internet telephone access (as % of per capita GDP), 2001	54
Affordability of Internet service provider fees (as % of per capita GDP), 2001	73
Ease of obtaining telephone lines, 2003	63
Cost of business telephone monthly subscription (as % of per capita GDP), 2002	72
Extent of staff training, 2003	48
Quality of business schools, 2003	38
Scientists and engineers in R&D (per 1,000 inhabitants), 2000	57
Government prioritization of ICT, 2003	27
Government online presence, 2003	79
Government procurement of ICT, 2003	35

Usage Component Index	**54**
Individual Usage	47
Business Usage	75
Government Usage	38
Personal computers (per 1,000 inhabitants), 2001	51
ISDN subscribers (per 1,000 inhabitants), 2001	46
Cable television subscribers (per 1,000 inhabitants), 2001	39
Internet users (per 1,000 inhabitants), 2001	55
Computers installed in businesses (per 1,000 inhabitants), 2002	57
Firm-level technology absorption, 2003	73
Prevalence of foreign technology licensing, 2003	73
Government success in ICT promotion, 2003	60
Government online services, 2003	29

Japan.jp

Key Indicators

Population, 2002	127,530,000
Main telephone lines in operation, 2002	71,149,000
growth (%) 1999–2002	1%
Cellular mobile telephone subscribers, 2002	81,118,000
growth (%) 1999–2002	43%
Personal computers, 2002	48,700,000
growth (%) 1999–2002	34%
Internet users (estimated), 2002	57,200,000
growth (%) 1999–2002	111%

Source: Data from International Telecommunication Union

RANK/102

Environment Component Index — 19

Market Environment	7
Political and Regulatory Environment	37
Infrastructure Environment	21
State of cluster development, 2003	5
Venture capital availability, 2003	45
Subsidies for firm-level R&D, 2003	10
Quality of scientific research institutions, 2003	11
Availability of scientists and engineers, 2003	9
Brain drain, 2003	8
Utility patents granted (per 1,000,000 inhabitants), 2002	2
ICT manufactured exports (per capita), 2001	19
ICT service exports (per capita), 2001	24
Overall administrative burden, 2003	50
Quality of the legal system, 2003	36
Laws relating to ICT, 2003	27
Competition in the ISP sector, 2003	14
Foreign ownership restrictions, 2003	85
Efficiency of the tax system, 2003	81
Freedom of the press, 2003	31
Overall infrastructure quality, 2003	18
Waiting time for telephone lines (years), 2000	1
Telephone mainlines (per 1,000 inhabitants), 2001	10
Public pay telephones (per 1,000 inhabitants), 2001	54
Internet servers (per 1,000,000 inhabitants), 2001	22

Networked Readiness Index Rank

2003–2004 (102 countries) — 12

2002–2003 (82 countries)	20
2001–2002 (75 countries)	21

Readiness Component Index — 11

Individual Readiness	14
Business Readiness	6
Government Readiness	17
Public expenditure on education (per capita), 2000	18
Adult illiteracy (%), 2001	17
Tertiary enrollment (gross %), 2001 or most recent available	29
Radios (per 1,000 inhabitants), 2001 or most recent available	16
Television sets (per 1,000 inhabitants), 2001	7
Households online (as % of households with computers), 2002	8
Quality of math and science education, 2003	24
Affordability of local fixed line calls (as % of per capita GDP), 2001	3
Affordability of Internet telephone access (as % of per capita GDP), 2001	78
Affordability of Internet service provider fees (as % of per capita GDP), 2001	11
Ease of obtaining telephone lines, 2003	6
Cost of business telephone monthly subscription (as % of per capita GDP), 2002	20
Extent of staff training, 2003	6
Quality of business schools, 2003	53
Scientists and engineers in R&D (per 1,000 inhabitants), 2000	1
Government prioritization of ICT, 2003	9
Government online presence, 2003	44
Government procurement of ICT, 2003	15

Usage Component Index — 11

Individual Usage	12
Business Usage	10
Government Usage	14
Personal computers (per 1,000 inhabitants), 2001	18
ISDN subscribers (per 1,000 inhabitants), 2001	6
Cable television subscribers (per 1,000 inhabitants), 2001	20
Internet users (per 1,000 inhabitants), 2001	8
Computers installed in businesses (per 1,000 inhabitants), 2002	14
Firm-level technology absorption, 2003	2
Prevalence of foreign technology licensing, 2003	27
Government success in ICT promotion, 2003	30
Government online services, 2003	8

Jordan.jo

Key Indicators

Population, 2002	5,329,000
Main telephone lines in operation, 2002	687,598
growth (%) 1999–2002	22%
Cellular mobile telephone subscribers, 2002	1,219,597
growth (%) 1999–2002	930%
Personal computers, 2002	200,000
growth (%) 1999–2002	122%
Internet users (estimated), 2002	307,000
growth (%) 1999–2002	156%

Source: Data from International Telecommunication Union

RANK/102

Environment Component Index	42
Market Environment	47
Political and Regulatory Environment	26
Infrastructure Environment	48
State of cluster development, 2003	52
Venture capital availability, 2003	62
Subsidies for firm-level R&D, 2003	54
Quality of scientific research institutions, 2003	46
Availability of scientists and engineers, 2003	12
Brain drain, 2003	63
Utility patents granted (per 1,000,000 inhabitants), 2002	57
ICT manufactured exports (per capita), 2001	56
ICT service exports (per capita), 2001	41
Overall administrative burden, 2003	9
Quality of the legal system, 2003	23
Laws relating to ICT, 2003	38
Competition in the ISP sector, 2003	19
Foreign ownership restrictions, 2003	47
Efficiency of the tax system, 2003	20
Freedom of the press, 2003	85
Overall infrastructure quality, 2003	23
Waiting time for telephone lines (years), 2000	40
Telephone mainlines (per 1,000 inhabitants), 2001	59
Public pay telephones (per 1,000 inhabitants), 2001	70
Internet servers (per 1,000,000 inhabitants), 2001	76

Networked Readiness Index Rank

2003–2004 (102 countries)　46

2002–2003 (82 countries)	51
2001–2002 (75 countries)	49

Readiness Component Index	51
Individual Readiness	54
Business Readiness	42
Government Readiness	67
Public expenditure on education (per capita), 2000	58
Adult illiteracy (%), 2001	60
Tertiary enrollment (gross %), 2001 or most recent available	48
Radios (per 1,000 inhabitants), 2001 or most recent available	58
Television sets (per 1,000 inhabitants), 2001	81
Households online (as % of households with computers), 2002	95
Quality of math and science education, 2003	31
Affordability of local fixed line calls (as % of per capita GDP), 2001	49
Affordability of Internet telephone access (as % of per capita GDP), 2001	41
Affordability of Internet service provider fees (as % of per capita GDP), 2001	66
Ease of obtaining telephone lines, 2003	29
Cost of business telephone monthly subscription (as % of per capita GDP), 2002	75
Extent of staff training, 2003	62
Quality of business schools, 2003	60
Scientists and engineers in R&D (per 1,000 inhabitants), 2000	28
Government prioritization of ICT, 2003	11
Government online presence, 2003	94
Government procurement of ICT, 2003	45

Usage Component Index	49
Individual Usage	70
Business Usage	52
Government Usage	33
Personal computers (per 1,000 inhabitants), 2001	62
ISDN subscribers (per 1,000 inhabitants), 2001	61
Cable television subscribers (per 1,000 inhabitants), 2001	90
Internet users (per 1,000 inhabitants), 2001	54
Computers installed in businesses (per 1,000 inhabitants), 2002	77
Firm-level technology absorption, 2003	48
Prevalence of foreign technology licensing, 2003	13
Government success in ICT promotion, 2003	8
Government online services, 2003	59

Kenya.ke

Key Indicators

Population, 2002	31,930,000
Main telephone lines in operation, 2002	328,104
growth (%) 1999–2002	8%
Cellular mobile telephone subscribers, 2002	1,325,222
growth (%) 1999–2002	5,478%
Personal computers, 2001	175,000
growth (%) 1999–2001	40%
Internet users (estimated), 2001	500,000
growth (%) 1999–2001	1,329%

Source: Data from International Telecommunication Union

Networked Readiness Index Rank

2003–2004 (102 countries) 84

RANK/102

Environment Component Index	91
Market Environment	63
Political and Regulatory Environment	75
Infrastructure Environment	98
State of cluster development, 2003	42
Venture capital availability, 2003	77
Subsidies for firm-level R&D, 2003	69
Quality of scientific research institutions, 2003	27
Availability of scientists and engineers, 2003	54
Brain drain, 2003	82
Utility patents granted (per 1,000,000 inhabitants), 2002	70
ICT manufactured exports (per capita), 2001	84
ICT service exports (per capita), 2001	82
Overall administrative burden, 2003	63
Quality of the legal system, 2003	84
Laws relating to ICT, 2003	67
Competition in the ISP sector, 2003	73
Foreign ownership restrictions, 2003	48
Efficiency of the tax system, 2003	49
Freedom of the press, 2003	79
Overall infrastructure quality, 2003	88
Waiting time for telephone lines (years), 2000	98
Telephone mainlines (per 1,000 inhabitants), 2001	88
Public pay telephones (per 1,000 inhabitants), 2001	88
Internet servers (per 1,000,000 inhabitants), 2001	99

Readiness Component Index	89
Individual Readiness	84
Business Readiness	89
Government Readiness	86
Public expenditure on education (per capita), 2000	82
Adult illiteracy (%), 2001	74
Tertiary enrollment (gross %), 2001 or most recent available	90
Radios (per 1,000 inhabitants), 2001 or most recent available	77
Television sets (per 1,000 inhabitants), 2001	92
Households online (as % of households with computers), 2002	73
Quality of math and science education, 2003	64
Affordability of local fixed line calls (as % of per capita GDP), 2001	90
Affordability of Internet telephone access (as % of per capita GDP), 2001	86
Affordability of Internet service provider fees (as % of per capita GDP), 2001	96
Ease of obtaining telephone lines, 2003	93
Cost of business telephone monthly subscription (as % of per capita GDP), 2002	95
Extent of staff training, 2003	63
Quality of business schools, 2003	73
Scientists and engineers in R&D (per 1,000 inhabitants), 2000	60
Government prioritization of ICT, 2003	81
Government online presence, 2003	77
Government procurement of ICT, 2003	67

Usage Component Index	76
Individual Usage	88
Business Usage	66
Government Usage	65
Personal computers (per 1,000 inhabitants), 2001	89
ISDN subscribers (per 1,000 inhabitants), 2001	95
Cable television subscribers (per 1,000 inhabitants), 2001	86
Internet users (per 1,000 inhabitants), 2001	71
Computers installed in businesses (per 1,000 inhabitants), 2002	93
Firm-level technology absorption, 2003	77
Prevalence of foreign technology licensing, 2003	28
Government success in ICT promotion, 2003	75
Government online services, 2003	59

Korea.kr

Key Indicators

Population, 2002	47,600,000
Main telephone lines in operation, 2002	23,257,000
growth (%) 1999–2002	13%
Cellular mobile telephone subscribers, 2002	32,342,000
growth (%) 1999–2002	38%
Personal computers, 2002	26,458,000
growth (%) 1999–2002	129%
Internet users (estimated), 2002	26,270,000
growth (%) 1999–2002	142%

Source: Data from International Telecommunication Union

Networked Readiness Index Rank

2003–2004 (102 countries) **20**

2002–2003 (82 countries)	14
2001–2002 (75 countries)	20

RANK/102

Environment Component Index	20
Market Environment	19
Political and Regulatory Environment	25
Infrastructure Environment	9
State of cluster development, 2003	8
Venture capital availability, 2003	16
Subsidies for firm-level R&D, 2003	15
Quality of scientific research institutions, 2003	26
Availability of scientists and engineers, 2003	40
Brain drain, 2003	32
Utility patents granted (per 1,000,000 inhabitants), 2002	14
ICT manufactured exports (per capita), 2001	18
ICT service exports (per capita), 2001	32
Overall administrative burden, 2003	23
Quality of the legal system, 2003	49
Laws relating to ICT, 2003	12
Competition in the ISP sector, 2003	1
Foreign ownership restrictions, 2003	68
Efficiency of the tax system, 2003	37
Freedom of the press, 2003	58
Overall infrastructure quality, 2003	21
Waiting time for telephone lines (years), 2000	1
Telephone mainlines (per 1,000 inhabitants), 2001	19
Public pay telephones (per 1,000 inhabitants), 2001	3
Internet servers (per 1,000,000 inhabitants), 2001	45

Readiness Component Index	19
Individual Readiness	21
Business Readiness	23
Government Readiness	9
Public expenditure on education (per capita), 2000	29
Adult illiteracy (%), 2001	33
Tertiary enrollment (gross %), 2001 or most recent available	2
Radios (per 1,000 inhabitants), 2001 or most recent available	11
Television sets (per 1,000 inhabitants), 2001	40
Households online (as % of households with computers), 2002	24
Quality of math and science education, 2003	35
Affordability of local fixed line calls (as % of per capita GDP), 2001	8
Affordability of Internet telephone access (as % of per capita GDP), 2001	9
Affordability of Internet service provider fees (as % of per capita GDP), 2001	24
Ease of obtaining telephone lines, 2003	23
Cost of business telephone monthly subscription (as % of per capita GDP), 2002	1
Extent of staff training, 2003	21
Quality of business schools, 2003	45
Scientists and engineers in R&D (per 1,000 inhabitants), 2000	19
Government prioritization of ICT, 2003	8
Government online presence, 2003	23
Government procurement of ICT, 2003	12

Usage Component Index	17
Individual Usage	15
Business Usage	18
Government Usage	10
Personal computers (per 1,000 inhabitants), 2001	22
ISDN subscribers (per 1,000 inhabitants), 2001	37
Cable television subscribers (per 1,000 inhabitants), 2001	15
Internet users (per 1,000 inhabitants), 2001	4
Computers installed in businesses (per 1,000 inhabitants), 2002	23
Firm-level technology absorption, 2003	10
Prevalence of foreign technology licensing, 2003	19
Government success in ICT promotion, 2003	4
Government online services, 2003	26

Latvia.lv

Key Indicators

Population, 2002	2,329,000
Main telephone lines in operation, 2002	701,211
growth (%) 1999–2002	-4%
Cellular mobile telephone subscribers, 2002	917,196
growth (%) 1999–2002	234%
Personal computers, 2002	400,000
growth (%) 1999–2002	100%
Internet users (estimated), 2002	310,000
growth (%) 1999–2002	195%

Source: Data from International Telecommunication Union

Networked Readiness Index Rank

2003–2004 (102 countries) **35**

2002–2003 (82 countries)	38
2001–2002 (75 countries)	39

RANK/102

Environment Component Index	**38**
Market Environment	32
Political and Regulatory Environment	33
Infrastructure Environment	46
State of cluster development, 2003	39
Venture capital availability, 2003	19
Subsidies for firm-level R&D, 2003	27
Quality of scientific research institutions, 2003	47
Availability of scientists and engineers, 2003	61
Brain drain, 2003	36
Utility patents granted (per 1,000,000 inhabitants), 2002	72
ICT manufactured exports (per capita), 2001	53
ICT service exports (per capita), 2001	42
Overall administrative burden, 2003	13
Quality of the legal system, 2003	47
Laws relating to ICT, 2003	28
Competition in the ISP sector, 2003	40
Foreign ownership restrictions, 2003	43
Efficiency of the tax system, 2003	24
Freedom of the press, 2003	59
Overall infrastructure quality, 2003	37
Waiting time for telephone lines (years), 2000	65
Telephone mainlines (per 1,000 inhabitants), 2001	37
Public pay telephones (per 1,000 inhabitants), 2001	67
Internet servers (per 1,000,000 inhabitants), 2001	30

Readiness Component Index	**36**
Individual Readiness	25
Business Readiness	41
Government Readiness	48
Public expenditure on education (per capita), 2000	42
Adult illiteracy (%), 2001	9
Tertiary enrollment (gross %), 2001 or most recent available	10
Radios (per 1,000 inhabitants), 2001 or most recent available	28
Television sets (per 1,000 inhabitants), 2001	5
Households online (as % of households with computers), 2002	90
Quality of math and science education, 2003	32
Affordability of local fixed line calls (as % of per capita GDP), 2001	59
Affordability of Internet telephone access (as % of per capita GDP), 2001	40
Affordability of Internet service provider fees (as % of per capita GDP), 2001	55
Ease of obtaining telephone lines, 2003	61
Cost of business telephone monthly subscription (as % of per capita GDP), 2002	51
Extent of staff training, 2003	37
Quality of business schools, 2003	33
Scientists and engineers in R&D (per 1,000 inhabitants), 2000	41
Government prioritization of ICT, 2003	52
Government online presence, 2003	59
Government procurement of ICT, 2003	23

Usage Component Index	**41**
Individual Usage	38
Business Usage	42
Government Usage	53
Personal computers (per 1,000 inhabitants), 2001	31
ISDN subscribers (per 1,000 inhabitants), 2001	33
Cable television subscribers (per 1,000 inhabitants), 2001	28
Internet users (per 1,000 inhabitants), 2001	45
Computers installed in businesses (per 1,000 inhabitants), 2002	51
Firm-level technology absorption, 2003	38
Prevalence of foreign technology licensing, 2003	18
Government success in ICT promotion, 2003	43
Government online services, 2003	59

Lithuania.lt

Key Indicators

Population, 2002	3,460,000
Main telephone lines in operation, 2002	935,899
growth (%) 1999–2002	-19%
Cellular mobile telephone subscribers, 2002	1,631,573
growth (%) 1999–2002	391%
Personal computers, 2002	380,000
growth (%) 1999–2002	73%
Internet users (estimated), 2002	500,000
growth (%) 1999–2002	385%

Source: Data from International Telecommunication Union

RANK/102

Environment Component Index	45
Market Environment	40
Political and Regulatory Environment	58
Infrastructure Environment	45
State of cluster development, 2003	46
Venture capital availability, 2003	22
Subsidies for firm-level R&D, 2003	46
Quality of scientific research institutions, 2003	38
Availability of scientists and engineers, 2003	28
Brain drain, 2003	69
Utility patents granted (per 1,000,000 inhabitants), 2002	49
ICT manufactured exports (per capita), 2001	45
ICT service exports (per capita), 2001	49
Overall administrative burden, 2003	52
Quality of the legal system, 2003	65
Laws relating to ICT, 2003	45
Competition in the ISP sector, 2003	58
Foreign ownership restrictions, 2003	63
Efficiency of the tax system, 2003	82
Freedom of the press, 2003	37
Overall infrastructure quality, 2003	39
Waiting time for telephone lines (years), 2000	57
Telephone mainlines (per 1,000 inhabitants), 2001	36
Public pay telephones (per 1,000 inhabitants), 2001	61
Internet servers (per 1,000,000 inhabitants), 2001	37

Networked Readiness Index Rank

2003–2004 (102 countries) **42**

2002–2003 (82 countries)	46
2001–2002 (75 countries)	42

Readiness Component Index	32
Individual Readiness	32
Business Readiness	32
Government Readiness	38
Public expenditure on education (per capita), 2000	40
Adult illiteracy (%), 2001	14
Tertiary enrollment (gross %), 2001 or most recent available	23
Radios (per 1,000 inhabitants), 2001 or most recent available	41
Television sets (per 1,000 inhabitants), 2001	33
Households online (as % of households with computers), 2002	32
Quality of math and science education, 2003	23
Affordability of local fixed line calls (as % of per capita GDP), 2001	62
Affordability of Internet telephone access (as % of per capita GDP), 2001	24
Affordability of Internet service provider fees (as % of per capita GDP), 2001	65
Ease of obtaining telephone lines, 2003	38
Cost of business telephone monthly subscription (as % of per capita GDP), 2002	46
Extent of staff training, 2003	67
Quality of business schools, 2003	49
Scientists and engineers in R&D (per 1,000 inhabitants), 2000	27
Government prioritization of ICT, 2003	54
Government online presence, 2003	33
Government procurement of ICT, 2003	47

Usage Component Index	53
Individual Usage	45
Business Usage	50
Government Usage	63
Personal computers (per 1,000 inhabitants), 2001	44
ISDN subscribers (per 1,000 inhabitants), 2001	44
Cable television subscribers (per 1,000 inhabitants), 2001	34
Internet users (per 1,000 inhabitants), 2001	47
Computers installed in businesses (per 1,000 inhabitants), 2002	54
Firm-level technology absorption, 2003	25
Prevalence of foreign technology licensing, 2003	66
Government success in ICT promotion, 2003	52
Government online services, 2003	63

Luxembourg.lu

Key Indicators

Population, 2002	449,000
Main telephone lines in operation, 2001	346,763
growth (%) 1999–2001	12%
Cellular mobile telephone subscribers, 2002	455,000
growth (%) 1999–2002	118%
Personal computers, 2001	230,000
growth (%) 1999–2001	35%
Internet users (estimated), 2002	165,000
growth (%) 1999–2002	120%

Source: Data from International Telecommunication Union

RANK/102

Environment Component Index — 9

Market Environment	8
Political and Regulatory Environment	10
Infrastructure Environment	18
State of cluster development, 2003	36
Venture capital availability, 2003	5
Subsidies for firm-level R&D, 2003	3
Quality of scientific research institutions, 2003	63
Availability of scientists and engineers, 2003	69
Brain drain, 2003	14
Utility patents granted (per 1,000,000 inhabitants), 2002	12
ICT manufactured exports (per capita), 2001	3
ICT service exports (per capita), 2001	1
Overall administrative burden, 2003	17
Quality of the legal system, 2003	18
Laws relating to ICT, 2003	20
Competition in the ISP sector, 2003	30
Foreign ownership restrictions, 2003	4
Efficiency of the tax system, 2003	7
Freedom of the press, 2003	18
Overall infrastructure quality, 2003	15
Waiting time for telephone lines (years), 2000	1
Telephone mainlines (per 1,000 inhabitants), 2001	26
Public pay telephones (per 1,000 inhabitants), 2001	80
Internet servers (per 1,000,000 inhabitants), 2001	4

Networked Readiness Index Rank

2003–2004 (102 countries) — **14**

2002–2003 (82 countries) — 27

Readiness Component Index — 25

Individual Readiness	28
Business Readiness	25
Government Readiness	28
Public expenditure on education (per capita), 2000	5
Adult illiteracy (%), 2001	1
Tertiary enrollment (gross %), 2001 or most recent available	76
Radios (per 1,000 inhabitants), 2001 or most recent available	56
Television sets (per 1,000 inhabitants), 2001	18
Households online (as % of households with computers), 2002	20
Quality of math and science education, 2003	41
Affordability of local fixed line calls (as % of per capita GDP), 2001	4
Affordability of Internet telephone access (as % of per capita GDP), 2001	63
Affordability of Internet service provider fees (as % of per capita GDP), 2001	2
Ease of obtaining telephone lines, 2003	19
Cost of business telephone monthly subscription (as % of per capita GDP), 2002	3
Extent of staff training, 2003	13
Quality of business schools, 2003	93
Scientists and engineers in R&D (per 1,000 inhabitants), 2000	15
Government prioritization of ICT, 2003	23
Government online presence, 2003	58
Government procurement of ICT, 2003	8

Usage Component Index — 8

Individual Usage	1
Business Usage	19
Government Usage	43
Personal computers (per 1,000 inhabitants), 2001	1
ISDN subscribers (per 1,000 inhabitants), 2001	2
Cable television subscribers (per 1,000 inhabitants), 2001	4
Internet users (per 1,000 inhabitants), 2001	7
Computers installed in businesses (per 1,000 inhabitants), 2001	19
Firm-level technology absorption, 2003	20
Prevalence of foreign technology licensing, 2003	46
Government success in ICT promotion, 2003	23
Government online services, 2003	54

Macedonia, FYR.mk

Key Indicators

Population, 2002	2,064,000
Main telephone lines in operation, 2001	538,507
growth (%) 1999–2001	14%
Cellular mobile telephone subscribers, 2001	223,275
growth (%) 1999–2001	358%
Personal computers, 2002	n/a
growth (%) 1999–2002	n/a
Internet users (estimated), 2001	70,000
growth (%) 1999–2001	133%

Source: Data from International Telecommunication Union

RANK/102

Environment Component Index	59
Market Environment	76
Political and Regulatory Environment	79
Infrastructure Environment	40
State of cluster development, 2003	95
Venture capital availability, 2003	36
Subsidies for firm-level R&D, 2003	79
Quality of scientific research institutions, 2003	84
Availability of scientists and engineers, 2003	42
Brain drain, 2003	98
Utility patents granted (per 1,000,000 inhabitants), 2002	72
ICT manufactured exports (per capita), 2001	73
ICT service exports (per capita), 2001	47
Overall administrative burden, 2003	69
Quality of the legal system, 2003	88
Laws relating to ICT, 2003	84
Competition in the ISP sector, 2003	76
Foreign ownership restrictions, 2003	86
Efficiency of the tax system, 2003	48
Freedom of the press, 2003	52
Overall infrastructure quality, 2003	85
Waiting time for telephone lines (years), 2000	76
Telephone mainlines (per 1,000 inhabitants), 2001	42
Public pay telephones (per 1,000 inhabitants), 2001	2
Internet servers (per 1,000,000 inhabitants), 2001	62

Networked Readiness Index Rank

2003–2004 (102 countries) 75

Readiness Component Index	75
Individual Readiness	50
Business Readiness	71
Government Readiness	91
Public expenditure on education (per capita), 2000	62
Adult illiteracy (%), 2001	45
Tertiary enrollment (gross %), 2001 or most recent available	53
Radios (per 1,000 inhabitants), 2001 or most recent available	80
Television sets (per 1,000 inhabitants), 2001	54
Households online (as % of households with computers), 2002	57
Quality of math and science education, 2003	39
Affordability of local fixed line calls (as % of per capita GDP), 2001	26
Affordability of Internet telephone access (as % of per capita GDP), 2001	5
Affordability of Internet service provider fees (as % of per capita GDP), 2001	48
Ease of obtaining telephone lines, 2003	55
Cost of business telephone monthly subscription (as % of per capita GDP), 2002	62
Extent of staff training, 2003	70
Quality of business schools, 2003	91
Scientists and engineers in R&D (per 1,000 inhabitants), 2000	61
Government prioritization of ICT, 2003	85
Government online presence, 2003	90
Government procurement of ICT, 2003	61

Usage Component Index	87
Individual Usage	59
Business Usage	90
Government Usage	88
Personal computers (per 1,000 inhabitants), 2001	57
ISDN subscribers (per 1,000 inhabitants), 2001	56
Cable television subscribers (per 1,000 inhabitants), 2001	57
Internet users (per 1,000 inhabitants), 2001	58
Computers installed in businesses (per 1,000 inhabitants), 2002	94
Firm-level technology absorption, 2003	93
Prevalence of foreign technology licensing, 2003	78
Government success in ICT promotion, 2003	89
Government online services, 2003	68

Madagascar.mg

Key Indicators

Population, 2002	15,910,600
Main telephone lines in operation, 2002	59,441
growth (%) 1999–2002	18%
Cellular mobile telephone subscribers, 2002	163,010
growth (%) 1999–2002	356%
Personal computers, 2001	40,000
growth (%) 1999–2001	33%
Internet users (estimated), 2002	55,000
growth (%) 1999–2002	120%

Source: Data from International Telecommunication Union

RANK/102

Environment Component Index	87
Market Environment	84
Political and Regulatory Environment	89
Infrastructure Environment	81
State of cluster development, 2003	92
Venture capital availability, 2003	82
Subsidies for firm-level R&D, 2003	87
Quality of scientific research institutions, 2003	86
Availability of scientists and engineers, 2003	60
Brain drain, 2003	77
Utility patents granted (per 1,000,000 inhabitants), 2002	72
ICT manufactured exports (per capita), 2001	69
ICT service exports (per capita), 2001	99
Overall administrative burden, 2003	101
Quality of the legal system, 2003	86
Laws relating to ICT, 2003	94
Competition in the ISP sector, 2003	79
Foreign ownership restrictions, 2003	74
Efficiency of the tax system, 2003	71
Freedom of the press, 2003	68
Overall infrastructure quality, 2003	96
Waiting time for telephone lines (years), 2000	28
Telephone mainlines (per 1,000 inhabitants), 2001	95
Public pay telephones (per 1,000 inhabitants), 2001	98
Internet servers (per 1,000,000 inhabitants), 2001	89

Networked Readiness Index Rank

2003–2004 (102 countries) **92**

Readiness Component Index	94
Individual Readiness	96
Business Readiness	97
Government Readiness	88
Public expenditure on education (per capita), 2000	90
Adult illiteracy (%), 2001	87
Tertiary enrollment (gross %), 2001 or most recent available	93
Radios (per 1,000 inhabitants), 2001 or most recent available	78
Television sets (per 1,000 inhabitants), 2001	93
Households online (as % of households with computers), 2002	77
Quality of math and science education, 2003	63
Affordability of local fixed line calls (as % of per capita GDP), 2001	99
Affordability of Internet telephone access (as % of per capita GDP), 2001	92
Affordability of Internet service provider fees (as % of per capita GDP), 2001	98
Ease of obtaining telephone lines, 2003	89
Cost of business telephone monthly subscription (as % of per capita GDP), 2002	99
Extent of staff training, 2003	86
Quality of business schools, 2003	74
Scientists and engineers in R&D (per 1,000 inhabitants), 2000	101
Government prioritization of ICT, 2003	44
Government online presence, 2003	95
Government procurement of ICT, 2003	75

Usage Component Index	90
Individual Usage	81
Business Usage	95
Government Usage	82
Personal computers (per 1,000 inhabitants), 2001	96
ISDN subscribers (per 1,000 inhabitants), 2001	85
Cable television subscribers (per 1,000 inhabitants), 2001	62
Internet users (per 1,000 inhabitants), 2001	94
Computers installed in businesses (per 1,000 inhabitants), 2002	95
Firm-level technology absorption, 2003	56
Prevalence of foreign technology licensing, 2003	98
Government success in ICT promotion, 2003	50
Government online services, 2003	93

Malawi.mw

Key Indicators

Population, 2002	10,436,800
Main telephone lines in operation, 2002	73,100
growth (%) 1999–2002	77%
Cellular mobile telephone subscribers, 2002	86,047
growth (%) 1999–2002	282%
Personal computers, 2001	13,000
growth (%) 1999–2001	30%
Internet users (estimated), 2002	27,000
growth (%) 1999–2002	170%

Source: Data from International Telecommunication Union

RANK/102

Environment Component Index · 88

Market Environment	82
Political and Regulatory Environment	49
Infrastructure Environment	100
State of cluster development, 2003	75
Venture capital availability, 2003	99
Subsidies for firm-level R&D, 2003	93
Quality of scientific research institutions, 2003	68
Availability of scientists and engineers, 2003	70
Brain drain, 2003	72
Utility patents granted (per 1,000,000 inhabitants), 2002	72
ICT manufactured exports (per capita), 2001	96
ICT service exports (per capita), 2001	88
Overall administrative burden, 2003	20
Quality of the legal system, 2003	40
Laws relating to ICT, 2003	90
Competition in the ISP sector, 2003	55
Foreign ownership restrictions, 2003	17
Efficiency of the tax system, 2003	32
Freedom of the press, 2003	73
Overall infrastructure quality, 2003	79
Waiting time for telephone lines (years), 2000	100
Telephone mainlines (per 1,000 inhabitants), 2001	93
Public pay telephones (per 1,000 inhabitants), 2001	97
Internet servers (per 1,000,000 inhabitants), 2001	96

Networked Readiness Index Rank

2003–2004 (102 countries) · 88

Readiness Component Index · 88

Individual Readiness	93
Business Readiness	78
Government Readiness	84
Public expenditure on education (per capita), 2000	96
Adult illiteracy (%), 2001	90
Tertiary enrollment (gross %), 2001 or most recent available	102
Radios (per 1,000 inhabitants), 2001 or most recent available	43
Television sets (per 1,000 inhabitants), 2001	100
Households online (as % of households with computers), 2002	84
Quality of math and science education, 2003	71
Affordability of local fixed line calls (as % of per capita GDP), 2001	91
Affordability of Internet telephone access (as % of per capita GDP), 2001	89
Affordability of Internet service provider fees (as % of per capita GDP), 2001	101
Ease of obtaining telephone lines, 2003	84
Cost of business telephone monthly subscription (as % of per capita GDP), 2002	85
Extent of staff training, 2003	69
Quality of business schools, 2003	68
Scientists and engineers in R&D (per 1,000 inhabitants), 2000	50
Government prioritization of ICT, 2003	89
Government online presence, 2003	67
Government procurement of ICT, 2003	80

Usage Component Index · 91

Individual Usage	100
Business Usage	88
Government Usage	87
Personal computers (per 1,000 inhabitants), 2001	99
ISDN subscribers (per 1,000 inhabitants), 2001	97
Cable television subscribers (per 1,000 inhabitants), 2001	n/a
Internet users (per 1,000 inhabitants), 2001	98
Computers installed in businesses (per 1,000 inhabitants), 2002	98
Firm-level technology absorption, 2003	92
Prevalence of foreign technology licensing, 2003	79
Government success in ICT promotion, 2003	76
Government online services, 2003	89

Malaysia.my

Key Indicators

Population, 2002	**24,370,000**
Main telephone lines in operation, 2002	**4,670,000**
growth (%) 1999–2002	5%
Cellular mobile telephone subscribers, 2002	**9,245,000**
growth (%) 1999–2002	209%
Personal computers, 2002	**3,600,000**
growth (%) 1999–2002	100%
Internet users (estimated), 2002	**7,500,000**
growth (%) 1999–2002	168%

Source: Data from International Telecommunication Union

RANK/102

Environment Component Index	**26**
Market Environment	26
Political and Regulatory Environment	31
Infrastructure Environment	27
State of cluster development, 2003	24
Venture capital availability, 2003	24
Subsidies for firm-level R&D, 2003	9
Quality of scientific research institutions, 2003	36
Availability of scientists and engineers, 2003	65
Brain drain, 2003	37
Utility patents granted (per 1,000,000 inhabitants), 2002	34
ICT manufactured exports (per capita), 2001	7
ICT service exports (per capita), 2001	30
Overall administrative burden, 2003	16
Quality of the legal system, 2003	41
Laws relating to ICT, 2003	7
Competition in the ISP sector, 2003	36
Foreign ownership restrictions, 2003	67
Efficiency of the tax system, 2003	5
Freedom of the press, 2003	98
Overall infrastructure quality, 2003	12
Waiting time for telephone lines (years), 2000	52
Telephone mainlines (per 1,000 inhabitants), 2001	53
Public pay telephones (per 1,000 inhabitants), 2001	6
Internet servers (per 1,000,000 inhabitants), 2001	47

Networked Readiness Index Rank

2003–2004 (102 countries) — **26**

2002–2003 (82 countries)	32
2001–2002 (75 countries)	36

Readiness Component Index	**29**
Individual Readiness	47
Business Readiness	38
Government Readiness	6
Public expenditure on education (per capita), 2000	37
Adult illiteracy (%), 2001	64
Tertiary enrollment (gross %), 2001 or most recent available	50
Radios (per 1,000 inhabitants), 2001 or most recent available	48
Television sets (per 1,000 inhabitants), 2001	60
Households online (as % of households with computers), 2002	26
Quality of math and science education, 2003	47
Affordability of local fixed line calls (as % of per capita GDP), 2001	19
Affordability of Internet telephone access (as % of per capita GDP), 2001	13
Affordability of Internet service provider fees (as % of per capita GDP), 2001	29
Ease of obtaining telephone lines, 2003	44
Cost of business telephone monthly subscription (as % of per capita GDP), 2002	37
Extent of staff training, 2003	18
Quality of business schools, 2003	46
Scientists and engineers in R&D (per 1,000 inhabitants), 2000	79
Government prioritization of ICT, 2003	2
Government online presence, 2003	43
Government procurement of ICT, 2003	2

Usage Component Index	**26**
Individual Usage	31
Business Usage	22
Government Usage	7
Personal computers (per 1,000 inhabitants), 2001	34
ISDN subscribers (per 1,000 inhabitants), 2001	48
Cable television subscribers (per 1,000 inhabitants), 2001	n/a
Internet users (per 1,000 inhabitants), 2001	26
Computers installed in businesses (per 1,000 inhabitants), 2002	33
Firm-level technology absorption, 2003	14
Prevalence of foreign technology licensing, 2003	2
Government success in ICT promotion, 2003	2
Government online services, 2003	20

Mali.ml

Key Indicators

Population, 2002	10,628,800
Main telephone lines in operation, 2002	49,730
growth (%) 1999–2002	47%
Cellular mobile telephone subscribers, 2002	52,639
growth (%) 1999–2002	724%
Personal computers, 2001	14,000
growth (%) 1999–2001	27%
Internet users (estimated), 2002	32,000
growth (%) 1999–2002	410%

Source: Data from International Telecommunication Union

RANK/102

Environment Component Index	80
Market Environment	87
Political and Regulatory Environment	70
Infrastructure Environment	77
State of cluster development, 2003	91
Venture capital availability, 2003	95
Subsidies for firm-level R&D, 2003	63
Quality of scientific research institutions, 2003	75
Availability of scientists and engineers, 2003	79
Brain drain, 2003	94
Utility patents granted (per 1,000,000 inhabitants), 2002	72
ICT manufactured exports (per capita), 2001	94
ICT service exports (per capita), 2001	91
Overall administrative burden, 2003	61
Quality of the legal system, 2003	63
Laws relating to ICT, 2003	96
Competition in the ISP sector, 2003	84
Foreign ownership restrictions, 2003	53
Efficiency of the tax system, 2003	58
Freedom of the press, 2003	36
Overall infrastructure quality, 2003	91
Waiting time for telephone lines (years), 2000	74
Telephone mainlines (per 1,000 inhabitants), 2001	95
Public pay telephones (per 1,000 inhabitants), 2001	31
Internet servers (per 1,000,000 inhabitants), 2001	92

Networked Readiness Index Rank

2003–2004 (102 countries) 96

Readiness Component Index	99
Individual Readiness	99
Business Readiness	98
Government Readiness	90
Public expenditure on education (per capita), 2000	94
Adult illiteracy (%), 2001	102
Tertiary enrollment (gross %), 2001 or most recent available	94
Radios (per 1,000 inhabitants), 2001 or most recent available	85
Television sets (per 1,000 inhabitants), 2001	95
Households online (as % of households with computers), 2002	78
Quality of math and science education, 2003	79
Affordability of local fixed line calls (as % of per capita GDP), 2001	96
Affordability of Internet telephone access (as % of per capita GDP), 2001	97
Affordability of Internet service provider fees (as % of per capita GDP), 2001	100
Ease of obtaining telephone lines, 2003	99
Cost of business telephone monthly subscription (as % of per capita GDP), 2002	92
Extent of staff training, 2003	102
Quality of business schools, 2003	96
Scientists and engineers in R&D (per 1,000 inhabitants), 2000	99
Government prioritization of ICT, 2003	21
Government online presence, 2003	101
Government procurement of ICT, 2003	72

Usage Component Index	98
Individual Usage	99
Business Usage	102
Government Usage	94
Personal computers (per 1,000 inhabitants), 2001	101
ISDN subscribers (per 1,000 inhabitants), 2001	90
Cable television subscribers (per 1,000 inhabitants), 2001	94
Internet users (per 1,000 inhabitants), 2001	91
Computers installed in businesses (per 1,000 inhabitants), 2002	84
Firm-level technology absorption, 2003	94
Prevalence of foreign technology licensing, 2003	102
Government success in ICT promotion, 2003	71
Government online services, 2003	99

Malta.mt

Key Indicators

Population, 2002	396,000
Main telephone lines in operation, 2002	207,269
growth (%) 1999–2002	5%
Cellular mobile telephone subscribers, 2002	276,859
growth (%) 1999–2002	637%
Personal computers, 2001	90,000
growth (%) 1999–2001	29%
Internet users (estimated), 2001	99,000
growth (%) 1999–2001	230%

Source: Data from International Telecommunication Union

RANK/102

Environment Component Index	29
Market Environment	41
Political and Regulatory Environment	20
Infrastructure Environment	29
State of cluster development, 2003	79
Venture capital availability, 2003	56
Subsidies for firm-level R&D, 2003	38
Quality of scientific research institutions, 2003	71
Availability of scientists and engineers, 2003	58
Brain drain, 2003	29
Utility patents granted (per 1,000,000 inhabitants), 2002	33
ICT manufactured exports (per capita), 2001	4
ICT service exports (per capita), 2001	19
Overall administrative burden, 2003	39
Quality of the legal system, 2003	21
Laws relating to ICT, 2003	29
Competition in the ISP sector, 2003	34
Foreign ownership restrictions, 2003	37
Efficiency of the tax system, 2003	8
Freedom of the press, 2003	35
Overall infrastructure quality, 2003	42
Waiting time for telephone lines (years), 2000	30
Telephone mainlines (per 1,000 inhabitants), 2001	30
Public pay telephones (per 1,000 inhabitants), 2001	20
Internet servers (per 1,000,000 inhabitants), 2001	24

Networked Readiness Index Rank

2003–2004 (102 countries) **27**

Readiness Component Index	31
Individual Readiness	35
Business Readiness	40
Government Readiness	23
Public expenditure on education (per capita), 2000	29
Adult illiteracy (%), 2001	53
Tertiary enrollment (gross %), 2001 or most recent available	58
Radios (per 1,000 inhabitants), 2001 or most recent available	26
Television sets (per 1,000 inhabitants), 2001	17
Households online (as % of households with computers), 2002	36
Quality of math and science education, 2003	30
Affordability of local fixed line calls (as % of per capita GDP), 2001	38
Affordability of Internet telephone access (as % of per capita GDP), 2001	8
Affordability of Internet service provider fees (as % of per capita GDP), 2001	33
Ease of obtaining telephone lines, 2003	32
Cost of business telephone monthly subscription (as % of per capita GDP), 2002	30
Extent of staff training, 2003	38
Quality of business schools, 2003	58
Scientists and engineers in R&D (per 1,000 inhabitants), 2000	47
Government prioritization of ICT, 2003	6
Government online presence, 2003	40
Government procurement of ICT, 2003	54

Usage Component Index	24
Individual Usage	20
Business Usage	29
Government Usage	17
Personal computers (per 1,000 inhabitants), 2001	30
ISDN subscribers (per 1,000 inhabitants), 2001	40
Cable television subscribers (per 1,000 inhabitants), 2001	8
Internet users (per 1,000 inhabitants), 2001	12
Computers installed in businesses (per 1,000 inhabitants), 2002	24
Firm-level technology absorption, 2003	45
Prevalence of foreign technology licensing, 2003	45
Government success in ICT promotion, 2003	7
Government online services, 2003	27

Mauritius.mu

Key Indicators

Population, 2002	**1,210,492**
Main telephone lines in operation, 2002	**327,225**
growth (%) 1999–2002	27%
Cellular mobile telephone subscribers, 2002	**350,000**
growth (%) 1999–2002	243%
Personal computers, 2001	**130,000**
growth (%) 1999–2001	18%
Internet users (estimated), 2002	**180,000**
growth (%) 1999–2002	227%

Source: Data from International Telecommunication Union

RANK/102

Environment Component Index	48
Market Environment	53
Political and Regulatory Environment	54
Infrastructure Environment	44
State of cluster development, 2003	31
Venture capital availability, 2003	31
Subsidies for firm-level R&D, 2003	50
Quality of scientific research institutions, 2003	78
Availability of scientists and engineers, 2003	66
Brain drain, 2003	62
Utility patents granted (per 1,000,000 inhabitants), 2002	72
ICT manufactured exports (per capita), 2001	60
ICT service exports (per capita), 2001	25
Overall administrative burden, 2003	87
Quality of the legal system, 2003	44
Laws relating to ICT, 2003	32
Competition in the ISP sector, 2003	99
Foreign ownership restrictions, 2003	87
Efficiency of the tax system, 2003	10
Freedom of the press, 2003	41
Overall infrastructure quality, 2003	35
Waiting time for telephone lines (years), 2000	59
Telephone mainlines (per 1,000 inhabitants), 2001	43
Public pay telephones (per 1,000 inhabitants), 2001	51
Internet servers (per 1,000,000 inhabitants), 2001	40

Networked Readiness Index Rank

2003–2004 (102 countries) **43**

2002–2003 (82 countries)	56
2001–2002 (75 countries)	51

Readiness Component Index	41
Individual Readiness	55
Business Readiness	49
Government Readiness	20
Public expenditure on education (per capita), 2000	50
Adult illiteracy (%), 2001	72
Tertiary enrollment (gross %), 2001 or most recent available	71
Radios (per 1,000 inhabitants), 2001 or most recent available	57
Television sets (per 1,000 inhabitants), 2001	47
Households online (as % of households with computers), 2002	46
Quality of math and science education, 2003	51
Affordability of local fixed line calls (as % of per capita GDP), 2001	34
Affordability of Internet telephone access (as % of per capita GDP), 2001	20
Affordability of Internet service provider fees (as % of per capita GDP), 2001	46
Ease of obtaining telephone lines, 2003	52
Cost of business telephone monthly subscription (as % of per capita GDP), 2002	29
Extent of staff training, 2003	31
Quality of business schools, 2003	69
Scientists and engineers in R&D (per 1,000 inhabitants), 2000	63
Government prioritization of ICT, 2003	4
Government online presence, 2003	32
Government procurement of ICT, 2003	66

Usage Component Index	37
Individual Usage	41
Business Usage	61
Government Usage	25
Personal computers (per 1,000 inhabitants), 2001	37
ISDN subscribers (per 1,000 inhabitants), 2001	51
Cable television subscribers (per 1,000 inhabitants), 2001	40
Internet users (per 1,000 inhabitants), 2001	36
Computers installed in businesses (per 1,000 inhabitants), 2002	56
Firm-level technology absorption, 2003	63
Prevalence of foreign technology licensing, 2003	51
Government success in ICT promotion, 2003	13
Government online services, 2003	44

Mexico.mx

Key Indicators

Population, 2002	101,877,000
Main telephone lines in operation, 2002	14,941,630
growth (%) 1999–2002	37%
Cellular mobile telephone subscribers, 2002	25,928,260
growth (%) 1999–2002	235%
Personal computers, 2001	6,900,000
growth (%) 1999–2001	60%
Internet users (estimated), 2002	4,663,364
growth (%) 1999–2002	156%

Source: Data from International Telecommunication Union

RANK/102

Environment Component Index	47
Market Environment	55
Political and Regulatory Environment	59
Infrastructure Environment	42
State of cluster development, 2003	47
Venture capital availability, 2003	76
Subsidies for firm-level R&D, 2003	51
Quality of scientific research institutions, 2003	52
Availability of scientists and engineers, 2003	82
Brain drain, 2003	31
Utility patents granted (per 1,000,000 inhabitants), 2002	41
ICT manufactured exports (per capita), 2001	27
ICT service exports (per capita), 2001	71
Overall administrative burden, 2003	82
Quality of the legal system, 2003	64
Laws relating to ICT, 2003	56
Competition in the ISP sector, 2003	49
Foreign ownership restrictions, 2003	26
Efficiency of the tax system, 2003	90
Freedom of the press, 2003	40
Overall infrastructure quality, 2003	52
Waiting time for telephone lines (years), 2000	33
Telephone mainlines (per 1,000 inhabitants), 2001	57
Public pay telephones (per 1,000 inhabitants), 2001	8
Internet servers (per 1,000,000 inhabitants), 2001	52

Networked Readiness Index Rank

2003–2004 (102 countries) — 44

2002–2003 (82 countries)	47
2001–2002 (75 countries)	44

Readiness Component Index	47
Individual Readiness	53
Business Readiness	50
Government Readiness	45
Public expenditure on education (per capita), 2000	35
Adult illiteracy (%), 2001	58
Tertiary enrollment (gross %), 2001 or most recent available	59
Radios (per 1,000 inhabitants), 2001 or most recent available	65
Television sets (per 1,000 inhabitants), 2001	53
Households online (as % of households with computers), 2002	28
Quality of math and science education, 2003	80
Affordability of local fixed line calls (as % of per capita GDP), 2001	52
Affordability of Internet telephone access (as % of per capita GDP), 2001	88
Affordability of Internet service provider fees (as % of per capita GDP), 2001	31
Ease of obtaining telephone lines, 2003	53
Cost of business telephone monthly subscription (as % of per capita GDP), 2002	52
Extent of staff training, 2003	42
Quality of business schools, 2003	35
Scientists and engineers in R&D (per 1,000 inhabitants), 2000	72
Government prioritization of ICT, 2003	41
Government online presence, 2003	47
Government procurement of ICT, 2003	59

Usage Component Index	36
Individual Usage	54
Business Usage	32
Government Usage	28
Personal computers (per 1,000 inhabitants), 2001	46
ISDN subscribers (per 1,000 inhabitants), 2001	26
Cable television subscribers (per 1,000 inhabitants), 2001	59
Internet users (per 1,000 inhabitants), 2001	57
Computers installed in businesses (per 1,000 inhabitants), 2002	37
Firm-level technology absorption, 2003	44
Prevalence of foreign technology licensing, 2003	8
Government success in ICT promotion, 2003	51
Government online services, 2003	24

Morocco.ma

Key Indicators

Population, 2002	**29,643,000**
Main telephone lines in operation, 2002	**1,127,447**
growth (%) 1999–2002	-23%
Cellular mobile telephone subscribers, 2002	**6,198,670**
growth (%) 1999–2002	1,579%
Personal computers, 2001	**400,000**
growth (%) 1999–2001	33%
Internet users (estimated), 2002	**500,000**
growth (%) 1999–2002	900%

Source: Data from International Telecommunication Union

RANK/102

Environment Component Index — 61

Market Environment	60
Political and Regulatory Environment	69
Infrastructure Environment	61
State of cluster development, 2003	40
Venture capital availability, 2003	53
Subsidies for firm-level R&D, 2003	36
Quality of scientific research institutions, 2003	66
Availability of scientists and engineers, 2003	53
Brain drain, 2003	90
Utility patents granted (per 1,000,000 inhabitants), 2002	72
ICT manufactured exports (per capita), 2001	54
ICT service exports (per capita), 2001	66
Overall administrative burden, 2003	36
Quality of the legal system, 2003	71
Laws relating to ICT, 2003	57
Competition in the ISP sector, 2003	74
Foreign ownership restrictions, 2003	31
Efficiency of the tax system, 2003	31
Freedom of the press, 2003	91
Overall infrastructure quality, 2003	65
Waiting time for telephone lines (years), 2000	32
Telephone mainlines (per 1,000 inhabitants), 2001	78
Public pay telephones (per 1,000 inhabitants), 2001	47
Internet servers (per 1,000,000 inhabitants), 2001	80

Networked Readiness Index Rank

2003–2004 (102 countries) 64

2002–2003 (82 countries)	52
2001–2002 (75 countries)	

Readiness Component Index — 70

Individual Readiness	78
Business Readiness	46
Government Readiness	82
Public expenditure on education (per capita), 2000	66
Adult illiteracy (%), 2001	94
Tertiary enrollment (gross %), 2001 or most recent available	73
Radios (per 1,000 inhabitants), 2001 or most recent available	74
Television sets (per 1,000 inhabitants), 2001	70
Households online (as % of households with computers), 2002	43
Quality of math and science education, 2003	50
Affordability of local fixed line calls (as % of per capita GDP), 2001	78
Affordability of Internet telephone access (as % of per capita GDP), 2001	70
Affordability of Internet service provider fees (as % of per capita GDP), 2001	78
Ease of obtaining telephone lines, 2003	33
Cost of business telephone monthly subscription (as % of per capita GDP), 2002	80
Extent of staff training, 2003	51
Quality of business schools, 2003	42
Scientists and engineers in R&D (per 1,000 inhabitants), 2000	45
Government prioritization of ICT, 2003	63
Government online presence, 2003	83
Government procurement of ICT, 2003	58

Usage Component Index — 59

Individual Usage	76
Business Usage	64
Government Usage	47
Personal computers (per 1,000 inhabitants), 2001	76
ISDN subscribers (per 1,000 inhabitants), 2001	62
Cable television subscribers (per 1,000 inhabitants), 2001	67
Internet users (per 1,000 inhabitants), 2001	72
Computers installed in businesses (per 1,000 inhabitants), 2002	79
Firm-level technology absorption, 2003	43
Prevalence of foreign technology licensing, 2003	69
Government success in ICT promotion, 2003	32
Government online services, 2003	54

Mozambique.mz

Key Indicators

Population, 2002	18,234,000
Main telephone lines in operation, 2001	89,488
growth (%) 1999–2001	15%
Cellular mobile telephone subscribers, 2002	297,000
growth (%) 1999–2002	2,326%
Personal computers, 2001	70,000
growth (%) 1999–2001	40%
Internet users (estimated), 2001	30,000
growth (%) 1999–2001	200%

Source: Data from International Telecommunication Union

RANK/102

Environment Component Index	95
Market Environment	95
Political and Regulatory Environment	86
Infrastructure Environment	93
State of cluster development, 2003	100
Venture capital availability, 2003	87
Subsidies for firm-level R&D, 2003	91
Quality of scientific research institutions, 2003	92
Availability of scientists and engineers, 2003	101
Brain drain, 2003	39
Utility patents granted (per 1,000,000 inhabitants), 2002	72
ICT manufactured exports (per capita), 2001	97
ICT service exports (per capita), 2001	73
Overall administrative burden, 2003	77
Quality of the legal system, 2003	85
Laws relating to ICT, 2003	89
Competition in the ISP sector, 2003	92
Foreign ownership restrictions, 2003	62
Efficiency of the tax system, 2003	51
Freedom of the press, 2003	81
Overall infrastructure quality, 2003	92
Waiting time for telephone lines (years), 2000	78
Telephone mainlines (per 1,000 inhabitants), 2001	95
Public pay telephones (per 1,000 inhabitants), 2001	91
Internet servers (per 1,000,000 inhabitants), 2001	83

Networked Readiness Index Rank

2003–2004 (102 countries) 97

Readiness Component Index	100
Individual Readiness	98
Business Readiness	102
Government Readiness	87
Public expenditure on education (per capita), 2000	99
Adult illiteracy (%), 2001	95
Tertiary enrollment (gross %), 2001 or most recent available	101
Radios (per 1,000 inhabitants), 2001 or most recent available	101
Television sets (per 1,000 inhabitants), 2001	99
Households online (as % of households with computers), 2002	83
Quality of math and science education, 2003	96
Affordability of local fixed line calls (as % of per capita GDP), 2001	100
Affordability of Internet telephone access (as % of per capita GDP), 2001	95
Affordability of Internet service provider fees (as % of per capita GDP), 2001	95
Ease of obtaining telephone lines, 2003	78
Cost of business telephone monthly subscription (as % of per capita GDP), 2002	102
Extent of staff training, 2003	83
Quality of business schools, 2003	99
Scientists and engineers in R&D (per 1,000 inhabitants), 2000	96
Government prioritization of ICT, 2003	55
Government online presence, 2003	91
Government procurement of ICT, 2003	73

Usage Component Index	82
Individual Usage	97
Business Usage	80
Government Usage	73
Personal computers (per 1,000 inhabitants), 2001	92
ISDN subscribers (per 1,000 inhabitants), 2001	97
Cable television subscribers (per 1,000 inhabitants), 2001	96
Internet users (per 1,000 inhabitants), 2001	100
Computers installed in businesses (per 1,000 inhabitants), 2002	96
Firm-level technology absorption, 2003	64
Prevalence of foreign technology licensing, 2003	84
Government success in ICT promotion, 2003	53
Government online services, 2003	81

Namibia.na

Key Indicators

Population, 2002	1,875,000
Main telephone lines in operation, 2001	117,398
growth (%) 1999–2001	9%
Cellular mobile telephone subscribers, 2002	150,000
growth (%) 1999–2002	400%
Personal computers, 2001	100,000
growth (%) 1999–2001	100%
Internet users (estimated), 2001	45,000
growth (%) 1999–2001	650%

Source: Data from International Telecommunication Union

RANK/102

Environment Component Index	37
Market Environment	71
Political and Regulatory Environment	44
Infrastructure Environment	23
State of cluster development, 2003	66
Venture capital availability, 2003	46
Subsidies for firm-level R&D, 2003	68
Quality of scientific research institutions, 2003	80
Availability of scientists and engineers, 2003	93
Brain drain, 2003	47
Utility patents granted (per 1,000,000 inhabitants), 2002	72
ICT manufactured exports (per capita), 2001	66
ICT service exports (per capita), 2001	55
Overall administrative burden, 2003	37
Quality of the legal system, 2003	32
Laws relating to ICT, 2003	68
Competition in the ISP sector, 2003	61
Foreign ownership restrictions, 2003	73
Efficiency of the tax system, 2003	17
Freedom of the press, 2003	65
Overall infrastructure quality, 2003	20
Waiting time for telephone lines (years), 2000	51
Telephone mainlines (per 1,000 inhabitants), 2001	70
Public pay telephones (per 1,000 inhabitants), 2001	1
Internet servers (per 1,000,000 inhabitants), 2001	58

Readiness Component Index	73
Individual Readiness	77
Business Readiness	67
Government Readiness	74
Public expenditure on education (per capita), 2000	52
Adult illiteracy (%), 2001	75
Tertiary enrollment (gross %), 2001 or most recent available	81
Radios (per 1,000 inhabitants), 2001 or most recent available	92
Television sets (per 1,000 inhabitants), 2001	88
Households online (as % of households with computers), 2002	59
Quality of math and science education, 2003	82
Affordability of local fixed line calls (as % of per capita GDP), 2001	47
Affordability of Internet telephone access (as % of per capita GDP), 2001	32
Affordability of Internet service provider fees (as % of per capita GDP), 2001	74
Ease of obtaining telephone lines, 2003	59
Cost of business telephone monthly subscription (as % of per capita GDP), 2002	54
Extent of staff training, 2003	53
Quality of business schools, 2003	92
Scientists and engineers in R&D (per 1,000 inhabitants), 2000	58
Government prioritization of ICT, 2003	70
Government online presence, 2003	71
Government procurement of ICT, 2003	69

Usage Component Index	79
Individual Usage	68
Business Usage	63
Government Usage	83
Personal computers (per 1,000 inhabitants), 2001	60
ISDN subscribers (per 1,000 inhabitants), 2001	49
Cable television subscribers (per 1,000 inhabitants), 2001	75
Internet users (per 1,000 inhabitants), 2001	66
Computers installed in businesses (per 1,000 inhabitants), 2002	69
Firm-level technology absorption, 2003	75
Prevalence of foreign technology licensing, 2003	33
Government success in ICT promotion, 2003	66
Government online services, 2003	89

Netherlands.nl

Key Indicators

Population, 2002	16,195,000
Main telephone lines in operation, 2002	10,000,000
growth (%) 1999–2002	4%
Cellular mobile telephone subscribers, 2002	12,100,000
growth (%) 1999–2002	79%
Personal computers, 2001	6,900,000
growth (%) 1999–2001	21%
Internet users (estimated), 2002	8,590,000
growth (%) 1999–2002	39%

Source: Data from International Telecommunication Union

RANK/102

Environment Component Index	15
Market Environment	12
Political and Regulatory Environment	14
Infrastructure Environment	20
State of cluster development, 2003	19
Venture capital availability, 2003	6
Subsidies for firm-level R&D, 2003	18
Quality of scientific research institutions, 2003	16
Availability of scientists and engineers, 2003	49
Brain drain, 2003	6
Utility patents granted (per 1,000,000 inhabitants), 2002	11
ICT manufactured exports (per capita), 2001	5
ICT service exports (per capita), 2001	7
Overall administrative burden, 2003	56
Quality of the legal system, 2003	5
Laws relating to ICT, 2003	26
Competition in the ISP sector, 2003	17
Foreign ownership restrictions, 2003	24
Efficiency of the tax system, 2003	23
Freedom of the press, 2003	3
Overall infrastructure quality, 2003	16
Waiting time for telephone lines (years), 2000	1
Telephone mainlines (per 1,000 inhabitants), 2001	8
Public pay telephones (per 1,000 inhabitants), 2001	77
Internet servers (per 1,000,000 inhabitants), 2001	20

Networked Readiness Index Rank

2003–2004 (102 countries) — 13

2002–2003 (82 countries)	11
2001–2002 (75 countries)	6

Readiness Component Index	14
Individual Readiness	12
Business Readiness	15
Government Readiness	19
Public expenditure on education (per capita), 2000	13
Adult illiteracy (%), 2001	17
Tertiary enrollment (gross %), 2001 or most recent available	20
Radios (per 1,000 inhabitants), 2001 or most recent available	14
Television sets (per 1,000 inhabitants), 2001	21
Households online (as % of households with computers), 2002	3
Quality of math and science education, 2003	25
Affordability of local fixed line calls (as % of per capita GDP), 2001	14
Affordability of Internet telephone access (as % of per capita GDP), 2001	69
Affordability of Internet service provider fees (as % of per capita GDP), 2001	9
Ease of obtaining telephone lines, 2003	13
Cost of business telephone monthly subscription (as % of per capita GDP), 2002	13
Extent of staff training, 2003	9
Quality of business schools, 2003	14
Scientists and engineers in R&D (per 1,000 inhabitants), 2000	17
Government prioritization of ICT, 2003	64
Government online presence, 2003	8
Government procurement of ICT, 2003	37

Usage Component Index	12
Individual Usage	3
Business Usage	15
Government Usage	40
Personal computers (per 1,000 inhabitants), 2001	11
ISDN subscribers (per 1,000 inhabitants), 2001	5
Cable television subscribers (per 1,000 inhabitants), 2001	1
Internet users (per 1,000 inhabitants), 2001	6
Computers installed in businesses (per 1,000 inhabitants), 2002	12
Firm-level technology absorption, 2003	51
Prevalence of foreign technology licensing, 2003	36
Government success in ICT promotion, 2003	54
Government online services, 2003	33

New Zealand.nz

Key Indicators

Population, 2002	3,939,100
Main telephone lines in operation, 2002	1,765,000
growth (%) 1999–2002	-4%
Cellular mobile telephone subscribers, 2002	2,436,000
growth (%) 1999–2002	75%
Personal computers, 2001	1,500,000
growth (%) 1999–2001	20%
Internet users (estimated), 2002	1,908,000
growth (%) 1999–2002	71%

Source: Data from International Telecommunication Union

Networked Readiness Index Rank

2003–2004 (102 countries) **23**

2002–2003 (82 countries)	23
2001–2002 (75 countries)	11

RANK/102

Environment Component Index	18
Market Environment	33
Political and Regulatory Environment	12
Infrastructure Environment	8
State of cluster development, 2003	44
Venture capital availability, 2003	17
Subsidies for firm-level R&D, 2003	72
Quality of scientific research institutions, 2003	17
Availability of scientists and engineers, 2003	50
Brain drain, 2003	55
Utility patents granted (per 1,000,000 inhabitants), 2002	22
ICT manufactured exports (per capita), 2001	36
ICT service exports (per capita), 2001	29
Overall administrative burden, 2003	60
Quality of the legal system, 2003	7
Laws relating to ICT, 2003	10
Competition in the ISP sector, 2003	22
Foreign ownership restrictions, 2003	8
Efficiency of the tax system, 2003	15
Freedom of the press, 2003	13
Overall infrastructure quality, 2003	22
Waiting time for telephone lines (years), 2000	1
Telephone mainlines (per 1,000 inhabitants), 2001	21
Public pay telephones (per 1,000 inhabitants), 2001	7
Internet servers (per 1,000,000 inhabitants), 2001	6

Readiness Component Index	20
Individual Readiness	15
Business Readiness	18
Government Readiness	29
Public expenditure on education (per capita), 2000	21
Adult illiteracy (%), 2001	17
Tertiary enrollment (gross %), 2001 or most recent available	7
Radios (per 1,000 inhabitants), 2001 or most recent available	13
Television sets (per 1,000 inhabitants), 2001	19
Households online (as % of households with computers), 2002	18
Quality of math and science education, 2003	44
Affordability of local fixed line calls (as % of per capita GDP), 2001	11
Affordability of Internet telephone access (as % of per capita GDP), 2001	37
Affordability of Internet service provider fees (as % of per capita GDP), 2001	20
Ease of obtaining telephone lines, 2003	16
Cost of business telephone monthly subscription (as % of per capita GDP), 2002	43
Extent of staff training, 2003	20
Quality of business schools, 2003	20
Scientists and engineers in R&D (per 1,000 inhabitants), 2000	22
Government prioritization of ICT, 2003	51
Government online presence, 2003	19
Government procurement of ICT, 2003	50

Usage Component Index	23
Individual Usage	25
Business Usage	13
Government Usage	22
Personal computers (per 1,000 inhabitants), 2001	13
ISDN subscribers (per 1,000 inhabitants), 2001	23
Cable television subscribers (per 1,000 inhabitants), 2001	80
Internet users (per 1,000 inhabitants), 2001	23
Computers installed in businesses (per 1,000 inhabitants), 2002	9
Firm-level technology absorption, 2003	22
Prevalence of foreign technology licensing, 2003	32
Government success in ICT promotion, 2003	59
Government online services, 2003	15

Nicaragua.ni

Key Indicators

Population, 2002	5,370,000
Main telephone lines in operation, 2002	171,632
growth (%) 1999–2002	14%
Cellular mobile telephone subscribers, 2002	239,927
growth (%) 1999–2002	442%
Personal computers, 2002	150,000
growth (%) 1999–2002	50%
Internet users (estimated), 2002	90,000
growth (%) 1999–2002	260%

Source: Data from International Telecommunication Union

RANK/102

Environment Component Index	98
Market Environment	97
Political and Regulatory Environment	81
Infrastructure Environment	101
State of cluster development, 2003	98
Venture capital availability, 2003	83
Subsidies for firm-level R&D, 2003	95
Quality of scientific research institutions, 2003	97
Availability of scientists and engineers, 2003	92
Brain drain, 2003	61
Utility patents granted (per 1,000,000 inhabitants), 2002	72
ICT manufactured exports (per capita), 2001	87
ICT service exports (per capita), 2001	61
Overall administrative burden, 2003	78
Quality of the legal system, 2003	99
Laws relating to ICT, 2003	88
Competition in the ISP sector, 2003	82
Foreign ownership restrictions, 2003	65
Efficiency of the tax system, 2003	74
Freedom of the press, 2003	38
Overall infrastructure quality, 2003	95
Waiting time for telephone lines (years), 2000	101
Telephone mainlines (per 1,000 inhabitants), 2001	82
Public pay telephones (per 1,000 inhabitants), 2001	82
Internet servers (per 1,000,000 inhabitants), 2001	63

Networked Readiness Index Rank

2003–2004 (102 countries) **94**

2002–2003 (82 countries)	79
2001–2002 (75 countries)	69

Readiness Component Index	86
Individual Readiness	87
Business Readiness	92
Government Readiness	80
Public expenditure on education (per capita), 2000	81
Adult illiteracy (%), 2001	88
Tertiary enrollment (gross %), 2001 or most recent available	70
Radios (per 1,000 inhabitants), 2001 or most recent available	71
Television sets (per 1,000 inhabitants), 2001	85
Households online (as % of households with computers), 2002	71
Quality of math and science education, 2003	90
Affordability of local fixed line calls (as % of per capita GDP), 2001	84
Affordability of Internet telephone access (as % of per capita GDP), 2001	84
Affordability of Internet service provider fees (as % of per capita GDP), 2001	88
Ease of obtaining telephone lines, 2003	88
Cost of business telephone monthly subscription (as % of per capita GDP), 2002	79
Extent of staff training, 2003	94
Quality of business schools, 2003	78
Scientists and engineers in R&D (per 1,000 inhabitants), 2000	91
Government prioritization of ICT, 2003	87
Government online presence, 2003	57
Government procurement of ICT, 2003	86

Usage Component Index	94
Individual Usage	80
Business Usage	91
Government Usage	97
Personal computers (per 1,000 inhabitants), 2001	83
ISDN subscribers (per 1,000 inhabitants), 2001	73
Cable television subscribers (per 1,000 inhabitants), 2001	74
Internet users (per 1,000 inhabitants), 2001	79
Computers installed in businesses (per 1,000 inhabitants), 2002	83
Firm-level technology absorption, 2003	91
Prevalence of foreign technology licensing, 2003	85
Government success in ICT promotion, 2003	92
Government online services, 2003	96

Nigeria.ng

Key Indicators

Population, 2002	120,079,000
Main telephone lines in operation, 2002	702,000
growth (%) 1999–2002	56%
Cellular mobile telephone subscribers, 2002	1,633,060
growth (%) 1999–2002	6,432%
Personal computers, 2001	800,000
growth (%) 1999–2001	14%
Internet users (estimated), 2002	200,000
growth (%) 1999–2002	300%

Source: Data from International Telecommunication Union

RANK/102

Environment Component Index	72
Market Environment	65
Political and Regulatory Environment	65
Infrastructure Environment	85
State of cluster development, 2003	22
Venture capital availability, 2003	66
Subsidies for firm-level R&D, 2003	64
Quality of scientific research institutions, 2003	81
Availability of scientists and engineers, 2003	55
Brain drain, 2003	97
Utility patents granted (per 1,000,000 inhabitants), 2002	68
ICT manufactured exports (per capita), 2001	101
ICT service exports (per capita), 2001	93
Overall administrative burden, 2003	76
Quality of the legal system, 2003	61
Laws relating to ICT, 2003	75
Competition in the ISP sector, 2003	77
Foreign ownership restrictions, 2003	21
Efficiency of the tax system, 2003	52
Freedom of the press, 2003	64
Overall infrastructure quality, 2003	99
Waiting time for telephone lines (years), 2000	64
Telephone mainlines (per 1,000 inhabitants), 2001	93
Public pay telephones (per 1,000 inhabitants), 2001	100
Internet servers (per 1,000,000 inhabitants), 2001	101

Networked Readiness Index Rank

2003–2004 (102 countries) **79**

2002–2003 (82 countries)	74
2001–2002 (75 countries)	75

Readiness Component Index	82
Individual Readiness	90
Business Readiness	81
Government Readiness	70
Public expenditure on education (per capita), 2000	88
Adult illiteracy (%), 2001	89
Tertiary enrollment (gross %), 2001 or most recent available	85
Radios (per 1,000 inhabitants), 2001 or most recent available	81
Television sets (per 1,000 inhabitants), 2001	63
Households online (as % of households with computers), 2002	102
Quality of math and science education, 2003	91
Affordability of local fixed line calls (as % of per capita GDP), 2001	88
Affordability of Internet telephone access (as % of per capita GDP), 2001	91
Affordability of Internet service provider fees (as % of per capita GDP), 2001	92
Ease of obtaining telephone lines, 2003	83
Cost of business telephone monthly subscription (as % of per capita GDP), 2002	78
Extent of staff training, 2003	68
Quality of business schools, 2003	77
Scientists and engineers in R&D (per 1,000 inhabitants), 2000	78
Government prioritization of ICT, 2003	67
Government online presence, 2003	78
Government procurement of ICT, 2003	32

Usage Component Index	75
Individual Usage	94
Business Usage	56
Government Usage	69
Personal computers (per 1,000 inhabitants), 2001	87
ISDN subscribers (per 1,000 inhabitants), 2001	101
Cable television subscribers (per 1,000 inhabitants), 2001	86
Internet users (per 1,000 inhabitants), 2001	99
Computers installed in businesses (per 1,000 inhabitants), 2002	81
Firm-level technology absorption, 2003	49
Prevalence of foreign technology licensing, 2003	34
Government success in ICT promotion, 2003	39
Government online services, 2003	86

Norway.no

Key Indicators

Population, 2002	**4,556,000**
Main telephone lines in operation, 2002	**3,325,000**
growth (%) 1999–2002	5%
Cellular mobile telephone subscribers, 2002	**3,842,000**
growth (%) 1999–2002	40%
Personal computers, 2001	**2,300,000**
growth (%) 1999–2001	15%
Internet users (estimated), 2002	**2,300,000**
growth (%) 1999–2002	28%

Source: Data from International Telecommunication Union

RANK/102

Environment Component Index	16
Market Environment	18
Political and Regulatory Environment	22
Infrastructure Environment	7
State of cluster development, 2003	23
Venture capital availability, 2003	10
Subsidies for firm-level R&D, 2003	16
Quality of scientific research institutions, 2003	19
Availability of scientists and engineers, 2003	25
Brain drain, 2003	5
Utility patents granted (per 1,000,000 inhabitants), 2002	19
ICT manufactured exports (per capita), 2001	23
ICT service exports (per capita), 2001	12
Overall administrative burden, 2003	32
Quality of the legal system, 2003	16
Laws relating to ICT, 2003	15
Competition in the ISP sector, 2003	25
Foreign ownership restrictions, 2003	69
Efficiency of the tax system, 2003	56
Freedom of the press, 2003	14
Overall infrastructure quality, 2003	34
Waiting time for telephone lines (years), 2000	1
Telephone mainlines (per 1,000 inhabitants), 2001	3
Public pay telephones (per 1,000 inhabitants), 2001	11
Internet servers (per 1,000,000 inhabitants), 2001	14

Networked Readiness Index Rank

2003–2004 (102 countries) **8**

2002–2003 (82 countries)	17
2001–2002 (75 countries)	5

Readiness Component Index	6
Individual Readiness	1
Business Readiness	8
Government Readiness	30
Public expenditure on education (per capita), 2000	1
Adult illiteracy (%), 2001	1
Tertiary enrollment (gross %), 2001 or most recent available	6
Radios (per 1,000 inhabitants), 2001 or most recent available	1
Television sets (per 1,000 inhabitants), 2001	3
Households online (as % of households with computers), 2002	1
Quality of math and science education, 2003	55
Affordability of local fixed line calls (as % of per capita GDP), 2001	10
Affordability of Internet telephone access (as % of per capita GDP), 2001	58
Affordability of Internet service provider fees (as % of per capita GDP), 2001	5
Ease of obtaining telephone lines, 2003	21
Cost of business telephone monthly subscription (as % of per capita GDP), 2002	5
Extent of staff training, 2003	22
Quality of business schools, 2003	12
Scientists and engineers in R&D (per 1,000 inhabitants), 2000	5
Government prioritization of ICT, 2003	48
Government online presence, 2003	27
Government procurement of ICT, 2003	27

Usage Component Index	4
Individual Usage	2
Business Usage	8
Government Usage	30
Personal computers (per 1,000 inhabitants), 2001	8
ISDN subscribers (per 1,000 inhabitants), 2001	1
Cable television subscribers (per 1,000 inhabitants), 2001	13
Internet users (per 1,000 inhabitants), 2001	1
Computers installed in businesses (per 1,000 inhabitants), 2002	4
Firm-level technology absorption, 2003	21
Prevalence of foreign technology licensing, 2003	62
Government success in ICT promotion, 2003	42
Government online services, 2003	29

Pakistan.pk

Key Indicators

Population, 2002	148,784,000
Main telephone lines in operation, 2002	3,690,000
growth (%) 1999–2002	24%
Cellular mobile telephone subscribers, 2002	1,219,000
growth (%) 1999–2002	337%
Personal computers, 2001	600,000
growth (%) 1999–2001	3%
Internet users (estimated), 2002	1,500,000
growth (%) 1999–2002	1,775%

Source: Data from International Telecommunication Union

RANK/102

Environment Component Index	76
Market Environment	75
Political and Regulatory Environment	74
Infrastructure Environment	78
State of cluster development, 2003	13
Venture capital availability, 2003	80
Subsidies for firm-level R&D, 2003	81
Quality of scientific research institutions, 2003	90
Availability of scientists and engineers, 2003	81
Brain drain, 2003	81
Utility patents granted (per 1,000,000 inhabitants), 2002	71
ICT manufactured exports (per capita), 2001	92
ICT service exports (per capita), 2001	98
Overall administrative burden, 2003	83
Quality of the legal system, 2003	77
Laws relating to ICT, 2003	77
Competition in the ISP sector, 2003	38
Foreign ownership restrictions, 2003	46
Efficiency of the tax system, 2003	93
Freedom of the press, 2003	65
Overall infrastructure quality, 2003	68
Waiting time for telephone lines (years), 2000	68
Telephone mainlines (per 1,000 inhabitants), 2001	85
Public pay telephones (per 1,000 inhabitants), 2001	84
Internet servers (per 1,000,000 inhabitants), 2001	98

Networked Readiness Index Rank

2003–2004 (102 countries) 76

Readiness Component Index	78
Individual Readiness	89
Business Readiness	77
Government Readiness	57
Public expenditure on education (per capita), 2000	93
Adult illiteracy (%), 2001	97
Tertiary enrollment (gross %), 2001 or most recent available	88
Radios (per 1,000 inhabitants), 2001 or most recent available	97
Television sets (per 1,000 inhabitants), 2001	73
Households online (as % of households with computers), 2002	100
Quality of math and science education, 2003	95
Affordability of local fixed line calls (as % of per capita GDP), 2001	69
Affordability of Internet telephone access (as % of per capita GDP), 2001	55
Affordability of Internet service provider fees (as % of per capita GDP), 2001	83
Ease of obtaining telephone lines, 2003	65
Cost of business telephone monthly subscription (as % of per capita GDP), 2002	88
Extent of staff training, 2003	76
Quality of business schools, 2003	56
Scientists and engineers in R&D (per 1,000 inhabitants), 2000	93
Government prioritization of ICT, 2003	29
Government online presence, 2003	64
Government procurement of ICT, 2003	78

Usage Component Index	62
Individual Usage	89
Business Usage	76
Government Usage	37
Personal computers (per 1,000 inhabitants), 2001	90
ISDN subscribers (per 1,000 inhabitants), 2001	79
Cable television subscribers (per 1,000 inhabitants), 2001	77
Internet users (per 1,000 inhabitants), 2001	89
Computers installed in businesses (per 1,000 inhabitants), 2002	101
Firm-level technology absorption, 2003	82
Prevalence of foreign technology licensing, 2003	61
Government success in ICT promotion, 2003	33
Government online services, 2003	36

Panama.pa

Key Indicators

Population, 2002	2,960,000
Main telephone lines in operation, 2001	376,499
growth (%) 1999–2001	-19%
Cellular mobile telephone subscribers, 2001	475,354
growth (%) 1999–2001	104%
Personal computers, 2001	110,000
growth (%) 1999–2001	22%
Internet users (estimated), 2001	120,000
growth (%) 1999–2001	167%

Source: Data from International Telecommunication Union

RANK/102

Environment Component Index	53
Market Environment	58
Political and Regulatory Environment	64
Infrastructure Environment	51
State of cluster development, 2003	57
Venture capital availability, 2003	34
Subsidies for firm-level R&D, 2003	73
Quality of scientific research institutions, 2003	82
Availability of scientists and engineers, 2003	83
Brain drain, 2003	25
Utility patents granted (per 1,000,000 inhabitants), 2002	51
ICT manufactured exports (per capita), 2001	83
ICT service exports (per capita), 2001	44
Overall administrative burden, 2003	71
Quality of the legal system, 2003	89
Laws relating to ICT, 2003	42
Competition in the ISP sector, 2003	37
Foreign ownership restrictions, 2003	45
Efficiency of the tax system, 2003	50
Freedom of the press, 2003	63
Overall infrastructure quality, 2003	46
Waiting time for telephone lines (years), 2000	49
Telephone mainlines (per 1,000 inhabitants), 2001	56
Public pay telephones (per 1,000 inhabitants), 2001	28
Internet servers (per 1,000,000 inhabitants), 2001	40

Networked Readiness Index Rank

2003–2004 (102 countries) **58**

2002–2003 (82 countries)	61
2001–2002 (75 countries)	48

Readiness Component Index	63
Individual Readiness	51
Business Readiness	64
Government Readiness	68
Public expenditure on education (per capita), 2000	39
Adult illiteracy (%), 2001	54
Tertiary enrollment (gross %), 2001 or most recent available	42
Radios (per 1,000 inhabitants), 2001 or most recent available	68
Television sets (per 1,000 inhabitants), 2001	65
Households online (as % of households with computers), 2002	45
Quality of math and science education, 2003	77
Affordability of local fixed line calls (as % of per capita GDP), 2001	41
Affordability of Internet telephone access (as % of per capita GDP), 2001	21
Affordability of Internet service provider fees (as % of per capita GDP), 2001	45
Ease of obtaining telephone lines, 2003	58
Cost of business telephone monthly subscription (as % of per capita GDP), 2002	57
Extent of staff training, 2003	59
Quality of business schools, 2003	67
Scientists and engineers in R&D (per 1,000 inhabitants), 2000	84
Government prioritization of ICT, 2003	91
Government online presence, 2003	38
Government procurement of ICT, 2003	91

Usage Component Index	57
Individual Usage	50
Business Usage	44
Government Usage	76
Personal computers (per 1,000 inhabitants), 2001	59
ISDN subscribers (per 1,000 inhabitants), 2001	34
Cable television subscribers (per 1,000 inhabitants), 2001	40
Internet users (per 1,000 inhabitants), 2001	60
Computers installed in businesses (per 1,000 inhabitants), 2002	50
Firm-level technology absorption, 2003	32
Prevalence of foreign technology licensing, 2003	25
Government success in ICT promotion, 2003	80
Government online services, 2003	63

Paraguay.py

Key Indicators

Population, 2002	5,782,000
Main telephone lines in operation, 2002	273,218
growth (%) 1999–2002	2%
Cellular mobile telephone subscribers, 2002	1,667,018
growth (%) 1999–2002	283%
Personal computers, 2002	200,000
growth (%) 1999–2002	233%
Internet users (estimated), 2002	100,000
growth (%) 1999–2002	400%

Source: Data from International Telecommunication Union

RANK/102

Environment Component Index — 92

Market Environment	100
Political and Regulatory Environment	87
Infrastructure Environment	75
State of cluster development, 2003	99
Venture capital availability, 2003	96
Subsidies for firm-level R&D, 2003	102
Quality of scientific research institutions, 2003	101
Availability of scientists and engineers, 2003	98
Brain drain, 2003	59
Utility patents granted (per 1,000,000 inhabitants), 2002	72
ICT manufactured exports (per capita), 2001	78
ICT service exports (per capita), 2001	46
Overall administrative burden, 2003	44
Quality of the legal system, 2003	100
Laws relating to ICT, 2003	98
Competition in the ISP sector, 2003	81
Foreign ownership restrictions, 2003	80
Efficiency of the tax system, 2003	34
Freedom of the press, 2003	69
Overall infrastructure quality, 2003	97
Waiting time for telephone lines (years), 2000	47
Telephone mainlines (per 1,000 inhabitants), 2001	74
Public pay telephones (per 1,000 inhabitants), 2001	73
Internet servers (per 1,000,000 inhabitants), 2001	70

Networked Readiness Index Rank

2003–2004 (102 countries) — 91

2002–2003 (82 countries)	76
2001–2002 (75 countries)	63

Readiness Component Index — 87

Individual Readiness	75
Business Readiness	87
Government Readiness	92
Public expenditure on education (per capita), 2000	69
Adult illiteracy (%), 2001	48
Tertiary enrollment (gross %), 2001 or most recent available	74
Radios (per 1,000 inhabitants), 2001 or most recent available	83
Television sets (per 1,000 inhabitants), 2001	58
Households online (as % of households with computers), 2002	64
Quality of math and science education, 2003	97
Affordability of local fixed line calls (as % of per capita GDP), 2001	81
Affordability of Internet telephone access (as % of per capita GDP), 2001	48
Affordability of Internet service provider fees (as % of per capita GDP), 2001	77
Ease of obtaining telephone lines, 2003	86
Cost of business telephone monthly subscription (as % of per capita GDP), 2002	60
Extent of staff training, 2003	96
Quality of business schools, 2003	82
Scientists and engineers in R&D (per 1,000 inhabitants), 2000	55
Government prioritization of ICT, 2003	101
Government online presence, 2003	52
Government procurement of ICT, 2003	102

Usage Component Index — 100

Individual Usage	73
Business Usage	97
Government Usage	99
Personal computers (per 1,000 inhabitants), 2001	75
ISDN subscribers (per 1,000 inhabitants), 2001	102
Cable television subscribers (per 1,000 inhabitants), 2001	60
Internet users (per 1,000 inhabitants), 2001	76
Computers installed in businesses (per 1,000 inhabitants), 2002	64
Firm-level technology absorption, 2003	100
Prevalence of foreign technology licensing, 2003	97
Government success in ICT promotion, 2003	102
Government online services, 2003	68

Peru.pe

Key Indicators

Population, 2002	26,748,970
Main telephone lines in operation, 2001	2,022,265
growth (%) 1999–2001	20%
Cellular mobile telephone subscribers, 2002	2,300,000
growth (%) 1999–2002	127%
Personal computers, 2001	1,250,000
growth (%) 1999–2001	39%
Internet users (estimated), 2001	2,000,000
growth (%) 1999–2001	300%

Source: Data from International Telecommunication Union

RANK/102

Environment Component Index	71
Market Environment	90
Political and Regulatory Environment	76
Infrastructure Environment	63
State of cluster development, 2003	85
Venture capital availability, 2003	85
Subsidies for firm-level R&D, 2003	97
Quality of scientific research institutions, 2003	91
Availability of scientists and engineers, 2003	71
Brain drain, 2003	70
Utility patents granted (per 1,000,000 inhabitants), 2002	67
ICT manufactured exports (per capita), 2001	75
ICT service exports (per capita), 2001	81
Overall administrative burden, 2003	91
Quality of the legal system, 2003	92
Laws relating to ICT, 2003	60
Competition in the ISP sector, 2003	66
Foreign ownership restrictions, 2003	57
Efficiency of the tax system, 2003	66
Freedom of the press, 2003	45
Overall infrastructure quality, 2003	83
Waiting time for telephone lines (years), 2000	61
Telephone mainlines (per 1,000 inhabitants), 2001	69
Public pay telephones (per 1,000 inhabitants), 2001	36
Internet servers (per 1,000,000 inhabitants), 2001	60

Networked Readiness Index Rank

2003–2004 (102 countries) — **70**

2002–2003 (82 countries)	67
2001–2002 (75 countries)	52

Readiness Component Index	66
Individual Readiness	63
Business Readiness	61
Government Readiness	65
Public expenditure on education (per capita), 2000	64
Adult illiteracy (%), 2001	61
Tertiary enrollment (gross %), 2001 or most recent available	47
Radios (per 1,000 inhabitants), 2001 or most recent available	72
Television sets (per 1,000 inhabitants), 2001	73
Households online (as % of households with computers), 2002	62
Quality of math and science education, 2003	93
Affordability of local fixed line calls (as % of per capita GDP), 2001	54
Affordability of Internet telephone access (as % of per capita GDP), 200	34
Affordability of Internet service provider fees (as % of per capita GDP), 200	58
Ease of obtaining telephone lines, 2003	37
Cost of business telephone monthly subscription (as % of per capita GDP), 200	82
Extent of staff training, 2003	78
Quality of business schools, 2003	47
Scientists and engineers in R&D (per 1,000 inhabitants), 2000	71
Government prioritization of ICT, 2003	82
Government online presence, 2003	41
Government procurement of ICT, 2003	91

Usage Component Index	72
Individual Usage	51
Business Usage	74
Government Usage	79
Personal computers (per 1,000 inhabitants), 2001	53
ISDN subscribers (per 1,000 inhabitants), 2001	52
Cable television subscribers (per 1,000 inhabitants), 2001	63
Internet users (per 1,000 inhabitants), 2001	39
Computers installed in businesses (per 1,000 inhabitants), 2002	55
Firm-level technology absorption, 2003	79
Prevalence of foreign technology licensing, 2003	72
Government success in ICT promotion, 2003	82
Government online services, 2003	53

Philippines.ph

Key Indicators

Population, 2002	**79,982,000**
Main telephone lines in operation, 2002	**3,338,926**
growth (%) 1999–2002	15%
Cellular mobile telephone subscribers, 2002	**14,216,230**
growth (%) 1999–2002	399%
Personal computers, 2002	**2,200,000**
growth (%) 1999–2002	75%
Internet users (estimated), 2001	**3,500,000**
growth (%) 1999–2001	221%

Source: Data from International Telecommunication Union

RANK/102

Environment Component Index	**82**
Market Environment	78
Political and Regulatory Environment	63
Infrastructure Environment	94
State of cluster development, 2003	43
Venture capital availability, 2003	71
Subsidies for firm-level R&D, 2003	78
Quality of scientific research institutions, 2003	89
Availability of scientists and engineers, 2003	72
Brain drain, 2003	87
Utility patents granted (per 1,000,000 inhabitants), 2002	58
ICT manufactured exports (per capita), 2001	28
ICT service exports (per capita), 2001	85
Overall administrative burden, 2003	98
Quality of the legal system, 2003	73
Laws relating to ICT, 2003	52
Competition in the ISP sector, 2003	41
Foreign ownership restrictions, 2003	83
Efficiency of the tax system, 2003	62
Freedom of the press, 2003	16
Overall infrastructure quality, 2003	89
Waiting time for telephone lines (years), 2000	88
Telephone mainlines (per 1,000 inhabitants), 2001	77
Public pay telephones (per 1,000 inhabitants), 2001	90
Internet servers (per 1,000,000 inhabitants), 2001	68

Networked Readiness Index Rank

2003–2004 (102 countries) **69**

2002–2003 (82 countries)	62
2001–2002 (75 countries)	58

Readiness Component Index	**72**
Individual Readiness	65
Business Readiness	80
Government Readiness	56
Public expenditure on education (per capita), 2000	73
Adult illiteracy (%), 2001	43
Tertiary enrollment (gross %), 2001 or most recent available	43
Radios (per 1,000 inhabitants), 2001 or most recent available	88
Television sets (per 1,000 inhabitants), 2001	69
Households online (as % of households with computers), 2002	97
Quality of math and science education, 2003	89
Affordability of local fixed line calls (as % of per capita GDP), 2001	76
Affordability of Internet telephone access (as % of per capita GDP), 2001	43
Affordability of Internet service provider fees (as % of per capita GDP), 2001	80
Ease of obtaining telephone lines, 2003	71
Cost of business telephone monthly subscription (as % of per capita GDP), 2002	101
Extent of staff training, 2003	41
Quality of business schools, 2003	32
Scientists and engineers in R&D (per 1,000 inhabitants), 2000	81
Government prioritization of ICT, 2003	61
Government online presence, 2003	49
Government procurement of ICT, 2003	84

Usage Component Index	**50**
Individual Usage	72
Business Usage	59
Government Usage	29
Personal computers (per 1,000 inhabitants), 2001	68
ISDN subscribers (per 1,000 inhabitants), 2001	88
Cable television subscribers (per 1,000 inhabitants), 2001	72
Internet users (per 1,000 inhabitants), 2001	64
Computers installed in businesses (per 1,000 inhabitants), 2002	63
Firm-level technology absorption, 2003	72
Prevalence of foreign technology licensing, 2003	23
Government success in ICT promotion, 2003	68
Government online services, 2003	20

Poland.pl

Key Indicators

Population, 2002	38,609,000
Main telephone lines in operation, 2001	11,400,000
growth (%) 1999–2001	12%
Cellular mobile telephone subscribers, 2002	14,000,000
growth (%) 1999–2002	254%
Personal computers, 2001	3,300,000
growth (%) 1999–2001	38%
Internet users (estimated), 2001	3,800,000
growth (%) 1999–2001	81%

Source: Data from International Telecommunication Union

RANK/102

Environment Component Index	50
Market Environment	46
Political and Regulatory Environment	56
Infrastructure Environment	56
State of cluster development, 2003	49
Venture capital availability, 2003	42
Subsidies for firm-level R&D, 2003	43
Quality of scientific research institutions, 2003	54
Availability of scientists and engineers, 2003	35
Brain drain, 2003	44
Utility patents granted (per 1,000,000 inhabitants), 2002	53
ICT manufactured exports (per capita), 2001	48
ICT service exports (per capita), 2001	50
Overall administrative burden, 2003	51
Quality of the legal system, 2003	51
Laws relating to ICT, 2003	46
Competition in the ISP sector, 2003	71
Foreign ownership restrictions, 2003	51
Efficiency of the tax system, 2003	87
Freedom of the press, 2003	50
Overall infrastructure quality, 2003	73
Waiting time for telephone lines (years), 2000	54
Telephone mainlines (per 1,000 inhabitants), 2001	38
Public pay telephones (per 1,000 inhabitants), 2001	50
Internet servers (per 1,000,000 inhabitants), 2001	44

Networked Readiness Index Rank

2003–2004 (102 countries) — 47

2002–2003 (82 countries)	39
2001–2002 (75 countries)	35

Readiness Component Index	43
Individual Readiness	39
Business Readiness	45
Government Readiness	46
Public expenditure on education (per capita), 2000	38
Adult illiteracy (%), 2001	11
Tertiary enrollment (gross %), 2001 or most recent available	19
Radios (per 1,000 inhabitants), 2001 or most recent available	42
Television sets (per 1,000 inhabitants), 2001	36
Households online (as % of households with computers), 2001	38
Quality of math and science education, 2003	36
Affordability of local fixed line calls (as % of per capita GDP), 2001	44
Affordability of Internet telephone access (as % of per capita GDP), 2001	100
Affordability of Internet service provider fees (as % of per capita GDP), 2001	36
Ease of obtaining telephone lines, 2003	68
Cost of business telephone monthly subscription (as % of per capita GDP), 2002	44
Extent of staff training, 2003	54
Quality of business schools, 2003	51
Scientists and engineers in R&D (per 1,000 inhabitants), 2001	35
Government prioritization of ICT, 2003	84
Government online presence, 2003	22
Government procurement of ICT, 2003	60

Usage Component Index	52
Individual Usage	42
Business Usage	41
Government Usage	78
Personal computers (per 1,000 inhabitants), 2001	42
ISDN subscribers (per 1,000 inhabitants), 2001	39
Cable television subscribers (per 1,000 inhabitants), 2001	32
Internet users (per 1,000 inhabitants), 2001	40
Computers installed in businesses (per 1,000 inhabitants), 2002	34
Firm-level technology absorption, 2003	54
Prevalence of foreign technology licensing, 2003	43
Government success in ICT promotion, 2003	81
Government online services, 2003	63

Portugal.pt

Key Indicators

Population, 2002	10,409,000
Main telephone lines in operation, 2002	4,361,000
growth (%) 1999–2002	3%
Cellular mobile telephone subscribers, 2002	8,528,900
growth (%) 1999–2002	83%
Personal computers, 2001	1,210,000
growth (%) 1999–2001	30%
Internet users (estimated), 2002	3,700,000
growth (%) 1999–2002	147%

Source: Data from International Telecommunication Union

RANK/102

Environment Component Index — 27

Market Environment	30
Political and Regulatory Environment	27
Infrastructure Environment	28
State of cluster development, 2003	41
Venture capital availability, 2003	33
Subsidies for firm-level R&D, 2003	24
Quality of scientific research institutions, 2003	41
Availability of scientists and engineers, 2003	48
Brain drain, 2003	27
Utility patents granted (per 1,000,000 inhabitants), 2002	40
ICT manufactured exports (per capita), 2001	35
ICT service exports (per capita), 2001	37
Overall administrative burden, 2003	54
Quality of the legal system, 2003	14
Laws relating to ICT, 2003	44
Competition in the ISP sector, 2003	35
Foreign ownership restrictions, 2003	59
Efficiency of the tax system, 2003	47
Freedom of the press, 2003	6
Overall infrastructure quality, 2003	30
Waiting time for telephone lines (years), 2000	39
Telephone mainlines (per 1,000 inhabitants), 2001	28
Public pay telephones (per 1,000 inhabitants), 2001	21
Internet servers (per 1,000,000 inhabitants), 2001	32

Networked Readiness Index Rank

2003–2004 (102 countries) — 31

2002–2003 (82 countries)	31
2001–2002 (75 countries)	27

Readiness Component Index — 35

Individual Readiness	38
Business Readiness	30
Government Readiness	42
Public expenditure on education (per capita), 2000	25
Adult illiteracy (%), 2001	52
Tertiary enrollment (gross %), 2001 or most recent available	24
Radios (per 1,000 inhabitants), 2001 or most recent available	67
Television sets (per 1,000 inhabitants), 2001	34
Households online (as % of households with computers), 2002	22
Quality of math and science education, 2003	76
Affordability of local fixed line calls (as % of per capita GDP), 2001	36
Affordability of Internet telephone access (as % of per capita GDP), 2001	83
Affordability of Internet service provider fees (as % of per capita GDP), 2001	30
Ease of obtaining telephone lines, 2003	24
Cost of business telephone monthly subscription (as % of per capita GDP), 2002	27
Extent of staff training, 2003	56
Quality of business schools, 2003	36
Scientists and engineers in R&D (per 1,000 inhabitants), 2000	31
Government prioritization of ICT, 2003	53
Government online presence, 2003	30
Government procurement of ICT, 2003	67

Usage Component Index — 30

Individual Usage	28
Business Usage	38
Government Usage	42
Personal computers (per 1,000 inhabitants), 2001	35
ISDN subscribers (per 1,000 inhabitants), 2001	18
Cable television subscribers (per 1,000 inhabitants), 2001	29
Internet users (per 1,000 inhabitants), 2001	28
Computers installed in businesses (per 1,000 inhabitants), 2002	30
Firm-level technology absorption, 2003	87
Prevalence of foreign technology licensing, 2003	9
Government success in ICT promotion, 2003	48
Government online services, 2003	36

Romania.ro

Key Indicators

Population, 2002	22,330,000
Main telephone lines in operation, 2001	4,116,000
growth (%) 1999–2001	10%
Cellular mobile telephone subscribers, 2001	3,845,116
growth (%) 1999–2001	184%
Personal computers, 2001	800,000
growth (%) 1999–2001	33%
Internet users (estimated), 2002	1,800,000
growth (%) 1999–2002	200%

Source: Data from International Telecommunication Union

RANK/102

Environment Component Index	75
Market Environment	61
Political and Regulatory Environment	88
Infrastructure Environment	70
State of cluster development, 2003	48
Venture capital availability, 2003	64
Subsidies for firm-level R&D, 2003	57
Quality of scientific research institutions, 2003	69
Availability of scientists and engineers, 2003	21
Brain drain, 2003	93
Utility patents granted (per 1,000,000 inhabitants), 2002	60
ICT manufactured exports (per capita), 2001	47
ICT service exports (per capita), 2001	60
Overall administrative burden, 2003	97
Quality of the legal system, 2003	82
Laws relating to ICT, 2003	50
Competition in the ISP sector, 2003	72
Foreign ownership restrictions, 2003	77
Efficiency of the tax system, 2003	100
Freedom of the press, 2003	76
Overall infrastructure quality, 2003	77
Waiting time for telephone lines (years), 2000	83
Telephone mainlines (per 1,000 inhabitants), 2001	54
Public pay telephones (per 1,000 inhabitants), 2001	59
Internet servers (per 1,000,000 inhabitants), 2001	53

Networked Readiness Index Rank

2003–2004 (102 countries) **61**

2002–2003 (82 countries)	72
2001–2002 (75 countries)	65

Readiness Component Index	56
Individual Readiness	41
Business Readiness	69
Government Readiness	62
Public expenditure on education (per capita), 2000	65
Adult illiteracy (%), 2001	29
Tertiary enrollment (gross %), 2001 or most recent available	52
Radios (per 1,000 inhabitants), 2001 or most recent available	60
Television sets (per 1,000 inhabitants), 2001	38
Households online (as % of households with computers), 2002	41
Quality of math and science education, 2003	5
Affordability of local fixed line calls (as % of per capita GDP), 2001	74
Affordability of Internet telephone access (as % of per capita GDP), 2001	38
Affordability of Internet service provider fees (as % of per capita GDP), 2001	54
Ease of obtaining telephone lines, 2003	75
Cost of business telephone monthly subscription (as % of per capita GDP), 2002	55
Extent of staff training, 2003	89
Quality of business schools, 2003	62
Scientists and engineers in R&D (per 1,000 inhabitants), 2000	43
Government prioritization of ICT, 2003	73
Government online presence, 2003	46
Government procurement of ICT, 2003	85

Usage Component Index	48
Individual Usage	46
Business Usage	68
Government Usage	39
Personal computers (per 1,000 inhabitants), 2001	61
ISDN subscribers (per 1,000 inhabitants), 2001	71
Cable television subscribers (per 1,000 inhabitants), 2001	27
Internet users (per 1,000 inhabitants), 2001	52
Computers installed in businesses (per 1,000 inhabitants), 2002	60
Firm-level technology absorption, 2003	65
Prevalence of foreign technology licensing, 2003	67
Government success in ICT promotion, 2003	49
Government online services, 2003	35

Russian Federation.ru

Part 2 Country Profiles | 189

Key Indicators

Population, 2002	146,586,000
Main telephone lines in operation, 2002	35,500,000
growth (%) 1999–2002	15%
Cellular mobile telephone subscribers, 2002	17,668,130
growth (%) 1999–2002	1,189%
Personal computers, 2002	13,000,000
growth (%) 1999–2002	136%
Internet users (estimated), 2002	6,000,000
growth (%) 1999–2002	300%

Source: Data from International Telecommunication Union

Networked Readiness Index Rank

2003–2004 (102 countries) **63**

2002–2003 (82 countries)	69
2001–2002 (75 countries)	61

RANK/102

Environment Component Index	73
Market Environment	48
Political and Regulatory Environment	95
Infrastructure Environment	68
State of cluster development, 2003	56
Venture capital availability, 2003	63
Subsidies for firm-level R&D, 2003	61
Quality of scientific research institutions, 2003	25
Availability of scientists and engineers, 2003	27
Brain drain, 2003	56
Utility patents granted (per 1,000,000 inhabitants), 2002	38
ICT manufactured exports (per capita), 2001	49
ICT service exports (per capita), 2001	74
Overall administrative burden, 2003	100
Quality of the legal system, 2003	81
Laws relating to ICT, 2003	76
Competition in the ISP sector, 2003	80
Foreign ownership restrictions, 2003	99
Efficiency of the tax system, 2003	96
Freedom of the press, 2003	82
Overall infrastructure quality, 2003	60
Waiting time for telephone lines (years), 2000	87
Telephone mainlines (per 1,000 inhabitants), 2001	44
Public pay telephones (per 1,000 inhabitants), 2001	56
Internet servers (per 1,000,000 inhabitants), 2001	55

Readiness Component Index	48
Individual Readiness	31
Business Readiness	43
Government Readiness	89
Public expenditure on education (per capita), 2000	56
Adult illiteracy (%), 2001	15
Tertiary enrollment (gross %), 2001 or most recent available	8
Radios (per 1,000 inhabitants), 2001 or most recent available	49
Television sets (per 1,000 inhabitants), 2001	24
Households online (as % of households with computers), 2002	54
Quality of math and science education, 2003	18
Affordability of local fixed line calls (as % of per capita GDP), 2001	56
Affordability of Internet telephone access (as % of per capita GDP), 2001	14
Affordability of Internet service provider fees (as % of per capita GDP), 2001	47
Ease of obtaining telephone lines, 2003	74
Cost of business telephone monthly subscription (as % of per capita GDP), 2002	66
Extent of staff training, 2003	79
Quality of business schools, 2003	61
Scientists and engineers in R&D (per 1,000 inhabitants), 2000	8
Government prioritization of ICT, 2003	78
Government online presence, 2003	82
Government procurement of ICT, 2003	77

Usage Component Index	69
Individual Usage	49
Business Usage	79
Government Usage	66
Personal computers (per 1,000 inhabitants), 2001	52
ISDN subscribers (per 1,000 inhabitants), 2001	54
Cable television subscribers (per 1,000 inhabitants), 2001	38
Internet users (per 1,000 inhabitants), 2001	61
Computers installed in businesses (per 1,000 inhabitants), 2002	42
Firm-level technology absorption, 2003	66
Prevalence of foreign technology licensing, 2003	93
Government success in ICT promotion, 2003	86
Government online services, 2003	44

Senegal.sn

Key Indicators

Population, 2002	**9,802,000**
Main telephone lines in operation, 2002	**224,623**
growth (%) 1999–2002	35%
Cellular mobile telephone subscribers, 2002	**553,427**
growth (%) 1999–2002	530%
Personal computers, 2002	**200,000**
growth (%) 1999–2002	43%
Internet users (estimated), 2002	**105,000**
growth (%) 1999–2002	250%

Source: Data from International Telecommunication Union

RANK/102

Environment Component Index	77
Market Environment	86
Political and Regulatory Environment	72
Infrastructure Environment	71
State of cluster development, 2003	96
Venture capital availability, 2003	92
Subsidies for firm-level R&D, 2003	60
Quality of scientific research institutions, 2003	67
Availability of scientists and engineers, 2003	84
Brain drain, 2003	85
Utility patents granted (per 1,000,000 inhabitants), 2002	72
ICT manufactured exports (per capita), 2001	77
ICT service exports (per capita), 2001	72
Overall administrative burden, 2003	89
Quality of the legal system, 2003	69
Laws relating to ICT, 2003	78
Competition in the ISP sector, 2003	86
Foreign ownership restrictions, 2003	44
Efficiency of the tax system, 2003	63
Freedom of the press, 2003	46
Overall infrastructure quality, 2003	87
Waiting time for telephone lines (years), 2000	55
Telephone mainlines (per 1,000 inhabitants), 2001	84
Public pay telephones (per 1,000 inhabitants), 2001	69
Internet servers (per 1,000,000 inhabitants), 2001	88

Networked Readiness Index Rank

2003–2004 (102 countries) 81

Readiness Component Index	85
Individual Readiness	95
Business Readiness	76
Government Readiness	85
Public expenditure on education (per capita), 2000	85
Adult illiteracy (%), 2001	100
Tertiary enrollment (gross %), 2001 or most recent available	87
Radios (per 1,000 inhabitants), 2001 or most recent available	94
Television sets (per 1,000 inhabitants), 2001	84
Households online (as % of households with computers), 2002	70
Quality of math and science education, 2003	78
Affordability of local fixed line calls (as % of per capita GDP), 2001	94
Affordability of Internet telephone access (as % of per capita GDP), 2001	82
Affordability of Internet service provider fees (as % of per capita GDP), 2001	81
Ease of obtaining telephone lines, 2003	62
Cost of business telephone monthly subscription (as % of per capita GDP), 2002	84
Extent of staff training, 2003	80
Quality of business schools, 2003	54
Scientists and engineers in R&D (per 1,000 inhabitants), 2000	102
Government prioritization of ICT, 2003	23
Government online presence, 2003	99
Government procurement of ICT, 2003	27

Usage Component Index	78
Individual Usage	86
Business Usage	62
Government Usage	71
Personal computers (per 1,000 inhabitants), 2001	72
ISDN subscribers (per 1,000 inhabitants), 2001	67
Cable television subscribers (per 1,000 inhabitants), 2001	100
Internet users (per 1,000 inhabitants), 2001	77
Computers installed in businesses (per 1,000 inhabitants), 2002	88
Firm-level technology absorption, 2003	12
Prevalence of foreign technology licensing, 2003	82
Government success in ICT promotion, 2003	36
Government online services, 2003	89

Serbia.yu

Key Indicators

Population, 2002	**10,720,000**
Main telephone lines in operation, 2002	**2,492,963**
growth (%) 1999–2002	9%
Cellular mobile telephone subscribers, 2002	**2,750,397**
growth (%) 1999–2002	354%
Personal computers, 2002	**290,000**
growth (%) 1999–2002	32%
Internet users (estimated), 2002	**640,000**
growth (%) 1999–2002	700%

Source: Data from International Telecommunication Union

RANK/102

Environment Component Index	79
Market Environment	69
Political and Regulatory Environment	92
Infrastructure Environment	66
State of cluster development, 2003	73
Venture capital availability, 2003	51
Subsidies for firm-level R&D, 2003	74
Quality of scientific research institutions, 2003	58
Availability of scientists and engineers, 2003	38
Brain drain, 2003	100
Utility patents granted (per 1,000,000 inhabitants), 2002	72
ICT manufactured exports (per capita), 2001	67
ICT service exports (per capita), 2001	54
Overall administrative burden, 2003	81
Quality of the legal system, 2003	80
Laws relating to ICT, 2003	65
Competition in the ISP sector, 2003	91
Foreign ownership restrictions, 2003	100
Efficiency of the tax system, 2003	46
Freedom of the press, 2003	86
Overall infrastructure quality, 2003	94
Waiting time for telephone lines (years), 2000	77
Telephone mainlines (per 1,000 inhabitants), 2001	48
Public pay telephones (per 1,000 inhabitants), 2001	29
Internet servers (per 1,000,000 inhabitants), 2001	79

Networked Readiness Index Rank

2003–2004 (102 countries) 77

Readiness Component Index	77
Individual Readiness	57
Business Readiness	88
Government Readiness	81
Public expenditure on education (per capita), 2000	68
Adult illiteracy (%), 2001	59
Tertiary enrollment (gross %), 2001 or most recent available	54
Radios (per 1,000 inhabitants), 2001 or most recent available	70
Television sets (per 1,000 inhabitants), 2001	62
Households online (as % of households with computers), 2002	63
Quality of math and science education, 2003	45
Affordability of local fixed line calls (as % of per capita GDP), 2001	67
Affordability of Internet telephone access (as % of per capita GDP), 2001	47
Affordability of Internet service provider fees (as % of per capita GDP), 2001	76
Ease of obtaining telephone lines, 2003	85
Cost of business telephone monthly subscription (as % of per capita GDP), 2002	69
Extent of staff training, 2003	88
Quality of business schools, 2003	84
Scientists and engineers in R&D (per 1,000 inhabitants), 2000	85
Government prioritization of ICT, 2003	45
Government online presence, 2003	86
Government procurement of ICT, 2003	62

Usage Component Index	77
Individual Usage	71
Business Usage	82
Government Usage	52
Personal computers (per 1,000 inhabitants), 2001	63
ISDN subscribers (per 1,000 inhabitants), 2001	76
Cable television subscribers (per 1,000 inhabitants), 2001	60
Internet users (per 1,000 inhabitants), 2001	78
Computers installed in businesses (per 1,000 inhabitants), 2002	73
Firm-level technology absorption, 2003	86
Prevalence of foreign technology licensing, 2003	86
Government success in ICT promotion, 2003	57
Government online services, 2003	49

Singapore.sg

Key Indicators

Population, 2002	4,163,700
Main telephone lines in operation, 2002	1,930,200
growth (%) 1999–2002	3%
Cellular mobile telephone subscribers, 2002	3,295,100
growth (%) 1999–2002	102%
Personal computers, 2001	2,100,000
growth (%) 1999–2001	24%
Internet users (estimated), 2002	2,247,000
growth (%) 1999–2002	137%

Source: Data from International Telecommunication Union

RANK/102

Environment Component Index	2
Market Environment	1
Political and Regulatory Environment	5
Infrastructure Environment	5
State of cluster development, 2003	4
Venture capital availability, 2003	12
Subsidies for firm-level R&D, 2003	1
Quality of scientific research institutions, 2003	10
Availability of scientists and engineers, 2003	16
Brain drain, 2003	15
Utility patents granted (per 1,000,000 inhabitants), 2002	10
ICT manufactured exports (per capita), 2001	1
ICT service exports (per capita), 2001	2
Overall administrative burden, 2003	1
Quality of the legal system, 2003	27
Laws relating to ICT, 2003	2
Competition in the ISP sector, 2003	18
Foreign ownership restrictions, 2003	5
Efficiency of the tax system, 2003	2
Freedom of the press, 2003	96
Overall infrastructure quality, 2003	1
Waiting time for telephone lines (years), 2000	1
Telephone mainlines (per 1,000 inhabitants), 2001	23
Public pay telephones (per 1,000 inhabitants), 2001	9
Internet servers (per 1,000,000 inhabitants), 2001	8

Networked Readiness Index Rank

2003–2004 (102 countries) — **2**

2002–2003 (82 countries)	3
2001–2002 (75 countries)	8

Readiness Component Index	4
Individual Readiness	22
Business Readiness	4
Government Readiness	1
Public expenditure on education (per capita), 2000	23
Adult illiteracy (%), 2001	51
Tertiary enrollment (gross %), 2001 or most recent available	32
Radios (per 1,000 inhabitants), 2001 or most recent available	34
Television sets (per 1,000 inhabitants), 2001	48
Households online (as % of households with computers), 2002	13
Quality of math and science education, 2003	1
Affordability of local fixed line calls (as % of per capita GDP), 2001	1
Affordability of Internet telephone access (as % of per capita GDP), 2001	1
Affordability of Internet service provider fees (as % of per capita GDP), 2001	21
Ease of obtaining telephone lines, 2003	2
Cost of business telephone monthly subscription (as % of per capita GDP), 2002	2
Extent of staff training, 2003	8
Quality of business schools, 2003	9
Scientists and engineers in R&D (per 1,000 inhabitants), 2000	4
Government prioritization of ICT, 2003	1
Government online presence, 2003	6
Government procurement of ICT, 2003	1

Usage Component Index	2
Individual Usage	18
Business Usage	2
Government Usage	1
Personal computers (per 1,000 inhabitants), 2001	7
ISDN subscribers (per 1,000 inhabitants), 2001	31
Cable television subscribers (per 1,000 inhabitants), 2001	43
Internet users (per 1,000 inhabitants), 2001	17
Computers installed in businesses (per 1,000 inhabitants), 2002	6
Firm-level technology absorption, 2003	5
Prevalence of foreign technology licensing, 2003	1
Government success in ICT promotion, 2003	1
Government online services, 2003	1

Slovak Republic.sk

Key Indicators

Population, 2002	5,378,000
Main telephone lines in operation, 2002	1,402,725
growth (%) 1999–2002	-15%
Cellular mobile telephone subscribers, 2002	2,923,383
growth (%) 1999–2002	340%
Personal computers, 2002	970,000
growth (%) 1999–2002	64%
Internet users (estimated), 2002	862,833
growth (%) 1999–2002	195%

Source: Data from International Telecommunication Union

RANK/102

Environment Component Index — 51

Market Environment	51
Political and Regulatory Environment	61
Infrastructure Environment	47
State of cluster development, 2003	54
Venture capital availability, 2003	55
Subsidies for firm-level R&D, 2003	67
Quality of scientific research institutions, 2003	59
Availability of scientists and engineers, 2003	15
Brain drain, 2003	68
Utility patents granted (per 1,000,000 inhabitants), 2002	36
ICT manufactured exports (per capita), 2001	38
ICT service exports (per capita), 2001	38
Overall administrative burden, 2003	86
Quality of the legal system, 2003	68
Laws relating to ICT, 2003	47
Competition in the ISP sector, 2003	67
Foreign ownership restrictions, 2003	13
Efficiency of the tax system, 2003	91
Freedom of the press, 2003	33
Overall infrastructure quality, 2003	57
Waiting time for telephone lines (years), 2000	48
Telephone mainlines (per 1,000 inhabitants), 2001	39
Public pay telephones (per 1,000 inhabitants), 2001	45
Internet servers (per 1,000,000 inhabitants), 2001	31

Networked Readiness Index Rank

2003–2004 (102 countries) **41**

2002–2003 (82 countries)	40
2001–2002 (75 countries)	33

Readiness Component Index — 34

Individual Readiness	37
Business Readiness	27
Government Readiness	43
Public expenditure on education (per capita), 2000	45
Adult illiteracy (%), 2001	1
Tertiary enrollment (gross %), 2001 or most recent available	44
Radios (per 1,000 inhabitants), 2001 or most recent available	15
Television sets (per 1,000 inhabitants), 2001	35
Households online (as % of households with computers), 2002	68
Quality of math and science education, 2003	11
Affordability of local fixed line calls (as % of per capita GDP), 2001	55
Affordability of Internet telephone access (as % of per capita GDP), 2001	26
Affordability of Internet service provider fees (as % of per capita GDP), 2001	34
Ease of obtaining telephone lines, 2003	35
Cost of business telephone monthly subscription (as % of per capita GDP), 2002	34
Extent of staff training, 2003	39
Quality of business schools, 2003	48
Scientists and engineers in R&D (per 1,000 inhabitants), 2000	30
Government prioritization of ICT, 2003	75
Government online presence, 2003	26
Government procurement of ICT, 2003	49

Usage Component Index — 39

Individual Usage	33
Business Usage	45
Government Usage	57
Personal computers (per 1,000 inhabitants), 2001	32
ISDN subscribers (per 1,000 inhabitants), 2001	30
Cable television subscribers (per 1,000 inhabitants), 2001	26
Internet users (per 1,000 inhabitants), 2001	37
Computers installed in businesses (per 1,000 inhabitants), 2002	46
Firm-level technology absorption, 2003	26
Prevalence of foreign technology licensing, 2003	48
Government success in ICT promotion, 2003	78
Government online services, 2003	40

Slovenia.si

Key Indicators

Population, 2002	**1,996,000**
Main telephone lines in operation, 2002	**811,435**
growth (%) 1999–2002	7%
Cellular mobile telephone subscribers, 2002	**1,667,000**
growth (%) 1999–2002	164%
Personal computers, 2002	**600,000**
growth (%) 1999–2002	20%
Internet users (estimated), 2002	**800,000**
growth (%) 1999–2002	220%

Source: Data from International Telecommunication Union

RANK/102

Environment Component Index	39
Market Environment	43
Political and Regulatory Environment	51
Infrastructure Environment	31
State of cluster development, 2003	66
Venture capital availability, 2003	61
Subsidies for firm-level R&D, 2003	29
Quality of scientific research institutions, 2003	29
Availability of scientists and engineers, 2003	64
Brain drain, 2003	34
Utility patents granted (per 1,000,000 inhabitants), 2002	26
ICT manufactured exports (per capita), 2001	31
ICT service exports (per capita), 2001	28
Overall administrative burden, 2003	55
Quality of the legal system, 2003	45
Laws relating to ICT, 2003	23
Competition in the ISP sector, 2003	59
Foreign ownership restrictions, 2003	90
Efficiency of the tax system, 2003	39
Freedom of the press, 2003	61
Overall infrastructure quality, 2003	36
Waiting time for telephone lines (years), 2000	29
Telephone mainlines (per 1,000 inhabitants), 2001	29
Public pay telephones (per 1,000 inhabitants), 2001	57
Internet servers (per 1,000,000 inhabitants), 2001	19

Networked Readiness Index Rank

2003–2004 (102 countries) **30**

2002–2003 (82 countries)	33
2001–2002 (75 countries)	29

Readiness Component Index	27
Individual Readiness	30
Business Readiness	24
Government Readiness	35
Public expenditure on education (per capita), 2000	27
Adult illiteracy (%), 2001	12
Tertiary enrollment (gross %), 2001 or most recent available	11
Radios (per 1,000 inhabitants), 2001 or most recent available	53
Television sets (per 1,000 inhabitants), 2001	39
Households online (as % of households with computers), 2002	29
Quality of math and science education, 2003	19
Affordability of local fixed line calls (as % of per capita GDP), 2001	17
Affordability of Internet telephone access (as % of per capita GDP), 2001	7
Affordability of Internet service provider fees (as % of per capita GDP), 2001	37
Ease of obtaining telephone lines, 2003	30
Cost of business telephone monthly subscription (as % of per capita GDP), 2002	9
Extent of staff training, 2003	29
Quality of business schools, 2003	31
Scientists and engineers in R&D (per 1,000 inhabitants), 2000	24
Government prioritization of ICT, 2003	58
Government online presence, 2003	28
Government procurement of ICT, 2003	44

Usage Component Index	28
Individual Usage	19
Business Usage	35
Government Usage	54
Personal computers (per 1,000 inhabitants), 2001	21
ISDN subscribers (per 1,000 inhabitants), 2001	14
Cable television subscribers (per 1,000 inhabitants), 2001	17
Internet users (per 1,000 inhabitants), 2001	22
Computers installed in businesses (per 1,000 inhabitants), 2002	27
Firm-level technology absorption, 2003	46
Prevalence of foreign technology licensing, 2003	60
Government success in ICT promotion, 2003	55
Government online services, 2003	54

South Africa.za

Key Indicators

Population, 2002	45,454,000
Main telephone lines in operation, 2002	4,895,000
growth (%) 1999–2002	-11%
Cellular mobile telephone subscribers, 2002	12,081,000
growth (%) 1999–2002	133%
Personal computers, 2002	3,300,000
growth (%) 1999–2002	27%
Internet users (estimated), 2002	3,100,000
growth (%) 1999–2002	70%

Source: Data from International Telecommunication Union

RANK/102

Environment Component Index	33
Market Environment	45
Political and Regulatory Environment	23
Infrastructure Environment	43
State of cluster development, 2003	28
Venture capital availability, 2003	32
Subsidies for firm-level R&D, 2003	39
Quality of scientific research institutions, 2003	24
Availability of scientists and engineers, 2003	74
Brain drain, 2003	67
Utility patents granted (per 1,000,000 inhabitants), 2002	31
ICT manufactured exports (per capita), 2001	51
ICT service exports (per capita), 2001	78
Overall administrative burden, 2003	48
Quality of the legal system, 2003	15
Laws relating to ICT, 2003	24
Competition in the ISP sector, 2003	50
Foreign ownership restrictions, 2003	30
Efficiency of the tax system, 2003	28
Freedom of the press, 2003	28
Overall infrastructure quality, 2003	19
Waiting time for telephone lines (years), 2000	60
Telephone mainlines (per 1,000 inhabitants), 2001	60
Public pay telephones (per 1,000 inhabitants), 2001	23
Internet servers (per 1,000,000 inhabitants), 2001	36

Networked Readiness Index Rank

2003–2004 (102 countries) — 37

2002–2003 (82 countries)	36
2001–2002 (75 countries)	40

Readiness Component Index	46
Individual Readiness	67
Business Readiness	33
Government Readiness	44
Public expenditure on education (per capita), 2000	51
Adult illiteracy (%), 2001	70
Tertiary enrollment (gross %), 2001 or most recent available	65
Radios (per 1,000 inhabitants), 2001 or most recent available	64
Television sets (per 1,000 inhabitants), 2001	72
Households online (as % of households with computers), 2002	42
Quality of math and science education, 2003	86
Affordability of local fixed line calls (as % of per capita GDP), 2001	57
Affordability of Internet telephone access (as % of per capita GDP), 2001	29
Affordability of Internet service provider fees (as % of per capita GDP), 2001	64
Ease of obtaining telephone lines, 2003	66
Cost of business telephone monthly subscription (as % of per capita GDP), 2002	64
Extent of staff training, 2003	25
Quality of business schools, 2003	18
Scientists and engineers in R&D (per 1,000 inhabitants), 2000	42
Government prioritization of ICT, 2003	35
Government online presence, 2003	54
Government procurement of ICT, 2003	38

Usage Component Index	33
Individual Usage	57
Business Usage	24
Government Usage	27
Personal computers (per 1,000 inhabitants), 2001	47
ISDN subscribers (per 1,000 inhabitants), 2001	59
Cable television subscribers (per 1,000 inhabitants), 2001	101
Internet users (per 1,000 inhabitants), 2001	46
Computers installed in businesses (per 1,000 inhabitants), 2002	26
Firm-level technology absorption, 2003	39
Prevalence of foreign technology licensing, 2003	4
Government success in ICT promotion, 2003	34
Government online services, 2003	29

Spain.es

Key Indicators

Population, 2002	40,683,000
Main telephone lines in operation, 2002	18,705,600
growth (%) 1999–2002	14%
Cellular mobile telephone subscribers, 2002	33,475,000
growth (%) 1999–2002	123%
Personal computers, 2001	6,800,000
growth (%) 1999–2001	42%
Internet users (estimated), 2002	7,856,000
growth (%) 1999–2002	178%

Source: Data from International Telecommunication Union

RANK/102

Environment Component Index	**30**
Market Environment	25
Political and Regulatory Environment	35
Infrastructure Environment	30
State of cluster development, 2003	35
Venture capital availability, 2003	23
Subsidies for firm-level R&D, 2003	23
Quality of scientific research institutions, 2003	51
Availability of scientists and engineers, 2003	30
Brain drain, 2003	4
Utility patents granted (per 1,000,000 inhabitants), 2002	27
ICT manufactured exports (per capita), 2001	32
ICT service exports (per capita), 2001	22
Overall administrative burden, 2003	61
Quality of the legal system, 2003	55
Laws relating to ICT, 2003	33
Competition in the ISP sector, 2003	48
Foreign ownership restrictions, 2003	27
Efficiency of the tax system, 2003	25
Freedom of the press, 2003	23
Overall infrastructure quality, 2003	24
Waiting time for telephone lines (years), 2000	25
Telephone mainlines (per 1,000 inhabitants), 2001	27
Public pay telephones (per 1,000 inhabitants), 2001	68
Internet servers (per 1,000,000 inhabitants), 2001	28

Networked Readiness Index Rank

2003–2004 (102 countries) **29**

2002–2003 (82 countries)	25
2001–2002 (75 countries)	26

Readiness Component Index	**24**
Individual Readiness	29
Business Readiness	22
Government Readiness	25
Public expenditure on education (per capita), 2000	24
Adult illiteracy (%), 2001	34
Tertiary enrollment (gross %), 2001 or most recent available	14
Radios (per 1,000 inhabitants), 2001 or most recent available	65
Television sets (per 1,000 inhabitants), 2001	15
Households online (as % of households with computers), 2002	48
Quality of math and science education, 2003	33
Affordability of local fixed line calls (as % of per capita GDP), 2001	15
Affordability of Internet telephone access (as % of per capita GDP), 2001	3
Affordability of Internet service provider fees (as % of per capita GDP), 2001	26
Ease of obtaining telephone lines, 2003	36
Cost of business telephone monthly subscription (as % of per capita GDP), 2002	14
Extent of staff training, 2003	32
Quality of business schools, 2003	11
Scientists and engineers in R&D (per 1,000 inhabitants), 2000	29
Government prioritization of ICT, 2003	37
Government online presence, 2003	29
Government procurement of ICT, 2003	31

Usage Component Index	**32**
Individual Usage	35
Business Usage	34
Government Usage	41
Personal computers (per 1,000 inhabitants), 2001	29
ISDN subscribers (per 1,000 inhabitants), 2001	19
Cable television subscribers (per 1,000 inhabitants), 2001	66
Internet users (per 1,000 inhabitants), 2001	32
Computers installed in businesses (per 1,000 inhabitants), 2002	31
Firm-level technology absorption, 2003	36
Prevalence of foreign technology licensing, 2003	55
Government success in ICT promotion, 2003	46
Government online services, 2003	36

Sri Lanka.lk

Key Indicators

Population, 2002	**18,947,000**
Main telephone lines in operation, 2002	**883,108**
growth (%) 1999–2002	31%
Cellular mobile telephone subscribers, 2002	**931,580**
growth (%) 1999–2002	263%
Personal computers, 2002	**250,000**
growth (%) 1999–2002	138%
Internet users (estimated), 2002	**200,000**
growth (%) 1999–2002	208%

Source: Data from International Telecommunication Union

RANK/102

Environment Component Index	**66**
Market Environment	54
Political and Regulatory Environment	62
Infrastructure Environment	73
State of cluster development, 2003	29
Venture capital availability, 2003	40
Subsidies for firm-level R&D, 2003	47
Quality of scientific research institutions, 2003	56
Availability of scientists and engineers, 2003	59
Brain drain, 2003	86
Utility patents granted (per 1,000,000 inhabitants), 2002	65
ICT manufactured exports (per capita), 2001	40
ICT service exports (per capita), 2001	70
Overall administrative burden, 2003	44
Quality of the legal system, 2003	66
Laws relating to ICT, 2003	69
Competition in the ISP sector, 2003	44
Foreign ownership restrictions, 2003	56
Efficiency of the tax system, 2003	30
Freedom of the press, 2003	83
Overall infrastructure quality, 2003	67
Waiting time for telephone lines (years), 2000	69
Telephone mainlines (per 1,000 inhabitants), 2001	76
Public pay telephones (per 1,000 inhabitants), 2001	81
Internet servers (per 1,000,000 inhabitants), 2001	77

Networked Readiness Index Rank

2003–2004 (102 countries) 66

2002–2003 (82 countries)	54
2001–2002 (75 countries)	62

Readiness Component Index	**64**
Individual Readiness	68
Business Readiness	66
Government Readiness	60
Public expenditure on education (per capita), 2000	80
Adult illiteracy (%), 2001	56
Tertiary enrollment (gross %), 2001 or most recent available	82
Radios (per 1,000 inhabitants), 2001 or most recent available	79
Television sets (per 1,000 inhabitants), 2001	78
Households online (as % of households with computers), 2002	66
Quality of math and science education, 2003	52
Affordability of local fixed line calls (as % of per capita GDP), 2001	70
Affordability of Internet telephone access (as % of per capita GDP), 2001	15
Affordability of Internet service provider fees (as % of per capita GDP), 2001	53
Ease of obtaining telephone lines, 2003	69
Cost of business telephone monthly subscription (as % of per capita GDP), 2002	71
Extent of staff training, 2003	60
Quality of business schools, 2003	52
Scientists and engineers in R&D (per 1,000 inhabitants), 2000	77
Government prioritization of ICT, 2003	47
Government online presence, 2003	62
Government procurement of ICT, 2003	65

Usage Component Index	**71**
Individual Usage	90
Business Usage	67
Government Usage	62
Personal computers (per 1,000 inhabitants), 2001	84
ISDN subscribers (per 1,000 inhabitants), 2001	77
Cable television subscribers (per 1,000 inhabitants), 2001	90
Internet users (per 1,000 inhabitants), 2001	82
Computers installed in businesses (per 1,000 inhabitants), 2002	100
Firm-level technology absorption, 2003	62
Prevalence of foreign technology licensing, 2003	44
Government success in ICT promotion, 2003	44
Government online services, 2003	68

Sweden.se

Key Indicators

Population, 2002	8,943,000
Main telephone lines in operation, 2002	6,441,000
growth (%) 1999–2002	-1%
Cellular mobile telephone subscribers, 2002	7,915,000
growth (%) 1999–2002	53%
Personal computers, 2001	5,000,000
growth (%) 1999–2001	25%
Internet users (estimated), 2002	5,125,000
growth (%) 1999–2002	40%

Source: Data from International Telecommunication Union

RANK/102

Environment Component Index	6
Market Environment	9
Political and Regulatory Environment	11
Infrastructure Environment	11
State of cluster development, 2003	15
Venture capital availability, 2003	7
Subsidies for firm-level R&D, 2003	30
Quality of scientific research institutions, 2003	6
Availability of scientists and engineers, 2003	10
Brain drain, 2003	11
Utility patents granted (per 1,000,000 inhabitants), 2002	4
ICT manufactured exports (per capita), 2001	11
ICT service exports (per capita), 2001	8
Overall administrative burden, 2003	11
Quality of the legal system, 2003	9
Laws relating to ICT, 2003	11
Competition in the ISP sector, 2003	12
Foreign ownership restrictions, 2003	6
Efficiency of the tax system, 2003	67
Freedom of the press, 2003	2
Overall infrastructure quality, 2003	7
Waiting time for telephone lines (years), 2000	1
Telephone mainlines (per 1,000 inhabitants), 2001	17
Public pay telephones (per 1,000 inhabitants), 2001	26
Internet servers (per 1,000,000 inhabitants), 2001	9

Networked Readiness Index Rank

2003–2004 (102 countries) **4**

2002–2003 (82 countries)	4
2001–2002 (75 countries)	4

Readiness Component Index	2
Individual Readiness	2
Business Readiness	2
Government Readiness	13
Public expenditure on education (per capita), 2000	3
Adult illiteracy (%), 2001	17
Tertiary enrollment (gross %), 2001 or most recent available	5
Radios (per 1,000 inhabitants), 2001 or most recent available	2
Television sets (per 1,000 inhabitants), 2001	1
Households online (as % of households with computers), 2002	2
Quality of math and science education, 2003	21
Affordability of local fixed line calls (as % of per capita GDP), 2001	13
Affordability of Internet telephone access (as % of per capita GDP), 2001	74
Affordability of Internet service provider fees (as % of per capita GDP), 2001	1
Ease of obtaining telephone lines, 2003	7
Cost of business telephone monthly subscription (as % of per capita GDP), 2002	17
Extent of staff training, 2003	3
Quality of business schools, 2003	7
Scientists and engineers in R&D (per 1,000 inhabitants), 2000	3
Government prioritization of ICT, 2003	14
Government online presence, 2003	17
Government procurement of ICT, 2003	24

Usage Component Index	5
Individual Usage	7
Business Usage	4
Government Usage	11
Personal computers (per 1,000 inhabitants), 2001	3
ISDN subscribers (per 1,000 inhabitants), 2001	15
Cable television subscribers (per 1,000 inhabitants), 2001	9
Internet users (per 1,000 inhabitants), 2001	3
Computers installed in businesses (per 1,000 inhabitants), 2002	3
Firm-level technology absorption, 2003	3
Prevalence of foreign technology licensing, 2003	63
Government success in ICT promotion, 2003	19
Government online services, 2003	11

Switzerland.ch

Key Indicators

Population, 2002	7,281,270
Main telephone lines in operation, 2002	5,335,000
growth (%) 1999–2002	5%
Cellular mobile telephone subscribers, 2002	5,734,000
growth (%) 1999–2002	88%
Personal computers, 2001	3,900,000
growth (%) 1999–2001	18%
Internet users (estimated), 2002	2,375,000
growth (%) 1999–2002	61%

Source: Data from International Telecommunication Union

RANK/102

Environment Component Index — 4

Market Environment	10
Political and Regulatory Environment	6
Infrastructure Environment	3
State of cluster development, 2003	18
Venture capital availability, 2003	26
Subsidies for firm-level R&D, 2003	41
Quality of scientific research institutions, 2003	3
Availability of scientists and engineers, 2003	7
Brain drain, 2003	7
Utility patents granted (per 1,000,000 inhabitants), 2002	5
ICT manufactured exports (per capita), 2001	6
ICT service exports (per capita), 2001	13
Overall administrative burden, 2003	4
Quality of the legal system, 2003	12
Laws relating to ICT, 2003	25
Competition in the ISP sector, 2003	15
Foreign ownership restrictions, 2003	36
Efficiency of the tax system, 2003	16
Freedom of the press, 2003	10
Overall infrastructure quality, 2003	2
Waiting time for telephone lines (years), 2000	1
Telephone mainlines (per 1,000 inhabitants), 2001	2
Public pay telephones (per 1,000 inhabitants), 2001	14
Internet servers (per 1,000,000 inhabitants), 2001	7

Networked Readiness Index Rank

2003–2004 (102 countries) — 7

2002–2003 (82 countries)	13
2001–2002 (75 countries)	16

Readiness Component Index — 13

Individual Readiness	10
Business Readiness	5
Government Readiness	33
Public expenditure on education (per capita), 2000	4
Adult illiteracy (%), 2001	17
Tertiary enrollment (gross %), 2001 or most recent available	34
Radios (per 1,000 inhabitants), 2001 or most recent available	12
Television sets (per 1,000 inhabitants), 2001	20
Households online (as % of households with computers), 2002	10
Quality of math and science education, 2003	6
Affordability of local fixed line calls (as % of per capita GDP), 2001	9
Affordability of Internet telephone access (as % of per capita GDP), 2001	75
Affordability of Internet service provider fees (as % of per capita GDP), 2001	7
Ease of obtaining telephone lines, 2003	3
Cost of business telephone monthly subscription (as % of per capita GDP), 2002	7
Extent of staff training, 2003	2
Quality of business schools, 2003	4
Scientists and engineers in R&D (per 1,000 inhabitants), 2000	7
Government prioritization of ICT, 2003	39
Government online presence, 2003	42
Government procurement of ICT, 2003	20

Usage Component Index — 7

Individual Usage	4
Business Usage	6
Government Usage	31
Personal computers (per 1,000 inhabitants), 2001	5
ISDN subscribers (per 1,000 inhabitants), 2001	3
Cable television subscribers (per 1,000 inhabitants), 2001	2
Internet users (per 1,000 inhabitants), 2001	20
Computers installed in businesses (per 1,000 inhabitants), 2002	5
Firm-level technology absorption, 2003	9
Prevalence of foreign technology licensing, 2003	58
Government success in ICT promotion, 2003	28
Government online services, 2003	33

Taiwan.tw

Key Indicators

Population, 2002	22,457,000
Main telephone lines in operation, 2002	13,099,420
growth (%) 1999–2002	9%
Cellular mobile telephone subscribers, 2002	23,905,410
growth (%) 1999–2002	107%
Personal computers, 2002	8,887,100
growth (%) 1999–2002	33%
Internet users (estimated), 2002	8,590,000
growth (%) 1999–2002	79%

Source: Data from International Telecommunication Union

RANK/102

Environment Component Index — 8

Market Environment	6
Political and Regulatory Environment	16
Infrastructure Environment	10
State of cluster development, 2003	3
Venture capital availability, 2003	18
Subsidies for firm-level R&D, 2003	2
Quality of scientific research institutions, 2003	18
Availability of scientists and engineers, 2003	17
Brain drain, 2003	16
Utility patents granted (per 1,000,000 inhabitants), 2002	3
ICT manufactured exports (per capita), 2001	34
ICT service exports (per capita), 2001	34
Overall administrative burden, 2003	7
Quality of the legal system, 2003	37
Laws relating to ICT, 2003	17
Competition in the ISP sector, 2003	23
Foreign ownership restrictions, 2003	58
Efficiency of the tax system, 2003	11
Freedom of the press, 2003	44
Overall infrastructure quality, 2003	27
Waiting time for telephone lines (years), 2000	36
Telephone mainlines (per 1,000 inhabitants), 2001	1
Public pay telephones (per 1,000 inhabitants), 2001	12
Internet servers (per 1,000,000 inhabitants), 2001	27

Networked Readiness Index Rank

2003–2004 (102 countries) — 17

2002–2003 (82 countries)	9
2001–2002 (75 countries)	15

Readiness Component Index — 17

Individual Readiness	17
Business Readiness	19
Government Readiness	12
Public expenditure on education (per capita), 2000	26
Adult illiteracy (%), 2001	46
Tertiary enrollment (gross %), 2001 or most recent available	3
Radios (per 1,000 inhabitants), 2001 or most recent available	55
Television sets (per 1,000 inhabitants), 2001	14
Households online (as % of households with computers), 2002	27
Quality of math and science education, 2003	12
Affordability of local fixed line calls (as % of per capita GDP), 2001	31
Affordability of Internet telephone access (as % of per capita GDP), 2001	59
Affordability of Internet service provider fees (as % of per capita GDP), 2001	32
Ease of obtaining telephone lines, 2003	28
Cost of business telephone monthly subscription (as % of per capita GDP), 2002	21
Extent of staff training, 2003	19
Quality of business schools, 2003	29
Scientists and engineers in R&D (per 1,000 inhabitants), 2000	18
Government prioritization of ICT, 2003	7
Government online presence, 2003	48
Government procurement of ICT, 2003	3

Usage Component Index — 22

Individual Usage	27
Business Usage	21
Government Usage	6
Personal computers (per 1,000 inhabitants), 2001	25
ISDN subscribers (per 1,000 inhabitants), 2001	45
Cable television subscribers (per 1,000 inhabitants), 2001	22
Internet users (per 1,000 inhabitants), 2001	30
Computers installed in businesses (per 1,000 inhabitants), 2002	28
Firm-level technology absorption, 2003	8
Prevalence of foreign technology licensing, 2003	14
Government success in ICT promotion, 2003	6
Government online services, 2003	11

Tanzania.tz

Key Indicators

Population, 2002	34,569,230
Main telephone lines in operation, 2001	148,464
growth (%) 1999–2001	-1%
Cellular mobile telephone subscribers, 2001	426,964
growth (%) 1999–2001	738%
Personal computers, 2001	120,000
growth (%) 1999–2001	50%
Internet users (estimated), 2001	100,000
growth (%) 1999–2001	300%

Source: Data from International Telecommunication Union

RANK/102

Environment Component Index — 65

Market Environment	64
Political and Regulatory Environment	52
Infrastructure Environment	76
State of cluster development, 2003	70
Venture capital availability, 2003	70
Subsidies for firm-level R&D, 2003	56
Quality of scientific research institutions, 2003	32
Availability of scientists and engineers, 2003	73
Brain drain, 2003	64
Utility patents granted (per 1,000,000 inhabitants), 2002	72
ICT manufactured exports (per capita), 2001	94
ICT service exports (per capita), 2001	95
Overall administrative burden, 2003	33
Quality of the legal system, 2003	38
Laws relating to ICT, 2003	55
Competition in the ISP sector, 2003	56
Foreign ownership restrictions, 2003	52
Efficiency of the tax system, 2003	55
Freedom of the press, 2003	80
Overall infrastructure quality, 2003	61
Waiting time for telephone lines (years), 2000	62
Telephone mainlines (per 1,000 inhabitants), 2001	95
Public pay telephones (per 1,000 inhabitants), 2001	99
Internet servers (per 1,000,000 inhabitants), 2001	89

Networked Readiness Index Rank
2003–2004 (102 countries) 71

Readiness Component Index — 76

Individual Readiness	94
Business Readiness	84
Government Readiness	36
Public expenditure on education (per capita), 2000	98
Adult illiteracy (%), 2001	79
Tertiary enrollment (gross %), 2001 or most recent available	99
Radios (per 1,000 inhabitants), 2001 or most recent available	52
Television sets (per 1,000 inhabitants), 2001	87
Households online (as % of households with computers), 2002	79
Quality of math and science education, 2003	74
Affordability of local fixed line calls (as % of per capita GDP), 2001	97
Affordability of Internet telephone access (as % of per capita GDP), 2001	98
Affordability of Internet service provider fees (as % of per capita GDP), 2001	99
Ease of obtaining telephone lines, 2003	76
Cost of business telephone monthly subscription (as % of per capita GDP), 2002	96
Extent of staff training, 2003	73
Quality of business schools, 2003	81
Scientists and engineers in R&D (per 1,000 inhabitants), 2000	68
Government prioritization of ICT, 2003	28
Government online presence, 2003	53
Government procurement of ICT, 2003	17

Usage Component Index — 65

Individual Usage	91
Business Usage	58
Government Usage	56
Personal computers (per 1,000 inhabitants), 2001	93
ISDN subscribers (per 1,000 inhabitants), 2001	90
Cable television subscribers (per 1,000 inhabitants), 2001	96
Internet users (per 1,000 inhabitants), 2001	81
Computers installed in businesses (per 1,000 inhabitants), 2002	97
Firm-level technology absorption, 2003	50
Prevalence of foreign technology licensing, 2003	35
Government success in ICT promotion, 2003	27
Government online services, 2003	74

Thailand.th

Key Indicators

Population, 2002	61,887,000
Main telephone lines in operation, 2002	6,499,842
growth (%) 1999–2002	25%
Cellular mobile telephone subscribers, 2002	16,117,000
growth (%) 1999–2002	589%
Personal computers, 2002	2,461,000
growth (%) 1999–2002	78%
Internet users (estimated), 2002	4,800,000
growth (%) 1999–2002	269%

Source: Data from International Telecommunication Union

RANK/102

Environment Component Index — 41

Market Environment	28
Political and Regulatory Environment	38
Infrastructure Environment	54
State of cluster development, 2003	10
Venture capital availability, 2003	39
Subsidies for firm-level R&D, 2003	25
Quality of scientific research institutions, 2003	43
Availability of scientists and engineers, 2003	63
Brain drain, 2003	12
Utility patents granted (per 1,000,000 inhabitants), 2002	46
ICT manufactured exports (per capita), 2001	30
ICT service exports (per capita), 2001	53
Overall administrative burden, 2003	25
Quality of the legal system, 2003	34
Laws relating to ICT, 2003	43
Competition in the ISP sector, 2003	29
Foreign ownership restrictions, 2003	75
Efficiency of the tax system, 2003	27
Freedom of the press, 2003	62
Overall infrastructure quality, 2003	29
Waiting time for telephone lines (years), 2000	66
Telephone mainlines (per 1,000 inhabitants), 2001	66
Public pay telephones (per 1,000 inhabitants), 2001	41
Internet servers (per 1,000,000 inhabitants), 2001	57

Networked Readiness Index Rank

2003–2004 (102 countries) — 38

2002–2003 (82 countries)	41
2001–2002 (75 countries)	43

Readiness Component Index — 37

Individual Readiness	44
Business Readiness	44
Government Readiness	22
Public expenditure on education (per capita), 2000	55
Adult illiteracy (%), 2001	42
Tertiary enrollment (gross %), 2001 or most recent available	41
Radios (per 1,000 inhabitants), 2001 or most recent available	76
Television sets (per 1,000 inhabitants), 2001	48
Households online (as % of households with computers), 2002	33
Quality of math and science education, 2003	42
Affordability of local fixed line calls (as % of per capita GDP), 2001	65
Affordability of Internet telephone access (as % of per capita GDP), 2001	50
Affordability of Internet service provider fees (as % of per capita GDP), 2001	42
Ease of obtaining telephone lines, 2003	41
Cost of business telephone monthly subscription (as % of per capita GDP), 2002	33
Extent of staff training, 2003	34
Quality of business schools, 2003	36
Scientists and engineers in R&D (per 1,000 inhabitants), 2000	90
Government prioritization of ICT, 2003	16
Government online presence, 2003	37
Government procurement of ICT, 2003	36

Usage Component Index — 40

Individual Usage	65
Business Usage	33
Government Usage	24
Personal computers (per 1,000 inhabitants), 2001	64
ISDN subscribers (per 1,000 inhabitants), 2001	69
Cable television subscribers (per 1,000 inhabitants), 2001	82
Internet users (per 1,000 inhabitants), 2001	48
Computers installed in businesses (per 1,000 inhabitants), 2002	49
Firm-level technology absorption, 2003	30
Prevalence of foreign technology licensing, 2003	5
Government success in ICT promotion, 2003	14
Government online services, 2003	40

Trinidad and Tobago.tt

Key Indicators

Population, 2002	1,301,500
Main telephone lines in operation, 2002	325,054
growth (%) 1999–2002	17%
Cellular mobile telephone subscribers, 2002	361,911
growth (%) 1999–2002	836%
Personal computers, 2002	103,500
growth (%) 1999–2002	48%
Internet users (estimated), 2002	138,000
growth (%) 1999–2002	84%

Source: Data from International Telecommunication Union

RANK/102

Environment Component Index — 49

Market Environment	56
Political and Regulatory Environment	47
Infrastructure Environment	50
State of cluster development, 2003	53
Venture capital availability, 2003	60
Subsidies for firm-level R&D, 2003	65
Quality of scientific research institutions, 2003	61
Availability of scientists and engineers, 2003	56
Brain drain, 2003	48
Utility patents granted (per 1,000,000 inhabitants), 2002	72
ICT manufactured exports (per capita), 2001	62
ICT service exports (per capita), 2001	36
Overall administrative burden, 2003	42
Quality of the legal system, 2003	24
Laws relating to ICT, 2003	80
Competition in the ISP sector, 2003	98
Foreign ownership restrictions, 2003	64
Efficiency of the tax system, 2003	14
Freedom of the press, 2003	47
Overall infrastructure quality, 2003	41
Waiting time for telephone lines (years), 2000	45
Telephone mainlines (per 1,000 inhabitants), 2001	45
Public pay telephones (per 1,000 inhabitants), 2001	60
Internet servers (per 1,000,000 inhabitants), 2001	42

Networked Readiness Index Rank

2003–2004 (102 countries) — 52

2002–2003 (82 countries)	58
2001–2002 (75 countries)	46

Readiness Component Index — 65

Individual Readiness	48
Business Readiness	68
Government Readiness	78
Public expenditure on education (per capita), 2000	34
Adult illiteracy (%), 2001	27
Tertiary enrollment (gross %), 2001 or most recent available	80
Radios (per 1,000 inhabitants), 2001 or most recent available	39
Television sets (per 1,000 inhabitants), 2001	42
Households online (as % of households with computers), 2002	40
Quality of math and science education, 2003	49
Affordability of local fixed line calls (as % of per capita GDP), 2001	27
Affordability of Internet telephone access (as % of per capita GDP), 2001	12
Affordability of Internet service provider fees (as % of per capita GDP), 2001	4
Ease of obtaining telephone lines, 2003	79
Cost of business telephone monthly subscription (as % of per capita GDP), 2002	63
Extent of staff training, 2003	44
Quality of business schools, 2003	43
Scientists and engineers in R&D (per 1,000 inhabitants), 2000	82
Government prioritization of ICT, 2003	76
Government online presence, 2003	81
Government procurement of ICT, 2003	39

Usage Component Index — 55

Individual Usage	44
Business Usage	47
Government Usage	70
Personal computers (per 1,000 inhabitants), 2001	45
ISDN subscribers (per 1,000 inhabitants), 2001	72
Cable television subscribers (per 1,000 inhabitants), 2001	33
Internet users (per 1,000 inhabitants), 2001	41
Computers installed in businesses (per 1,000 inhabitants), 2002	43
Firm-level technology absorption, 2003	47
Prevalence of foreign technology licensing, 2003	42
Government success in ICT promotion, 2003	70
Government online services, 2003	68

Tunisia.tn

Key Indicators

Population, 2002	9,815,000
Main telephone lines in operation, 2002	1,148,000
growth (%) 1999–2002	35%
Cellular mobile telephone subscribers, 2002	503,911
growth (%) 1999–2002	812%
Personal computers, 2002	300,000
growth (%) 1999–2002	107%
Internet users (estimated), 2002	505,500
growth (%) 1999–2002	237%

Source: Data from International Telecommunication Union

RANK/102

Environment Component Index	36
Market Environment	29
Political and Regulatory Environment	34
Infrastructure Environment	52
State of cluster development, 2003	63
Venture capital availability, 2003	25
Subsidies for firm-level R&D, 2003	7
Quality of scientific research institutions, 2003	45
Availability of scientists and engineers, 2003	13
Brain drain, 2003	41
Utility patents granted (per 1,000,000 inhabitants), 2002	62
ICT manufactured exports (per capita), 2001	58
ICT service exports (per capita), 2001	52
Overall administrative burden, 2003	10
Quality of the legal system, 2003	33
Laws relating to ICT, 2003	19
Competition in the ISP sector, 2003	60
Foreign ownership restrictions, 2003	40
Efficiency of the tax system, 2003	18
Freedom of the press, 2003	87
Overall infrastructure quality, 2003	33
Waiting time for telephone lines (years), 2000	58
Telephone mainlines (per 1,000 inhabitants), 2001	62
Public pay telephones (per 1,000 inhabitants), 2001	40
Internet servers (per 1,000,000 inhabitants), 2001	75

Networked Readiness Index Rank

2003–2004 (102 countries) **40**

2002–2003 (82 countries)   34

Readiness Component Index	42
Individual Readiness	56
Business Readiness	35
Government Readiness	37
Public expenditure on education (per capita), 2000	49
Adult illiteracy (%), 2001	83
Tertiary enrollment (gross %), 2001 or most recent available	57
Radios (per 1,000 inhabitants), 2001 or most recent available	90
Television sets (per 1,000 inhabitants), 2001	64
Households online (as % of households with computers), 2002	60
Quality of math and science education, 2003	10
Affordability of local fixed line calls (as % of per capita GDP), 2001	37
Affordability of Internet telephone access (as % of per capita GDP), 2001	19
Affordability of Internet service provider fees (as % of per capita GDP), 2001	61
Ease of obtaining telephone lines, 2003	49
Cost of business telephone monthly subscription (as % of per capita GDP), 2002	25
Extent of staff training, 2003	26
Quality of business schools, 2003	24
Scientists and engineers in R&D (per 1,000 inhabitants), 2000	64
Government prioritization of ICT, 2003	5
Government online presence, 2003	85
Government procurement of ICT, 2003	5

Usage Component Index	45
Individual Usage	56
Business Usage	46
Government Usage	36
Personal computers (per 1,000 inhabitants), 2001	65
ISDN subscribers (per 1,000 inhabitants), 2001	78
Cable television subscribers (per 1,000 inhabitants), 2001	48
Internet users (per 1,000 inhabitants), 2001	53
Computers installed in businesses (per 1,000 inhabitants), 2002	68
Firm-level technology absorption, 2003	23
Prevalence of foreign technology licensing, 2003	29
Government success in ICT promotion, 2003	3
Government online services, 2003	81

Turkey.tr

Key Indicators

Population, 2002	67,272,000
Main telephone lines in operation, 2002	18,914,860
growth (%) 1999–2002	5%
Cellular mobile telephone subscribers, 2002	23,374,360
growth (%) 1999–2002	188%
Personal computers, 2001	2,700,000
growth (%) 1999–2001	23%
Internet users (estimated), 2002	4,900,000
growth (%) 1999–2002	227%

Source: Data from International Telecommunication Union

RANK/102

Environment Component Index	**58**
Market Environment	57
Political and Regulatory Environment	73
Infrastructure Environment	55
State of cluster development, 2003	32
Venture capital availability, 2003	84
Subsidies for firm-level R&D, 2003	40
Quality of scientific research institutions, 2003	79
Availability of scientists and engineers, 2003	47
Brain drain, 2003	52
Utility patents granted (per 1,000,000 inhabitants), 2002	56
ICT manufactured exports (per capita), 2001	57
ICT service exports (per capita), 2001	45
Overall administrative burden, 2003	66
Quality of the legal system, 2003	57
Laws relating to ICT, 2003	86
Competition in the ISP sector, 2003	54
Foreign ownership restrictions, 2003	66
Efficiency of the tax system, 2003	94
Freedom of the press, 2003	70
Overall infrastructure quality, 2003	54
Waiting time for telephone lines (years), 2000	42
Telephone mainlines (per 1,000 inhabitants), 2001	40
Public pay telephones (per 1,000 inhabitants), 2001	79
Internet servers (per 1,000,000 inhabitants), 2001	51

Networked Readiness Index Rank

2003–2004 (102 countries) **56**

2002–2003 (82 countries)	50
2001–2002 (75 countries)	41

Readiness Component Index	**61**
Individual Readiness	58
Business Readiness	56
Government Readiness	66
Public expenditure on education (per capita), 2000	57
Adult illiteracy (%), 2001	71
Tertiary enrollment (gross %), 2001 or most recent available	66
Radios (per 1,000 inhabitants), 2001 or most recent available	44
Television sets (per 1,000 inhabitants), 2001	45
Households online (as % of households with computers), 2002	35
Quality of math and science education, 2003	54
Affordability of local fixed line calls (as % of per capita GDP), 2001	68
Affordability of Internet telephone access (as % of per capita GDP), 2001	90
Affordability of Internet service provider fees (as % of per capita GDP), 2001	60
Ease of obtaining telephone lines, 2003	60
Cost of business telephone monthly subscription (as % of per capita GDP), 2002	39
Extent of staff training, 2003	58
Quality of business schools, 2003	55
Scientists and engineers in R&D (per 1,000 inhabitants), 2000	66
Government prioritization of ICT, 2003	90
Government online presence, 2003	45
Government procurement of ICT, 2003	83

Usage Component Index	**56**
Individual Usage	63
Business Usage	49
Government Usage	45
Personal computers (per 1,000 inhabitants), 2001	56
ISDN subscribers (per 1,000 inhabitants), 2001	70
Cable television subscribers (per 1,000 inhabitants), 2001	70
Internet users (per 1,000 inhabitants), 2001	56
Computers installed in businesses (per 1,000 inhabitants), 2002	52
Firm-level technology absorption, 2003	54
Prevalence of foreign technology licensing, 2003	23
Government success in ICT promotion, 2003	87
Government online services, 2003	20

Uganda.ug

Key Indicators

Population, 2002	24,700,000
Main telephone lines in operation, 2002	54,976
growth (%) 1999–2002	-4%
Cellular mobile telephone subscribers, 2002	393,310
growth (%) 1999–2002	598%
Personal computers, 2001	70,000
growth (%) 1999–2001	27%
Internet users (estimated), 2001	60,000
growth (%) 1999–2001	140%

Source: Data from International Telecommunication Union

RANK/102

Environment Component Index — 78

Market Environment	62
Political and Regulatory Environment	67
Infrastructure Environment	88
State of cluster development, 2003	51
Venture capital availability, 2003	57
Subsidies for firm-level R&D, 2003	48
Quality of scientific research institutions, 2003	33
Availability of scientists and engineers, 2003	77
Brain drain, 2003	83
Utility patents granted (per 1,000,000 inhabitants), 2002	66
ICT manufactured exports (per capita), 2001	90
ICT service exports (per capita), 2001	101
Overall administrative burden, 2003	41
Quality of the legal system, 2003	58
Laws relating to ICT, 2003	66
Competition in the ISP sector, 2003	53
Foreign ownership restrictions, 2003	32
Efficiency of the tax system, 2003	64
Freedom of the press, 2003	93
Overall infrastructure quality, 2003	80
Waiting time for telephone lines (years), 2000	80
Telephone mainlines (per 1,000 inhabitants), 2001	101
Public pay telephones (per 1,000 inhabitants), 2001	94
Internet servers (per 1,000,000 inhabitants), 2001	86

Readiness Component Index — 90

Individual Readiness	97
Business Readiness	93
Government Readiness	55
Public expenditure on education (per capita), 2000	97
Adult illiteracy (%), 2001	85
Tertiary enrollment (gross %), 2001 or most recent available	91
Radios (per 1,000 inhabitants), 2001 or most recent available	93
Television sets (per 1,000 inhabitants), 2001	91
Households online (as % of households with computers), 2002	81
Quality of math and science education, 2003	68
Affordability of local fixed line calls (as % of per capita GDP), 2001	102
Affordability of Internet telephone access (as % of per capita GDP), 2001	99
Affordability of Internet service provider fees (as % of per capita GDP), 2001	93
Ease of obtaining telephone lines, 2003	73
Cost of business telephone monthly subscription (as % of per capita GDP), 2002	100
Extent of staff training, 2003	77
Quality of business schools, 2003	70
Scientists and engineers in R&D (per 1,000 inhabitants), 2000	96
Government prioritization of ICT, 2003	39
Government online presence, 2003	70
Government procurement of ICT, 2003	41

Usage Component Index — 64

Individual Usage	95
Business Usage	65
Government Usage	46
Personal computers (per 1,000 inhabitants), 2001	95
ISDN subscribers (per 1,000 inhabitants), 2001	97
Cable television subscribers (per 1,000 inhabitants), 2001	96
Internet users (per 1,000 inhabitants), 2001	92
Computers installed in businesses (per 1,000 inhabitants), 2001	92
Firm-level technology absorption, 2003	60
Prevalence of foreign technology licensing, 2003	40
Government success in ICT promotion, 2003	25
Government online services, 2003	59

Ukraine.ua

Key Indicators

Population, 2002	**50,137,000**
Main telephone lines in operation, 2001	**10,669,600**
growth (%) 1999–2001	6%
Cellular mobile telephone subscribers, 2001	**2,224,600**
growth (%) 1999–2001	927%
Personal computers, 2001	**920,000**
growth (%) 1999–2001	15%
Internet users (estimated), 2001	**600,000**
growth (%) 1999–2001	200%

Source: Data from International Telecommunication Union

RANK/102

Environment Component Index — 93

Market Environment	67
Political and Regulatory Environment	98
Infrastructure Environment	82
State of cluster development, 2003	88
Venture capital availability, 2003	73
Subsidies for firm-level R&D, 2003	66
Quality of scientific research institutions, 2003	57
Availability of scientists and engineers, 2003	45
Brain drain, 2003	74
Utility patents granted (per 1,000,000 inhabitants), 2002	47
ICT manufactured exports (per capita), 2001	40
ICT service exports (per capita), 2001	84
Overall administrative burden, 2003	72
Quality of the legal system, 2003	83
Laws relating to ICT, 2003	85
Competition in the ISP sector, 2003	75
Foreign ownership restrictions, 2003	89
Efficiency of the tax system, 2003	98
Freedom of the press, 2003	101
Overall infrastructure quality, 2003	59
Waiting time for telephone lines (years), 2000	97
Telephone mainlines (per 1,000 inhabitants), 2001	51
Public pay telephones (per 1,000 inhabitants), 2001	49
Internet servers (per 1,000,000 inhabitants), 2001	67

Networked Readiness Index Rank

2003–2004 (102 countries) — 78

2002–2003 (82 countries)	70
2001–2002 (75 countries)	66

Readiness Component Index — 58

Individual Readiness	36
Business Readiness	72
Government Readiness	73
Public expenditure on education (per capita), 2000	75
Adult illiteracy (%), 2001	13
Tertiary enrollment (gross %), 2001 or most recent available	33
Radios (per 1,000 inhabitants), 2001 or most recent available	18
Television sets (per 1,000 inhabitants), 2001	30
Households online (as % of households with computers), 2002	47
Quality of math and science education, 2003	27
Affordability of local fixed line calls (as % of per capita GDP), 2001	79
Affordability of Internet telephone access (as % of per capita GDP), 2001	11
Affordability of Internet service provider fees (as % of per capita GDP), 2001	57
Ease of obtaining telephone lines, 2003	80
Cost of business telephone monthly subscription (as % of per capita GDP), 2002	91
Extent of staff training, 2003	95
Quality of business schools, 2003	65
Scientists and engineers in R&D (per 1,000 inhabitants), 2000	26
Government prioritization of ICT, 2003	69
Government online presence, 2003	66
Government procurement of ICT, 2003	82

Usage Component Index — 85

Individual Usage	60
Business Usage	92
Government Usage	85
Personal computers (per 1,000 inhabitants), 2001	73
ISDN subscribers (per 1,000 inhabitants), 2001	63
Cable television subscribers (per 1,000 inhabitants), 2001	49
Internet users (per 1,000 inhabitants), 2001	75
Computers installed in businesses (per 1,000 inhabitants), 2002	72
Firm-level technology absorption, 2003	67
Prevalence of foreign technology licensing, 2003	94
Government success in ICT promotion, 2003	82
Government online services, 2003	74

United Kingdom.uk

Key Indicators

Population, 2002	59,088,000
Main telephone lines in operation, 2002	35,145,000
growth (%) 1999–2002	3%
Cellular mobile telephone subscribers, 2002	49,921,000
growth (%) 1999–2002	84%
Personal computers, 2001	22,000,000
growth (%) 1999–2001	22%
Internet users (estimated), 2002	24,000,000
growth (%) 1999–2002	92%

Source: Data from International Telecommunication Union

RANK/102

Environment Component Index	14
Market Environment	13
Political and Regulatory Environment	9
Infrastructure Environment	19
State of cluster development, 2003	14
Venture capital availability, 2003	2
Subsidies for firm-level R&D, 2003	19
Quality of scientific research institutions, 2003	5
Availability of scientists and engineers, 2003	37
Brain drain, 2003	13
Utility patents granted (per 1,000,000 inhabitants), 2002	18
ICT manufactured exports (per capita), 2001	13
ICT service exports (per capita), 2001	14
Overall administrative burden, 2003	38
Quality of the legal system, 2003	10
Laws relating to ICT, 2003	8
Competition in the ISP sector, 2003	8
Foreign ownership restrictions, 2003	1
Efficiency of the tax system, 2003	35
Freedom of the press, 2003	15
Overall infrastructure quality, 2003	26
Waiting time for telephone lines (years), 2000	1
Telephone mainlines (per 1,000 inhabitants), 2001	11
Public pay telephones (per 1,000 inhabitants), 2001	53
Internet servers (per 1,000,000 inhabitants), 2001	10

Networked Readiness Index Rank

2003–2004 (102 countries) — **15**

2002–2003 (82 countries)	7
2001–2002 (75 countries)	10

Readiness Component Index	10
Individual Readiness	7
Business Readiness	14
Government Readiness	10
Public expenditure on education (per capita), 2000	16
Adult illiteracy (%), 2001	17
Tertiary enrollment (gross %), 2001 or most recent available	13
Radios (per 1,000 inhabitants), 2001 or most recent available	6
Television sets (per 1,000 inhabitants), 2001	2
Households online (as % of households with computers), 2002	16
Quality of math and science education, 2003	43
Affordability of local fixed line calls (as % of per capita GDP), 2001	32
Affordability of Internet telephone access (as % of per capita GDP), 2001	67
Affordability of Internet service provider fees (as % of per capita GDP), 2001	13
Ease of obtaining telephone lines, 2003	22
Cost of business telephone monthly subscription (as % of per capita GDP), 2002	26
Extent of staff training, 2003	11
Quality of business schools, 2003	5
Scientists and engineers in R&D (per 1,000 inhabitants), 2000	16
Government prioritization of ICT, 2003	25
Government online presence, 2003	5
Government procurement of ICT, 2003	42

Usage Component Index	21
Individual Usage	21
Business Usage	20
Government Usage	18
Personal computers (per 1,000 inhabitants), 2001	17
ISDN subscribers (per 1,000 inhabitants), 2001	22
Cable television subscribers (per 1,000 inhabitants), 2001	46
Internet users (per 1,000 inhabitants), 2001	13
Computers installed in businesses (per 1,000 inhabitants), 2002	17
Firm-level technology absorption, 2003	34
Prevalence of foreign technology licensing, 2003	57
Government success in ICT promotion, 2003	47
Government online services, 2003	8

United States.us

Key Indicators

Population, 2002	288,368,700
Main telephone lines in operation, 2002	190,000,000
growth (%) 1999–2002	4%
Cellular mobile telephone subscribers, 2002	140,766,800
growth (%) 1999–2002	64%
Personal computers, 2001	178,000,000
growth (%) 1999–2001	26%
Internet users (estimated), 2002	155,000,000
growth (%) 1999–2002	52%

Source: Data from International Telecommunication Union

RANK/102

Environment Component Index — 1

Market Environment	2
Political and Regulatory Environment	8
Infrastructure Environment	2
State of cluster development, 2003	6
Venture capital availability, 2003	3
Subsidies for firm-level R&D, 2003	12
Quality of scientific research institutions, 2003	1
Availability of scientists and engineers, 2003	8
Brain drain, 2003	1
Utility patents granted (per 1,000,000 inhabitants), 2002	1
ICT manufactured exports (per capita), 2001	21
ICT service exports (per capita), 2001	20
Overall administrative burden, 2003	19
Quality of the legal system, 2003	13
Laws relating to ICT, 2003	5
Competition in the ISP sector, 2003	2
Foreign ownership restrictions, 2003	9
Efficiency of the tax system, 2003	45
Freedom of the press, 2003	7
Overall infrastructure quality, 2003	8
Waiting time for telephone lines (years), 2000	1
Telephone mainlines (per 1,000 inhabitants), 2001	6
Public pay telephones (per 1,000 inhabitants), 2001	19
Internet servers (per 1,000,000 inhabitants), 2001	2

Networked Readiness Index Rank

2003–2004 (102 countries) — **1**

2002–2003	(82 countries)	2
2001–2002	(75 countries)	1

Readiness Component Index — 3

Individual Readiness	5
Business Readiness	3
Government Readiness	3
Public expenditure on education (per capita), 2000	19
Adult illiteracy (%), 2001	37
Tertiary enrollment (gross %), 2001 or most recent available	4
Radios (per 1,000 inhabitants), 2001 or most recent available	3
Television sets (per 1,000 inhabitants), 2001	6
Households online (as % of households with computers), 2002	4
Quality of math and science education, 2003	37
Affordability of local fixed line calls (as % of per capita GDP), 2001	7
Affordability of Internet telephone access (as % of per capita GDP), 2001	17
Affordability of Internet service provider fees (as % of per capita GDP), 2001	3
Ease of obtaining telephone lines, 2003	18
Cost of business telephone monthly subscription (as % of per capita GDP), 2002	36
Extent of staff training, 2003	5
Quality of business schools, 2003	1
Scientists and engineers in R&D (per 1,000 inhabitants), 2000	6
Government prioritization of ICT, 2003	15
Government online presence, 2003	4
Government procurement of ICT, 2003	10

Usage Component Index — 1

Individual Usage	8
Business Usage	1
Government Usage	2
Personal computers (per 1,000 inhabitants), 2001	2
ISDN subscribers (per 1,000 inhabitants), 2001	29
Cable television subscribers (per 1,000 inhabitants), 2001	7
Internet users (per 1,000 inhabitants), 2001	5
Computers installed in businesses (per 1,000 inhabitants), 2002	1
Firm-level technology absorption, 2003	6
Prevalence of foreign technology licensing, 2003	23
Government success in ICT promotion, 2003	18
Government online services, 2003	2

Uruguay.uy

Key Indicators

Population, 2002	3,385,000
Main telephone lines in operation, 2002	946,533
growth (%) 1999–2002	6%
Cellular mobile telephone subscribers, 2002	652,000
growth (%) 1999–2002	104%
Personal computers, 2001	370,000
growth (%) 1999–2001	12%
Internet users (estimated), 2001	400,000
growth (%) 1999–2001	21%

Source: Data from International Telecommunication Union

RANK/102

Environment Component Index	52
Market Environment	81
Political and Regulatory Environment	53
Infrastructure Environment	41
State of cluster development, 2003	90
Venture capital availability, 2003	100
Subsidies for firm-level R&D, 2003	84
Quality of scientific research institutions, 2003	74
Availability of scientists and engineers, 2003	44
Brain drain, 2003	78
Utility patents granted (per 1,000,000 inhabitants), 2002	42
ICT manufactured exports (per capita), 2001	71
ICT service exports (per capita), 2001	65
Overall administrative burden, 2003	74
Quality of the legal system, 2003	31
Laws relating to ICT, 2003	79
Competition in the ISP sector, 2003	64
Foreign ownership restrictions, 2003	71
Efficiency of the tax system, 2003	78
Freedom of the press, 2003	27
Overall infrastructure quality, 2003	48
Waiting time for telephone lines (years), 2000	1
Telephone mainlines (per 1,000 inhabitants), 2001	41
Public pay telephones (per 1,000 inhabitants), 2001	32
Internet servers (per 1,000,000 inhabitants), 2001	39

Networked Readiness Index Rank

2003–2004 (102 countries) — 54

2002–2003 (82 countries)	55
2001–2002 (75 countries)	37

Readiness Component Index	53
Individual Readiness	42
Business Readiness	54
Government Readiness	71
Public expenditure on education (per capita), 2000	61
Adult illiteracy (%), 2001	35
Tertiary enrollment (gross %), 2001 or most recent available	39
Radios (per 1,000 inhabitants), 2001 or most recent available	35
Television sets (per 1,000 inhabitants), 2001	26
Households online (as % of households with computers), 2002	53
Quality of math and science education, 2003	56
Affordability of local fixed line calls (as % of per capita GDP), 2001	75
Affordability of Internet telephone access (as % of per capita GDP), 2001	46
Affordability of Internet service provider fees (as % of per capita GDP), 2001	63
Ease of obtaining telephone lines, 2003	25
Cost of business telephone monthly subscription (as % of per capita GDP), 2002	56
Extent of staff training, 2003	84
Quality of business schools, 2003	39
Scientists and engineers in R&D (per 1,000 inhabitants), 2000	73
Government prioritization of ICT, 2003	71
Government online presence, 2003	55
Government procurement of ICT, 2003	88

Usage Component Index	61
Individual Usage	37
Business Usage	78
Government Usage	81
Personal computers (per 1,000 inhabitants), 2001	36
ISDN subscribers (per 1,000 inhabitants), 2001	58
Cable television subscribers (per 1,000 inhabitants), 2001	25
Internet users (per 1,000 inhabitants), 2001	38
Computers installed in businesses (per 1,000 inhabitants), 2000	39
Firm-level technology absorption, 2003	96
Prevalence of foreign technology licensing, 2003	76
Government success in ICT promotion, 2003	79
Government online services, 2003	73

Venezuela.ve

Key Indicators

Population, 2002	25,300,000
Main telephone lines in operation, 2002	2,841,771
growth (%) 1999–2002	11%
Cellular mobile telephone subscribers, 2002	6,463,561
growth (%) 1999–2002	71%
Personal computers, 2001	1,300,000
growth (%) 1999–2001	30%
Internet users (estimated), 2002	1,274,429
growth (%) 1999–2002	87%

Source: Data from International Telecommunication Union

RANK/102

Environment Component Index	81
Market Environment	83
Political and Regulatory Environment	96
Infrastructure Environment	59
State of cluster development, 2003	80
Venture capital availability, 2003	93
Subsidies for firm-level R&D, 2003	85
Quality of scientific research institutions, 2003	77
Availability of scientists and engineers, 2003	67
Brain drain, 2003	84
Utility patents granted (per 1,000,000 inhabitants), 2002	39
ICT manufactured exports (per capita), 2001	74
ICT service exports (per capita), 2001	83
Overall administrative burden, 2003	102
Quality of the legal system, 2003	101
Laws relating to ICT, 2003	58
Competition in the ISP sector, 2003	62
Foreign ownership restrictions, 2003	76
Efficiency of the tax system, 2003	92
Freedom of the press, 2003	88
Overall infrastructure quality, 2003	62
Waiting time for telephone lines (years), 2000	49
Telephone mainlines (per 1,000 inhabitants), 2001	62
Public pay telephones (per 1,000 inhabitants), 2001	34
Internet servers (per 1,000,000 inhabitants), 2001	50

Networked Readiness Index Rank

2003–2004 (102 countries) **72**

2002–2003 (82 countries) 66
2001–2002 (75 countries) 50

Readiness Component Index	62
Individual Readiness	60
Business Readiness	63
Government Readiness	63
Public expenditure on education (per capita), 2000	41
Adult illiteracy (%), 2001	49
Tertiary enrollment (gross %), 2001 or most recent available	49
Radios (per 1,000 inhabitants), 2001 or most recent available	69
Television sets (per 1,000 inhabitants), 2001	68
Households online (as % of households with computers), 2002	52
Quality of math and science education, 2003	94
Affordability of local fixed line calls (as % of per capita GDP), 2001	53
Affordability of Internet telephone access (as % of per capita GDP), 2001	23
Affordability of Internet service provider fees (as % of per capita GDP), 2001	51
Ease of obtaining telephone lines, 2003	54
Cost of business telephone monthly subscription (as % of per capita GDP), 2002	74
Extent of staff training, 2003	71
Quality of business schools, 2003	50
Scientists and engineers in R&D (per 1,000 inhabitants), 2000	76
Government prioritization of ICT, 2003	93
Government online presence, 2003	20
Government procurement of ICT, 2003	87

Usage Component Index	70
Individual Usage	53
Business Usage	57
Government Usage	86
Personal computers (per 1,000 inhabitants), 2001	49
ISDN subscribers (per 1,000 inhabitants), 2001	34
Cable television subscribers (per 1,000 inhabitants), 2001	52
Internet users (per 1,000 inhabitants), 2001	50
Computers installed in businesses (per 1,000 inhabitants), 2002	44
Firm-level technology absorption, 2003	74
Prevalence of foreign technology licensing, 2003	50
Government success in ICT promotion, 2003	99
Government online services, 2003	47

Vietnam.vn

Key Indicators

Population, 2002	81,248,500
Main telephone lines in operation, 2002	3,664,752
growth (%) 1999–2002	74%
Cellular mobile telephone subscribers, 2002	1,902,388
growth (%) 1999–2002	479%
Personal computers, 2002	800,000
growth (%) 1999–2002	60%
Internet users (estimated), 2002	1,500,000
growth (%) 1999–2002	1,400%

Source: Data from International Telecommunication Union

RANK/102

Environment Component Index	74
Market Environment	38
Political and Regulatory Environment	78
Infrastructure Environment	92
State of cluster development, 2003	45
Venture capital availability, 2003	58
Subsidies for firm-level R&D, 2003	34
Quality of scientific research institutions, 2003	35
Availability of scientists and engineers, 2003	32
Brain drain, 2003	43
Utility patents granted (per 1,000,000 inhabitants), 2002	72
ICT manufactured exports (per capita), 2001	85
ICT service exports (per capita), 2001	79
Overall administrative burden, 2003	40
Quality of the legal system, 2003	53
Laws relating to ICT, 2003	54
Competition in the ISP sector, 2003	85
Foreign ownership restrictions, 2003	84
Efficiency of the tax system, 2003	61
Freedom of the press, 2003	97
Overall infrastructure quality, 2003	76
Waiting time for telephone lines (years), 2000	85
Telephone mainlines (per 1,000 inhabitants), 2001	79
Public pay telephones (per 1,000 inhabitants), 2001	95
Internet servers (per 1,000,000 inhabitants), 2001	94

Networked Readiness Index Rank

2003–2004 (102 countries) **68**

2002–2003 (82 countries)	71
2001–2002 (75 countries)	74

Readiness Component Index	67
Individual Readiness	73
Business Readiness	74
Government Readiness	52
Public expenditure on education (per capita), 2000	86
Adult illiteracy (%), 2001	50
Tertiary enrollment (gross %), 2001 or most recent available	75
Radios (per 1,000 inhabitants), 2001 or most recent available	96
Television sets (per 1,000 inhabitants), 2001	67
Households online (as % of households with computers), 2002	96
Quality of math and science education, 2003	57
Affordability of local fixed line calls (as % of per capita GDP), 2001	71
Affordability of Internet telephone access (as % of per capita GDP), 2001	66
Affordability of Internet service provider fees (as % of per capita GDP), 2001	85
Ease of obtaining telephone lines, 2003	70
Cost of business telephone monthly subscription (as % of per capita GDP), 2002	67
Extent of staff training, 2003	64
Quality of business schools, 2003	85
Scientists and engineers in R&D (per 1,000 inhabitants), 2000	70
Government prioritization of ICT, 2003	34
Government online presence, 2003	84
Government procurement of ICT, 2003	11

Usage Component Index	58
Individual Usage	79
Business Usage	53
Government Usage	50
Personal computers (per 1,000 inhabitants), 2001	81
ISDN subscribers (per 1,000 inhabitants), 2001	86
Cable television subscribers (per 1,000 inhabitants), 2001	73
Internet users (per 1,000 inhabitants), 2001	74
Computers installed in businesses (per 1,000 inhabitants), 2001	75
Firm-level technology absorption, 2003	15
Prevalence of foreign technology licensing, 2003	68
Government success in ICT promotion, 2003	15
Government online services, 2003	81

Zambia.zm

Key Indicators

Population, 2002	10,696,000
Main telephone lines in operation, 2002	88,475
growth (%) 1999–2002	6%
Cellular mobile telephone subscribers, 2002	139,092
growth (%) 1999–2002	393%
Personal computers, 2002	80,000
growth (%) 1999–2002	23%
Internet users (estimated), 2002	52,420
growth (%) 1999–2002	249%

Source: Data from International Telecommunication Union

Networked Readiness Index Rank

2003–2004 (102 countries) 85

RANK/102

Environment Component Index	86
Market Environment	88
Political and Regulatory Environment	55
Infrastructure Environment	96
State of cluster development, 2003	69
Venture capital availability, 2003	86
Subsidies for firm-level R&D, 2003	86
Quality of scientific research institutions, 2003	76
Availability of scientists and engineers, 2003	78
Brain drain, 2003	99
Utility patents granted (per 1,000,000 inhabitants), 2002	72
ICT manufactured exports (per capita), 2001	79
ICT service exports (per capita), 2001	102
Overall administrative burden, 2003	47
Quality of the legal system, 2003	56
Laws relating to ICT, 2003	72
Competition in the ISP sector, 2003	78
Foreign ownership restrictions, 2003	28
Efficiency of the tax system, 2003	26
Freedom of the press, 2003	77
Overall infrastructure quality, 2003	82
Waiting time for telephone lines (years), 2000	94
Telephone mainlines (per 1,000 inhabitants), 2001	90
Public pay telephones (per 1,000 inhabitants), 2001	96
Internet servers (per 1,000,000 inhabitants), 2001	100

Readiness Component Index	81
Individual Readiness	83
Business Readiness	86
Government Readiness	75
Public expenditure on education (per capita), 2000	92
Adult illiteracy (%), 2001	77
Tertiary enrollment (gross %), 2001 or most recent available	92
Radios (per 1,000 inhabitants), 2001 or most recent available	86
Television sets (per 1,000 inhabitants), 2001	80
Households online (as % of households with computers), 2002	74
Quality of math and science education, 2003	69
Affordability of local fixed line calls (as % of per capita GDP), 2001	92
Affordability of Internet telephone access (as % of per capita GDP), 2001	79
Affordability of Internet service provider fees (as % of per capita GDP), 2001	87
Ease of obtaining telephone lines, 2003	82
Cost of business telephone monthly subscription (as % of per capita GDP), 2002	81
Extent of staff training, 2003	81
Quality of business schools, 2003	80
Scientists and engineers in R&D (per 1,000 inhabitants), 2000	59
Government prioritization of ICT, 2003	79
Government online presence, 2003	68
Government procurement of ICT, 2003	70

Usage Component Index	84
Individual Usage	92
Business Usage	84
Government Usage	74
Personal computers (per 1,000 inhabitants), 2001	86
ISDN subscribers (per 1,000 inhabitants), 2001	95
Cable television subscribers (per 1,000 inhabitants), 2001	88
Internet users (per 1,000 inhabitants), 2001	93
Computers installed in businesses (per 1,000 inhabitants), 2002	91
Firm-level technology absorption, 2003	88
Prevalence of foreign technology licensing, 2003	77
Government success in ICT promotion, 2003	67
Government online services, 2003	74

Zimbabwe.zw

Key Indicators

Population, 2002	11,634,660
Main telephone lines in operation, 2002	287,854
growth (%) 1999–2002	20%
Cellular mobile telephone subscribers, 2002	353,000
growth (%) 1999–2002	103%
Personal computers, 2002	600,000
growth (%) 1999–2002	300%
Internet users (estimated), 2002	500,000
growth (%) 1999–2002	2400%

Source: Data from International Telecommunication Union

RANK/102

Environment Component Index	97
Market Environment	80
Political and Regulatory Environment	100
Infrastructure Environment	95
State of cluster development, 2003	60
Venture capital availability, 2003	52
Subsidies for firm-level R&D, 2003	76
Quality of scientific research institutions, 2003	72
Availability of scientists and engineers, 2003	88
Brain drain, 2003	101
Utility patents granted (per 1,000,000 inhabitants), 2002	63
ICT manufactured exports (per capita), 2001	70
ICT service exports (per capita), 2001	58
Overall administrative burden, 2003	94
Quality of the legal system, 2003	97
Laws relating to ICT, 2003	82
Competition in the ISP sector, 2003	87
Foreign ownership restrictions, 2003	101
Efficiency of the tax system, 2003	33
Freedom of the press, 2003	102
Overall infrastructure quality, 2003	63
Waiting time for telephone lines (years), 2000	102
Telephone mainlines (per 1,000 inhabitants), 2001	86
Public pay telephones (per 1,000 inhabitants), 2001	37
Internet servers (per 1,000,000 inhabitants), 2001	93

Networked Readiness Index Rank

2003–2004 (102 countries) **95**

2002–2003 (82 countries)	80
2001–2002 (75 countries)	70

Readiness Component Index	91
Individual Readiness	70
Business Readiness	82
Government Readiness	101
Public expenditure on education (per capita), 2000	48
Adult illiteracy (%), 2001	62
Tertiary enrollment (gross %), 2001 or most recent available	86
Radios (per 1,000 inhabitants), 2001 or most recent available	59
Television sets (per 1,000 inhabitants), 2001	76
Households online (as % of households with computers), 2001	61
Quality of math and science education, 2003	60
Affordability of local fixed line calls (as % of per capita GDP), 2001	54
Affordability of Internet telephone access (as % of per capita GDP), 2001	39
Affordability of Internet service provider fees (as % of per capita GDP), 2001	84
Ease of obtaining telephone lines, 2003	97
Cost of business telephone monthly subscription (as % of per capita GDP), 2002	59
Extent of staff training, 2003	35
Quality of business schools, 2003	89
Scientists and engineers in R&D (per 1,000 inhabitants), 2000	67
Government prioritization of ICT, 2003	99
Government online presence, 2003	98
Government procurement of ICT, 2003	90

Usage Component Index	93
Individual Usage	78
Business Usage	70
Government Usage	100
Personal computers (per 1,000 inhabitants), 2001	80
ISDN subscribers (per 1,000 inhabitants), 2001	84
Cable television subscribers (per 1,000 inhabitants), 2001	65
Internet users (per 1,000 inhabitants), 2001	84
Computers installed in businesses (per 1,000 inhabitants), 2002	87
Firm-level technology absorption, 2003	80
Prevalence of foreign technology licensing, 2003	39
Government success in ICT promotion, 2003	97
Government online services, 2003	99

Part 3
Data Presentation

The Networked Readiness Index: Methodology

Michele Hibon, Mark Yung, and Amit Jain

INSEAD

The Networked Readiness Index (NRI) is defined as the degree of preparation of a nation or community to participate in and benefit from information and communication technologies (ICT) development. By looking at the overall index of a country, one can get an idea of how a country compares to other countries; specifically, to countries facing similar global and ICT challenges. In calculating the NRI the overriding aim was to provide the most scientific and credible interpretation of reality. The process included selecting qualitatively relevant variables, estimating missing data and, finally, calculating the index by averaging the normalized data. The main steps are shown in Figure 1 and are explained in greater detail in the following text.

Choosing Variables

The first step in the study was to collect the most complete and high quality set of data possible relating to ICT. At the outset, 91 variables were chosen based on their qualitative relevance to the Networked Readiness Framework. These variables were then divided into three component indexes: Environment, Readiness, and Usage. Next, the variables were further categorized into three different subindexes (e.g., within Environment the three subindexes are: Market, Political/Regulatory and Infrastructure), leading to a total of three component indexes and nine subindexes.

There were two types of short-listed variables, namely, soft data and hard data. For the purposes of this study, the subjective data gathered from survey questionnaires are termed "soft" data, and statistical data collected by independent agencies are termed "hard" data. The soft data initially selected for the study were extracted from the 2002 and 2003 Executive Opinion Survey conducted by the World Economic Forum. The hard data were extracted from six different sources: World Development Indicators (WDI), the World Information Technology and Service Alliance (WITSA), International Telecommunication Union (ITU), Pyramid, and the World Economic Forum. While soft data are critical in establishing the opinions of decision makers and influencers who are intimately familiar with a particular economy, the hard data captures fundamental elements related to the development of infrastructure, human capital, and e-commerce.

Selecting the Countries

The main criteria used in selecting countries were the extent of data available as well as the reliability of the data being considered. Limitations in the availability of reliable data led us to consider only 102 countries for the study—82 countries from last year's *Global Information Technology Report* and 20 additional countries. All 20 additional countries have also been included in this year's *Global Competitiveness Report* (GCR). The scope of the study was limited to the GCR

Figure 1. **Steps in NRI Calculation**

Variable selection and country selection → Data modification → Data estimation using regression → Data estimation using clustering → Further data modification → Data reduction and normalization → Final index calculation

countries because of the importance of the GCR data in the calculation of the NRI.

A number of the 102 countries considered in the study are not covered by some of the data collection agencies. For countries with missing data, one had to utilize several estimation techniques in order to derive appropriate data points. These estimation techniques are described in the ensuing sections.

Dropping Variables

After the data were extracted from different data sources, variables with less than 65 observations were dropped. Soft data variables whose survey results appeared to be questionable were also dropped. Finally, the highly correlated variables within each block were dropped. For pairs of variables that had a correlation coefficient higher than 0.8, the one that was qualitatively less relevant and/or had fewer observations was dropped. Approximately seven variables were dropped due to the 65 observation threshold, another 13 due to the weakness of the underlying raw data, and a further 23 variables because of their high correlation to another variable within the same block. As a result, only 48 variables remained for the computation of the NRI from the original 91 selected variables.

Data Transformation
Step 1: Making the data comparable

In order to compare the data across the 102 selected countries, a number of variables that could not be used in their absolute form to calculate the NRI were transformed. These variables were identified and then weighed against an external variable, such as GDP, population, or GDP per capita, to make them comparable across the countries. Table 1 lists the transformed variables.

Soft data such as that of GCR 2003 did not require transformation. Other hard data variables not listed above also did not require transformation as the data had been previously weighted by the data collection agencies (either as a percentage or by a common denominator such as population).

Estimating Data
Step 1: Regression method

Despite reducing the number of variables from 91 to 48 as described in the preceding choosing Variables section, there were still a number of missing observations that had to be estimated. It was decided to estimate the missing data rather than have missing values because missing values would have led to a bias in calculating the index and limited the ability to make comparisons across the countries. Different approaches were used in order to estimate the missing data.

Table 1. **Transforming Variables to Make Them Comparable**

Variable Name	Variable Explanation	Denominator
ICT service exports, 2001	Communications and computer service exports	Population
Utility patents, 2002	Number of utility patents granted	Population
ICT manufactured exports, 2001	High technology manufactured exports	Population
Public pay telephones, 2001	Number of public pay telephones	Population
Internet servers, 2001	Number of secure Internet servers	Population
Affordability of local fixed line calls, 2001	Cost of local 3-minute call at peak rate (US$)	GDP per capita
Affordability of Internet service provider, 2001	Cost per 30 off-peak hours (US$)	GDP per capita
Affordability of Internet telephone access, 2001	Cost per 30 off-peak hours (US$)	GDP per capita
Cost of business phone subscription, 2002	Cost of business telephone monthly subscription (US$)	GDP per capita
Internet users, 2001	Number of Internet users	Population
ISDN subscribers, 2001	Number of ISDN subscribers	Population
Computers installed in businesses, 2001	Computers installed in businesses	Population

Table 2. Estimating Data Through Regression

Variable Name	Description of Dependent Variable	Description of Independent Variable
Telephone mainlines, 2001	Telephone mainlines per 1,000 inhabitants, 2001	Quality of public schools
Public pay telephones, 2001	Public pay telephones per 1,000 inhabitants, 2001	Population
Television receivers, 2001	Television receivers per 1,000 inhabitants, 2001 or most recent available	Internet access at school
Households online, 2002	Households online as percent of households with personal computers, 2002	GDP per capita
Scientists and engineers in R&D, 2000	Scientists and engineers in R&D per 1,000 inhabitants, 2000 or most recent	Capacity for innovation
ISDN subscribers, 2001	ISDN subscribers per 1,000 inhabitants, 2001	ISDN, DSL and CATV Accounts
Personal computers, 2001	Personal computers per 1,000 inhabitants, 2001	GDP per capita

In the first approach, the missing values were estimated using a regression analysis. The process involved picking a variable (X) that was highly correlated to another variable (Y) with the missing values. X was then used as the independent variable to estimate the dependent variable (Y) in the linear regression Y = a + bX.

In a more extensive form, as a first step a bi-variate correlation analysis was conducted of the 90 short-listed variables and three external variables. The three external variables chosen were GDP, GDP per capita, and population. In case there was more than one highly correlated variable, the variable with all 102 observations and the highest coefficient of correlation was chosen as the independent variable (X). In the event that there was no highly correlated variable that had all 102 observations, the most highly correlated independent variable that had data for the missing countries with missing observations was used.

If the variable used in the regression analysis was not an external variable, but one of the 91 variables, it was dropped in the final calculation of the NRI. Table 2 lists the variables for which data were estimated using this approach. This method, however, was not sufficient to estimate all the missing values; a second approach was therefore used at a later stage in the study to estimate the rest of the missing data.

Estimating Data
Step 2: Clustering

The variables that could not be estimated using the regression method were estimated using a clustering technique. The countries were clustered or grouped according to their GDP per capita. In most cases, countries were grouped with other countries that were within the range of GDP +/- 20 percent. However, in the case of three countries, namely, Ethiopia, Mozambique, and Malawi, the GDP range was broadened in order to obtain an estimate. Therefore, for the three aforementioned countries, the clustering technique overestimates the missing data.

Table 3. Variables Needing Transformation

Variable Number	Title of the Variable	Description of the Variable
I 1.07	Utility patents granted	Number of utility patents (i.e., patents for invention) granted
I 3.02	Telephone wait	Waiting time for telephone mainlines (in years)
II 1.08	Cost of local call	Cost of local call (USD per 3 minutes)
II 1.10	ISP access charge	Internet service provider access charges (US$ per 30 off-peak hours)
II 1.09	Internet telephone access charge	Internet telephone access charges (US$ per 30 off-peak hours)
II 1.02	Illiteracy	Illiteracy rate, adult total (% of people ages 15 and above)
II 2.02	Business telephone cost	Cost of business telephone subscription (US$ per month)

Estimating Data
Step 3: Pro-rata

For the one variable where data provided by WITSA was used, the missing observations had to be estimated using a pro-rata allocation method. Although WITSA provided specific raw data for 53 countries, the remaining data were lumped into five regional sub-categories termed "Rest of [Region]," namely, Western Europe, Central and Eastern Europe, Asia-Pacific, Latin America, and Mid-East Africa. In order to estimate country-specific data for the missing 49 countries, the Rest of Region data were allocated to a country based on that country's GDP relative to the region's combined GDP, net of the GDPs of the 53 countries with reported data.

Special care was taken not to estimate data using other estimated data.

Data Transformation
Step 2: Making the variables consistent

The next step in calculating the NRI required further transformation of variables to make the variables consistent. While a high score on most of the variables would lead to a higher index score, a few variables had a reverse effect on the index and it was necessary to transform them to make them consistent with the other variables. The data of these variables were multiplied by a factor of -1. The soft data did not require modification as the questions were worded similarly and made the data consistent. Table 3 lists the variables that required transformation.

Standardization of the Variables

Once the final list of variables was determined, the data were converted on a scale of 1 to 7, using linear transformation. The formula used to standardize the data was:

$6 \times ((\text{country value} - \text{sample min})/(\text{sample max} - \text{sample min})) + 1$

The soft data did not need this standardization as they were originally collected from respondents using a 7-point scale.

Calculation of the Index

The final step was the calculation of the NRI. First, each subindex was calculated by taking an average of all the variables in each block. Next, the average of the three subindexes was taken to calculate the three component indexes, namely, Environment, Readiness, and Usage. Finally, the average of the three component indexes was used to arrive at the NRI.

How to Read the Data Tables

The data ranking section provides a list of all the variables with detailed data for all 102 countries included in the study.

Following a set of key indicators, the data are divided into the nine sections of the Networked Readiness Framework:

I.1. Environment–Market

I.2. Environment–Political/Regulatory

I.3. Environment–Infrastructure

II.1. Readiness–Individual

II.2. Readiness–Business

II.3. Readiness–Government

III.1. Usage–Individual

III.2. Usage–Business

III.3. Usage–Government

As mentioned in the Methodology section, two types of variables are used in our analysis: hard data variables and "soft," or survey data variables. For each variable, the short name and a description are listed at the beginning of each table.

Hard variables. Some hard variables had to be "transformed" to ensure that they were comparable across countries; the hard data presented in the tables are transformed data. For more details on how the data were modified, please see the preceding section, NRI Index: Methodology.

Soft variables. For each survey variable, the original question is included in the description of the variable. The values for these variables range from one to seven, where a response of one corresponds to a lower relative performance, and a response of seven corresponds to the highest level of relative performance. The values are responses to questionnaires and represent the average score of different respondents in a country. Variable I.3.01 for example, corresponds to a question about overall infrastructure quality; here, a low score means that the general infrastructure is poorly developed and

inefficient, while a high score shows that it is on the level of the most advanced countries. The survey data are drawn from the Executive Opinion Survey conducted annually by the World Economic Forum during the first half of the year.

Missing Data. The missing data were estimated to complete the data set. This was done primarily because the missing values would have led to a bias in calculating the index, and would limit us in making comparisons across countries. Estimated data are indicated by an asterisk (*). For more details, please refer to the preceding section, NRI Index: Methodology, in the book.

Ranking. The countries have been ranked using the complete data set for each variable. The country responses shown in the tables are rounded off to two decimal places. Two countries with the same listed variable value can have different rankings. The differences in the rankings exist because exact figures, not rounded numbers, were used to rank the countries. If two countries have exactly the same value then they will have the same rank.

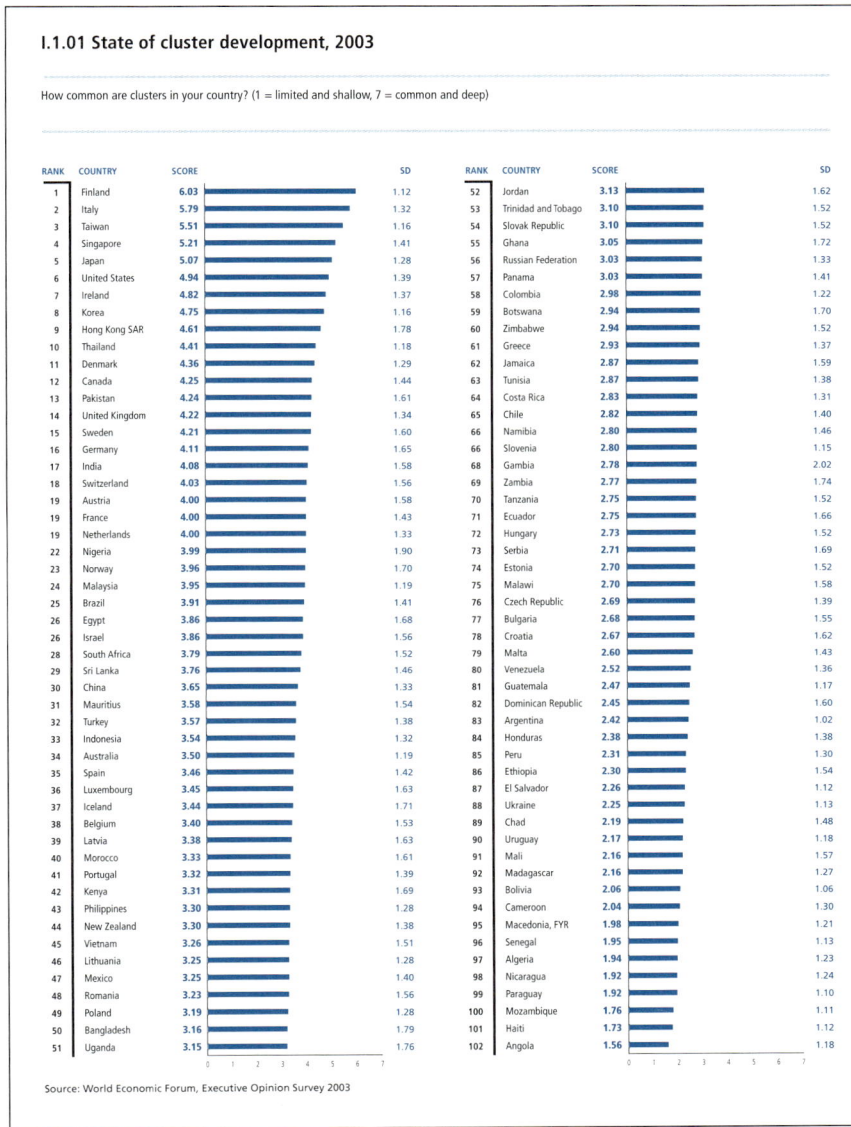

I.1.01 State of cluster development, 2003

How common are clusters in your country? (1 = limited and shallow, 7 = common and deep)

RANK	COUNTRY	SCORE	SD		RANK	COUNTRY	SCORE	SD
1	Finland	6.03	1.12		52	Jordan	3.13	1.62
2	Italy	5.79	1.32		53	Trinidad and Tobago	3.10	1.52
3	Taiwan	5.51	1.16		54	Slovak Republic	3.10	1.52
4	Singapore	5.21	1.41		55	Ghana	3.05	1.72
5	Japan	5.07	1.28		56	Russian Federation	3.03	1.33
6	United States	4.94	1.39		57	Panama	3.03	1.41
7	Ireland	4.82	1.37		58	Colombia	2.98	1.22
8	Korea	4.75	1.16		59	Botswana	2.94	1.70
9	Hong Kong SAR	4.61	1.78		60	Zimbabwe	2.94	1.52
10	Thailand	4.41	1.18		61	Greece	2.93	1.37
11	Denmark	4.36	1.29		62	Jamaica	2.87	1.59
12	Canada	4.25	1.44		63	Tunisia	2.87	1.38
13	Pakistan	4.24	1.61		64	Costa Rica	2.83	1.31
14	United Kingdom	4.22	1.34		65	Chile	2.82	1.40
15	Sweden	4.21	1.60		66	Namibia	2.80	1.46
16	Germany	4.11	1.65		66	Slovenia	2.80	1.15
17	India	4.08	1.58		68	Gambia	2.78	2.02
18	Switzerland	4.03	1.56		69	Zambia	2.77	1.74
19	Austria	4.00	1.58		70	Tanzania	2.75	1.52
19	France	4.00	1.43		71	Ecuador	2.75	1.66
19	Netherlands	4.00	1.33		72	Hungary	2.73	1.52
22	Nigeria	3.99	1.90		73	Serbia	2.71	1.69
23	Norway	3.96	1.70		74	Estonia	2.70	1.52
24	Malaysia	3.95	1.19		75	Malawi	2.70	1.58
25	Brazil	3.91	1.41		76	Czech Republic	2.69	1.39
26	Egypt	3.86	1.68		77	Bulgaria	2.68	1.55
26	Israel	3.86	1.56		78	Croatia	2.67	1.62
28	South Africa	3.79	1.52		79	Malta	2.60	1.43
29	Sri Lanka	3.76	1.46		80	Venezuela	2.52	1.36
30	China	3.65	1.33		81	Guatemala	2.47	1.17
31	Mauritius	3.58	1.54		82	Dominican Republic	2.45	1.60
32	Turkey	3.57	1.38		83	Argentina	2.42	1.02
33	Indonesia	3.54	1.32		84	Honduras	2.38	1.38
34	Australia	3.50	1.19		85	Peru	2.31	1.30
35	Spain	3.46	1.42		86	Ethiopia	2.30	1.54
36	Luxembourg	3.45	1.63		87	El Salvador	2.26	1.12
37	Iceland	3.44	1.71		88	Ukraine	2.25	1.13
38	Belgium	3.40	1.53		89	Chad	2.19	1.48
39	Latvia	3.38	1.63		90	Uruguay	2.17	1.18
40	Morocco	3.33	1.61		91	Mali	2.16	1.57
41	Portugal	3.32	1.39		92	Madagascar	2.16	1.27
42	Kenya	3.31	1.69		93	Bolivia	2.06	1.06
43	Philippines	3.30	1.28		94	Cameroon	2.04	1.30
44	New Zealand	3.30	1.38		95	Macedonia, FYR	1.98	1.21
45	Vietnam	3.26	1.51		96	Senegal	1.95	1.13
46	Lithuania	3.25	1.28		97	Algeria	1.94	1.23
47	Mexico	3.25	1.40		98	Nicaragua	1.92	1.24
48	Romania	3.23	1.56		99	Paraguay	1.92	1.10
49	Poland	3.19	1.28		100	Mozambique	1.76	1.11
50	Bangladesh	3.16	1.79		101	Haiti	1.73	1.12
51	Uganda	3.15	1.76		102	Angola	1.56	1.18

Source: World Economic Forum, Executive Opinion Survey 2003

List of Data Tables

List of Key Indicators

Market Environment

I.1.01 State of cluster development, 2003

How common are clusters in your country? (1 = limited and shallow, 7 = common and deep)

RANK	COUNTRY	SCORE	SD	RANK	COUNTRY	SCORE	SD
1	Finland	6.03	1.12	52	Jordan	3.13	1.62
2	Italy	5.79	1.32	53	Trinidad and Tobago	3.10	1.52
3	Taiwan	5.51	1.16	54	Slovak Republic	3.10	1.52
4	Singapore	5.21	1.41	55	Ghana	3.05	1.72
5	Japan	5.07	1.28	56	Russian Federation	3.03	1.33
6	United States	4.94	1.39	57	Panama	3.03	1.41
7	Ireland	4.82	1.37	58	Colombia	2.98	1.22
8	Korea	4.75	1.16	59	Botswana	2.94	1.70
9	Hong Kong SAR	4.61	1.78	60	Zimbabwe	2.94	1.52
10	Thailand	4.41	1.18	61	Greece	2.93	1.37
11	Denmark	4.36	1.29	62	Jamaica	2.87	1.59
12	Canada	4.25	1.44	63	Tunisia	2.87	1.38
13	Pakistan	4.24	1.61	64	Costa Rica	2.83	1.31
14	United Kingdom	4.22	1.34	65	Chile	2.82	1.40
15	Sweden	4.21	1.60	66	Namibia	2.80	1.46
16	Germany	4.11	1.65	66	Slovenia	2.80	1.15
17	India	4.08	1.58	68	Gambia	2.78	2.02
18	Switzerland	4.03	1.56	69	Zambia	2.77	1.74
19	Austria	4.00	1.58	70	Tanzania	2.75	1.52
19	France	4.00	1.43	71	Ecuador	2.75	1.66
19	Netherlands	4.00	1.33	72	Hungary	2.73	1.52
22	Nigeria	3.99	1.90	73	Serbia	2.71	1.69
23	Norway	3.96	1.70	74	Estonia	2.70	1.52
24	Malaysia	3.95	1.19	75	Malawi	2.70	1.58
25	Brazil	3.91	1.41	76	Czech Republic	2.69	1.39
26	Egypt	3.86	1.68	77	Bulgaria	2.68	1.55
26	Israel	3.86	1.56	78	Croatia	2.67	1.62
28	South Africa	3.79	1.52	79	Malta	2.60	1.43
29	Sri Lanka	3.76	1.46	80	Venezuela	2.52	1.36
30	China	3.65	1.33	81	Guatemala	2.47	1.17
31	Mauritius	3.58	1.54	82	Dominican Republic	2.45	1.60
32	Turkey	3.57	1.38	83	Argentina	2.42	1.02
33	Indonesia	3.54	1.32	84	Honduras	2.38	1.38
34	Australia	3.50	1.19	85	Peru	2.31	1.30
35	Spain	3.46	1.42	86	Ethiopia	2.30	1.54
36	Luxembourg	3.45	1.63	87	El Salvador	2.26	1.12
37	Iceland	3.44	1.71	88	Ukraine	2.25	1.13
38	Belgium	3.40	1.53	89	Chad	2.19	1.48
39	Latvia	3.38	1.63	90	Uruguay	2.17	1.18
40	Morocco	3.33	1.61	91	Mali	2.16	1.57
41	Portugal	3.32	1.39	92	Madagascar	2.16	1.27
42	Kenya	3.31	1.69	93	Bolivia	2.06	1.06
43	Philippines	3.30	1.28	94	Cameroon	2.04	1.30
44	New Zealand	3.30	1.38	95	Macedonia, FYR	1.98	1.21
45	Vietnam	3.26	1.51	96	Senegal	1.95	1.13
46	Lithuania	3.25	1.28	97	Algeria	1.94	1.23
47	Mexico	3.25	1.40	98	Nicaragua	1.92	1.24
48	Romania	3.23	1.56	99	Paraguay	1.92	1.10
49	Poland	3.19	1.28	100	Mozambique	1.76	1.11
50	Bangladesh	3.16	1.79	101	Haiti	1.73	1.12
51	Uganda	3.15	1.76	102	Angola	1.56	1.18

Source: World Economic Forum, Executive Opinion Survey 2003

I.1.02 Venture capital availability, 2003

Entrepreneurs with innovative but risky projects can generally find venture capital in your country (1 = not true, 7 = true)

Part 3 Data Presentation

RANK	COUNTRY	SCORE		SD
1	Finland	5.36		0.96
2	United Kingdom	5.29		1.34
3	United States	5.25		1.55
4	Israel	4.95		1.24
5	Luxembourg	4.91		1.23
6	Netherlands	4.87		1.55
7	Australia	4.75		1.65
7	Sweden	4.75		1.21
9	Ireland	4.68		1.40
10	Norway	4.62		1.53
11	Canada	4.59		1.52
12	Singapore	4.53		1.41
13	Denmark	4.46		1.57
14	France	4.42		1.48
15	Hong Kong SAR	4.42		1.37
16	Korea	4.40		1.25
17	New Zealand	4.39		1.39
18	Taiwan	4.37		1.13
19	Latvia	4.36		1.58
20	Iceland	4.26		1.29
21	Belgium	4.20		1.44
22	Lithuania	4.12		1.31
23	Spain	4.06		1.41
24	Malaysia	4.04		1.29
25	Tunisia	3.90		1.63
26	Switzerland	3.89		1.63
27	Estonia	3.86		1.38
28	India	3.82		1.49
29	Italy	3.75		1.31
30	Germany	3.66		1.50
31	Mauritius	3.65		1.28
32	South Africa	3.61		1.55
33	Portugal	3.61		1.44
34	Panama	3.61		1.56
35	Greece	3.51		1.44
36	Macedonia, FYR	3.47		2.18
37	Chile	3.43		1.47
38	Czech Republic	3.42		1.58
39	Thailand	3.38		1.31
40	Sri Lanka	3.35		1.42
41	Hungary	3.30		1.57
42	Botswana	3.28		1.62
42	Poland	3.28		1.32
44	Egypt	3.26		1.86
45	Japan	3.22		1.31
46	Namibia	3.21		1.33
47	Austria	3.18		1.52
48	Dominican Republic	3.18		1.77
49	Indonesia	3.17		1.38
50	El Salvador	3.15		1.43
51	Serbia	3.12		1.71
52	Zimbabwe	3.12		1.58
53	Morocco	3.07		1.74
54	Brazil	3.05		1.34
55	Slovak Republic	3.03		1.33
56	Malta	3.03		1.34
57	Uganda	3.01		1.89
58	China	3.00		1.22
58	Vietnam	3.00		1.62
60	Trinidad and Tobago	2.98		1.40
61	Slovenia	2.95		1.25
62	Jordan	2.94		1.35
63	Russian Federation	2.92		1.46
64	Romania	2.86		1.63
65	Croatia	2.79		1.63
66	Nigeria	2.72		1.50
67	Guatemala	2.70		1.55
68	Costa Rica	2.70		1.52
69	Colombia	2.69		1.30
70	Tanzania	2.68		1.40
71	Philippines	2.63		1.24
72	Ghana	2.62		1.51
73	Ukraine	2.59		1.34
74	Jamaica	2.53		1.57
75	Bulgaria	2.42		1.35
76	Mexico	2.41		1.29
77	Kenya	2.40		1.45
78	Cameroon	2.40		1.55
79	Gambia	2.38		1.62
80	Pakistan	2.36		1.28
81	Ecuador	2.36		1.59
82	Madagascar	2.31		1.49
83	Nicaragua	2.25		1.46
84	Turkey	2.24		1.23
85	Peru	2.23		1.19
86	Zambia	2.14		1.23
87	Mozambique	2.11		1.35
88	Bolivia	2.09		1.27
89	Haiti	2.08		1.19
90	Ethiopia	2.06		1.65
91	Honduras	2.05		1.25
92	Senegal	2.04		0.98
93	Venezuela	2.03		1.09
94	Bangladesh	2.01		1.28
95	Mali	1.97		1.50
96	Paraguay	1.97		1.43
97	Angola	1.93		1.35
98	Argentina	1.92		1.11
99	Malawi	1.91		1.16
100	Uruguay	1.84		1.12
101	Algeria	1.77		1.26
102	Chad	1.52		1.06

Source: World Economic Forum, Executive Opinion Survey 2003

I.1.03 Subsidies for firm-level R&D, 2003

For firms conducting research and development (R&D) in your country, direct government subsidies to individual companies or R&D tax credits
(1 = never occur, 7 = are widespread and large)

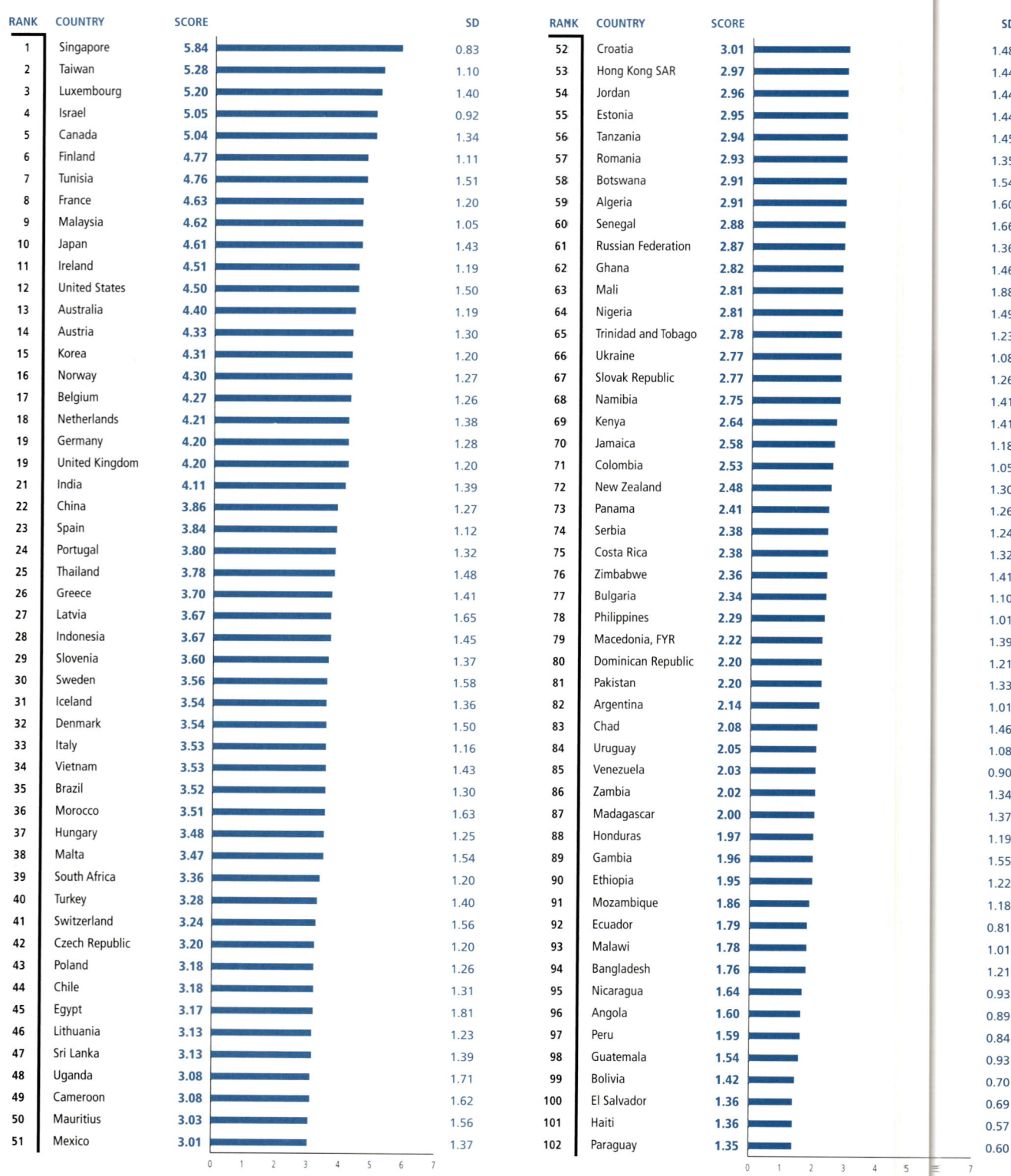

RANK	COUNTRY	SCORE	SD	RANK	COUNTRY	SCORE	SD
1	Singapore	5.84	0.83	52	Croatia	3.01	1.48
2	Taiwan	5.28	1.10	53	Hong Kong SAR	2.97	1.44
3	Luxembourg	5.20	1.40	54	Jordan	2.96	1.44
4	Israel	5.05	0.92	55	Estonia	2.95	1.44
5	Canada	5.04	1.34	56	Tanzania	2.94	1.45
6	Finland	4.77	1.11	57	Romania	2.93	1.35
7	Tunisia	4.76	1.51	58	Botswana	2.91	1.54
8	France	4.63	1.20	59	Algeria	2.91	1.60
9	Malaysia	4.62	1.05	60	Senegal	2.88	1.66
10	Japan	4.61	1.43	61	Russian Federation	2.87	1.36
11	Ireland	4.51	1.19	62	Ghana	2.82	1.46
12	United States	4.50	1.50	63	Mali	2.81	1.88
13	Australia	4.40	1.19	64	Nigeria	2.81	1.49
14	Austria	4.33	1.30	65	Trinidad and Tobago	2.78	1.23
15	Korea	4.31	1.20	66	Ukraine	2.77	1.08
16	Norway	4.30	1.27	67	Slovak Republic	2.77	1.26
17	Belgium	4.27	1.26	68	Namibia	2.75	1.41
18	Netherlands	4.21	1.38	69	Kenya	2.64	1.41
19	Germany	4.20	1.28	70	Jamaica	2.58	1.18
19	United Kingdom	4.20	1.20	71	Colombia	2.53	1.05
21	India	4.11	1.39	72	New Zealand	2.48	1.30
22	China	3.86	1.27	73	Panama	2.41	1.26
23	Spain	3.84	1.12	74	Serbia	2.38	1.24
24	Portugal	3.80	1.32	75	Costa Rica	2.38	1.32
25	Thailand	3.78	1.48	76	Zimbabwe	2.36	1.41
26	Greece	3.70	1.41	77	Bulgaria	2.34	1.10
27	Latvia	3.67	1.65	78	Philippines	2.29	1.01
28	Indonesia	3.67	1.45	79	Macedonia, FYR	2.22	1.39
29	Slovenia	3.60	1.37	80	Dominican Republic	2.20	1.21
30	Sweden	3.56	1.58	81	Pakistan	2.20	1.33
31	Iceland	3.54	1.36	82	Argentina	2.14	1.01
32	Denmark	3.54	1.50	83	Chad	2.08	1.46
33	Italy	3.53	1.16	84	Uruguay	2.05	1.08
34	Vietnam	3.53	1.43	85	Venezuela	2.03	0.90
35	Brazil	3.52	1.30	86	Zambia	2.02	1.34
36	Morocco	3.51	1.63	87	Madagascar	2.00	1.37
37	Hungary	3.48	1.25	88	Honduras	1.97	1.19
38	Malta	3.47	1.54	89	Gambia	1.96	1.55
39	South Africa	3.36	1.20	90	Ethiopia	1.95	1.22
40	Turkey	3.28	1.40	91	Mozambique	1.86	1.18
41	Switzerland	3.24	1.56	92	Ecuador	1.79	0.81
42	Czech Republic	3.20	1.20	93	Malawi	1.78	1.01
43	Poland	3.18	1.26	94	Bangladesh	1.76	1.21
44	Chile	3.18	1.31	95	Nicaragua	1.64	0.93
45	Egypt	3.17	1.81	96	Angola	1.60	0.89
46	Lithuania	3.13	1.23	97	Peru	1.59	0.84
47	Sri Lanka	3.13	1.39	98	Guatemala	1.54	0.93
48	Uganda	3.08	1.71	99	Bolivia	1.42	0.70
49	Cameroon	3.08	1.62	100	El Salvador	1.36	0.69
50	Mauritius	3.03	1.56	101	Haiti	1.36	0.57
51	Mexico	3.01	1.37	102	Paraguay	1.35	0.60

Source: World Economic Forum, Executive Opinion Survey 2003

I.1.04 Quality of scientific research institutions, 2003

Scientific research institutions in your country (e.g., university laboratories, government laboratories) are (1 = nonexistent, 7 = the best in their fields)

RANK	COUNTRY	SCORE	SD		RANK	COUNTRY	SCORE	SD
1	United States	6.23	1.35		52	Mexico	3.93	1.31
2	Israel	5.86	0.79		53	Botswana	3.93	1.36
3	Switzerland	5.84	1.01		54	Poland	3.90	1.18
4	Finland	5.75	0.65		55	Greece	3.89	1.15
5	United Kingdom	5.68	0.95		56	Sri Lanka	3.87	1.38
6	Sweden	5.63	0.69		57	Ukraine	3.85	1.27
7	Denmark	5.50	0.71		58	Serbia	3.81	1.54
8	France	5.46	0.88		59	Slovak Republic	3.80	1.29
9	Australia	5.45	0.76		60	Egypt	3.76	1.69
10	Singapore	5.44	0.90		61	Trinidad and Tobago	3.74	1.14
11	Japan	5.38	0.96		62	Indonesia	3.74	1.29
12	Germany	5.36	0.81		63	Luxembourg	3.73	1.28
13	Canada	5.32	0.98		64	Colombia	3.68	1.34
14	Ireland	5.20	0.97		65	Ethiopia	3.66	1.49
15	Belgium	5.15	1.11		66	Morocco	3.66	1.63
16	Netherlands	5.13	1.10		67	Senegal	3.65	1.85
17	New Zealand	5.11	0.99		68	Malawi	3.64	1.52
18	Taiwan	5.02	1.12		69	Romania	3.62	1.65
19	Norway	4.93	1.07		70	Bulgaria	3.62	1.36
20	India	4.86	1.35		71	Malta	3.58	1.38
21	Iceland	4.85	0.95		72	Zimbabwe	3.58	1.39
22	Hungary	4.79	1.07		73	Argentina	3.54	1.37
23	Austria	4.72	1.02		74	Uruguay	3.54	1.34
24	South Africa	4.69	1.20		75	Mali	3.51	1.79
25	Russian Federation	4.69	1.52		76	Zambia	3.51	1.42
26	Korea	4.69	1.11		77	Venezuela	3.47	1.28
27	Kenya	4.63	1.33		78	Mauritius	3.47	1.32
28	China	4.58	1.12		79	Turkey	3.41	1.15
29	Slovenia	4.55	0.98		80	Namibia	3.40	1.30
30	Costa Rica	4.51	1.21		81	Nigeria	3.39	1.43
31	Estonia	4.49	1.13		82	Panama	3.35	1.26
32	Tanzania	4.47	1.44		83	Dominican Republic	3.20	1.39
33	Uganda	4.42	1.62		84	Macedonia, FYR	3.20	1.59
34	Czech Republic	4.41	1.27		85	Bangladesh	3.18	1.32
35	Vietnam	4.37	1.31		86	Madagascar	3.16	1.29
36	Malaysia	4.33	1.02		87	Gambia	3.10	1.93
37	Jamaica	4.31	1.25		88	Algeria	3.06	1.23
38	Lithuania	4.29	1.33		89	Philippines	3.02	1.29
39	Hong Kong SAR	4.25	1.28		90	Pakistan	3.02	1.28
40	Ghana	4.25	1.55		91	Peru	2.99	1.14
41	Portugal	4.24	0.97		92	Mozambique	2.88	1.42
42	Croatia	4.24	1.31		93	Guatemala	2.87	1.34
43	Thailand	4.22	1.04		94	Ecuador	2.83	1.28
44	Italy	4.21	1.38		95	Honduras	2.61	1.29
45	Tunisia	4.16	1.30		96	El Salvador	2.52	1.05
46	Jordan	4.15	1.32		97	Nicaragua	2.48	1.19
47	Latvia	4.15	1.29		98	Bolivia	2.44	1.08
48	Chile	4.15	1.34		99	Angola	2.43	1.22
49	Brazil	4.11	1.12		100	Chad	2.42	1.52
50	Cameroon	4.02	1.46		101	Paraguay	2.19	1.01
51	Spain	3.99	1.19		102	Haiti	1.60	0.71

Source: World Economic Forum, Executive Opinion Survey 2003

I.1.05 Availability of scientists and engineers, 2003

Scientists and engineers in your country are (1 = nonexistent or rare, 7 = widely available)

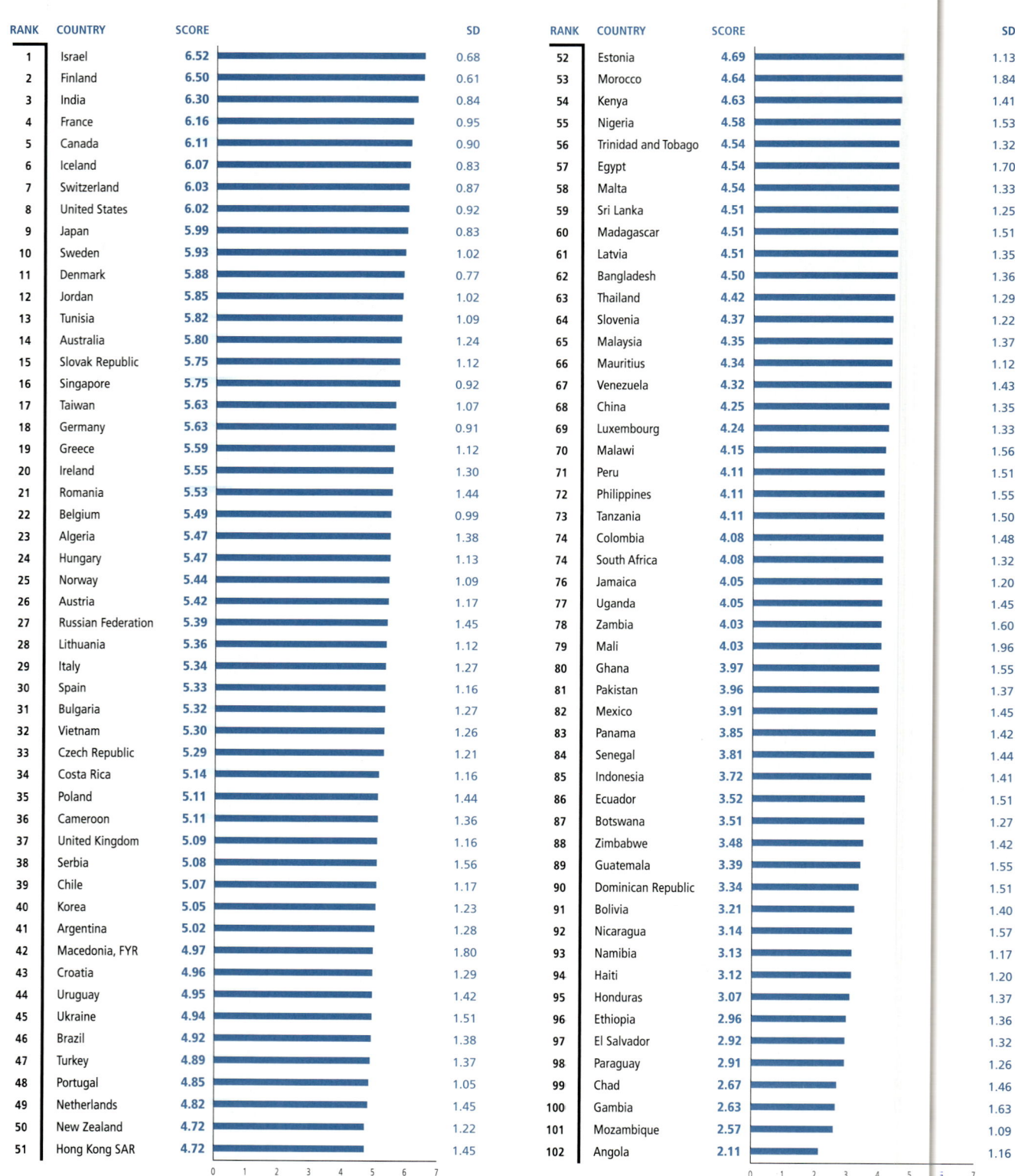

RANK	COUNTRY	SCORE	SD	RANK	COUNTRY	SCORE	SD
1	Israel	6.52	0.68	52	Estonia	4.69	1.13
2	Finland	6.50	0.61	53	Morocco	4.64	1.84
3	India	6.30	0.84	54	Kenya	4.63	1.41
4	France	6.16	0.95	55	Nigeria	4.58	1.53
5	Canada	6.11	0.90	56	Trinidad and Tobago	4.54	1.32
6	Iceland	6.07	0.83	57	Egypt	4.54	1.70
7	Switzerland	6.03	0.87	58	Malta	4.54	1.33
8	United States	6.02	0.92	59	Sri Lanka	4.51	1.25
9	Japan	5.99	0.83	60	Madagascar	4.51	1.51
10	Sweden	5.93	1.02	61	Latvia	4.51	1.35
11	Denmark	5.88	0.77	62	Bangladesh	4.50	1.36
12	Jordan	5.85	1.02	63	Thailand	4.42	1.29
13	Tunisia	5.82	1.09	64	Slovenia	4.37	1.22
14	Australia	5.80	1.24	65	Malaysia	4.35	1.37
15	Slovak Republic	5.75	1.12	66	Mauritius	4.34	1.12
16	Singapore	5.75	0.92	67	Venezuela	4.32	1.43
17	Taiwan	5.63	1.07	68	China	4.25	1.35
18	Germany	5.63	0.91	69	Luxembourg	4.24	1.33
19	Greece	5.59	1.12	70	Malawi	4.15	1.56
20	Ireland	5.55	1.30	71	Peru	4.11	1.51
21	Romania	5.53	1.44	72	Philippines	4.11	1.55
22	Belgium	5.49	0.99	73	Tanzania	4.11	1.50
23	Algeria	5.47	1.38	74	Colombia	4.08	1.48
24	Hungary	5.47	1.13	74	South Africa	4.08	1.32
25	Norway	5.44	1.09	76	Jamaica	4.05	1.20
26	Austria	5.42	1.17	77	Uganda	4.05	1.45
27	Russian Federation	5.39	1.45	78	Zambia	4.03	1.60
28	Lithuania	5.36	1.12	79	Mali	4.03	1.96
29	Italy	5.34	1.27	80	Ghana	3.97	1.55
30	Spain	5.33	1.16	81	Pakistan	3.96	1.37
31	Bulgaria	5.32	1.27	82	Mexico	3.91	1.45
32	Vietnam	5.30	1.26	83	Panama	3.85	1.42
33	Czech Republic	5.29	1.21	84	Senegal	3.81	1.44
34	Costa Rica	5.14	1.16	85	Indonesia	3.72	1.41
35	Poland	5.11	1.44	86	Ecuador	3.52	1.51
36	Cameroon	5.11	1.36	87	Botswana	3.51	1.27
37	United Kingdom	5.09	1.16	88	Zimbabwe	3.48	1.42
38	Serbia	5.08	1.56	89	Guatemala	3.39	1.55
39	Chile	5.07	1.17	90	Dominican Republic	3.34	1.51
40	Korea	5.05	1.23	91	Bolivia	3.21	1.40
41	Argentina	5.02	1.28	92	Nicaragua	3.14	1.57
42	Macedonia, FYR	4.97	1.80	93	Namibia	3.13	1.17
43	Croatia	4.96	1.29	94	Haiti	3.12	1.20
44	Uruguay	4.95	1.42	95	Honduras	3.07	1.37
45	Ukraine	4.94	1.51	96	Ethiopia	2.96	1.36
46	Brazil	4.92	1.38	97	El Salvador	2.92	1.32
47	Turkey	4.89	1.37	98	Paraguay	2.91	1.26
48	Portugal	4.85	1.05	99	Chad	2.67	1.46
49	Netherlands	4.82	1.45	100	Gambia	2.63	1.63
50	New Zealand	4.72	1.22	101	Mozambique	2.57	1.09
51	Hong Kong SAR	4.72	1.45	102	Angola	2.11	1.16

Source: World Economic Forum, Executive Opinion Survey 2003

I.1.06 Brain drain, 2003

Your country's talented people (1 = normally leave to pursue opportunities in other countries, 7 = almost always remain in the country)

RANK	COUNTRY	SCORE		SD	RANK	COUNTRY	SCORE		SD
1	United States	6.31		1.11	52	Turkey	3.33		1.22
2	Finland	5.61		1.20	53	Guatemala	3.33		1.26
3	Chile	5.60		1.06	54	Egypt	3.31		1.76
4	Spain	5.44		1.28	55	New Zealand	3.23		1.05
5	Norway	5.37		1.01	56	Russian Federation	3.08		1.43
6	Netherlands	5.31		1.13	57	Angola	3.06		1.36
7	Switzerland	5.29		1.09	58	Colombia	3.05		1.30
8	Japan	5.25		1.08	59	Paraguay	3.03		1.36
9	Costa Rica	5.17		1.42	60	Honduras	3.02		1.34
10	Iceland	5.11		0.89	61	Nicaragua	3.01		1.56
11	Sweden	5.11		1.23	62	Mauritius	2.97		1.18
12	Thailand	5.05		1.10	63	Jordan	2.93		1.27
13	United Kingdom	5.02		1.07	64	Tanzania	2.88		1.51
14	Luxembourg	5.00		1.09	65	India	2.83		1.24
15	Singapore	4.92		1.24	66	Chad	2.82		1.56
16	Taiwan	4.77		1.04	67	South Africa	2.81		1.17
17	Botswana	4.76		1.64	68	Slovak Republic	2.79		1.18
18	Israel	4.76		1.00	69	Lithuania	2.75		1.26
19	Belgium	4.76		1.43	70	Peru	2.73		1.16
20	Ireland	4.73		1.22	71	Croatia	2.71		1.38
21	Hong Kong SAR	4.70		1.34	72	Malawi	2.71		1.14
22	Brazil	4.60		1.41	73	Argentina	2.66		1.11
23	Austria	4.57		1.42	74	Ukraine	2.60		1.27
24	Denmark	4.57		1.25	75	Ecuador	2.57		1.33
25	Panama	4.43		1.54	76	Bolivia	2.57		1.09
26	Canada	4.39		1.52	77	Madagascar	2.54		1.34
27	Portugal	4.33		1.30	78	Uruguay	2.52		1.35
28	Germany	4.31		1.56	79	Jamaica	2.52		0.98
29	Malta	4.26		1.31	80	Cameroon	2.50		1.54
30	Australia	4.25		1.12	81	Pakistan	2.48		1.34
31	Mexico	4.24		1.43	82	Kenya	2.47		1.41
32	Korea	4.17		1.39	83	Uganda	2.46		1.50
33	Dominican Republic	4.17		1.56	84	Venezuela	2.32		1.07
34	Slovenia	4.15		1.41	85	Senegal	2.26		1.32
35	Czech Republic	4.10		1.41	86	Sri Lanka	2.26		1.10
36	Latvia	4.09		1.50	87	Philippines	2.23		1.07
37	Malaysia	4.03		1.14	88	Algeria	2.23		1.19
38	Estonia	3.89		1.15	89	Gambia	2.23		1.38
39	Mozambique	3.84		1.81	90	Morocco	2.15		1.42
40	France	3.82		1.48	91	Bulgaria	2.10		1.09
41	Tunisia	3.81		1.54	92	Ethiopia	2.08		1.31
42	Greece	3.75		1.35	93	Romania	2.06		1.13
43	Vietnam	3.75		1.57	94	Mali	2.06		1.27
44	Poland	3.66		1.27	95	Bangladesh	2.01		1.00
45	Indonesia	3.63		1.21	96	Ghana	2.01		0.98
46	Hungary	3.61		1.30	97	Nigeria	1.96		1.02
47	Namibia	3.61		1.31	98	Macedonia, FYR	1.95		1.31
48	Trinidad and Tobago	3.57		1.31	99	Zambia	1.92		1.13
49	El Salvador	3.56		1.44	100	Serbia	1.88		0.95
50	Italy	3.48		1.40	101	Zimbabwe	1.79		1.11
51	China	3.40		1.34	102	Haiti	1.60		0.71

Source: World Economic Forum, Executive Opinion Survey 2003

I.1.07 Utility patents, 2002

Utility patents granted (per 1,000,000 inhabitants), 2002

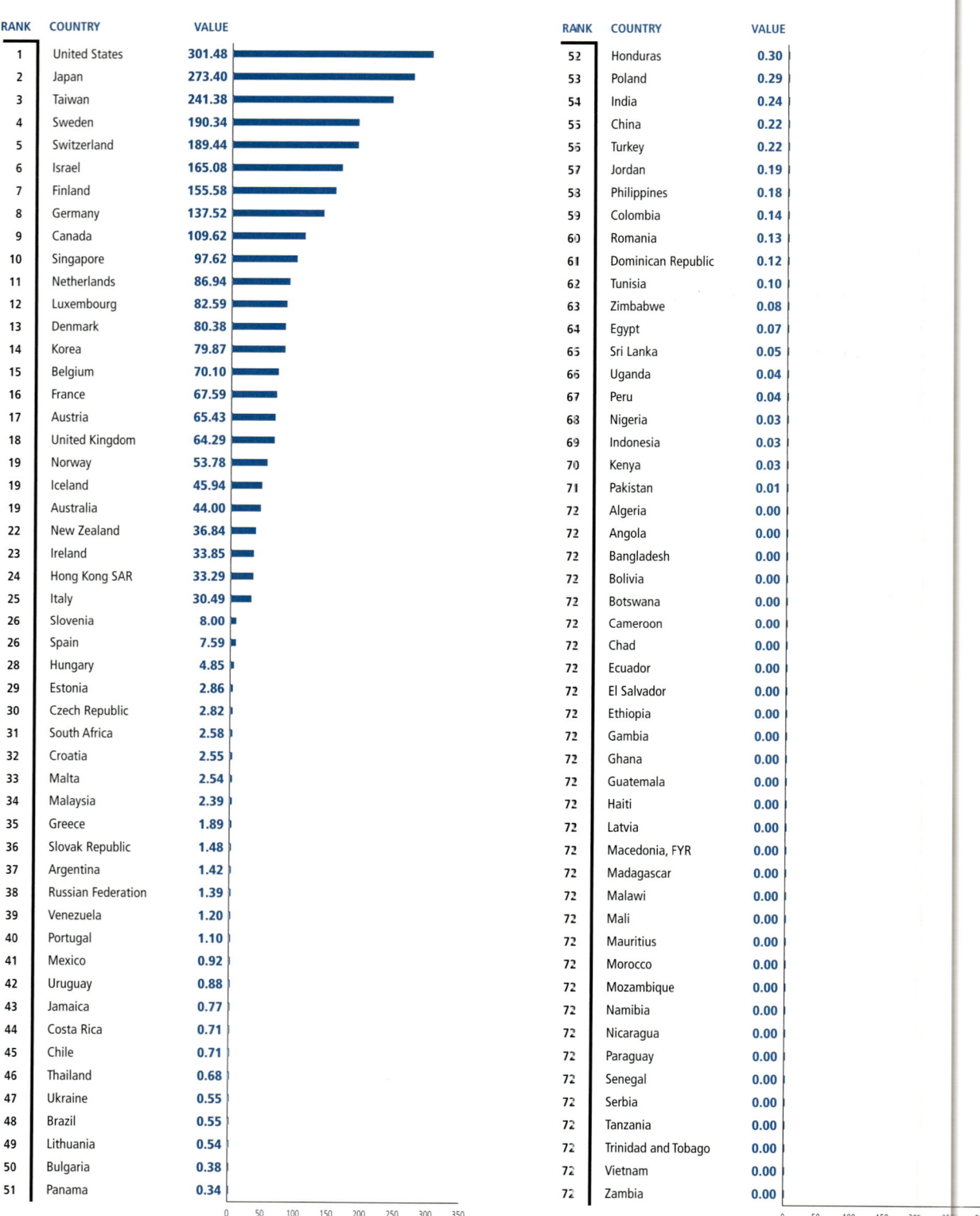

RANK	COUNTRY	VALUE
1	United States	301.48
2	Japan	273.40
3	Taiwan	241.38
4	Sweden	190.34
5	Switzerland	189.44
6	Israel	165.08
7	Finland	155.58
8	Germany	137.52
9	Canada	109.62
10	Singapore	97.62
11	Netherlands	86.94
12	Luxembourg	82.59
13	Denmark	80.38
14	Korea	79.87
15	Belgium	70.10
16	France	67.59
17	Austria	65.43
18	United Kingdom	64.29
19	Norway	53.78
19	Iceland	45.94
19	Australia	44.00
22	New Zealand	36.84
23	Ireland	33.85
24	Hong Kong SAR	33.29
25	Italy	30.49
26	Slovenia	8.00
26	Spain	7.59
28	Hungary	4.85
29	Estonia	2.86
30	Czech Republic	2.82
31	South Africa	2.58
32	Croatia	2.55
33	Malta	2.54
34	Malaysia	2.39
35	Greece	1.89
36	Slovak Republic	1.48
37	Argentina	1.42
38	Russian Federation	1.39
39	Venezuela	1.20
40	Portugal	1.10
41	Mexico	0.92
42	Uruguay	0.88
43	Jamaica	0.77
44	Costa Rica	0.71
45	Chile	0.71
46	Thailand	0.68
47	Ukraine	0.55
48	Brazil	0.55
49	Lithuania	0.54
50	Bulgaria	0.38
51	Panama	0.34

RANK	COUNTRY	VALUE
52	Honduras	0.30
53	Poland	0.29
54	India	0.24
55	China	0.22
56	Turkey	0.22
57	Jordan	0.19
58	Philippines	0.18
59	Colombia	0.14
60	Romania	0.13
61	Dominican Republic	0.12
62	Tunisia	0.10
63	Zimbabwe	0.08
64	Egypt	0.07
65	Sri Lanka	0.05
66	Uganda	0.04
67	Peru	0.04
68	Nigeria	0.03
69	Indonesia	0.03
70	Kenya	0.03
71	Pakistan	0.01
72	Algeria	0.00
72	Angola	0.00
72	Bangladesh	0.00
72	Bolivia	0.00
72	Botswana	0.00
72	Cameroon	0.00
72	Chad	0.00
72	Ecuador	0.00
72	El Salvador	0.00
72	Ethiopia	0.00
72	Gambia	0.00
72	Ghana	0.00
72	Guatemala	0.00
72	Haiti	0.00
72	Latvia	0.00
72	Macedonia, FYR	0.00
72	Madagascar	0.00
72	Malawi	0.00
72	Mali	0.00
72	Mauritius	0.00
72	Morocco	0.00
72	Mozambique	0.00
72	Namibia	0.00
72	Nicaragua	0.00
72	Paraguay	0.00
72	Senegal	0.00
72	Serbia	0.00
72	Tanzania	0.00
72	Trinidad and Tobago	0.00
72	Vietnam	0.00
72	Zambia	0.00

Source: US Patent and Trademark Office, February 2003

I.1.08 ICT manufactured exports, 2001

High technology manufactured exports per capita, 2001

RANK	COUNTRY	VALUE		RANK	COUNTRY	VALUE
1	Singapore	14,898.1		52	Indonesia	20.6
2	Ireland	9,204.6		53	Latvia	18.8
3	Luxembourg	3,044.4		54	Morocco	17.3
4	Malta	2,656.4		55	Botswana	* 17.1
5	Netherlands	2,435.0		56	Jordan	17.0
6	Switzerland	2,410.2		57	Turkey	16.0
7	Malaysia	1,780.0		58	Tunisia	15.9
8	Finland	1,779.6		59	Dominican Republic	* 15.8
9	Belgium	1,571.2		60	Mauritius	11.7
10	Denmark	1,304.2		61	Bulgaria	10.1
11	Sweden	1,215.7		62	Trinidad and Tobago	8.7
12	Israel	1,183.5		63	Colombia	* 8.0
13	United Kingdom	1,129.2		64	El Salvador	7.9
14	France	1,125.5		65	Chile	6.9
15	Germany	1,048.3		66	Namibia	* 6.3
16	Austria	922.4		67	Serbia	* 6.2
17	Canada	862.6		68	Guatemala	5.9
18	Korea	852.9		69	Madagascar	* 5.7
19	Japan	779.5		70	Zimbabwe	* 5.5
20	Hungary	636.2		71	Uruguay	5.5
21	United States	620.1		72	Bolivia	4.3
22	Hong Kong SAR	530.9		73	Macedonia, FYR	4.2
23	Norway	462.7		74	Venezuela	3.8
24	Estonia	418.2		75	Peru	2.1
25	Italy	374.3		76	Ecuador	1.9
26	Czech Republic	297.7		77	Senegal	1.2
27	Mexico	292.3		78	Paraguay	1.2
28	Philippines	267.6		79	Zambia	1.0
29	Costa Rica	255.0		80	Algeria	0.7
30	Thailand	237.7		81	Honduras	0.6
31	Slovenia	221.1		82	India	* 0.6
32	Spain	178.1		83	Panama	0.5
33	Australia	137.0		84	Kenya	0.4
34	Taiwan	* 135.7		85	Haiti	* 0.4
35	Portugal	134.3		85	Vietnam	* 0.4
36	New Zealand	122.6		87	Nicaragua	0.4
37	Iceland	95.8		88	Bangladesh	* 0.4
38	Slovak Republic	87.6		89	Jamaica	0.2
39	Croatia	75.9		90	Uganda	0.2
40	Angola	* 66.3		91	Egypt	0.2
40	Sri Lanka	* 66.3		92	Pakistan	0.2
40	Ukraine	* 66.3		93	Chad	* 0.1
43	Greece	51.7		94	Mali	* 0.1
44	China	38.2		94	Tanzania	* 0.1
45	Lithuania	36.1		96	Malawi	* 0.1
46	Brazil	35.0		97	Mozambique	0.1
47	Romania	25.4		98	Ghana	0.1
48	Poland	24.3		99	Gambia	0.1
49	Russian Federation	22.6		100	Cameroon	0.1
50	Argentina	21.3		101	Nigeria	0.0
51	South Africa	21.2		102	Ethiopia	0.0

Note: *estimate
Source: WITSA, 2003

I.1.09 ICT service exports, 2001

Communications and computer service exports per capita, 2001

RANK	COUNTRY	VALUE		RANK	COUNTRY	VALUE
1	Luxembourg	7504.43		52	Tunisia	47.72
2	Singapore	3623.48		53	Thailand	43.62
3	Ireland	3071.93		54	Serbia	*43.01
4	Hong Kong SAR	2459.23		55	Namibia	*42.59
5	Austria	1944.59		56	Egypt	37.55
6	Belgium	1835.48		57	Algeria	*37.48
7	Netherlands	1597.28		58	Zimbabwe	*33.00
8	Sweden	1300.08		59	Brazil	32.47
9	Israel	1173.83		60	Romania	31.93
10	Denmark	1159.61		61	Nicaragua	31.77
11	Iceland	1055.12		62	El Salvador	28.40
12	Norway	1003.99		63	Dominican Republic	28.13
13	Switzerland	984.05		64	Guatemala	27.56
14	United Kingdom	837.65		65	Uruguay	27.26
15	Finland	551.75		66	Morocco	24.42
16	Germany	537.73		67	Cameroon	*22.82
17	France	500.83		68	Argentina	22.11
18	Canada	495.21		69	Honduras	22.04
19	Malta	469.29		70	Sri Lanka	17.18
20	United States	432.06		71	Mexico	16.37
21	Italy	383.49		72	Senegal	*16.30
22	Spain	362.91		73	Mozambique	16.12
23	Hungary	298.88		74	Russian Federation	16.07
24	Japan	271.33		75	Angola	15.53
25	Mauritius	235.28		76	Ecuador	13.97
26	Estonia	233.31		77	India	13.86
27	Czech Republic	220.69		78	South Africa	13.69
28	Slovenia	220.22		79	Haiti	*11.96
29	New Zealand	214.25		79	Vietnam	*11.96
30	Malaysia	194.29		81	Peru	11.36
31	Croatia	189.34		82	Kenya	10.88
32	Korea	188.97		83	Venezuela	9.72
33	Australia	188.27		84	Ukraine	8.97
34	Taiwan	*186.59		85	Philippines	8.74
35	Greece	183.30		86	Colombia	8.42
36	Trinidad and Tobago	*178.65		87	China	8.17
37	Portugal	156.24		88	Malawi	6.85
38	Slovak Republic	141.54		89	Bolivia	6.20
39	Jamaica	111.65		90	Chad	*5.58
40	Costa Rica	109.50		91	Gambia	*5.12
41	Jordan	100.90		91	Mali	*5.12
42	Latvia	98.75		93	Nigeria	*4.63
43	Chile	75.90		94	Bangladesh	4.37
44	Panama	70.31		95	Tanzania	4.01
45	Turkey	69.37		96	Ethiopia	3.47
46	Paraguay	67.05		97	Ghana	3.28
47	Macedonia, FYR	62.10		98	Pakistan	3.26
48	Bulgaria	61.53		99	Madagascar	1.24
49	Lithuania	60.32		100	Indonesia	1.03
50	Poland	53.69		101	Uganda	0.95
51	Botswana	*51.09		102	Zambia	0.01

Note: *estimate
Source: International Monetary Fund and the World Bank

Political/Regulatory Environment

I.2.01 Overall administrative burden, 2003

Administrative regulations in your country are (1 = burdensome, 7 = not burdensome)

RANK	COUNTRY	SCORE		SD
1	Singapore	5.12		1.42
2	Hong Kong SAR	5.03		1.34
3	Finland	4.69		1.47
4	Switzerland	4.25		1.43
5	Iceland	4.19		1.30
6	Estonia	4.17		1.34
7	Taiwan	4.09		1.31
8	Gambia	4.09		2.11
9	Jordan	3.86		1.53
10	Tunisia	3.76		1.52
11	Sweden	3.75		1.46
12	Austria	3.69		1.40
13	Latvia	3.68		1.55
14	Denmark	3.64		1.53
15	Indonesia	3.63		1.53
16	Malaysia	3.59		1.21
17	Luxembourg	3.56		1.62
18	Ireland	3.43		1.52
19	United States	3.37		1.63
20	Malawi	3.35		1.35
21	China	3.32		1.26
22	Australia	3.30		1.59
23	Korea	3.23		1.31
24	Germany	3.22		1.50
25	Thailand	3.16		1.40
26	Botswana	3.13		1.67
27	Ghana	3.11		1.60
28	Costa Rica	3.09		1.42
29	El Salvador	3.09		1.33
30	Chile	3.08		1.40
31	Israel	3.05		1.56
32	Norway	3.04		1.51
33	Tanzania	3.03		1.53
34	Canada	3.03		1.52
35	Angola	3.00		2.00
36	Morocco	2.98		2.08
37	Namibia	2.96		1.47
38	United Kingdom	2.95		1.39
39	Malta	2.95		1.31
40	Vietnam	2.94		1.57
41	Uganda	2.94		1.69
42	Trinidad and Tobago	2.92		1.41
43	Chad	2.92		2.15
44	Paraguay	2.90		1.64
44	Sri Lanka	2.90		1.32
46	Dominican Republic	2.88		1.69
47	Zambia	2.86		1.48
48	South Africa	2.85		1.19
49	Egypt	2.83		2.13
50	Japan	2.82		1.42
51	Poland	2.82		1.31

RANK	COUNTRY	SCORE		SD
52	Lithuania	2.81		1.12
53	Brazil	2.77		1.44
54	Portugal	2.76		1.20
55	Slovenia	2.76		1.09
56	Netherlands	2.75		1.17
57	Czech Republic	2.71		1.32
58	Hungary	2.69		1.32
59	Haiti	2.68		1.77
60	New Zealand	2.67		1.14
61	Mali	2.67		1.60
61	Spain	2.67		1.16
63	Kenya	2.64		1.35
64	Colombia	2.56		1.24
65	Bulgaria	2.53		1.29
66	Turkey	2.50		1.22
67	India	2.49		1.23
68	Ethiopia	2.45		1.49
69	Macedonia, FYR	2.41		1.68
70	Honduras	2.39		1.32
71	Panama	2.39		1.32
72	Ukraine	2.38		1.25
73	Italy	2.37		1.25
74	Uruguay	2.37		1.22
75	Greece	2.36		1.32
76	Nigeria	2.35		1.44
77	Mozambique	2.32		1.38
78	Nicaragua	2.30		1.17
79	Cameroon	2.29		1.40
80	Bolivia	2.28		1.23
81	Serbia	2.28		1.28
82	Mexico	2.26		1.08
83	Pakistan	2.26		1.24
84	Guatemala	2.25		1.16
85	Croatia	2.24		1.22
86	Slovak Republic	2.23		1.00
87	Mauritius	2.22		1.29
88	Ecuador	2.21		1.22
89	Senegal	2.19		1.39
90	France	2.14		1.18
91	Peru	2.08		1.08
92	Jamaica	2.07		1.14
93	Belgium	2.07		1.18
94	Zimbabwe	2.06		1.12
95	Argentina	2.05		1.09
96	Bangladesh	2.03		1.10
97	Romania	1.96		1.20
98	Philippines	1.96		0.95
99	Algeria	1.94		1.11
100	Russian Federation	1.87		1.17
101	Madagascar	1.85		1.04
102	Venezuela	1.58		0.97

Source: World Economic Forum, Executive Opinion Survey 2003

I.2.02 Quality of the legal system, 2003

The judiciary in your country is independent from political influences of members of government, citizens, or firms (1 = no, heavily influenced, 7 = yes, entirely independent)

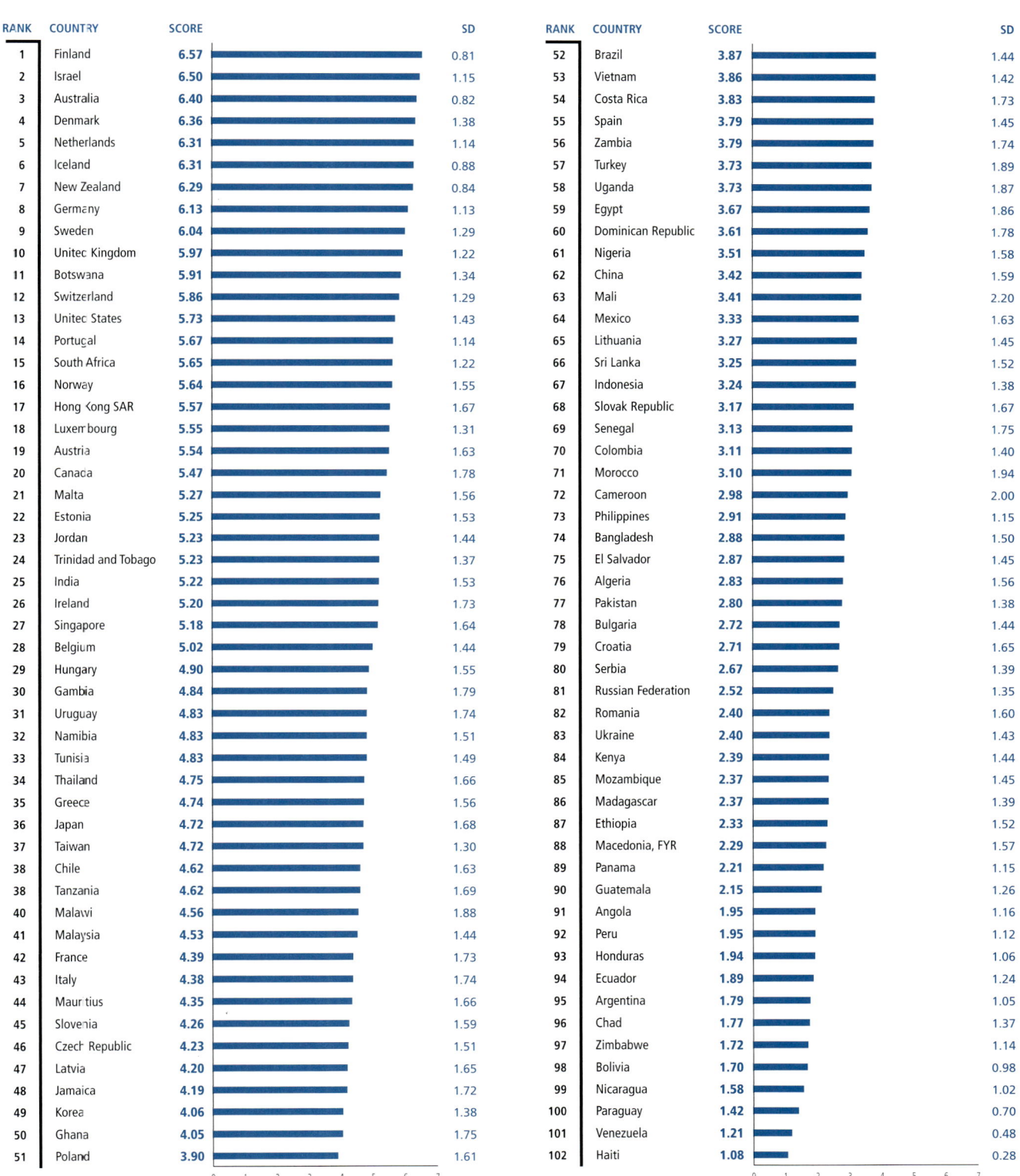

RANK	COUNTRY	SCORE	SD		RANK	COUNTRY	SCORE	SD
1	Finland	6.57	0.81		52	Brazil	3.87	1.44
2	Israel	6.50	1.15		53	Vietnam	3.86	1.42
3	Australia	6.40	0.82		54	Costa Rica	3.83	1.73
4	Denmark	6.36	1.38		55	Spain	3.79	1.45
5	Netherlands	6.31	1.14		56	Zambia	3.79	1.74
6	Iceland	6.31	0.88		57	Turkey	3.73	1.89
7	New Zealand	6.29	0.84		58	Uganda	3.73	1.87
8	Germany	6.13	1.13		59	Egypt	3.67	1.86
9	Sweden	6.04	1.29		60	Dominican Republic	3.61	1.78
10	United Kingdom	5.97	1.22		61	Nigeria	3.51	1.58
11	Botswana	5.91	1.34		62	China	3.42	1.59
12	Switzerland	5.86	1.29		63	Mali	3.41	2.20
13	United States	5.73	1.43		64	Mexico	3.33	1.63
14	Portugal	5.67	1.14		65	Lithuania	3.27	1.45
15	South Africa	5.65	1.22		66	Sri Lanka	3.25	1.52
16	Norway	5.64	1.55		67	Indonesia	3.24	1.38
17	Hong Kong SAR	5.57	1.67		68	Slovak Republic	3.17	1.67
18	Luxembourg	5.55	1.31		69	Senegal	3.13	1.75
19	Austria	5.54	1.63		70	Colombia	3.11	1.40
20	Canada	5.47	1.78		71	Morocco	3.10	1.94
21	Malta	5.27	1.56		72	Cameroon	2.98	2.00
22	Estonia	5.25	1.53		73	Philippines	2.91	1.15
23	Jordan	5.23	1.44		74	Bangladesh	2.88	1.50
24	Trinidad and Tobago	5.23	1.37		75	El Salvador	2.87	1.45
25	India	5.22	1.53		76	Algeria	2.83	1.56
26	Ireland	5.20	1.73		77	Pakistan	2.80	1.38
27	Singapore	5.18	1.64		78	Bulgaria	2.72	1.44
28	Belgium	5.02	1.44		79	Croatia	2.71	1.65
29	Hungary	4.90	1.55		80	Serbia	2.67	1.39
30	Gambia	4.84	1.79		81	Russian Federation	2.52	1.35
31	Uruguay	4.83	1.74		82	Romania	2.40	1.60
32	Namibia	4.83	1.51		83	Ukraine	2.40	1.43
33	Tunisia	4.83	1.49		84	Kenya	2.39	1.44
34	Thailand	4.75	1.66		85	Mozambique	2.37	1.45
35	Greece	4.74	1.56		86	Madagascar	2.37	1.39
36	Japan	4.72	1.68		87	Ethiopia	2.33	1.52
37	Taiwan	4.72	1.30		88	Macedonia, FYR	2.29	1.57
38	Chile	4.62	1.63		89	Panama	2.21	1.15
38	Tanzania	4.62	1.69		90	Guatemala	2.15	1.26
40	Malawi	4.56	1.88		91	Angola	1.95	1.16
41	Malaysia	4.53	1.44		92	Peru	1.95	1.12
42	France	4.39	1.73		93	Honduras	1.94	1.06
43	Italy	4.38	1.74		94	Ecuador	1.89	1.24
44	Mauritius	4.35	1.66		95	Argentina	1.79	1.05
45	Slovenia	4.26	1.59		96	Chad	1.77	1.37
46	Czech Republic	4.23	1.51		97	Zimbabwe	1.72	1.14
47	Latvia	4.20	1.65		98	Bolivia	1.70	0.98
48	Jamaica	4.19	1.72		99	Nicaragua	1.58	1.02
49	Korea	4.06	1.38		100	Paraguay	1.42	0.70
50	Ghana	4.05	1.75		101	Venezuela	1.21	0.48
51	Poland	3.90	1.61		102	Haiti	1.08	0.28

Source: World Economic Forum, Executive Opinion Survey 2003

I.2.03 Laws relating to ICT, 2003

Laws relating to information and communication technologies (ICT) (electronic commerce, digital signatures, consumer protection) are
(1 = nonexistent, 7 = well developed and enforced)

RANK	COUNTRY	SCORE	SD
1	Finland	5.86	0.88
2	Singapore	5.75	0.94
3	Australia	5.55	0.94
4	Denmark	5.54	1.10
5	United States	5.48	1.09
6	Estonia	5.46	1.13
7	Malaysia	5.42	1.10
8	United Kingdom	5.38	1.16
9	Iceland	5.15	0.99
10	New Zealand	5.06	1.10
11	Sweden	5.04	0.96
12	Korea	4.99	1.10
13	France	4.99	1.23
14	Germany	4.96	1.42
15	Norway	4.78	1.15
16	Canada	4.77	1.58
17	Taiwan	4.70	1.12
18	Hong Kong SAR	4.69	1.34
19	Tunisia	4.69	1.47
20	Luxembourg	4.68	1.25
21	Israel	4.67	1.14
22	Ireland	4.63	1.26
23	Slovenia	4.60	1.18
24	South Africa	4.58	1.14
25	Switzerland	4.56	1.48
26	Netherlands	4.55	1.24
27	Japan	4.44	1.31
28	Latvia	4.35	1.51
29	Malta	4.33	1.38
30	Chile	4.32	1.27
31	Austria	4.26	1.49
32	Mauritius	4.25	1.14
33	Spain	4.23	1.06
34	Italy	4.22	1.40
35	Czech Republic	4.16	1.16
36	India	4.08	1.48
37	Brazil	4.06	1.34
38	Jordan	4.05	1.46
39	Belgium	4.02	1.28
40	Dominican Republic	4.00	1.30
41	Colombia	3.92	1.31
42	Panama	3.84	1.61
43	Thailand	3.80	1.27
44	Portugal	3.79	1.28
45	Lithuania	3.74	1.31
46	Poland	3.74	1.28
47	Slovak Republic	3.74	1.22
48	Indonesia	3.73	1.35
49	Hungary	3.67	1.28
50	Romania	3.65	1.49
51	China	3.65	1.32

RANK	COUNTRY	SCORE	SD
52	Philippines	3.62	1.29
53	Ghana	3.59	1.65
54	Vietnam	3.54	1.50
55	Tanzania	3.53	1.68
56	Mexico	3.53	1.30
57	Morocco	3.49	1.70
58	Venezuela	3.47	1.33
59	Jamaica	3.44	1.36
60	Peru	3.43	1.36
61	Croatia	3.41	1.55
62	Costa Rica	3.39	1.47
63	Egypt	3.35	1.81
64	Greece	3.33	1.39
65	Serbia	3.28	1.38
65	Uganda	3.27	1.86
67	Kenya	3.24	1.38
63	Namibia	3.20	1.47
63	Sri Lanka	3.18	1.37
70	Bulgaria	3.16	1.39
71	Argentina	3.16	1.22
72	Zambia	3.16	1.42
73	Botswana	3.13	1.39
74	El Salvador	3.06	1.41
75	Nigeria	3.06	1.53
76	Russian Federation	3.05	1.38
77	Pakistan	3.04	1.20
78	Senegal	3.04	1.86
79	Uruguay	3.02	1.27
80	Trinidad and Tobago	2.98	1.28
81	Ecuador	2.97	1.30
82	Zimbabwe	2.84	1.39
83	Gambia	2.84	1.94
84	Macedonia, FYR	2.83	1.63
85	Ukraine	2.76	1.35
86	Turkey	2.75	1.16
87	Cameroon	2.73	1.55
88	Nicaragua	2.72	1.33
89	Mozambique	2.68	1.44
90	Malawi	2.58	1.65
91	Honduras	2.54	1.34
92	Guatemala	2.51	1.32
93	Chad	2.33	1.47
94	Madagascar	2.27	1.28
95	Bolivia	2.27	1.27
96	Mali	2.21	1.45
97	Angola	2.16	1.15
98	Paraguay	2.13	1.26
99	Bangladesh	2.08	1.19
100	Algeria	1.97	1.20
101	Ethiopia	1.94	1.22
102	Haiti	1.52	0.92

Source: World Economic Forum, Executive Opinion Survey 2003

I.2.04 Competition in the ISP sector, 2003

Is there sufficient competition among Internet service providers (ISPs) in your country to ensure high quality, infrequent interruptions, and low prices?
(1 = no, 7 = yes, equal to the best in the world)

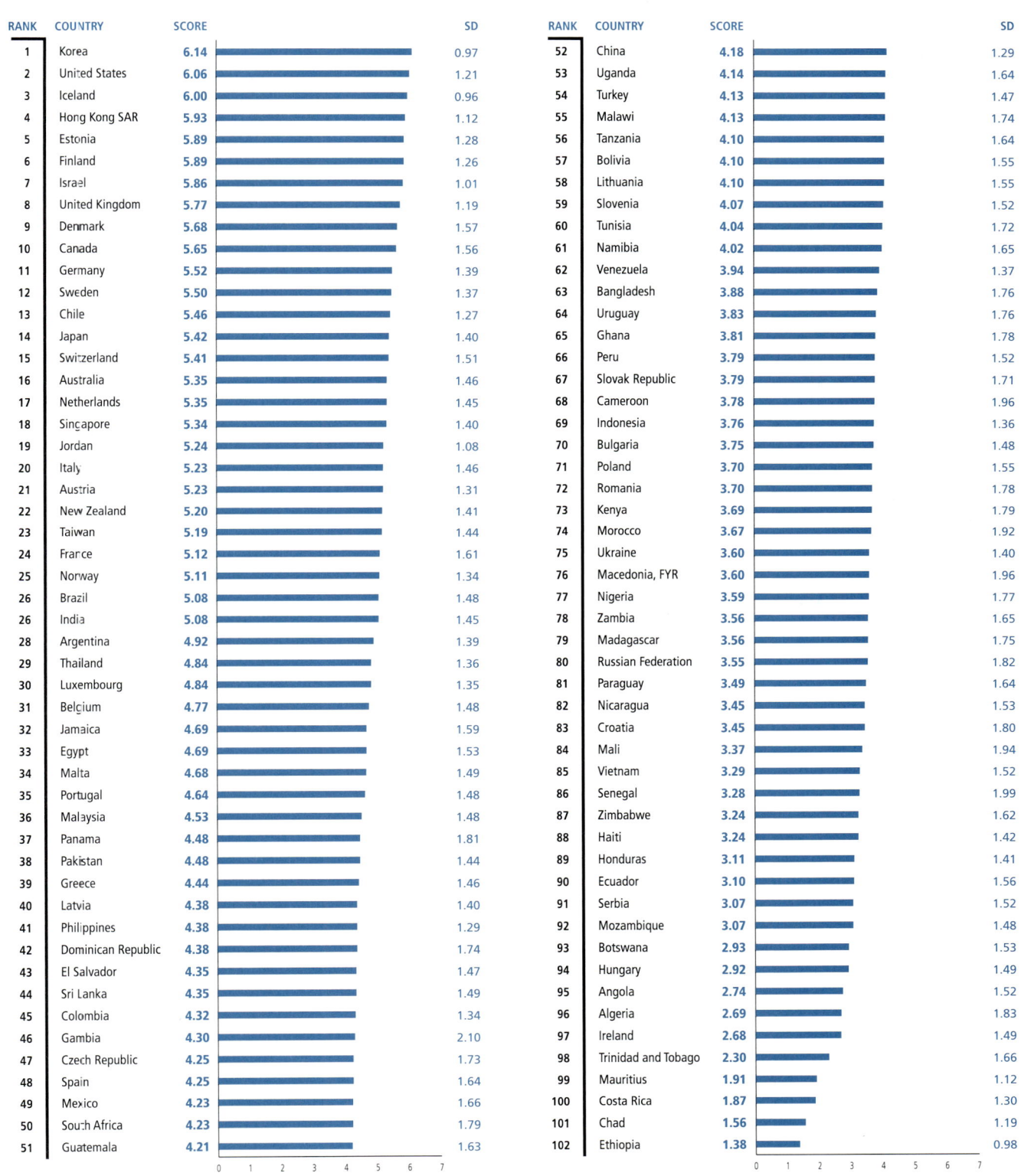

RANK	COUNTRY	SCORE	SD	RANK	COUNTRY	SCORE	SD
1	Korea	6.14	0.97	52	China	4.18	1.29
2	United States	6.06	1.21	53	Uganda	4.14	1.64
3	Iceland	6.00	0.96	54	Turkey	4.13	1.47
4	Hong Kong SAR	5.93	1.12	55	Malawi	4.13	1.74
5	Estonia	5.89	1.28	56	Tanzania	4.10	1.64
6	Finland	5.89	1.26	57	Bolivia	4.10	1.55
7	Israel	5.86	1.01	58	Lithuania	4.10	1.55
8	United Kingdom	5.77	1.19	59	Slovenia	4.07	1.52
9	Denmark	5.68	1.57	60	Tunisia	4.04	1.72
10	Canada	5.65	1.56	61	Namibia	4.02	1.65
11	Germany	5.52	1.39	62	Venezuela	3.94	1.37
12	Sweden	5.50	1.37	63	Bangladesh	3.88	1.76
13	Chile	5.46	1.27	64	Uruguay	3.83	1.76
14	Japan	5.42	1.40	65	Ghana	3.81	1.78
15	Switzerland	5.41	1.51	66	Peru	3.79	1.52
16	Australia	5.35	1.46	67	Slovak Republic	3.79	1.71
17	Netherlands	5.35	1.45	68	Cameroon	3.78	1.96
18	Singapore	5.34	1.40	69	Indonesia	3.76	1.36
19	Jordan	5.24	1.08	70	Bulgaria	3.75	1.48
20	Italy	5.23	1.46	71	Poland	3.70	1.55
21	Austria	5.23	1.31	72	Romania	3.70	1.78
22	New Zealand	5.20	1.41	73	Kenya	3.69	1.79
23	Taiwan	5.19	1.44	74	Morocco	3.67	1.92
24	France	5.12	1.61	75	Ukraine	3.60	1.40
25	Norway	5.11	1.34	76	Macedonia, FYR	3.60	1.96
26	Brazil	5.08	1.48	77	Nigeria	3.59	1.77
26	India	5.08	1.45	78	Zambia	3.56	1.65
28	Argentina	4.92	1.39	79	Madagascar	3.56	1.75
29	Thailand	4.84	1.36	80	Russian Federation	3.55	1.82
30	Luxembourg	4.84	1.35	81	Paraguay	3.49	1.64
31	Belgium	4.77	1.48	82	Nicaragua	3.45	1.53
32	Jamaica	4.69	1.59	83	Croatia	3.45	1.80
33	Egypt	4.69	1.53	84	Mali	3.37	1.94
34	Malta	4.68	1.49	85	Vietnam	3.29	1.52
35	Portugal	4.64	1.48	86	Senegal	3.28	1.99
36	Malaysia	4.53	1.48	87	Zimbabwe	3.24	1.62
37	Panama	4.48	1.81	88	Haiti	3.24	1.42
38	Pakistan	4.48	1.44	89	Honduras	3.11	1.41
39	Greece	4.44	1.46	90	Ecuador	3.10	1.56
40	Latvia	4.38	1.40	91	Serbia	3.07	1.52
41	Philippines	4.38	1.29	92	Mozambique	3.07	1.48
42	Dominican Republic	4.38	1.74	93	Botswana	2.93	1.53
43	El Salvador	4.35	1.47	94	Hungary	2.92	1.49
44	Sri Lanka	4.35	1.49	95	Angola	2.74	1.52
45	Colombia	4.32	1.34	96	Algeria	2.69	1.83
46	Gambia	4.30	2.10	97	Ireland	2.68	1.49
47	Czech Republic	4.25	1.73	98	Trinidad and Tobago	2.30	1.66
48	Spain	4.25	1.64	99	Mauritius	1.91	1.12
49	Mexico	4.23	1.66	100	Costa Rica	1.87	1.30
50	South Africa	4.23	1.79	101	Chad	1.56	1.19
51	Guatemala	4.21	1.63	102	Ethiopia	1.38	0.98

Source: World Economic Forum, Executive Opinion Survey 2003

I.2.05 Foreign ownership restrictions, 2003

Foreign ownership of companies in your country is (1 = rare, limited to few cases, and prohibited in key sectors, 7 = prevalent and encouraged)

RANK	COUNTRY	SCORE		SD
1	United Kingdom	6.31		1.03
2	Hong Kong SAR	6.25		1.05
2	Ireland	6.25		0.63
4	Luxembourg	6.15		0.71
5	Singapore	6.07		1.03
6	Sweden	6.04		0.81
7	Finland	5.97		0.94
8	New Zealand	5.90		0.89
9	United States	5.86		1.06
10	Chile	5.84		0.85
11	Germany	5.79		1.02
12	Hungary	5.74		0.98
13	Slovak Republic	5.72		1.24
14	Gambia	5.71		1.45
15	Denmark	5.64		1.10
16	Jamaica	5.64		0.99
17	Malawi	5.64		1.22
18	Belgium	5.63		0.88
19	France	5.62		0.96
20	Austria	5.61		0.99
21	Dominican Republic	5.60		1.22
21	Nigeria	5.60		1.26
23	Israel	5.55		1.19
24	Netherlands	5.55		1.07
25	Botswana	5.55		1.07
26	Mexico	5.53		1.22
27	Spain	5.53		0.86
28	Zambia	5.50		1.34
29	Estonia	5.49		1.03
30	South Africa	5.48		1.08
31	Morocco	5.47		1.49
32	Uganda	5.47		1.68
33	Costa Rica	5.44		1.11
34	Ghana	5.42		1.36
35	Czech Republic	5.39		0.98
36	Switzerland	5.37		1.16
37	Malta	5.36		1.34
38	Argentina	5.36		1.02
39	Australia	5.35		1.23
40	Tunisia	5.31		1.51
41	India	5.30		1.32
42	Brazil	5.25		0.95
43	Latvia	5.24		0.94
44	Senegal	5.23		1.21
45	Panama	5.23		1.19
46	Pakistan	5.23		1.55
47	Jordan	5.23		1.28
48	Kenya	5.22		1.26
49	Cameroon	5.20		1.19
50	El Salvador	5.20		1.39
51	Poland	5.16		1.19

RANK	COUNTRY	SCORE		SD
52	Tanzania	5.15		1.47
53	Mali	5.15		1.48
54	Greece	5.14		1.29
55	Canada	5.11		1.37
56	Sri Lanka	5.09		1.40
57	Peru	5.08		1.19
58	Taiwan	5.07		1.32
59	Portugal	5.07		1.18
60	Angola	5.02		1.56
61	Bangladesh	4.99		1.77
62	Mozambique	4.97		1.38
63	Lithuania	4.92		1.18
64	Trinidad and Tobago	4.88		1.34
65	Nicaragua	4.87		1.45
66	Turkey	4.85		1.52
67	Malaysia	4.83		1.38
68	Korea	4.83		1.23
69	Norway	4.81		0.92
70	Egypt	4.74		1.66
71	Uruguay	4.72		1.53
72	Italy	4.71		1.01
73	Namibia	4.70		1.40
74	Madagascar	4.66		1.47
75	Thailand	4.61		1.45
76	Venezuela	4.56		1.52
77	Romania	4.55		1.64
78	Honduras	4.54		1.58
79	Colombia	4.54		1.29
80	Paraguay	4.47		1.66
81	China	4.45		1.58
82	Bolivia	4.43		1.44
83	Philippines	4.34		1.74
84	Vietnam	4.34		1.65
85	Japan	4.33		1.23
86	Macedonia, FYR	4.22		1.73
87	Mauritius	4.16		1.44
88	Guatemala	4.14		1.32
89	Ukraine	4.05		1.22
90	Slovenia	4.02		1.02
91	Ecuador	4.00		1.39
92	Croatia	3.97		1.37
93	Iceland	3.96		1.65
94	Bulgaria	3.93		1.33
95	Indonesia	3.86		1.29
96	Algeria	3.86		1.82
97	Chad	3.81		2.04
98	Haiti	3.75		1.59
99	Russian Federation	3.75		1.41
100	Serbia	3.58		1.44
101	Zimbabwe	3.44		1.29
102	Ethiopia	3.30		1.92

Source: World Economic Forum, Executive Opinion Survey 2003

I.2.06 Efficiency of the tax system, 2003

Your country's tax system is (1 = highly complex and distortive on business decisions, 7 = simple and transparent)

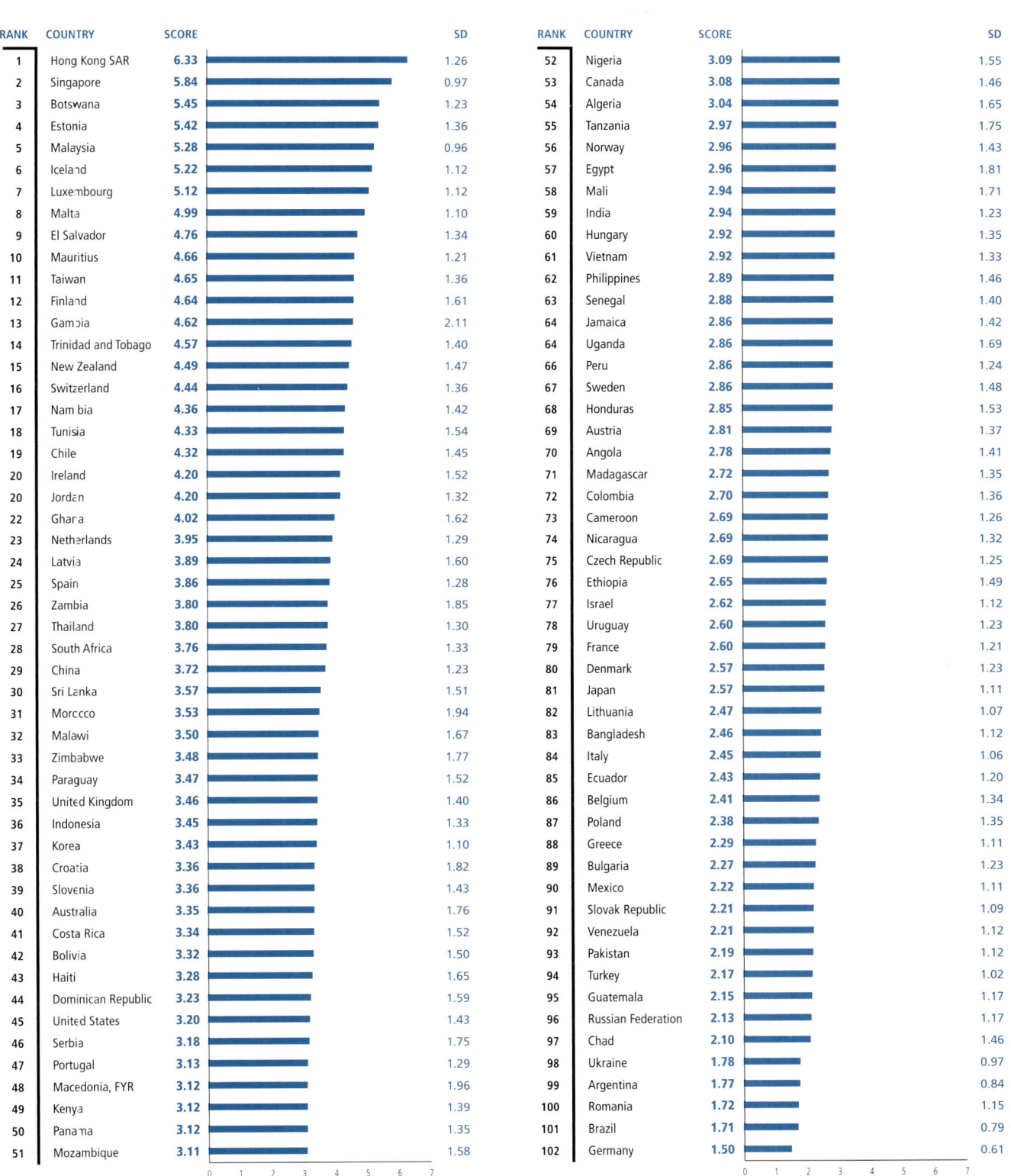

RANK	COUNTRY	SCORE		SD	RANK	COUNTRY	SCORE		SD
1	Hong Kong SAR	6.33		1.26	52	Nigeria	3.09		1.55
2	Singapore	5.84		0.97	53	Canada	3.08		1.46
3	Botswana	5.45		1.23	54	Algeria	3.04		1.65
4	Estonia	5.42		1.36	55	Tanzania	2.97		1.75
5	Malaysia	5.28		0.96	56	Norway	2.96		1.43
6	Iceland	5.22		1.12	57	Egypt	2.96		1.81
7	Luxembourg	5.12		1.12	58	Mali	2.94		1.71
8	Malta	4.99		1.10	59	India	2.94		1.23
9	El Salvador	4.76		1.34	60	Hungary	2.92		1.35
10	Mauritius	4.66		1.21	61	Vietnam	2.92		1.33
11	Taiwan	4.65		1.36	62	Philippines	2.89		1.46
12	Finland	4.64		1.61	63	Senegal	2.88		1.40
13	Gambia	4.62		2.11	64	Jamaica	2.86		1.42
14	Trinidad and Tobago	4.57		1.40	64	Uganda	2.86		1.69
15	New Zealand	4.49		1.47	66	Peru	2.86		1.24
16	Switzerland	4.44		1.36	67	Sweden	2.86		1.48
17	Namibia	4.36		1.42	68	Honduras	2.85		1.53
18	Tunisia	4.33		1.54	69	Austria	2.81		1.37
19	Chile	4.32		1.45	70	Angola	2.78		1.41
20	Ireland	4.20		1.52	71	Madagascar	2.72		1.35
20	Jordan	4.20		1.32	72	Colombia	2.70		1.36
22	Ghana	4.02		1.62	73	Cameroon	2.69		1.26
23	Netherlands	3.95		1.29	74	Nicaragua	2.69		1.32
24	Latvia	3.89		1.60	75	Czech Republic	2.69		1.25
25	Spain	3.86		1.28	76	Ethiopia	2.65		1.49
26	Zambia	3.80		1.85	77	Israel	2.62		1.12
27	Thailand	3.80		1.30	78	Uruguay	2.60		1.23
28	South Africa	3.76		1.33	79	France	2.60		1.21
29	China	3.72		1.23	80	Denmark	2.57		1.23
30	Sri Lanka	3.57		1.51	81	Japan	2.57		1.11
31	Morocco	3.53		1.94	82	Lithuania	2.47		1.07
32	Malawi	3.50		1.67	83	Bangladesh	2.46		1.12
33	Zimbabwe	3.48		1.77	84	Italy	2.45		1.06
34	Paraguay	3.47		1.52	85	Ecuador	2.43		1.20
35	United Kingdom	3.46		1.40	86	Belgium	2.41		1.34
36	Indonesia	3.45		1.33	87	Poland	2.38		1.35
37	Korea	3.43		1.10	88	Greece	2.29		1.11
38	Croatia	3.36		1.82	89	Bulgaria	2.27		1.23
39	Slovenia	3.36		1.43	90	Mexico	2.22		1.11
40	Australia	3.35		1.76	91	Slovak Republic	2.21		1.09
41	Costa Rica	3.34		1.52	92	Venezuela	2.21		1.12
42	Bolivia	3.32		1.50	93	Pakistan	2.19		1.12
43	Haiti	3.28		1.65	94	Turkey	2.17		1.02
44	Dominican Republic	3.23		1.59	95	Guatemala	2.15		1.17
45	United States	3.20		1.43	96	Russian Federation	2.13		1.17
46	Serbia	3.18		1.75	97	Chad	2.10		1.46
47	Portugal	3.13		1.29	98	Ukraine	1.78		0.97
48	Macedonia, FYR	3.12		1.96	99	Argentina	1.77		0.84
49	Kenya	3.12		1.39	100	Romania	1.72		1.15
50	Panama	3.12		1.35	101	Brazil	1.71		0.79
51	Mozambique	3.11		1.58	102	Germany	1.50		0.61

Source: World Economic Forum, Executive Opinion Survey 2003

I.2.07 Freedom of the press, 2003

In your country, can newspapers publish stories of their choosing without fear of censorship or retaliation? (1 = no, 7 = yes, whatever they want)

RANK	COUNTRY	SCORE		SD	RANK	COUNTRY	SCORE		SD
1	Denmark	6.98		0.15	52	Macedonia, FYR	5.48		2.03
2	Sweden	6.89		0.31	53	Jamaica	5.47		1.81
3	Netherlands	6.79		0.76	54	Argentina	5.44		1.63
4	Germany	6.76		0.60	55	Botswana	5.39		1.50
5	Australia	6.75		0.44	56	Algeria	5.36		1.62
6	Portugal	6.72		0.62	57	Bolivia	5.29		1.62
7	United States	6.71		0.54	58	Korea	5.27		1.37
8	Finland	6.57		1.22	59	Latvia	5.24		1.25
9	Belgium	6.57		0.75	60	Dominican Republic	5.24		1.56
10	Switzerland	6.56		0.71	61	Slovenia	5.20		1.57
11	Austria	6.51		0.94	62	Thailand	5.11		1.70
12	Iceland	6.50		0.76	63	Panama	5.07		1.70
13	New Zealand	6.49		0.80	64	Nigeria	5.06		1.76
14	Norway	6.44		1.22	65	Namibia	5.04		1.69
15	United Kingdom	6.40		1.12	65	Pakistan	5.04		1.81
16	Philippines	6.38		1.09	67	Honduras	5.04		1.82
17	Brazil	6.35		0.93	68	Madagascar	5.01		1.71
18	Luxembourg	6.32		0.84	69	Paraguay	4.98		1.95
19	Canada	6.32		1.15	70	Turkey	4.93		1.80
20	Estonia	6.31		1.07	71	Gambia	4.85		1.82
21	Costa Rica	6.24		1.42	72	Guatemala	4.83		1.86
22	Israel	6.24		1.51	73	Malawi	4.76		2.15
23	Spain	6.24		1.02	74	Croatia	4.74		2.02
24	Greece	6.22		1.14	75	Bangladesh	4.66		1.87
25	France	6.19		1.19	76	Romania	4.66		2.06
26	India	6.19		1.01	77	Zambia	4.64		2.00
27	Uruguay	6.17		1.11	78	Bulgaria	4.61		1.84
28	South Africa	6.16		1.22	79	Kenya	4.59		1.95
29	El Salvador	6.15		1.18	80	Tanzania	4.57		1.84
30	Chile	6.07		1.14	81	Mozambique	4.43		1.78
31	Japan	6.07		1.15	82	Russian Federation	4.31		1.84
32	Czech Republic	6.05		1.20	83	Sri Lanka	4.15		1.86
33	Slovak Republic	5.91		1.37	84	Haiti	4.12		1.81
34	Italy	5.85		1.52	85	Jordan	4.11		1.63
35	Malta	5.85		1.41	86	Serbia	4.09		2.03
36	Mali	5.84		1.79	87	Tunisia	3.97		1.80
37	Lithuania	5.84		1.41	88	Venezuela	3.82		1.91
38	Nicaragua	5.81		1.77	89	Indonesia	3.82		1.31
39	Hong Kong SAR	5.80		1.73	90	Egypt	3.77		2.00
40	Mexico	5.79		1.22	91	Morocco	3.51		1.99
41	Mauritius	5.78		1.52	92	Cameroon	3.45		1.92
42	Hungary	5.77		1.44	93	Uganda	3.43		2.10
43	Ghana	5.75		1.49	94	Ethiopia	3.40		2.01
44	Taiwan	5.72		1.24	95	Chad	3.27		2.36
45	Peru	5.70		1.49	96	Singapore	3.25		1.71
46	Senegal	5.69		1.29	97	Vietnam	3.15		1.55
47	Trinidad and Tobago	5.67		1.48	98	Malaysia	3.06		1.56
48	Ireland	5.63		1.85	99	China	3.05		1.40
49	Colombia	5.62		1.20	100	Angola	2.95		1.96
50	Poland	5.58		1.31	101	Ukraine	2.94		1.63
51	Ecuador	5.48		1.50	102	Zimbabwe	2.85		2.00

Source: World Economic Forum, Executive Opinion Survey 2003

Infrastructure Environment

I.3.01 Overall infrastructure quality, 2003

General infrastructure in your country is (1 = poorly developed and inefficient, 7 = among the best in the world)

RANK	COUNTRY	SCORE	SD		RANK	COUNTRY	SCORE	SD
1	Singapore	6.77	0.44		52	Mexico	3.59	1.17
2	Switzerland	6.73	0.79		53	Gambia	3.55	1.50
3	Denmark	6.67	0.62		54	Turkey	3.48	1.33
4	Germany	6.64	0.81		55	China	3.47	1.23
5	Finland	6.56	0.69		56	Jamaica	3.45	1.23
6	France	6.46	0.68		57	Slovak Republic	3.35	1.36
7	Sweden	6.39	0.74		58	Hungary	3.34	1.21
8	United States	6.35	1.08		59	Ukraine	3.28	1.49
9	Australia	6.30	0.66		60	Russian Federation	3.25	1.29
10	Hong Kong SAR	6.27	1.10		61	Tanzania	3.21	1.29
11	Iceland	6.20	0.65		62	Venezuela	3.21	1.32
12	Malaysia	6.08	0.74		63	Zimbabwe	3.19	1.31
13	Austria	6.06	1.06		64	Ireland	3.15	1.33
14	Canada	6.04	1.13		65	Morocco	3.10	1.31
15	Luxembourg	5.97	0.83		66	Colombia	3.10	1.00
16	Netherlands	5.95	1.20		67	Sri Lanka	3.06	1.27
17	Belgium	5.91	0.90		68	Pakistan	3.00	1.25
18	Japan	5.64	1.27		69	Algeria	2.96	1.13
19	South Africa	5.24	0.97		70	India	2.92	1.31
20	Namibia	5.21	1.00		71	Ghana	2.92	1.21
21	Korea	5.20	0.97		72	Costa Rica	2.89	1.12
22	New Zealand	5.20	1.23		73	Poland	2.83	1.12
23	Jordan	5.17	0.87		74	Bulgaria	2.79	1.18
24	Spain	5.03	0.93		75	Guatemala	2.75	1.19
25	Israel	5.00	0.95		76	Vietnam	2.75	1.16
26	United Kingdom	4.95	1.26		77	Romania	2.71	1.46
27	Taiwan	4.95	1.05		78	Ecuador	2.69	0.93
28	Botswana	4.92	1.17		79	Malawi	2.68	1.27
29	Thailand	4.89	1.07		80	Uganda	2.63	1.35
30	Portugal	4.85	0.89		81	Croatia	2.62	1.25
31	Chile	4.75	0.83		82	Zambia	2.56	1.19
32	Estonia	4.75	1.01		83	Peru	2.53	1.07
33	Tunisia	4.70	1.09		84	Cameroon	2.52	0.97
34	Norway	4.70	1.46		85	Macedonia, FYR	2.48	1.31
35	Mauritius	4.63	1.10		86	Honduras	2.48	1.02
36	Slovenia	4.55	1.04		87	Senegal	2.37	1.04
37	Latvia	4.38	1.21		88	Kenya	2.33	1.00
38	Czech Republic	4.34	1.32		89	Philippines	2.32	1.04
39	Lithuania	4.22	1.32		90	Bangladesh	2.09	0.92
40	Italy	4.21	1.40		91	Mali	2.05	1.00
41	Trinidad and Tobago	4.03	1.18		92	Mozambique	1.97	0.96
42	Malta	3.99	1.23		93	Ethiopia	1.96	1.03
43	Egypt	3.89	1.36		94	Serbia	1.93	0.90
44	Dominican Republic	3.86	1.12		95	Nicaragua	1.91	0.91
45	Argentina	3.85	1.26		96	Madagascar	1.91	0.90
46	Panama	3.81	1.22		97	Paraguay	1.86	0.88
47	Brazil	3.81	1.23		98	Bolivia	1.86	0.81
48	Uruguay	3.78	1.11		99	Nigeria	1.79	0.86
49	Greece	3.78	1.10		100	Angola	1.51	0.59
50	El Salvador	3.75	1.06		101	Haiti	1.33	0.56
51	Indonesia	3.68	1.32		102	Chad	1.23	0.57

Source: World Economic Forum, Executive Opinion Survey 2003

I.3.02 Waiting time for telephone lines, 2000

Waiting time for telephone lines in years, 2000

RANK	COUNTRY	VALUE
1	Australia	0.00
1	Austria	0.00
1	Belgium	*0.00
1	Canada	0.00
1	Denmark	0.00
1	Finland	0.00
1	France	0.00
1	Germany	0.00
1	Hong Kong SAR	0.00
1	Iceland	0.00
1	Ireland	*0.00
1	Italy	0.00
1	Japan	0.00
1	Korea	0.00
1	Luxembourg	0.00
1	Netherlands	0.00
1	New Zealand	0.00
1	Norway	0.00
1	Singapore	0.00
1	Sweden	0.00
1	Switzerland	0.00
1	United Kingdom	0.00
1	United States	0.00
1	Uruguay	0.00
25	Israel	*0.01
25	Spain	0.01
27	Chile	0.04
28	Madagascar	0.06
29	Slovenia	0.08
30	Malta	0.08
31	Hungary	0.12
32	Morocco	0.12
33	Mexico	0.13
34	Czech Republic	0.16
35	Argentina	0.17
36	Taiwan	*0.17
37	Greece	0.19
38	Bolivia	0.19
39	Portugal	0.25
40	Jordan	0.25
41	Costa Rica	0.33
42	Turkey	0.47
43	Chad	0.47
44	Brazil	0.52
45	Trinidad and Tobago	0.54
46	Botswana	0.55
47	Paraguay	0.66
48	Slovak Republic	0.68
49	Panama	*0.70
49	Venezuela	*0.70
51	Namibia	0.70

RANK	COUNTRY	VALUE
52	Malaysia	0.74
53	India	0.75
54	Poland	0.81
55	Senegal	0.82
56	Croatia	0.88
57	Lithuania	0.94
58	Tunisia	0.95
59	Mauritius	0.98
60	South Africa	1.10
61	Peru	1.25
62	Tanzania	1.30
63	Estonia	1.36
64	Nigeria	1.37
65	Latvia	*1.56
66	Thailand	1.63
67	Dominican Republic	1.65
68	Pakistan	1.80
69	Sri Lanka	1.90
70	Egypt	1.92
71	Colombia	1.96
72	El Salvador	2.22
73	Ecuador	2.33
74	Mali	2.44
75	Ghana	3.12
76	Macedonia, FYR	3.12
77	Serbia	3.17
78	Mozambique	*3.18
79	Bangladesh	3.29
80	Uganda	*3.61
81	Bulgaria	3.62
82	Guatemala	3.69
83	Romania	3.83
84	Indonesia	4.64
85	Haiti	*4.64
85	Vietnam	*4.64
87	Russian Federation	*5.13
88	China	*5.27
88	Philippines	*5.27
90	Algeria	*5.37
91	Gambia	5.98
92	Cameroon	6.24
93	Jamaica	6.53
94	Zambia	6.73
95	Honduras	7.82
96	Ethiopia	7.83
97	Ukraine	7.91
98	Kenya	8.10
99	Angola	8.55
100	Malawi	9.10
101	Nicaragua	9.10
102	Zimbabwe	10.00

Note: *estimate
Source: International Telecommunication Union

I.3.03 Telephone mainlines, 2001

Telephone mainlines per 1,000 inhabitants, 2001

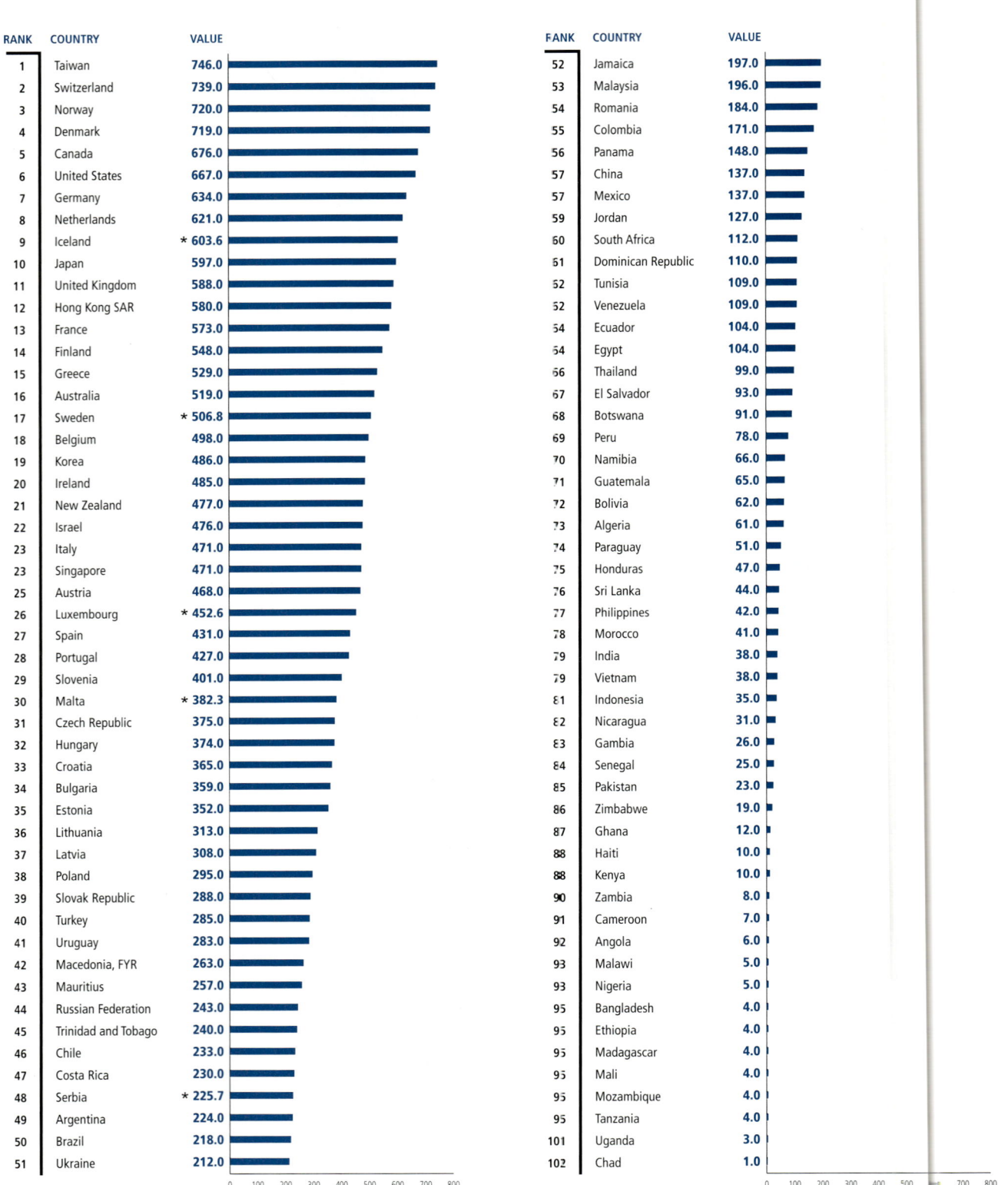

RANK	COUNTRY	VALUE		RANK	COUNTRY	VALUE
1	Taiwan	746.0		52	Jamaica	197.0
2	Switzerland	739.0		53	Malaysia	196.0
3	Norway	720.0		54	Romania	184.0
4	Denmark	719.0		55	Colombia	171.0
5	Canada	676.0		56	Panama	148.0
6	United States	667.0		57	China	137.0
7	Germany	634.0		57	Mexico	137.0
8	Netherlands	621.0		59	Jordan	127.0
9	Iceland	* 603.6		60	South Africa	112.0
10	Japan	597.0		61	Dominican Republic	110.0
11	United Kingdom	588.0		62	Tunisia	109.0
12	Hong Kong SAR	580.0		62	Venezuela	109.0
13	France	573.0		64	Ecuador	104.0
14	Finland	548.0		64	Egypt	104.0
15	Greece	529.0		66	Thailand	99.0
16	Australia	519.0		67	El Salvador	93.0
17	Sweden	* 506.8		68	Botswana	91.0
18	Belgium	498.0		69	Peru	78.0
19	Korea	486.0		70	Namibia	66.0
20	Ireland	485.0		71	Guatemala	65.0
21	New Zealand	477.0		72	Bolivia	62.0
22	Israel	476.0		73	Algeria	61.0
23	Italy	471.0		74	Paraguay	51.0
23	Singapore	471.0		75	Honduras	47.0
25	Austria	468.0		76	Sri Lanka	44.0
26	Luxembourg	* 452.6		77	Philippines	42.0
27	Spain	431.0		78	Morocco	41.0
28	Portugal	427.0		79	India	38.0
29	Slovenia	401.0		79	Vietnam	38.0
30	Malta	* 382.3		81	Indonesia	35.0
31	Czech Republic	375.0		82	Nicaragua	31.0
32	Hungary	374.0		83	Gambia	26.0
33	Croatia	365.0		84	Senegal	25.0
34	Bulgaria	359.0		85	Pakistan	23.0
35	Estonia	352.0		86	Zimbabwe	19.0
36	Lithuania	313.0		87	Ghana	12.0
37	Latvia	308.0		88	Haiti	10.0
38	Poland	295.0		88	Kenya	10.0
39	Slovak Republic	288.0		90	Zambia	8.0
40	Turkey	285.0		91	Cameroon	7.0
41	Uruguay	283.0		92	Angola	6.0
42	Macedonia, FYR	263.0		93	Malawi	5.0
43	Mauritius	257.0		93	Nigeria	5.0
44	Russian Federation	243.0		95	Bangladesh	4.0
45	Trinidad and Tobago	240.0		95	Ethiopia	4.0
46	Chile	233.0		95	Madagascar	4.0
47	Costa Rica	230.0		95	Mali	4.0
48	Serbia	* 225.7		95	Mozambique	4.0
49	Argentina	224.0		95	Tanzania	4.0
50	Brazil	218.0		101	Uganda	3.0
51	Ukraine	212.0		102	Chad	1.0

Note: *estimate
Source: World Bank, World Development Indicators 2003 using International Telecommunication Union data

I.3.04 Public pay telephones, 2001

Public pay telephones per 1,000 inhabitants, 2001

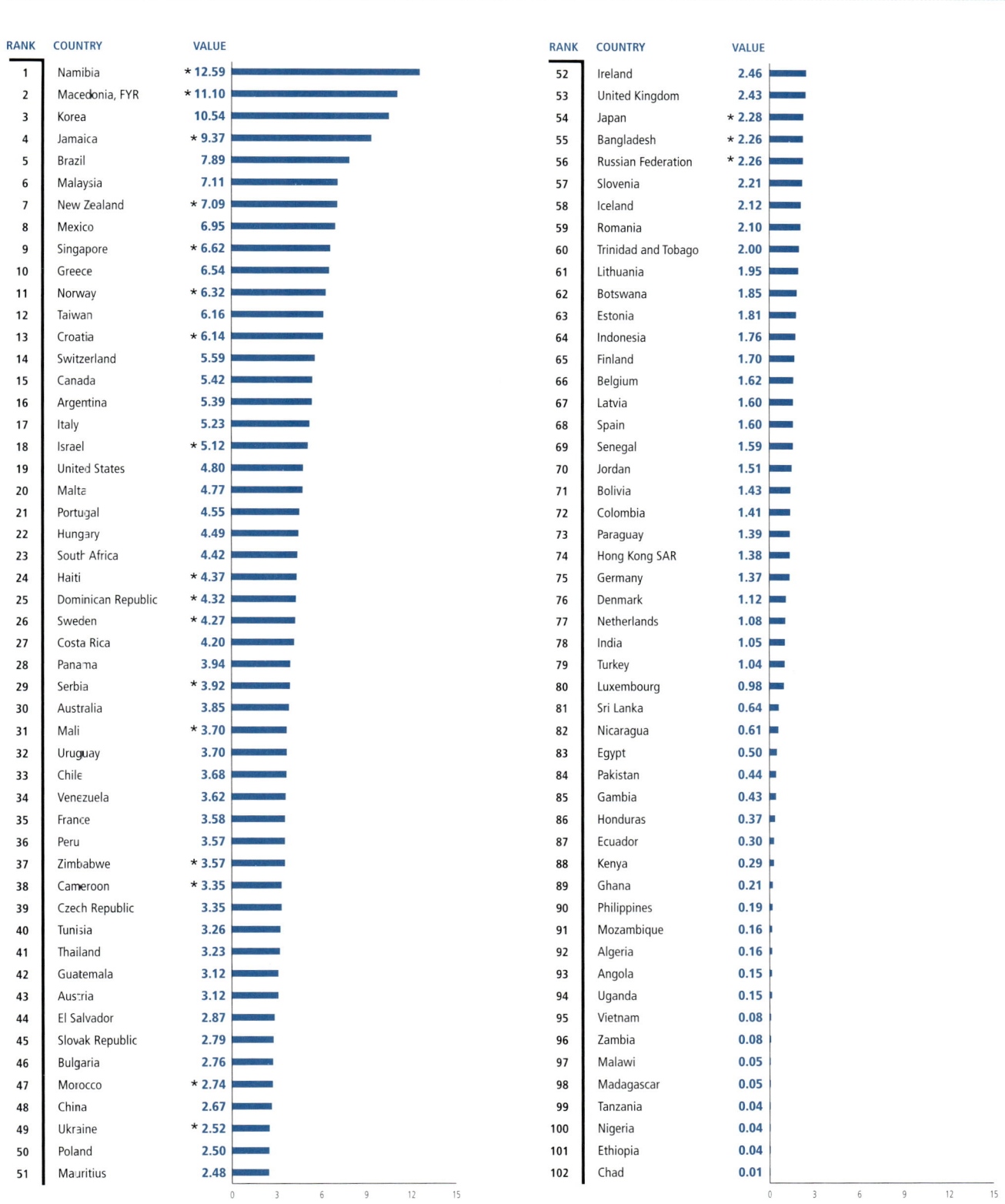

RANK	COUNTRY	VALUE		RANK	COUNTRY	VALUE
1	Namibia	* 12.59		52	Ireland	2.46
2	Macedonia, FYR	* 11.10		53	United Kingdom	2.43
3	Korea	10.54		54	Japan	* 2.28
4	Jamaica	* 9.37		55	Bangladesh	* 2.26
5	Brazil	7.89		56	Russian Federation	* 2.26
6	Malaysia	7.11		57	Slovenia	2.21
7	New Zealand	* 7.09		58	Iceland	2.12
8	Mexico	6.95		59	Romania	2.10
9	Singapore	* 6.62		60	Trinidad and Tobago	2.00
10	Greece	6.54		61	Lithuania	1.95
11	Norway	* 6.32		62	Botswana	1.85
12	Taiwan	6.16		63	Estonia	1.81
13	Croatia	* 6.14		64	Indonesia	1.76
14	Switzerland	5.59		65	Finland	1.70
15	Canada	5.42		66	Belgium	1.62
16	Argentina	5.39		67	Latvia	1.60
17	Italy	5.23		68	Spain	1.60
18	Israel	* 5.12		69	Senegal	1.59
19	United States	4.80		70	Jordan	1.51
20	Malta	4.77		71	Bolivia	1.43
21	Portugal	4.55		72	Colombia	1.41
22	Hungary	4.49		73	Paraguay	1.39
23	South Africa	4.42		74	Hong Kong SAR	1.38
24	Haiti	* 4.37		75	Germany	1.37
25	Dominican Republic	* 4.32		76	Denmark	1.12
26	Sweden	* 4.27		77	Netherlands	1.08
27	Costa Rica	4.20		78	India	1.05
28	Panama	3.94		79	Turkey	1.04
29	Serbia	* 3.92		80	Luxembourg	0.98
30	Australia	3.85		81	Sri Lanka	0.64
31	Mali	* 3.70		82	Nicaragua	0.61
32	Uruguay	3.70		83	Egypt	0.50
33	Chile	3.68		84	Pakistan	0.44
34	Venezuela	3.62		85	Gambia	0.43
35	France	3.58		86	Honduras	0.37
36	Peru	3.57		87	Ecuador	0.30
37	Zimbabwe	* 3.57		88	Kenya	0.29
38	Cameroon	* 3.35		89	Ghana	0.21
39	Czech Republic	3.35		90	Philippines	0.19
40	Tunisia	3.26		91	Mozambique	0.16
41	Thailand	3.23		92	Algeria	0.16
42	Guatemala	3.12		93	Angola	0.15
43	Austria	3.12		94	Uganda	0.15
44	El Salvador	2.87		95	Vietnam	0.08
45	Slovak Republic	2.79		96	Zambia	0.08
46	Bulgaria	2.76		97	Malawi	0.05
47	Morocco	* 2.74		98	Madagascar	0.05
48	China	2.67		99	Tanzania	0.04
49	Ukraine	* 2.52		100	Nigeria	0.04
50	Poland	2.50		101	Ethiopia	0.04
51	Mauritius	2.48		102	Chad	0.01

Note: *estimate
Source: World Bank, World Development Indicators 2003 using International Telecommunication Union data

I.3.05 Internet servers, 2001

Secure Internet servers per 1,000,000 inhabitants, 2001

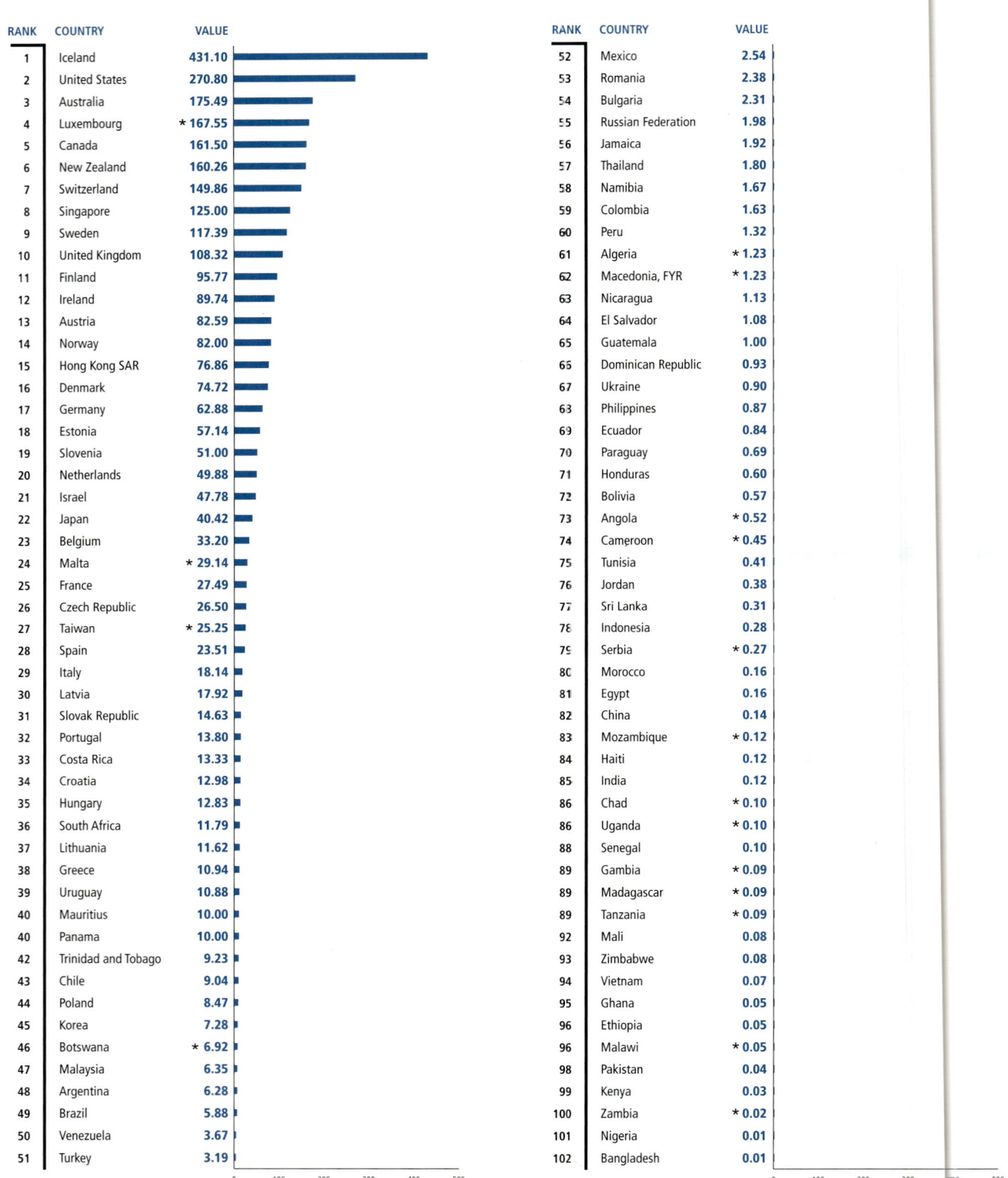

RANK	COUNTRY	VALUE		RANK	COUNTRY	VALUE
1	Iceland	431.10		52	Mexico	2.54
2	United States	270.80		53	Romania	2.38
3	Australia	175.49		54	Bulgaria	2.31
4	Luxembourg	*167.55		55	Russian Federation	1.98
5	Canada	161.50		56	Jamaica	1.92
6	New Zealand	160.26		57	Thailand	1.80
7	Switzerland	149.86		58	Namibia	1.67
8	Singapore	125.00		59	Colombia	1.63
9	Sweden	117.39		60	Peru	1.32
10	United Kingdom	108.32		61	Algeria	*1.23
11	Finland	95.77		62	Macedonia, FYR	*1.23
12	Ireland	89.74		63	Nicaragua	1.13
13	Austria	82.59		64	El Salvador	1.08
14	Norway	82.00		65	Guatemala	1.00
15	Hong Kong SAR	76.86		65	Dominican Republic	0.93
16	Denmark	74.72		67	Ukraine	0.90
17	Germany	62.88		63	Philippines	0.87
18	Estonia	57.14		69	Ecuador	0.84
19	Slovenia	51.00		70	Paraguay	0.69
20	Netherlands	49.88		71	Honduras	0.60
21	Israel	47.78		72	Bolivia	0.57
22	Japan	40.42		73	Angola	*0.52
23	Belgium	33.20		74	Cameroon	*0.45
24	Malta	*29.14		75	Tunisia	0.41
25	France	27.49		76	Jordan	0.38
26	Czech Republic	26.50		77	Sri Lanka	0.31
27	Taiwan	*25.25		78	Indonesia	0.28
28	Spain	23.51		79	Serbia	*0.27
29	Italy	18.14		80	Morocco	0.16
30	Latvia	17.92		81	Egypt	0.16
31	Slovak Republic	14.63		82	China	0.14
32	Portugal	13.80		83	Mozambique	*0.12
33	Costa Rica	13.33		84	Haiti	0.12
34	Croatia	12.98		85	India	0.12
35	Hungary	12.83		86	Chad	*0.10
36	South Africa	11.79		86	Uganda	*0.10
37	Lithuania	11.62		88	Senegal	0.10
38	Greece	10.94		89	Gambia	*0.09
39	Uruguay	10.88		89	Madagascar	*0.09
40	Mauritius	10.00		89	Tanzania	*0.09
40	Panama	10.00		92	Mali	0.08
42	Trinidad and Tobago	9.23		93	Zimbabwe	0.08
43	Chile	9.04		94	Vietnam	0.07
44	Poland	8.47		95	Ghana	0.05
45	Korea	7.28		96	Ethiopia	0.05
46	Botswana	*6.92		96	Malawi	*0.05
47	Malaysia	6.35		98	Pakistan	0.04
48	Argentina	6.28		99	Kenya	0.03
49	Brazil	5.88		100	Zambia	*0.02
50	Venezuela	3.67		101	Nigeria	0.01
51	Turkey	3.19		102	Bangladesh	0.01

Note: *estimate
Source: World Bank, World Development Indicators 2003 using International Telecommunication Union data

Individual Readiness

II.1.01 Public expenditure on education, 2000

Public expenditure on education per capita, 2000

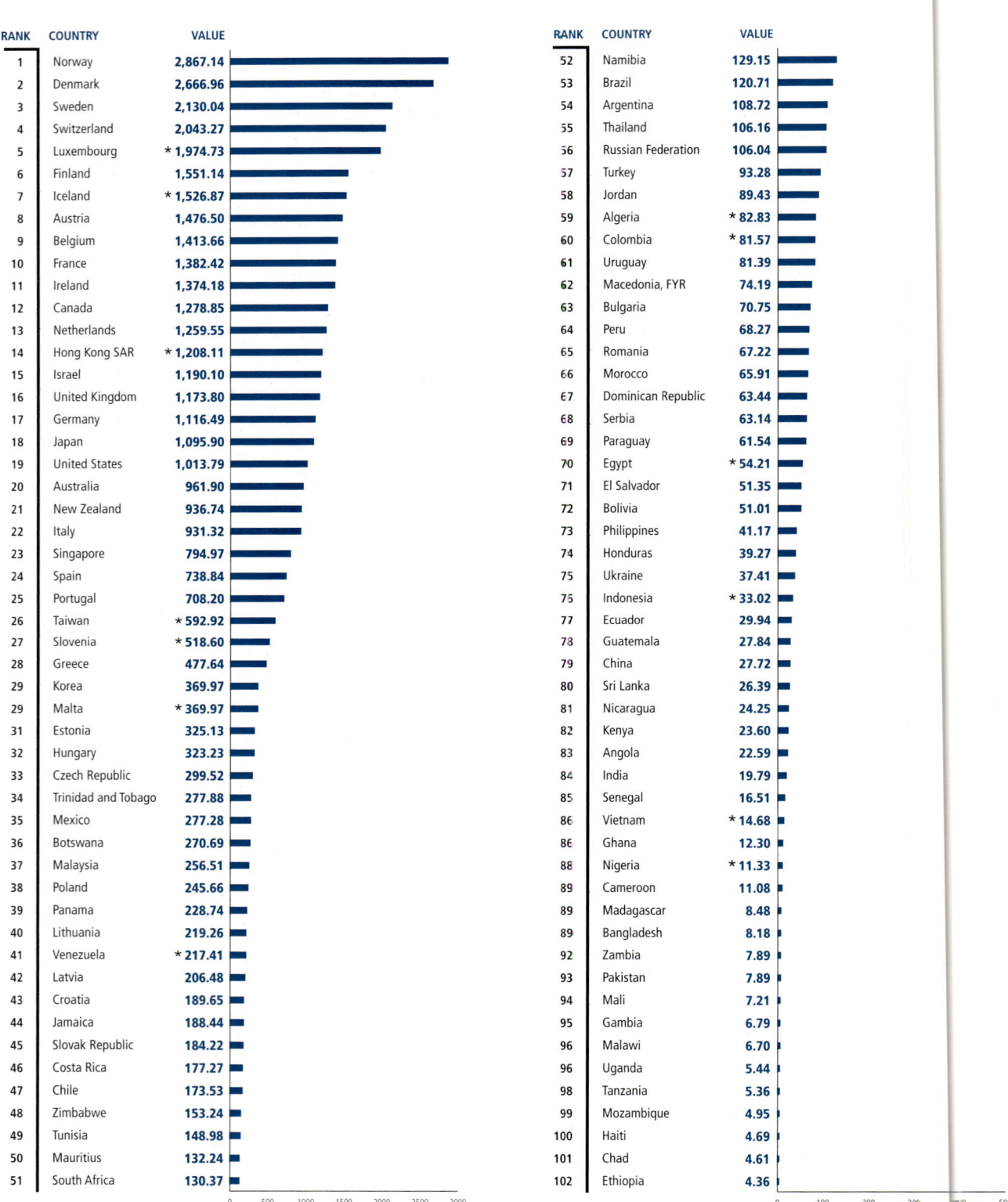

RANK	COUNTRY	VALUE
1	Norway	2,867.14
2	Denmark	2,666.96
3	Sweden	2,130.04
4	Switzerland	2,043.27
5	Luxembourg	* 1,974.73
6	Finland	1,551.14
7	Iceland	* 1,526.87
8	Austria	1,476.50
9	Belgium	1,413.66
10	France	1,382.42
11	Ireland	1,374.18
12	Canada	1,278.85
13	Netherlands	1,259.55
14	Hong Kong SAR	* 1,208.11
15	Israel	1,190.10
16	United Kingdom	1,173.80
17	Germany	1,116.49
18	Japan	1,095.90
19	United States	1,013.79
20	Australia	961.90
21	New Zealand	936.74
22	Italy	931.32
23	Singapore	794.97
24	Spain	738.84
25	Portugal	708.20
26	Taiwan	* 592.92
27	Slovenia	* 518.60
28	Greece	477.64
29	Korea	369.97
29	Malta	* 369.97
31	Estonia	325.13
32	Hungary	323.23
33	Czech Republic	299.52
34	Trinidad and Tobago	277.88
35	Mexico	277.28
36	Botswana	270.69
37	Malaysia	256.51
38	Poland	245.66
39	Panama	228.74
40	Lithuania	219.26
41	Venezuela	* 217.41
42	Latvia	206.48
43	Croatia	189.65
44	Jamaica	188.44
45	Slovak Republic	184.22
46	Costa Rica	177.27
47	Chile	173.53
48	Zimbabwe	153.24
49	Tunisia	148.98
50	Mauritius	132.24
51	South Africa	130.37

RANK	COUNTRY	VALUE
52	Namibia	129.15
53	Brazil	120.71
54	Argentina	108.72
55	Thailand	106.16
56	Russian Federation	106.04
57	Turkey	93.28
58	Jordan	89.43
59	Algeria	* 82.83
60	Colombia	* 81.57
61	Uruguay	81.39
62	Macedonia, FYR	74.19
63	Bulgaria	70.75
64	Peru	68.27
65	Romania	67.22
66	Morocco	65.91
67	Dominican Republic	63.44
68	Serbia	63.14
69	Paraguay	61.54
70	Egypt	* 54.21
71	El Salvador	51.35
72	Bolivia	51.01
73	Philippines	41.17
74	Honduras	39.27
75	Ukraine	37.41
75	Indonesia	* 33.02
77	Ecuador	29.94
78	Guatemala	27.84
79	China	27.72
80	Sri Lanka	26.39
81	Nicaragua	24.25
82	Kenya	23.60
83	Angola	22.59
84	India	19.79
85	Senegal	16.51
86	Vietnam	* 14.68
86	Ghana	12.30
88	Nigeria	* 11.33
89	Cameroon	11.08
89	Madagascar	8.48
89	Bangladesh	8.18
92	Zambia	7.89
93	Pakistan	7.89
94	Mali	7.21
95	Gambia	6.79
96	Malawi	6.70
96	Uganda	5.44
98	Tanzania	5.36
99	Mozambique	4.95
100	Haiti	4.69
101	Chad	4.61
102	Ethiopia	4.36

Note: *estimate
Source: UNESCO Institute for Statistics

II.1.02 Adult illiteracy, 2001

Adult Illiteracy rate in percent, 2001

RANK	COUNTRY	VALUE
1	Australia	*0.00
1	Denmark	*0.00
1	Finland	*0.00
1	Luxembourg	*0.00
1	Norway	*0.00
1	Slovak Republic	*0.00
7	Czech Republic	*0.10
7	Iceland	*0.10
9	Latvia	0.20
10	Estonia	0.22
11	Poland	0.26
12	Slovenia	0.35
13	Ukraine	0.38
14	Lithuania	0.42
15	Russian Federation	0.43
16	Hungary	0.66
17	France	*1.00
17	Germany	*1.00
17	Japan	*1.00
17	Netherlands	*1.00
17	New Zealand	*1.00
17	Sweden	*1.00
17	Switzerland	*1.00
17	United Kingdom	*1.00
25	Bulgaria	1.51
26	Italy	1.52
27	Trinidad and Tobago	1.61
28	Croatia	1.64
29	Romania	1.78
30	Austria	*2.00
30	Belgium	*2.00
30	Ireland	*2.00
33	Korea	2.14
34	Spain	2.28
35	Uruguay	2.36
36	Greece	2.74
37	Canada	*3.00
37	United States	*3.00
39	Argentina	3.09
40	Chile	4.10
41	Costa Rica	4.32
42	Thailand	4.35
43	Philippines	4.85
44	Israel	4.93
45	Macedonia, FYR	*5.00
46	Taiwan	*6.00
47	Hong Kong SAR	6.49
48	Paraguay	6.50
49	Venezuela	7.17
50	Vietnam	7.32
51	Singapore	7.45

RANK	COUNTRY	VALUE
52	Portugal	7.47
53	Malta	7.71
54	Panama	7.93
55	Colombia	8.11
56	Sri Lanka	8.14
57	Ecuador	8.16
58	Mexico	8.57
59	Serbia	*9.00
60	Jordan	9.66
61	Peru	9.80
62	Zimbabwe	10.66
63	Angola	*11.24
64	Malaysia	12.12
65	Indonesia	12.66
66	Brazil	12.70
67	Jamaica	12.72
68	Bolivia	14.00
69	China	14.23
70	South Africa	14.39
71	Turkey	14.49
72	Mauritius	15.17
73	Dominican Republic	15.99
74	Kenya	16.66
75	Namibia	17.35
76	El Salvador	20.84
77	Zambia	20.96
78	Botswana	21.94
79	Tanzania	23.95
80	Honduras	24.44
81	Ghana	27.31
82	Cameroon	27.61
83	Tunisia	27.89
84	Guatemala	30.79
85	Uganda	32.03
86	Algeria	32.20
87	Madagascar	32.69
88	Nicaragua	33.18
89	Nigeria	34.61
90	Malawi	39.02
91	India	41.99
92	Egypt	43.88
93	Haiti	49.17
94	Morocco	50.22
95	Mozambique	54.76
96	Chad	55.77
97	Pakistan	55.96
98	Bangladesh	59.45
99	Ethiopia	59.69
100	Senegal	61.70
101	Gambia	62.20
102	Mali	73.60

Note: *estimate
Source: UNESCO Institute for Statistics

II.1.03 Tertiary enrollment, 2001

Gross tertiary enrollment rate in percent, 2001 or most recent available

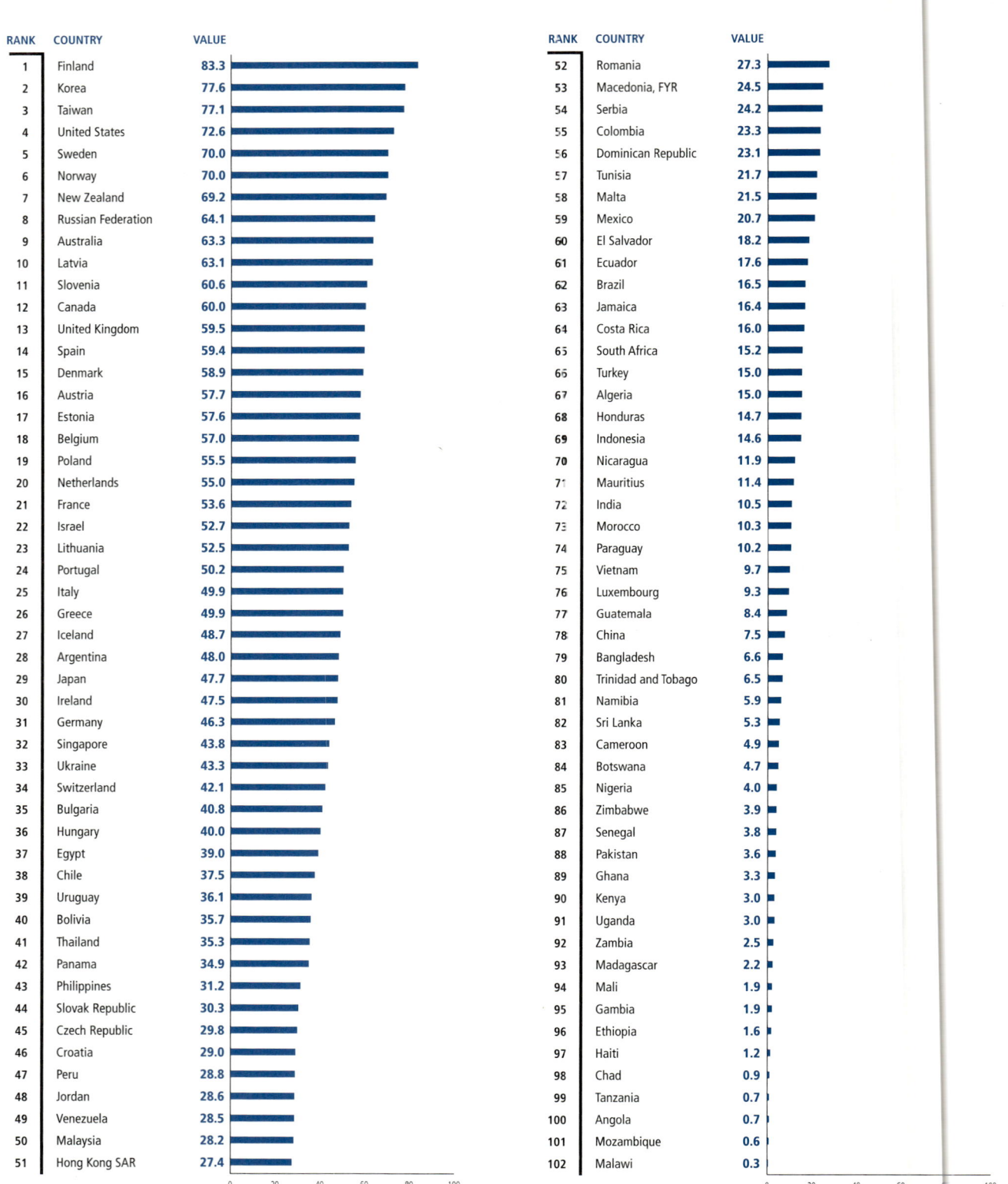

RANK	COUNTRY	VALUE
1	Finland	83.3
2	Korea	77.6
3	Taiwan	77.1
4	United States	72.6
5	Sweden	70.0
6	Norway	70.0
7	New Zealand	69.2
8	Russian Federation	64.1
9	Australia	63.3
10	Latvia	63.1
11	Slovenia	60.6
12	Canada	60.0
13	United Kingdom	59.5
14	Spain	59.4
15	Denmark	58.9
16	Austria	57.7
17	Estonia	57.6
18	Belgium	57.0
19	Poland	55.5
20	Netherlands	55.0
21	France	53.6
22	Israel	52.7
23	Lithuania	52.5
24	Portugal	50.2
25	Italy	49.9
26	Greece	49.9
27	Iceland	48.7
28	Argentina	48.0
29	Japan	47.7
30	Ireland	47.5
31	Germany	46.3
32	Singapore	43.8
33	Ukraine	43.3
34	Switzerland	42.1
35	Bulgaria	40.8
36	Hungary	40.0
37	Egypt	39.0
38	Chile	37.5
39	Uruguay	36.1
40	Bolivia	35.7
41	Thailand	35.3
42	Panama	34.9
43	Philippines	31.2
44	Slovak Republic	30.3
45	Czech Republic	29.8
46	Croatia	29.0
47	Peru	28.8
48	Jordan	28.6
49	Venezuela	28.5
50	Malaysia	28.2
51	Hong Kong SAR	27.4

RANK	COUNTRY	VALUE
52	Romania	27.3
53	Macedonia, FYR	24.5
54	Serbia	24.2
55	Colombia	23.3
56	Dominican Republic	23.1
57	Tunisia	21.7
58	Malta	21.5
59	Mexico	20.7
60	El Salvador	18.2
61	Ecuador	17.6
62	Brazil	16.5
63	Jamaica	16.4
64	Costa Rica	16.0
65	South Africa	15.2
66	Turkey	15.0
67	Algeria	15.0
68	Honduras	14.7
69	Indonesia	14.6
70	Nicaragua	11.9
71	Mauritius	11.4
72	India	10.5
73	Morocco	10.3
74	Paraguay	10.2
75	Vietnam	9.7
76	Luxembourg	9.3
77	Guatemala	8.4
78	China	7.5
79	Bangladesh	6.6
80	Trinidad and Tobago	6.5
81	Namibia	5.9
82	Sri Lanka	5.3
83	Cameroon	4.9
84	Botswana	4.7
85	Nigeria	4.0
86	Zimbabwe	3.9
87	Senegal	3.8
88	Pakistan	3.6
89	Ghana	3.3
90	Kenya	3.0
91	Uganda	3.0
92	Zambia	2.5
93	Madagascar	2.2
94	Mali	1.9
95	Gambia	1.9
96	Ethiopia	1.6
97	Haiti	1.2
98	Chad	0.9
99	Tanzania	0.7
100	Angola	0.7
101	Mozambique	0.6
102	Malawi	0.3

Source: UNESCO Institute for Statistics; World Bank, World Development Indicators 2003; National sources

II.1.04 Radios, 2001

Radios per 1,000 inhabitants, 2001 or most recent available

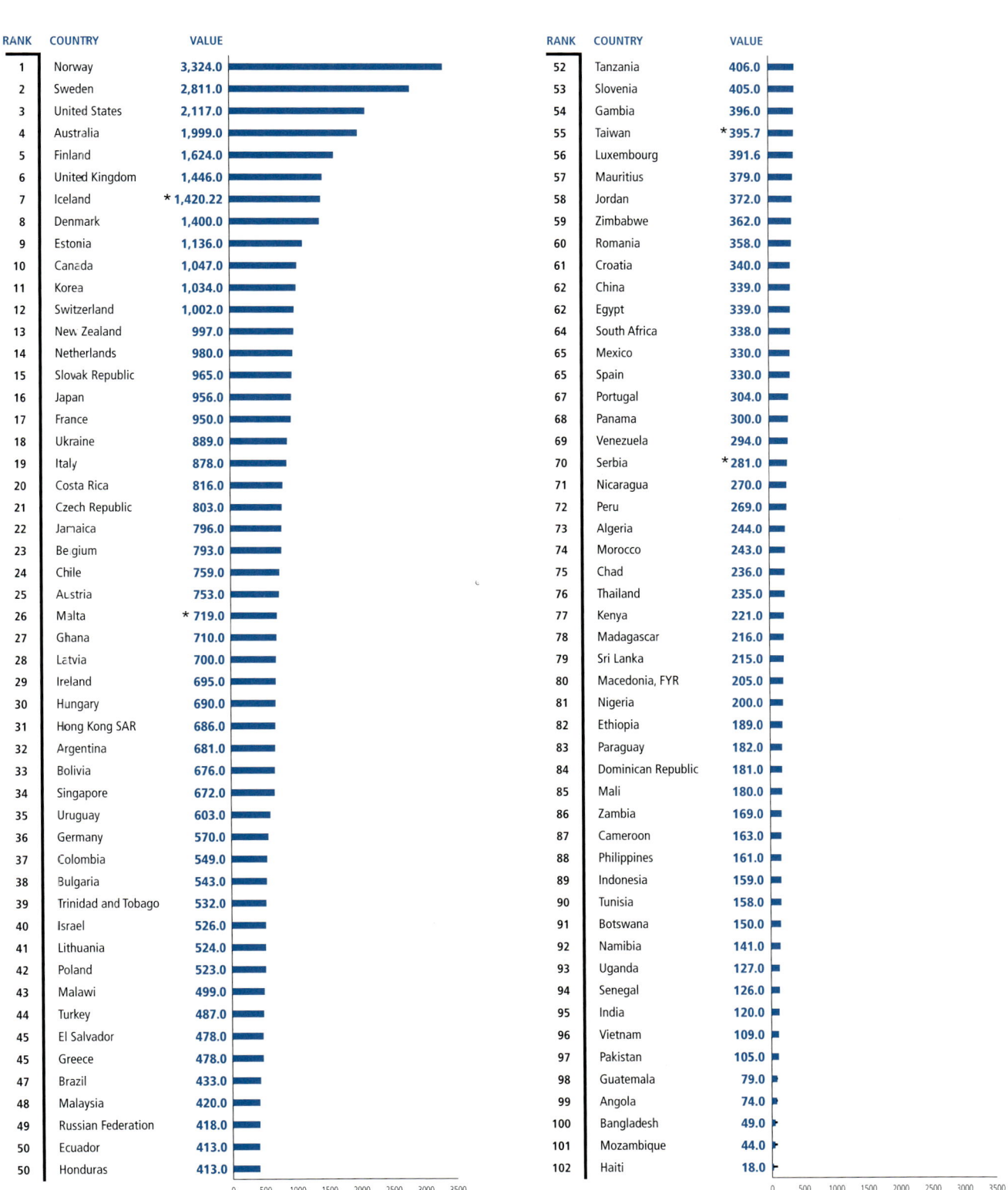

RANK	COUNTRY	VALUE
1	Norway	3,324.0
2	Sweden	2,811.0
3	United States	2,117.0
4	Australia	1,999.0
5	Finland	1,624.0
6	United Kingdom	1,446.0
7	Iceland	*1,420.22
8	Denmark	1,400.0
9	Estonia	1,136.0
10	Canada	1,047.0
11	Korea	1,034.0
12	Switzerland	1,002.0
13	New Zealand	997.0
14	Netherlands	980.0
15	Slovak Republic	965.0
16	Japan	956.0
17	France	950.0
18	Ukraine	889.0
19	Italy	878.0
20	Costa Rica	816.0
21	Czech Republic	803.0
22	Jamaica	796.0
23	Belgium	793.0
24	Chile	759.0
25	Austria	753.0
26	Malta	*719.0
27	Ghana	710.0
28	Latvia	700.0
29	Ireland	695.0
30	Hungary	690.0
31	Hong Kong SAR	686.0
32	Argentina	681.0
33	Bolivia	676.0
34	Singapore	672.0
35	Uruguay	603.0
36	Germany	570.0
37	Colombia	549.0
38	Bulgaria	543.0
39	Trinidad and Tobago	532.0
40	Israel	526.0
41	Lithuania	524.0
42	Poland	523.0
43	Malawi	499.0
44	Turkey	487.0
45	El Salvador	478.0
45	Greece	478.0
47	Brazil	433.0
48	Malaysia	420.0
49	Russian Federation	418.0
50	Ecuador	413.0
50	Honduras	413.0

RANK	COUNTRY	VALUE
52	Tanzania	406.0
53	Slovenia	405.0
54	Gambia	396.0
55	Taiwan	*395.7
56	Luxembourg	391.6
57	Mauritius	379.0
58	Jordan	372.0
59	Zimbabwe	362.0
60	Romania	358.0
61	Croatia	340.0
62	China	339.0
62	Egypt	339.0
64	South Africa	338.0
65	Mexico	330.0
65	Spain	330.0
67	Portugal	304.0
68	Panama	300.0
69	Venezuela	294.0
70	Serbia	*281.0
71	Nicaragua	270.0
72	Peru	269.0
73	Algeria	244.0
74	Morocco	243.0
75	Chad	236.0
76	Thailand	235.0
77	Kenya	221.0
78	Madagascar	216.0
79	Sri Lanka	215.0
80	Macedonia, FYR	205.0
81	Nigeria	200.0
82	Ethiopia	189.0
83	Paraguay	182.0
84	Dominican Republic	181.0
85	Mali	180.0
86	Zambia	169.0
87	Cameroon	163.0
88	Philippines	161.0
89	Indonesia	159.0
90	Tunisia	158.0
91	Botswana	150.0
92	Namibia	141.0
93	Uganda	127.0
94	Senegal	126.0
95	India	120.0
96	Vietnam	109.0
97	Pakistan	105.0
98	Guatemala	79.0
99	Angola	74.0
100	Bangladesh	49.0
101	Mozambique	44.0
102	Haiti	18.0

Note: *estimate
Source: UNESCO Institute for Statistics

II.1.05 Television sets, 2001

Television sets per 1,000 inhabitants, 2001 or most recent available

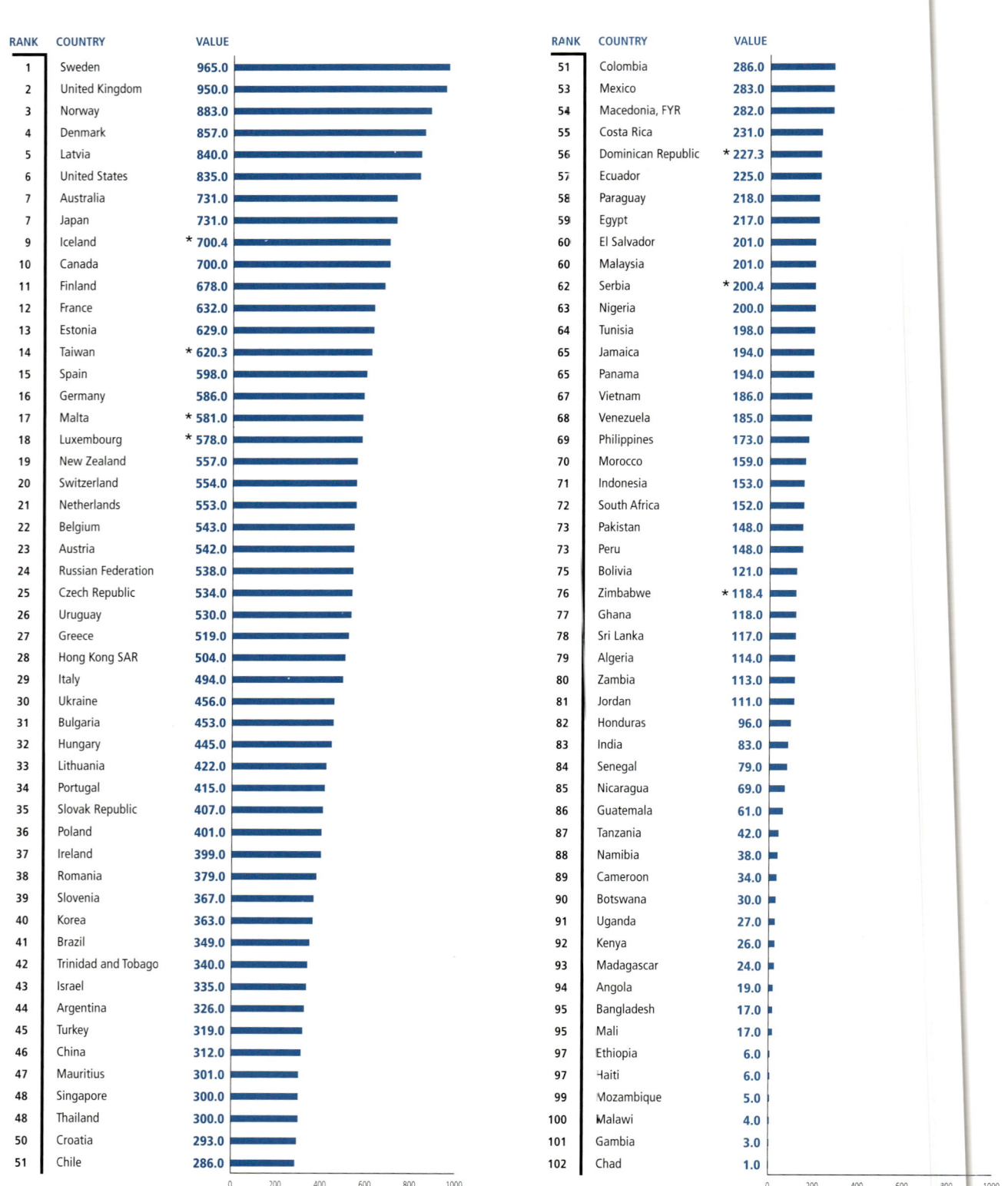

RANK	COUNTRY	VALUE
1	Sweden	965.0
2	United Kingdom	950.0
3	Norway	883.0
4	Denmark	857.0
5	Latvia	840.0
6	United States	835.0
7	Australia	731.0
7	Japan	731.0
9	Iceland	* 700.4
10	Canada	700.0
11	Finland	678.0
12	France	632.0
13	Estonia	629.0
14	Taiwan	* 620.3
15	Spain	598.0
16	Germany	586.0
17	Malta	* 581.0
18	Luxembourg	* 578.0
19	New Zealand	557.0
20	Switzerland	554.0
21	Netherlands	553.0
22	Belgium	543.0
23	Austria	542.0
24	Russian Federation	538.0
25	Czech Republic	534.0
26	Uruguay	530.0
27	Greece	519.0
28	Hong Kong SAR	504.0
29	Italy	494.0
30	Ukraine	456.0
31	Bulgaria	453.0
32	Hungary	445.0
33	Lithuania	422.0
34	Portugal	415.0
35	Slovak Republic	407.0
36	Poland	401.0
37	Ireland	399.0
38	Romania	379.0
39	Slovenia	367.0
40	Korea	363.0
41	Brazil	349.0
42	Trinidad and Tobago	340.0
43	Israel	335.0
44	Argentina	326.0
45	Turkey	319.0
46	China	312.0
47	Mauritius	301.0
48	Singapore	300.0
48	Thailand	300.0
50	Croatia	293.0
51	Chile	286.0

RANK	COUNTRY	VALUE
51	Colombia	286.0
53	Mexico	283.0
54	Macedonia, FYR	282.0
55	Costa Rica	231.0
56	Dominican Republic	* 227.3
57	Ecuador	225.0
58	Paraguay	218.0
59	Egypt	217.0
60	El Salvador	201.0
60	Malaysia	201.0
62	Serbia	* 200.4
63	Nigeria	200.0
64	Tunisia	198.0
65	Jamaica	194.0
65	Panama	194.0
67	Vietnam	186.0
68	Venezuela	185.0
69	Philippines	173.0
70	Morocco	159.0
71	Indonesia	153.0
72	South Africa	152.0
73	Pakistan	148.0
73	Peru	148.0
75	Bolivia	121.0
76	Zimbabwe	* 118.4
77	Ghana	118.0
78	Sri Lanka	117.0
79	Algeria	114.0
80	Zambia	113.0
81	Jordan	111.0
82	Honduras	96.0
83	India	83.0
84	Senegal	79.0
85	Nicaragua	69.0
86	Guatemala	61.0
87	Tanzania	42.0
88	Namibia	38.0
89	Cameroon	34.0
90	Botswana	30.0
91	Uganda	27.0
92	Kenya	26.0
93	Madagascar	24.0
94	Angola	19.0
95	Bangladesh	17.0
95	Mali	17.0
97	Ethiopia	6.0
97	Haiti	6.0
99	Mozambique	5.0
100	Malawi	4.0
101	Gambia	3.0
102	Chad	1.0

Note: *estimate
Source: International Telecommunication Union

II.1.06 Households online, 2002

Households online as percent of households with personal computers, 2002

RANK	COUNTRY	VALUE
1	Norway	94.10
2	Sweden	92.34
3	Netherlands	87.11
4	United States	85.86
5	Denmark	85.13
6	Germany	84.55
7	Iceland	* 82.10
8	Japan	81.89
9	Greece	81.79
10	Switzerland	81.67
11	Finland	81.65
12	Canada	81.26
13	Singapore	* 81.15
14	Hong Kong SAR	80.58
15	Austria	78.28
16	United Kingdom	76.91
17	France	76.82
18	New Zealand	75.92
19	Italy	74.54
20	Luxembourg	74.08
21	Ireland	74.00
22	Portugal	71.67
23	Australia	71.39
24	Korea	71.05
25	Israel	68.68
26	Malaysia	67.84
27	Taiwan	67.77
28	Mexico	66.61
29	Slovenia	65.51
30	Hungary	64.80
31	Estonia	64.42
32	Lithuania	63.81
33	Thailand	63.71
34	Czech Republic	63.66
35	Turkey	62.97
36	Malta	* 62.87
37	Croatia	62.26
38	Poland	61.35
39	Belgium	60.66
40	Trinidad and Tobago	* 60.06
41	Romania	59.35
42	South Africa	58.51
43	Morocco	58.09
44	Costa Rica	* 57.34
45	Panama	* 57.20
46	Mauritius	* 57.11
47	Ukraine	57.04
48	Spain	56.77
49	Botswana	* 56.52
50	Jamaica	* 56.38
51	Chile	56.34

RANK	COUNTRY	VALUE
52	Venezuela	56.33
53	Uruguay	* 56.30
54	Russian Federation	56.04
55	Dominican Republic	* 55.96
56	El Salvador	* 55.67
57	Macedonia, FYR	* 55.28
58	Guatemala	* 55.12
59	Namibia	* 55.08
60	Tunisia	55.00
61	Zimbabwe	* 54.97
62	Peru	54.96
63	Serbia	* 54.75
64	Paraguay	* 54.74
65	Honduras	* 54.51
66	Sri Lanka	* 54.39
67	Angola	* 54.37
68	Slovak Republic	54.36
69	Cameroon	* 54.14
70	Senegal	* 54.07
71	Nicaragua	* 54.05
72	Haiti	* 53.99
73	Kenya	* 53.94
74	Zambia	* 53.91
75	Bangladesh	* 53.90
76	Ghana	* 53.87
77	Madagascar	* 53.84
78	Mali	* 53.83
79	Tanzania	* 53.83
80	Gambia	* 53.83
81	Uganda	* 53.81
82	Chad	* 53.81
83	Mozambique	* 53.79
84	Malawi	* 53.75
85	Bulgaria	53.73
86	Ethiopia	* 53.68
87	Brazil	53.60
88	Algeria	53.57
89	China	53.03
90	Latvia	53.02
91	Colombia	52.89
92	Indonesia	51.68
93	Argentina	50.66
94	Bolivia	50.52
95	Jordan	50.48
96	Vietnam	50.08
97	Philippines	49.32
98	Ecuador	48.33
99	Egypt	46.17
100	Pakistan	42.45
101	India	38.29
102	Nigeria	31.06

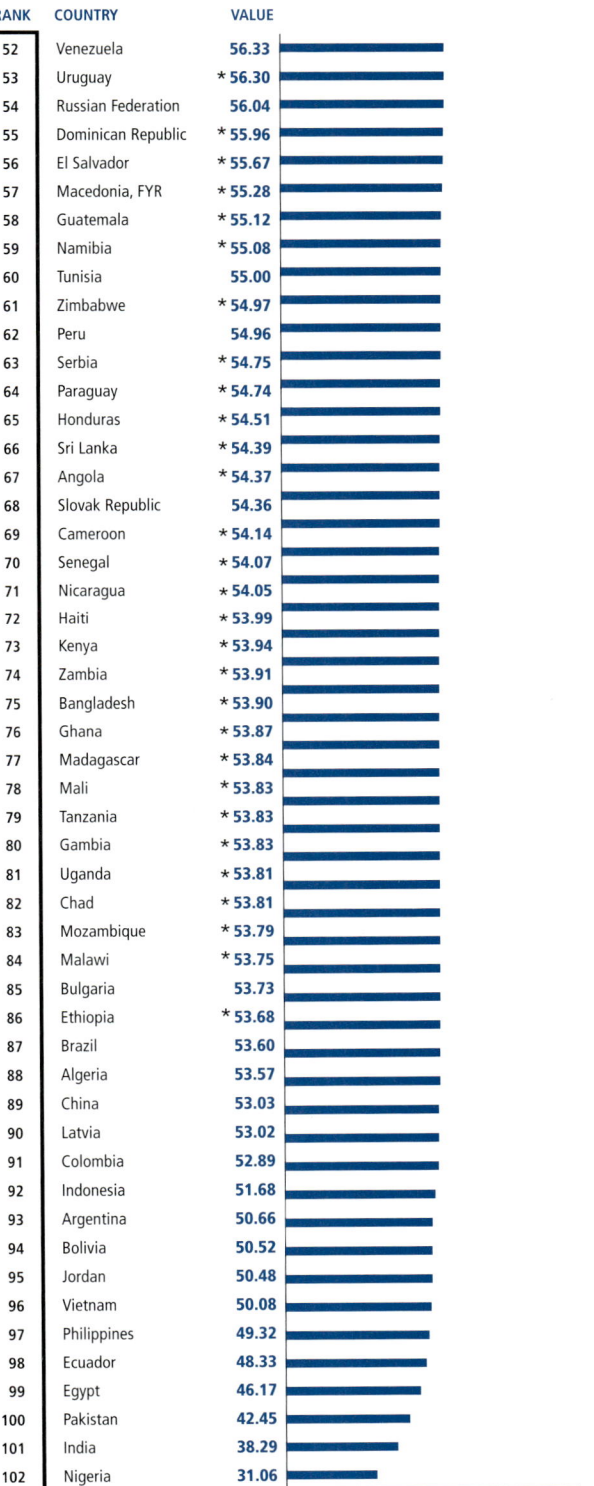

Note: *estimate
Source: Euromonitor, 2003

II.1.07 Quality of math and science education, 2003

Math and science education in your country's schools (1 = lag far behind most other countries, 7 = are among the best in the world)

RANK	COUNTRY	SCORE		SD	RANK	COUNTRY	SCORE		SD
1	Singapore	6.48		0.64	52	Sri Lanka	4.17		1.56
2	Belgium	6.07		0.96	53	Germany	4.11		1.49
3	France	6.07		1.01	54	Turkey	4.05		1.61
4	Finland	5.89		0.85	55	Norway	4.04		1.81
5	Romania	5.89		1.46	56	Uruguay	3.88		1.49
6	Switzerland	5.86		1.05	57	Vietnam	3.86		1.54
7	Austria	5.84		1.05	58	Colombia	3.85		1.51
8	Hungary	5.70		1.05	59	Botswana	3.85		1.41
9	Australia	5.70		1.22	60	Zimbabwe	3.79		1.52
10	Tunisia	5.65		1.07	61	Cameroon	3.73		1.57
11	Slovak Republic	5.64		0.97	62	Indonesia	3.71		1.43
12	Taiwan	5.63		1.07	63	Madagascar	3.70		1.34
13	Canada	5.54		1.26	64	Kenya	3.68		1.48
14	India	5.54		1.22	65	Argentina	3.68		1.20
15	Estonia	5.52		0.87	66	Egypt	3.59		1.60
16	Hong Kong SAR	5.49		1.07	67	Chile	3.56		1.27
17	Czech Republic	5.48		1.26	68	Uganda	3.55		1.46
18	Russian Federation	5.35		1.37	69	Zambia	3.52		1.47
19	Slovenia	5.30		1.16	70	Ghana	3.51		1.67
20	Ireland	5.30		1.44	71	Malawi	3.38		1.63
21	Israel	5.29		0.78	72	Jamaica	3.36		1.50
21	Sweden	5.29		1.18	73	Algeria	3.34		1.48
23	Lithuania	5.23		1.16	74	Tanzania	3.32		1.46
24	Japan	5.19		1.18	75	Brazil	3.32		1.32
25	Netherlands	5.19		1.42	76	Portugal	3.22		1.33
26	Iceland	5.15		0.86	77	Panama	3.20		1.44
27	Ukraine	5.10		1.29	78	Senegal	3.15		1.38
28	Denmark	5.10		1.05	79	Mali	3.14		1.62
29	Bulgaria	4.95		1.47	80	Mexico	3.14		1.44
30	Malta	4.91		1.31	81	El Salvador	3.06		1.37
31	Jordan	4.90		1.20	82	Namibia	3.02		1.38
32	Latvia	4.83		1.14	83	Gambia	2.99		1.77
33	Spain	4.79		1.20	84	Dominican Republic	2.91		1.25
34	Croatia	4.75		1.59	85	Ethiopia	2.83		1.26
35	Korea	4.75		1.49	86	South Africa	2.82		1.40
36	Poland	4.75		1.38	87	Bangladesh	2.80		1.38
37	United States	4.65		1.60	88	Bolivia	2.79		1.19
38	Greece	4.64		1.32	89	Philippines	2.78		1.30
39	Macedonia, FYR	4.63		1.90	90	Nicaragua	2.77		1.19
40	Italy	4.63		1.33	91	Nigeria	2.72		1.52
41	Luxembourg	4.53		1.11	92	Ecuador	2.69		1.27
42	Thailand	4.52		1.17	93	Peru	2.65		1.08
43	United Kingdom	4.48		1.31	94	Venezuela	2.65		1.10
44	New Zealand	4.46		1.36	95	Pakistan	2.65		1.06
45	Serbia	4.42		1.80	96	Mozambique	2.61		1.34
46	China	4.39		1.48	97	Paraguay	2.31		1.06
47	Malaysia	4.36		1.32	98	Haiti	2.28		1.24
48	Costa Rica	4.30		1.23	99	Honduras	2.14		1.08
49	Trinidad and Tobago	4.28		1.59	100	Chad	2.06		1.16
50	Morocco	4.25		1.94	101	Guatemala	2.02		1.05
51	Mauritius	4.23		1.14	102	Angola	1.91		0.97

Source: World Economic Forum, Executive Opinion Survey 2003

II.1.08 Affordability of local fixed line calls, 2001

Cost of a local 3-minute call at peak rate as percent of per capita GDP (*100,000), 2001

RANK	COUNTRY	VALUE		RANK	COUNTRY	VALUE
1	Singapore	0.09		52	Mexico	2.54
2	Israel	0.12		53	Venezuela	2.66
3	Japan	0.22		54	Zimbabwe	2.71
4	Luxembourg	0.24		55	Slovak Republic	2.74
5	Denmark	0.25		56	Russian Federation	* 2.85
6	Iceland	0.29		57	South Africa	2.95
7	United States	* 0.29		58	El Salvador	3.14
8	Korea	0.31		59	Latvia	3.14
9	Switzerland	0.32		60	Jamaica	* 3.15
10	Norway	0.33		61	Dominican Republic	* 3.20
11	New Zealand	* 0.37		62	Lithuania	3.21
12	Germany	0.37		63	Argentina	3.31
13	Sweden	0.40		64	Peru	3.38
14	Netherlands	0.42		65	Thailand	3.56
15	Spain	0.43		66	India	4.14
16	Ireland	0.45		67	Serbia	* 4.44
17	Slovenia	0.47		68	Turkey	4.50
18	Finland	0.47		69	Pakistan	4.57
19	Malaysia	0.48		70	Sri Lanka	4.70
20	Hong Kong SAR	* 0.49		71	Vietnam	4.71
21	Canada	* 0.49		72	Guatemala	4.89
22	Austria	0.51		73	Bulgaria	* 5.19
23	Italy	0.53		74	Romania	5.73
24	Australia	0.54		75	Uruguay	5.85
25	Belgium	0.54		76	Philippines	6.12
26	Macedonia, FYR	0.55		77	China	6.28
27	Trinidad and Tobago	0.58		78	Morocco	6.68
28	France	0.59		79	Ukraine	7.06
29	Botswana	0.64		80	Honduras	7.13
30	Greece	0.64		81	Paraguay	7.31
31	Taiwan	* 0.64		82	Haiti	7.50
32	United Kingdom	0.65		83	Bangladesh	9.17
33	Costa Rica	0.74		84	Nicaragua	9.48
34	Mauritius	0.79		85	Angola	9.56
35	Egypt	0.82		86	Bolivia	9.70
36	Portugal	0.90		87	Ghana	10.00
37	Tunisia	0.91		88	Nigeria	10.11
38	Malta	1.10		89	Cameroon	10.28
39	Algeria	1.16		90	Kenya	10.85
40	Hungary	1.39		91	Malawi	12.24
41	Panama	1.55		92	Zambia	17.49
42	Brazil	1.56		93	Gambia	19.89
43	Czech Republic	1.62		94	Senegal	21.32
44	Poland	1.63		95	Ethiopia	22.03
45	Croatia	1.77		96	Mali	27.19
46	Colombia	1.83		97	Tanzania	27.43
47	Namibia	1.88		98	Ecuador	32.07
48	Estonia	2.08		99	Madagascar	33.94
49	Jordan	2.24		100	Mozambique	33.95
50	Chile	2.42		101	Chad	43.34
51	Indonesia	2.51		102	Uganda	54.97

Note: *estimate
Source: World Bank, World Development Indicators 2003 using International Telecommunication Union data

II.1.09 Affordability of Internet telephone access, 2001

Cost per 30 off-peak hours as percent of per capita GDP, 2001

RANK	COUNTRY	VALUE		RANK	COUNTRY	VALUE
1	Singapore	0.00		52	Greece	0.04
2	Bulgaria	0.00		53	Iceland	0.05
3	Spain	* 0.00		54	Jamaica	* 0.05
4	Israel	0.00		55	Pakistan	0.05
5	Macedonia, FYR	0.00		56	Brazil	* 0.05
6	Costa Rica	* 0.00		57	Dominican Republic	* 0.05
7	Slovenia	0.00		58	Norway	0.05
8	Malta	* 0.00		59	Taiwan	* 0.05
9	Korea	* 0.00		60	Germany	* 0.05
10	Botswana	0.00		61	Ireland	0.05
11	Ukraine	0.00		62	France	* 0.05
12	Trinidad and Tobago	0.01		63	Luxembourg	0.05
13	Malaysia	0.01		64	Hong Kong SAR	* 0.05
14	Russian Federation	0.01		65	Canada	* 0.05
15	Sri Lanka	0.01		66	Vietnam	0.06
16	Croatia	0.01		67	United Kingdom	0.06
17	United States	0.01		68	Honduras	0.06
18	Algeria	0.01		69	Netherlands	0.06
19	Tunisia	0.01		70	Morocco	0.06
20	Mauritius	0.01		71	Denmark	* 0.06
21	Panama	* 0.01		72	Austria	0.07
22	Chile	* 0.01		73	Angola	0.07
23	Venezuela	* 0.01		74	Sweden	0.08
24	Lithuania	0.01		75	Switzerland	0.08
25	Egypt	0.01		76	Haiti	* 0.08
26	Slovak Republic	0.01		77	Italy	0.09
27	Australia	0.01		78	Japan	0.09
28	Estonia	0.01		79	Zambia	0.09
29	South Africa	0.01		80	Cameroon	0.10
30	China	0.01		81	Bangladesh	0.10
31	Colombia	0.02		82	Senegal	0.10
32	Namibia	* 0.02		83	Portugal	0.11
33	Ecuador	* 0.02		84	Nicaragua	0.11
34	Peru	* 0.02		85	Belgium	0.11
35	Guatemala	* 0.02		86	Kenya	0.12
36	Argentina	0.02		87	Ghana	0.13
37	New Zealand	* 0.02		88	Mexico	0.14
38	Romania	0.02		89	Malawi	0.15
39	Zimbabwe	0.02		90	Turkey	0.15
40	Latvia	0.02		91	Nigeria	0.16
41	Jordan	0.02		92	Madagascar	0.17
42	Indonesia	0.03		93	Czech Republic	0.17
43	Philippines	* 0.03		94	Hungary	0.21
44	El Salvador	0.03		95	Mozambique	0.26
45	Bolivia	* 0.03		96	Ethiopia	0.26
46	Uruguay	* 0.03		97	Mali	0.28
47	Serbia	* 0.03		98	Tanzania	0.31
48	Paraguay	* 0.03		99	Uganda	0.35
49	India	0.04		100	Poland	0.37
50	Thailand	0.04		101	Chad	0.47
51	Finland	0.04		102	Gambia	1.07

Note: *estimate
Source: World Bank, World Development Indicators 2003 using International Telecommunication Union data

II.1.10 Affordability of Internet service provider fees, 2001

Cost per 30 off-peak hours as percent of per capita GDP, 2001

RANK	COUNTRY	VALUE
1	Sweden	0.01
2	Luxembourg	0.01
3	United States	0.02
4	Trinidad and Tobago	0.02
5	Norway	0.03
6	Iceland	0.03
7	Switzerland	* 0.04
8	Ireland	* 0.04
9	Netherlands	* 0.05
10	Canada	0.05
11	Japan	0.05
12	Germany	0.05
13	United Kingdom	0.05
14	Austria	* 0.06
15	Finland	* 0.06
16	Belgium	* 0.06
17	Australia	0.06
18	Denmark	0.06
19	Israel	0.07
20	New Zealand	0.07
21	Singapore	* 0.07
22	Italy	* 0.07
23	Hong Kong SAR	0.08
24	Korea	0.08
25	France	0.08
26	Spain	0.10
27	Greece	0.12
28	Czech Republic	* 0.12
29	Malaysia	0.13
30	Portugal	* 0.14
31	Mexico	0.17
32	Taiwan	* 0.18
33	Malta	* 0.19
34	Slovak Republic	0.19
35	Hungary	0.20
36	Poland	* 0.26
37	Slovenia	0.28
38	Bulgaria	0.37
39	Costa Rica	0.40
40	Estonia	* 0.42
41	Croatia	0.45
42	Thailand	0.46
43	Botswana	0.47
44	Chile	* 0.52
45	Panama	* 0.54
46	Mauritius	0.61
47	Russian Federation	0.61
48	Macedonia, FYR	0.67
49	China	0.68
50	Dominican Republic	0.71
51	Venezuela	0.71

RANK	COUNTRY	VALUE
52	Egypt	0.71
53	Sri Lanka	0.76
54	Romania	0.78
55	Latvia	0.81
56	Ecuador	* 0.84
57	Ukraine	0.85
58	Peru	* 0.94
59	Brazil	* 0.99
60	Turkey	* 1.09
61	Tunisia	1.13
62	El Salvador	1.16
63	Uruguay	* 1.22
64	South Africa	1.25
65	Lithuania	1.31
66	Jordan	1.34
67	Bolivia	* 1.41
68	Guatemala	* 1.50
69	Colombia	* 1.50
70	Honduras	1.53
71	Algeria	1.54
72	Indonesia	1.57
73	Jamaica	1.65
74	Namibia	* 1.70
75	India	2.07
76	Serbia	* 2.17
77	Paraguay	* 2.18
78	Morocco	2.20
79	Angola	2.39
80	Philippines	2.44
81	Senegal	2.72
82	Argentina	2.87
83	Pakistan	2.88
84	Zimbabwe	3.09
85	Vietnam	4.64
86	Bangladesh	5.28
87	Zambia	5.54
88	Nicaragua	6.18
89	Haiti	* 6.73
90	Gambia	7.15
91	Ghana	12.00
92	Nigeria	12.41
93	Uganda	12.69
94	Cameroon	13.24
95	Mozambique	14.55
96	Kenya	17.78
97	Chad	21.99
98	Madagascar	25.08
99	Tanzania	27.04
100	Mali	27.28
101	Malawi	37.95
102	Ethiopia	103.56

Note: *estimate
Source: World Bank, World Development Indicators 2003 using International Telecommunication Union data

Business Readiness

II.2.01 Ease of obtaining telephone lines, 2003

New telephone lines for your business are (1 = scarce and difficult to obtain, 7 = widely available and highly reliable)

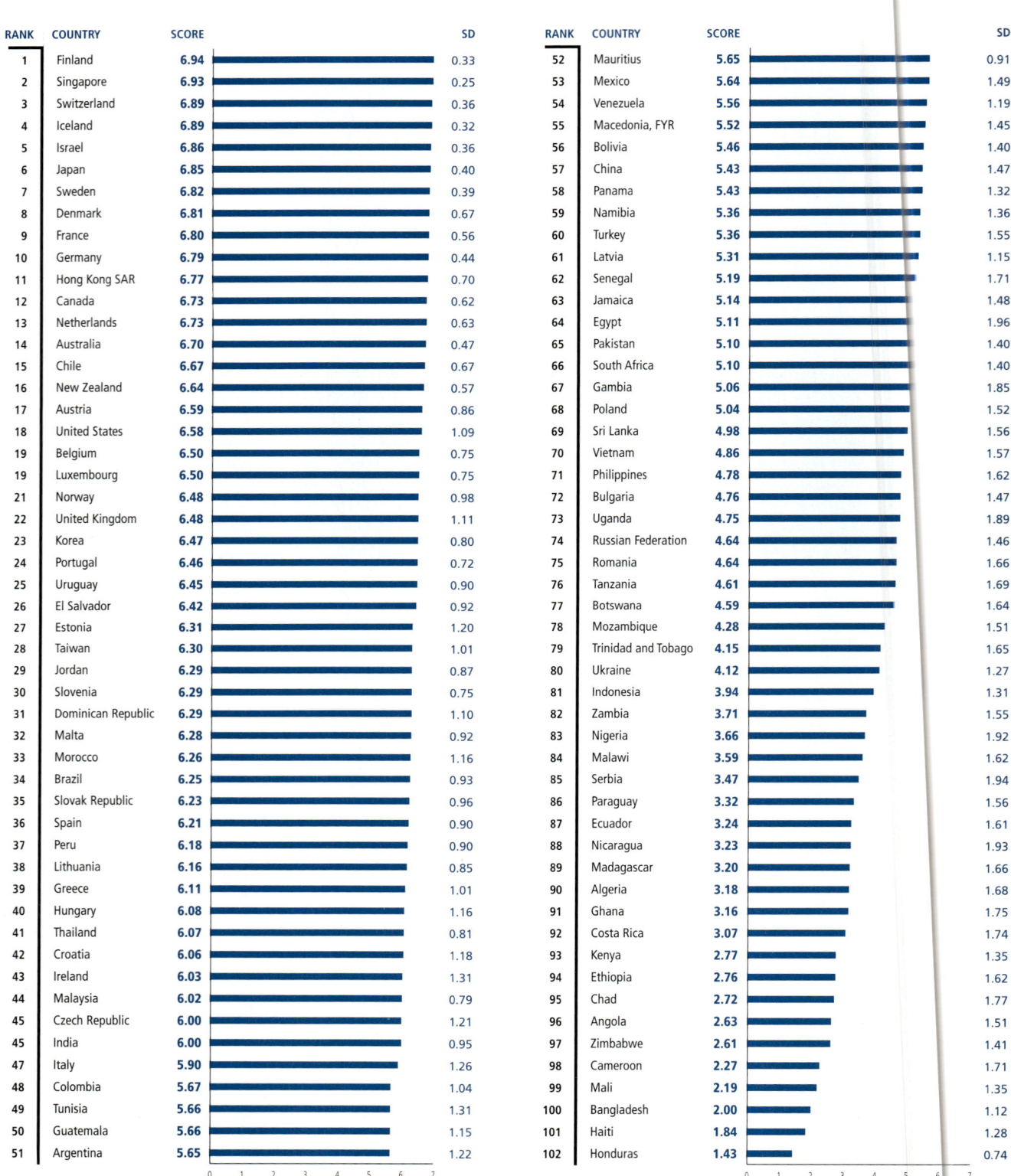

RANK	COUNTRY	SCORE	SD	RANK	COUNTRY	SCORE	SD
1	Finland	6.94	0.33	52	Mauritius	5.65	0.91
2	Singapore	6.93	0.25	53	Mexico	5.64	1.49
3	Switzerland	6.89	0.36	54	Venezuela	5.56	1.19
4	Iceland	6.89	0.32	55	Macedonia, FYR	5.52	1.45
5	Israel	6.86	0.36	56	Bolivia	5.46	1.40
6	Japan	6.85	0.40	57	China	5.43	1.47
7	Sweden	6.82	0.39	58	Panama	5.43	1.32
8	Denmark	6.81	0.67	59	Namibia	5.36	1.36
9	France	6.80	0.56	60	Turkey	5.36	1.55
10	Germany	6.79	0.44	61	Latvia	5.31	1.15
11	Hong Kong SAR	6.77	0.70	62	Senegal	5.19	1.71
12	Canada	6.73	0.62	63	Jamaica	5.14	1.48
13	Netherlands	6.73	0.63	64	Egypt	5.11	1.96
14	Australia	6.70	0.47	65	Pakistan	5.10	1.40
15	Chile	6.67	0.67	66	South Africa	5.10	1.40
16	New Zealand	6.64	0.57	67	Gambia	5.06	1.85
17	Austria	6.59	0.86	68	Poland	5.04	1.52
18	United States	6.58	1.09	69	Sri Lanka	4.98	1.56
19	Belgium	6.50	0.75	70	Vietnam	4.86	1.57
19	Luxembourg	6.50	0.75	71	Philippines	4.78	1.62
21	Norway	6.48	0.98	72	Bulgaria	4.76	1.47
22	United Kingdom	6.48	1.11	73	Uganda	4.75	1.89
23	Korea	6.47	0.80	74	Russian Federation	4.64	1.46
24	Portugal	6.46	0.72	75	Romania	4.64	1.66
25	Uruguay	6.45	0.90	76	Tanzania	4.61	1.69
26	El Salvador	6.42	0.92	77	Botswana	4.59	1.64
27	Estonia	6.31	1.20	78	Mozambique	4.28	1.51
28	Taiwan	6.30	1.01	79	Trinidad and Tobago	4.15	1.65
29	Jordan	6.29	0.87	80	Ukraine	4.12	1.27
30	Slovenia	6.29	0.75	81	Indonesia	3.94	1.31
31	Dominican Republic	6.29	1.10	82	Zambia	3.71	1.55
32	Malta	6.28	0.92	83	Nigeria	3.66	1.92
33	Morocco	6.26	1.16	84	Malawi	3.59	1.62
34	Brazil	6.25	0.93	85	Serbia	3.47	1.94
35	Slovak Republic	6.23	0.96	86	Paraguay	3.32	1.56
36	Spain	6.21	0.90	87	Ecuador	3.24	1.61
37	Peru	6.18	0.90	88	Nicaragua	3.23	1.93
38	Lithuania	6.16	0.85	89	Madagascar	3.20	1.66
39	Greece	6.11	1.01	90	Algeria	3.18	1.68
40	Hungary	6.08	1.16	91	Ghana	3.16	1.75
41	Thailand	6.07	0.81	92	Costa Rica	3.07	1.74
42	Croatia	6.06	1.18	93	Kenya	2.77	1.35
43	Ireland	6.03	1.31	94	Ethiopia	2.76	1.62
44	Malaysia	6.02	0.79	95	Chad	2.72	1.77
45	Czech Republic	6.00	1.21	96	Angola	2.63	1.51
45	India	6.00	0.95	97	Zimbabwe	2.61	1.41
47	Italy	5.90	1.26	98	Cameroon	2.27	1.71
48	Colombia	5.67	1.04	99	Mali	2.19	1.35
49	Tunisia	5.66	1.31	100	Bangladesh	2.00	1.12
50	Guatemala	5.66	1.15	101	Haiti	1.84	1.28
51	Argentina	5.65	1.22	102	Honduras	1.43	0.74

Source: World Economic Forum, Executive Opinion Survey 2003

II.2.02 Cost of business phone subscription, 2002

Cost of business telephone monthly subscription as percent of per capita GDP, 2002

RANK	COUNTRY	VALUE
1	Korea	0.03
2	Singapore	0.03
3	Luxembourg	0.04
4	Denmark	0.04
5	Norway	0.04
6	Finland	0.04
7	Switzerland	0.04
8	Germany	0.04
9	Slovenia	0.05
10	Ireland	0.05
11	Israel	0.05
12	Iceland	0.06
13	Netherlands	0.06
14	Spain	0.06
15	France	0.06
16	Greece	0.06
17	Sweden	0.06
18	Austria	0.06
19	Belgium	0.06
20	Japan	0.07
21	Taiwan	0.07
22	Hong Kong SAR	0.07
23	Italy	0.08
24	Australia	0.08
25	Tunisia	0.08
26	United Kingdom	0.09
27	Portugal	0.09
28	Czech Republic	0.09
29	Mauritius	0.09
30	Malta	0.10
31	Botswana	0.10
32	Canada	0.11
33	Thailand	0.11
34	Slovak Republic	0.12
35	Ghana	0.12
36	United States	0.12
37	Malaysia	0.13
38	Egypt	0.13
39	Turkey	0.15
40	Algeria	0.15
41	Costa Rica	0.15
42	Estonia	0.16
43	New Zealand	0.16
44	Poland	0.17
45	Croatia	0.19
46	Lithuania	0.20
47	Hungary	0.21
48	Colombia	0.22
49	Chile	0.23
50	Bulgaria	0.26
51	Latvia	0.27

RANK	COUNTRY	VALUE
52	Mexico	0.34
53	Guatemala	0.34
54	Namibia	0.35
55	Romania	0.38
56	Uruguay	0.38
57	Panama	0.39
58	Brazil	0.39
59	Zimbabwe	0.39
60	Paraguay	0.40
61	Indonesia	0.40
62	Macedonia, FYR	0.40
63	Trinidad and Tobago	0.40
64	South Africa	0.41
65	Cameroon	0.41
66	Russian Federation	0.42
67	Vietnam	0.43
68	Dominican Republic	0.43
69	Serbia	0.44
70	China	0.44
71	Sri Lanka	0.47
72	Jamaica	0.54
73	El Salvador	0.57
74	Venezuela	0.59
75	Jordan	0.63
76	Ecuador	0.64
77	Honduras	0.66
78	Nigeria	0.68
79	Nicaragua	0.73
80	Morocco	0.80
81	Zambia	0.81
82	Peru	0.82
83	Bangladesh	0.82
84	Senegal	0.83
85	Malawi	0.85
86	Haiti	0.86
87	Gambia	0.89
88	Pakistan	0.90
89	Bolivia	0.92
90	Argentina	1.00
91	Ukraine	1.01
92	Mali	1.02
93	Angola	1.02
94	India	1.10
95	Kenya	1.22
96	Tanzania	1.37
97	Chad	2.09
98	Ethiopia	2.21
99	Madagascar	2.39
100	Uganda	2.41
101	Philippines	2.54
102	Mozambique	4.06

Source: International Telecommunication Union, World Telecommunication Indicators Database, accessed July 2003

II.2.03 Extent of staff training, 2003

The general approach of companies in your country to human resources is (1 = to invest little in training and employee development, 7 = to invest heavily to attract, train, and retain employees)

RANK	COUNTRY	SCORE		SD	RANK	COUNTRY	SCORE		SD
1	Denmark	6.00		0.73	52	Colombia	3.70		1.00
2	Switzerland	5.97		0.90	53	Namibia	3.66		1.10
3	Sweden	5.89		0.92	54	Poland	3.64		1.18
4	Germany	5.86		0.91	55	China	3.64		1.17
5	United States	5.86		1.14	56	Portugal	3.61		0.98
6	Japan	5.83		0.97	57	Argentina	3.59		1.04
7	Finland	5.78		0.76	58	Turkey	3.59		1.18
8	Singapore	5.67		0.99	59	Panama	3.57		1.22
9	Netherlands	5.51		0.97	60	Sri Lanka	3.51		1.39
10	Belgium	5.46		1.00	61	Botswana	3.50		1.48
11	United Kingdom	5.37		1.14	62	Jordan	3.49		1.44
12	Australia	5.30		0.98	63	Kenya	3.46		1.38
13	Luxembourg	5.29		1.07	64	Vietnam	3.46		1.44
14	Iceland	5.26		1.13	65	Hungary	3.45		1.23
15	France	5.23		1.04	66	Egypt	3.45		1.53
16	Austria	5.22		1.13	67	Lithuania	3.38		1.38
17	Canada	5.15		1.13	68	Nigeria	3.38		1.59
18	Malaysia	5.11		1.20	69	Malawi	3.31		1.45
19	Taiwan	5.07		1.03	70	Macedonia, FYR	3.29		1.87
20	New Zealand	5.01		1.14	71	Venezuela	3.26		1.31
21	Korea	4.93		1.16	72	Ghana	3.24		1.55
22	Norway	4.93		1.04	73	Tanzania	3.14		1.43
23	Ireland	4.93		1.46	74	Croatia	3.10		1.43
24	Israel	4.55		1.23	75	Guatemala	3.07		1.22
25	South Africa	4.53		1.20	76	Pakistan	2.98		1.10
26	Tunisia	4.48		1.52	77	Uganda	2.97		1.71
27	Brazil	4.46		1.16	78	Peru	2.96		1.20
28	Hong Kong SAR	4.43		1.27	79	Russian Federation	2.95		1.36
29	Slovenia	4.42		1.16	80	Senegal	2.92		1.32
30	Costa Rica	4.37		1.38	81	Zambia	2.91		1.27
31	Mauritius	4.32		1.05	82	Gambia	2.88		1.78
32	Spain	4.32		1.29	83	Mozambique	2.86		1.49
33	Italy	4.28		1.21	84	Uruguay	2.86		1.16
34	Thailand	4.27		1.32	85	Cameroon	2.81		1.45
35	Zimbabwe	4.24		1.28	86	Madagascar	2.77		1.30
36	Chile	4.21		1.18	87	Algeria	2.73		1.45
37	Latvia	4.18		1.28	88	Serbia	2.73		1.33
38	Malta	4.17		1.30	89	Romania	2.73		1.55
39	Slovak Republic	4.07		1.25	90	Ecuador	2.72		1.00
40	Estonia	4.02		1.40	91	Bulgaria	2.60		1.19
41	Philippines	3.91		1.15	92	Honduras	2.60		1.20
42	Mexico	3.87		1.33	93	Angola	2.52		1.36
43	Dominican Republic	3.85		1.37	94	Nicaragua	2.50		1.11
44	Trinidad and Tobago	3.82		1.16	95	Ukraine	2.49		1.21
45	India	3.80		1.26	96	Paraguay	2.42		0.88
46	Greece	3.80		1.20	97	Chad	2.37		1.60
47	Indonesia	3.74		1.48	98	Bangladesh	2.30		0.97
48	Jamaica	3.74		1.13	99	Haiti	2.28		1.17
49	El Salvador	3.73		1.32	100	Bolivia	2.25		0.91
50	Czech Republic	3.72		1.29	101	Ethiopia	2.15		1.07
51	Morocco	3.72		1.82	102	Mali	2.11		1.41

Source: World Economic Forum, Executive Opinion Survey 2003

II.2.04 Quality of business schools, 2003

Management or business schools in your country are (1 = limited or of poor quality, 7 = the best in the world)

RANK	COUNTRY	SCORE		SD	RANK	COUNTRY	SCORE		SD
1	United States	6.55		0.92	52	Sri Lanka	4.14		1.33
2	France	6.25		0.97	53	Japan	4.14		1.41
3	Canada	6.23		0.56	54	Senegal	4.12		1.37
4	Switzerland	6.03		0.76	55	Turkey	4.11		1.37
5	United Kingdom	5.94		0.75	56	Pakistan	4.10		1.15
6	Finland	5.81		0.62	57	Greece	4.09		1.28
7	Sweden	5.75		0.59	58	Malta	4.06		1.33
8	India	5.75		1.03	59	Ghana	4.01		1.52
9	Singapore	5.67		0.75	60	Jordan	3.94		1.52
10	Israel	5.65		0.75	61	Russian Federation	3.93		1.55
11	Spain	5.64		0.77	62	Romania	3.87		1.64
12	Norway	5.59		0.80	63	Dominican Republic	3.86		1.35
13	Australia	5.55		1.05	64	El Salvador	3.85		1.37
14	Netherlands	5.52		1.01	65	Ukraine	3.76		1.33
15	Belgium	5.49		0.89	66	Guatemala	3.66		1.21
16	Ireland	5.45		1.26	67	Panama	3.65		1.20
17	Chile	5.44		0.87	68	Malawi	3.65		1.50
18	South Africa	5.37		1.04	69	Mauritius	3.65		1.17
19	Germany	5.33		0.71	70	Uganda	3.60		1.34
20	New Zealand	5.30		0.99	71	Indonesia	3.58		1.58
21	Iceland	5.30		0.99	72	China	3.56		1.25
22	Austria	5.24		1.18	73	Kenya	3.56		1.34
23	Denmark	5.19		0.83	74	Madagascar	3.54		1.32
24	Tunisia	5.14		1.00	75	Egypt	3.52		1.46
25	Argentina	5.13		0.90	76	Cameroon	3.52		1.43
26	Costa Rica	5.06		0.92	77	Nigeria	3.51		1.43
27	Italy	5.00		1.17	78	Nicaragua	3.38		1.33
28	Estonia	4.92		0.96	79	Croatia	3.35		1.40
29	Taiwan	4.91		1.00	80	Zambia	3.34		1.52
30	Hong Kong SAR	4.83		1.32	81	Tanzania	3.34		1.54
31	Slovenia	4.83		1.06	82	Paraguay	3.32		1.20
32	Philippines	4.80		1.09	83	Botswana	3.27		1.45
33	Latvia	4.74		1.08	84	Serbia	3.24		1.19
34	Brazil	4.73		1.10	85	Vietnam	3.21		1.26
35	Mexico	4.59		1.10	86	Algeria	3.20		1.22
36	Portugal	4.56		0.87	87	Bulgaria	3.19		1.21
36	Thailand	4.56		1.34	88	Gambia	3.13		1.56
38	Jamaica	4.55		1.29	89	Zimbabwe	3.09		1.21
39	Uruguay	4.49		0.99	90	Ecuador	3.08		1.10
40	Hungary	4.49		1.11	91	Macedonia, FYR	3.04		1.61
41	Colombia	4.48		1.00	92	Namibia	3.02		1.44
42	Morocco	4.38		1.92	93	Bangladesh	3.00		1.33
43	Trinidad and Tobago	4.31		1.22	93	Luxembourg	3.00		1.56
44	Czech Republic	4.28		1.26	95	Bolivia	2.90		1.10
45	Korea	4.25		1.09	96	Mali	2.84		1.30
46	Malaysia	4.23		1.22	97	Ethiopia	2.80		1.31
47	Peru	4.22		1.13	98	Honduras	2.79		1.23
48	Slovak Republic	4.21		1.15	99	Mozambique	2.63		1.18
49	Lithuania	4.17		1.15	100	Haiti	2.52		0.82
50	Venezuela	4.15		1.48	101	Chad	1.98		1.18
51	Poland	4.14		1.17	102	Angola	1.94		0.89

Source: World Economic Forum, Executive Opinion Survey 2003

II.2.05 Scientists and engineers in R&D, 2000

Scientists and engineers in R&D per 1,000 inhabitants, 2000 or most recent

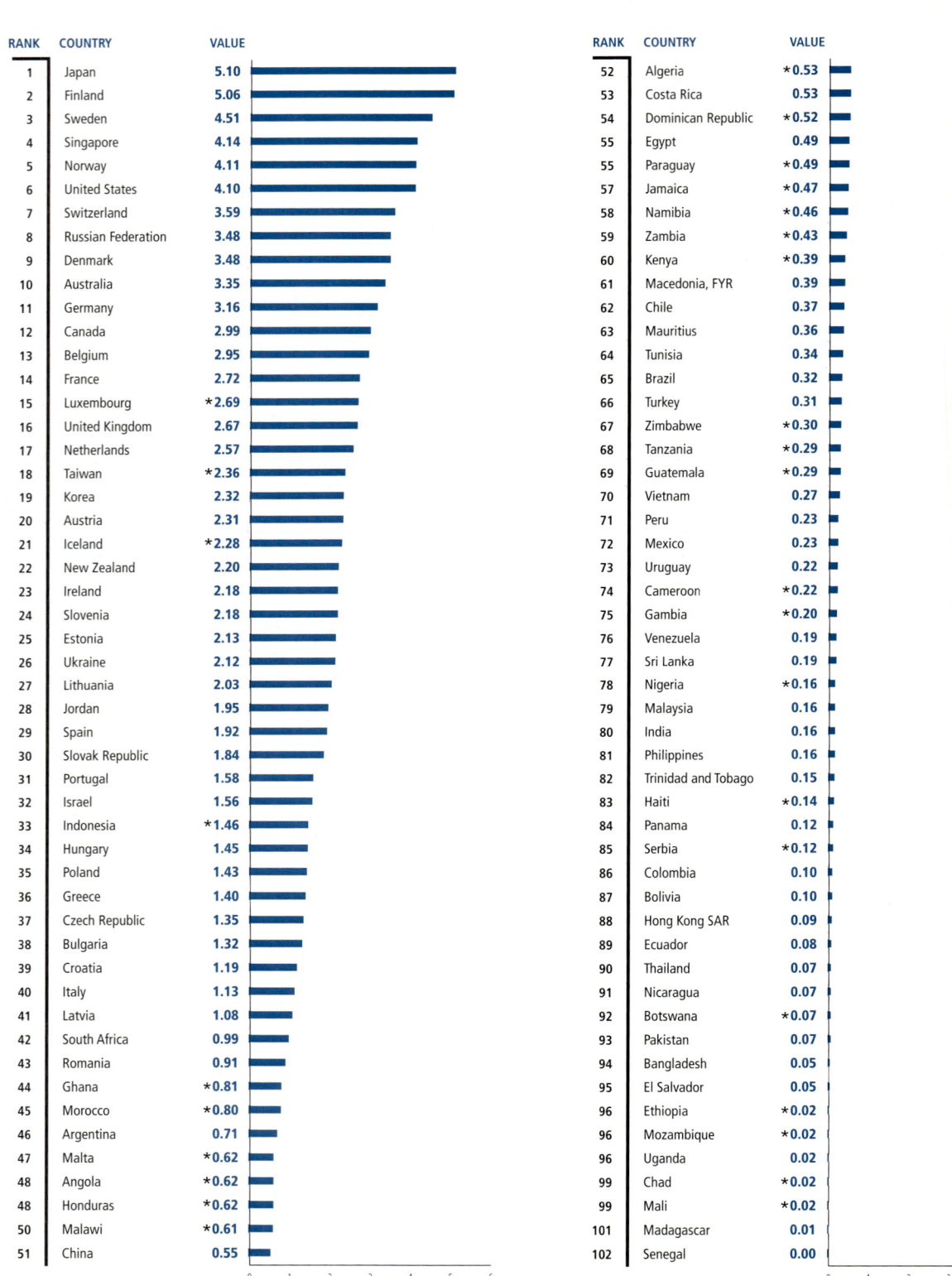

RANK	COUNTRY	VALUE
1	Japan	5.10
2	Finland	5.06
3	Sweden	4.51
4	Singapore	4.14
5	Norway	4.11
6	United States	4.10
7	Switzerland	3.59
8	Russian Federation	3.48
9	Denmark	3.48
10	Australia	3.35
11	Germany	3.16
12	Canada	2.99
13	Belgium	2.95
14	France	2.72
15	Luxembourg	*2.69
16	United Kingdom	2.67
17	Netherlands	2.57
18	Taiwan	*2.36
19	Korea	2.32
20	Austria	2.31
21	Iceland	*2.28
22	New Zealand	2.20
23	Ireland	2.18
24	Slovenia	2.18
25	Estonia	2.13
26	Ukraine	2.12
27	Lithuania	2.03
28	Jordan	1.95
29	Spain	1.92
30	Slovak Republic	1.84
31	Portugal	1.58
32	Israel	1.56
33	Indonesia	*1.46
34	Hungary	1.45
35	Poland	1.43
36	Greece	1.40
37	Czech Republic	1.35
38	Bulgaria	1.32
39	Croatia	1.19
40	Italy	1.13
41	Latvia	1.08
42	South Africa	0.99
43	Romania	0.91
44	Ghana	*0.81
45	Morocco	*0.80
46	Argentina	0.71
47	Malta	*0.62
48	Angola	*0.62
48	Honduras	*0.62
50	Malawi	*0.61
51	China	0.55

RANK	COUNTRY	VALUE
52	Algeria	*0.53
53	Costa Rica	0.53
54	Dominican Republic	*0.52
55	Egypt	0.49
55	Paraguay	*0.49
57	Jamaica	*0.47
58	Namibia	*0.46
59	Zambia	*0.43
60	Kenya	*0.39
61	Macedonia, FYR	0.39
62	Chile	0.37
63	Mauritius	0.36
64	Tunisia	0.34
65	Brazil	0.32
66	Turkey	0.31
67	Zimbabwe	*0.30
68	Tanzania	*0.29
69	Guatemala	*0.29
70	Vietnam	0.27
71	Peru	0.23
72	Mexico	0.23
73	Uruguay	0.22
74	Cameroon	*0.22
75	Gambia	*0.20
76	Venezuela	0.19
77	Sri Lanka	0.19
78	Nigeria	*0.16
79	Malaysia	0.16
80	India	0.16
81	Philippines	0.16
82	Trinidad and Tobago	0.15
83	Haiti	*0.14
84	Panama	0.12
85	Serbia	*0.12
86	Colombia	0.10
87	Bolivia	0.10
88	Hong Kong SAR	0.09
89	Ecuador	0.08
90	Thailand	0.07
91	Nicaragua	0.07
92	Botswana	*0.07
93	Pakistan	0.07
94	Bangladesh	0.05
95	El Salvador	0.05
96	Ethiopia	*0.02
96	Mozambique	*0.02
96	Uganda	0.02
99	Chad	*0.02
99	Mali	*0.02
101	Madagascar	0.01
102	Senegal	0.00

Note: *estimate
Source: UNESCO Institute for Statistics

Government Readiness

II.3.01 Government prioritization of ICT, 2003

Information and communication technologies (ICT) are an overall priority for the government (1 = strongly disagree, 7 = strongly agree)

RANK	COUNTRY	SCORE		SD
1	Singapore	6.37		0.79
2	Malaysia	6.33		0.69
3	Finland	5.94		0.97
4	Mauritius	5.84		1.25
5	Tunisia	5.80		1.10
6	Malta	5.65		1.18
7	Taiwan	5.60		0.93
8	Korea	5.60		1.24
9	Japan	5.60		1.16
10	Denmark	5.54		0.98
11	Jordan	5.44		1.34
12	India	5.37		1.32
13	Gambia	5.35		1.83
14	Sweden	5.32		1.19
15	United States	5.32		1.28
16	Thailand	5.29		1.32
17	Ghana	5.28		1.46
18	Estonia	5.22		1.31
19	Canada	5.16		1.41
20	Iceland	5.11		1.28
21	Mali	5.11		1.56
22	Hong Kong SAR	5.05		1.26
23	Luxembourg	5.00		1.32
23	Senegal	5.00		1.72
25	United Kingdom	4.97		1.22
26	France	4.91		1.15
27	Jamaica	4.89		1.60
28	Tanzania	4.88		1.38
29	Pakistan	4.88		1.36
30	Australia	4.85		1.18
31	Ireland	4.83		1.58
32	China	4.82		1.63
33	Chile	4.81		1.28
34	Vietnam	4.79		1.57
35	South Africa	4.79		1.42
36	Botswana	4.76		1.40
37	Spain	4.75		1.35
38	Germany	4.70		1.31
39	Switzerland	4.62		1.25
39	Uganda	4.62		1.81
41	Mexico	4.62		1.44
42	Egypt	4.62		1.54
43	Bangladesh	4.61		1.74
44	Madagascar	4.61		1.67
45	Serbia	4.59		1.65
46	Cameroon	4.49		2.08
47	Sri Lanka	4.48		1.45
48	Norway	4.48		1.12
49	Croatia	4.43		1.66
50	Hungary	4.43		1.49
51	New Zealand	4.41		1.46

RANK	COUNTRY	SCORE		SD
52	Latvia	4.40		1.35
53	Portugal	4.40		1.25
54	Lithuania	4.38		1.61
55	Mozambique	4.36		1.81
56	Austria	4.34		1.53
57	Colombia	4.30		1.50
58	Israel	4.29		1.61
58	Slovenia	4.29		1.28
60	Belgium	4.27		1.56
61	Philippines	4.26		1.85
62	Czech Republic	4.25		1.54
63	Morocco	4.19		1.85
64	Netherlands	4.18		1.51
65	Italy	4.17		1.17
66	Brazil	4.15		1.35
67	Nigeria	4.10		1.83
68	Greece	4.08		1.31
69	Ukraine	4.06		1.68
70	Namibia	4.05		1.58
71	Uruguay	3.98		1.53
72	El Salvador	3.98		1.45
73	Romania	3.95		1.69
74	Dominican Republic	3.94		1.71
75	Slovak Republic	3.93		1.52
76	Trinidad and Tobago	3.85		1.48
77	Costa Rica	3.84		1.54
78	Russian Federation	3.78		1.68
79	Zambia	3.78		1.62
80	Algeria	3.77		1.74
81	Kenya	3.74		1.67
82	Peru	3.72		1.51
83	Indonesia	3.70		1.29
84	Poland	3.61		1.24
85	Macedonia, FYR	3.52		2.15
86	Ethiopia	3.52		1.97
87	Nicaragua	3.51		1.71
88	Bulgaria	3.49		1.67
89	Malawi	3.48		1.60
90	Turkey	3.37		1.34
91	Panama	3.34		1.52
92	Honduras	3.01		1.52
93	Venezuela	3.00		1.58
94	Bolivia	2.96		1.46
95	Ecuador	2.95		1.54
96	Chad	2.85		2.07
97	Angola	2.81		1.47
98	Argentina	2.81		1.43
99	Zimbabwe	2.52		1.33
100	Haiti	2.48		1.29
101	Paraguay	2.28		1.28
102	Guatemala	2.25		1.35

Source: World Economic Forum, Executive Opinion Survey 2003

II.3.02 Government procurement of ICT, 2003

Government purchase decisions for the procurement of advanced technology products are (1 = based solely on price, 7 = based on technology and encourage innovation)

RANK	COUNTRY	SCORE		SD	RANK	COUNTRY	SCORE		SD
1	Singapore	5.38		1.24	52	Algeria	3.62		1.51
2	Malaysia	5.20		1.04	53	Brazil	3.62		1.21
3	Taiwan	4.98		0.96	54	Malta	3.60		1.37
4	Finland	4.97		0.90	55	Chile	3.60		1.35
5	Tunisia	4.93		1.48	56	Belgium	3.60		1.33
6	France	4.82		1.13	57	El Salvador	3.49		1.42
7	Israel	4.78		1.11	58	Morocco	3.47		1.75
8	Luxembourg	4.77		1.03	59	Mexico	3.47		1.49
9	China	4.71		1.33	60	Poland	3.46		1.42
10	United States	4.69		1.12	61	Macedonia, FYR	3.45		1.94
11	Vietnam	4.53		1.57	62	Serbia	3.45		1.63
12	Korea	4.52		1.24	63	Dominican Republic	3.44		1.56
13	Denmark	4.45		1.28	64	Colombia	3.43		1.24
14	Germany	4.38		1.26	65	Sri Lanka	3.40		1.51
15	Japan	4.36		1.32	66	Mauritius	3.39		1.31
16	Canada	4.30		1.48	67	Kenya	3.38		1.56
17	Tanzania	4.21		1.50	67	Portugal	3.38		1.17
18	Ireland	4.20		1.05	69	Namibia	3.33		1.57
19	Ghana	4.17		1.60	70	Zambia	3.32		1.57
20	Switzerland	4.16		1.36	71	India	3.31		1.18
21	Iceland	4.07		1.49	72	Mali	3.30		1.88
22	Cameroon	4.06		1.78	73	Mozambique	3.30		1.41
23	Latvia	4.05		1.46	74	Croatia	3.29		1.60
24	Sweden	4.04		1.11	75	Madagascar	3.29		1.66
25	Botswana	4.02		1.66	76	Greece	3.20		1.16
26	Hong Kong SAR	4.02		1.38	77	Russian Federation	3.18		1.48
27	Australia	4.00		1.05	78	Pakistan	3.12		1.40
27	Indonesia	4.00		1.37	79	Bulgaria	3.10		1.48
27	Norway	4.00		1.06	80	Malawi	3.10		1.54
27	Senegal	4.00		1.41	81	Gambia	3.06		1.94
31	Spain	3.94		1.29	82	Ukraine	3.06		1.46
32	Nigeria	3.94		1.49	83	Turkey	3.04		1.21
33	Estonia	3.93		1.35	84	Philippines	2.96		1.30
34	Hungary	3.88		1.37	85	Romania	2.91		1.54
35	Jamaica	3.88		1.39	86	Nicaragua	2.86		1.39
36	Thailand	3.86		1.32	87	Venezuela	2.86		1.09
37	Netherlands	3.82		1.34	88	Uruguay	2.85		1.21
38	South Africa	3.82		1.06	89	Argentina	2.80		1.12
39	Trinidad and Tobago	3.82		1.12	90	Zimbabwe	2.79		1.03
40	Italy	3.81		1.30	91	Panama	2.77		1.46
41	Uganda	3.81		1.86	92	Peru	2.76		1.35
42	United Kingdom	3.80		1.36	93	Haiti	2.73		1.24
43	Austria	3.78		1.46	94	Ecuador	2.66		1.29
44	Slovenia	3.77		1.33	95	Ethiopia	2.66		1.54
45	Jordan	3.77		1.51	96	Angola	2.61		1.59
46	Costa Rica	3.76		1.52	97	Bangladesh	2.60		1.50
47	Lithuania	3.72		1.28	98	Honduras	2.53		1.35
48	Egypt	3.69		1.80	99	Chad	2.51		1.68
49	Slovak Republic	3.69		1.44	100	Guatemala	2.48		1.27
50	New Zealand	3.68		1.07	101	Bolivia	2.28		1.08
51	Czech Republic	3.67		1.21	102	Paraguay	2.14		1.12

Source: World Economic Forum, Executive Opinion Survey 2003

II.3.03 Government online presence, 2003

Web presence of the various branches of government (1–7 scale), 2003

RANK	COUNTRY	SCORE
1	Canada	7.00
2	Germany	6.99
3	France	6.96
4	United States	6.84
5	United Kingdom	6.79
6	Singapore	6.76
7	Austria	6.73
8	Netherlands	6.53
9	Australia	6.42
10	Ireland	6.40
11	Brazil	6.32
12	Finland	6.25
13	Italy	6.18
14	Chile	6.17
15	Denmark	6.11
16	Argentina	6.09
17	Sweden	5.94
18	Estonia	5.85
19	New Zealand	5.85
20	Venezuela	5.72
21	Czech Republic	5.68
22	Poland	5.68
23	Korea	5.64
24	Colombia	5.58
25	Croatia	5.48
26	Slovak Republic	5.46
27	Norway	5.45
28	Slovenia	5.45
29	Spain	5.44
30	Portugal	5.38
31	Belgium	5.37
32	Mauritius	5.24
33	Lithuania	5.22
34	India	5.18
35	Israel	5.18
36	Dominican Republic	5.10
37	Thailand	5.06
38	Panama	5.02
39	Hong Kong SAR	4.99
40	Malta	4.92
41	Peru	4.88
42	Switzerland	4.86
43	Malaysia	4.86
44	Japan	4.81
45	Turkey	4.81
46	Romania	4.76
47	Mexico	4.73
48	Taiwan	4.73
49	Philippines	4.67
50	Iceland	4.62
51	El Salvador	4.59

RANK	COUNTRY	SCORE
52	Paraguay	4.56
53	Tanzania	4.42
54	South Africa	4.33
55	Uruguay	4.25
56	Bulgaria	4.24
57	Nicaragua	4.20
58	Luxembourg	4.19
59	Latvia	4.12
60	Hungary	4.00
61	Costa Rica	3.93
62	Sri Lanka	3.92
63	Guatemala	3.91
64	Pakistan	3.87
65	Greece	3.86
66	Ukraine	3.80
67	Malawi	3.78
68	Zambia	3.76
69	Cameroon	3.65
70	Uganda	3.53
71	Namibia	3.52
72	Bolivia	3.51
73	Indonesia	3.36
74	Haiti	3.35
75	Botswana	3.23
76	China	3.16
77	Kenya	3.13
78	Nigeria	3.10
79	Jamaica	3.09
80	Algeria	3.04
81	Trinidad and Tobago	3.04
82	Russian Federation	2.83
83	Morocco	2.82
84	Vietnam	2.78
85	Tunisia	2.77
86	Serbia	2.53
87	Ecuador	2.46
88	Ghana	2.41
89	Egypt	2.40
90	Macedonia, FYR	2.39
91	Mozambique	2.26
92	Gambia	2.20
93	Angola	2.04
94	Jordan	1.97
95	Madagascar	1.89
96	Bangladesh	1.71
97	Honduras	1.46
98	Zimbabwe	1.35
99	Senegal	1.29
100	Ethiopia	1.16
101	Mali	1.11
102	Chad	1.00

Source: World Economic Forum, 2003

Individual Readiness

III.1.01 Personal computers, 2001

Personal computers per 1,000 inhabitants, 2001

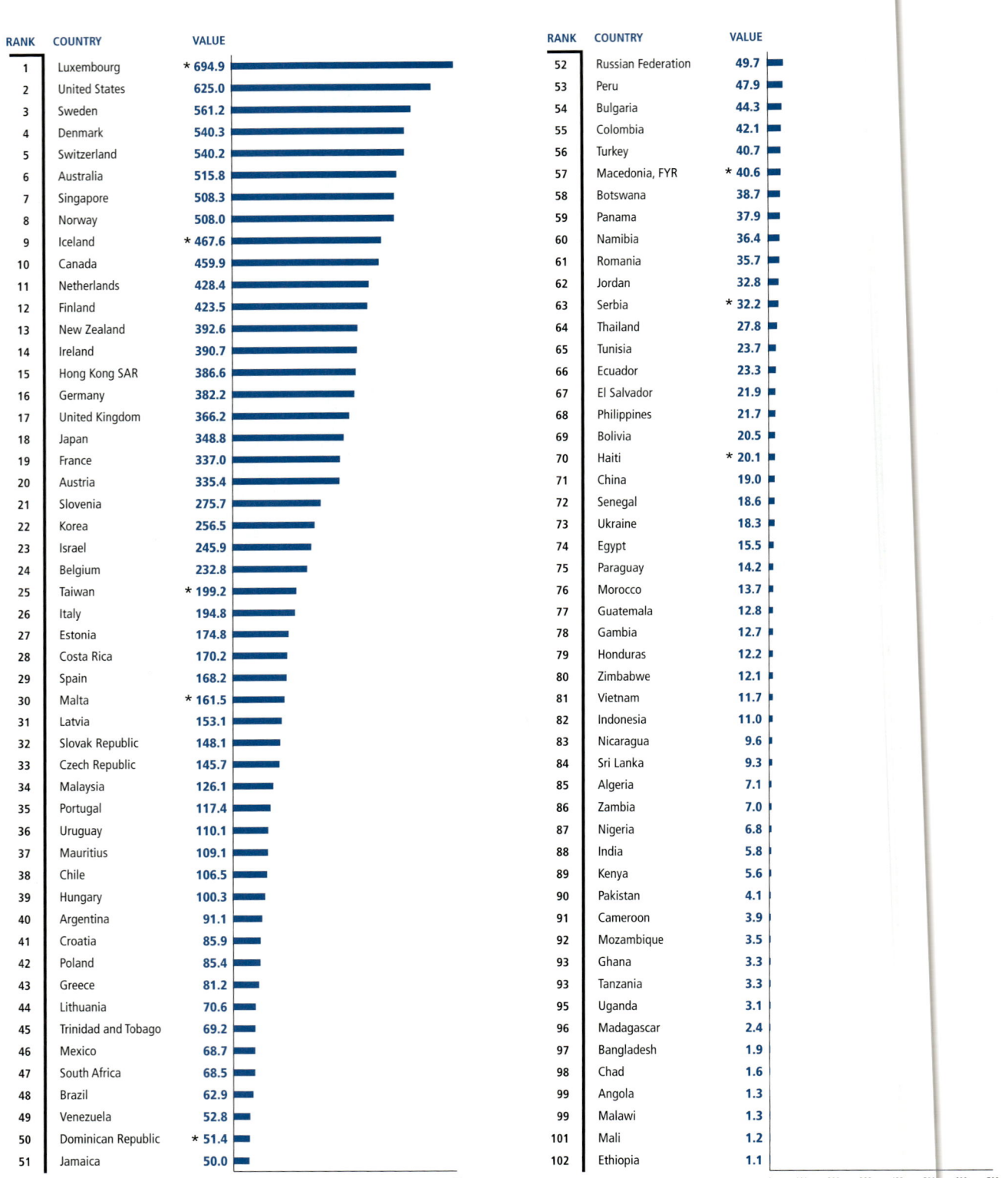

RANK	COUNTRY	VALUE
1	Luxembourg	* 694.9
2	United States	625.0
3	Sweden	561.2
4	Denmark	540.3
5	Switzerland	540.2
6	Australia	515.8
7	Singapore	508.3
8	Norway	508.0
9	Iceland	* 467.6
10	Canada	459.9
11	Netherlands	428.4
12	Finland	423.5
13	New Zealand	392.6
14	Ireland	390.7
15	Hong Kong SAR	386.6
16	Germany	382.2
17	United Kingdom	366.2
18	Japan	348.8
19	France	337.0
20	Austria	335.4
21	Slovenia	275.7
22	Korea	256.5
23	Israel	245.9
24	Belgium	232.8
25	Taiwan	* 199.2
26	Italy	194.8
27	Estonia	174.8
28	Costa Rica	170.2
29	Spain	168.2
30	Malta	* 161.5
31	Latvia	153.1
32	Slovak Republic	148.1
33	Czech Republic	145.7
34	Malaysia	126.1
35	Portugal	117.4
36	Uruguay	110.1
37	Mauritius	109.1
38	Chile	106.5
39	Hungary	100.3
40	Argentina	91.1
41	Croatia	85.9
42	Poland	85.4
43	Greece	81.2
44	Lithuania	70.6
45	Trinidad and Tobago	69.2
46	Mexico	68.7
47	South Africa	68.5
48	Brazil	62.9
49	Venezuela	52.8
50	Dominican Republic	* 51.4
51	Jamaica	50.0

RANK	COUNTRY	VALUE
52	Russian Federation	49.7
53	Peru	47.9
54	Bulgaria	44.3
55	Colombia	42.1
56	Turkey	40.7
57	Macedonia, FYR	* 40.6
58	Botswana	38.7
59	Panama	37.9
60	Namibia	36.4
61	Romania	35.7
62	Jordan	32.8
63	Serbia	* 32.2
64	Thailand	27.8
65	Tunisia	23.7
66	Ecuador	23.3
67	El Salvador	21.9
68	Philippines	21.7
69	Bolivia	20.5
70	Haiti	* 20.1
71	China	19.0
72	Senegal	18.6
73	Ukraine	18.3
74	Egypt	15.5
75	Paraguay	14.2
76	Morocco	13.7
77	Guatemala	12.8
78	Gambia	12.7
79	Honduras	12.2
80	Zimbabwe	12.1
81	Vietnam	11.7
82	Indonesia	11.0
83	Nicaragua	9.6
84	Sri Lanka	9.3
85	Algeria	7.1
86	Zambia	7.0
87	Nigeria	6.8
88	India	5.8
89	Kenya	5.6
90	Pakistan	4.1
91	Cameroon	3.9
92	Mozambique	3.5
93	Ghana	3.3
93	Tanzania	3.3
95	Uganda	3.1
96	Madagascar	2.4
97	Bangladesh	1.9
98	Chad	1.6
99	Angola	1.3
99	Malawi	1.3
101	Mali	1.2
102	Ethiopia	1.1

Note: *estimate
Source: World Bank, World Development Indicators 2003 using International Telecommunication Union data

III.1.02 ISDN subscribers, 2001

ISDN subscribers per 1,000 inhabitants, 2001

RANK	COUNTRY	VALUE		RANK	COUNTRY	VALUE
1	Norway	170.81		52	Peru	0.85
2	Luxembourg	130.57		53	China	0.84
3	Switzerland	119.56		54	Russian Federation	* 0.78
4	Germany	111.22		55	Ecuador	* 0.76
5	Netherlands	88.50		56	Algeria	* 0.61
6	Japan	80.92		56	Macedonia, FYR	* 0.61
7	Denmark	76.75		58	Uruguay	0.56
8	Iceland	63.60		59	South Africa	0.55
9	Ireland	* 58.66		60	Costa Rica	0.45
10	Finland	53.15		61	Jordan	0.35
11	Austria	50.25		62	Morocco	0.32
12	Belgium	43.47		63	Angola	* 0.24
13	Italy	39.72		63	Bolivia	* 0.24
14	Slovenia	38.69		63	Honduras	* 0.24
15	Sweden	32.53		63	Ukraine	* 0.24
16	Australia	* 32.00		67	Senegal	0.17
17	France	30.15		68	El Salvador	0.14
18	Portugal	25.07		69	Thailand	0.13
19	Spain	20.70		70	Turkey	0.13
20	Greece	19.28		71	Romania	0.12
21	Hungary	17.56		72	Trinidad and Tobago	0.12
22	United Kingdom	14.32		73	Cameroon	* 0.10
23	New Zealand	* 12.67		73	Nicaragua	* 0.10
24	Israel	9.02		75	Guatemala	0.10
25	Estonia	8.82		76	Serbia	* 0.10
26	Mexico	* 8.62		77	Sri Lanka	0.07
27	Chile	* 8.49		78	Tunisia	0.07
28	Czech Republic	8.19		79	Pakistan	* 0.05
29	United States	7.04		80	Egypt	0.04
30	Slovak Republic	5.75		81	Dominican Republic	0.03
31	Singapore	5.37		82	India	0.03
32	Croatia	* 4.08		83	Indonesia	0.02
33	Latvia	4.04		84	Zimbabwe	0.02
34	Panama	* 3.97		85	Madagascar	0.02
34	Venezuela	* 3.97		86	Haiti	* 0.01
36	Canada	3.52		86	Vietnam	* 0.01
37	Korea	2.84		88	Philippines	0.01
38	Argentina	* 2.80		89	Chad	* 0.01
39	Poland	2.65		90	Gambia	* 0.01
40	Malta	2.20		90	Mali	* 0.01
41	Colombia	2.04		90	Tanzania	* 0.01
42	Brazil	* 1.90		93	Bangladesh	* 0.01
43	Hong Kong SAR	1.85		94	Ghana	0.01
44	Lithuania	1.77		95	Kenya	* 0.00
45	Taiwan	1.67		95	Zambia	* 0.00
46	Botswana	* 1.61		97	Ethiopia	* 0.00
46	Jamaica	* 1.61		97	Malawi	* 0.00
48	Malaysia	1.26		97	Mozambique	* 0.00
49	Namibia	1.24		97	Uganda	0.00
50	Bulgaria	1.21		101	Nigeria	0.00
51	Mauritius	1.18		102	Paraguay	0.00

Note: *estimate
Source: International Telecommunication Union, World Telecommunication Indicators Database, accessed July 2003

III.1.03 Cable television subscribers, 2001

Cable television subscribers per 1,000 inhabitants, 2001

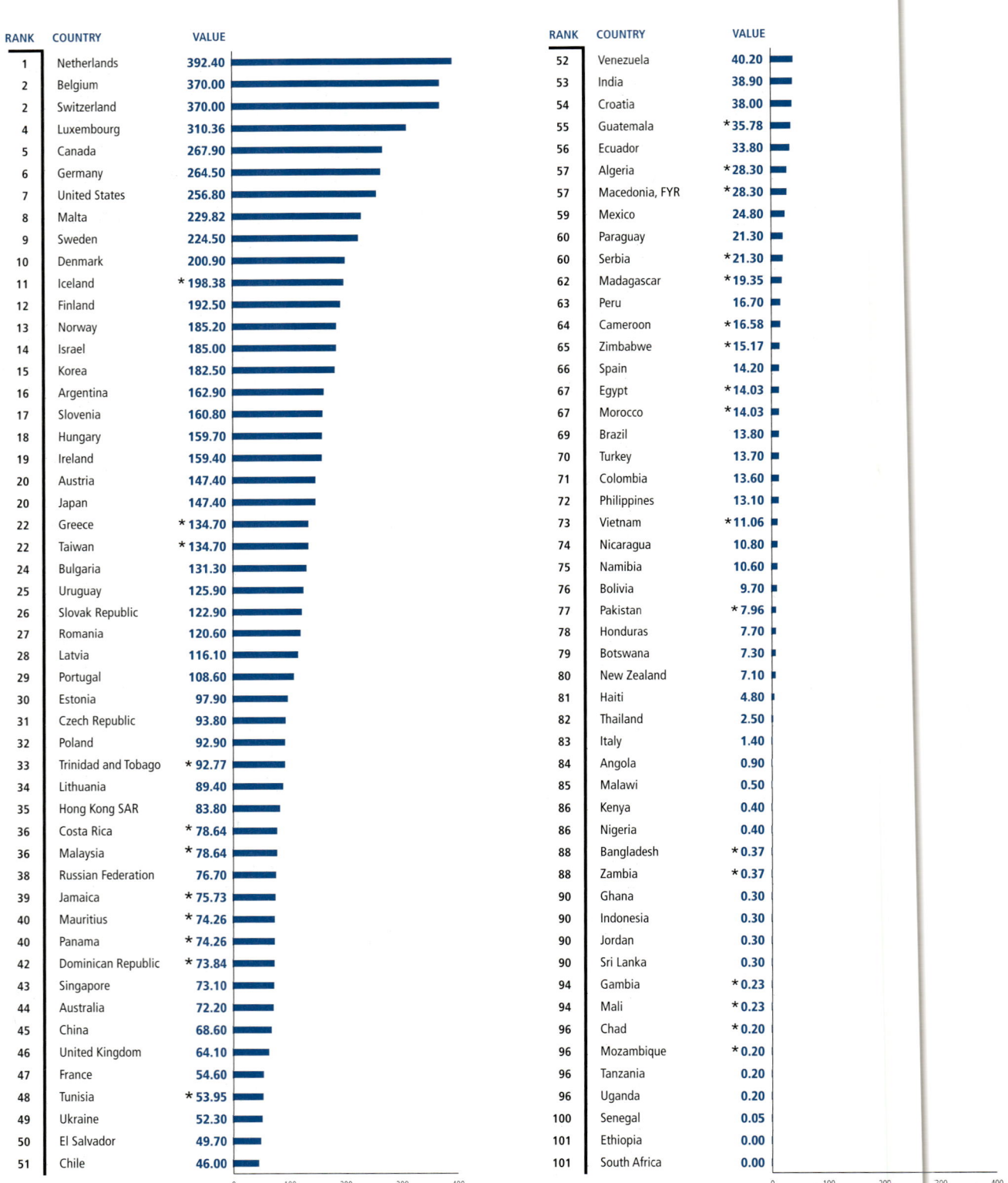

RANK	COUNTRY	VALUE		RANK	COUNTRY	VALUE
1	Netherlands	392.40		52	Venezuela	40.20
2	Belgium	370.00		53	India	38.90
2	Switzerland	370.00		54	Croatia	38.00
4	Luxembourg	310.36		55	Guatemala	*35.78
5	Canada	267.90		56	Ecuador	33.80
6	Germany	264.50		57	Algeria	*28.30
7	United States	256.80		57	Macedonia, FYR	*28.30
8	Malta	229.82		59	Mexico	24.80
9	Sweden	224.50		60	Paraguay	21.30
10	Denmark	200.90		60	Serbia	*21.30
11	Iceland	*198.38		62	Madagascar	*19.35
12	Finland	192.50		63	Peru	16.70
13	Norway	185.20		64	Cameroon	*16.58
14	Israel	185.00		65	Zimbabwe	*15.17
15	Korea	182.50		66	Spain	14.20
16	Argentina	162.90		67	Egypt	*14.03
17	Slovenia	160.80		67	Morocco	*14.03
18	Hungary	159.70		69	Brazil	13.80
19	Ireland	159.40		70	Turkey	13.70
20	Austria	147.40		71	Colombia	13.60
20	Japan	147.40		72	Philippines	13.10
22	Greece	*134.70		73	Vietnam	*11.06
22	Taiwan	*134.70		74	Nicaragua	10.80
24	Bulgaria	131.30		75	Namibia	10.60
25	Uruguay	125.90		76	Bolivia	9.70
26	Slovak Republic	122.90		77	Pakistan	*7.96
27	Romania	120.60		78	Honduras	7.70
28	Latvia	116.10		79	Botswana	7.30
29	Portugal	108.60		80	New Zealand	7.10
30	Estonia	97.90		81	Haiti	4.80
31	Czech Republic	93.80		82	Thailand	2.50
32	Poland	92.90		83	Italy	1.40
33	Trinidad and Tobago	*92.77		84	Angola	0.90
34	Lithuania	89.40		85	Malawi	0.50
35	Hong Kong SAR	83.80		86	Kenya	0.40
36	Costa Rica	*78.64		86	Nigeria	0.40
36	Malaysia	*78.64		88	Bangladesh	*0.37
38	Russian Federation	76.70		88	Zambia	*0.37
39	Jamaica	*75.73		90	Ghana	0.30
40	Mauritius	*74.26		90	Indonesia	0.30
40	Panama	*74.26		90	Jordan	0.30
42	Dominican Republic	*73.84		90	Sri Lanka	0.30
43	Singapore	73.10		94	Gambia	*0.23
44	Australia	72.20		94	Mali	*0.23
45	China	68.60		96	Chad	*0.20
46	United Kingdom	64.10		96	Mozambique	*0.20
47	France	54.60		96	Tanzania	0.20
48	Tunisia	*53.95		96	Uganda	0.20
49	Ukraine	52.30		100	Senegal	0.05
50	El Salvador	49.70		101	Ethiopia	0.00
51	Chile	46.00		101	South Africa	0.00

Note: *estimate
Source: World Bank, World Development Indicators 2003 using International Telecommunication Union data

III.1.04 Internet users, 2001

Internet users per 1,000 inhabitants, 2001

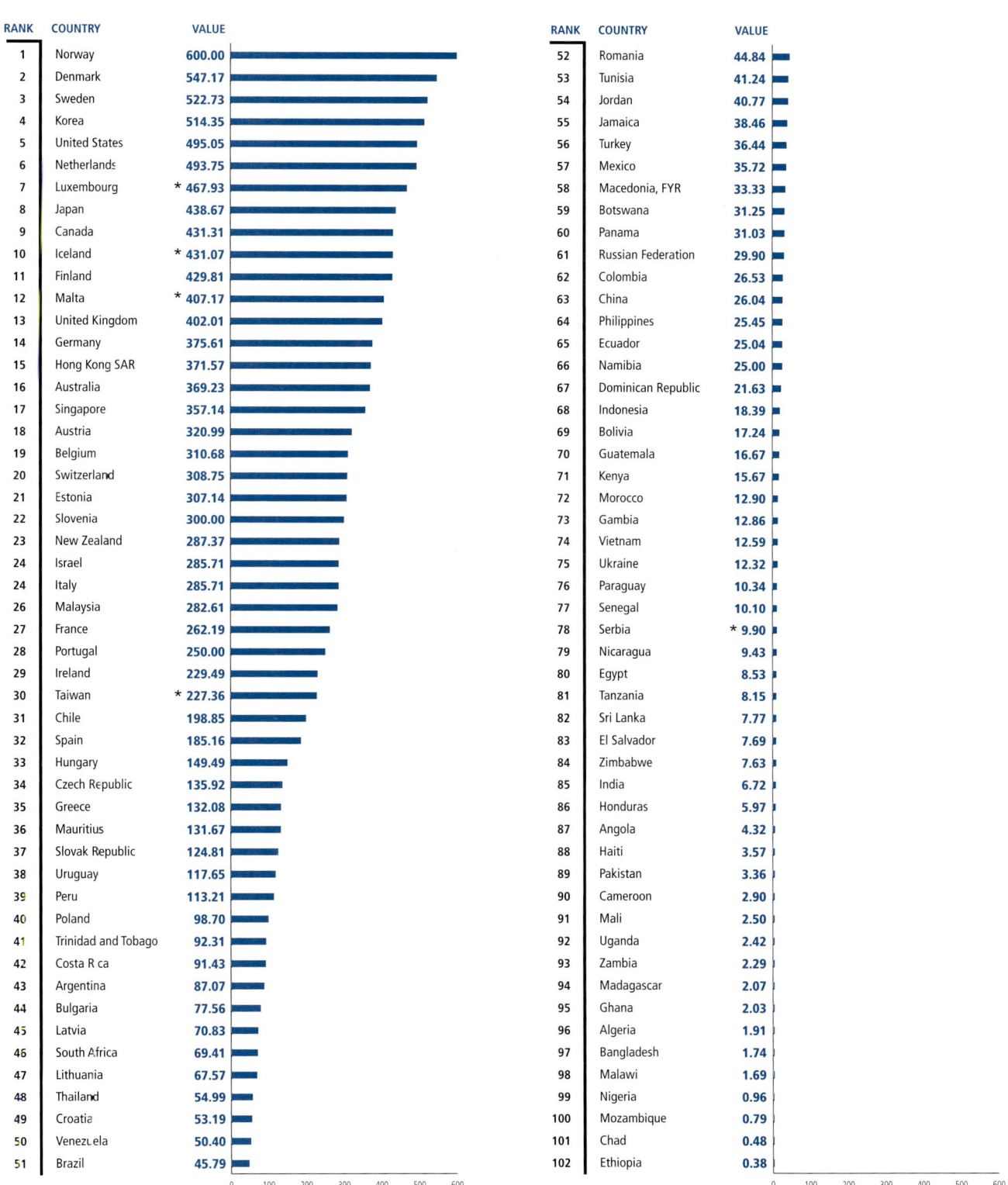

RANK	COUNTRY	VALUE
1	Norway	600.00
2	Denmark	547.17
3	Sweden	522.73
4	Korea	514.35
5	United States	495.05
6	Netherlands	493.75
7	Luxembourg	* 467.93
8	Japan	438.67
9	Canada	431.31
10	Iceland	* 431.07
11	Finland	429.81
12	Malta	* 407.17
13	United Kingdom	402.01
14	Germany	375.61
15	Hong Kong SAR	371.57
16	Australia	369.23
17	Singapore	357.14
18	Austria	320.99
19	Belgium	310.68
20	Switzerland	308.75
21	Estonia	307.14
22	Slovenia	300.00
23	New Zealand	287.37
24	Israel	285.71
24	Italy	285.71
26	Malaysia	282.61
27	France	262.19
28	Portugal	250.00
29	Ireland	229.49
30	Taiwan	* 227.36
31	Chile	198.85
32	Spain	185.16
33	Hungary	149.49
34	Czech Republic	135.92
35	Greece	132.08
36	Mauritius	131.67
37	Slovak Republic	124.81
38	Uruguay	117.65
39	Peru	113.21
40	Poland	98.70
41	Trinidad and Tobago	92.31
42	Costa Rica	91.43
43	Argentina	87.07
44	Bulgaria	77.56
45	Latvia	70.83
46	South Africa	69.41
47	Lithuania	67.57
48	Thailand	54.99
49	Croatia	53.19
50	Venezuela	50.40
51	Brazil	45.79

RANK	COUNTRY	VALUE
52	Romania	44.84
53	Tunisia	41.24
54	Jordan	40.77
55	Jamaica	38.46
56	Turkey	36.44
57	Mexico	35.72
58	Macedonia, FYR	33.33
59	Botswana	31.25
60	Panama	31.03
61	Russian Federation	29.90
62	Colombia	26.53
63	China	26.04
64	Philippines	25.45
65	Ecuador	25.04
66	Namibia	25.00
67	Dominican Republic	21.63
68	Indonesia	18.39
69	Bolivia	17.24
70	Guatemala	16.67
71	Kenya	15.67
72	Morocco	12.90
73	Gambia	12.86
74	Vietnam	12.59
75	Ukraine	12.32
76	Paraguay	10.34
77	Senegal	10.10
78	Serbia	* 9.90
79	Nicaragua	9.43
80	Egypt	8.53
81	Tanzania	8.15
82	Sri Lanka	7.77
83	El Salvador	7.69
84	Zimbabwe	7.63
85	India	6.72
86	Honduras	5.97
87	Angola	4.32
88	Haiti	3.57
89	Pakistan	3.36
90	Cameroon	2.90
91	Mali	2.50
92	Uganda	2.42
93	Zambia	2.29
94	Madagascar	2.07
95	Ghana	2.03
96	Algeria	1.91
97	Bangladesh	1.74
98	Malawi	1.69
99	Nigeria	0.96
100	Mozambique	0.79
101	Chad	0.48
102	Ethiopia	0.38

Note: *estimate
Source: World Bank, World Development Indicators 2003 using International Telecommunication Union data

Business Readiness

III.2.01 Computers installed in businesses, 2002

Computers installed in businesses per 1,000 inhabitants, 2002

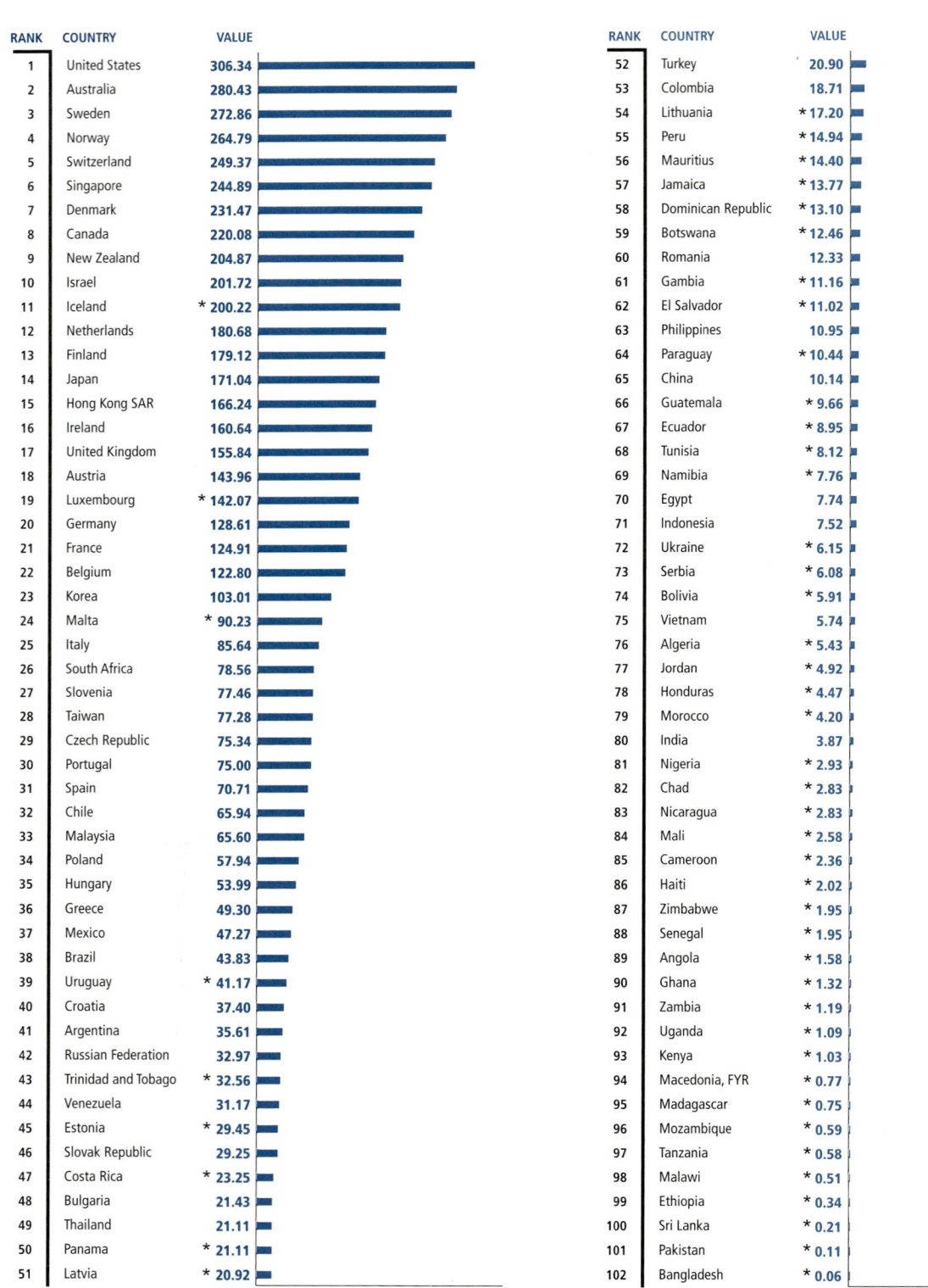

RANK	COUNTRY	VALUE
1	United States	306.34
2	Australia	280.43
3	Sweden	272.86
4	Norway	264.79
5	Switzerland	249.37
6	Singapore	244.89
7	Denmark	231.47
8	Canada	220.08
9	New Zealand	204.87
10	Israel	201.72
11	Iceland	* 200.22
12	Netherlands	180.68
13	Finland	179.12
14	Japan	171.04
15	Hong Kong SAR	166.24
16	Ireland	160.64
17	United Kingdom	155.84
18	Austria	143.96
19	Luxembourg	* 142.07
20	Germany	128.61
21	France	124.91
22	Belgium	122.80
23	Korea	103.01
24	Malta	* 90.23
25	Italy	85.64
26	South Africa	78.56
27	Slovenia	77.46
28	Taiwan	77.28
29	Czech Republic	75.34
30	Portugal	75.00
31	Spain	70.71
32	Chile	65.94
33	Malaysia	65.60
34	Poland	57.94
35	Hungary	53.99
36	Greece	49.30
37	Mexico	47.27
38	Brazil	43.83
39	Uruguay	* 41.17
40	Croatia	37.40
41	Argentina	35.61
42	Russian Federation	32.97
43	Trinidad and Tobago	* 32.56
44	Venezuela	31.17
45	Estonia	* 29.45
46	Slovak Republic	29.25
47	Costa Rica	* 23.25
48	Bulgaria	21.43
49	Thailand	21.11
50	Panama	* 21.11
51	Latvia	* 20.92

RANK	COUNTRY	VALUE
52	Turkey	20.90
53	Colombia	18.71
54	Lithuania	* 17.20
55	Peru	* 14.94
56	Mauritius	* 14.40
57	Jamaica	* 13.77
58	Dominican Republic	* 13.10
59	Botswana	* 12.46
60	Romania	12.33
61	Gambia	* 11.16
62	El Salvador	* 11.02
63	Philippines	10.95
64	Paraguay	* 10.44
65	China	10.14
66	Guatemala	* 9.66
67	Ecuador	* 8.95
68	Tunisia	* 8.12
69	Namibia	* 7.76
70	Egypt	7.74
71	Indonesia	7.52
72	Ukraine	* 6.15
73	Serbia	* 6.08
74	Bolivia	* 5.91
75	Vietnam	5.74
76	Algeria	* 5.43
77	Jordan	* 4.92
78	Honduras	* 4.47
79	Morocco	* 4.20
80	India	3.87
81	Nigeria	* 2.93
82	Chad	* 2.83
83	Nicaragua	* 2.83
84	Mali	* 2.58
85	Cameroon	* 2.36
86	Haiti	* 2.02
87	Zimbabwe	* 1.95
88	Senegal	* 1.95
89	Angola	* 1.58
90	Ghana	* 1.32
91	Zambia	* 1.19
92	Uganda	* 1.09
93	Kenya	* 1.03
94	Macedonia, FYR	* 0.77
95	Madagascar	* 0.75
96	Mozambique	* 0.59
97	Tanzania	* 0.58
98	Malawi	* 0.51
99	Ethiopia	* 0.34
100	Sri Lanka	* 0.21
101	Pakistan	* 0.11
102	Bangladesh	* 0.06

Note: *estimate
Sources: IDC and the World Bank, 2003

III.2.02 Firm-level technology absorption, 2003

Companies in your country are (1 = not interested in absorbing new technology, 7 = aggressive in absorbing new technology)

RANK	COUNTRY	SCORE		SD	RANK	COUNTRY	SCORE		SD
1	Finland	6.42		0.60	52	El Salvador	4.83		1.36
2	Japan	6.28		0.61	53	Czech Republic	4.76		1.22
3	Sweden	6.26		0.66	54	Poland	4.76		1.08
4	Israel	6.19		0.81	54	Turkey	4.76		1.20
5	Singapore	6.10		0.79	56	Madagascar	4.75		1.40
6	United States	6.06		1.42	57	Ghana	4.74		1.56
7	Iceland	6.00		0.62	58	China	4.72		1.46
8	Taiwan	5.86		1.08	59	Colombia	4.70		1.21
9	Switzerland	5.78		1.10	60	Uganda	4.66		1.79
10	Korea	5.76		1.04	61	Italy	4.66		1.26
11	Germany	5.74		1.05	62	Sri Lanka	4.66		1.44
12	Senegal	5.70		1.27	63	Mauritius	4.66		0.87
13	Denmark	5.69		0.64	64	Mozambique	4.61		1.43
14	Malaysia	5.55		0.77	65	Romania	4.58		1.39
15	Vietnam	5.51		1.28	66	Russian Federation	4.58		1.41
16	Australia	5.45		0.60	67	Ukraine	4.57		1.26
17	Costa Rica	5.43		1.15	68	Hungary	4.57		0.94
18	Canada	5.43		1.00	69	Botswana	4.55		1.25
19	Estonia	5.42		1.03	70	Argentina	4.49		1.18
20	Luxembourg	5.38		0.95	71	Egypt	4.49		1.61
21	Norway	5.37		0.84	72	Philippines	4.49		1.12
22	New Zealand	5.34		0.88	73	Jamaica	4.48		1.25
23	Tunisia	5.34		1.17	74	Venezuela	4.47		1.31
24	Chile	5.34		0.99	75	Namibia	4.47		1.18
25	Lithuania	5.32		0.90	76	Algeria	4.46		1.65
26	Slovak Republic	5.30		1.12	77	Kenya	4.45		1.24
27	France	5.28		0.88	78	Greece	4.42		1.20
28	Hong Kong SAR	5.27		1.25	79	Peru	4.42		1.28
29	Ireland	5.25		0.98	80	Zimbabwe	4.36		1.22
30	Thailand	5.22		0.97	81	Guatemala	4.33		1.30
31	India	5.19		1.09	82	Pakistan	4.31		1.21
32	Panama	5.15		1.11	83	Bangladesh	4.29		1.46
33	Dominican Republic	5.14		1.09	84	Cameroon	4.27		1.60
34	United Kingdom	5.14		1.04	85	Angola	4.26		1.85
35	Croatia	5.14		1.51	86	Serbia	4.25		1.30
36	Spain	5.13		1.06	87	Portugal	4.20		1.24
37	Austria	5.12		1.17	88	Zambia	4.19		1.38
38	Latvia	5.09		0.95	89	Haiti	4.16		1.40
39	South Africa	5.08		0.96	90	Ecuador	4.12		1.39
40	Brazil	5.06		1.06	91	Nicaragua	4.11		1.65
41	Belgium	5.04		1.07	92	Malawi	4.09		1.52
42	Gambia	5.01		1.55	93	Macedonia, FYR	4.04		1.76
43	Morocco	5.00		1.70	94	Mali	4.03		1.92
44	Mexico	4.99		1.13	95	Bulgaria	4.01		1.23
45	Malta	4.96		1.01	96	Indonesia	4.00		1.54
46	Slovenia	4.95		0.96	96	Uruguay	4.00		1.05
47	Trinidad and Tobago	4.92		1.00	98	Ethiopia	3.99		1.60
48	Jordan	4.86		1.25	99	Chad	3.98		2.13
49	Nigeria	4.85		1.35	100	Paraguay	3.85		1.35
50	Tanzania	4.85		1.28	101	Honduras	3.77		1.40
51	Netherlands	4.85		1.17	102	Bolivia	3.72		1.32

0 1 2 3 4 5 6 7   0 1 2 3 4 5 6 7

Source: World Economic Forum, Executive Opinion Survey 2003

III.2.03 Prevalence of foreign technology licensing, 2003

In your country, licensing foreign technology is (1 = uncommon, 7 = a common means of acquiring new technology)

RANK	COUNTRY	SCORE	SD		RANK	COUNTRY	SCORE	SD
1	Singapore	5.71	1.15		52	Canada	4.63	1.61
2	Malaysia	5.60	0.86		53	Belgium	4.62	1.66
3	Australia	5.60	1.05		54	Ireland	4.62	1.52
4	South Africa	5.59	0.81		55	France	4.62	1.22
5	Thailand	5.51	1.10		55	Spain	4.62	1.69
6	India	5.48	1.38		57	United Kingdom	4.62	1.71
7	Brazil	5.32	1.41		58	El Salvador	4.61	1.54
8	Mexico	5.24	1.41		58	Switzerland	4.61	1.59
9	Portugal	5.21	1.25		60	Slovenia	4.58	1.24
10	Greece	5.20	1.41		61	Pakistan	4.56	1.65
11	Costa Rica	5.16	1.39		62	Norway	4.56	1.19
12	Botswana	5.13	1.56		63	Sweden	4.52	1.61
13	Jordan	5.12	1.54		64	Egypt	4.52	1.68
14	Taiwan	5.12	1.58		65	Hungary	4.51	1.54
15	Italy	5.11	1.24		66	Lithuania	4.49	1.47
16	Denmark	5.10	1.16		67	Romania	4.48	1.62
17	Czech Republic	5.09	1.31		68	Vietnam	4.44	1.71
18	Latvia	5.08	1.15		69	Morocco	4.42	1.85
19	Korea	5.08	1.42		70	China	4.36	1.57
20	Israel	5.05	1.10		71	Ghana	4.29	1.73
21	Croatia	5.05	1.71		72	Peru	4.27	1.55
22	Iceland	5.04	1.22		73	Jamaica	4.21	1.58
23	Philippines	5.00	1.26		74	Austria	4.16	1.50
23	Turkey	5.00	1.45		75	Colombia	4.10	1.60
23	United States	5.00	1.31		76	Uruguay	4.02	1.46
26	Panama	4.99	1.43		77	Zambia	3.91	1.84
27	Japan	4.99	1.50		78	Macedonia, FYR	3.91	2.19
28	Kenya	4.96	1.66		79	Malawi	3.90	1.94
29	Tunisia	4.92	1.34		80	Ecuador	3.84	1.53
30	Chile	4.91	1.40		81	Indonesia	3.82	1.35
31	Dominican Republic	4.90	1.42		82	Senegal	3.81	2.08
32	New Zealand	4.89	1.30		83	Bangladesh	3.80	1.90
33	Namibia	4.88	1.42		84	Mozambique	3.79	1.86
34	Nigeria	4.87	1.71		85	Nicaragua	3.78	1.54
35	Tanzania	4.86	1.63		86	Serbia	3.78	1.90
36	Netherlands	4.85	1.40		87	Guatemala	3.74	1.77
37	Hong Kong SAR	4.85	1.74		88	Cameroon	3.72	1.86
38	Germany	4.83	1.43		89	Honduras	3.72	1.59
39	Zimbabwe	4.82	1.47		90	Gambia	3.60	2.07
40	Uganda	4.82	2.01		91	Bulgaria	3.57	1.59
41	Estonia	4.78	1.34		92	Algeria	3.35	1.97
42	Trinidad and Tobago	4.77	1.58		93	Russian Federation	3.27	1.62
43	Poland	4.75	1.41		94	Ukraine	3.25	1.49
44	Sri Lanka	4.71	1.65		95	Bolivia	3.11	1.53
45	Malta	4.70	1.64		96	Angola	3.09	1.79
46	Luxembourg	4.69	1.49		97	Paraguay	2.94	1.31
47	Finland	4.68	1.45		98	Madagascar	2.79	1.72
48	Slovak Republic	4.67	1.57		99	Ethiopia	2.76	1.72
49	Argentina	4.65	1.54		100	Chad	2.73	1.90
50	Venezuela	4.65	1.41		101	Haiti	2.58	1.74
51	Mauritius	4.63	1.30		102	Mali	2.57	1.82

Source: World Economic Forum, Executive Opinion Survey 2003

Government Readiness

III.3.01 Government success in ICT promotion, 2003

Government programs promoting the use of information and communication technologies (ICT) are (1 = not very successful, 7 = highly successful)

RANK	COUNTRY	SCORE	SD	RANK	COUNTRY	SCORE	SD
1	Singapore	5.90	0.86	52	Lithuania	3.72	1.36
2	Malaysia	5.32	0.91	53	Mozambique	3.71	1.53
3	Tunisia	5.29	1.19	54	Netherlands	3.70	1.33
4	Korea	5.29	1.15	55	Slovenia	3.70	1.32
5	Finland	5.23	0.91	56	Colombia	3.70	1.32
6	Taiwan	5.19	1.18	57	Serbia	3.65	1.43
7	Malta	5.05	1.31	58	Italy	3.65	1.25
8	Jordan	4.94	1.26	59	New Zealand	3.65	1.27
9	Gambia	4.89	1.64	60	Jamaica	3.62	1.28
10	Denmark	4.83	1.11	61	Belgium	3.61	1.50
11	Iceland	4.81	1.27	62	El Salvador	3.59	1.22
12	Estonia	4.77	1.07	63	Costa Rica	3.59	1.40
13	Mauritius	4.77	0.97	64	Croatia	3.58	1.53
14	Thailand	4.64	1.19	65	Hungary	3.58	1.45
15	Vietnam	4.64	1.31	66	Namibia	3.57	1.35
16	India	4.59	1.28	67	Zambia	3.55	1.56
17	Canada	4.56	1.63	68	Philippines	3.55	1.53
18	United States	4.55	1.29	69	Indonesia	3.54	1.19
19	Sweden	4.43	1.40	70	Trinidad and Tobago	3.51	1.30
20	Ireland	4.41	1.48	71	Mali	3.49	1.56
21	Israel	4.38	1.59	72	Greece	3.47	1.26
22	Ghana	4.37	1.56	73	Cameroon	3.44	1.57
23	Luxembourg	4.33	1.19	74	Dominican Republic	3.39	1.50
24	China	4.30	1.39	75	Kenya	3.37	1.51
25	Uganda	4.26	1.90	76	Malawi	3.34	1.26
26	France	4.26	1.20	77	Czech Republic	3.27	1.40
27	Tanzania	4.22	1.59	78	Slovak Republic	3.25	1.31
28	Switzerland	4.15	1.39	79	Uruguay	3.25	1.34
29	Botswana	4.15	1.23	80	Panama	3.21	1.44
30	Japan	4.12	1.32	81	Poland	3.13	1.37
31	Hong Kong SAR	4.11	1.40	82	Peru	3.11	1.41
32	Morocco	4.08	1.61	82	Ukraine	3.11	1.37
33	Pakistan	4.06	1.37	84	Ethiopia	3.06	1.52
34	South Africa	4.03	1.28	85	Bulgaria	2.95	1.31
35	Egypt	4.01	1.54	86	Russian Federation	2.94	1.31
36	Senegal	4.00	1.70	87	Turkey	2.87	1.07
37	Germany	3.99	1.33	88	Bangladesh	2.82	1.26
38	Brazil	3.98	1.31	89	Macedonia, FYR	2.79	1.65
39	Nigeria	3.91	1.76	90	Angola	2.78	1.29
40	Austria	3.90	1.36	91	Algeria	2.78	1.24
41	Chile	3.89	1.33	92	Nicaragua	2.78	1.31
42	Norway	3.89	1.19	93	Bolivia	2.65	1.35
43	Latvia	3.89	1.45	94	Ecuador	2.46	1.26
44	Sri Lanka	3.87	1.36	95	Honduras	2.44	1.21
45	Australia	3.85	0.93	96	Argentina	2.43	1.18
46	Spain	3.82	1.26	97	Zimbabwe	2.42	1.26
47	United Kingdom	3.80	1.30	98	Chad	2.33	1.64
48	Portugal	3.80	1.14	99	Venezuela	2.21	1.17
49	Romania	3.77	1.54	100	Haiti	1.96	1.00
50	Madagascar	3.77	1.51	101	Guatemala	1.95	1.01
51	Mexico	3.74	1.47	102	Paraguay	1.81	1.11

Source: World Economic Forum, Executive Opinion Survey 2003

III.3.02 Government online services, 2003

Sophistication of government online services (1–7 scale), 2003

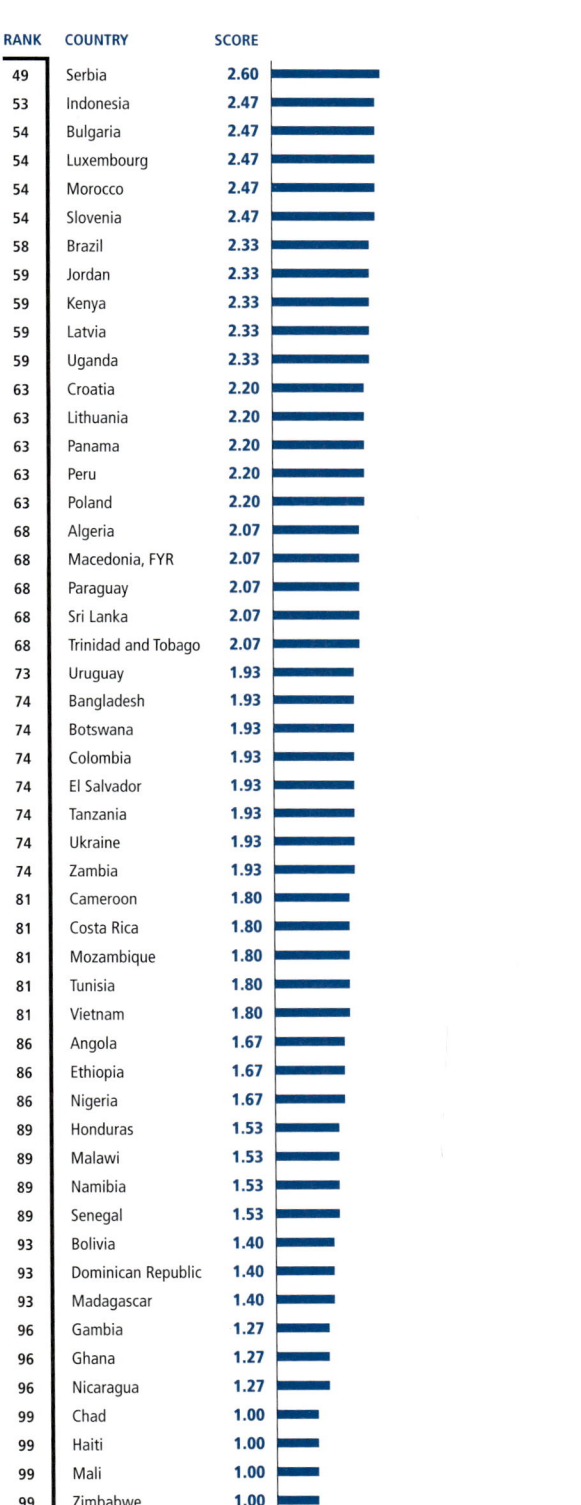

RANK	COUNTRY	SCORE
1	Singapore	7.00
2	Hong Kong SAR	6.47
2	United States	6.47
4	Canada	6.20
5	Denmark	5.27
6	Germany	4.87
7	Austria	4.73
8	Israel	4.60
8	Japan	4.60
8	United Kingdom	4.60
11	Australia	4.47
11	Sweden	4.47
11	Taiwan	4.47
14	France	4.33
15	New Zealand	4.20
16	Estonia	4.07
17	Argentina	4.07
18	China	3.93
18	Ireland	3.93
20	Finland	3.80
20	Malaysia	3.80
20	Philippines	3.80
20	Turkey	3.80
24	Belgium	3.67
24	Mexico	3.67
26	Korea	3.67
27	Italy	3.53
27	Malta	3.53
29	Jamaica	3.40
29	Norway	3.40
29	South Africa	3.40
32	Chile	3.27
33	Netherlands	3.13
33	Switzerland	3.13
35	Romania	3.13
36	Pakistan	3.00
36	Portugal	3.00
36	Spain	3.00
39	Iceland	2.87
40	Hungary	2.87
40	India	2.87
40	Slovak Republic	2.87
40	Thailand	2.87
44	Egypt	2.73
44	Mauritius	2.73
44	Russian Federation	2.73
47	Czech Republic	2.73
47	Venezuela	2.73
49	Ecuador	2.60
49	Greece	2.60
49	Guatemala	2.60

RANK	COUNTRY	SCORE
49	Serbia	2.60
53	Indonesia	2.47
54	Bulgaria	2.47
54	Luxembourg	2.47
54	Morocco	2.47
54	Slovenia	2.47
58	Brazil	2.33
59	Jordan	2.33
59	Kenya	2.33
59	Latvia	2.33
59	Uganda	2.33
63	Croatia	2.20
63	Lithuania	2.20
63	Panama	2.20
63	Peru	2.20
63	Poland	2.20
68	Algeria	2.07
68	Macedonia, FYR	2.07
68	Paraguay	2.07
68	Sri Lanka	2.07
68	Trinidad and Tobago	2.07
73	Uruguay	1.93
74	Bangladesh	1.93
74	Botswana	1.93
74	Colombia	1.93
74	El Salvador	1.93
74	Tanzania	1.93
74	Ukraine	1.93
74	Zambia	1.93
81	Cameroon	1.80
81	Costa Rica	1.80
81	Mozambique	1.80
81	Tunisia	1.80
81	Vietnam	1.80
86	Angola	1.67
86	Ethiopia	1.67
86	Nigeria	1.67
89	Honduras	1.53
89	Malawi	1.53
89	Namibia	1.53
89	Senegal	1.53
93	Bolivia	1.40
93	Dominican Republic	1.40
93	Madagascar	1.40
96	Gambia	1.27
96	Ghana	1.27
96	Nicaragua	1.27
99	Chad	1.00
99	Haiti	1.00
99	Mali	1.00
99	Zimbabwe	1.00

Source: World Economic Forum, 2003

Key Indicators

1. Total GDP, 2002

RANK	COUNTRY	GROSS DOMESTIC PRODUCT IN BILLIONS OF US DOLLARS, 2002	RANK	COUNTRY	GROSS DOMESTIC PRODUCT IN BILLIONS OF US DOLLARS, 2002
1	United States	10,445.6	52	Ukraine	41.4
2	Japan	3,992.2	53	Morocco	37.2
3	Germany	1,990.3	54	Vietnam	34.1
4	United Kingdom	1,557.2	55	Ecuador	24.5
5	France	1,422.9	56	Slovak Republic	23.7
6	China	1,237.2	57	Dominican Republic	21.8
7	Italy	1,188.0	58	Tunisia	21.3
8	Canada	727.8	59	Croatia	21.2
9	Spain	655.1	60	Slovenia	21.2
10	Mexico	641.5	61	Luxembourg	20.6
11	India	502.4	62	Guatemala	19.6
12	Korea	461.5	63	Zimbabwe	9.3
13	Brazil	448.7	64	Costa Rica	6.9
14	Netherlands	419.9	65	Sri Lanka	16.4
15	Australia	399.1	66	Bulgaria	16.2
16	Russian Federation	346.6	67	El Salvador	4.5
17	Taiwan	281.5	68	Serbia	3.0
18	Switzerland	267.5	69	Lithuania	2.7
19	Belgium	246.8	70	Kenya	1.8
20	Sweden	240.3	71	Angola	1.6
21	Austria	206.2	72	Panama	.2
22	Norway	189.7	73	Uruguay	9.9
23	Poland	189.2	74	Tanzania	.4
24	Turkey	182.8	75	Jordan	.3
25	Indonesia	173.2	76	Cameroon	3.0
26	Denmark	172.4	77	Trinidad and Tobago	.0
27	Hong Kong SAR	163.0	78	Iceland	7
28	Greece	133.2	79	Latvia	4
29	Finland	132.2	80	Bolivia	.1
30	Thailand	126.4	81	Jamaica	.8
31	Portugal	122.1	82	Paraguay	1
32	Ireland	121.8	83	Honduras	6
33	South Africa	104.8	84	Estonia	
34	Argentina	103.0	85	Ghana	
35	Israel	102.7	86	Ethiopia	
36	Malaysia	95.2	87	Uganda	
37	Venezuela	94.3	88	Senegal	
38	Singapore	90.2	89	Botswana	
39	Egypt	85.5	90	Mauritius	4.
40	Philippines	77.1	91	Madagascar	4.
41	Colombia	71.2	92	Malta	3.
42	Czech Republic	70.1	93	Mozambique	3.
43	Pakistan	65.1	94	Macedonia, FYR	3.8
44	Chile	64.5	95	Zambia	3.7
45	Hungary	64.0	96	Haiti	3.6
46	New Zealand	58.4	97	Mali	3.1
47	Peru	54.8	98	Namibia	2.9
48	Algeria	54.1	99	Nicaragua	2.6
49	Bangladesh	46.9	100	Chad	1.9
50	Romania	42.8	101	Malawi	1.9
51	Nigeria	42.7	102	Gambia	0.4

Source: IMF World Economic Outlook Database, April 2002

2. GDP per capita, 2002

RANK	COUNTRY	GROSS DOMESTIC PRODUCT PER CAPITA IN US DOLLARS, 2002	RANK	COUNTRY	GROSS DOMESTIC PRODUCT PER CAPITA IN US DOLLARS, 2002
1	Luxembourg	45,975	52	Brazil	2,568
2	Norway	42,164	53	Dominican Republic	2,538
3	Switzerland	37,150	54	Russian Federation	2,410
4	United States	36,207	55	South Africa	2,370
5	Denmark	32,524	56	El Salvador	2,233
6	Japan	31,312	57	Tunisia	2,191
7	Ireland	31,231	58	Bulgaria	2,081
8	Iceland	30,633	59	Peru	2,069
9	Sweden	27,308	60	Thailand	1,966
10	Netherlands	26,241	61	Romania	1,920
11	United Kingdom	26,084	62	Ecuador	1,871
12	Austria	25,457	63	Macedonia, FYR	1,810
13	Finland	25,428	64	Jordan	1,789
14	Germany	24,272	65	Algeria	1,724
15	Belgium	23,960	66	Guatemala	1,637
16	France	23,835	67	Colombia	1,637
17	Hong Kong SAR	23,283	68	Namibia	1,594
18	Canada	23,252	69	Zimbabwe	1,473
19	Singapore	21,486	70	Serbia	1,238
20	Italy	20,696	71	Paraguay	1,231
21	Australia	20,466	72	Egypt	1,217
22	Spain	16,419	73	Morocco	1,198
23	Israel	16,303	74	Honduras	982
24	New Zealand	15,356	75	Philippines	980
25	Greece	12,570	76	China	956
26	Taiwan	12,512	77	Bolivia	927
27	Portugal	12,210	78	Sri Lanka	851
28	Slovenia	10,607	79	Ukraine	850
29	Malta	9,969	80	Angola	837
30	Korea	9,736	81	Indonesia	796
31	Trinidad and Tobago	6,947	82	Cameroon	583
32	Czech Republic	6,807	83	Senegal	516
33	Hungary	6,465	84	Nicaragua	485
34	Mexico	6,302	85	India	483
35	Poland	4,913	86	Pakistan	438
36	Croatia	4,516	87	Haiti	427
37	Slovak Republic	4,386	88	Vietnam	425
38	Estonia	4,335	89	Kenya	369
39	Malaysia	4,137	90	Nigeria	356
40	Chile	4,132	91	Zambia	343
41	Costa Rica	4,029	92	Bangladesh	327
42	Panama	3,877	93	Ghana	300
43	Mauritius	3,778	94	Madagascar	265
44	Venezuela	3,759	95	Mali	257
45	Latvia	3,500	96	Tanzania	255
46	Lithuania	3,426	97	Gambia	251
47	Botswana	3,148	98	Uganda	236
48	Jamaica	2,991	99	Chad	231
49	Uruguay	2,907	100	Mozambique	206
50	Argentina	2,718	101	Malawi	163
51	Turkey	2,665	102	Ethiopia	91

Sources: Calculation based on GDP data from the IMF World Economic Outlook Database, April 2002 and Population data from the UNFPA State of the World Population 2002.

Part 3   Data Presentation

3. Population, 2002

RANK	COUNTRY	TOTAL POPULATION, 2002	RANK	COUNTRY	TOTAL POPULATION, 2002
1	China	1,284,530,000	52	Greece	11,018,000
2	India	1,041,846,000	53	Serbia	10,720,000
3	United States	288,368,700	54	Zambia	10,656,000
4	Indonesia	212,110,000	55	Mali	10,643,800
5	Brazil	173,879,000	56	Malawi	10,455,800
6	Pakistan	148,784,000	57	Portugal	10,409,000
7	Russian Federation	146,586,000	58	Belgium	10,336,000
8	Bangladesh	133,132,000	59	Hungary	10,122,000
9	Japan	127,530,000	60	Czech Republic	10,145,000
10	Nigeria	120,079,000	61	Tunisia	9,815,000
11	Mexico	101,877,000	62	Senegal	9,802,000
12	Germany	82,600,000	63	Sweden	8,945,000
13	Vietnam	81,248,500	64	Dominican Republic	8,707,500
14	Philippines	79,982,000	65	Bolivia	8,340,000
15	Ethiopia	67,347,000	66	Haiti	8,290,000
16	Turkey	67,272,000	67	Austria	8,151,000
17	Egypt	65,643,000	68	Chad	7,871,778
18	Thailand	61,887,000	69	Bulgaria	7,801,000
19	France	59,637,000	70	Switzerland	7,281,270
20	United Kingdom	59,088,000	71	Hong Kong SAR	6,773,000
21	Italy	56,464,000	72	Honduras	6,712,000
22	Ukraine	50,137,000	73	Israel	6,635,000
23	Korea	47,600,000	74	El Salvador	6,457,000
24	South Africa	45,454,000	75	Paraguay	5,782,000
25	Colombia	43,290,000	76	Slovak Republic	5,378,000
26	Spain	40,683,000	77	Denmark	5,374,355
27	Poland	38,609,000	78	Nicaragua	5,370,000
28	Argentina	36,600,000	79	Jordan	5,329,000
29	Tanzania	34,569,230	80	Finland	5,207,000
30	Kenya	31,930,000	81	Croatia	4,844,000
31	Canada	31,414,000	82	Norway	4,556,000
32	Algeria	31,293,000	83	Singapore	4,163,000
33	Morocco	29,643,000	84	Costa Rica	4,143,000
34	Peru	26,748,970	85	New Zealand	3,939,100
35	Venezuela	25,300,000	86	Ireland	3,931,000
36	Uganda	24,700,000	87	Lithuania	3,460,000
37	Malaysia	24,370,000	88	Uruguay	3,385,000
38	Taiwan	22,457,000	89	Panama	2,960,000
39	Romania	22,330,000	90	Jamaica	2,618,000
40	Ghana	21,674,000	91	Latvia	2,329,000
41	Australia	19,662,780	92	Macedonia, FYR	2,064,000
42	Sri Lanka	18,947,000	93	Slovenia	1,996,000
43	Mozambique	18,234,000	94	Namibia	1,875,000
44	Netherlands	16,195,000	95	Botswana	1,720,000
45	Madagascar	15,910,600	96	Gambia	1,372,000
46	Cameroon	15,752,000	97	Estonia	1,355,000
47	Chile	15,050,340	98	Trinidad and Tobago	1,301,500
48	Angola	13,937,000	99	Mauritius	1,210,492
49	Ecuador	12,941,500	100	Luxembourg	449,000
50	Guatemala	11,997,000	101	Malta	396,000
51	Zimbabwe	11,634,660	102	Iceland	288,000

Source: International Telecommunication Union, World Telecommunication Indicators database, accessed July 2003

4. Households, 2002

RANK	COUNTRY	NUMBER OF HOUSEHOLDS, 2002	
1	China	347,663,000	
2	India	192,816,000	
3	United States	108,291,000	
4	Indonesia	53,972,000	
5	Russian Federation	52,000,000	b
6	Japan	48,105,000	
7	Brazil	46,103,000	
8	Germany	38,456,000	a
9	Bangladesh	25,673,000	
10	Pakistan	24,703,000	
11	France	24,582,000	a
12	Nigeria	24,554,000	
13	United Kingdom	24,410,000	a
14	Mexico	21,800,000	a
15	Italy	21,176,000	b
16	Vietnam	16,386,000	
17	Ukraine	16,300,000	b
18	Philippines	15,967,000	
19	Thailand	15,889,000	
20	Korea	14,852,000	
21	Turkey	14,820,000	
22	Egypt	14,033,000	
23	Spain	13,548,000	a
24	Poland	13,130,100	b
25	Ethiopia	12,874,000	
26	Canada	12,105,000	
27	South Africa	10,200,000	
28	Argentina	10,106,300	a
29	Colombia	8,679,000	a
30	Australia	7,393,000	a
31	Romania	7,392,131	a
32	Netherlands	7,041,000	a
33	Tanzania	6,996,036	
34	Kenya	6,938,000	
35	Taiwan	6,818,000	
36	Peru	5,855,000	a
37	Malaysia	5,389,000	
38	Morocco	5,354,000	a
39	Venezuela	5,261,202	a
40	Uganda	5,255,319	
41	Algeria	5,000,000	a
42	Sri Lanka	4,741,000	
43	Ghana	4,463,000	
44	Sweden	4,300,000	a
45	Belgium	4,277,670	a
46	Mozambique	4,270,000	
47	Chile	4,250,000	a
48	Czech Republic	3,828,912	a
49	Hungary	3,726,000	a
50	Greece	3,600,000	a
51	Portugal	3,567,983	a
52	Dominican Republic	3,448,000	b
53	Austria	3,311,000	a
54	Madagascar	3,098,459	a
55	Switzerland	3,035,125	
56	Bulgaria	2,901,600	b
57	Ecuador	2,848,000	a
58	Angola	2,787,400	
59	Cameroon	2,765,000	a
60	Zimbabwe	2,644,200	
61	Guatemala	2,600,000	a
62	Denmark	2,466,693	
63	Malawi	2,426,000	
64	Finland	2,400,000	a
65	Serbia	2,350,000	a
66	Hong Kong SAR	2,133,700	
67	Zambia	2,080,000	
68	Tunisia	2,055,200	a
69	Norway	1,955,000	a
70	Bolivia	1,923,000	a
71	Israel	1,856,000	
72	Mali	1,756,826	
73	Slovak Republic	1,665,535	a
74	Croatia	1,623,732	b
75	Haiti	1,621,569	a
76	Chad	1,574,355	
77	Honduras	1,487,319	a
78	El Salvador	1,467,000	a
79	New Zealand	1,382,000	
80	Paraguay	1,368,204	a
81	Lithuania	1,350,335	b
82	Ireland	1,305,000	
83	Senegal	1,125,660	a
84	Uruguay	1,000,000	a
85	Latvia	998,000	a
86	Singapore	991,000	
87	Nicaragua	937,000	a
88	Costa Rica	935,273	b
89	Jordan	919,000	
90	Jamaica	727,000	
91	Panama	691,600	a
92	Slovenia	640,195	a
93	Estonia	580,000	a
94	Macedonia, FYR	561,000	b
95	Botswana	414,000	
96	Namibia	357,000	
97	Trinidad and Tobago	347,000	
98	Mauritius	310,000	
99	Gambia	175,000	
100	Luxembourg	174,775	
101	Malta	131,341	a
102	Iceland	102,000	a

Note: a=2001 data, b=2000 data
Source: International Telecommunication Union, World Telecommunication Indicators database, accessed July 2003

5. Telephone lines, 2002

RANK	COUNTRY	NUMBER OF MAIN TELEPHONE LINES IN OPERATION, 2002	
1	China	214,420,000	
2	United States	190,000,000	
3	Japan	71,149,000	
4	Germany	53,720,000	
5	India	41,420,000	
6	Brazil	38,810,000	
7	Russian Federation	35,500,000	
8	United Kingdom	35,145,000	
9	France	33,928,740	
10	Italy	27,451,950	
11	Korea	23,257,000	
12	Canada	19,962,070	
13	Turkey	18,914,860	
14	Spain	18,705,600	
15	Mexico	14,941,630	
16	Taiwan	13,099,420	
17	Poland	11,400,000	a
18	Ukraine	10,669,600	a
19	Australia	10,590,000	
20	Netherlands	10,000,000	
21	Argentina	8,009,446	
22	Colombia	7,766,000	
23	Indonesia	7,750,035	
24	Egypt	7,430,000	
25	Thailand	6,499,842	
26	Sweden	6,441,000	
27	Greece	5,607,726	a
28	Switzerland	5,335,000	
29	Belgium	5,132,427	
30	South Africa	4,895,000	
31	Malaysia	4,670,000	
32	Portugal	4,361,000	
33	Romania	4,116,000	a
34	Austria	3,988,000	
35	Czech Republic	3,860,843	a
36	Hong Kong SAR	3,842,943	
37	Denmark	3,739,247	
38	Pakistan	3,690,000	
39	Hungary	3,666,443	
40	Vietnam	3,664,752	
41	Chile	3,467,202	
42	Philippines	3,338,926	
43	Norway	3,325,000	
44	Israel	3,100,000	
45	Bulgaria	2,922,028	
46	Finland	2,850,000	
47	Venezuela	2,841,771	
48	Serbia	2,492,963	
49	Peru	2,022,265	a
50	Ireland	1,975,000	
51	Singapore	1,930,200	

RANK	COUNTRY	NUMBER OF MAIN TELEPHONE LINES IN OPERATION, 2002	
52	Algeria	1,808,000	
53	Croatia	1,779,000	
54	New Zealand	1,755,000	
55	Ecuador	1,426,188	
56	Slovak Republic	1,422,725	
57	Tunisia	1,218,000	
58	Morocco	1,127,447	
59	Costa Rica	1,037,986	
60	Dominican Republic	935,145	a
61	Uruguay	955,533	
62	Lithuania	935,899	
63	Sri Lanka	883,108	
64	Guatemala	845,968	
65	Slovenia	811,435	
66	Nigeria	700,000	
67	Latvia	701,211	
68	Jordan	687,598	
69	Bangladesh	682,000	
70	El Salvador	665,699	
71	Bolivia	565,941	
72	Macedonia, FYR	533,507	a
73	Estonia	471,000	
74	Jamaica	450,000	
75	Panama	376,499	a
76	Ethiopia	368,199	
77	Luxembourg	346,763	a
78	Kenya	328,404	
79	Mauritius	327,825	
80	Trinidad and Tobago	325,054	
81	Honduras	322,497	
82	Zimbabwe	287,654	
83	Paraguay	273,218	
84	Ghana	242,122	a
85	Senegal	224,223	
86	Malta	207,669	
87	Iceland	180,890	
88	Nicaragua	171,832	
89	Tanzania	148,454	a
90	Botswana	142,600	a
91	Haiti	130,000	
92	Namibia	117,338	a
93	Cameroon	101,412	a
94	Mozambique	89,443	a
95	Zambia	88,435	
96	Angola	85,000	
97	Malawi	73,100	
98	Madagascar	59,441	
99	Uganda	54,975	
100	Mali	49,732	
101	Gambia	38,350	
102	Chad	11,834	

Note: a=2001 data

Source: International Telecommunication Union, World Telecommunication Indicators database, accessed July 2003

6. Cellular phones, 2002

RANK	COUNTRY	NUMBER OF CELLULAR MOBILE TELEPHONE SUBSCRIBERS, 2002	RANK	COUNTRY	NUMBER OF CELLULAR MOBILE TELEPHONE SUBSCRIBERS, 2002
1	China	206,620,000	52	Ukraine	2,224,600
2	United States	140,766,800	53	Vietnam	1,902,388
3	Japan	81,118,000	54	Paraguay	1,667,018
4	Germany	59,200,000	55	Slovenia	1,667,000
5	Italy	52,316,000	56	Nigeria	1,633,060
6	United Kingdom	49,921,000	57	Lithuania	1,631,573
7	France	38,585,300	58	Guatemala	1,577,085
8	Brazil	34,881,000	59	Ecuador	1,560,861
9	Spain	33,475,000	60	Bulgaria	1,550,000
10	Korea	32,342,000	61	Jamaica	1,400,000
11	Mexico	25,928,260	62	Kenya	1,325,222
12	Taiwan	23,905,410	63	Dominican Republic	1,270,082
13	Turkey	23,374,360	64	Jordan	1,219,597
14	Russian Federation	17,668,130	65	Pakistan	1,219,000
15	Thailand	16,117,000	66	Bangladesh	1,075,000
16	Philippines	14,216,230	67	Sri Lanka	931,580
17	Poland	14,000,000	68	Latvia	917,196
18	India	12,687,640	69	El Salvador	888,818
19	Australia	12,579,000	70	Estonia	881,000
20	Netherlands	12,100,000	71	Bolivia	872,676
21	South Africa	12,081,000	72	Uruguay	652,000
22	Canada	11,849,020	73	Cameroon	563,000
23	Indonesia	11,700,000	74	Senegal	553,427
24	Greece	9,314,260	75	Costa Rica	528,047
25	Malaysia	9,245,000	76	Tunisia	503,911
26	Czech Republic	8,610,177	77	Panama	475,354
27	Portugal	8,528,900	78	Luxembourg	455,000
28	Belgium	8,135,512	79	Tanzania	426,964
29	Sweden	7,915,000	80	Botswana	415,000
30	Hungary	6,561,998	81	Ghana	405,000
31	Argentina	6,500,000	82	Algeria	400,000
32	Venezuela	6,463,561	83	Uganda	393,310
33	Chile	6,445,698	84	Trinidad and Tobago	361,911
34	Austria	6,415,000	85	Zimbabwe	353,000
35	Israel	6,334,000	86	Mauritius	350,000
36	Hong Kong SAR	6,297,541	87	Honduras	326,508
37	Morocco	6,198,670	88	Mozambique	297,000
38	Switzerland	5,734,000	89	Malta	276,859
39	Colombia	4,597,000	90	Iceland	256,000
40	Egypt	4,494,700	91	Nicaragua	239,927
41	Denmark	4,478,145	92	Macedonia, FYR	223,275
42	Finland	4,400,000	93	Madagascar	163,010
43	Romania	3,845,116	94	Namibia	150,000
44	Norway	3,842,000	95	Haiti	140,000
45	Singapore	3,295,100	96	Zambia	139,092
46	Ireland	2,969,000	97	Angola	130,000
47	Slovak Republic	2,923,383	98	Gambia	100,000
48	Serbia	2,750,397	99	Malawi	86,047
49	New Zealand	2,436,000	100	Mali	52,639
50	Peru	2,300,000	101	Ethiopia	50,369
51	Croatia	2,278,000	102	Chad	34,200

Source: International Telecommunication Union, World Telecommunication Indicators database, accessed July 2003

7. Personal computers, 2002

RANK	COUNTRY	NUMBER OF PERSONAL COMPUTERS, 2002	
1	United States	178,000,000	a
2	Japan	48,700,000	
3	Germany	35,920,940	
4	Korea	26,458,000	
5	China	25,000,000	a
6	United Kingdom	22,000,000	a
7	France	20,700,000	
8	Canada	15,300,000	
9	Italy	13,025,000	
10	Brazil	13,000,000	
10	Russian Federation	13,000,000	
12	Australia	10,000,000	a
13	Taiwan	8,887,100	
14	Mexico	6,900,000	a
14	Netherlands	6,900,000	a
16	Spain	6,800,000	a
17	India	6,000,000	a
18	Sweden	5,000,000	a
19	Switzerland	3,900,000	a
20	Malaysia	3,600,000	
21	Poland	3,300,000	a
21	South Africa	3,300,000	
23	Denmark	3,100,000	
24	Austria	3,013,000	
25	Argentina	3,000,000	
26	Turkey	2,700,000	a
27	Hong Kong SAR	2,600,000	a
28	Belgium	2,500,000	
29	Thailand	2,461,000	
30	Finland	2,300,000	
30	Indonesia	2,300,000	a
30	Norway	2,300,000	a
33	Philippines	2,200,000	
34	Colombia	2,133,000	
35	Singapore	2,100,000	a
36	Chile	1,795,814	
37	Israel	1,600,000	a
38	Czech Republic	1,500,000	a
38	Ireland	1,500,000	a
38	New Zealand	1,500,000	a
41	Venezuela	1,300,000	a
42	Peru	1,250,000	a
43	Portugal	1,210,000	a
44	Egypt	1,120,000	
45	Hungary	1,100,000	
46	Slovak Republic	970,000	
47	Ukraine	920,000	a
48	Greece	860,000	a
49	Nigeria	800,000	a
49	Romania	800,000	a
49	Vietnam	800,000	
52	Croatia	760,000	
53	Costa Rica	700,000	a
54	Pakistan	600,000	a
54	Slovenia	600,000	
54	Zimbabwe	600,000	
57	Bangladesh	450,000	
58	Bulgaria	405,000	
59	Ecuador	402,652	
60	Latvia	400,000	
60	Morocco	400,000	a
62	Lithuania	380,000	
63	Uruguay	370,000	a
64	Tunisia	300,000	
65	Serbia	290,000	
66	Estonia	285,000	
67	Sri Lanka	250,000	
68	Luxembourg	230,000	a
69	Algeria	220,000	a
70	Jordan	200,000	
70	Paraguay	200,000	
70	Senegal	200,000	
73	Bolivia	190,000	
74	Kenya	175,000	a
75	Guatemala	150,000	a
75	Nicaragua	150,000	
77	El Salvador	140,000	a
78	Iceland	130,000	
78	Jamaica	130,000	a
78	Mauritius	130,000	a
81	Tanzania	120,000	a
82	Panama	110,000	a
83	Trinidad and Tobago	103,500	
84	Ethiopia	100,000	
84	Namibia	100,000	a
86	Malta	90,000	a
87	Honduras	80,000	a
87	Zambia	80,000	
89	Ghana	70,000	a
89	Mozambique	70,000	a
89	Uganda	70,000	a
92	Botswana	65,000	a
93	Cameroon	60,000	a
94	Madagascar	40,000	a
95	Angola	27,000	
96	Gambia	17,000	a
97	Mali	14,000	a
98	Malawi	13,000	a
99	Chad	12,000	a

Note: a=2001 data
Source: International Telecommunication Union, World Telecommunication Indicators database, accessed July 2003

8. Internet users, 2001

RANK	COUNTRY	NUMBER OF INTERNET USERS (ESTIMATED), 2001	
1	United States	155,000,000	
2	China	59,100,000	
3	Japan	57,200,000	
4	Germany	35,000,000	
5	Korea	26,270,000	
6	United Kingdom	24,000,000	
7	France	18,716,000	
8	Italy	17,000,000	
9	India	16,580,000	
10	Canada	15,200,000	
11	Brazil	14,300,000	
12	Netherlands	8,590,000	
12	Taiwan	8,590,000	
14	Australia	8,400,000	
15	Indonesia	8,000,000	
16	Spain	7,856,000	
17	Malaysia	7,500,000	
18	Russian Federation	6,000,000	
19	Sweden	5,125,000	
20	Turkey	4,900,000	
21	Thailand	4,800,000	
22	Mexico	4,663,364	
23	Argentina	4,100,000	
24	Poland	3,800,000	a
25	Portugal	3,700,000	
26	Chile	3,575,000	
27	Philippines	3,500,000	
28	Belgium	3,400,000	
29	Austria	3,340,000	
30	South Africa	3,100,000	
31	Hong Kong SAR	2,918,800	
32	Finland	2,650,000	
33	Czech Republic	2,500,000	
33	Denmark	2,500,000	
35	Switzerland	2,375,000	
36	Norway	2,300,000	
37	Singapore	2,247,000	
38	Israel	2,000,000	
38	Peru	2,000,000	a
40	Colombia	1,982,000	
41	New Zealand	1,908,000	
42	Romania	1,800,000	
43	Greece	1,704,936	
44	Hungary	1,600,000	
45	Egypt	1,500,000	
45	Pakistan	1,500,000	
45	Vietnam	1,500,000	
48	Venezuela	1,274,429	
49	Ireland	1,065,000	
50	Slovak Republic	862,833	
51	Slovenia	800,000	

RANK	COUNTRY	NUMBER OF INTERNET USERS (ESTIMATED), 2001	
52	Croatia	789,000	
53	Bulgaria	700,000	
54	Serbia	640,000	
55	Ukraine	600,000	a
56	Estonia	560,000	
57	Tunisia	505,500	
58	Ecuador	503,315	
59	Algeria	500,000	
59	Kenya	500,000	a
59	Lithuania	500,000	
59	Morocco	500,000	
59	Zimbabwe	500,000	
64	Guatemala	400,000	
64	Uruguay	400,000	a
66	Costa Rica	384,000	a
67	Latvia	310,000	
68	Jordan	307,000	
69	El Salvador	300,000	
70	Bolivia	270,000	
71	Bangladesh	204,000	
72	Honduras	200,000	
72	Nigeria	200,000	
72	Sri Lanka	200,000	
75	Dominican Republic	186,000	a
76	Mauritius	180,000	
77	Iceland	175,000	
78	Luxembourg	165,000	
79	Trinidad and Tobago	138,000	
80	Panama	120,000	a
81	Senegal	105,000	
82	Jamaica	100,000	a
82	Paraguay	100,000	
82	Tanzania	100,000	a
85	Malta	99,000	a
86	Nicaragua	90,000	
87	Haiti	80,000	
88	Macedonia, FYR	70,000	a
89	Uganda	60,000	a
90	Madagascar	55,000	
91	Zambia	52,420	
92	Botswana	50,000	a
92	Ethiopia	50,000	
94	Cameroon	45,000	a
94	Namibia	45,000	a
96	Angola	41,000	
97	Ghana	40,520	a
98	Mali	32,000	
99	Mozambique	30,000	a
100	Malawi	27,000	
101	Gambia	18,000	a
102	Chad	15,000	

Note: a=2001 data
Source: International Telecommunication Union, World Telecommunication Indicators database, accessed July 2003

9. Television, 2002

RANK	COUNTRY	NUMBER OF TELEVISION RECEIVERS, 2002	
1	China	410,000,000	a
2	United States	267,000,000	a
3	Japan	100,000,000	
4	India	85,000,000	a
5	Russian Federation	79,000,000	b
6	Brazil	60,000,000	a
7	United Kingdom	57,100,000	a
8	Germany	48,300,000	a
9	France	37,500,000	a
10	Indonesia	32,000,000	a
11	Turkey	28,461,090	
12	Italy	28,300,000	b
12	Mexico	28,300,000	a
14	Ukraine	23,000,000	b
15	Spain	22,800,000	a
16	Canada	21,486,000	a
17	Pakistan	21,390,000	a
18	Thailand	18,400,000	a
19	Korea	17,000,000	a
20	Poland	16,298,000	a
21	Egypt	15,400,000	
22	Vietnam	15,109,000	a
23	Philippines	14,500,000	
24	Australia	14,168,000	a
25	Colombia	13,111,980	
26	Nigeria	12,000,000	a
27	Argentina	11,800,000	a
28	Netherlands	10,500,000	
29	Taiwan	9,960,000	
30	Sweden	8,600,000	a
31	Romania	8,500,000	b
32	South Africa	8,053,000	
33	Chile	7,868,711	
34	Bangladesh	7,850,200	
35	Belgium	5,600,000	a
36	Czech Republic	5,500,000	a
36	Greece	5,500,000	a
38	Austria	5,200,000	
39	Morocco	4,861,667	a
40	Malaysia	4,773,000	a
41	Denmark	4,600,000	a
41	Venezuela	4,600,000	a
43	Hungary	4,451,000	b
44	Portugal	4,273,000	a
45	Norway	4,000,000	a
45	Switzerland	4,000,000	a
47	Peru	3,900,000	a
48	Bulgaria	3,691,600	b
49	Finland	3,520,000	a
50	Algeria	3,500,000	a
51	Hong Kong SAR	3,390,000	a
52	Ecuador	3,061,633	
53	Serbia	3,000,000	b
54	Slovak Republic	2,200,000	a
54	Sri Lanka	2,200,000	a
56	Israel	2,150,000	a
57	New Zealand	2,131,000	a
58	Tunisia	2,000,000	a
59	Latvia	1,980,000	
60	Uruguay	1,770,000	b
61	Guatemala	1,700,000	a
62	Lithuania	1,685,000	
63	Ireland	1,515,000	a
64	Tanzania	1,500,000	a
65	El Salvador	1,490,000	a
66	Croatia	1,310,000	b
67	Singapore	1,260,000	
68	Paraguay	1,200,000	b
69	Cameroon	1,150,000	a
70	Ghana	1,100,000	a
71	Bolivia	990,000	b
72	Jamaica	971,000	a
73	Jordan	944,000	
74	Costa Rica	930,000	b
75	Kenya	812,983	a
76	Honduras	800,000	
77	Senegal	760,000	a
78	Slovenia	730,000	
79	Angola	710,000	a
80	Estonia	630,000	
81	Nicaragua	640,000	a
81	Zimbabwe	640,000	a
83	Panama	574,469	
84	Macedonia, FYR	570,000	b
85	Zambia	540,000	a
86	Namibia	504,480	
87	Trinidad and Tobago	443,000	a
88	Madagascar	390,000	a
89	Ethiopia	370,000	a
90	Mauritius	359,000	a
91	Mali	350,000	
92	Luxembourg	295,000	a
93	Uganda	275,000	a
94	Mozambique	250,000	
95	Malta	221,945	a
96	Iceland	143,000	b
97	Botswana	74,000	a
98	Haiti	50,000	a
99	Malawi	40,000	a
100	Gambia	20,000	a
101	Chad	15,000	

Note: a=2001 data, b=2000 data
Source: International Telecommunication Union, World Telecommunication Indicators database, accessed July 2003

10. Cable television, 2002

RANK	COUNTRY	NUMBER OF CABLE TELEVISION SUBSCRIBERS, 2002	
1	China	96,380,000	
2	United States	73,147,600	a
3	India	40,000,000	a
4	Japan	23,332,220	
5	Germany	21,800,000	a
6	Russian Federation	11,274,570	b
7	Korea	8,392,000	b
8	Canada	7,868,000	a
9	Netherlands	6,500,000	
10	Argentina	5,900,000	a
11	Taiwan	4,642,000	
12	United Kingdom	3,850,000	a
13	Belgium	3,814,949	a
14	Bangladesh	3,600,000	
15	Poland	3,529,448	
16	France	3,239,411	a
17	Philippines	2,940,000	
18	Romania	2,700,000	a
19	Switzerland	2,671,330	a
20	Ukraine	2,640,000	b
21	Mexico	2,487,000	a
22	Brazil	2,368,000	a
23	Sweden	2,200,000	
24	Hungary	1,592,866	a
25	Australia	1,400,000	a
26	Israel	1,221,000	
27	Portugal	1,119,342	a
28	Bulgaria	1,100,000	a
29	Denmark	1,078,483	a
30	Austria	1,076,750	
31	Finland	1,000,000	a
32	Venezuela	977,375	a
33	Czech Republic	965,000	a
34	Turkey	954,612	
35	Chile	864,024	
36	Norway	838,707	a
37	Thailand	800,000	
38	Slovak Republic	684,492	
39	Ireland	615,000	a
40	Spain	587,829	a
41	Colombia	577,112	b
42	Hong Kong SAR	563,512	a
43	Ecuador	437,638	
44	Peru	429,778	b
45	Uruguay	420,000	b
46	Slovenia	320,000	
47	El Salvador	312,000	b
48	Latvia	308,000	
49	Singapore	302,000	a
50	Lithuania	260,000	
51	Croatia	170,000	b
52	Estonia	145,000	
53	Luxembourg	138,000	a
54	Paraguay	120,000	a
55	Malta	90,091	a
56	Bolivia	80,000	b
56	Italy	80,000	a
58	Indonesia	70,000	a
59	Nigeria	59,000	a
60	Nicaragua	55,000	b
61	Honduras	50,000	b
62	Haiti	40,000	a
63	Namibia	30,000	
64	New Zealand	27,300	a
65	Pakistan	25,000	b
66	Zimbabwe	24,001	b
67	Kenya	15,000	a
68	Zambia	13,000	a
69	Angola	12,085	b
70	Tanzania	8,000	a
71	Sri Lanka	6,500	a
72	Ghana	6,000	a
72	Uganda	6,000	a
74	Jordan	1,400	b
75	Iceland	1,300	b
76	Senegal	500	a
77	Ethiopia	0	b
77	Greece	0	a
77	Malawi	0	a
77	Malaysia	0	a
77	Egypt	0	
77	South Africa	0	

Note: a=2001 data, b=2000 data
Source: International Telecommunication Union, World Telecommunication Indicators database, accessed July 2003

11. Public pay telephones, 2002

RANK	COUNTRY	NUMBER OF PUBLIC PAY PHONES, 2002	
1	China	3,462,000	a
2	United States	1,384,935	a
3	Brazil	1,378,000	a
4	India	1,092,000	a
5	Japan	714,772	b
6	Mexico	708,000	a
7	Korea	499,566	a
8	Indonesia	402,869	
9	Italy	300,000	a
10	France	213,965	a
11	Thailand	207,606	a
12	Argentina	204,329	a
13	South Africa	195,399	a
14	Russian Federation	192,800	b
15	Canada	169,626	a
16	Malaysia	163,528	a
17	United Kingdom	145,000	a
18	Taiwan	138,629	a
19	Germany	112,000	a
20	Poland	96,061	a
21	Peru	94,596	a
22	Venezuela	90,211	
23	Pakistan	83,000	
24	Australia	80,000	
25	Turkey	71,149	a
26	Greece	69,296	a
27	Ukraine	64,400	b
28	Spain	63,866	a
29	Colombia	61,309	a
30	Chile	57,465	a
31	Morocco	46,843	b
32	Romania	46,838	a
33	Egypt	45,786	
34	Portugal	45,467	a
35	Hungary	44,490	a
36	Switzerland	40,215	a
37	Guatemala	37,487	a
38	Czech Republic	34,458	a
39	Tunisia	31,613	a
40	Austria	25,300	a
41	Israel	22,000	c
41	Singapore	22,000	c
43	Bulgaria	21,512	a
44	El Salvador	18,670	a
45	Costa Rica	17,659	a
46	Netherlands	17,300	a
47	Belgium	16,736	a
48	Senegal	15,727	a
49	Philippines	15,200	a
50	Slovak Republic	15,060	a
51	Uruguay	12,578	a
52	Bolivia	12,465	a
53	Sri Lanka	12,281	a
54	Dominican Republic	12,161	b
55	Panama	11,439	a
56	Norway	10,640	b
57	Hong Kong SAR	9,683	a
58	Kenya	9,604	
59	Ireland	9,575	a
60	Finland	8,851	a
61	Paraguay	8,049	a
62	Jordan	7,851	a
63	Lithuania	7,223	a
64	Cameroon	6,555	c
65	Vietnam	6,500	a
66	Denmark	5,930	a
67	Namibia	5,300	b
68	Algeria	5,000	a
69	Nigeria	4,866	a
70	Serbia	4,673	a
71	Slovenia	4,410	a
72	Ghana	4,295	a
73	Jamaica	3,979	b
74	Ecuador	3,976	a
75	Latvia	3,845	a
76	Uganda	3,700	a
77	Zimbabwe	3,234	b
78	Nicaragua	3,208	a
79	Mozambique	3,105	a
80	Mauritius	2,981	a
81	Botswana	2,964	a
82	Trinidad and Tobago	2,595	a
83	Ethiopia	2,554	a
84	Estonia	2,531	a
85	Honduras	2,509	a
86	Mali	1,365	b
87	Bangladesh	1,128	b
88	Angola	1,110	a
89	Macedonia, FYR	1,034	b
90	Malta	874	a
91	Tanzania	592	a
92	Zambia	375	a
93	Madagascar	267	a
94	Iceland	200	a
95	Gambia	195	a
96	Malawi	171	a
97	Luxembourg	141	a
98	Chad	54	a

Note: a=2001 data, b=2000 data, c=1999 data
Source: International Telecommunication Union, World Telecommunication Indicators database, accessed July 2003

12. Household Internet penetration, 2001

RANK	COUNTRY	INTERNET ACCOUNTS AS % OF TOTAL HOUSEHOLDS, 2001
1	Singapore	140.74
2	Hong Kong SAR	84.08
3	Korea	79.15
4	Taiwan	74.54
5	Switzerland	53.63
6	Israel	52.49
7	Netherlands	52.41
8	United States	49.90
9	Austria	43.14
10	United Kingdom	39.52
11	Malaysia	37.79
12	Japan	37.25
13	Spain	34.65
14	Italy	31.43
15	Belgium	30.79
16	Germany	27.49
17	France	26.93
18	Portugal	26.36
19	Chile	17.06
20	Poland	11.26
21	Czech Republic	11.07
22	Uruguay	10.63
23	Turkey	9.61
24	Slovak Republic	8.62
25	Thailand	7.99
26	Hungary	7.85
27	Mexico	7.68
28	South Africa	7.10
29	Argentina	6.67
30	Brazil	6.66
31	Venezuela	6.01
32	Colombia	6.00
33	Panama	5.20
34	Peru	3.89
35	Costa Rica	3.81
36	Guatemala	3.80
37	China	3.75
38	Honduras	2.60
39	Philippines	2.53
40	Ecuador	2.40
41	Romania	2.20
42	Bulgaria	2.15
43	Bolivia	1.74
44	India	1.38
45	Paraguay	1.23
46	Egypt	1.18
47	Nicaragua	1.11
48	Ukraine	1.06
49	Indonesia	1.00
50	Russian Federation	0.94
51	Vietnam	0.81
52	El Salvador	0.65
53	Morocco	0.53
54	Nigeria	0.03

Source: Pyramid, 2003

13. Business Internet penetration, 2001

RANK	COUNTRY	INTERNET ACCOUNTS AS % OF TOTAL NUMBER OF BUSINESSES, 2001
1	Singapore	905.4
2	Israel	381.8
3	Austria	227.0
4	Netherlands	218.3
5	Hong Kong SAR	164.2
6	Taiwan	150.9
7	United Kingdom	137.6
8	Switzerland	137.1
9	Korea	118.2
10	Uruguay	105.4
11	Germany	97.4
12	France	96.5
13	Italy	87.2
14	Thailand	86.6
15	Spain	85.8
16	Malaysia	80.6
17	United States	69.9
18	Portugal	65.8
19	China	65.4
20	Nigeria	47.6
21	Panama	41.7
22	Morocco	39.3
23	Belgium	37.4
24	Argentina	35.5
25	South Africa	35.0
26	Slovak Republic	34.2
27	Chile	29.9
28	Guatemala	28.7
29	Brazil	25.5
30	Costa Rica	25.5
31	Romania	22.8
32	Philippines	21.9
33	Paraguay	19.5
34	Russian Federation	19.0
35	Bolivia	15.5
36	Poland	14.6
37	Colombia	13.4
38	Bulgaria	12.4
39	Japan	11.6
40	India	11.1
41	Turkey	11.1
42	Mexico	9.9
43	Czech Republic	9.7
44	El Salvador	8.9
45	Honduras	7.6
46	Vietnam	7.1
47	Ecuador	6.1
48	Nicaragua	5.1
49	Ukraine	4.5
50	Peru	4.3
51	Venezuela	4.1
52	Hungary	3.5
53	Indonesia	1.7
54	Egypt	1.6

Source: Pyramid, 2003

14. Broadband subscriber lines, 2001

RANK	COUNTRY	NUMBER OF BROADBAND SUBSCRIBERS, 2001
1	United States	12,298,613
2	Korea	8,197,290
3	United Kingdom	5,221,400
4	China	2,711,107
5	Japan	2,702,987
6	Germany	1,920,050
7	Taiwan	1,139,248
8	Netherlands	948,630
9	France	776,217
10	Belgium	661,398
11	Hong Kong SAR	633,765
12	Spain	481,977
13	Italy	442,418
14	Austria	425,145
15	Brazil	335,831
16	Singapore	166,121
17	Mexico	127,926
18	Switzerland	123,750
19	Portugal	97,452
20	Argentina	96,509
21	Chile	64,455
22	Malaysia	60,452
23	India	55,353
24	Israel	47,629
25	Czech Republic	35,450
26	Poland	34,000
27	Hungary	30,884
28	Venezuela	30,459
29	Russian Federation	23,376
30	Colombia	23,245
31	Turkey	17,902
32	Ukraine	15,032
33	Indonesia	12,804
34	Philippines	12,716
35	Slovak Republic	11,777
36	South Africa	10,550
37	Thailand	10,332
38	Peru	9,661
39	Bulgaria	9,582
40	Nigeria	7,028
41	Guatemala	5,772
42	Panama	5,100
43	El Salvador	5,031
44	Uruguay	4,000
45	Bolivia	3,951
46	Romania	2,200
47	Costa Rica	1,950
48	Paraguay	1,800
49	Nicaragua	1,600
50	Ecuador	1,269
51	Vietnam	393
52	Morocco	266
53	Egypt	189

Source: Pyramid, 2003

15. Broadband penetration, 2001

RANK	COUNTRY	BROADBAND SUBSCRIBERS AS % OF TOTAL POPULATION, 2001
1	Korea	1?.19
2	Hong Kong SAR	?.42
3	United Kingdom	?.71
4	Belgium	6.45
5	Netherlands	5.94
6	Austria	5.20
7	Taiwan	5.09
8	United States	4.32
9	Singapore	4.?5
10	Germany	2.?4
11	Japan	2.?3
12	Switzerland	1.?0
13	France	1.?0
14	Spain	1.?0
15	Portugal	0.?7
16	Italy	0.?
17	Israel	0.?
18	Chile	0.?
19	Czech Republic	0.3?
20	Hungary	0.3
21	Argentina	0.2?
22	Malaysia	0.2
23	Slovak Republic	0.2
24	China	0.2
25	Brazil	0.19
26	Panama	0.18
27	Mexico	0.13
28	Venezuela	0.12
29	Bulgaria	0.12
30	Uruguay	0.12
31	Poland	0.09
32	El Salvador	0.08
33	Colombia	0.05
34	Costa Rica	0.05
35	Guatemala	0.05
36	Bolivia	0.05
37	Peru	0.04
38	Paraguay	0.03
39	Ukraine	0.03
40	Nicaragua	0.03
41	Turkey	0.03
42	South Africa	0.02
43	Thailand	0.02
44	Russian Federation	0.02
45	Philippines	0.02
46	Ecuador	0.01
47	Romania	0.01
48	Indonesia	0.01
49	Nigeria	0.01
50	India	0.01

Source: Pyramid, 2003

16. B2C e-commerce, 2002

RANK	COUNTRY	VALUE IN US DOLLARS, 2002
1	United States	79,856,747,389
2	Japan	12,773,329,698
3	United Kingdom	8,696,991,265
4	Germany	8,458,448,757
5	Canada	6,936,429,552
6	Korea	6,597,874,674
7	Australia	4,390,914,799
8	France	4,076,098,578
9	Italy	3,084,490,569
10	China	2,693,375,225
11	Taiwan	1,726,237,028
12	Spain	1,645,216,624
13	Netherlands	1,560,213,683
14	Sweden	1,416,580,215
15	Switzerland	1,125,506,078
16	Hong Kong SAR	855,115,917
17	Norway	822,906,787
18	Austria	805,550,289
19	Brazil	752,639,814
20	Singapore	733,665,345
21	Denmark	699,398,211
22	Finland	680,121,522
23	South Africa	626,600,000
24	Belgium	540,503,390
25	New Zealand	422,046,377
26	Malaysia	417,031,955
27	Ireland	327,465,234
28	Philippines	285,386,222
29	Portugal	254,952,880
30	Greece	250,832,758
31	Indonesia	233,322,891
32	Thailand	200,201,727
33	Argentina	189,594,191
34	Mexico	179,252,419
35	Poland	135,945,676
36	Israel	118,000,000
37	Czech Republic	80,849,900
38	Chile	52,632,099
39	India	48,572,065
40	Russian Federation	40,491,030
41	Hungary	40,236,576
42	Venezuela	37,993,873
43	Turkey	35,000,000
44	Colombia	25,223,282
45	Slovenia	16,169,912
46	Bulgaria	16,010,515
47	Romania	11,730,419
48	Egypt	8,674,000
49	Slovak Republic	4,211,257
50	Vietnam	3,720,186
51	Croatia	1,887,675

Source: IDC and the World Bank, 2003

17. B2B e-commerce, 2002

RANK	COUNTRY	VALUE IN US DOLLARS, 2002
1	United States	305,034,013,703
2	Japan	121,926,898,348
3	Germany	69,912,466,926
4	United Kingdom	43,536,006,463
5	France	30,482,073,010
6	Canada	29,184,780,122
7	Italy	25,782,401,963
8	Korea	14,840,146,368
9	Taiwan	12,035,665,167
10	Australia	11,859,950,670
11	Spain	10,999,047,414
12	Netherlands	10,603,173,493
13	China	9,657,030,855
14	Sweden	9,060,663,515
15	Switzerland	8,786,150,296
16	Denmark	6,479,890,365
17	Belgium	5,839,729,758
18	Austria	5,522,590,911
19	Brazil	5,424,351,687
20	Norway	5,343,710,083
21	Mexico	5,321,678,830
22	Singapore	3,844,242,866
23	Finland	3,724,608,336
24	Hong Kong SAR	2,531,445,039
25	South Africa	2,506,400,000
26	India	2,092,621,166
27	Greece	1,854,600,742
28	Poland	1,788,379,341
29	Ireland	1,763,625,958
30	New Zealand	1,726,047,125
31	Portugal	1,669,069,274
32	Chile	1,595,999,623
33	Venezuela	1,190,839,594
34	Russian Federation	1,001,864,931
35	Malaysia	982,122,190
36	Colombia	894,392,145
37	Indonesia	767,891,570
38	Czech Republic	745,504,789
39	Argentina	715,108,305
40	Thailand	700,075,733
41	Philippines	614,015,544
42	Israel	603,200,000
43	Hungary	528,628,347
44	Turkey	85,000,000
45	Romania	36,791,779
46	Egypt	34,696,000
47	Croatia	23,087,309
48	Slovak Republic	21,601,191
49	Vietnam	10,033,218
50	Slovenia	8,950,765
51	Bulgaria	2,517,782

Source: IDC and the World Bank, 2003

18. ICT spending, 2001

RANK	COUNTRY	VALUE IN US DOLLARS, 2001
1	United States	546,680,536,828
2	Japan	188,011,945,077
3	Germany	98,260,222,945
4	United Kingdom	91,355,793,169
5	France	81,221,001,801
6	Canada	39,629,720,308
7	Italy	32,450,297,469
8	Netherlands	23,987,974,805
9	China	22,591,207,608
10	Australia	19,288,806,323
11	Brazil	18,328,205,806
12	Sweden	17,487,485,935
13	Switzerland	17,025,204,573
14	Korea	16,173,613,981
15	Spain	15,180,153,055
16	Belgium	11,956,000,408
17	Denmark	10,258,428,196
18	Austria	8,891,974,702
19	Mexico	8,404,813,899
20	Norway	7,626,404,143
21	India	7,130,865,891
22	South Africa	6,975,398,787
23	Taiwan	6,633,776,395
24	Finland	6,630,368,648
25	Russian Federation	5,256,654,462
26	Singapore	4,898,681,945
27	Hong Kong SAR	4,234,935,557
28	Israel	4,191,513,674
29	Poland	4,031,168,573
30	Argentina	4,012,026,326
31	New Zealand	3,380,548,405
32	Ireland	3,365,305,486
33	Portugal	3,269,653,564
34	Malaysia	2,809,403,841
35	Czech Republic	2,722,340,910
36	Greece	2,381,169,789
37	Colombia	2,188,861,581
38	Venezuela	2,071,936,370
39	Hungary	1,957,806,502
40	Turkey	1,955,093,729
41	Thailand	1,941,127,682
42	Chile	1,704,155,336
43	Philippines	1,467,778,807
44	Indonesia	1,228,494,005
45	Egypt	1,045,994,855
46	Slovak Republic	683,955,356
47	Slovenia	490,030,601
48	Romania	416,292,685
49	Vietnam	414,778,471
50	Bulgaria	269,064,533

Source: IDC and the World Bank, 2003

19. PC units in business/government, 2001

RANK	COUNTRY	INSTALLED BASE OF PC UNITS IN THE BUSINESS & GOVERNMENT MARKETS, 2001
1	United States	129,868,318
2	Japan	22,791,100
3	China	17,295,121
4	Germany	12,762,242
5	Canada	9,091,336
6	United Kingdom	8,906,137
7	Brazil	7,947,101
8	France	7,683,140
9	Australia	7,586,12
10	Korea	5,366,09
11	Mexico	5,118,69
12	Russian Federation	4,387,11
13	India	3,874,222
14	Italy	3,574,839
15	South Africa	3,395,215
16	Spain	2,748,719
17	Taiwan	2,427,51
18	Poland	2,352,513
19	Netherlands	2,284,86
20	Malaysia	2,196,17
21	Argentina	1,958,817
22	Sweden	1,943,955
23	Indonesia	1,906,77
24	Switzerland	1,757,03
25	Thailand	1,610,32
26	Hong Kong SAR	1,446,84
27	Norway	1,284,970
28	Singapore	1,274,419
29	Denmark	1,178,162
30	Turkey	1,153,483
31	Belgium	1,126,853
32	Philippines	1,119,634
33	Israel	1,118,077
34	Austria	1,045,132
35	Czech Republic	926,787
36	New Zealand	901,419
37	Chile	890,099
38	Finland	887,838
39	Venezuela	822,201
40	Colombia	787,960
41	Portugal	780,419
42	Hungary	714,312
43	Vietnam	664,517
44	Greece	586,178
45	Ireland	568,905
46	Egypt	454,441
47	Romania	342,149
48	Slovenia	268,499
49	Slovak Republic	258,134
50	Bulgaria	205,527

Source: IDC and the World Bank, 2003

List of Authors

Scott Beardsley

Scott Beardsley is a director in McKinsey & Company's Brussels office. He is a global leader of McKinsey's telecommunications practice, has led the European wireline practice for five years, and is currently leading a special initiative on broadband. Prior to joining McKinsey, Mr Beardsley was an editor and marketing manager at the Sloan Management Review; he has also worked in strategic sales and product marketing for the semiconductor industry's Advanced Micro Devices and Analog Devices. Mr Beardsley was recently honored as a Fellow at the Institut d'Administration et de Gestion at the Université Catholique de Louvain in Belgium for outstanding contributions to management, and is a guest lecturer at the Business School. He was a Henry S. Dupont III Scholar (highest honors) at the Massachusetts Institute of Technology (MIT) Sloan School of Management where he graduated with an MBA in corporate strategy and marketing, and he holds a BSc in electrical engineering, magna cum laude, from Tufts University where he was a Kodak Scholar, elected a member of Tau Beta Pi, and was president of Eta Kappa Nu.
e-mail: scott_beardsley@mckinsey.com

Ingo Beyer von Morgenstern

Dr Ingo Beyer von Morgenstern holds a PhD in process engineering from the Technical University in Munich and an MBA from INSEAD, Fontainebleau. After working in North America, he later joined McKinsey Munich in 1985. He leads McKinsey's European High Tech Practice and co-leads its Global High Tech Practice; in these positions he serves clients in computer and data communications, industrial electronics, and aerospace and defense on strategic, operational, and organizational projects. The main focus of his work is value creation, profit improvement, governance, and growth. He lectures regularly at the physics department of the Technical University in Munich.
e-mail: Ingo_Beyer_von_Morgenstern@mckinsey.com

Soumitra Dutta

Dr Soumitra Dutta is the Roland Berger Professor of Business and Technology and Dean for Executive Education at INSEAD. He is also the faculty director of eLab, INSEAD's initiative in building a center of excellence in teaching and research in the digital economy (http://elab.insead.edu/). Prior to joining the faculty of INSEAD, he was employed with Schlumberger in Japan and General Electric in the United States. Professor Dutta obtained his PhD in computer science and his MS in business administration from the University of California at Berkeley.

Dr Dutta's research and consulting have focused on the interrelationships between innovation, technology strategy, and organizational design. His most recent book is entitled, *The Global Information Technology Report: Readiness for the Networked World* (Oxford University Press, January 2003). Previous works include, *The Bright Stuff: How Innovative People and Technology Can Make the Old Economy New* (Financial Times/Prentice Hall 2002), *Embracing the Net: Get.Competitive* (Financial Times/Prentice Hall 2001), and *Process Reengineering, Organizational Change and Performance Improvement* (Mc-Graw Hill 1999). In addition, he has published more than 50 articles in leading international journals.

A Fellow of the World Economic Forum, Dr Dutta has won several awards for research and pedagogy. His research has been showcased in prominent international media and he has also been the project leader in a number of high-impact global research projects. He has taught in and consulted with leading international corporations across the world. His personal URL is: http://www.insead.edu/facultyresearch/tm/dutta/.
e-mail: Soumitra.Dutta@insead.edu

Luis Enriquez

Luis Enriquez is an associate principal in McKinsey & Company's London office. He has extensive experience serving cable, mobile, and fixed operators in the telecommunications industry in the United States, Europe, and Latin America. He is one of the practice's global regulatory experts, and has led McKinsey's regulatory knowledge initiative. Prior to McKinsey, Mr Enriquez worked extensively in regulation both in the United States and Latin America, and assisted Eastern European governments with liberalization and European Union accession issues. Mr Enriquez holds a BA in economics magna cum laude from Harvard University and has done doctoral work in economics at the University of California at Berkeley.
e-mail: Luis_Enriques@mckinsey.com

José María Figueres-Olsen

José María Figueres-Olsen is the Co-Chief Executive Officer of the World Economic Forum. Under his leadership, the World Economic Forum has greatly expanded its offerings for its members and communities, actively engaging actors from business, politics, academia, and civil society in examining, understanding, and addressing many of the key issues that affect the world.

During his political career he served in positions of leadership, including that of president of Costa Rica from 1994 until 1998. During his presidency, he ushered the incorporation of the principles of sustainable development into Costa Rica's development platform, while stressing the importance of maintaining and enhancing sound macroeconomic and human development policies. In the international arena, he was the proponent of the Central American Alliance for Sustainable Development, signed by regional heads of state in late 1994. Prior to becoming president, he served as director of the Costa Rican Railways, as well as Minister of Trade and Minister of Agriculture for Costa Rica. Former President Figueres has a keen interest in issues pertaining to the environment and access to information technology in the developing world. Outside of his official duties at the World Economic Forum, he currently holds leadership roles in major international organizations and initiatives. Among his multiple appointments, he serves as the personal representative of the United Nations Secretary General on issues pertaining to technology and the digital divide, as well as senior advisor of the Global Environment Facility of The World Bank. Additionally, he chairs the United Nations Information and Communication Technologies Task Force and is a board member of the Digital Nations Consortium, a project launched by the Media Lab at MIT.

A recipient of numerous major awards and distinctions, he is a graduate of the United States Military Academy at West Point and the John F. Kennedy School of Government at Harvard University, where he was a Mason Fellow.
e-mail: Jose-Maria_Figueres@weforum.org.

Amit Jain

Amit Jain is the research program manager for the Global Information Technology Project with the World Economic Forum at INSEAD. He has worked at INSEAD on various research projects in information and communication technology and knowledge management, and has been the technical director of INSEAD Online, INSEAD's e-learning effort. Prior to joining INSEAD, he worked with Schlumberger in the Middle East and pursued several entrepreneurial opportunities in information technology. Mr Jain obtained his MBA from INSEAD, and a bachelor of technology degree in mechanical engineering from the Indian Institute of Technology.
e-mail: Amit.Jain@insead.edu

Bruno Lanvin

At the World Bank, Bruno Lanvin is the manager of the Information for Development Programme (*info*Dev), a multidonor program focusing on extending digital opportunities for all (see http://www.infodev.org) So far, *info*Dev has financed more than 170 projects in some 85 countries around the world. In 2000, Mr Lanvin was appointed Executive Secretary of DOT Force, the G-8 initiative launched by the Okinawa Summit of July 2000 to bridge the digital divide (see http://www.dotforce.org). The World Bank recruited him in September 2000 to be senior advisor for e-commerce and e-government. Prior to these appointments, he was Head of Electronic Commerce in the United Nations Conference on Trade and Development (UNCTAD) in Geneva. Mr Lanvin has spent 20 years in the United Nations system and has occupied various senior positions, including management from 1999–2000 of UNCTAD's component of the United Nations "Development Account," which was devoted to e-commerce and development. In this position he organized a series of regional and interregional workshops on e-commerce, allowing more than 2,000 representatives from governments and enterprises to exchange experience and best practices in the area of e-commerce. A frequent keynote speaker and participant in international conferences on the "new economy," he has published a large number of articles and books on ICT and development. He was the main drafter, team leader, and editor of *Building Confidence: Electronic Commerce and Development*, published in January 2000 (http://www.unctad.org/ecommerce). Bruno Lanvin has worked in more than 60 countries. He holds a BA in mathematics and physics from the University of Valenciennes (France), an MBA from Ecole des Hautes Etudes Commerciales (HEC) in Paris, and a PhD in economics from the Université of Paris I (La Sorbonne) in France. His mother tongue is French and he speaks and writes English and Spanish; he also has a working knowledge of Italian, Portuguese, and Russian.
e-mail: blanvin@worldbank.org.

Fiona Paua

Fiona Paua is an economist with the Global Competitiveness Programme at the World Economic Forum and the co-editor of the Global Information Technology Report series. Previously, she was Vice President and the Country Head of Research for Citibank Philippines and a financial analyst at Goldman Sachs in the United States, Hong Kong, and Singapore. She has also served in various capacities at several institutions including the World Bank and the United States Agency for International Development, and worked on

ICT policy-related projects at Harvard University. She is the co-founder of b2bpricenow.com, winner of the 2001 Development Marketplace Award of the World Bank. Ms Paua is a graduate of Dartmouth College and Harvard University.
e-mail: Fiona.Paua@weforum.org.

Petri Rouvinen

Petri Rouvinen is a research director at ETLA, The Research Institute of the Finnish Economy. He holds a PhD in economics from Vanderbilt University as well as several other degrees. His research interests include ICT and technology in general, innovation, R&D, globalization, competitiveness, and economic policy. He has recently participated in international ICT-related projects at OECD and UNU/WIDER has served as a referee for several scholarly journals, such as *Economics of Innovation and New Technology* and *Journal of Economic Behavior and Organization*. Mr Rouvinen has also been a consultant for The Ministry of Trade and Industry in Finland (Business Environment Policy in the New Economy), DG Enterprise (Competitiveness Report 2003: ICT and Reorganization) and World Bank (Knowledge Economies in EU Accession Countries). He has published many books and contributed to several collective volumes by well-known publishers. His academic work has been published in *Applied Economics Letters*, *Economics of Innovation and New Technology*, *Information Economics and Policy*, and *Journal of Applied Economics*, among others. Mr Rouvinen currently heads a major national project on entrepreneurship.
e-mail: pro@etla.fi

Christine Zhen-Wei Qiang

Christine Zhen-Wei Qiang is an economist at the Global ICT Department at the World Bank. Her main responsibilities include ICT policy and strategy development, design and preparation, and supervision of information infrastructure projects. She has written and published a number of articles on ICT and development, with a focus on policy. She was the author of the ICT chapter in *China and the Knowledge Economy: Seizing the 21st Century* (World Bank 2001) and co-authored the chapter "Liberalization, Investment and Beyond—An ICT Reform Agenda for Universal Access and the Networked Economy" in *Issues in Telecommunications Development III* (ITU, forthcoming) and *Investment and Growth of the Information Infrastructure: Summary Results of a Global Survey* (Telecom Policy 2000). Ms Qiang holds a PhD in economics and an MSE in computer science and engineering from the Johns Hopkins University.
e-mail: cqiang@worldbank.org

Walter Verbeke

Walter Verbeke is an engagement manager in McKinsey & Company's Brussels office, and is affiliated to the McKinsey Telecom and Media Practice. He has extensive experience serving telecommunications, media, and cable clients. He is one of the practice's global regulatory experts and has been involved in several knowledge initiatives. Prior to joining McKinsey, Mr Verbeke worked in the telecom industry, where he served telecommunications and cable operators during the liberalization of the markets in Europe. Mr Verbeke holds a master in law and complementary studies in economics at the University of Antwerp (Belgium).
e-mail: Walter_Verbeke@mckinsey.com.

Pekka Ylä-Anttila

Pekka Ylä-Anttila is research director at ETLA (The Research Institute of the Finnish Economy) and managing director of Etlatieto Ltd (a project research and information services unit of ETLA). He has authored and co-authored some 25 books and dozens of articles in the fields of competitiveness analysis, industrial and technology policies, industrial economics, technological change, and internationalization of business. A participant in international ICT-related projects at OECD and UNU/WIDER, Mr Ylä-Anttila is also a team leader of ETLA–BRIE (Berkeley Roundtable on the International Economy at the University of California, Berkeley), a collaborative research program on wireless economy. From 1984–1992, he served as Executive Committee member of EARIE (European Association for Research in Industrial Economics) and from 1996–2002 was a member of the Scientific Advisory Board of Statistics Finland (Central Statistical Office). Mr Ylä-Anttila was also the director of the major cluster study program, Advantage Finland: the Future of Finnish Industries conducted between 1992 and 1995. He was the main advisor for the Ministry of Trade and Industry in preparing National Industrial Strategy for Finland in 1992 and 1993 and a consultant in industrial and innovation policy guidelines in 2001. Mr Ylä-Anttila earned his BSc degree in 1970, MSc in economics in 1973, and LicSc in economics in 1987, all from the Helsinki School of Economics.
e-mail: Pekka.Yla-Anttila@etla.fi

List of Partner Institutes

Algeria

Centre de Recherche en Economie Appliquée pour le Développement (CREAD)

Professor Yassine Ferfera

Angola

SOF—Serviços de Organização e Finanças

Marcolino Meireles, Manager

Manuel José Alves Da Rocha, Consultant

Emil Moreso Grion, Consultant

Argentina

IAE—Universidad Austral

Marcelo Paladino, Research Director

Alberto Willi, Research Assistant

Australia

Business Council of Australia

Katie Lahey, Chief Executive

Melinda Ciento, Chief Economist

Austria

WIFO—Austrian Institute of Economic Research

Professor Karl Aiginger, Deputy Director

Bangladesh

Centre for Policy Dialogue (CPD)

Dr Debapriya Bhattacharya, Executive Director

Dr Uttam Kumar Deb, Research Fellow

Kazi Mahmudur Rahman, Research Associate

Belgium

Vlerick Leuven Gent Management School

Professor Dr Lutgart Van den Berghe, Executive Director, Chairman Competence Centre—Entrepreneurship, Governance & Strategy

Harry Bowen, Professor, Economics and International Business

Lucy Amez, Research Assistant

Bolivia

Universidad Catolica Boliviana

Lic. Marcela A. De Guzman, Directora, Depto. Economia

Botswana

Botswana Institute for Development Policy Analysis (BIDPA)

Dr N.H. Fidzani, Executive Director

Kedikilwe P. Maroba, Programme Coordinator

Brazil

Fundação Dom Cabral

Professor Carlos Arruda, Associate Dean for Development

Fabiana Santos

Bulgaria

Center for Economic Development

Anelia Damianova, PhD, Senior Expert

Cameroon

Centre d'Etudes et de Recherches en Economie et Gestion

Professor Seraphin Magloire Fouda, Director

Canada

Institute for Competitiveness and Prosperity

Roger Martin, Dean of the Rotman School of Management, University of Toronto and Chairman of the Institute for Competitiveness and Prosperity

James Milway, Executive Director of the Institute for Competitiveness and Prosperity

Chad

Groupe de Recherches Alternatives et de Monitoring du Projet Pétrole-Tchad-Cameroun (GRAMP-TC)

Professor Gilbert Maoundonodji, Director

Chile

Universidad Adolfo Ibañez

Andres Allamand Zavala, Dean of the School of Government

Victoria Hurtado Larrain, Academic Coordinator of the School of Government

China

Institute of Economics Systems and Management

State Council Office for Restructuring Economic Systems

Chen Li, Executive Deputy Director

Dr Gao Shi-Ji, Deputy Director for Research

Zhou Mei, Assistant Fellow

Colombia

National Planning Department

María Isabel Agudelo

Fernando J. Estupiñan V.

Croatia

National Competitiveness Council

Mira Lenardic, Secretary General

Ivana Cesljas, Advisor

Czech Republic

CMC—Graduate School of Business

Peter Loewenguth, President

Professor Jaroslav A. Jirasek, Honorary Dean

Denmark

Copenhagen Business School

Heather Alison Hazard, Associate Professor, Program Director, Vice President for International Affairs

Mette Reerbirk, Programme Administrator

Ecuador

Escuela Superior Politecnica del Litoral (ESPOL)

Escuela de Postgrado en Administracion de Empresas (ESPAE)

Virginia Lasio, Acting Director

Karina Astudillo, Project Assistant

Egypt

Egyptian Center for Economic Studies

Dr Ahmed Galal, Executive Director

Estonia

Estonian Chamber of Commerce and Industry

Siim Raie, Director General

Ethiopia

Ethiopian Economic Association/Ethiopian Economic Policy Research Institute

Berhanu Nega, Director

Kibre Moges, Senior Researcher

Worku Gebeyehu, Assistant Researcher

Finland

ETLA—The Research Institute of the Finnish Economy

Pentti Vartia, President

Pekka Ylä-Anttila, Managing Director

Petri Rouvinen, Research Director

France

HEC School of Management—Paris

Bernard Ramanantsoa, Professor, Dean of HEC School of Management

Bertrand Moingeon, Professor, Associate Dean for Executive Education

Gambia

Gambia Economic and Social Development
Research Institute (GESDRI)

Makaireh A. Njie, Director

Germany

Wissenschaftliche Hochschule für
Unternehmensführung Koblenz

WHU—Otto Beisheim Graduate School of
Management

Professor Michael Frenkel

Ghana

The International Institute for IT (INIIT)

Professor Clement Dzidonu, President and
Senior Research Fellow

Eliza Sam, Projects Officer

Greece

Federation of Greek Industries

Antonis Tortopidis, Co-ordinator, Research
and Analysis

Theodora Aivazoglou, Economist, Research
and Analysis

Haiti

SOGEBANK—Société Général Haïtienne de
Banque S.A.

Claude Pierre-Louis, General Manager

Pierre-Marie Boisson, Chief Economist

Reginald Saint-Fleur, Economist

Hong Kong SAR

The Hong Kong General Chamber
of Commerce

David O'Rear, Chief Economist

Federation of Hong Kong Industries

Alexandra Poon, Director

Hungary

Kopint-Datorg, Economic Research

Dr Éva Palócz, Deputy General Director

Ágnes Nagy, Project Manager

Iceland

ICETEC

Hallgrimur Jonasson, General Director

India

Confederation of Indian Industry

Tarun Das, Director General

Indonesia

LP3E-Kadin Indonesia

Dr Tulus Tambunan

Ireland

Department of Economics, University
College of Cork

Dr Eleanor Doyle

Rosemary Kelleher

Niall O'Sullivan

Bernadette Power

Israel

Manufacturers Association of Israel,
Foreign Trade and International Relations
Division

Moshe Nahum, Director

Italy

SDA Bocconi

Claudio Dematté, Full Professor of Strategic
Management and Entrepreneurship
Bocconi University—SDA Bocconi

Paola Dubini, Associate Professor Strategic
Management and Entrepreneurship
Bocconi University—SDA Bocconi

Elena Grassi, Research Assistant, SDA
Bocconi

Jamaica

Private Sector Organisation of Jamaica (PSOJ)

Greta Bogues, Chief Executive Officer
Mona School of Business at the University
of the West Indies (MSB)

Gordon Shirley, Professor

Japan

Hitotsubashi University Graduate School of
International Corporate Strategy (ICS)

Hirotaka Takeuchi, Dean

Jordan

Ministry of Planning, Competitiveness Unit

Naseem Al-Rahahleh, Director

Kenya

Institute of Policy Analysis and Research
(IPAR)

Dr T. Nzioki Kibua, Executive Director

John Omiti, Senior Research Fellow and
Coordinator, Real Sector

R. Njeri Chacha, Resource Centre Manager

Korea

Korea Development Institute

Dr Cho Byung-Koo, Chief of Information
and Computing Center

Latvia

Institute of Economics, Latvian Academy of
Sciences, Riga

Dr Raite Karnite, Director

Lithuania

Statistikos Tyrimai—Statistical Surveys,
Vilnius

Benonas Miksas, Director

Luxembourg

Chamber of Commerce of the Grand Duchy
of Luxembourg

Carlo Thelen, Member of the Management
Committee

Macedonia, FYR

National Entrepreneurship and
Competitiveness Council

Ilija Filipovski, Minister of Economy,
Co-Chairman of the Council

Svetozar Janevski, CEO, "Pivara," Skopje,
Co-Chairman of the Council

Madagascar

University of Antananarivo

Pépé Andrianomanana, Director, Centre of
Economic Studies

Malawi

Malawi Investment Promotion Agency

Alick C.E. Sukasuka, Director of Operations

Malaysia

Institute of Strategic and International
Studies (ISIS)

Tan Sri Dato'
Dr Mohamed Noordin Sopiee, Chairman
and Chief Executive Officer

Mali

Groupe de Recherche en Economie
Appliquée et Théorique (GREAT)

Massa Coulibaly, Coordinator

Malta

Foundation for National Competitiveness

Dr John C. Grech, President

Adrian Said, Chief Coordinator

Wilfred Kenely, Policy and Programs
Coordinator

Dr Jennifer Cassingena Harper,
International Relations Coordinator

Mauritius

Joint Economic Council of Mauritius

Raj Makoond, Director

Mexico

Ministry of the Economy

Dr Eduardo J. Solis Sanchez, Chief of the Office for the Co-ordination of International Trade and Investment Promotion

Lic. Veronica Orendain De Los Santos, Assistant in the Office for the Co-ordination of International Trade and Investment Promotion

Center for Intellectual Capital and Competitiveness

Dr Rene Villarreal, President

Dra Rocio Ramos de Villarreal, Vice-President

Mexican Institute of Competitiveness (IMCO)

Valentín Díez Morodo, Chairman of the Board and President

Emilio Carrillo Gamboa, Secretary

Morocco

Université Hassan II

Fouzi Mourji, Professor of Economics

Mozambique

EconPolicy Research Group, Lda

Dr Peter Coughlin, Partner

Professor Dr Paulo N. Mole, Partner

Namibia

Namibian Economic Policy Research Unit

Dr Christoph Stork, Senior Researcher

Antony N. Masarakufa, Researcher

Netherlands

Erasmus Strategic Renewal Center, Erasmus University Rotterdam

Professor Frans A. J. van den Bosch

Professor Henk W. Volberda

New Zealand

Business New Zealand

Anne Knowles, Executive Director

Nigeria

Nigerian Economic Summit Group (NESG)

Chris Onyemenam, Director, Operations and Administration

Dr Felix Ogbera, Associate Director, Research

Mayowa Obilade, Research Consultant

Norway

Norwegian School of Management BI, Centre for Value Creation

Dr Erik W. Jakobsen, Associate Professor

Dr Torger Reve, Professor

Anne Fossum, Analyst

Pakistan

Pakistan Institute of Development Economics

Dr A.R. Kemal

Paraguay

Centro de Analisis y Difusion de Economia Paraguaya (CADEP)

Fernando Masi, Director

Dionisio Borda, Research Member

Nelson Aguilera Alfred, Research Member

Peru

Centro de Desarrollo Industrial (CDI)— Sociedad Nacional de Industrias

Luis Tenorio, Executive Director

Néstor Asto, Project Director

Philippines

Makati Business Club

Guillermo M. Luz, Executive Director

Marc P. Opulencia, Deputy Director

Michael B. Mundo, Chief Economist

Poland

Warsaw School of Economics

Professor Bogdan Radomski, Associate Professor

Portugal

PROFORUM, Associação Para o Desenvolvimento da Engenharia

Ilídio António de Ayala Serôdio, Member of the Board of Directors

Romania

Romanian Economics Society (SOREC)

Professor Daniel Daianu; President SOREC, Professor of Economics, Academy of Economic Studies Bucharest

Dr Liviu Voinea, Senior Lecturer, Romanian-American University

Dragos N. Pislaru, Research Fellow, Romanian Center for Economic Policies

Russian Federation

Bauman Technical University (BMSTU)

Dr Alexei Prazdnitchnyk, Project Coordinator, BMSTU Russian Regional Competitiveness Survey Project

Institute for Private Sector Development and Socio-Economic Analysis (IPSSA)

Irina Evseyeva

Stockholm School of Economics in Saint Petersburg

Professor Carl F. Fey, Associate Dean of Research

Dr Igor Dukeov, Research Fellow

Senegal

Centre de Recherches Economiques Appliquées (CREA)

Abdoulaye Diagne, Director

Dr Gaye Daffé, Scientific Coordinator

Serbia

Serbia National Competitiveness Council

Dragoljub Vukadinovic, Chairman

Goran Pitic, Member of the Executive Committee

Professor Boris Begovic, Member of the Executive Committee

Singapore

Economic Development Board

Shirley Chen, Assistant Managing Director, Corporate Services

Slovak Republic

Business Alliance of Slovakia (PAS)

Robert Kicina, Project Manager

Institute for Economic and Social Reforms (INEKO)

Eugen Jurzyca, Director

Slovenia

Institute for Economic Research
Dr Peter Stanovnik, Director
Dr Mateja Drnovšek, Faculty of Economics
Professor Aleš Vahčič, Faculty of Economics

South Africa

Business South Africa
Ben Van Der Ross, Chief Executive Officer
Friede Dowie, Secretary General

Spain

IESE Business School-Anselmo Rubiralta
Center for Globalization and Strategy
Professor Eduardo Ballarín
María Luisa Blázquez, Research Associate

Sri Lanka

Institute of Policy Studies
Indika Siriwardena, Database Manager

Sweden

Stockholm School of Economics, Institute
of International Business
Professor Örjan Sölvell

Switzerland

University of St. Gallen
Professor Dr Franz Jaeger, Director,
Research Institute for Empirical Economics
and Economic Policy

Taiwan

Council for Economic Planning and
Development
Economic Research Department
Dr C.Y. Hu, Director
Chung-Chung Shieh, Researcher

Tanzania

Economic and Social Research Foundation
Professor Haidari Amani, Executive Director
John Ulanga, Coordinator, Commissioned
Studies Department
Moses Msuya, Research Assistant,
Commissioned Studies Department

Thailand

National Economic and Social Development
Board
Arkhom Termpittayapaisith, Senior Advisor
in Policy and Planning

Trinidad and Tobago

University of the West Indies: Institute
of Business
Dr Rolph Balgobin, Executive Director
Vashti G. Guyadeen, Senior Research
Associate
Sasha Rampersad, Research Analyst

Tunisia

Institut Arabe des Chefs d'Entreprises
Faycal Lakhoua, Conseiller

Turkey

Turkish Economic and Social Studies
Foundation (TESEV)
Can Paker, Chairman

Uganda

Makarere Institute for Social Research
Professor J.C. Munene

Ukraine

CASE—Ukraine, Center for Social and
Economic Research
Vladimir Dubrovskiy, Project Manager

United Kingdom

Interdisciplinary Institute of
Management, London School of
Economics and Political Science
Sir Geoffrey Owen, Senior Fellow

United States

Council on Competitiveness
Deborah Wince-Smith, President
Chad Evans, Vice President, Research
and Analysis

Uruguay

Universidad ORT
Professor Isidoro Hodara

Venezuela

CONAPRI, National Council for
Investment Promotion
María Eugenia Labrador, Special Projects
Manager
Camilo Daza, Investor Service
Kitys Gil, Communication Assistant

Vietnam

Institute for Economic Research
Nguyen Xuan Thanh, Research Fellow

Zambia

INESOR: Institute of Economic and Social
Research, University of Zambia
Chileshe L. Mulenga, Director

Zimbabwe

University of Zimbabwe
Professor A.M. Hawkins, Director, Graduate
School of Management

Bolivia, Costa Rica, Dominican Republic, Ecuador, El Salvador, Guatemala, Honduras, Nicaragua, Panama

Latin American Center for Competitiveness
and Sustainable Development (INCAE)
Roberto Artavia, Rector
Arturo Condo, Associate Dean
Marlene de Estrella, Administrative
Director

Estonia, Latvia, Lithuania

Stockholm School of Economics in Riga
Dr Anders Paalzow, Rector
Dr Karlis Kreslins, Associate Professor